The Art of SHAKESPEARE'S SONNETS

The Art of
SHAKESPEARE'S SONNETS

HELEN VENDLER

The Belknap Press of
HARVARD UNIVERSITY PRESS
CAMBRIDGE, MASSACHUSETTS
LONDON, ENGLAND

Printed in the United States of America

Designed by Marianne Perlak

First Harvard University Press paperback edition, 1999

Publication of this book has been aided by a grant from the Hyder Edward Rollins Fund.

Library of Congress Cataloging-in-Publication Data

Vendler, Helen Hennessy.
The art of Shakespeare's sonnets / Helen Vendler.
p. cm.
Includes bibliographical references and index.
ISBN 0–674–63711–9 (cloth)
ISBN 0-674-63712-7 (pbk.)
1. Shakespeare, William, 1564–1616. Sonnets. 2. Sonnets, English—History and criticism. I. Title.
PR2848.V46 1997
821′.3—dc21 97–15306

For Joan Weitzner Levine

Those friends thou hast, and their adoption tried,
Grapple them unto thy soul with hoops of steel.

—*Hamlet*

ACKNOWLEDGMENTS

I am sincerely grateful to those who have preceded me in writing about the *Sonnets*. Though I mention only recent scholars in my Introduction, I am of course also indebted to all those, from the eighteenth century onward, who have reflected on these poems. My understanding of individual sonnets has been helped over the years by the editions and commentaries and books and articles and translations I have absorbed. The sheer volume of comment on Shakespeare precludes my footnoting work by others on individual sonnets, but I regard my own writing as part of a long collaborative effort to take the measure of Shakespeare—an effort that shows no sign of waning.

Over the nine years of work on this commentary, I was funded for residence at various places, to all of which I am grateful. To the Rockefeller Foundation for a residency in 1987 at the Villa Serbelloni in Bellagio, where I began my work on this commentary; to read and annotate the *Sonnets* in that most generous of atmospheres was a distinct happiness. To the National Humanities Center in North Carolina, where for two months the staff assisted me in getting an unwieldy manuscript under computer control, and where the Fellows provided absorbing conversation on many subjects; I thank Robert Connor, Director of the Center, for inviting his Trustees (of whom I was then one) to come for short stays at the Center. To Drue Heinz and the Hawthornden Foundation for a memorable five-week stay at Hawthornden Castle, Edinburgh, Scotland; the poet Daniel Halpern encouraged me to apply, and I owe him gratitude for the company (and solitude) I found there. To the Wilson Center, where (though I was funded for work on Yeats) I also began revisions of the first complete draft of this work; my semester stay was enlivened by the company of James Morris, Director of the Literature and Culture Division. To Magdalene College, Cambridge University, where, as the Parnell Fellow, I spent three months in eloquently beautiful surroundings working on various projects, of which this was one; I thank the Master, Sir John Gurdon, and the Fellows for their hospitality and friendship. And finally, to Harvard University, which granted me sabbatical leave in 1994–95, a leave the more deeply appreciated because it came in the wake of illness.

Though I do not normally show work in progress to others, the long evolution of this commentary led to my giving parts of it as lectures, and to printing four essays deriving from it (see Bibliography). I thank especially Professor Ruth Stevenson and the Department of English at Union College for my time spent there as Lamont Professor; the lecture and workshop on the *Sonnets* that I gave there has appeared in a collection of essays on teaching Shakespeare of which Professor Stevenson is coeditor. When Professor Sylvan Barnet of Tufts University requested a short essay to include in his revised *Sonnets* for the Signet Shakespeare, he caused me to think further about synecdoche; he also has been unstintingly helpful on many other occasions. Professor Russ MacDonald of the University of Rochester solicited an essay from me for his collection *Shakespeare Reread.* And the American Academy of Arts and Sciences, by inviting me to speak, generated an essay printed in its *Bulletin.* Professor Jonathan Bennett of the Department of Philosophy at Syracuse University evoked another effort, a lecture, given at Syracuse, which later became one of three Messenger Lectures on Shakespeare's *Sonnets* at Cornell University, where my kindly host was the poet A. R. Ammons. The genesis of the commentary came from a 1973 essay on sonnet 129 that I wrote in honor of I. A. Richards, at the invitation of the late Professor Reuben Brower of Harvard University; the delights of thinking about sonnet 129 were such that I found I could not forgo thinking about the other sonnets. I also wish to thank Professor Massimo Bacigalupo of the University of Genoa for sending me a photocopy of Basil Bunting's copy of Shakespeare's *Sonnets* (altered under Ezra Pound's direction), and for alerting me to the existence of Bunting's Shakespeare. Two poets—my former colleague at Boston University, George Starbuck, and Howard Moss of *The New Yorker*—by their inspired parodies of the *Sonnets*, helped me see (or see through) the poems with a poet's eye; I am sorry that they did not live to receive my thanks. Professor Emeritus George T. Wright of the University of Minnesota was kind enough to take pleasure in my writing on Shakespeare as he saw it evolve over several years, and gave me much-needed support when my ideas were still sketchy ones. Elsie Duncan-Jones, scholar of Hopkins and Marvell, by her friendship, her love of poetry, and her spirited interest in literary criticism, encouraged me by example.

I owe debts of gratitude to colleagues close to home: to President Neil Rudenstine, who permitted an extra sabbatical term and a reduced teaching load in one semester in order to let this work go forward, and who visited my undergraduate seminar to discuss the *Sonnets* with us; to Professor

Gwynne Evans, editor of the Cambridge Shakespeare, who, in an act of extraordinary generosity, read my manuscript and offered numerous annotations, additions, and corrections from his exemplary knowledge of the texts; errors remaining are mine. The late Professor Hyder Rollins, editor of the *Variorum Sonnets*, left a bequest to the Harvard English Department which helped me to meet research expenses. I warmly thank Margaretta Fulton of the Harvard Press, my impeccable editor since 1960, for her long sponsorship of this project; Maria Ascher, my erudite copyeditor, who contributed the anagram-insight noted of sonnet 8; and my former assistant Susan Welby, who resiliently coped with computer conversion and successive manuscripts.

I am grateful to the Getty Foundation for permission to reproduce on my book jacket a Renaissance panel painting incorporating a quotation from Petrarch's *Canzoniere;* the painting is thought to be by Holbein, and was once owned by Prince Henry (the son of James I). The Harvard Library, the Library of Congress, and the Folger Shakespeare Library were places indispensable to me, as they have been to so many others. The Quarto *Sonnets* are reproduced by permission of the Folger Library.

My mother was the first person to introduce me to Shakespeare's sonnets. She quoted them often, and had memorized many of them. Her last pieces of writing (which we found after Alzheimer's disease had robbed her of memory) were fragments of the *Sonnets* which, either from fear of forgetting or as a means of self-reassurance, she had written down on scraps of paper. It is no mean tribute to the *Sonnets* that they, of the hundreds of poems she knew by heart, were the last to fade. I remain grateful to her and to my father (my first teachers), and to the university instructors who enlarged my knowledge of poetry: among the dead, Sister Marie Barry, I. A. Richards, Douglas Bush, Reuben Brower, Northrop Frye, and Rosemond Tuve; among the living, Morton Berman and John Kelleher. Their minds formed mine, and I hear their voices when I read the poems they taught me.

In affection and admiration, I have dedicated this book to Joan Levine. We met in 1960 as young mothers at Cornell, and we were colleagues for many years in the Department of English at Boston University. Evenings of talk and laughter we have spent together are now so many as to be innumerable; because many of our conversations were about the *Sonnets*, I feel her presence throughout this commentary.

Finally, I must thank Shakespeare himself, whose poems have kept me company for so many decades. His envoi to the young man of the *Sonnets* seems strangely applicable to himself:

[Thou] hast by waning grown, and therein show'st
Thy lovers withering, as thy sweet self grow'st.

The culture and rhetorical practice that gave rise to the Renaissance sonnet have almost disappeared, yet the intense lyric energy stored in Shakespeare's poems, made visible I hope in this Commentary, gives me confidence that the *Sonnets* will remain intelligible, moving, and beautiful to contemporary and future readers.

CONTENTS

CONVENTIONS OF REFERENCE

I HAVE reprinted both the 1609 Quarto *Sonnets* and a modernized version of my own. All editors repunctuate according to their own understanding of the connection among the lines and quatrains of a given sonnet. While considering, and often adopting, the choices made by such editors as Booth and Evans, I have finally followed my own best understanding of the articulation of a sonnet in modernizing its punctuation. The emendations in my modernized sonnets are chosen from emendations already proposed by others. In each dubious case, my comments explain my choice among available emendations. Because some of Shakespeare's linguistic play depends on Quarto spelling, I specify whenever an interpretive remark requires reference to the Quarto. Otherwise, it can be assumed that whatever I say in the Commentary is as true of the Quarto as of the modern text.

In the comment on each sonnet, I aim to disclose some of the sonnet's significant features—imaginative, structural, semantic, syntactic, phonemic, graphic—and to point out their cooperation in a mimetic aesthetic result. That is, I assume that the features of these poems are designed to cooperate with, reinforce, meaningfully contradict, and play with one another. I also assume that such interplay has a psychologically mimetic end (to enact, by linguistic means, moves engaged in by the human heart and mind). I assume, too, that all of this play and enacting would be of no use unless the result were aesthetic novelty with respect to lyric tradition—by which I mean that something striking, memorable, beautiful, disturbing, surprising, etc. has been created.

Though many of the *Sonnets* play (often in blasphemous or subversive ways) with ideas central to their culture, I assume that a poem is not an essay, and that its paraphrasable propositional content is merely the jumping-off place for its real work. As I say in my Introduction, I do not regard as literary criticism any set of remarks about a poem which would be equally true of its paraphrasable propositional content. The poetics from which Shakespeare's sonnets issue is not the only poetics from which poems can be constructed, but the Aristotelian conventions about the unity of the literary work seem to apply particularly well to a form so tightly structured as the Shakespearean sonnet. However, there are ways in which most of the sonnets are self-contradicting, as I will say below; and the sequence itself, with its two main subsequences and its several subsubsequences, is a powerful dispersive structure. Nonetheless, it would be absurd to believe that Shakespeare, the most hyperconscious of writers, was inscribing lines and words in a given sonnet more or less at random. Since another set of words would have done equally well to transmit the propositional or paraphrasable content of the poem, content by itself (as it is usually defined) cannot possibly be the guide at work in determining the author's choice of words and syntactic features. If at first I seem excessive in finding orders and structurings, I hope readers will become convinced of the existence of such structurings as they read further in the Commentary.

My comments vary in length. Some amount to small essays on the sonnet in question (a temptation not to be resisted in the case of the most complex poems, such as 73, 116, and 129). Others are brief sketches of linguistic features that would need to be accounted for in any critical examination of the sonnet. In the past, I have often wished, as I was reading a poem, that I could know what another reader had noticed in it; and I leave a record here of what one person has remarked so that others can compare their own noticings with mine. In such a way, we may advance our understanding of Shakespeare's procedures as a working poet—that is, as a master of aesthetic strategy. In no case does my commentary exhaust any given sonnet. These are sketches, not completions. And yet, since the sonnets are still the least investigated, aesthetically speaking, of Shakespeare's works, there is room for a first sketch of the salient stylistic self-presentation of each of these poems.

I have not followed a single expository scheme for each sonnet. For variety's sake, I have taken up different aesthetic problems at different times; and I have deliberately changed topics for the first twenty sonnets, so that anyone reading straight on would find many of Shakespeare's concerns raised early. After that, I have let each sonnet dictate what seemed most essential to discuss. I cannot pretend to understand all the sonnets equally well; some still elude me (and my instinct in such cases is to think I have not found the spring that will open the box, rather than to judge that Shakespeare had nothing interesting in mind).

At the end of each sonnet-commentary, I have consistently pointed out what I call (for want of a better name) the Couplet Tie—the words appearing in the body of the sonnet (ll. 1–12) which are repeated in the couplet (ll. 13–14). By "words" I really mean "a word and its variants"; for example, in this context, *live*, *lives*, and *outlive* count as the same "word." Shakespeare expended real effort in creating verbal connections between the body of a sonnet and its couplet, and the words he chose to reiterate in this way are almost always thematically highly significant ones. (It is this repetition which has caused some readers—who seem to read only for theme—to assert that the couplets are superflous; but see my comments on the problem of the Shakespearean couplet in the Introduction.) After giving the root version of each word of the Couplet Tie, I print, in brackets, the variants in which it appears: *live* [*outlive*] [*-s*]. If the root word itself does *not* appear in the poem, I print it in brackets: if, for instance, "being" and "been" were the Couplet Tie, I would print [*be*] [*-ing*] [*been*]. After each Couplet Tie "word," I print in parentheses the line numbers in which it appears.

Often, Shakespeare used a more complex form of repetition than the Couplet Tie. He frequently firmly connected the four units of his sonnet—three quatrains and a couplet (Q_1, Q_2, Q_3, and C, in my abbreviated form of reference)—by repeating in each of these units a single "word" (as defined above). That single "word" appears (at least) four times in the sonnet, (at least) once in each part. In sonnet 7, for instance, Q_1 contains the word *looks*, Q_2 the word *looks* again, Q_3 the word *look*, and C the word *unlooked-on*. I call the root word that is so used—in this case, the root word *look*—a KEY WORD, and register it at the end of my commentary, preceding the Couplet Tie (which of course contains it). It is easy for an author writing a sonnet to use a given word in Q_1, and still fairly easy in Q_2; but as the vortex of meaning and development tightens, Q_3 puts a greater demand on ingenuity to insert the word; and C—with only two lines to work within instead of four, and with closure necessary—is the hardest of all.

Sometimes Shakespeare plays games with his KEY WORD. In sonnet 55 *(Not marble nor the gilded monuments)*, we find *outlive* in Q_1, *living* in Q_2, and *live* in C. Though we began by thinking (as we read the octave and couplet) that we might be about to find the fourth use that would make *live* a KEY WORD, we are momentarily "disappointed" as we look back on Q_3 and find no mention of anything "living" or "outliving" anything else:

> 'Gainst death and all oblivious enmity
> Shall you pace forth; your praise shall still find room
> Even in the eyes of all posterity
> That wear this world out to the ending doom.

It is only on a second reading that we notice, with distinct amusement, the "tucked-away" KEY WORD *live* in *ob**livi**ous*, making the pattern phonetically (if not graphically) complete in all four units of the poem. There are other such instances (e.g., 106, where instead of *praise* in a fourth appearance, for instance, we find *press*). The most complex such game occurs in 105, where the key word *one* appears (sometimes in phonemic, sometimes in graphic, form) *twice* in each of the four units. Without a sense of Shakespeare's wish to put the KEY WORD into each of the three quatrains and the couplet, one misses the ingenuity of *oblivious* in 55 and of *expressed* in 106, and one does not see the reason for their location in their respective poems.

Once a potential KEY WORD has been spotted in three of the members of a given sonnet, one feels it "ought" to appear in the fourth. When it doesn't, one suspects that the expected word has been designedly suppressed in the part where it is missing. I register here, in addition to any KEY WORD, the existence (when it occurs) of a DEFECTIVE KEY WORD, because I think we are meant to notice the *absence* of the expected word; it is, I find, almost always thematically relevant that the word is "suppressed" in the quatrain or couplet where we (alerted by its appearance in each of the other three units of the poem) have supposed it would appear. See Appendixes 1 and 2, on KEY WORDS and DEFECTIVE KEY WORDS.

Throughout, I have italicized phrases from the *Sonnets* in order to avoid a page littered with quotation marks. Any word here italicized comes directly from the sonnet in question. I have occasionally, for syntactic coherence, rearranged the words of a phrase: discussing the line *O how much more doth beauty beauteous seem* (sonnet 54), I might say, "The speaker says that *beauty seem[s] beauteous* when accompanied by truth." The convention of italicizing is meant to indicate that these words actually occur in the poem, even if not in this order, whereas in my sentence the word "accompanied" does not form part of the poem. Usually, however, I keep the cited words in the order in which they appear in the sonnet. On the occasions when I wish to summarize quickly the plot of a sonnet, or quote a string of connected phrases, I have omitted the usual ellipses signifying omission and the virgules signifying line-breaks. Of 147, for instance, I might write, "The speaker says, in rapid succession, *My love is as a fever, reason hath left me, past cure I am.*" This choice, too, is made to avoid excess punctuational distraction.

Sometimes, when I wish to make a point about a single word and that word alone, I enclose the relevant line of the sonnet in quotation marks and italicize only the word which is the object of attention. I might say, "In writing 'But thy *eternal* summer shall not fade,' Shakespeare attaches to an innately demarcated concept—a season (summer)—a word *(eternal)* cognitively inapplicable to it." In this way, I sequester the word *eternal* from the rest of its line, in order to make a point about it. When I wish to indicate how Shakespeare might alternatively have written a given line (though he did not), I use italics within brackets: [*But thy delightful summer shall not wane*].

In many cases in the Commentary, I have resorted to a diagram of some feature of a sonnet so that it can be grasped at a glance. These patterns can be phonetic (see 126), syntactic (129), relational (144), or conceptual (43)—but they always have ideational import, on which the specific commentary usually remarks. I know that diagrams are offensive to some readers, who feel that algebra is being substituted for explanatory language; but the density of Shakespeare's sonnet-structure is often so dense that it can be best untangled through giving a separate diagram for each subordinate structure. (One structure—say, a logical one—may divide up the sonnet in three parts: eight lines for a thesis, four lines for an antithesis, two lines for a synthesis. A second structure visible in the same sonnet—say, a pronominal one—may divide up the sonnet in two parts: six lines of reflection, eight lines of direct address. Yet a third structure in the same sonnet—say, a change from religious to secular diction—may divide up the sonnet into two entirely different parts: twelve lines of the religious, two lines of the secular. Each of these structures may need a separate map to demonstrate its own inner complexity.) Irritated readers can skip my schemes, and simply read the Commentary without them. But the shorthand of a scheme has often been useful to me, and I include diagrams for those to whom they appeal. In diagrams, when I want to refer to *line numbers*, I place them in parentheses: (4–6) means "lines 4 through 6 of the sonnet." When I want to sum up the *number of lines* devoted to a certain topic, in order to show its proportional space in the sonnet, I attach in the diagram the number unbracketed, placing it beside the portion of the diagram to which it refers.

Diagrams sometimes entail abbreviations. I use, as I have said above, the abbreviations Q_1, Q_2, Q_3, and C for the four units of each sonnet; the abbreviation Quarto for the 1609 *Sonnets;* and occasionally the abbreviations YM for the young man of the poems, and S for the speaker of the poems. I usually refer to the person uttering the sonnet as "the speaker," but when he represents himself in the poem as a poet, I sometimes call him "the poet." When I refer to "Shakespeare," I mean the author who invented the text spoken by the fictive speaker, and who structured and ornamented that text for his own aesthetic ends. "Shakespeare" stands always in an ironic relation to the fictive speaker, since the written poem exists on a plane other than the temporal "now" of the imagined speaker's moment.

In printing compound words—e.g., *myself*—I have used sometimes the two-word form *my self,* sometimes the compound one, as the sense of the sonnet seems to require. *My self* is the separable self objectified; *myself* can substitute for "I" or "me."

I use the acute accent for stress, the grave accent to show an *e* that is pronounced. And I have used boldface to emphasize one portion of an italicized word.

Biblical quotations are taken from the Geneva Bible, since the Authorized Version was published after the *Sonnets* appeared.

And I'll be sworn upon't that he loves her;
For here's a paper written in his hand,
A halting sonnet of his own pure brain.

—William Shakespeare, *Much Ado about Nothing*, V, iv, 85–87

There lives within the very flame of love
A kind of wick or snuff that will abate it.

—William Shakespeare, *Hamlet*, IV, vii, 114–115

Through torrid entrances, past icy poles
A hand moves on the page!
Sheets that mock lust and thorns that scribble hate
Are lifted from torn flesh with human rue.

—Hart Crane, "To Shakespeare"

I neer found so many beauties in the sonnets—they seem to be full of fine things said unintentionally—in the intensity of working out conceits.

—John Keats to J. H. Reynolds, 22 November 1817

Our talking about poetry is a part of, an extension of, our experience of it, and as a good deal of thinking has gone to the making of poetry, so a good deal may well go to the study of it.

—T. S. Eliot, *The Use of Poetry and the Use of Criticism*

When Shakespeare wrote, "Two loves I have," reader, he was *not kidding*.

—John Berryman, *The Freedom of the Poet*

INTRODUCTION

> There are indeed a sort of underlying auxiliars to the difficulty of work, call'd Commentators and Critics, who wou'd frighten many people by their number and bulk, and perplex our progress under pretense of fortifying their author.
>
> —Alexander Pope to Joseph Addison, 1714

> In fact, every poem has the right to ask for a new poetics. This is created only once to express the contents, also given only once, of a poem.
>
> —Anna Swir, quoted by Czeslaw Milosz in his introduction to *Talking to My Body*, by Anna Swir

Writing on the Sonnets

Before I begin to describe my own intentions in commenting on Shakespeare's *Sonnets*, I must say a few prefatory words. I intend this work for those who already know the *Sonnets*, or who have beside them the sort of lexical annotation found in the current editions (for example, those of Booth, Kerrigan, or Evans). A brief account of the reception history of the *Sonnets* can be found in these editions, as well as a more comprehensive bibliography than I can offer here. The older reception history in Hyder Rollins' *Variorum Sonnets* is still the most complete—and the most sobering to anyone hazarding a new addition to that history. Perhaps total immersion in the *Sonnets*—that is to say, in Shakespeare's mind—is a mildly deranging experience to anyone, and I cannot hope, I suppose, to escape the obsessive features characterizing Shakespearean sonnet criticism.

How are the *Sonnets* being written about nowadays? And why should I add another book to those already available? I want to do so because I admire the *Sonnets*, and wish to defend the high value I put on them, since they are being written about these days with considerable jaundice.[1] The spheres from which most of the current criticisms are generated are social and psychological ones. Contemporary emphasis on the participation of literature in a social matrix balks at acknowledging how lyric, though it may *refer to* the social, remains the genre that directs its *mimesis* toward the performance of the mind in *solitary* speech. Because lyric is intended to be voiceable by anyone reading it, in its normative form it deliberately strips away most social specification (age, regional location, sex, class, even race). A social reading is better directed at a novel or a play: the abstraction desired by the writer of, and the willing reader of, normative lyric frustrates the mind that wants social fictions or biographical revelations.

Even the best sociopsychological critic to write on the *Sonnets*, Eve Sedgwick, says "Shakespeare's Sonnets seem to offer a single, discursive, deeply felt *narrative* of the dangers and vicissitudes of one male homosocial adventure" [49]; "It is here that *one most wishes the Sonnets were a novel, that readers have most treated it as a novel*, and that we are, instead, going to bring the Sonnets' preoccupation to bear on *real novels*" [46] (italics mine). The persistent wish to turn the sequence into a novel (or a drama) speaks to the interests of the sociopsychological critic, whose aim is less to inquire into the successful carrying-out of a literary project than to investigate the representation of gender relations. It is perhaps a tribute to Shakespeare's "reality-effect" that "one most wishes the Sonnets were a novel," but it does no good to act as if these lyrics were either a novel or a documentary of a lived life.

Other critics (Barrell, Marotti, Kernan) have brought the *Sonnets* into the realm of the social by drawing analogies between the language of the poetry and the language of solicitations addressed to patrons and requesting patronage. This is a reasonable semantic (if not poetic) investigation, and reminds us that lyric language in any given epoch draws on all available sociolects of that epoch. The *Sonnets*, however (as Kernan makes clear), go far outside the originating discourse: no patron was ever addressed *qua* patron in language like that of sonnet 20 *(A woman's face with Nature's own hand painted)*. Aesthetically speaking, it is what a lyric *does with* its borrowed social languages—i.e., how it casts them into new permutational and combinatorial forms—that is important. Shakespeare is unusually rich in his borrowings of diction and formulas from patronage, from religion, from law, from courtship, from diplomacy, from astronomy, and so on; but he tends to be a blasphemer in all of these realms. He was a master subverter of the languages he borrowed, and the point of *literary* interest is not the fact of his borrowings but how he turned them inside out. (See, in the commentary, sonnets 20, 33, 105, 135, or 144.)[2] One of Shakespeare's most frequent means of subversion is the total redefinition, within a single sonnet, of a word initially borrowed from a defined social realm (such as *state* in sonnet 33); there is no social discourse which he does not interrogate and ironize.

The sonnets have also been investigated by psychoanalytically minded critics, of whom the most formidable was the late Joel Fineman. Fineman, fundamentally disappointed by the Young Man sonnets, much preferred the Dark Lady sequence, where "difference" (read: the Lacanian Symbolic) replaces "sameness" (read: the Lacanian Imaginary).[3] Anyone who prizes drama above other genres delights in conflict, the structural principle of drama; and for Shakespeareans the Dark Lady sequence is, give or take a few details, a proto-sketch for a drama rather like *Othello*, with its jealousy, its sexuality, its ambiguous "darkness," its betrayals, and so on. It is much harder to imagine the Young Man sequence as a play. Yet, if one judges not by the criteria proper to drama but by those appropriate to lyric—"How well does the structure of this poem mimic the structure of thinking?" and "How well does the linguistic play of the poem embody that structural mimesis?"—Shakespeare's first subsequence is at least as good as (and in my view better than) the second. A psychological view of the *Sonnets* (whether psychoanalytically oriented or not) stresses motivation, will, and other characterological features, and above all needs a story on which to hang motivation. The "story" of the *Sonnets* continues to fascinate readers, but lyric is both more and less than story. And, in any case, the story of the *Sonnets* will always exhibit those "gaps" and that "indeterminacy" [Kuin, 251] intrinsic to the sonnet sequence as a genre. A coherent psychological account of the *Sonnets* is what the *Sonnets* exist to frustrate. They do not fully reward psychological criticism (or gender criticism, motivated by many of the same characterological aims) any more than they do political criticism. Too much of their activity escapes the large sieves of both psychology and politics, disciplines not much concerned to examine the basic means of lyric: subgenre, structure, syntax, and linguistic play.

The true "actors" in lyric are words, not "dramatic persons"; and the drama of any lyric is constituted by the successive entrances of new sets of words, or new stylistic arrangements (grammatic, syntactical, phonetic) which are visibly in conflict with previous arrangements used with reference to the "same" situation. (See, for example, my comments on sonnet 73 or sonnet 116.) Thus, the introduction of a new linguistic strategy is, in a sonnet, as interruptive and interesting as the entrance of a new character in a play. And any internal change in topic (from autumn to twilight to glowing fire in sonnet 73, for instance) or any change in syntactic structure (say, from parallel placement of items to chiastic placement) are among the strategies which—because they mimic changes of mind—constitute vivid drama within the lyric genre. Read in the light of these lyric criteria, the first subsequence is fully as dramatic (in the form proper to lyric) as the second. The art of seeing drama in linguistic action proper (action that may be as simple as the grammatical change in a given passage from nouns to verbals and back again—see sonnet 129) is an art that has lapsed, even in interpreters whose criteria appear to be literary rather than political or psychological.[4]

What, then, am I attempting in the Commentary below? Chiefly, a supplement to the accounts of the *Sonnets* in current editions (Ingram and Redpath, Booth,[5] Kerrigan, Evans) and in the books of the last thirty years (notably those by Leishman, Melchiori, Trousdale, Booth, Dubrow, Fineman, Vickers, de Grazia, Roche, Pequigney, Sedgwick, Weiser, and Martin). These editorial and critical accounts do not, to my mind, pay enough attention to the sonnets as poems—that is, as a writer's projects invented to amuse and challenge his own capacity for inventing artworks. Formal mimeses of the mind and heart in action are of course representative of human reality, but it is not enough to show that the moves of their language "chart . . . the ways we may be affected, morally and emotionally, by our own rhetoric" [Dubrow, 213]. A poem must be beautiful, too, exhibiting the double beauty that Stevens called "the poetry of the idea" and "the poetry of the words." That is, the theme must be freshly imagined, the genre must be renewed, and the words must surprise and satisfy from the point of view of proportion, musicality, and lexical vivacity.

The Architecture of the Sonnet

What, then, is a Shakespearean sonnet and what can we say about it as a poem? Here is a sonnet of which every word was written by Shakespeare:

O how I faint when I of you do write,
Knowing a better spirit doth use your name,
And in the praise thereof spends all his might,
To make me tongue-tied speaking of your fame.
I never saw that you did painting need,
And therefore to your fair no painting set;
I found, or thought I found, you did exceed
The barren tender of a poet's debt.
Lean penury within that pen doth dwell,
That to his subject lends not some small glory,
But he that writes of you, if he can tell
That you are you, so dignifies his story.

You still shall live—such virtue hath my pen—
Where breath most breathes, even in the mouths of men.
(sonnets 80, 83, 84, 81)

This pastiche, however, is not "a Shakespearean sonnet," even though it is composed of three quatrains and a couplet in iambic pentameter, and even though it rehearses, in the familiar tones of adoration, humility, and boast, familiar themes of the poet's inadequacy, the young man's excellence, and the rivalries of poets. It is not a Shakespearean sonnet because it shows no structural coherence, no logical development, and no unity of play. It is, in the sense in which I use the term, not even a "poem," because it is not engaged in the fundamental act of a Shakespearean poem, which is to unfold itself in a developing dynamic of thought and feeling marked by a unifying play of mind and language. No such development or unifying play is visible in these fourteen lines.

Next, for purposes of comparison, consider this genuine sonnet, written by Shakespeare, which serves as the epilogue to *Henry V:*

Thus far with rough, and all-unable pen,
Our bending author hath pursued the story,
In little room confining mighty men,
Mangling by starts the full course of their glory.
Small time: but in that small, most greatly lived
This star of England. Fortune made his sword;
By which, the world's best garden he achieved;
And of it left his son imperial lord.
Henry the Sixth, in infant bands crowned king
Of France and England, did this king succeed;
Whose state so many had the managing,
That they lost France, and made his England bleed:
Which oft our stage hath shown; and for their sake,
In your fair minds let this acceptance take.

Though we recognize the Shakespearean rhyme-scheme, this poem is nothing like the poems published in the 1609 *Sonnets.* Those are inward, meditative, and lyrical; this is outward, expository, and narrative. Nothing in this Commentary would illuminate the sonnet from *Henry V* (or the comparable expository ones opening Acts I and II of *Romeo and Juliet*). Even the sonnets uttered within plays by dramatic characters (Romeo and Juliet, Longaville, Berowne) are shaped by the themes of the drama and by the actions taking place on the stage; they do not show the successive intellectual position-taking that is such a striking feature of the *Sonnets.*

Here, for instance, is Berowne's charming sonnet repudiating "figures pedantical" in favor of plainness in language. It is evident that it is a reiterative sonnet: each of its four units repeats the same antirhetorical stance. Berowne's outburst, because it is chiefly reiterative, lacks those dynamic reversals of thought and feeling indispensable to the true Shakespearean sonnet:

O, never will I trust to speeches penned,
Nor to the motion of a schoolboy's tongue,
Nor never come in vizard to my friend,
Nor woo in rhyme, like a blind harper's song!
Taffeta phrases, silken terms precise,
Three-piled hyperboles, spruce affectation,
Figures pedantical—these summer flies
Have blown me full of maggot ostentation.
I do forswear them; and I here protest
By this white glove (how white the hand, God knows!)
Henceforth my wooing mind shall be expressed
In russet yeas and honest kersey noes.
And to begin, wench—so God help me, law!—
My love to thee is sound, sans crack or flaw.

(*Love's Labor's Lost,* V, ii, 405–419)

The essential function of such a sonnet is to advance the plot and represent Berowne's repentance.

There is, on the other hand, a real evolution in the inventive dialogue-sonnet of Romeo and Juliet, but it is an evolution of dramatic interaction rather than of inward psychic reevaluation:

Romeo
If I profane with my unworthiest hand
   This holy shrine, the gentle sin is this:
My lips, two blushing pilgrims, ready stand
   To smooth that rough touch with a tender kiss.

Juliet
Good pilgrim, you do wrong your hand too much,
   Which mannerly devotion shows in this;

For saints have hands that pilgrims' hands do touch,
  And palm to palm is holy palmers' kiss.

Romeo
Have not saints lips, and holy palmers too?

Juliet
Ay, pilgrim, lips that they must use in prayer.

Romeo
O, then, dear saint, let lips do what hands do!
They pray; grant thou, lest faith turn to despair.

Juliet
Saints do not move, though grant for prayers' sake.

Romeo
Then move not while my prayer's effect I take.
(*Romeo and Juliet* I, v, 95–108)

Precisely because he was a dramatist by temperament and by training, Shakespeare could, in the 1609 Quarto, turn the external dramatic enactment we see here into the interior meditative drama of lyric. Because the drama of the 1609 poems has less to do with their themes than with the way those themes are stylistically dramatized through grammar, syntax, and word choice, any treatment of the *Sonnets* that focuses chiefly on their themes loses almost all of their aesthetic richness.

Consider, for instance, what is left of a genuine Shakespearean sonnet when its themes are preserved but its language is altered. Here is Shakespeare's sonnet 29, followed by George Santayana's "translation" of it into modern English:

When in disgrace with Fortune and men's eyes,
I all alone beweep my outcast state,
And trouble deaf heaven with my bootless cries,
And look upon myself and curse my fate,
Wishing me like to one more rich in hope,
Featured like him, like him with friends possessed,
Desiring this man's art, and that man's scope,
With what I most enjoy contented least;
Yet in these thoughts myself almost despising,
Haply I think on thee, and then my state

(Like to the lark at break of day arising
From sullen earth) sings hymns at heaven's gate,
  For thy sweet love rememb'red such wealth brings,
  That then I scorn to change my state with kings.

When times are hard and old friends fall away
And all alone I lose my hope and pluck,
Doubting if God can hear me when I pray,
And brood upon myself and curse my luck,
Envying some stranger for his handsome face,
His wit, his wealth, his chances, or his friends,
Desiring this man's brains and that man's place,
And vexed with all I have that makes amends,
Yet in these thoughts myself almost despising,—
By chance I think of you; and then my mind,
Like music from deep sullen murmurs rising
To peals and raptures, leaves the earth behind;
  For if you care for me, what need I care
  To own the world or be a millionaire?

In spite of its resemblance to the original in theme, sentiments, and rhyme, this is not a Shakespearean sonnet. "The experiment," says Santayana in *The Genteel Tradition,* "is meant only to make evident how much old finery there is in our literary baggage" [70–71]. It is the "old finery" as well as the internal psychological dynamic (retained in Santayana's version) that makes a Shakespeare sonnet what it is. It is not theme as such (since, as is evident, much Shakespearean thematic material is present in my opening collage-pastiche or in Santayana's "translation"). Because a comprehension of the internal logic and the "old finery" of Elizabethan lyric has now almost vanished, I have written this Commentary to restore them to view as they appear in Shakespeare's *Sonnets.* I hope, of course, that the logic and the finery will be relished as soon as seen.

The modernist lyric aesthetic has been, on the whole, hostile to finery of Shakespeare's sort. One of the more bizarre moments in the reception history of the *Sonnets* occurred when the English poet Basil Bunting went to study with Ezra Pound at the "Ezuversity" in Rapallo.[6] The task Pound set the young Bunting was to go through Shakespeare's *Sonnets* correcting the inversions, and removing all the "superfluous words." There is a spirit of beginner's bravado in Bunting's compliance: sonnet 87, for instance, is briskly reduced to a mere two lines;

Farewell! Thou art too dear for my possessing;
And like enough thou know'st thy estimate.

That says it all, if one accepts the Poundian aesthetic. But perhaps more instructive with respect to modern distaste for Elizabethan rhetoric is a somewhat less mutilated sonnet. Here is Shakespeare's original sonnet 30:

When to the sessions of sweet silent thought
I summon up remembrance of things past,
I sigh the lack of many a thing I sought,
And with old woes new wail my dear time's waste:
Then can I drown an eye, unus'd to flow,
For precious friends hid in death's dateless night,
And weep afresh love's long since cancell'd woe,
And moan th'expense of many a vanish'd sight:
Then can I grieve at grievances foregone,
And heavily from woe to woe tell o'er
The sad account of fore-bemoanèd moan,
Which I new pay as if not paid before.
  But if the while I think on thee, dear friend,
  All losses are restor'd, and sorrows end.
(Quoted from Bunting's copy)

And here it is after Bunting's blue-penciling:

When I summon up remembrance of things past
To the sessions of silent thought,
I sigh the lack of many a thing I sought,
And wail time's waste:
I can drown an eye
For precious friends hid in dateless night,
And weep afresh love's long since cancell'd woe,
And many a vanish'd sight:
I can tell o'er
The sad account
As if not paid before.
But if I think on thee,
All losses are restor'd.

My transcription lacks of course what a facsimile reproduction would convey—how much the youthful Bunting enjoyed the literary vandalism of crossing out, with heavy pen-strokes, such a large number of "superfluous" words, how he reveled in "correcting," with his loops and arrows, Shakespeare's old-fashioned syntactic inversions. Nothing could better clarify twentieth-century impatience with *copia*, apparent reduplication, and elaboration. Naturally, the entire implicit aesthetic of the Renaissance poem, and its cunning enactment of its woe as the lines unwind, is lost in Bunting's version (see my description in the Commentary of the necessary and functional nature of all that Bunting deletes).

The logical termination of the modernist reduction in a comic-populist mode may be seen in George Starbuck's witty 1986 *Space-Saver Sonnets*, where sonnet 29, reduced to its (slightly tampered-with) rhyme scheme, becomes:

The Sessions

To
think.

Lou,
Dink,
and
Miss
Land-
is,
dead.

You
do
stead-
y
me.

It is in the hope of showing that Shakespeare's sonnets contain more than is to be found in their translations or reductions or paraphrases that I have compiled this Commentary.

"A Verbal Contraption"

Shakespeare is a poet who matches technique to content in a stunningly exemplary way, and his poems deserve to be asked the two questions formulated by Auden in *The Dyer's Hand:*

> The questions which interest me most when reading a poem are two. The first is technical: "Here is a verbal contraption. How

> does it work?" The second is, in the broadest sense, moral: "What kind of a guy inhabits this poem? What is his notion of the good life or the good place? His notion of the Evil One? What does he conceal from the reader? What does he conceal even from himself?" [50–51].

Like any poet, Auden knows that the second question cannot be responded to correctly until the first has been answered. It is the workings of the verbal construct that give evidence of the moral stance of the poet. Auden here separates the technical from the moral, and perhaps believes that the answer about the "verbal contraption" must be distinct from the answer about personality, ethics, and what we would now call "unconscious" and "deconstructive" moments in the poem. I believe that the deepest insights into the moral world of the poem, and into its constructive and deconstructive energies, come precisely from understanding it as a contraption made of "words," by which I mean not only the semantic units we call "words" but all the language games in which words can participate. Because many essays on the sonnets attempt moral and ethical discussion without any close understanding of how the poems are put together, I have emphasized in this Commentary the total "contraptionness" of any given sonnet as the first necessary level of understanding. I hope that my comments on the famous "moral" sonnets (such as 66, 94, 116, 129) will not disappoint readers who are looking for Shakespeare's "notion of the good life . . . the Evil One" and so on. As to what Shakespeare may conceal from the reader, or even from himself, such a supremely conscious writer conceals, it seems to me, very little.

I regret the absence, except in occasional cases below, of metrical commentary.[7] I don't doubt that a careful examination of Shakespeare's prosody in the sonnets (which can't be separated from a study of phrasal segmentation in the lines) would reveal repeated patterns of substantial interest. But that would make another book, and one that I (not yet having found an acceptably subtle and yet communicable theory of scansion) am not competent to write. I have tried to notice exceptional moments of prosodic originality that occur outside the common practices of prosodic variation (such as reversed initial feet).

To arrive at the understandings proposed in my Commentary, I found it necessary to learn the *Sonnets* by heart. I would often think I "knew" a sonnet; but then, scanning it in memory, I would find lacunae. Those gaps made me realize that some pieces of the whole must not yet have been integrated into my understanding of the intent of the work, since I was able to forget them. The recovery of the missing pieces always brought with it a further understanding of the design of that sonnet, and made me aware of what I had not initially perceived about the function of those words. No pianist or violinist would omit to learn a sonata by heart before interpreting it in public performance, but the equal habit of knowing poetry by heart before interpreting it has been lost. I first memorized many of the *Sonnets* (from my mother's copy) in the heartfelt way of youth, and I hope I have not lost that "heartfelt" sense of the poems. But I have since learned to love in a more conscious way Shakespeare's elated variety of invention, his ironic capacity, his astonishing refinement of technique, and, above all, the reach of his skeptical imaginative intent. I hope in this Commentary to illustrate these qualities, as well as, from time to time, the pathos, reflectiveness, and moral urgency already well described by previous readers.

Evidence and Import

This Commentary consists primarily of what might be called "evidential" criticism: that is, I wanted to write down remarks for which I attempt to supply instant and sufficient linguistic evidence. This, like all Platonic aims, must be imperfectly achieved, but I've tried to remember it at every point. There must of course be conjecture and speculation in divining the poetic laws which are being obeyed by a particular series of words, but I have given the reasons for my conjectures in as plain a way as I could find. One can write convincing evidential criticism only on fairly short texts (in longer texts, the permutations become too numerous). The *Sonnets* are ideal for such a purpose; and they deserve detailed and particular commentary because they comprise a virtual anthology of lyric possibility—in the poet's choice of subgenres, in arrangements of words, in tone, in dramatic modeling of the inner life, in speech-acts. In every case, I wanted to delineate whatever the given sonnet offered that seemed aesthetically most provocative: if there is an interesting change of address, it will be remarked, while a predictable change of address may not be commented on at all. The presence of unexpected (or inexplicable) words will be dwelt on; other words may go unnoticed. I have tried to point out problems that I have not been able to solve to my own satisfaction.

I come to Shakespeare's *Sonnets* as a critic of lyric poetry, interested in how successful poems are put together, ideationally, structurally, and linguistically; or, to put it another way, what ideational and structural and linguistic acts by a poet result in a successful poem. The brilliant beginnings in this direction by William Empson (on individual words and images), Winifred Nowottny (on formal arrangement), Stephen Booth (on overlapping structures), and Brian Vickers and Heather Dubrow (on rhetorical figuration) suggest that such efforts are particularly rewarding. Inevitably, rather few sonnets have been examined in detail, since critics tend to dwell on the most famous ten or fifteen out of the total 154; in fact, the *Sonnets* represent the largest tract of unexamined Shakespearean lines left open to scrutiny. As A. Nejgebauer remarked in his recapitulation (in the 1962 *Shakespeare Survey)* of work on the *Sonnets:* "Criticism of the sonnets will not stand comparison with that of the plays. . . . It has largely been amateurish and misplaced. . . . As regards the use of language, stanzaic structure, metre, tropes, and imagery, these demand the full tilth and husbandry of criticism." [18] Nejgebauer's complaint could not be made with quite the same vehemence today, largely because of Stephen Booth's massive intervention with his *Essay on Shakespeare's Sonnets* (1969) and his provocative edition of the *Sonnets* (1977). Yet Booth's critical stance—that the critic, helpless before the plurisignification of language and overlapping of multiple structures visible in a Shakespearean sonnet, must be satisfied with irresolution with respect to its fundamental gestalt—seems to me too ready a surrender to hermeneutic suspicion.

On the other hand, the wish of interpreters of poems to arrive at something they call "meaning" seems to me misguided. However important "meaning" may be to a theological hermeneutic practice eager to convey accurately the Word of God, it cannot have that importance in lyric. Lyric poetry, especially highly conventionalized lyric of the sort represented by the *Sonnets*, has almost no significant freight of "meaning" at all, in our ordinary sense of the word. "I have insomnia because I am far away from you" is the gist of one sonnet; "Even though Nature wishes to prolong your life, Time will eventually demand that she render you to death" is the "meaning" of another. These are not taxing or original ideas, any more than other lyric "meanings" ("My love is like a rose," "London in the quiet of dawn is as beautiful as any rural scene," etc.). Very few lyrics offer the sort of philosophical depth that stimulates meaning-seekers in long, complex, and self-contradicting texts like Shakespeare's plays or Dostoevsky's novels. In an effort to make lyrics more meaning-full, even linguistically minded critics try to load every rift with ore, inventing and multiplying ambiguities, plural meanings, and puns as if in a desperate attempt to add adult interest to what they would otherwise regard as banal sentiment. This is Booth's path, and it is also that of Joseph Pequigney, who would read the words of the *Sonnets* as an elaborate code referring to homosexual activity. Somehow, Shakespeare's words and images (most of the latter, taken singly, fully conventional) do not seem interesting enough as "meaning" to scholarly critics; and so an argument for additional "ambiguous" import is presented, if only to prop up Shakespeare's reputation. The poet Frank O'Hara had a better sense for the essential semantic emptiness of love lyrics when he represented them (in his poem "Blocks") as "saying" "I need you, you need me, yum yum." The appeal of lyric lies elsewhere than in its paraphrasable statement. Where, then, does the charm of lyric lie? The answers given in this Commentary are as various as the sonnets examined, since Shakespeare almost never repeats a strategy. However, they can be summed up in the phrase "the arrangement of statement." Form is content-as-arranged; content is form-as-deployed.

The Dramatis Personae

The new broom sweeping clean in Margreta de Grazia's *Shakespeare Verbatim* has cleared away the early editorial contextualizing of the *Sonnets* by Benson, Malone, and others; the construction of a story "behind" the sequence has been rebuked by critics pointing out how few of the sonnets include gendered pronouns; and the new purity of anti-intentional criticism (stemming in part from the postmodern wish to dispense with "the author function") is salutary as a defense against the search for biographical origins of the *Sonnets.* Still, there is a factual minimum account of Shakespeare's compositional acts in any given poem on which all readers of a text must agree. In my comment on each sonnet, I give this minimal account (of Shakespeare's lexical, grammatical, syntactic, and sequential choices) on which any interpretation must found itself. Even such a minimal narrative is not a simple one. Any commentator must—given Shakespeare's frequent authorial irony—make a division between Shakespeare the author and his fictive self, whom we name the speaker of the sonnets. Yet often the two are designedly blurred, since the fictive self, too, is an author. It is difficult, as well, to settle on a word for the object of the speaker's affections. Each word prejudices the case. The "beloved"? The "object"? The "friend"? The "lover"? The "mistress"? The "young man"? The "dark lady"? I use whatever seems best suited to the sonnet at hand, and aim at some variety of reference to avoid boredom.

I have also decided, in the interests of common sense, to hold to the convention which assumes that the order of the sonnets as we have them is Shakespearean. In this convention, we take the first 126 sonnets as ones concerning a young man, and the rest as ones concerning a dark-haired and dark-eyed woman; I therefore say "him" or "her" in my sentences about the love-object in ungendered sonnets according to the subsequence in which they occur. I say "Shakespeare" when I mean "the writer of these poems." I say "the speaker" when I mean the fictive person uttering the poem; and I sometimes say "the poet" when the fictional speaker identifies himself in the sonnet as a poet. Though the terms "dark lady" and "mistress" are now offensive to some modern ears, the blunt word "woman," used of the tormenting betrayer of the second cycle, often rings false to the historical language-conventions of the *Sonnets* themselves.

The *Sonnets* raise powerful sexual anxieties not only by representing a sexual triangle (as other sequences, European and English, did not) but by making the speaker's erotic relationships unusual ones. Though most reviewers found unconvincing Pequigney's insistence on a concealed linguistic code of homosexual acts, over time there has evolved—in the work of Blackmur, Sedgwick, Pequigney, Stallybrass, and others—an increasing willingness to admit, about the first subsequence, that its controlling motive is sexual infatuation. (The motive of sexual desire has never been doubted in the second subsequence.) The infatuation of the speaker with the young man is so entirely an infatuation of the eye—which makes a fetish of the beloved's countenance rather than of his entire body—that gazing is this infatuation's chief (and perhaps best and only) form of intercourse. Shakespeare's insistence on the eye as the chief sexual organ is everywhere present in the *Sonnets*, as in the plays:

Tell me where is fancy bred,
Or in the heart, or in the head?
How begot, how nourishèd?
    Reply, reply.
It is engend'red in the eyes
With gazing fed, and fancy dies
In the cradle where it lies.
(*The Merchant of Venice*, III, ii, 63ff.)

I don't mean to slight the aura of privilege surrounding the young man as an enhancement of his beauty; but everything in the sonnets suggests that it was the youth's beauty of countenance (remarked upon, and attractive to others) which caused the helpless attachment recorded in the poems. Shakespeare was, after all, a man subdued to the aesthetic.

The perplexing case of the second subsequence seems to contradict what I have just said. If the speaker is so susceptible to conventional beauty, how is it he becomes entangled with a woman *colour'd ill?* Freud describes, in an essay called "A Special Type of Choice of Object Made by Men" (1910), the case of men who can be sexually aroused (when the object is a woman) only by a woman known to be promiscuous. Though the *Sonnets* can't offer conclusive proof of such a leaning in the speaker, it is suggestive that the speaker repeatedly and obsessively dwells on the promiscuity of his mistress, and that he remains baffled, almost until the end of this subsequence, by her power to arouse him. A psychoanalytic argument can be made that in having intercourse with a woman who has betrayed him with the young man, the speaker is in effect having vicariously that homosexual intercourse which he desires (but is frustrated of) in sonnet 20; and the meeting of the author's and the young man's "wills" in the woman's "will" supports such an argument. Yet one feels that evidence from literature is not the same as evidence from life; and it is certain that the speaker never introduces a self-analysis of the latter motive (vicarious homosexual intercourse), while he does understand, eventually, that it is precisely the promiscuity of his mistress that is the prerequisite for his own troubling sexual arousal in her presence. It is this latter understanding which causes the anguished self-division (the *perjur'd I* of which Fineman makes so much) in the second subsequence.

Because two different causes of sexual passion—homosexual infatuation consummated in the eye's intercourse with an image, and heterosexual infatuation consummated in the penis' intercourse within *the bay where all men ride*—are so idiosyncratically present together in Shakespeare's speaker, it seems at first extraordinary that they should have been euphemized by so many commentators into conventional friendship and conventional (if adulterous) heterosexual practice. But the reason these passions were susceptible to such euphemizing is that the *feelings* attached to fetishistic or anomalous sexual attraction are identical to the feelings attached to more conventional sexual practice, and it is essential feelings, not love-objects, which are traced in lyric.

Allegations of misogyny have arisen with respect to Shakespeare's speaker's discourse about his mistress and about *false women* (sonnet 20) in general. There is a philosophical impropriety in anachronistic reproaches to speakers of earlier centuries whose theological, ethical, and socially regulative concepts are alien to ours. But such accusations make us ask ourselves how we conceive an author's duty as a writer of lyric. As I see it, the poet's duty is to create aesthetically convincing representations of feelings felt and thoughts thought. Readers have certainly found the feelings and thoughts of Shakespeare's speaker with respect to his mistress convincingly represented. Whether or not we believe that such *should* have been the speaker's feelings and thoughts is entirely irrelevant to the aesthetic success of the poem, as irrelevant as whether the fictive speaker *should* have found himself sexually aroused by the knowledge that his mistress was promiscuous. Whether he should have experienced self-loathing once he discovered the motive for his arousal is equally irrelevant. What *is* important, for the advance of the representational powers of lyric as it historically evolved, is that Shakespeare discovered a newly complex system of expression, unprecedented in the Renaissance lyric, through which he could, accurately and convincingly, represent and enact that arousal and that self-loathing—just as he had found strategic ways in the first subsequence to represent and enact his speaker's abject infatuation with a beautiful face. The ethics of lyric writing lies in the accuracy of its representation of inner life, and in that alone. Shakespeare's duty as a poet of the inner life was not to be fair to women but to be accurate in the representation of the feelings of his speaker. If the fictive speaker is a man tormented by his self-enslavement to a flagrantly unfaithful mistress, we can scarcely expect from him, at this moment, a judiciousness about women. The "poetic justice" of the sequence comes in the objectivity of Shakespeare's representation of his speaker in all his irrationality and wildness of language.

The Art of the Sonnets, and the Speaker They Create

With respect to the *Sonnets*—a text now almost four hundred years old—what can a commentary offer that is new? It can, I think, approach the sonnets, as I have chosen to do, from the vantage point of the poet who wrote them, asking the questions that a poet would ask about any poem. What was the aesthetic challenge for Shakespeare in writing these poems, of confining himself (with a few exceptions) to a single architectural form? (I set aside, as not of essential importance, the money or privileges he may have earned from his writing.) A writer of Shakespeare's seriousness writes from internal necessity—to do the best he can under his commission (if he was commissioned) and to perfect his art. What is the inner agenda of the *Sonnets?* What are their compositional motivations? What does a writer gain from working, over and over, in one subgenre? My brief answer is that Shakespeare learned to find strategies to enact feeling in form, feelings in forms, multiplying both to a superlative degree through 154 poems. No poet has ever found more linguistic forms by which to replicate human responses than Shakespeare in the *Sonnets.*

Shakespeare comes late in the sonnet tradition, and he is challenged by that very fact to a display of virtuosity, since he is competing against great predecessors. His thematic originality in his *dramatis personae* makes the sequence new in Western lyric. Though the sharing of the speaker by the young man and the lady, and the sharing of the young man by the lady and the rival poet, could in other hands become the material of farce, the "plot" is treated by Shakespeare elegiacally, sardonically, ironically, and tragically, making the *Sonnets* a repository of relationships and moods wholly without peer in the sonnet tradition. However, thematic originality alone never yet made a memorable artwork. Nor did psychological depth—though that is at least a prerequisite for lyric profundity.

No sufficient description exists in the critical literature of how Shakespeare makes his speaker "real." (The speaker is the only "person" interiorized in the *Sonnets*, though there are other *dramatis personae.*) The act of the lyric is to offer its reader a script to say. The words of a poem are not "overheard" (as in the formulations of J. S. Mill and T. S. Eliot); this would make the reader an eavesdropping voyeur of the writer's sensations. Nor is the poet "speaking to himself" without reference to a reader (if so, there would be no need to write the poem down, and all communicative action would be absent). While the social genres "build in" the reader either as listener (to a narrator of a novel) or as audience (to a play), the private literary genres—such as the Psalms, or prayers printed in prayer books, or secular lyrics—are scripted for repeated personal recitation. One is to utter them as one's own words, not as the words of another. Shakespeare's sonnets, with their unequaled idiomatic language-contours (written, after all, by a master in dramatic speech who shaped that speech into what C. S. Lewis called their lyric *cantabile*), are preeminently utterances for us to utter as ours. It is indispensable, then, if we are to be made to want to enter the lyric script, that the voice offered for our use be "believable" to us, resembling a "real voice" coming from a "real mind" like our own.

It is hard to achieve such "realness." Many lyrics are content with a very generalized and transient voice, one of no determinate length of life or depth of memory. In a drama, the passage of time and the interlocking of the web of events in which a character participates allow for a gradual deepening of the constructed personality of even minor characters. But Shakespeare must render his sonnet-speaker convincing in a mere fourteen lines. He is helped, to this end, by the fact that a "thick description" of his speaker accretes as the sequence progresses; but since few readers read the sequence straight through, the demand for evident "realness" in each poem, even were it to stand alone in an anthology, remains. The

Sonnets cannot be "dramatic" in the ordinary sense because in them, as in every lyric of a normative sort, there is only one authorized voice. True drama requires at least two voices (so that even Beckett's monologues often include an offstage voice, or a tape of a voice, to fulfill this requirement). Some feminist critics, mistaking lyric for a social genre, have taken offense that the women who figure as *dramatis personae* within sonnet sequences are "silenced," meaning that they are not allowed to expostulate or reply. In that (mistaken) sense one would have to see *all* addressees in lyric as "silenced" (God by George Herbert, Robert Browning by E. B. Browning) since no addressee, in normative lyric, is given a counter and equal voice responding to that of the speaker.[8] Since the person uttering a lyric is always represented as alone with his thoughts, his imagined addressee can by definition never be present. The lyric (in contrast to the dramatic monologue, where there is always a listener present in the room), gives us the mind alone with itself. Lyric can present no "other" as alive and listening or responding in the same room as the solitary speaker. (One of Herbert's witty genre-inventions, depending on this very genre-constraint, was to assert that since God is everywhere, God could be present in the room even in the speaker's "solitariness" and could thus offer a reply, as God the Father does in "The Collar" and as Jesus does in "Dialogue.")

Shakespeare's speaker, alone with his thoughts, is the greatest achievement, imaginatively speaking, of the sequence. He is given "depth" of character in each individual sonnet by several compositional strategies on Shakespeare's part. These will be more fully described and demonstrated in the individual commentaries below, but in brief they are:

1. *Temporal.* The establishment of several retreating "panels" of time, representing episodes or epochs in the speaker's past, gives him a continuous, nontransient existence and a continuity of memory. (See, for example, sonnet 30, *When to the sessions of sweet silent thought.*)

2. *Emotional.* The reflection, within the same poem, of sharply conflicting moods with respect to the same topic (see, e.g., sonnet 148, *O me! what eyes hath love put in my head*). This can be abetted by contradictory or at least nonhomogeneous discourses rendering a topic complicated (see, e.g., sonnet 125, *Wer't aught to me I bore the canopy*). The volatility of moods in the speaker (symbolized by the famous *lark at break of day arising* of sonnet 29) suggests a flexibility—even an instability—of response verbally "guaranteeing" the presence of passion.

3. *Semantic.* The speaker's mind has a great number of compartments of discourse (theological, legal, alchemical, medicinal, political, aesthetic,

etc.). These compartments are semipervious to each other, and the osmosis between them is directed by an invisible discourse-master, who stands for the intellectual imagination.

4. *Conceptual.* The speaker resorts to many incompatible models of existence (described in detail in the commentary) even within the same poem; for example, sonnet 60 first describes life as a homogeneous steady-state succession of identical waves/minutes (a stoic model); then as a sharply delineated rise-and-eclipse of a sun (a tragic model); and next as a series of incessant violent extinctions (a brutal model). These models, unreconciled, convey a disturbing cognitive dissonance, one which is, in a philosophical sense, intolerable. The alert and observant mind that constructs these models asserts the "truth" of each for a particular occasion or aspect of life, but finds no "supramodel" under which they can be intelligibly grouped, and by which they can be intelligibly contained. In this way, the mind of the speaker is represented as one in the grip of philosophical conflict.

5. *Philosophical.* The speaker is a rebel against received ideas. He is well aware of the received topoi of his culture, but he subjects them to interrogation, as he counters neo-Platonic courtly love with Pauline marital love (116), or the Christian Trinity with the Platonic Triad (105), or analogizes sacred hermeneutics to literary tradition (106). No topics are more sharply scrutinized than those we now subsume under the phrase "gender relations": the speaker interrogates androgyny of appearance by evoking a comic myth of Nature's own dissatisfaction with her creation (20); he criticizes hyperbolic praise of female beauty in 130; he condones adultery throughout the "will" sonnets and elsewhere (and sees adultery as less criminal than adulterated discourse, e.g., in 152). This is not even to mention the interrogations of "love" and "lust" in 116 and 129 (sonnets of which the moral substance has not been properly understood because they have not been described in formal terms). No received idea of sexuality goes uninvestigated; and the thoroughly unconventional sexual attachments represented in both parts of the sequence stand as profound (if sometimes unwilling) critiques of the ideals of heterosexual desire, chastity, continence, marital fidelity, and respect for the character of one's sexual partner. What "ought to be" in the way of gender relations (by Christian and civic standards) is represented as an ideal in the "marriage sonnets" with which the sequence opens, but never takes on existential or "realist" lived validation. Shakespeare's awareness of norms is as complete as his depiction, in his speaker, of experiential violation of those norms.

6. *Perceptual.* The speaker is also given depth by the things he notices,

from damask roses to the odor of marjoram to a canopy of state. Though the sonnets are always openly drifting toward emblematic or allegorical language, they are plucked back (except in extreme cases like 66) into the perceptual, as their symbolic rose is distilled into "real" perfume (54) or as an emblematic April is *burned* by *hot* June (104). The speaker stands poised between a medieval emblematic tendency and a more modern empirical posture; within his moral and philosophical systems, he savors the tang of the "sensual feast."

7. *Dramatic.* The speaker indirectly quotes his antagonist. Though no one but the speaker "speaks" in a lyric, Shakespeare exploits the usefulness of having the speaker, in private, quote in indirect discourse something one or the other of the *dramatis personae* previously said. Many of the sonnets (e.g., 76 and 116) have been misunderstood because they have been thought to be free-standing statements on the speaker's part rather than replies to the antagonist's implicitly quoted words. Again, I support this statement below in detail; but one can see what a difference it makes to interpretation whether in sonnet 76 the poet-speaker means to criticize his own verse—"Why is my verse so barren of new pride?"—or whether he is repeating, by quoting, an anterior criticism by the young man: "Why [you ask] is my verse so [in your words] 'barren of new pride'?" In the (often bitter) give-and-take of prior-criticism-answered-by-the-speaker (in such rebuttal-sonnets as 105,117,151, and the previously mentioned 76 and 116), we come closest, in the sonnets, to Shakespeare the dramatist.

More could be said of the strategies that create a credible speaker with a complex and imaginative mind (a mind which we take on as our own when stepping into the voice); but I want to pass on to the greatest strength of the sonnets as "contraptions," their multiple armatures. Booth sees these "overlapping structures" as a principle of irresoluble indeterminacy; I, by contrast, see them as mutually reinforcing, and therefore as principles of authorial instruction.

Organizing Structures

When lyric poems are boring, it is frequently because they possess only one organizing structure, which reveals itself unchanged each time the poem is read. *If* the poet has decided to employ a single structure (in, say, a small two-part song such as "When daisies pied and violets blue"), then the poem needs some other principle of interest to sustain rereading (in that song, a copious set of aspects—vegetative, human, and avian—of the spring). Shakespeare abounds in such discourse-variety, and that in part sustains rereadings of the sonnets; but I have found that rereading is even better sustained by his wonderful fertility in structural complexity. The Shakespearean sonnet form, though not invented by Shakespeare, is manipulated by him in ways unknown to his predecessors. Because it has four parts—three isomorphic ones (the quatrains) and one anomalous one (the couplet), it is far more flexible than the two-part Italian sonnet. The four units of the Shakespearean sonnet can be set in any number of logical relations to one another:

successive and equal;
hierarchical;
contrastive;
analogous;
logically contradictory;
successively "louder" or "softer."

This list is merely suggestive, and by no means exhaustive. The four "pieces" of any given sonnet may also be distinguished from one another by changes of agency ("I do this; you do that"), of rhetorical address ("O Muse"; "O beloved"), of grammatical form (a set of nouns in one quatrain, a set of adjectives in another), or of discursive texture (as the descriptive changes to the philosophical), or of speech act (as denunciation changes to exhortation). Each of these has its own poetic import and effect. The four "pieces" of the sonnet may be distinguished, again, by different phonemic clusters or metrical effects. Booth rightly remarks on the presence of such patternings, but he refuses to establish hierarchy among them, or to subordinate minor ones to major ones, as I think one can often do.

I take it that a Shakespearean sonnet is fundamentally structured by an evolving inner emotional dynamic, as the fictive speaker is shown to "see more," "change his mind," "pass from description to analysis," "move from negative refutation to positive refutation," and so on. There can be a surprisingly large number of such "moves" in any one sonnet. The impression of an evolving dynamic within the speaker's mind and heart is of course created by a large "law of form" obeyed by the words in each sonnet. Other observable structural patterns play a subordinate role to this largest one. In its Shakespearean incarnation, the sonnet is a system in motion, never immobile for long, and with several subsystems going their way within the whole.

The chief defect in critical readings of the *Sonnets* has been the critics' propensity to take the first line of a sonnet as a "topic sentence" which the rest of the poem merely illustrates and reiterates (a model visible in Berowne's sonnet quoted above). Only in the plays does Shakespeare write nondramatic sonnets in this expository mode. In his lyrics, he sees structure itself as motion, as a composer of music would imagine it. Once the dynamic curve of a given sonnet is perceived, the lesser structuring principles "fall into place" beneath it. See, e.g., my commentary on 129 for a textbook example of a trajectory of changing feelings in the speaker about a single topic (lust); it is the patterns and underpatterns of the sonnet that enable us to see the way those feelings change. If the feeling were unchanging, the patterns would also remain invariable. The crucial rule of thumb in understanding any lyric is that every significant change of linguistic pattern represents a motivated change in feeling in the speaker. Or, to put it differently, if we sense a change of feeling in the speaker, we must look to see whether, and how, it is stylistically "guaranteed." Unless it is deflected by some new intensity, the poem continues by inertia in its original groove.

I deliberately do not dwell in this Commentary on Shakespeare's imagery as such, since it is a topic on which good criticism has long existed. Although large allegorical images *(beauty's rose)* are relatively stable in the *Sonnets,* imagery is meaningful only in context; it cannot be assigned secure symbolic import except with respect to the poem in which it occurs. The point, e.g., of the fire in sonnet 73 *(That time of year)* is that it is a stratified image: the glowing of the fire *lies upon* the ashes of youth. The previous images in the sonnet have been linear ones (*time of year* and *twilight*) referring to an extension in time (a year, a day), rather than superposition in space. By itself, the image "fire" does not call up the notion of stratification, nor does it in the other sonnets in which it appears; but in this poem, because of the poet's desire for variance from a previously established linear structure, the fire is called upon to play this spatial role, by which youth appears as exhausted subpositioned ashes rather than as an idyllic era *(the sweet birds; sunset)* lost at an earlier point in a timeline. Previous thematic commentators have often missed such contextual determination of imagistic meaning.

In trying to see the chief aesthetic "game" being played in each sonnet, I depart from the isolated registering of figures—a paradox here, an antimetabole there—to which the practice of word-by-word or phrase-by-phrase commentary inevitably leads. I wish to point out instead the larger imaginative or structural patterns in which such rhetorical figures take on functional (by contrast to purely decorative) significance. I do not intend, by this procedure, to minimize the sonnets' ornamental "excess" (so reprehensible to Pound); no art is more pointedly ornamental (see Puttenham) than the Renaissance lyric. Yet Shakespeare is happiest when an ornamental flourish can be seen to have a necessary poetic function. His changes in discursive texture, and his frequent consciousness of etymological roots as he plays on Anglo-Saxon and Latin versions of the "same" meaning ("with my *extern* the *outward* honoring"), all become more striking when incorporated into a general and dynamic theory of the poem. (Rather than invoke the terms of Renaissance rhetoric, which do not convey much to the modern reader, I use ordinary language to describe Shakespeare's rhetorical figuration.)

To give an illustration: I myself find no real functional significance in Shakespeare's alliteration when the speaker says that in *the* ***sw****art com****pl****ex-ioned night, /* ***W****hen* ***sp****arkling* ***st****ars* ***tw****ire not, thou [the young man] gild****st*** *the even.* Such phonetic effects seem to have a purely decorative intent. But an alliterative "meaning-string"—such as sonnet 25's *favour*, *fortune*, *trium****ph***, *favourites*, *fair*, *frown*, *painful*, *famousèd*, *fight (an emendation)*, *foiled*, and *forgot*—encapsulates the argument of the poem in little, and helps to create and sustain that argument as it unfolds. Grammar and syntax, too, can be functionally significant to argument; see, for instance, the way in which 66 uses phrases of agency, or the way in which 129 uses its many verbals. In his edition of the *Sonnets*, Booth leaves it up to the reader to construct the poem; I have hoped to help the reader actively to that construction by laying out evidence that no interpretation can afford to ignore. Any number of interpretations, guided by any number of interests, can be built on the same foundation of evidence; but an interpretation ignoring that evidence can never be a defensible one.

I believe that anyone seriously contemplating the interior structures and interrelations of these sonnets is bound to conclude that many were composed in the order in which they are arranged. However, given the poems' variation in aesthetic success, it seems probable that some sonnets—perhaps written in youth (as Andrew Gurr suggested of the tetrameter sonnet 145, with its pun on "Hathaway") or composed before the occurrence of the triangular plot—were inserted *ad libitum* for publication. (I am inclined to believe Katherine Duncan-Jones's argument that the *Sonnets* may have been an authorized printing.) The more trifling sonnets—those that place ornament above imaginative gesture, or fancifulness above depth (such as 4, 6, 7, 9, 145, 153, and 154)—do seem to be less experienced trial-pieces. The greater sonnets achieve an effortless combination of imaginative reach with high technical invention (18, 73, 124, 138), or a quintessence of grace (104, 106, 132), or a power of dramatic condensation (121, 147) that we have come to call "Shakespearean," even if, as Kent Hieatt (1991) has persuasively shown, they were composed in groups over time.

The speaker of Shakespeare's sonnets scorns the consolations of Christianity—an afterlife in heaven for himself, a Christian resurrection of his body after death—as fully as he refuses (except in a few sonnets) the learned adornment of classical references—a staple of the continental sonnet. The sonnets stand as the record of a mind working out positions without the help of any pantheon or any systematic doctrine. Shakespeare's speaker often considers, in rapid succession, any number of intellectual or ideological positions, but he does not move among them at random. To the contrary: in the first quatrain of any given sonnet he has a wide epistemological field in which to play, but in the second quatrain he generally queries or contradicts or subverts his first position (together with its discourse-field). By the third quatrain, he must (usually) advance to his subtlest or most comprehensive or most truthful position (Q_3 therefore taking on, in the Shakespearean sonnet, the role of the sestet in the Petrarchan sonnet). And the couplet—placed not as resolution (which is the function of Q_3) but as coda—can then stand in any number of relations (summarizing, ironic, expansive) to the preceding argument. The gradually straitened possibilities as the speaker advances in his considerations give the Shakespearean sonnet a funnel-shape, narrowing in Q_3 to a vortex of condensed perceptual and intellectual force, and either constricting or expanding that vortex via the couplet.

The Couplet

The Shakespearean couplet has often been a stumbling block to readers. Rosalie Colie's helpful distinction (in *Shakespeare's Living Art*) between the *mel* (honey) of love-poetry and the *sal* (salt) of epigram—a genre conventionally used for satiric purposes—represents a real insight into the mind of Shakespeare's speaker: the speaker is a person who wishes to analyze and summarize his experience as well as to describe and enact it. The distance from one's own experience necessitated by an analytic stance is symbolized most fully by the couplet, whereas the empathetic perception necessary to display one's state of mind is symbolized by the quatrains. In speaking about the relation of quatrain to couplet, one must distinguish the fictive speaker (even when he represents himself as a poet) from Shakespeare the author. The fictive speaker gradually becomes, over the course of the poem, more analytic about his situation (and therefore more distanced from his first self-pathos) until he finally reaches the couplet, in which he often expresses a self-ironizing turn:

> For thee watch I, whilst thou dost wake elsewhere,
> From me far off, with others all too near.
>
> (sonnet 61)

This we can genuinely call intrapsychic irony in the fictive speaker. But the author, who is arranging the whole poem, has from the moment of conception a relation of irony to his fictive persona. The persona lives in the "real time" of the poem, in which he feels, thinks, and changes his mind; the author has planned the whole evolution of the poem before writing the first line, and "knows" conceptually the gyrations which he plans to represent taking place over time in his fictive speaker. There is thus a perpetual ironizing of the living temporality of the speaker by the coordinating spatial overview of the author. Although the speaker seems "spontaneous" in his utterance, the cunning arrangements of the utterance belong primarily to Shakespeare (even if dramatically ascribed to the speaker). It is at the moment of the couplet that the view of the speaker and the view of the author come nearest to convergence.

One of Shakespeare's strategies for the couplet which has disappointed some readers is the turn of the speaker to the *consensus gentium*, either via a known proverb or via a discourse which resembles the characteristic idiom of proverb:

> For sweetest things turn sourest by their deeds;
> Lilies that fester smell far worse than weeds.
>
> (sonnet 94)

Such a turn toward the proverbial always represents the speaker's despair at solving by himself, in personally formulated language, the conundrum presented by the sonnet. "*I* don't know; what does the common wisdom say about this situation?" Unless one senses the reason for the speaker's turn to the proverbial, and of course "hears" the proverbial tone lurking "under" the "personal" language of the speaker, one is at a loss to know how to utter the couplet. It should be uttered with implied quotation marks around each of its proverbial sayings:

> For [as everyone says] "Sweetest things turn sourest by their deeds";
> [And it is also said] "Lilies that fester smell far worse than weeds."

The "meaning" carried by such a turn to the *consensus gentium* is that the speaker has run out, absolutely, of things to say from his own heart. He has to turn to old saws to console himself in his rejection, and to warn the young man that no good can come of his infidelities.

It might be thought that the couplet is the likeliest place for proverbial expression. Yet, knowing that the proverbial implies that the speaker "gives up" on the conundrum as insoluble, we are glad to see the displacement upward of proverbial closure into the body of the poem. I insert the mental quotation marks and emphasis implied by the following displaced-upward "closures":

> [Everyone knows that] "It is a greater grief
> To bear love's wrong than hate's known injury."
>
> (sonnet 40)

> No marvel then that *I* mistake *my* view,
> "The sun itself sees not till heaven clears."
>
> (sonnet 148)

When proverbial matter—implying a desire for unquestionable closure—is displaced upward into Q_3, it makes room for a new departure in the couplet, such as the fresh sensual address in sonnet 40 (*Lascivious grace*, etc.). Or, as in 148, the upward displacement of the proverbial idiom into lines 11–12 can enable a change of reference from third-person *love* (meaning successively "Cupid" or "the experience of love" or "emblematic Love") to a more mordantly "aware" second-person use of *love* in the couplet to mean the dark lady (a meaning certified by the obscenely punning adjective "cunning"):

> O me! what eyes hath *love* put in my head
> . . . . .
> *love* doth well denote
> *Love's eye* is not so true as all men's: no,
> . . . . .
> No marvel then though I mistake my view;
> The sun itself sees not till heaven clears.
> O *cunning love*, with tears thou keep'st me blind,
> Lest eyes well seeing thy foul faults should find.

A reader alert to the way that boilerplate idiom, when it is found in the couplet (*as black as hell, as dark as night*, sonnet 147), carries the speaker's despair of a solution, and who sees how in other sonnets the speaker finds a "way out" by displacing despair from the couplet to a few lines above (thereby providing room in the couplet for a fresh view), will not find couplets of either sort uninteresting.

Readers intent only on the propositional statement made by the couplet have often found it redundant. When one looks at what a given couplet permits by way of functional agency, one sees more. A telling comment on the couplet was made by Jan Kott in his introduction to Jerzy Sito's edition of the *Sonnets:* "The closing couplet of each sonnet is addressed directly to the protagonist [by himself]. It is almost spoken. It is an actor's line." While this is not true of the couplets in all the sonnets, Kott's remark shows us a critic perceiving a crucial *tonal* difference between the body of the sonnet and the couplet, even if what they "say" is "the same." A theory of interpretation that is interested only in the paraphrasable "meaning" of a poem tends to find Shakespeare's couplets uninteresting; but such a theory merely betrays its own inadequacy. It is more productive to look for what Shakespeare might have had in mind to make his couplets "work" than to assume that, because they "restate" semantically the body of the sonnet, they are superfluous. Poetically speaking, Shakespeare was not given to idle superfluity. In the Commentary following, I have pointed out, for each sonnet, the significant words from the body of the poem that are repeated in the couplet, calling the aggregate of such words the Couplet Tie. These words are usually thematically central, and to see Shakespeare's careful reiteration of them is to be directed in one's interpretation by them. There are very few sonnets that do not exhibit such a Couplet Tie. Shakespeare clearly depended on this device not only to point up the thematic intensities of a sonnet, but also to show how the same words take on different emotional import as the poem progresses.

Reading the Sonnets

Shakespeare encourages alertness in his reader. Because he is especially occupied with literary consolidation (resuming the topics, the images, the consecrated adjectives, and the repertoire of tones of previous sonneteers), one can miss his subversive moves: the "shocking" elements of the sonnets in both subsequences; the parodies, by indirect quotation, of Petrarchan praise in sonnets 21 and 130 (though the latter has been sometimes read as denigration of the mistress, it is no such thing); the satire on learned language (78, 85); on sycophantic poets (79) and newfangled poets (76); the revisionism with respect to Christian views of lust (129) and continence (94) and with respect to Petrarchan views of love (116); the querying of eternizing boasts (122), of the Platonic conventions (95), of dramatic plot (144), of enumerative praise (84), of "idolatry" (105), of the Lord's Prayer (108) and of love-pursuit (143). That is, readers of the sonnets find themselves encountering—and voicing—both the most conventional images *(rose, time, fair, stars, love)* and the most unsettling statements. Many quatrains, taken singly, could well be called conventional, and paraphrases of them by critics make them sound stultifying. What is *not* conventional is the sonnet's (invisibly predicated) set of relations—of the quatrains to one another and to the couplet; of the words and images to one another; of the individual grammatical and syntactic units to one another. Even though the appearance of logic is often smoothly maintained by a string of logical connectives *(When . . . When . . . Then)*, some disruptive or contradictory force will enter the poem to pull one quatrain in two directions at once—toward its antecedent quatrain by one set of words, toward its consequent by another; toward the couplet by its temporality; toward a preceding quatrain by its spatiality. Since quatrains often participate in several patterns simultaneously, their true "meaning" is chartable only by charting their pattern-sets.

Though antithesis is Shakespeare's major figure for constructing the world in the sonnets, it is safe to say that the ever antithetically minded Shakespeare permitted his antitheses to breed and bring to birth a third thing (see sonnet 66). His second preferred figure, chiasmus, contends in the sonnets against the "natural" formulation of a sentence (linear, temporal, ongoing). Chiasmus refuses to let a phrase or a sentence dilate "naturally": instead, it makes the syntax round on itself. Not "Least contented with what I most enjoy" (the linear or parallel formation), but rather *With what I most enjoy contented least* (the chiastic formulation). The chiastic formulation always implies an analytic moment in the speaker. "Spontaneous" moments say things "naturally"; but when the speaker has had time to think things out and judge them, he speaks chiastically. *Consumed with that which it was nourished by*—where *consumed* and *nourished* bracket *that* and *which*—is a formulation that simply could not occur in Q_1 or Q_2 of 73. The first two quatrains of that sonnet are the epitome of linearity, as phrase follows phrase in a "natural" imitation of life's gradual leakage:

> In me thou seest the twilight of such day
> As after sunset fadeth in the west,

Which by and by black night doth take away,
Death's second self that seals up all in rest.

On this narrative of pathos, there supervenes the superb analytic moment of Q_3: the stratified fire does not fade, it glows; and the analytic law of consumption and nourishment refuses a linear statement of itself: "As the fire was nourished by heat, so it is consumed by heat". Between the glowing fire and the physical law, however, there is one line of linear "leakage": *As the death-bed whereon it must expire.* If that were the last line of the poem, the speaker's stoic resolve could be said to have left him, and he would have submitted to a "natural" dying fall. But he pulls himself up from that moment of expiring linearity into his great chiastic law, that we die from the very same vital heat which has nourished us in life. It is (as this example shows) always worth noting whether a Shakespearean statement is being made "linearly," in a first-order experiential and "spontaneous" way, or whether it is being made chiastically, in a second-order analytic way. These represent very different stances within the speaker.

Strategies of Unfolding

One of the strategies making many sonnets odd is that the utterances of the speaker are being generated by invisible strings "behind" the poem—the concurrent deducible actions or remarks of an implied other. Such poems are like the rebuttal sonnets mentioned earlier, except that the invisible prompt is not an earlier speech-act by another but rather a series of actions or speech-acts which are, imaginatively speaking, *in process while* the sonnet is being uttered. (See my comments on 34, which explain why the changes of metaphor in the poem—storm, rain, slave, physic, cross, pearl, ransom—are not inexplicable or unintelligible.) And then there are the "shadow-poems" (as I think of them), where one can deduce, from the speaker's actual statements, what he would really like to say to the young man (in the case of the "slavery" sonnet, 57) or to the mistress (in, say, 138) if he could speak clearly.

Yet another recurrent strategy for Shakespeare is to "mix up" the order of narration so that it departs from the normal way in which such an event would be unfolded. It would be "normal" to say, "He abandoned me; and what did that feel like? It felt like seeing the sun go behind a cloud." In "normal" narration, the literal event is recounted first, and then a metaphor is sought to explain what the narrator felt like. But in sonnet 33 *(Full many a glorious morning have I seen)*, the metaphor—not perceived as such because not introduced by "Just as"—precedes the literal event. After seeing the sunny landscape clouded, and thinking we have been admitted to the literal level of the poem, we hear *Even so my sun one early morn did shine.* In order to understand such a poem, we must ask why the poet has rearranged the normal order of narration. In 97, for example, it would be "normal" to state literal perception first, and let an emotional contradiction follow—to say, "It was summertime, *and yet* it seemed like winter to me with you away." Instead, the poet puts the speaker's emotional perception ahead of his sense-perception: "How like a winter hath my absence been / From thee. . . ! / *And yet* this time removed was summer's time." Similarly, the very peculiar order of narration in 62 *(Sin of self-love)* has to be both noticed and interpreted.

I want to say a word here about Shakespeare's fancifulness. It ought not surprise us that the author of *A Midsummer Night's Dream* might also be fanciful in his poems. Modern readers have shown little admiration for the sonnets that play with the convention of the contest between eye and heart (such as 46 or 47) or the sonnet about flowers stealing their odor and hue from the young man (99, *The forward violet*), or the sonnets of elaborate wordplay (43, *When most I wink*), or the more whimsical complimentary sonnets, such as 78 *(So oft have I invoked thee).* Such sonnets may be fanciful, but they are not frivolous, as I hope to have shown in the Commentary. Read from the right angle, so to speak, they can be very beautiful, or at least delightful; and in them, as elsewhere, Shakespeare is inventing some game or other and playing it out to its conclusion in deft and surprising ways.

Shakespeare the Writer

The purpose of my Commentary is to point out strategies of the sort I have been enumerating—strategies that make the speaker credible, that generate an evolutionary dynamic, that suggest interaction among the linguistic ingredients of the lines, that "use" the couplet, that beguile by fancifulness, and so on. There are hundreds of such strategies in the sonnets, since Shakespeare rarely amuses himself the same way twice. He is a poet acutely conscious of grammatical and syntactic possibility as one of the ingredients in "invention," and he routinely, but not idly, varies tense, mood, subject-position, and clause-patterns in order to make conceptual or rhetorical points. These *differentia* contribute to our sense that his mind was discriminating as well as copious. His inventories are sometimes exhaustive (as he reels off the forms of prognostication in sonnet 14, or the forms of social trespass by *lust till action* in 129) but at other times rigidly repetitive (as in the implication, by the almost invariant organization of 66, that the anatomy of evil is less complex than the world would like to believe). In any given case of enumeration in the *Sonnets*, an implicit table of organization is constructed, frequently through the "places" of logic ("who," "where," "when," "in what manner," "by what means," "with what aid," etc.). Items may then be further accumulated, contrasted, subtracted, and so forth, either from this table of organization or from another organizational grid superimposed on it as a corrective (as love and its obligations are superimposed on the masque of social evil in 66). A formidable intellectual command of phenomena (both physical and moral), of means (both human and cosmic), of categories (both quotidian and philosophical), and of discourses (both learned and popular) lies behind the *Sonnets* in the person of their invisible author. It is this intellectual command which accounts for the *Sonnets*' serene and unfaltering air of poetic resource, even (or perhaps especially) in the moments of the speaker's greatest psychological distraction. Though I cannot hope to have caught all of Shakespeare's strategies, or to have understood them all properly, or to have assigned them their proper weight with respect to one another, I do hope that I will have shown Shakespeare as a poet constantly inventing new permutations of internal form, designed to match what he was recording—the permutations of emotional response.

Sometimes I have not been sure of the "game" of a given sonnet, but I am happy to ask others to try their wits after me. There is always something cryptographic in Shakespeare's sonnet-surfaces—sometimes literally so, as in the anagrams of 7, or as in the play on *vile* and *evil* in 121, but more often merely an oddness that catches the eye and begs explanation. The obviousness of the *Sonnets*' "content"—love, jealousy, time's depredations—simply leaves readers obscurely conscious that their reactions to these poems exceed the rather commonplace matter they have understood. Poetry is not generally in the matter of its utterance philosophical; but it is philosophical insofar as its dynamic (when well constructed) represents in abstract or "geometric" form one or several of the infinite curves of human response. Shakespeare's *Sonnets* are philosophical insofar as they display interrelationships among their parts which, as they unfold, trace a conflict in human cognitive and affective motions. The surface of any poem is what John Ashbery calls its "visible core" ("Self-Portrait in a Convex Mirror"), and I have tried, by examining the surfaces of these poems as a writer would see and interpret them, to make the core visible. And though my main concern has been to show the unifying forces in each sonnet, the whole sequence displays, when taken as a single object, dispersive gaps and uncertainties between its individual units. It is on just such large uncertainties that the smaller certainties of single sonnets float and collide.

Shakespeare the Poet

What sort of poet is Shakespeare, as we meet him at work composing sonnets? The answer generated by each sonnet, or even by each part of a sonnet, is a particular one. Consider for a moment sonnet 54:

O how much more doth beauty beauteous seem
By that sweet ornament which truth doth give!
The rose looks fair, but fairer we it deem
For that sweet odour which doth in it live.
The canker blooms have full as deep a dye
As the perfumèd tincture of the roses,
Hang on such thorns, and play as wantonly,
When summer's breath their maskèd buds discloses;
But for their virtue only is their show,
They live unwooed, and unrespected fade,
Die to themselves. Sweet roses do not so,
Of their sweet deaths are sweetest odours made:
  And so of you, beauteous and lovely youth,
  When that shall vade, my verse distils your truth.

"What sort of poet?" "A poet of deep sensuous relish," one might say after reading the second quatrain of 54, with its play of deep-dyed maskèd rosebuds. Yet, reading the first two lines of the same sonnet, one might have said that the author was a metaphysical homilist, discoursing on truth and beauty. And, reading the couplet of the same poem (as generally emended), we might simply say: "This is a love-poet." Looking to the third quatrain, seeing the roses used as figures of human vice and virtue, we might see the author as a writer of ethical emblems, contrasting inner virtue to outward show. And yet each of these descriptions is inadequate. A poet of pure sensuous relish would not have needed to insert the moral pointer of *wanton play* into his descriptive attention to the roses. A metaphysical homilist would not have referred to truth as an *ornament* to beauty. A love-poet does not, unless he is also a poet of moral emphasis, give death-warnings to his beloved. An emblematic poet usually cancels from the interpretation of his emblem the lingering sensual overtones which Shakespeare retains in the word *unwooed* and the repetition *sweet . . . sweet . . . sweetest.* What is always unsettling in Shakespeare is the way that he places only a very permeable osmotic membrane between the compartments holding his separate languages—pictorial description, philosophical analysis, emblematic application, erotic pleading—and lets words "leak " from one compartment to the other in each direction. Rather than creating "full-fledged" metaphor, this practice creates a constant fluidity of reference, which produces not so much the standard disruptive effect of catachresis ("mixed metaphor") as an almost unnoticed rejuvenation of diction at each moment. The most famous example of this unexampled fluidity arrives in sonnet 60:

> Nativity, once in the main of light,
> Crawls to maturity, wherewith being crowned,
> Crookèd eclipses 'gainst his glory fight.

This passage, in which Shakespeare allows free passage of language from compartment to compartment, behaves as though the discourses of astrology, seamanship, astronomy, child development, political theory, deformity, religion, and warfare were (or could be) one. Such freedom of lexical range suggests forcefully an *ur*-language (occurring in time after the Kristevan *chora* but before even the imaginary in the Lacanian order of things) in which these discourses *were* all one, before what Blake would call their fall into division. As Shakespeare performs their resurrection into unity, we recognize most fully that this heady mix of discourses *is* (as with the peculiar interfusion of spaniels and candy once noticed by Caroline Spurgeon) Shakespeare's "native language" when his powers of expression are most on their mettle.

And yet there is no "ambiguity" in this passage. A lesser poet would have clung to one or two chief discourses: "Man, once born onto the earth, crawls to maturity, but at that very moment falls, finding his strength failing him"; or "Our sun, once in its dawn of light, ascends to its zenith, whereupon crooked eclipses obscure it." The inertial tendency of language to remain within the discourse-category into which it has first launched itself seems grandly abrogated by Shakespeare. Yet we know he was aware of that inertial tendency because he exploited it magisterially; every time a discourse shifts, it is (he lets us know) because the mind has shifted its angle of vision. Unpacked, the three lines above from sonnet 60 show us that the speaker first thinks of a child's horoscope, cast at birth; then he thinks of dawn as an image for the beginning of human life, because the life-span seems but a day; then he reverts to the biological reality of the crawling infant; then he likens the human being to a king (a dauphin perhaps in adolescence, but crowned when he reaches maturity); then (knowing the necessity of human fate) he leaves the image of a king behind (since the uncrowning of a king is contingent—on, say, a revolution—but death is a necessary event) and returns to the natural world. We assume the speaker will predict, as his emblem of necessity (as he does in 73), the darkness of night overtaking the sun that rose at dawn; but instead, feeling the "wrongness" of death's striking down a human being just at maturity, the poet shows nature in its "wicked" guise, as the eclipse "wrongfully" obscuring the sun in the "glory" of his noon. Yet, remembering how death is not without struggle, the speaker shows the man being "fought against," not simply blotted out, by the dark. If we do not see each of these shifts in discourse as evidence of a change of mental direction by the speaker, and seek the motivation for each change of direction, we will not participate in the activity of the poem as its surface instructs us to do.

In conceptual matters, Shakespeare displays an exceptionally firm sense of categories (logical, philosophical, religious), together with a willingness to let them succeed each other in total aspectual contradiction. Within the process of invention itself, as I have said above, his mind operates always by antithesis. As soon as he thinks one thing, he thinks of something that is different from it (though perhaps assimilable to it under a larger rubric). If one believes, as I do, that in many of the sonnets successive quatrains "correct" each other, and that in the "philosophical" sonnets Q_3 generally offers an ampler, subtler, or truer view of the problem than those voiced in Q_1 or Q_2, then it is true to say that these aspectual contradictions—like those offered by 60 as it presents models of life that are successively stoic, tragic, and brutal—are ranked hierarchically and climactically with respect to their "truth-value." The stratified erotic fire in Q_3 of sonnet 73 *(That time of year)* is therefore a "truer" picture of human life *(Consumed with that which it was nourished by)* than the earlier "pathetic" autumnal tree or the subsequent "rest-awaiting" twilight. And yet Q_1 and Q_2 are not repudiated as *un*true: in 73, the whole question of how we picture our life has been thrice answered (once physically, once emblematically, and once philosophically). If the third formulation is better than the others, because intellectually more comprehensive (no villain robs us of life, we die of having lived, and our *calor vitae*, even in old age, makes us "glowing" rather than "ruined" or "fading"), it does not invalidate the psychological "truth" of the two earlier models. The proffering and hierarchizing of several conceptual models at once is, as I see it, Shakespeare's main intellectual and poetic achievement in the *Sonnets.*

Yet conceptual models, though necessary for the architectonics of poems, do not guarantee poetic interest. Although the conceptual models ("conceits") govern the working-out of compositional order, they do not repress other poetic energies, but rather act to stimulate them. As Keats put it (in a letter to J. H. Reynolds of November 22, 1817): "I neer found so many beauties in the sonnets—they seem to be full of fine things said unintentionally—in the intensity of working out conceits." The passage that drew this comment from Keats (Q_2 of sonnet 12) struck him so powerfully, we may suppose, because its theme—one that never failed to move him—was the consuming of beautiful and benevolent nature by death ("Is this to be borne?" Keats wrote in the margin; "Hark ye!"):

> When lofty trees I see barren of leaves,
> Which erst from heat did canopy the herd,
> And summer's green all girded up in sheaves
> Borne on the bier with white and bristly beard . . .

Even transfixed as he was by Shakespeare's theme of autumnal mortality, what Keats comments on is the "fine things" said (as if unintentionally) as the conception is worked out. Here, Shakespeare's metaphorical "leakages" occur in the words *barren, canopy, green, girded up, bier,* and *beard,* which "replace," with anthropomorphic emphasis, plausible words either more literal or more abstractly all-embracing, such as *shed, shade, corn, gathered into, wagon,* and *awn.* Here (with apologies) is a "literal" version of the quatrain:

> When lofty trees I see have shed the leaves
> Which erst from sultry heat did shade the fawn,
> And summer's corn all gathered into sheaves,
> Borne on the wain with white and bristly awn . . .

One can see the lessening of pathos in such a formulation.

But it was not merely the anthropomorphic reference in the metaphorical leakages that so affected Keats. I believe he was also moved by the apparently gratuitous insertion of *herd* (perhaps conceived "in the intensity of working out" the rhyme for *beard,* a word necessary to the bier-deathbed scene underlying the close of the quatrain). The trees at the opening of the quatrain are not only beautiful in their foliage, they are also virtuous (if unconsciously so) in the benefit they confer on the herd by their *canopy* (the Shakespeare Concordance shows that Shakespeare uses *herd* to mean *flock* rather than *shepherd*). That Shakespeare had the virtue as well as the beauty of the trees in mind is proved by the summary in line 11, "*sweets* and beauties do themselves forsake," in which the only conceptual antecedent in the sonnet for *sweets* is the charitable trees. In the sonnets, while *beauty* is used of appearance, *sweet* is used of substance and virtue. To Keats, the fact that Shakespeare wanted his trees kind as well as beautiful answered to his deepest wish that his "Presider" (as he called Shakespeare) be as exemplary in breadth of vision as in talent of execution.

The complex effect of this single quatrain, as it evoked Keats's comment on Shakespeare's procedures in writing, suggests that many, if not all, of the sonnets deserve close and writerly scrutiny, more than I can give in my much-reduced comments below. I regret not being able to write at more length about the successive emotional tonalities of the *Sonnets*, from abjectness to solitary triumph, from perplexity to self-loathing, from comedy to pathos—but tribute to their tonal variety has been a staple of criticism, and is not likely to go unobserved by any reader.

Of course this Commentary is not intended to be read straight through. I think of it as a work that those interested in the *Sonnets*, or students of the lyric, or poets hungry for resource, may want to browse in. The elation of seeing what Shakespeare is up to is, I hope, a contagious feeling. I have included a recording of some of the *Sonnets* read aloud because the three readings available on tape are done by actors who, so far as I can judge, did not invest much time in studying the texts, and who therefore speak the lines with constant mis-emphases, destroying the meaning of many of the sonnets by not observing inner antitheses and parallels. Though I am acutely conscious that for both textual and acoustic reasons the ideal reading of the sonnets would be done by a male voice, in another sense a helpful reading-aloud can be done by one who sees the *allure de la phrase* in each poem, and has thought about how the poem develops intellectually and tonally. With the aim of being useful to a reader who wants (reasonably enough) to hear the sonnets as well as to read them and think about them, I have recorded a selection of the *Sonnets* as best I could. I did not want to deprive Shakespeare of his full voice, one still alive throughout the world after almost four centuries.

Notes

1. The most recent book considering them in some detail—Christopher Martin's *Policy in Love: Lyric and Public in Ovid, Petrarch and Shakespeare* (Pittsburgh: Duquesne University Press, 1994)—may serve to prove my assertion. Here are some quotations:

On the initial seventeen sonnets: "[The poet's] rigid alignment with a legitimizing community exhausts the technical resources of his discourse as it exposes the emotional sterility of the conventions in which he invests" [134–135].

"While the procreation subsequence's tight focus insures coherence, it simultaneously threatens a monotony that has also taken its toll on the poetry's modern audience. Even Wordsworth . . . was put off by a general 'sameness,' a feature most damagingly concentrated in this introductory series" [145].

"Lars Engle is right to suggest that the initial quatrain:

> [From fairest creatures we desire increase,
> That thereby beauty's rose might never die,
> But as the riper should by time decease
> His tender heir might bear his memory . . .]

'might be the voice-over of a Sierra Club film in which California condors soar over their eggless nest'" [148].

"The poet betrays himself [in the early sonnets] as one uneager to focus on human beings in any precise manner, much less upon the potentially messy emotions which join them to one another. . . . Questions of detail make him nervous, and he would just as soon stick to the homey blur of abstracted tradition" [148].

"On sonnets 124 ("If my dear love were but the child of state") and 125 ("Were't aught to me I bore the canopy"): "Posing as sonnets about discovery and liberation, these poems are overtaken by a spirit of persecution and resentment. . . . He resorts to a fantasy isolation . . . He lapses, moreover, by the final couplet's arch renunciation ["Hence, thou suborned informer! A true soul / When most impeached stands least in thy control"], from anxious vigilance to paranoia" [175].

2. Because of Shakespeare's subversion of any discourse he adapts, it seems to me inadequate to suggest, as John Barrell does, that sonnet 29 ("When in disgrace with fortune and men's eyes") "may be actively concealing . . . a meaning that runs like this: 'when I'm pushed for money, with all the degradation that poverty involves, I sometimes remember you, and you're always good for a couple of quid'" [30]. Barrell prefers to conceive of Shakespeare as attempting the language of transcendent love, but unable to achieve it, "because the historical moment he seeks to transcend is represented by a discourse [of patronage] whose nature and function is to contaminate the very language by which that assertion of transcendence must try to find expression. For me, the pathos of the poem—I can repeat here my earlier point—is that the narrator can find no words to assert the transcendent power of true love, which cannot be interpreted as making a request for a couple of quid" [42].

A poet is not quite so helpless before his discourses as Barrell believes. In the first place, the very playfulness of the poem (see my comments below on the chiasmus "most enjoy contented least" and the puns on "state") prevents its being an actual speech-act of either "transcendent love" or "a request for a couple of quid." The sonnet, taken entire, is a fictional speech-act, of which the intent is to mimic the motions of the mind when it rises from low to high. In mimicking, in the octave, the movement of the mind in agitated depression and, in the sestet, the movement of the mind in relieved elation, the sonnet is fulfilling its purpose as a lyric. Shakespeare's skill in such psychological mimicry ensures the continuing power of the poem. A poet (as the contrast between octave and sestet shows) is the master of his discourses, not (as in Barrell's scenario) their helpless performer.

3. According to Fineman's theory, the object of desire as mirror image cannot generate dramatic conflict, and so the poetry of the speaker's same-sex object-relation remains mired in narcissism; but when the object of desire changes gender, and is no longer worshipfully desired but rather is abhorred, a fruitful dissonance arises that generates a new subjectivity. Fineman's more extravagant claims for the historical newness of the subject-position in the Dark Lady sequence have generally not been adopted; but his psychoanalytic criterion of value for poetry—that "difference" is better than "sameness"—has apparently gone unquestioned. It is naturally typical of Shakespeareans to prefer drama to lyric: after all, they became Shakespeareans because they were drawn to drama. And Fineman's book on the *Sonnets* was not fundamentally concerned with lyric, any more than his essay on *The Rape of Lucrece* was about complaint; both were prefatory, in their concern with character and will, to the book on Shakespeare's plays he did not live, alas, to write.

4. One editor of the *Sonnets*, John Kerrigan, betrays his restricted criterion of lyric value—chiefly, that metaphor is necessary for a good poem—as he writes of sonnet 105 that it is "scrupulously and Shakespearianly dull, but it is dull nonetheless. . . . The text is stripped of metaphor. . . . The result is a poem which, for all its charm [unspecified by Kerrigan] (and integrity), lacks the compelling excitement of a metaphoric sonnet such as 60, 'Like as the waves make toward the pebbled shore.' In so far as Shakespeare exceeds the Erasmian *copia*, shunning 'variation' for the sake of tautologous recurrence, his verse palls" [29]. See my commentary on sonnet 105 for a demonstration of how interesting the poem becomes once one admits criteria for lyric excellence besides the presence or absence of metaphor (though 105 is also one continued metaphor comparing erotic worship to Christian worship, and blasphemously equating them).

To take another instance of Kerrigan's misreading (springing from his lack of interest in linguistic variation), I cite his description of sonnet 129 ("Th'expense of spirit in a waste of shame"). He, like other critics preceding him, takes a single-minded expository view of the poem, as though it were a self-consistent sermon: "While 116 deals with Love complexly, however, questioning the absolute which it erects, 129 describes and enacts with single-minded, though cynically quibbling, forcefulness the distemperature of phallocentric lust. Fitful and fretting, such a passion squanders the moral powers along with the semen, committing both to a 'waste of shame' and 'shameful waist.' . . . It goads men towards satisfaction, yet, once sated in the irrational frenzy of orgasm, it is queasy, woeful, and full of remorse. . . . Lust is fixated by the moment: yearning towards emission, it lies sullied and futile in its wake, sourly foretasting hell, with nothing to hope for but further 'pursuit.' Its imaginative field is vorticose, centripetal, obsessive" [56]. Such a passage allows for no change of mind in the course of the poem—but if there is one thing the poem *does* mimic, it is successive changes of mind in the cycle of desire, changes of mind impossible in a homiletic diatribe such as Kerrigan represents the sonnet to be (see my comments on 129).

5. Every writer on the *Sonnets* owes gratitude to Stephen Booth's giant edition, which spells out in more detail the principles guiding his critical book on the *Sonnets.* Yet in stressing the richness of implication of Shakespeare's language over the firmness of implied authorial instruction, Booth gives up on the possibility of reliable internal guides for interpretation. Of course every interpretive act brings special interests to the poem, so that a psychoanalytic interpretation foregrounds aspects that a historical interpretation may overlook. But any respectable account of a poem ought to have considered closely its chief formal features. A set of remarks on a poem which would be equally true of a prose paraphrase of that poem is not, by my standards, interpretation at all. Commentary on the propositional content of the poem is something entirely different from the interpretation of a poem, which must take into account the poem's linguistic strategies as well as its propositional statements.

The extent of authorial instruction retrievable from a text is also disputed. Yet authorial instruction is embedded, for instance, in the mere fact that one metaphor follows another. Sonnet 73 would have to be interpreted differently if we were given the twilight in quatrain 1, the fire in quatrain 2, and the autumn in quatrain 3. Shakespeare's arrangement of his metaphors is both cognitively and morally meaningful; quatrains cannot be reordered at will. Authorial instruction is also embedded in smaller units of every sonnet. To give one instance, it can be found in the parallels drawn between one part of the poem and another. The grammatical parallel linking the four "moral nouns"—*expense, spirit, waste,* and *shame*—that open sonnet 129 to the four "emotional" nouns—*bliss, woe, joy,* and *dream*—replacing them in its sestet is an "authorial instruction" telling us to notice the contrast between the two sets, and to infer a change of mind in the speaker who is uttering them about one and the same experience.

Any account of a poem ought to contemplate such implicit authorial instructions. Booth gives up too easily on interpretation. Even in the richness of Shakespeare's language, we are not left afloat on an uninterpretable set of "ideational static," not when the formal features of the *Sonnets* are there to guide us. It was her awareness of those formal features that made the late Winifred Nowottny the best guide to the sequence; it is a matter of deep regret to me that she did not complete the Arden edition which she had undertaken, and left only a few brilliant essays as tokens of that effort. It is equally a matter for rejoicing that the new Arden *Sonnets* will soon appear, edited by Katherine Duncan-Jones.

6. The tale of Pound, Bunting, and Shakespeare's *Sonnets* is contained in Mas-

simo Bacigalupo's *Pound in Rapallo*. Bunting's reductions are quoted from a xerox of his copy of Shakespeare's *Sonnets*, kindly sent to me by Professor Bacigalupo of the University of Genoa.

7. The best account of Shakespeare's metrical practice is to be found in George T. Wright, *Shakespeare's Metrical Art*, 75–90; but see my critique of his scansion of 116 in my comments on that sonnet.

8. I do not include eclogues, debate-poems, etc. in the definition of normative single-speaker lyric. Such poems are constructed against the norm, and derive their originality from bringing into the public (dramatic) arena of shared speech thoughts that in normative lyric remain intrapsychic.

The Sonnets

1

FRom fairest creatures we desire increase,
That thereby beauties *Rose* might neuer die,
But as the riper should by time decease,
His tender heire might beare his memory:
But thou contracted to thine owne bright eyes,
Feed'st thy lights flame with selfe substantiall fewell,
Making a famine where aboundance lies,
Thy selfe thy foe,to thy sweet selfe too cruell:
Thou that art now the worlds fresh ornament,
And only herauld to the gaudy spring,
Within thine owne bud buriest thy content,
And tender chorle makst wast in niggarding:
  Pitty the world,or else this glutton be,
  To eate the worlds due,by the graue and thee.

From fairest creatures we desire increase,
That thereby beauty's rose might never die,
But as the riper should by time decease,
His tender heir might bear his memory:
But thou, contracted to thine own bright eyes,
Feed'st thy light's flame with self-substantial fuel,
Making a famine where abundance lies,
Thyself thy foe, to thy sweet self too cruel.
Thou that art now the world's fresh ornament,
And only herald to the gaudy spring,
Within thine own bud buriest thy content,
And, tender churl, mak'st waste in niggarding:
  Pity the world, or else this glutton be,
  To eat the world's due, by the grave and thee.

WHEN GOD saw his creatures, he commanded them to increase and multiply. Shakespeare, in this first sonnet of the sequence, suggests we have internalized the paradisal command in an aestheticized form: *From fairest creatures we desire increase.* The sonnet begins, so to speak, in the desire for an Eden where beauty's rose will never die; but the fall quickly arrives with *decease* (where we expect, by parallel with *increase*, the milder *decrease*). Unless the young man pities the world, and consents to his own increase, even a successively self-renewing Eden is unavailable.

Here we first meet the Shakespearean speaker, and begin to be acquainted with his range of tones. He can speak philosophically, or rise to an urgent vocative, or can turn to a diction drawn from "common sense" (aphorisms, epigrams, proverbs, and biblical tags). All are in play throughout the sequence: the sorrowing disinterestedness of his philosophical voice, the increasingly interested passion of his direct address, and the pathos of his frequent invoking of common wisdom in the hope of persuading a recalcitrant addressee. The different rhetorical moments of this sonnet (generalizing reflection, reproach, injunction, prophecy) are permeable to one another's metaphors, so that the *rose* of philosophical reflection yields the *bud* of direct address, and the *famine* of address yields the *glutton* who, in epigram, eats the world's due. The reappearance of a previous metaphor in a moment of different rhetoricity makes us believe that behind all the speaker's instances of particular rhetorical usage there lies in his mind a storehouse or bank of fundamental images to be drawn on. We are thereby made to believe throughout the sequence in the sustained and real existential being of the speaker.

We are also educated in the speaker's culture—here, in such stock figures as the medieval Rose of beauty, gluttony as one of the seven deadly sins, an allusion to Isaiah [32.5], the command from Genesis to increase and multiply, the dynastic obligation to produce heirs, and so on. Our education continues throughout the sequence, until the speaker's mind creates our own. With rare exceptions, the speaker draws on the common coin of his culture. It is not to his imagery in itself that an aesthetic inquiry must look, but rather to his juxtapositions that test one image against another for adequacy.

There are two distinguishing features in this originating (but perhaps late-composed) sonnet, both of which we might not expect in such a brief poem: the first is the sheer abundance of values, images, and concepts important in the sequence which are called into play, and the second is the number of significant words brought to our attention. Such a wide sweep leads me to think that the sonnet may have been deliberately composed late, as a "preface" to the others. The sonnet can be seen, in sum, as an index to the rest of the sonnets, or as a diapason of the notes of the sequence. A quick enumeration of values considered by the speaker as axiomatic and self-evidently good would include beauty, increase, inheritance, memory, light, abundance, sweetness, freshness, ornament, springtime, tenderness, and the world's rights. The salient images include fair creatures, the rose, bright eyes, flame and light, fuel, famine, abundance, foe, ornament, herald, spring, bud, burial, and (the oxymoronic) tender churl. The concepts—because Shakespeare's mind works by contrastive taxonomy—tend to be summoned in pairs: increase and decease, ripening and dying; beauty and immortality versus memory and inheritance; expansion and contraction; inner spirit (eyes) and outward show (bud); self-consumption and dispersal, famine and abundance, hoarding and waste; gluttony, debt. This sonnet is unusual in bringing into play such a plethora of conceptual material; it seems a self-conscious groundwork laid for the rest of an edifice. Words appearing here which will take on special resonance in the sequence are numerous: *fair*, *beauty*, *ripe*, *time*, *tender*, *heir*, *bear*, *memory*, *bright*, *eyes*, *feed*, *light*, *flame*, *self*, *substance*, *make*, *abundance*, *foe*, *sweet*, *cruel*, *world*, *fresh*, *ornament*, *spring*, *bud*, *bury*, *content*, *waste*, *pity*, *eat*, *due*, and *grave*.

In short, we may say that this sonnet makes an aesthetic investment in profusion. Its indexing function for the sequence allows it to be seen as a packed bud from which many subsequent petals will spring. It is a sonnet that best bears rereading in the context of the sequence, when one is prepared to hear to the full the resonance of all its concepts, values, images, and words. Since its aesthetic display is intended to evoke profusion, the poem enacts its own reproach to the niggardliness it describes; as the heralding bud of the sequence, it displays the same potential for self-replicating increase as natural creatures. But Shakespeare will abandon this easy parallel between aesthetic and natural increase in favor of a different aesthetic, that of distillation. The style of profusion will soon alternate with a style of metaphysical wit and concentration.

Shakespeare's commitment to profusion in this sonnet is visible as well in the way in which two alternate readings, one inorganic and one organic, are given of the young man's refusal to breed: he is a candle contracted to the flame of his bright eyes; or he is a rose refusing to unfold his bud. The first symbolizes the refusal of the spirit; the second, the refusal of the flesh. The first creates famine; the second, waste. The juxtaposing of two incompatible categories—here, the inorganic and the organic—is one of Shakespeare's most reliable techniques for provoking thought in the reader. When two incompatible categories are combined in the *same* metaphor—"a candle which refuses to bud forth"—we say we have mixed metaphor, or catachresis, a figure which vigorously calls attention to itself. Shakespeare's use of metaphors from incompatible categories applied to the same object (here, the young man) does not immediately call attention to itself; it can pass almost unnoticed. Yet the candle-value (light and heat should be diffused as a social good, not consumed only by the candle) derives perhaps from a New Testament source (hiding one's light under a bushel), and is in any case parabolic and moral in import. But the organic metaphor *(Thou . . . Within thine own bud buriest thy content)*, though offered as a moral reproach, suggests a weakness of a biological sort, such as we infer in a bud that does not blossom, perhaps because it cannot. Since neither of these metaphors, organic or inorganic, is drawn from the human realm, they both exist in dissonance with human metaphors like *foe* or *glutton*, the first suggesting self-war (by contrast to the self-nurturing implied in *self-substantial fuel*), the second self-cannibalism. As the poem glides from metaphor to metaphor, it "makes sense" on the argumentative level, while revealing, on the metaphorical level, the author's struggle through thickets of metaphor seeking relevant (if contradictory) categorizations of the young man's culpable inertia—which is alternately seen as a sin of omission *(buriest)* and a sin of commission *(foe)*. The cognitive dissonance of the metaphors presses the reader into reflection; and this technique, recurrent throughout the sonnets, is the chief source of their intellectual provocativeness.

A willed profusion of the sort remarked in the diction and metaphors of the sonnet is also evident in the many speech-acts of the poem (the number here is greater than the norm in the sequence). An appeal to the *consensus gentium* ("we") is followed by an exemplum: *as the riper should decease, his heir might bear his memory.* With the rise of temperature always implicit in the turn to direct address, the rapidity of speech-acts increases with the vocative second quatrain: the little narrative *(thou feed'st thy light's flame with self-substantial fuel)* is succeeded by dependent paradoxes of famine in abundance and cruelty in sweetness. Praise has turned to reproach, and the two are combined in the oxymoron and paradox of the *tender churl* who makes *waste in niggarding*. An exhortation—*Pity the world*—is followed by a prophetic threat *(or else)*. These speech-acts will be among those most frequent in the speaker's repertory throughout the sequence; in fact, we tend to define the speaker as one given to paradox, to exempla, to appeals to the *consensus gentium*, to volatile changes from praise to reproach, and to exhortation and prophecy. By showing us the speaker in many of his characteristic speech-acts, Shakespeare continues the display of profusion, initiates in us a further sense (beyond his fund of metaphors) of the speaker's typical behavior, and prepares us for the rest of the sequence.

If we take profusion as the aesthetic intent of the sonnet, we can justly ask whether the intent fails in any respect. An honest answer might be that the human alternatives offered by the logic of the sonnet ("breed or sin") seem incomplete when measured against the reaches of Shakespeare's imagination elsewhere. The narrowing of profusion to these bare alternatives makes the close of the sonnet purely conceptual and rhetorical, rather than truly imaginative. And these dynastic alternatives are not relevant to Shakespeare himself (who had already married and begotten children). The issue of a good poem must be urgent to the poet. When Shakespeare, after sonnet 17, abandons the dynastic question in favor of issues of mortality and corruption, his imagination can come fully into play.

Primary Structure of Sonnet 1

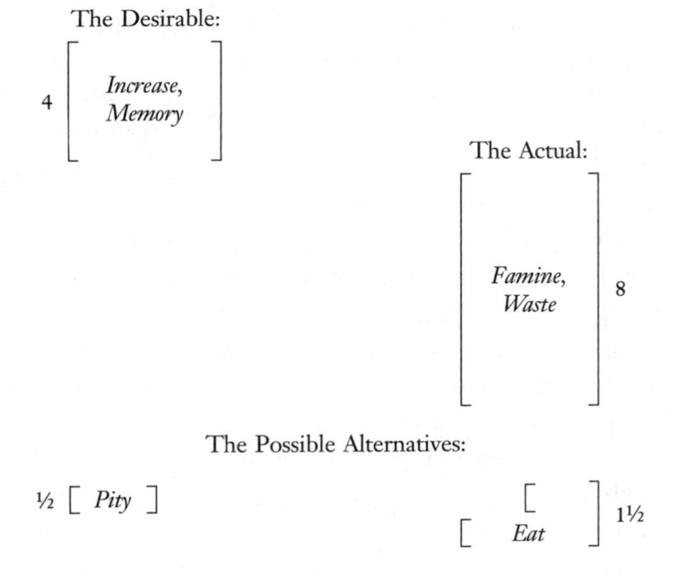

Most of the sonnets lend themselves to more than one schematic representation. This one is no exception, but we may say that its primary structure seems to be as shown in the diagram. The unexpectedness of such a structure, in which the reproachful narrative of actuality (lines 5–12) straddles the octave and sestet, shows Shakespeare's inventiveness with respect to the continental sonnet structure. Many of Shakespeare's sonnets preserve (except for rhyme) the two-part structure of the Italian sonnet, in which the first eight lines are logically or metaphorically set against the last six. An octave-generalization will be followed by a particular sestet-application, an octave-question will be followed by a sestet-answer (or at least by a quatrain-answer before a summarizing couplet). In such poems, we can see to what an extent Shakespeare had internalized the two-part structure of so many of his predecessors, Italian, French, and English. On the other hand, he finds a strenuous pleasure in inventing as many ways as possible to construct a fourteen-line poem; and I think it is no accident that the first sonnet in his sequence avoids the two structures a reader might expect—the binary structure of the Italian sonnet, and the quatrains-in-parallel of the English sonnet. (The quatrains here are not parallel, since direct address does not appear until after the first-quatrain, which, unlike the other two quatrains, is phrased in the first person plural.)

Because the ghost of the Italian sonnet can be said to underlie all the sonnets in the sequence, a "shadow sonnet" often can be intuited behind the sonnet we are reading. To give only one example of how such a ghost is felt here, let us imagine a sonnet more equally balanced, in which the initial reproaches to the young man are followed by a sestet of positive exhortations: [*So thou, fair youth, must bear an heir to be / An ornament, as thou wert, to the spring*]. The place of such expectable lines of positive injunction is usurped, as it were, by the reiteration in Q_3 of the narrative of reproach already heard in Q_2; and the "fact" of such usurpation is made evident by the tormented brevity of the single positive exhortation, *Pity the world.* The profusion so "normal" in this sonnet (as we have seen) is thus sharply prevented from exhibiting itself in positive terms at the close by the distorting "overabundance" of the narrative of reproach.

A confidence in the social norm of reproduction (from which the young man's deviancy is measured) exists, here as later, in tension with a confidence in the young man, so that even in the two small reproach-narratives, the terms of reproach *(famine, waste)* are preceded, as if involuntarily, by a rhetoric of praise. It is as though, before coming to the point, the speaker had to delay in wonder and admiration: "Thou—*that art now the world's fresh ornament and only herald to the gaudy spring*—buriest thy content." It is easy to imagine a more mitigated praise; but here the praise is unqualified, as though social morality might reproach, but not dim, beauty. If Shakespeare (and the social *world* linking the third quatrain and the couplet) are here the owners and deployers of judgmental language, the young man is the sovereign over descriptive usage: he compels it to be beautiful, even when it is describing a sinner.

Couplet Tie: *world* [-'s] (9, 13, 14)

2

VV Hen fortie Winters ſhall beſeige thy brow,
And digge deep trenches in thy beauties field,
Thy youthes proud liuery ſo gaz'd on now,
Wil be a totter'd weed of ſmal worth held:
Then being askt, where all thy beautie lies,
Where all the treaſure of thy luſty daies;
To ſay within thine owne deepe ſunken eyes,
Were an all-eating ſhame, and thriftleſſe praiſe.
How much more praiſe deſeru'd thy beauties vſe,
If thou couldſt anſwere this faire child of mine
Shall ſum my count, and make my old excuſe
Proouing his beautie by ſucceſſion thine.
This were to be new made when thou art ould,
And ſee thy blood warme when thou feel'ſt it could,

When forty winters shall besiege thy brow,
And dig deep trenches in thy beauty's field,
Thy youth's proud livery so gazed on now
Will be a tottered weed of small worth held:
Then being asked, where all thy beauty lies,
Where all the treasure of thy lusty days,
To say within thine own deep-sunken eyes
Were an all-eating shame, and thriftless praise.
How much more praise deserved thy beauty's use,
If thou couldst answer, "This fair child of mine
Shall sum my count, and make my old excuse,"
Proving his beauty by succession thine.
This were to be new made when thou art old,
And see thy blood warm when thou feel'st it cold.

THIS sonnet raises the question of the locus of self-worth: Does it lie in the self, or in the world's opinion of the self? We see for the first time in the sequence the technique of double exposure, by which Shakespeare offers two alternative scenarios both responding to the same situation. The structure may be roughly mapped as shown in the diagram.

Q_2 says, in indirect discourse, that the young man may give, at forty, two possible answers to the question ["*Where lies thy beauty, / Where all the treasure of thy lusty days?*"]. The two answers are unequally sketched in Q_2 and Q_3. The first brief answer, ["*Within [my] own deep-sunken eyes*"], is summarily dismissed in a reported judgment by the world echoing the gluttony and waste of sonnet 1: To answer thus *were an all-eating shame and thriftless praise.* The second, better, longer answer, "*This fair child . . . ,*" evokes a two-part judgment, one from the world, one from the speaker. Should the young man give the second answer, he would deserve *more praise* from the world, first of all; then the speaker adds a judgment perhaps more persuasive, because of its narcissistic interest to the young man (repeating the subjunctive *were* to parallel the world's earlier judgment): *This were to be new made.* Shakespeare experiments here with a "bottom-heavy" structure, in which the alternative scenarios of young man's answer / others' judgment are linked powerfully together by parallelism and chiasmus: *say, were shame, praise, // more praise, answer, were to be new made.* This renders the answers and judgments (of lines 7–14) the "long sestet," so to speak, responding to the "short octave" of the future question put in lines 1–6. Or one could say that the opening lines (1–6) of prophecy/question are an initial sestet followed by an octave of answers/judgments (lines 7–14): an indication, in its topsy-turvy structure, that Shakespeare intends to experiment with the conventional Italian structure, here by turning it upside down and writing the "sestet" first.

Since the young man's two answers, like the world's putative question, are hypothetical, they are phantoms of the future. The world's and the narrator's *judgments* on these answers are, however, transcendental and based on values assumed to be permanent; and the necessitarian prophecy of the eventual dimming of physical beauty is likewise certain.

SONNET 2

Primary Structure of Sonnet 2

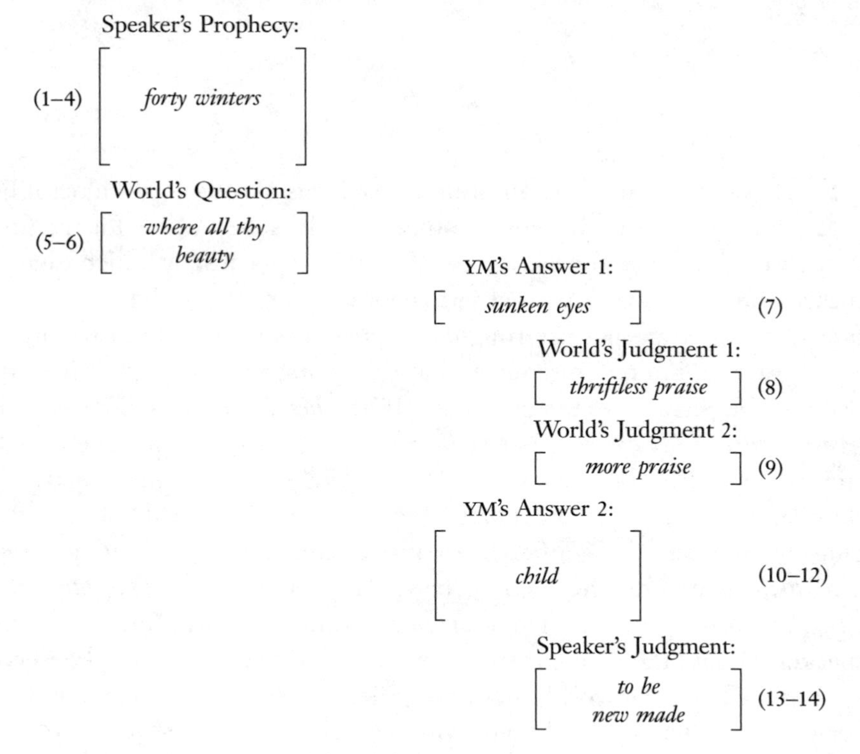

Alternative Structure for Sonnet 2

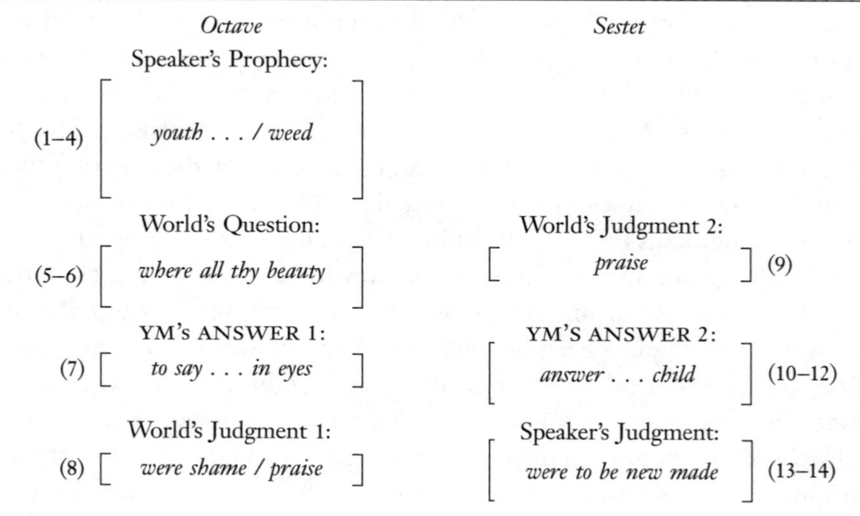

In this respect, another mapping of the sonnet becomes possible, as shown here; uppercase is used for suppositional or hypothetical events, and one should read down on the left, then on the right. Both the opening eight-line "octave" and the closing six-line "sestet" would then each exhibit a hypothetical middle answer (here in uppercase), framed by unhypothetical parts (statements of natural fact or transcendental judgment). To unfold a purely hypothetical future situation is a frequent enterprise in the sonnets, assuring the literally infinite possibility of their continuance. Whether anyone would ever actually ask the unmarried young man, in his fortieth year, where all his beauty and youth lie, scarcely matters. The extrapolation of mutually exclusive future alternatives is, after all, a guide for the present.

The words put in the young man's mouth, both indirectly *(To say . . .)* and directly *(This fair child of mine . . .)* are the first of a great many to be ascribed to him in the course of the sequence. Ascribing words to him or, later, to the "dark lady," is one way of building up a credible existential character for these *dramatis personae* over time.

The sonnet offers two motives for action. The first arises from a social morality dependent on others' response, in which one acts so as to avoid *shame*, or receive *praise*, or *make excuse*. The social morality of the body of the poem, however, is displaced in the closing couplet by an appeal to individual pleasure: the reward for reproducing and the source of self-worth is now narcissistic (warm blood, new self) rather than social, and, if not purely intrinsic, at least entirely self-referential.

This sonnet derives its aesthetic claim on us by the variousness of its suppositional moves. The variables (social / personal; right answer / wrong answer; favorable judgment / unfavorable judgment) make for those rapid conceptual shifts of which poetry is enamored. Are we to be in the social world of shame and praise or the world of narcissistic happiness? Of childlessness or reproduction? Of waste or of treasure? Of growing old or being new-made? As the alternative scenarios are expounded by the speaker, they are made, by their parallel constructions, palimpsests of each other rather than side-by-side pictures. What we see is a double exposure: the forty-year-old sunken-eyed bachelor feeling his blood cold in his veins superimposed on the forty-year-old proud father seeing his blood warm in his son. The poem exerts aesthetic power in compelling us to see both at once.

Finally, this sonnet introduces into the sequence those metaphors of seasonal destruction *(winters besiege thy brow)*, Time's delving *(dig deep trenches)*, and usury *(thy beauty's use)* that will be elaborated in other sonnets.

Couplet Tie: *were* (8, 13)
old (11, 13)
make [*made*] (11, 13)

3

LOoke in thy glaſſe and tell the face thou veweſt,
Now is the time that face ſhould forme an other,
Whoſe freſh repaire if now thou not reneweſt,
Thou doo'ſt beguile the world, vnbleſſe ſome mother.
For where is ſhe ſo faire whoſe vn-eard wombe
Diſdaines the tillage of thy husbandry?
Or who is he ſo fond will be the tombe,
Of his ſelfe loue to ſtop poſterity?
Thou art thy mothers glaſſe and ſhe in thee
Calls backe the louely Aprill of her prime,
So thou through windowes of thine age ſhalt ſee,
Diſpight of wrinkles this thy goulden time.
  But if thou liue remembred not to be,
  Die ſingle and thine Image dies with thee.

Look in thy glass and tell the face thou viewest,
Now is the time that face should form another,
Whose fresh repair if now thou not renewest,
Thou dost beguile the world, unbless some mother.
For where is she so fair whose uneared womb
Disdains the tillage of thy husbandry?
Or who is he so fond will be the tomb
Of his self-love to stop posterity?
Thou art thy mother's glass, and she in thee
Calls back the lovely April of her prime;
So thou through windows of thine age shalt see,
Despite of wrinkles, this thy golden time.
  But if thou live rememb'red not to be,
  Die single, and thine image dies with thee.

NO SINGLE repeated significant word links the couplet of sonnet 3 to the body of the poem; this absence is very unusual. Shakespeare is thus at pains to emphasize here the logical disjunction between the body of the sonnet and its couplet; and even a hasty reading shows that the sonnet falls logically into an exhortation to breed (in the quatrains) followed by the couplet-result—phrased almost as a death-curse—if the advice is not followed:

But if thou live rememb'red not to be,
Die single, and thine image dies with thee.

On the *But* of the couplet the whole poem appears to turn; the body of the poem would seem to be devoted to life, the couplet to death.

However, a second reading shows smaller "deaths" scattered throughout the poem; and the sonnet, instead of being mapped,

(1–12) [Reproduce]

[If not, die] (13–14)

can also be seen as a continuing offering of alternatives, both life-giving and death-dealing, as italicized in the diagram opposite. However, to divide the complicated second quatrain into the simple alternatives of husbandry/tomb does not do it justice. A better mapping of the second quatrain would show how each of its two rhetorical questions embodies both death (to *disdain husbandry*, to *stop posterity*) and life (since no woman, it is presumed, will be so mistaken as to scorn the young man, nor will any man be so fond as to make himself his own tomb). The second quatrain, then, is the "knot" thematizing in little the larger contrast between life and death, between the body of the sonnet and its couplet. In acting as a mini-thematizer of the whole, the second quatrain draws attention to the *dédoublement*, or aesthetic self-reflection, so frequent in the sonnets.

In this sonnet, the young man's face is compared to that of his mother; one might more properly expect a comparison with that of his father:

Alternatives Offered in Sonnet 3

	Life		*Death*	
2	*Tell face in glass time to make another*	If not	*beguile, unbless*	2
2	*fair womb . . . husbandry*	Or	*tomb . . . stop posterity*	2
4	*Mother sees self in you; you see self in son*	But if not	*die single, image dies*	2

[*Thou art thy father's glass, and he in thee*
Calls back the lovely April of his prime.]

It has been suggested (mistakenly, I think) that the young man's father must be dead (*you had a father*, sonnet 13), and that this fact explains the invoking of his mother as his model. It seems more likely that Shakespeare transforms the putative future bride-*mother* of line 4 into the actual *mother* of line 9 in order ostensibly to connect octave and sestet; the analogy with the mother's face is also relevant to the young man's possession of *a woman's face* (sonnet 20). The octave and sestet are connected not only by the word *mother*, but also by the word *glass (Look in thy glass . . . thy mother's glass)* and by the idea of regarding one's face in a mirror. To the idea of replication-by-breeding this sonnet adds the idea of replication-in-a-mirror, combining the two in a single image of dynastic representation *(Thou art thy mother's glass)*. The image is further complicated by the idea of an adult *see[ing] through windows* of his aged eyes his own child, the incarnate image of his youth. It is as though two forms of glass—the unsilvered one of the cornea permitting a mental representation, the silvered one of the mirror permitting a visual replication—were to confront each other. Already Shakespeare is classifying forms of representation, an interest reaching its apogee in the eye/heart sonnets.

Sonnet 3 reads like a series of sketches for future sonnets. *The lovely April of her prime* is a sketch for the seasonal poems, *the tomb* a foretaste of the *memento mori* sonnets; the chain of alliterative or prefix-iterated signifiers *(face, form, fresh, fair, fond; be-guile, be, be; un-bless, un-eared; re-pair, re-newest, re-memb'red)* and the graphic or phonetic puns *(till-**age**/**age**/im-**age**; **husband**-ry; g-**old**-en time)* betoken better efforts to come. The public-gesturing rhetorical questions about disdainful maidens and foolish self-entombers presage far more agonizing "real" questions to come: *Ah, wherefore with infection should he live?* or *Wherefore says she not she is unjust?* The principle of predictable dynastic recurrence in breeding *(thou . . . shalt see [again] . . . thy golden time)* is of no permanent interest to Shakespeare, and will soon fade from the sequence in favor of the contemplation of unique beauty. The couplet—which speaks not of breeding but of being remembered—hints at the emphasis on memory that will replace, after sonnet 17, the emphasis on physical reproduction (itself subordinately present in re-mem-***bred*** in the Quarto spelling). And the separation, in line 14, of the young man into himself and his image is one of the most fruitful strategies of the sequence, generating a score of poems in which image and embodiment shadow each other in aesthetic play.

Couplet Tie: None (see opening of commentary). But there are couplet ties of a hidden sort, such as *til**lage**/**age**/im**age*** (6, 11, 14), and ***re**pair*, ***re**newest*, ***re**memb'red* (3, 3, 13).

4

VNthrifty louelineſſe why doſt thou ſpend,
Vpon thy ſelfe thy beauties legacy?
Natures bequeſt giues nothing but doth lend,
And being franck ſhe lends to thoſe are free:
Then beautious nigard why dooſt thou abuſe,
The bountious largeſſe giuen thee to giue?
Profitles vſerer why dooſt thou vſe
So great a ſumme of ſummes yet can'ſt not liue?
For hauing traffike with thy ſelfe alone,
Thou of thy ſelfe thy ſweet ſelfe doſt deceaue,
Then how when nature calls thee to be gone,
What acceptable *Audit* can'ſt thou leaue?
  Thy vnuſ'd beauty muſt be tomb'd with thee,
  Which vſed liues th'executor to be.

Unthrifty loveliness, why dost thou spend
Upon thyself thy beauty's legacy?
Nature's bequest gives nothing, but doth lend,
And being frank she lends to those are free:
Then, beauteous niggard, why dost thou abuse
The bounteous largess given thee to give?
Profitless usurer, why dost thou use
So great a sum of sums yet canst not live?
For having traffic with thyself alone,
Thou of thyself thy sweet self dost deceive:
Then how when Nature calls thee to be gone,
What acceptable audit canst thou leave?
  Thy unused beauty must be tombed with thee,
  Which usèd lives th'executor to be.

CAPITULATING to paradox, Shakespeare produces a series of showy compound epithets characterizing the young man: *unthrifty loveliness, beauteous niggard, profitless usurer.* The three nouns, charged (like all nouns) with bearing essence, establish the beloved's beauty, his miserliness, and his (figurative) financial profligacy; the three adjectives, charged (like all adjectives) with bearing qualities, establish his (figurative) financial profligacy, his beauty, and his profitlessness. We are hard put to know whether he is a beauteous niggard or a niggardly beauty, and the very uncertainty as to essence and accident contributes to the confusion attending on any definition of the young man's ethical status.

The model of ethical value set up in the sonnet is drawn from the behavior of Nature, who benevolently circulates her currency: she *lends . . . bounteous largess,* or she *gives* it to the young man for him to *give* in turn; *being frank,* nature *lends* to those who are *free,* and her legacy is to be freely bequeathed to others. The young man's unacceptable behavior is both usurious and profitless; he unjustly hoards his beauty *unused* and *spends* it on himself. Like an unprofitable steward, he cannot leave an *acceptable audit,* and he has no *executors.* The speaker's "innocent" introduction of legal and banking language, especially when he speaks about Nature's loans, suggests that he can appeal to the young man only in the contaminated language the young man understands—the language of social, not natural, exchange.

This sonnet is a homily, and behind its vocatives, its hectoring questions, and its final proposing of strict alternatives for choice, lies the religious genre of the reproach of the cleric to the sinner. But of course true homiletic vocatives ("O miserable sinner") would not melt into the relenting dazzled oxymorons of *unthrifty loveliness* and *beauteous niggard.* Only the third vocative, *profitless usurer,* is a true homiletic vocative-to-the-sinner, in which both essence *and* accident are reproved. In this poem, homily has been secularized. Not God, with the divine command "Increase and multiply" as in sonnet 1, but rather organic Nature here provides the motive for reproduction; and the speaker's own ethical double standard in judging the "sinner" is visible in the first two vocatives of perplexed adoration and in the reference to "thy sweet self"—a double standard unthinkable in a priest. The recommended normative behavior of this secularized homily is not even ethically derived: it is drawn partly from the biologically normative circulation of life (visible in Nature's actions) and partly from the self-serving prudential counsel of worldliness (which advises an *acceptable audit*).

This sonnet, like others appearing early in the sequence, forecasts problems to come. The increasingly uncomfortable attempts of the speaker to sort out his own principles (and attendant questions both ethical and aesthetic) will motivate, psychologically speaking, many future sonnets. The sequence will contain other "homilies," and more interesting ones (such as sonnet 129). The boy's autoerotic *traffic with [himself] alone* is an early parody of the many true reciprocities envisaged in the sequence (those between mother and child, father and son, lover and beloved, poet and subject of celebration, friend and friend). The formal mark of reciprocity here is the reflexive verb-sequence *having traffic with thy self alone thou dost deceive thy sweet self of thyself*, an "enacting" process bettered in later sonnets. The rhyme *use-abuse* will turn up later, as will the subject of usury; and the *audit* will recur in the last of the sonnets to the young man (126), where it must be *answered* with Nature's surrendering of the young man to Time.

The aesthetic value proposed here is a rigid isomorphism (each of the four hectoring questions occupies two lines, and three of the questions use the same phrase, *why dost thou*). In the *Sonnets*, Shakespeare varies between being pleased with the idea of isomorphism (see, e.g., the repeated one-line indictments in 66, *Tired with all these*) and being driven by it to cunning variations within it; here, after an almost perfect isomorphism in the first three questions, to wit:

Adjective + noun, *why dost thou* verb
- *abuse*
- *spend*
- *use*

he turns impatiently in the fourth question (lines 11–12) to a different form, omitting the vocative and asking *how* and *what* instead of *why*, but retaining still the two-line frame. The scattering of isomorphic questions through the three quatrains of the sonnet (1–2; 5–6; 7–8; 11–12) means that in its rhetorical structure this sonnet is distributively "Shakespearean" rather than contrastively "Italian"; but the "Italian" residue remains present in the fact that the first three "perfectly" isomorphic questions, which occur in the octave, have to do with spending, whereas the last question, which occurs in the sestet, has to do with nature's calling in her accounts—an audit instead of an expenditure. The "Shakespearean" distributed syntactic structure of the four questions, then, offers itself against the "Italian" two-part thematic structure of expense and audit; and one of the perpetual sources of aesthetic play in the sonnets is precisely this offer, to the attentive reader, of two sonnets in one. The anomalies in phrasing and content of the fourth question disturb the very syntactic isomorphism which seems at first to be the structuring plot of the poem—which we at last see to be a double plot in which repetitive querying reproach for spending meets profligacy finally called to account. The double plot is mimed in the macaronic pun on ***use*/*exec*utor** in line 14 (representing a satisfactory audit) versus the other appearances of evil *use*, *abuse*, *unused*, and *usurer*.

Couplet Tie: *beauty* [-'*s*], [*beauteous*] (2, 5, 13)
use (7, 14), *abuse* (5), *usurer* (7), *unused* (13), *usèd*, *exec***utor** (14)
live [-*s*] (8, 14)

5

THose howers that with gentle worke did frame,
The louely gaze where euery eye doth dwell
Will play the tirants to the very ſame,
And that vnfaire which fairely doth excell:
For neuer reſting time leads Summer on,
To hidious winter and confounds him there,
Sap checkt with froſt and luſtie leau's quite gon,
Beauty ore-ſnow'd and barenes euery where,
Then were not ſummers diſtillation left
A liquid priſoner pent in walls of glaſſe,
Beauties effect with beauty were bereft,
Nor it nor noe remembrance what it was.
  But flowers diſtil'd though they with winter meete,
  Leeſe but their ſhow,their ſubſtance ſtill liues ſweet.

Those hours that with gentle work did frame
The lovely gaze where every eye doth dwell
Will play the tyrants to the very same,
And that unfair which fairly doth excel;
For never-resting time leads summer on
To hideous winter and confounds him there,
Sap checked with frost and lusty leaves quite gone,
Beauty o'ersnowed and bareness every where:
Then were not summer's distillation left
A liquid prisoner pent in walls of glass,
Beauty's effect with beauty were bereft,
Nor it nor no remembrance what it was.
  But flowers distilled, though they with winter meet,
  Leese but their show; their substance still lives sweet.

THIS beautiful sonnet is the first to exploit the powerful seasonal metaphor which will animate other sonnets like 73 *(That time of year)* and 97 *(How like a winter)*, setting the inexorable destructions of time against an apparently available defense here named "distillation." Sonnet 5 is also the first impersonal sonnet, deliberately eschewing any personal pronouns *(I, you, we);* in this respect it may be compared with 129 *(Th'expense of spirit)*. Wholly impersonal sonnets are very rare in the sequence, and are all the more telling when they appear, since the *Sonnets* is a volume dominated by personal shifters, especially by *thou, you,* and *I.* ("Shifters" are pronouns whose reference depends on the person uttering them.)

Sonnet 5 experiments with falling silent before it has reached its logical end in an expected hortatory direct address (which is postponed to the beginning of the linked sonnet 6). One may choose to regard sonnets 5 and 6 as a single, logically complete, poem; but since it is true that 5 is certainly a complete poem in itself, I prefer to see it as a poem requiring from its reader a silent extrapolation of its syllogistic warning logic into completion-by-exhortation, thereby generating sonnet 6. Let me sketch it, and the hortatory extrapolation (in brackets) that it calls for:

1. The same hours that framed a lovely gaze will unfair it,
2. (For time leads summer on to winter and its destructions):
3. Then were not summer's distillation left, beauty would cease to exist;
4. But flowers distilled keep their substance (if not their show) after winter has come.

[5.] [So you, too, must be distilled before your winter comes.]

The fifth of my units above, missing in the poem, makes explicit, in vocative address, the parallel that lies implicit in the threatening exemplum of the flower. This missing fifth unit becomes the opening of sonnet 6:

Then let not winter's ragged hand deface
In thee thy summer ere thou be distilled:
Make sweet some vial.

The aesthetic advantage to sonnet 5 of *not* ending with the explicit direct address is that of closing with metaphor rather than with literal biological advice. Even the extrapolation in 6 remains at the level of metaphor: *make sweet some vial* is not translated into the crude bodily terms, "impregnate some woman."

It must quickly be added that the flowers of the couplet of sonnet 5 are not metaphorical in the same way that the earlier sap, leaves, and perfume of lines 7, 8, and 10 are metaphorical. The couplet imitates the pointed brevity of proverb ("Flowers distilled lose show, not substance"); and since nouns in proverbs are already generalized into analogical fixities (the eggs all in one basket having lost any of the pictorial or culinary particularity of real eggs), one wants to distinguish the proverb-flowers of the couplet from the pictorial ingredients of the poem—sap, frost, lusty leaves, snow, and bareness—as well as from the stunning phrasing of the *liquid prisoner pent in walls of glass,* a self-reflexive figure literally picturing perfume, but analogically picturing the emotionally labile contents of any sonnet as they preserve their mobility within the transparent walls of prescribed length, meter, and rhyme. Degrees of metaphoricity in the *Sonnets,* from the sensuously pictorial to the proverbially emblematic to the analogously symbolic, are very gradually nuanced. They vary from the most strikingly individual *(liquid prisoner)* through the sufficiently-particularized-but-conventional *(sap, frost)* to the proverbially fossilized *(lilies that fester)*. The latter are meant not as visual images but as mnemonic adages.

Shakespeare is attracted to all levels of the metaphorical, from the fanciful through the sublime, not excepting the fossilized, the mythical, and the figure referred to as the pathetic fallacy. Even his returns to a discursive mode are likely to bring with them some lingering fragrance of the metaphorical, as, indeed, in the ending of sonnet 54 where one reads not:

> And so of you, beauteous and lovely youth,
> When that shall *die*, my verse *will show* your truth,

but rather *vade* (or *fade*) and *distils.* Thus, in 54, the couplet's initial literal drawing of the analogy from flower to youth *(and so of you)* is itself by *vade* and *distils* made metaphorical, thereby suggesting the mutual permeability of the literal and figurative, and forbidding any too-easy distinguishing of tenor and vehicle. Flowers and beauty both *fade* and go; perfumes and verse both *distil.*

In sonnet 5, we can see Shakespeare experimenting with a technique very frequent in the sequence—having his speaker say "the same thing" twice. The first time, the speaker says it fairly "neutrally," "objectively," or "scientifically"; the second time he says it with emphatic emotionality.

What was repressed in the first account bursts out, with sudden power, in the second:

1. *Those hours . . . will play the tyrants* and will *unfair* the *lovely gaze.*
2. *For never-resting time leads summer on to hideous winter and confounds him there . . . bareness every where.*

To *play the tyrants* and to *unfair* are fairly colorless phrases for temporal destruction; but the more radically metaphorical second formulation—with its seasonal decline into catastrophe and its suggestions of deception and torture on the part of time—puts back into the poem the anguish concealed under the previous verbal play of unfairing the fair. There is, we feel, an equable rhythmic measure to the balanced early lines in which the hours

Will play the tyrants to the very same
And that unfair which fairly doth excel.

But the second quatrain shows its distress by its enjambment *(leads summer on / To hideous winter);* and its initial iambics of ritual inevitability are followed by "wintry" rhythmic irregularities (initial and final spondees—*sap checked* and *quite gone*—and an initial trochee—*beauty*). The distress is enacted as well by parallel "wintry" events in Q_2, in which the initial noun of the first three meets with catastrophe:

sap *checked with frost*
lusty leaves *quite gone*
beauty *o'ersnowed*
bareness every where.

We remark the "false parallel" of the fourth phrase, *bareness every where,* which lacks either a "good" natural noun like *sap* or *leaves* or a "good" abstract noun like *beauty.* It also lacks a participial adjective of the sort possessed by its three predecessors; the first three phrases enact a presence denied, while the fourth exhibits an absence now absolute.

It is also true that the speaker's first, neutral statement in Q_2 is enunciated in a demarcated tense-structure: the hours once *did frame* the gaze which now *doth excel,* and they *will unfair* it in the future. But the speaker's second, far more intense enunciation, in Q_2, by resorting to the present tense of habitual action, makes the destructive process ever-present: *time leads summer on* (always) *to hideous winter.*

In both quatrains, no possibility is envisaged other than a destructive slope ending in confounding catastrophe. Since Nature is being used here as a figure for human life (which is not reborn), the poem exhibits no upward slope in seasonal change. It cannot be too strongly emphasized that nothing can be said to happen in a poem which is not there suggested. If *summer is confounded in hideous winter*, one is not permitted to add, irrelevantly, "But can spring be far behind?" If the poet had wanted to provoke such an extrapolation, he would by some means have suggested it. Here, by the insistence on instrumental distillation as the *only* possible preserving of beauty, he explicitly forbids any recourse to the idea of a recurring organic spring. Though *nature* is in fact cyclical, not all metaphorical *uses* of nature in poetry invoke its cyclicity, not by any means. Context controls the extent of reference, both here and, e.g., in sonnet 73.

The splendidly achieved aesthetic shape of sonnet 5 is conferred by the speaker's stereoptical comprehension (with "divining eyes") of past, present, and future time in one gaze. Schematically, the shape of the poem looks like that shown in the diagram below.

As the apparently inexorable prophecy of future destruction in lines 1–8 yields to a hypothesis of an alternate future, the speaker's stereoptical gaze turns out to be also an optative one, with an optimistic shadow-future glimmering beyond his pessimistic prediction in Q_2.

Shakespeare's description in Q_3 of the predicted future without distillation is radically stripped of metaphor, stripped of anything but that *bareness everywhere* which it enacts. If distillation were not to occur,

Beauty's effect with beauty were bereft,
Nor it nor no remembrance what it was.

The almost total semantic bleakness of that empty language is yet ornamented by the alliteration and word-repetition characteristic of almost all the *Sonnets*.

The emptiness is at last countered and redeemed by the mimetic play of ***distilled* / *still** lives* in the couplet, and by the sonnet's lingering liquid close on the assertion that beauty's *substance still lives sweet*. But this assurance is won only by the principled sacrifice of the sentimental—with respect to human beings—hope for the natural rebirth of a loved form. Distillation destroys form, says the speaker, asserting the nonmimetic nature of even "mimetic" art. *Show* cannot be preserved, but *substance* can—a hope that successive sonnets will continue to explore.

Aesthetic Shape of Sonnet 5

Time (lines 1–8)

Past	*Present*	*Future*
hours did frame gaze	lovely gaze where every eye doth dwell	hours will play tyrants
	gaze fairly excels	hours will unfair gaze
[spring]	summer	hideous winter summer confounded
sap	sap	frost checks sap
lusty leaves	leaves	leaves gone
beauty	beauty	o'ersnowed
vegetation	vegetation	bareness every where

Beauty's Future (lines 9–14)

Future without distillation	*Future with distillation*
beauty bereft	summer's distillation
beauty's effect bereft as well	beauty's effect remains
no remembrance	remembrance of beauty
lost show	living substance
	sweet [odor]

Couplet Tie: *winter* (6, 13)
distillation/distilled/still (9, 13, 14)

THen let not winters wragged hand deface,
In thee thy ſummer ere thou be diſtil'd:
Make ſweet ſome viall; treaſure thou ſome place,
With beautits treaſure ere it be ſelfe kil'd:
That vſe is not forbidden vſery,
Which happies thoſe that pay the willing lone;
That's for thy ſelfe to breed an other thee,
Or ten times happier be it ten for one,
Ten times thy ſelfe were happier then thou art,
If ten of thine ten times refigur'd thee,
Then what could death doe if thou ſhould'ſt depart,
Leauing thee liuing in poſterity?
  Be not ſelfe-wild for thou art much too faire,
  To be deaths conqueſt and make wormes thine heire.

Then let not winter's ragged hand deface
In thee thy summer ere thou be distilled:
Make sweet some vial; treasure thou some place
With beauty's treasure ere it be self-killed:
That use is not forbidden usury
Which happies those that pay the willing loan;
That's for thyself to breed another thee,
Or ten times happier be it ten for one;
Ten times thyself were happier than thou art,
If ten of thine ten times refigured thee:
Then what could death do if thou shouldst depart,
Leaving thee living in posterity?
  Be not self-willed, for thou art much too fair
  To be death's conquest and make worms thine heir.

SONNET 6 takes its origin directly from 5, and begins by completing the analogy between natural summer and a human summer, evoking the prospect of the de-facing of the lovely gaze by the hand of winter. (The odd *ragged hand* of winter may be partially explained by the fact that in the Quarto spelling, *ragged* and *winter* visually alliterate: *winters wragged hand.*) However, 6 then departs entirely from the organic ground of distillation from nature to take up the inorganic metaphor of treasure. This strange move (repeated in sonnet 65) is perhaps explicable here by the difficulty of manipulating perfume into any interesting activity, whereas treasure—as a metaphor for the semen that can invisibly act (*treasure*, verb) to create a child (*treasure*, noun)—*can* be put to use, and (literally) is, in the enacting of money's breeding money in lines 5–10. *Happies, happier, happier,* goes the breeding; forbid*den, ten, ten, ten, ten, ten; times, times; leaving, living.*

In this rather labored conceit of interest-bearing funds, a play—deliberately situated in the tenth line—on a posterity of *ten* producing a posterity of *ten* times that number reveals the degree to which Shakespeare could be entranced by fancifulness. The poem's opposed alternatives—make sweet some vial or make worms thine heir; make a willing loan or be self-willed; be distilled or be self-killed—are not very interesting, and the climax *Then what could death do* (had you ensured your posterity) is less than convincing.

These are the projections of interest-production:

another thee
ten for one
ten times thyself
ten of thine ten times refigured thee.

They "breed" the young man in an astonishing growth of an economic base; Shakespeare here reverses the one-in-ten rate of highest permitted interest, as Kerrigan suggests. This growth is permitted because the young mother is happy, as is posterity, to pay the young man back in biological interest—children. These operations of the fancy will not detain

Shakespeare long. The formal scheme, frequently found in homily, frames positive exhortations (lines 3–12) with opening and closing negative brackets *Let not* (1–2) and *Be not* (13–14)—a firm if uninventive structure.

Couplet Tie: *make* (3, 14)
will [-*ing*] [-*ed*] (6, 13)
death [-*'s*] (11, 14)

7

Loe in the Orient when the gracious light,
Lifts vp his burning head,each vnder eye
Doth homage to his new appearing ſight,
Seruing with lookes his ſacred maieſty,
And hauing climb'd the ſteepe vp heauenly hill,
Reſembling ſtrong youth in his middle age,
Yet mortall lookes adore his beauty ſtill,
Attending on his goulden pilgrimage:
But when from high-moſt pich with wery car,
Like feeble age he reeleth from the day,
The eyes(fore dutious)now conuerted are
From his low tract and looke an other way:
So thou,thy ſelfe out-going in thy noon:
Vnlok'd on dieſt vnleſſe thou get a ſonne.

Lo in the orient when the gracious light
Lifts up his burning head, each under eye
Doth homage to his new-appearing sight,
Serving with looks his sacred majesty;
And having climbed the steep-up heavenly hill,
Resembling strong youth in his middle age,
Yet mortal looks adore his beauty still,
Attending on his golden pilgrimage:
But when from highmost pitch with weary car
Like feeble age he reeleth from the day,
The eyes (fore duteous) now converted are
From his low tract and look another way:
So thou, thyself outgoing in thy noon,
Unlooked on diest unless thou get a son.

LIKE MANY of the *Sonnets*, this one is organized around a principle that for convenience of reference I call the use of a KEY WORD. In its simplest form, this principle requires that each of the four units of the sonnet contain (at least once per unit) the same (meaningful) word, a thematically significant one. The word may appear in its root form or a variant thereof. In 7, the word is LOOK, and it appears in the forms LOOKs (Q_1), LOOKs (Q_2), LOOK (Q_3), and unLOOKed (C). Here in 7 (and in 32 as well), the principle has an added constraint: The KEY WORD must appear in the *latter half* of each unit in which it appears; and so we find it in lines 4, 7, 12, and 14, rather, say, than in lines 2, 5, 9, and 13. Absurd though such principles of composition may seem to nonpoetic eyes, poets find them appealing (as such forms as sestinas and pantoums bear witness). Shakespeare often brings the KEY WORD to several elaborate heights of ingenuity (see, e.g., sonnets 50, 55, and 105, and the total list in Appendixes 1 and 2).

Structure of Sonnet 7

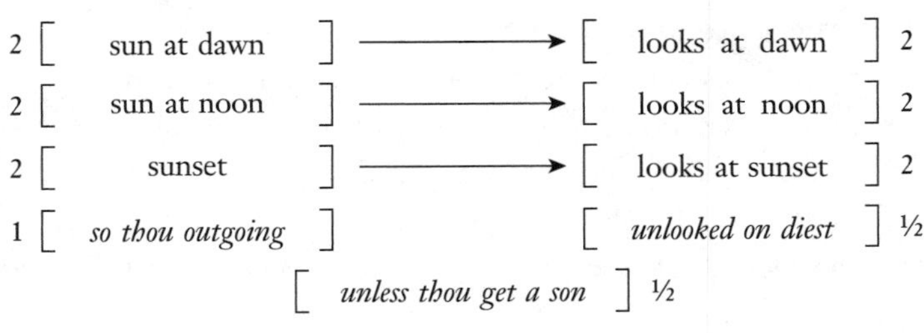

There are, besides the KEY WORD, other forms of wordplay in this sonnet, but it is perhaps better to sketch first its double structure, in which a little narrative about the sun—its rising, its noon glory, and its setting—is matched by a second little narrative in tandem with it—one which recounts the changes in human looks that follow the sun's course, as they at first render homage and adore, gradually lose interest, and finally look away. After every two lines about the sun (the word *sun* is never, for reasons we shall come to, used in the poem) there are two lines about LOOKS. Finally, the witty couplet, with its quick bolthole pun *(son)*, offers a last-minute escape from the doom of solar analogy (by which a childless man would set, like the sun, and be found by onlookers to be of no social consequence). The poem can be mapped as shown in the diagram.

There are some odd words in the poem—among them *fore duteous* and *tract*—which beg for explanation. It becomes evident, as one reads the sonnets, that as Shakespeare begins to follow out a given verbal scheme, the constraints on language grow as the sonnet in question progresses to its end. Nothing in the requirements of meaning or sound alone would have prevented Shakespeare from writing:

> The eyes [***once***] duteous now converted are
> From his low [***path***] and look another way.

Neither *fore* nor *tract* can be explained by semantic, alliterative, or phonetic needs. At the risk of seeming overingenious, I can only suggest that the golden sun generates, throughout the sonnet, French puns on *or*: ***or****ient*, *ad****or****e*, *m****or****tal*, and—our point of origin—*f****or****e*; and that the central image of the sun's ***car*** generates anagrammatically scrambled cars elsewhere: in ***g****r****a****c****ious*, ***s****a****c****r****ed*, and—our point of origin—*t****rac****t*. The aging of the sun in the poem seems to generate *hom****age***, ***age***, *gold****en*** *pilgrim****age***, and (once again) ***age***; and the long and (to the reader, intolerable) suppression of the word ***sun*** of course makes the word ***son***, when it finally leaps off the page as the closing word, entirely inevitable.

The rigid left-right optical symmetry of the poem, as the sun visible in the "left" half of each quatrain is mirrored by the LOOKS on the "right" (explaining why the KEY WORD appears always in the second half of each member), perhaps suggested some of the mirror-resembling acts with words. I do not believe anagrams to be common in the *Sonnets*, but neither do I believe they were beneath Shakespeare's interest (see 20 for *hue/hew*, another example). The degree of verbal fancifulness in the sonnets to the young man lessens as the subsequence advances and imagination supervenes on mechanical fancy. (This is perhaps one reason for believing that most of the sonnets in this initial subsequence were composed in the order in which they appear, even if later revised.)

Sonnet 7 has little to recommend it, imaginatively; both the conceit of the sun's predictable day-long *jour*-ney (another French pun) and the conceit of the fall of favorites from public respect are well-worn topics. It was perhaps because his topics here were so entirely conventional that Shakespeare looked to word-games to put him on his mettle in composing the poem. He certainly enjoyed the obstacle of shaping his four parts around a single KEY WORD enough to propose it to himself later many times.

KEY WORD: LOOK [-S] [unLOOKed]

Couplet Tie: *look* [*-s*] [*un**look**ed*] (4, 7, 12, 14)

8

Musick to heare, why hear'st thou musick sadly,
Sweets with sweets warre not, ioy delights in ioy:
Why lou'st thou that which thou receaust not gladly,
Or else receau'st with pleasure thine annoy?
If the true concord of well tuned sounds,
By vnions married do offend thine eare,
They do but sweetly chide thee, who confounds
In singlenesse the parts that thou should'st beare:
Marke how one string sweet husband to an other,
Strikes each in each by mutuall ordering;
Resembling sier, and child, and happy mother,
Who all in one, one pleasing note do sing:
  Whose speechlesse song being many, seeming one,
  Sings this to thee thou single wilt proue none.

Music to hear, why hear'st thou music sadly?
Sweets with sweets war not, joy delights in joy:
Why lov'st thou that which thou receiv'st not gladly,
Or else receiv'st with pleasure thine annoy?
If the true concord of well-tunèd sounds
By unions married do offend thine ear,
They do but sweetly chide thee, who confounds
In singleness the parts that thou shouldst bear;
Mark how one string, sweet husband to another,
Strikes each in each by mutual ordering;
Resembling sire, and child, and happy mother,
Who all in one, one pleasing note do sing;
  Whose speechless song being many, seeming one,
  Sings this to thee, "Thou single wilt prove none."

IT IS NOT Shakespeare’s use of the commonplace conceit *single life : married life : : single string : consort* (see Evans on its use in *Arcadia*, etc.) that here requires comment, but rather the increasingly fantastic prolongation of this commonplace through the last ten lines of the sonnet. The conceit is made the more fantastic by being elaborated not in solitary meditation or sustained public oratorical argument (where a conceit can easily take on a growth disproportionate to its origins), but rather in the intimate address of one person to another.

The pretext for the conceit is the young man’s uneasiness as he listens to sweet music. This untoward response gives Shakespeare the opportunity (more stringently practiced in sonnet 40) to give his speaker balanced half-lines enacting the figure of opposition. I show in parentheses the number of syllables per half-line:

Music to hear (4)	*why hear’st thou music sadly?* (7)
Sweets with sweets war not (5)	*joy delights in joy* (5)
Why lov’st thou that (4)	*which thou receiv’st not gladly* (7)
Or else receiv’st with pleasure (7)	*thine annoy?* (3)

It is clear that Shakespeare is here intent on deliberate caesural variation (which would be evident even if my placing of the caesura were slightly modified). The rocky disequilibrium of this quatrain could be charted metrically in the initial trochees of the first two (or three) lines and in the spondees of *sweets war not;* or it could be shown phonetically in the cacophony of *lov**st thou that** which **thou** receiv**’st***, etc. The metrical and phonetic disequilibrium is meant to enact the dis-ease of bachelorhood. By contrast, the family harmony which would exist were the young man to marry and beget a child generates the flurry of puns on harmonic unison, the graphic anagram of “unions”: ***tun**èd*, ***unions***, ***one** string*, *all in* ***one, one*** *pleasing note*, *seeming* ***one***. Bachelorhood contrasted with marriage generates the contrastive monodic pun on ***single*** and ***sing (sing**leness*, *do* ***sing***, ***song***, ***sings***, ***single)***. A fundamental appeal wants to turn the young man’s *not* (line 2) to a *note* (line 12).

The “invention” at work in the elaborate conceit of harmony (lines 5–14) is the decision to divide music into its three parts: its *sounds* or aural effect (lines 5–8); its *strings* or medium (lines 9–12); and its *song* or content (lines 13–14). This sort of logical division of a single entity into multiple (and therefore elaboratable) aspects is one of Shakespeare's most common inventive moves, widely shared with his contemporaries and borrowed of course from commonplace logical training. (For Shakespeare's most searching critique of the belief that everything can be classified by aspectual definition into parts, see sonnet 129.) Here, although the division of music into sounds, strings, and song is an intrinsically and materially rational one, the insistently developed conceit of married (and childbearing) strings is not. Shakespeare's procedure thus foregrounds the extent to which interpretation of a phenomenon (here, music) is determined by the context in which it is investigated. Were it not for the speaker's wish (whether commissioned or not) to incite the young man to marry, he would scarcely continue to insist, when hearing music, on the conceit of "married" sounds. As it is, his preexisting concern shapes his analysis of the aspects of music into his conceit. As sounds, the ingredients of music are simply *married.* As strings, one first becomes *sweet husband to another* and, as another instrument is added, they resemble *sire, and child, and happy mother* (where the happiness of the "mother" and the presence of the "child" are equally preposterous). Finally, as song, they are "lent" by the speaker a putative message for their literally *speechless* song, a message which taunts the young man for his nullity ("one," being *single,* cannot be a *number*; the concept "number" being regarded as solely plural). The projection of human motive onto the sounds *(They do but sweetly chide thee)* is a step up in invention from the young man's being (apparently irrationally but really understandably) annoyed by their "married" presence; and the projection into the sounds of chiding words (line 14)—words which, we are given to understand, they have been singing to the young man from the very beginning, causing his sadness and "annoy"—is a further escalation of invention.

The original dramatic situation of paradox (lines 1–4), in which sweets meet sweets sadly, seems more successfully worked than the rather tortured subsequent explanatory conceit. However, the resolution of many parts in one unison / *(being many, seeming one)* is of obvious relevance as an aesthetic principle for the Shakespearean sonnet, which, because of its four discrete parts, runs an inherently greater risk of disunity than does the Italian sonnet.

The assumed preestablished harmony between music and a harmoniously ordered human soul exists in the young man; he loves music, and normally receives pleasure from hearing it. Shakespeare (characteristically) gives several verbal formulations of reciprocity to the philosophical dissonance which provokes the sonnet:

1. The young man, though his effect is the same as that of music, *hears* music *sadly*.
2. The young man (a "sweet") *wars with* another "sweet" (music).
3. The young man (a "joy" to others) normally would *delight in* music (a "joy" to him) [but does not].
4. The young man, hearing music, *receives pleasure*, yes, but along with it, *annoy[ance]*.
5. Concord *offends [his] ear.*

Equally characteristically, Shakespeare varies the rhetorical form: a single question, two proverbs, a double question, a hypothesis. Both of these tactics—giving several conceptually different formulations of a problem, and embedding them in different rhetorical formats—are well-known strategies in persuasive oratory. They are made fresh here by the psychological presence of the philosophical problem of the Many and the One, as embodied in the young man's sulk at the prospect of his Oneness having to turn into Manyness. Shakespeare's reconciliation of the problem via music (perhaps borrowed from the *Arcadia*) is not new, but his straddling of the solution is: the strings sing *one* note, in truth, but the *sound* they make only *seems* one, and *is* many. Both oneness and manyness exist, existentially, in the music, in equal dominance. This is (or ought to be) reassuring to the young man; it clearly is to Shakespeare.

Shakespeare's strategies for unifying sonnet-parts into a true *concord . . . by unions married* are enormously varied, and can be clarified by a diagram. Here, one strategy of unification is to continue the musical lexicon

Structure of Sonnet 8

1						)		)		)	
2			composition by			)		)		)	
3			half-lines			)		)		)	
4						)		)		)	implied
5						)		)	direct	)	direct
6						)	musical	)	address	)	address
7						)	lexicon	)	(speaker	)	(strings
8				)		)		)	to young	)	to young
9		)		)	marrige	)		)	man)	)	man)
10		)		)	conceit	)		)		)	
11	*one/*	)	*sing/*	)		)		)		)	
12	*none*	)	*single/*	)		)		)		)	
13		)	*song*	)		)		)		)	
14		)		)		)		)		)	

through all fourteen lines; another is to sustain till the end the initial speech-act of direct address. The conceit of married sounds chiding singleness unifies lines 5–14; lines 8–14 are connected by the pun on *single* and *sing;* and lines 9–14 are connected by the puns on *one/none.* This principle of overlapping connections is one of the strongest and most frequently used in the composition of the *Sonnets.* A map of 8 (see the diagram) will clarify its overlaps.

Shakespeare's persistent willingness to be fanciful (frequently criticized by modern critics in, e.g., 99) represents delight in invention for its own sake. Shakespeare is careless, almost, of where fancifulness might lead. Its whimsical excesses are an index to the nature of imagination in its most visually accessible form, the fanciful (the sublime imagination, by contrast, is harder to track). Dr. Johnson's acute remark in his *Preface* on Shakespeare's fondness for a quibble can be enlarged to extend to more than puns: Shakespeare, for a moment, can treat any fantastical element of invention as all-important. It could be a conceit, as here; it could be the talismanic letters in *car,* as in sonnet 7; it could be the fascination of a symmetrical word like *widdow* (Quarto spelling), as in 9; or it could be the false "etymological" resemblance of *sing* [< *singan*] to *single* [< *singulus*]. (For another instance of this latter practice, see 24, where *the **sun** de**lights** to peep,* although *delight* [< *delectare*] has no etymology in common with *light* [< *lux, leukos*].) In short, any linguistic phenomenon can "distract" the verbal imagination from its supposed message.

Dr. Johnson's simile of Atalanta shows that he regarded as a distraction this glancing-aside of the Shakespearean imagination. I would suggest, by contrast, that the true intent of the verbal imagination is always to *make a chain of interesting signifiers,* with the "message" tucked in as best the poet can. My formulation is as exaggerated, in its way, as Dr. Johnson's, but it represents a serious view—that the verbal imagination lives in and by engagement with its medium. As the painter must serve color, and the sculptor volume, the poet must serve language. A poem that does not serve language is no poem, and when the opportunity for servitude to *w*—or mastery of the use of *w,* since the two come to the same thing—presents itself as a possible exercise, the verbal imagination cannot resist it, as we shall see in the next sonnet.

Couplet Tie: *sing,* [*song*], *sing* [*-s*] (12, 13, 14); *sing* [*-le*] [*-leness*] (8, 14)
one (9, 12, 13)

IS it for feare to wet a widdowes eye,
That thou consum'st thy selfe in single life?
Ah;if thou issulesse shalt hap to die,
The world will waile thee like a makelesse wife,
The world wilbe thy widdow and still weepe,
That thou no forme of thee hast left behind,
When euery priuat widdow well may keepe,
By childrens eyes,her husbands shape in minde:
Looke what an vnthrift in the world doth spend
Shifts but his place,for still the world inioyes it
But beauties waste, hath in the world an end,
And kept vnvsde the vser so destroyes it:
  No loue toward others in that bosome sits
  That on himselfe such murdrous shame commits.

Is it for fear to wet a widow's eye
That thou consum'st thyself in single life?
Ah! if thou issueless shalt hap to die,
The world will wail thee like a makeless wife,
The world will be thy widow and still weep,
That thou no form of thee hast left behind,
When every private widow well may keep,
By children's eyes, her husband's shape in mind:
Look what an unthrift in the world doth spend
Shifts but his place, for still the world enjoys it,
But beauty's waste hath in the world an end,
And kept unused, the user so destroys it:
  No love toward others in that bosom sits
  That on himself such murd'rous shame commits.

THIS "Fantasy on the Letter W" (as it could be entitled) arises, I believe, from Shakespeare's fascinated observation of the shape of the word *widdow* (the Quarto spelling):

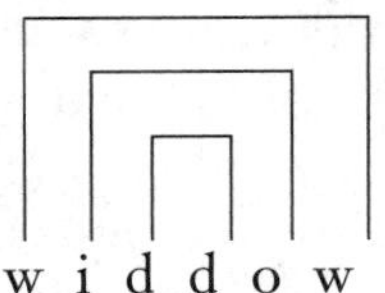

The initial and final *w*'s of *widdow* are mirror images of each other, and its middle letter is repeated—*dd*—in self-identity. The only letters in the alphabet which are mirror images of themselves are (roughly speaking, and disregarding serifs) *i, m, o, u, v, w,* and *x*. A word having *i, o, u, v,* or *x* both fore and aft is almost impossible to find, unless it is a proper name, an invented word, or slang (e.g., *Ubu, Xerox,* or *obbo* [for "observation," as in the idiom "keeping obbo"]). A word with a mirror-letter fore and aft and a middle repeated letter is even harder to find. The word *willow* (which Shakespeare uses in *Othello*) is another one of the rare natural instances of almost perfect symmetry. Shakespeare, delighted with the properties of the word *widdow,* and with the fact that *w* is a double *u* (and that *v* is internally printed *u,* and v is used for initial *u* in Elizabethan printing), sets off in a flurry of *w*'s, *u*'s, and *v*'s. Words containing more or less symmetrical parts like *issulesse* and *makelesse* and *unused* and *bosome* arise in the train of *widdow.* The poem needs to be read in the Quarto spelling, since in modern spelling some of the symmetries disappear (compare *widow* and *widdow, issueless and issulesse*). I have put the *w*'s, letters that would be *v*'s in modern spelling, and *u*'s in boldface; it will be seen that every line has at least one of these, and most lines have several:

Is it for feare to ***w****et a* ***w****iddo***w****es eye,*
*That tho***u** *cons***u***m'st thy selfe in single life?*
*Ah; if tho***u** *iss***u***lesse shalt hap to die,*
The ***w****orld* ***w****ill* ***w****aile thee like a makelesse* ***w****ife,*
The ***w****orld* ***w****ilbe thy* ***w****iddo***w** *and still* ***w****eepe,*

That thou no forme of thee hast left behind,
When euery priuat widdow well may keepe,
By childrens eyes, her husbands shape in minde:
Looke what an vnthrift in the world doth spend
Shifts but his place, for still the world inioyes it
But beauties waste hath in the world an end,
And kept vnvsde the vser so destroyes it:
No loue toward others in that bosome sits
That on himselfe such murdrous shame commits.

Whatever the charms of mirror-image letters and symmetrical words, the poem has to mean something too, and has to have a general shape. Categories familiar in the age of Shakespeare have now often fallen into desuetude; it has not, I think, been recognized that the shape of this sonnet depends on the contrast between a *sin of omission* (octave) and a *sin of commission* (sestet). This theological contrast (see the *New Catholic Encyclopedia*, 1967, *s.v.* "Omission") is foregrounded by the octave-words of negativity or absence (issue*less*, make*less*, *no form*) contrasted with sestet-words implying action *(spend, waste, user, destroys, murd'rous, commits).* The change in metaphor from the octave (a husband who leaves his widow childless) to the sestet (a hoarder who destroys beauty and murders himself) reinforces the distinction between omission and commission, as does the change from the octave's second-person address *(thou consum'st thyself)* to the sestet's third-person examples *(an unthrift . . . the user . . . on himself).* In sonnet 9, with its many differences demarcating octave from sestet, Shakespeare comes as close as he ever does to approximating the internal form of the Italian sonnet.

The sonnet at first presumes a *love toward others* (mentioned in line 13) as a natural quality in the young man, preposterously suggesting that he may have chosen to refrain from marriage so as not to make his future widow unhappy if he dies. One can read this as a reply sonnet:

Young Man: I'm not going to marry: how could I forgive myself if I were to die and leave my wife a widow? I love others too much to do that to her.

Speaker: Is it really for fear of grieving your widow that you don't marry? *Is* it really love of others? Whether or not you leave a widow, the whole world will mourn your death, so you'll be grieving people by your death whether you're married or not. *No love toward others* sits in your bosom, because self-love (according to the commandment to

> love others as yourself) has to precede love of others, and you commit murder[-ous shame] on yourself.

The "sin of omission" in the octave *(thou consum'st thyself)* advances toward the "sin of commission" in the couplet (the man refusing marriage *commits murd'rous shame on himself*) via the odd modulatory metaphor of circulating capital in Q_3. Money, because it is a medium of exchange, is always afloat in society as a value. But beauty—another form of social capital—cannot be transferred, and can be spent only by its owner. Shakespeare's interesting perception of the comparability of different forms of social capital, tangible (money) and intangible (beauty), brings them together only to divide them: [*use*]/[*money*]/*enjoy* ≠ *unuse/beauty/destroy*, a difference foregrounded by the rhyme *enjoys it / destroys it*.

Couplet Tie: *no* (6, 13). Normally, such a small and insignificant word would not "count" as a Couplet Tie. However, since one of the themes of the sonnet is omission, the adjective *no* is a strongly thematic word. Also, in its two occurrences it appears in the same sort of phrase (No X + preposition + personal pronoun)—*no form of thee* (6) and *no love toward others* (13), so that the word *no* becomes mnemonically foregrounded by patterning.

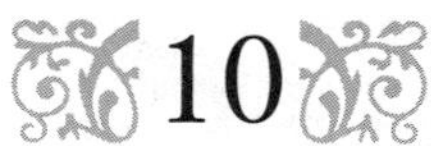

FOr ſhame deny that thou bear'ſt loue to any
Who for thy ſelfe art ſo vnprouident
Graunt if thou wilt,thou art belou'd of many,
But that thou none lou'ſt is moſt euident:
For thou art ſo poſſeſt with murdrous hate,
That gainſt thy ſelfe thou ſtickſt not to conſpire,
Seeking that beautious roofe to ruinate
Which to repaire ſhould be thy chiefe deſire :
O change thy thought,that I may change my minde,
Shall hate be fairer log'd then gentle loue?
Be as thy preſence is gracious and kind,
Or to thy ſelfe at leaſt kind harted proue,
  Make thee an other ſelfe for loue of me,
  That beauty ſtill may liue in thine or thee.

For shame deny that thou bear'st love to any,
Who for thy self art so unprovident.
Grant, if thou wilt, thou art beloved of many,
But that thou none lov'st is most evident;
For thou art so possessed with murd'rous hate,
That 'gainst thy self thou stick'st not to conspire,
Seeking that beauteous roof to ruinate
Which to repair should be thy chief desire:
O change thy thought, that I may change my mind!
Shall hate be fairer lodged than gentle love?
Be as thy presence is, gracious and kind,
Or to thy self at least kind-hearted prove:
  Make thee another self for love of me,
  That beauty still may live in thine or thee.

SHAKESPEARE is especially concerned, I think, to punctuate his sequence with moments of visible drama. It is on these dramatic "turns" that all putative reconstructions of the "narratives" behind the sequence have been based. Sonnet 10 is the first poem to use the first-person singular, *I* and *me.* Such a moment in lyric is the equivalent of the entry of a new *dramatis persona* on the stage: its effect cannot be overestimated. In what asks to be taken (because of the contrast with preceding sonnets voiced in a generalized "we") as a startling moment of personal sentiment, the speaker cries at the *volta, O change thy thought, that I may change my mind!* Later he asks the young man to breed, *for love of me.* Since the aim of the poem is to enact the speaker's plea that the young man change from hate to love, it has recourse to such matched pairs as *art beloved / none lov'st, ruinate/repair, hate/love.* The Quarto spelling of *thyself* as two words, *thy* and *selfe,* allows for the presence of the KEY WORD "SELF" (lines 2, 6, 12, 13), distributed between *thy self* and *another self,* so as to enact the identity-in-difference of father and child.

The logical quibble on which this (rather uninteresting) sonnet turns is the distinction between love of self and love of others (continued from sonnet 9), and depends on the injunction, "Thou shall love thy neighbor *as thyself.*" This moral obligation stems from the concept of distributive justice, by which we are forbidden to hoard goods to which others have a right. The speaker's sophistical argument, which wishes to force the young man to admit that he is moved to single life not by self-love but by self-hatred, runs through the following changes of hortatory verb:

> [*Admit* that thou dost not love anyone at all]
> *Deny* that thou bear'st love to any
> Since thou art so unprovident even toward [what should be the first object of thy love] thy self.
> *Grant* thou art beloved of many,
> But [*grant* also that] thou lov'st none at all.
> For thou art so possessed with murd'rous hate,
> That thou dost not hesitate to conspire even against thy self . . .
> *Change* thy thought from hate to love (that I may change my opinion of thee)

Be [to all] gracious and kind,
Or at least to thyself *prove* kind-hearted:
Make thee another self for love of me,
That beauty still may live in { thine or thee.

Sonnet 10 serves as a means to absolve the young man from the accusation that he loves himself alone. Sonnet 9 had accused him of having no love *for others,* with the implication that he spent his love on himself (as had been said explicitly in 4, where he was accused of *having traffic with [him]self alone*). Sonnet 10, by contrast, "proves" sophistically that the young man cannot be accused of self-love, since he exhibits a self-hatred leading to self-murder. This fiction marks the beginning of much sophistry about the young man's deeds. It is, among other things, the cunning verbal management of such sophistical arguments by the speaker of the *Sonnets* that leads us to distinguish Shakespeare the ironic author from his (deceived-and-self-deceiving) speaker.

KEY WORD: SELF

Couplet Tie: *self* (2, 6, 12, 13)
love (10, 13)
beauty [*beauteous*] (7, 14)

11

A S faſt as thou ſhalt wane ſo faſt thou grow'ſt,
In one of thine, from that which thou departeſt,
And that freſh bloud which yongly thou beſtow'ſt,
Thou maiſt call thine, when thou from youth conuerteſt,
Herein liues wiſdome, beauty, and increaſe,
Without this follie, age, and could decay,
If all were minded ſo, the times ſhould ceaſe,
And threeſcoore yeare would make the world away:
Let thoſe whom nature hath not made for ſtore,
Harſh, featureleſſe, and rude, barrenly perriſh,
Looke whom ſhe beſt indow'd, ſhe gaue the more;
Which bountious guift thou ſhouldſt in bounty cherriſh,
  She caru'd thee for her ſeale, and ment therby,
  Thou ſhouldſt print more, not let that coppy die.

As fast as thou shalt wane, so fast thou grow'st,
In one of thine, from that which thou departest,
And that fresh blood which youngly thou bestow'st
Thou mayst call thine, when thou from youth convertest:
Herein lives wisdom, beauty, and increase,
Without this, folly, age, and cold decay;
If all were minded so, the times should cease,
And threescore year would make the world away.
Let those whom Nature hath not made for store,
Harsh, featureless, and rude, barrenly perish:
Look whom she best endowed she gave the more;
Which bounteous gift thou shouldst in bounty cherish:
  She carved thee for her seal, and meant thereby
  Thou shouldst print more, not let that copy die.

THE early sonnets represent begetting both by organic metaphors and by inorganic ones. The organic metaphors are self-evident: they are drawn from vegetation, agriculture, husbandry, and physiology (flowers in sonnets 1, 3 and 16; corn in 12; the *store* of 11 and 14; the *blood* of 11). Among the inorganic metaphors, at least two are scarcely avoidable by any poet treating begetting: the first is the dynastically conventional one of the *house* that the young man should repair, not ruinate (10, 13); the other is the punning conceit on *son* and sun (7). Other inorganic metaphors give freer play to Shakespeare's invention: they include the looking *glass* of 3; the *vial* of perfume of 5 and 6; the "good" *use* of money of 4, 6, and 9; the musical *strings* of 8; and the *seal* of the present sonnet. "Generation" of a second object (these inorganic metaphors tell us) can come about through various processes: mirror-reflection, distillation, money-lending, musical harmonization, printing. It is typical of Shakespeare's constantly analytic mind that he would press into use so many different inorganic as well as organic categories by which one thing "begets" another, and that he would discriminate tonally among (a) those happy instances which produce the new without themselves being diminished (e.g., the happy strings in their married concord); (b) the happier instances where the original is augmented (as in the loan repayment by which *ten of thine ten times refigured thee*, in sonnet 6); and (c) those elegiac instances which introduce nostalgia (as the mother's glass in 3 *calls back the lovely April of her prime*).

Shakespeare often works to bring his inorganic metaphors to life; frequently, though he creates them inanimate, he animates them by metaphorizing his metaphor (as the inorganic instrument-strings are made to *marry* each other and beget new sounds, or as the inorganic distillate becomes a *liquid prisoner pent*). In 11, however, the inorganic metaphor of the *seal* remains inanimate: the young man is urged to use himself as a seal to *print copies* of himself. The *seal* itself is not animated by any anthropomorphic device comparable to marriage or imprisonment. And because the rest of 11 is so resolutely biological (as the fresh *blood* of the descendant replaces the progenitor, and nature's biological intent of *store* is expounded), the intransigently inorganic *seal* of the couplet comes as a shock. How, then, is the action of copy-printing to be made vividly reproductive?

To answer this question—which represents the aesthetic problem Shakespeare here set himself—we must look, for a moment, at the whole of 11. The closing image—by which the *seal* prints *copies* of itself—is a steady-state image of reduplication; the seal is not diminished or added to by its copies. However, the governing image of the body of the sonnet is that of inversely proportional decline and increase. (As 12 will shortly put it, sweets and beauties die *as fast as* they see others grow.) Sonnet 11 says, "*As fast as* thou shalt wane, *so fast* thou grow'st." As the young man wanes, he will grow in the person of his child. The metaphor of waning and growing is very far from the metaphor of undiminished copy-printing. The two metaphors—organic and inorganic—exist in tension with each other, and the poem has obligations to enact each of them. Shakespeare will "do" waning-and-growing first; then he will "do" printing. If it is entertaining to watch him doing them, as I believe it is, it must have been far more entertaining for him to think up how to do them; sonnets such as this rejoice in their own athleticism.

The waning-and-growing is done three times over. The first time, it is done triply in small—wane/grow/wane/grow/wane—in a personal narrative: "As fast as *thou shalt wane* so fast *thou grow'st* [from what] *thou departest; fresh blood thou bestowest* when *thou from youth convertest.*" The second time it is done more slowly as grow/wane in impersonal and epigrammatic terms:

> *Herein lives wisdom, beauty, and increase,* [grow]
> *Without this, folly, age, and cold decay.* [wane]

The third time it is done yet more expansively as wane/grow in generalized terms referring to men in general:

> *If all were minded so, the times should cease,*
> *And threescore year would make the world away.*
> *Let those whom Nature hath not made for store,*
> *Harsh, featureless, and rude, barrenly perish.* } [wane]
>
> *Look whom she best endowed she gave the more.* [grow]

The poem now returns to the personal narrative with which it began, but it does so while largely abandoning the constitutive organic metaphor of waning and growing which it has been so patently enacting. It turns instead to a "better" metaphor which will not require the disagreeable *waning* of the beloved—the inorganic metaphor of the seal that prints successive copies. And in its last four lines, the sonnet begins to print copies of its own words: *gave*, *gift; bounteous*, *bounty; more*, *more; shouldst*, *shouldst; carved*, *copy;* ***meant***, ***print***. The process of "copying" is enacted before the reader's eyes.

However, the inorganic process of copying does not entirely efface the initial organic metaphor of waning and growing, breeding and perishing; rather, it is ultimately subsumed within the larger structure of that organic metaphor. The initial biological model of a selective group of superior beings kept by nature as *store* (breeding-stock for future generations) and the subsequent aesthetic model of a carved *seal* are brought together in the final adjuration: "[Do not] let that *copy die.*" Printed copies do not die. "Copy" in this sense forcibly recalls its etymological root, *copia*, and thus puns on the semantic import of *increase* and *bounty*, those signs of nature's cornu*copia*.

The whole poem can be divided under the two heads *Increase* and *Perish:*

Increase	Perish
	As fast as thou shalt wane,
so fast thou grow'st / In one of thine	*from that which thou departest,*
And that fresh blood which youngly thou bestow'st	
Thou mayst call thine	*when thou from youth convertest:*
Herein lives wisdom, beauty, and increase	*Without this, folly, age, and cold decay;*
	If all were minded so, the times should cease,
	And threescore year would make the world away.
	Let those whom Nature hath not made for store,
	Harsh, featureless, and rude, barrenly perish:
Look whom she best endowed she gave the more;	
Which bounteous gift thou shouldst in bounty cherish:	

Increase	Perish
She carved thee for her seal, and meant thereby	
Thou shouldst print more,	*not let that copy die.*

Printing (and reading) the sonnet in this way emphasizes how much it is a piece of *verse*, in the old etymological meaning of the back-and-forth turning of the plough *(versus)*. The successive turns—from *increasing* to *perishing* and back again—become visible, establishing the conclusive persistence of the metaphor *waning/growing* as a structuring principle. At the same time, printing out the sonnet in this way makes us realize how early its own reduplicative copy-printing is inserted in the sonnet, long before the copy-metaphor is voiced: we notice *as fast, so fast; from that, from youth;* and, most strikingly, the three parallel triads: *wisdom, beauty, and increase; folly, age, and cold decay; harsh, featureless, and rude.*

Shakespeare introduces the ruling goddess Natura in the sestet as a contrast to his concentration in the octave on reproductive decision-making by human beings. Natura's interest in keeping the world going makes her do two things: in her capacity as generation-goddess she selects a breeding stock, and in her capacity as supreme artist she carves a seal. (We shall see Natura as artist again in sonnet 20). It is a more serious thing, we gather, to disobey Natura than to indulge one's own wish not to breed; and it is (the climax suggests) more serious to disobey Natura the artist than Natura the engenderer. Natura the artist has transferred her own initial agency ("she carved thee") to the young man ("and meant thereby / *Thou shouldst print* more"); this transfer imposes on the young man the responsibility of *Natura naturans.* With the introduction of the word *print*, we begin to approach the emphasis on the eternizing power of art which will, after sonnet 17, supplant breeding altogether.

A few remarks on verbal and technical interconnections of 11 to other sonnets may be useful. The words *increase* and *cease* echo sonnet 1 *(increase, decease)* and anticipate 13 *(lease, decease)* and 15 *(increase, decrease)*. I believe Shakespeare could not have been unconscious of the anagram *seale/lease*, since *lease* (13) springs into view so shortly after *seale* (11, Quarto spelling). Because *seale* is in every way a surprise when it occurs (in its inorganic nature, its failure to seem necessitated by alliteration or rhyme), it is foregrounded, and provokes special attention. It is because we are forced to pay attention to it that we are led to perceive the contrast between the organic and the inorganic, between man's proposing and Natura's disposing. And we are led by it as well into perceiving the poem as a seal which generates within itself copies of its own stylistic features. Whether the foregrounding of *seale* is remembered when one encounters *that beauty which you hold in lease* in 13 perhaps depends on whether the reader shares with Shakespeare the Renaissance fascination with the way words look when printed. A purely oral poetry can have no interest in anagrams; but Shakespeare belongs to the world of print, a world in which anagrams were recognized and enjoyed.

Finally, a word on feminine rhymes. They are relatively rare in the *Sonnets*, and I think have no strong aesthetic import unless they dominate (as they do in 20 and 87). However, because feminine rhymes such as those here *(departest*, *convertest; perish*, *cherish)* are more undulant or pliant than stiff monosyllabic masculine rhymes, they convey something of a dying fall, appropriate both here and in their occurrence *(pleasure*, *treasure)* in 126.

Couplet Tie: *more* (11, 14) The sonnet in little.

12

VV Hen I doe count the clock that tels the time,
And ſee the braue day ſunck in hidious night,
When I behold the violet paſt prime,
And ſable curls or ſiluer'd ore with white:
When lofty trees I ſee barren of leaues,
Which erſt from heat did canopie the herd
And Sommers greene all girded vp in ſheaues
Borne on the beare with white and briſtly beard:
Then of thy beauty do I queſtion make
That thou among the waſtes of time muſt goe,
Since ſweets and beauties do them-ſelues forſake,
And die as faſt as they ſee others grow,
And nothing gainſt Times ſieth can make defence
Saue breed to braue him, when he takes thee hence.

When I do count the clock that tells the time,
And see the brave day sunk in hideous night,
When I behold the violet past prime,
And sable curls all silvered o'er with white;
When lofty trees I see barren of leaves,
Which erst from heat did canopy the herd,
And summer's green all girded up in sheaves
Borne on the bier with white and bristly beard:
Then of thy beauty do I question make
That thou among the wastes of time must go,
Since sweets and beauties do themselves forsake
And die as fast as they see others grow,
And nothing 'gainst Time's scythe can make defence
Save breed to brave him, when he takes thee hence.

FOR the first time, the speaker's first-person pronoun dominates a poem. (In sonnet 10, the "I" fell into a subordinate syntactic position: "O [do thou] change thy thought, that *I may change my mind . . .* / [Do thou] make thee another self *for love of me.*") With this poem, there enters into the sequence the animating speaker-and-meditator whom earlier readers like Wordsworth called "Shakespeare." Our age wishes rather to call him "the speaker" or—when he represents himself as a writer—"the poet," reserving the name "Shakespeare" for the writer who invented these fictions and figures, a writer aware—as his speaker seems often not to be—of various sophistries and self-deceptions in his speaker's words. "Shakespeare" is the proper name for the author who, by imaginative and writerly means (from structure to puns to meter to syntactic schemes) renders the utterance of his fictional protagonist a literary one. Here, the *I* of the speaker begins its ascendancy in the drama of the sequence which it will come to dominate.

To my mind, the phrase in sonnet 12 that most demands explanation and rewards attention (one can unravel the whole poem from it) is the cluster *sweets and beauties. Beauties* is clear enough from many anterior references in the sonnet; but what does Shakespeare mean us to understand by *sweets?* To answer this question, I must glance at the organization of the whole.

Sonnet 12 opposes two models of Time. The first is the gradually vanishing conceptual entity registered by the poem's aurally and visually ticking clock *(When I do **count** the **clock that tells** the time).* The second model is represented by the aggressive emblem-figure of Time with his scythe. These models of Time in turn call up two models of death—an intransitive one in which things, as the clock ticks, all by themselves sink, go among the wastes of Time, grow barren, and die; and a transitive one in which Time the reaper actively cuts them down and takes them away. In the first death-model, death occurs of itself, gradually and innocently, if sadly; in the second, death occurs because life has been murdered.

The innocence of the first death-model accounts for the elegiac submission that characterizes the first twelve lines of the poem. The extraordinary poignancy of these lines arises from the list of intransitively fading *beauties* (the brave day, the violet, sable curls, summer's green). For the moment, we tend to assimilate to this list of *beauties* the lofty trees that come between the sable curls and summer's green, and we rather skip over those unexpected *dramatis personae*, the herd (sheep or cows). The sestet continues the emphasis on *beauty:* "Then of *thy beauty* do I question make." It is only in line 11 that we come to a phrase that is clearly intended as a summary of what has gone before: *sweets and beauties.* We expected the summary noun *beauties*, but we did not expect to find it prefaced by another summary noun, *sweets.*

Sweetness and *beauty* are two of Shakespeare's constituting categories of value, standing respectively for inward *virtue* and outward *show* (see 54). We recognize that they occur in sonnet 12 as a compliment to the young man. If the speaker were reminded of the young man's fate only by things that resembled him in *beauty* (as first seems likely in the coordinating emphasis on *thy* in "Then of *thy* beauty do I question make") he would be treating the young man solely as an aesthetic object, not as (also) a moral subject. By adding *sweets* as a category which reminds him of the young man, the speaker tells us that he is struck by *good* things that disappear as well as beautiful ones; and when we look back to see what proof we have of that interest in the poem, we behold, as if for the first time, the kindly trees sheltering the grateful herd. Kindness to a flock of animals on the part of trees is a strange *sweet*, but it was aesthetically necessary that the subtly proffered proleptic example of a *sweet* not appear to break the list of *beauties;* and trees keep company unobtrusively with the day, the violet, and summer's green growth. Insofar as the lofty trees are now barren of leaves, they participate fully in the list of fading beauties; insofar as they canopied the herd from heat, they stand for something "sweet" (virtuous) as well as beautiful.

The two involuntary models of death alluded to above—the innocently declining one (expressed in the adjectives *sunk*, *past*, *silvered*, *barren*, and *borne*) and the murderous one (caused by Time's *taking* of victims) are both compatible with the disappearance of *beauties.* The two models are in tension, surprisingly, with a third model, one making the candidate for destruction a moral subject, able to *choose* to disappear. In this third model, death is freely and reflexively elected in response to the sight of a new generation growing up:

> . . . sweets and beauties *do themselves forsake* [the only enjambment]
> *And die as fast as they see others grow.*

Those *others* are able to grow not only because their progenitors have chosen to forsake themselves and die, but also because the progenitors have chosen to breed, so that Death's power may be at least braved, if not evaded. Had the young man not been created a moral subject by the inclusion of the trees' sweet kindliness to the herd, and its retroactive foregrounding by the subsequent appearance of the category *sweets*, he could not be expected to undertake the inward free moral choices of breeding and accepting his own mortality.

The major aesthetic inventions of sonnet 12 are thus the decision to add *sweets* to *beauties*, and its corollary, the model of freely chosen acquiescence in one's own death in favor of one's children's life. I call the second the corollary of the first because both arise from a moral perception deeper than that generating earlier conventional reproaches addressed to the young man. If the young man is to be a creature of human worth, he must be virtuous, must not rail against but must acquiesce morally in his own extermination, and must defy, by biologically reinforcing Nature's increase, the power of Time to decrease value. Against the euphemistic view of Time by which things are said merely to sink or fade past their prime, the poem bravely faces up to the aggressive destructive power manifesting itself through Time the reaper; and against an aestheticism that would deplore only aging and the loss of beauty, the poem sets a moral elegy that deplores the eventual disappearance of sweet virtue, as well. In the pun connecting the body of the poem to the couplet, the intransitive sinking of the *brave* day is *braved* by the transitive act of beauty voluntarily bred anew.

Sonnet 12 is unlike some later sonnets in allowing its three models of dying—vanishing, being scythed down, and freely choosing to breed and be willing to die—to melt insensibly from one to the next (the *scythe*, e.g., being anticipated by the *sheaves*), without harsh juxtaposition or acknowledged conflict. Sharply juxtaposed and conflicting models of Time, life, and death will arise later in the sequence (in sonnets 60 and 73, for instance).

Shakespeare's lists almost always exhibit disproportion in verbal quantity as well as variety in example, and the list of beauties and sweets here is no exception to the rule. The first quatrain gives each of its three items *(day, violet, curls)* only one line apiece, but the second, broadening, quatrain gives each of its items *(trees, green)* two lines. The items in Q_1 are seen only in their present decayed state *(sunk, past prime, silvered o'er);* but Q_2 accords a full backward glance away from decrepitude *(barren, bier)* to Nature's prime *(leaves which erst . . . did canopy . . . summer's green.)* The degree to which the more leisurely sketch of a pastoral landscape in Q_2 broadens and extends the rapid inventory of Q_1 is itself a sign of nostalgia and maturing reflection, as is the checking of the initial indulgence in affective language *(brave, hideous)* by a more philosophical and resigned meditation *(Then of thy beauty do I question make)*. The repeated linguistic sign in the poem is the phrase Noun + Past Participle (or Adjective), enacting the collapse of value: *day sunk, violet past, curls silvered, trees barren, green borne.* But the horror of this collapse is eventually subdued into moral necessity: *thou . . . must go.* The pained farewell to the paternal *white and bristly beard* seen for the last time is, by the end of the poem, converted into a generational energy which, though it cannot yet find a visual counterweight to *borne on the bier*, can be announced as a conceptual counterforce: *breed to brave* Death.

The sonnet embodies a precarious moment of pure regret, a precious moment when, as yet, the young man is still all virtue, all beauty, and the speaker all tenderness, all grief. The anthropomorphizing of nature—in which trees are *barren* (not "bereft"), the day is *brave*, the sheaves borne on a *bier* (which in the Quarto spelling, *beare*, so resembles the anthropomorphic *beard*)—arises from this suffusing regret, a regret as ready to humanize vegetation as to sympathize with the uncomfortable shade-seeking herd. The doubly-orphaned Keats wrote in anguished protest, in the margin of his copy of the sonnets, now in Harvard's Houghton Library, next to the account of summer's bier, "Is this to be borne? Hark ye!"

Couplet Tie: *brave* (2, 14)
time (1, 10, 13)

O That you were your ſelfe,but loue you are
No longer yours,then you your ſelfe here liue,
Againſt this cumming end you ſhould prepare,
And your ſweet ſemblance to ſome other giue.
So ſhould that beauty which you hold in leaſe
Find no determination,then you were
You ſelfe again after your ſelfes deceaſe,
When your ſweet iſſue your ſweet forme ſhould beare.
Who lets ſo faire a houſe fall to decay,
Which husbandry in honour might vphold,
Againſt the ſtormy guſts of winters day
And barren rage of deaths eternall cold?
O none but vnthrifts,deare my loue you know,
You had a Father,let your Son ſay ſo.

O that you were your self! but, love, you are
No longer yours than you yourself here live;
Against this coming end you should prepare,
And your sweet semblance to some other give:
So should that beauty which you hold in lease
Find no determination; then you were
Your self again after yourself's decease,
When your sweet issue your sweet form should bear.
Who lets so fair a house fall to decay,
Which husbandry in honour might uphold
Against the stormy gusts of winter's day
And barren rage of death's eternal cold?
O none but unthrifts: dear my love, you know
You had a father, let your son say so.

IN THE drama of the *Sonnets*, this poem marks the momentous instant in which the speaker first uses vocatives of love: he addresses the young man as *love* and *dear my love*. It is an unforgettable change of address even from the earlier vocatives such as *tender churl* (sonnet 1), *unthrifty loveliness* (4), and *music to hear* (8); and although the injunction to breed (still the putative motive for the speaker's utterance) will persist for a few poems yet, this poem sets a new tone of personal intensity with respect to an envisaged personal loss.

The sonnet is an Italianate one, in which the octave argues for preservation of the individual self, the sestet for preservation of family lineage. The word linking octave and sestet is *hold*, and its initial *h* is graphically foregrounded as well; *t**h**e beauty w**h**ich you **hold** in lease* (individual) becomes in the sestet the dynastic ***h**ouse . . ./W**h**ich **h**usbandry in **h**onor mig**h**t up**hold**.)* Argument links the two parts of the poem, argument pulling out so many stops that we feel uncertain which parts of it are intended to carry the most weight. The speaker offers the young man many competing arguments for breeding, and inserts in them a flurry of parallel phrases *(your self, your . . . semblance, your . . . issue, your . . . form)*, a play on *decease* and *decay*, a play on *should* (obligation and probable future), and even such graphic overlaps as the one in *de**ter**mination* and *e**ter**nal:*

1. Religious: *Prepare / Against this coming end*
2. Ethical/Altruistic: *You should give your semblance to some other*
3. Narcissistic: *So should that beauty which you hold in lease / Find no determination*
4. Resurrective: *You [would be] your self again after yourself's decease*
5. Aesthetic: *Your sweet issue your sweet form [would] bear*
6. Dynastic: *Who lets so fair a house fall to decay*
7. Aristocratic: *Which husbandry in honor might uphold*
8. Prudential: *husbandry . . . none but unthrifts*
9. Erotic: *dear my love*
10. Paternal: *let your son say so*

All these positive arguments taken together are less persuasive than the single chilling phrase (marked in Keats's copy of the *Sonnets*), *barren rage of death's eternal cold.* The fulcrum-word, *death*, stands out as it balances the futile energy of *barren rage* to its left with the ghostly numbness of *eternal cold* to its right.

As I understand this poem, it is the first of many "reply-sonnets," poems which respond to an implied anterior utterance from the young man. We are to imagine that the young man has said, in response to earlier reproaches, "I am myself, sufficient to myself." The speaker replies, as the sonnet opens, "Oh that that were true! *O that you were your self [in some permanent fashion]; but, love, you are / No longer yours than you yourself here live.*" Such "replies" to implied remarks by the young man reach their apogee in sonnets 76 *(Why is my verse)*, 110 *(Alas 'tis true)*, 116 *(Let me not)*, and 117 *(Accuse me thus)*, as will be seen below. The flurry of arguments which I have spelled out above suggests a speaker uncertain which of his competing discourses of persuasion will best convince his interlocutor.

Though fertility of invention in argument may be the logical aim of the poem, the sudden glacial current of the *voix d'outre-tombe* speaking of *death's eternal cold* is its imaginative excuse for being, and represents the sudden thrust of the participatory Shakespearean imagination triumphing over the cleverness of position-taking.

Couplet Tie: *love* (1, 13). Normally, this would represent a weak Couplet Tie, the word *love* being such a frequent and expectable one in the sequence. However, used as it is here, as the first-encountered instance of the vocative of personal intensity, it is, of course, unusually visible; and the two pleadings of direct address are foregrounded positionally as well, since they open and close the poem.

14

NOt fro n the ſtars do I my iudgement plucke,
And yet me thinkes I haue Aſtronomy,
But not to tell of good,or euil lucke,
Of plagues,of dearths,or ſeaſons quallity,
Nor can I fortune to breefe mynuits tell;
Pointing to each his thunder, raine and winde,
Or ſay with Princes if it ſhal go wel
By oft predict that I in heauen finde.
But from thine eies my knowledge I deriue,
And conſtant ſtars in them I read ſuch art
As truth and beautie ſhal together thriue
If from thy ſelfe,to ſtore thou wouldſt conuert:
Or elſe of thee this I prognoſticate,
Thy end is Truthes and Beauties doome and date.

Not from the stars do I my judgement pluck,
And yet methinks I have astronomy,
But not to tell of good or evil luck,
Of plagues, of dearths, or seasons' quality;
Nor can I fortune to brief minutes tell,
Pointing to each his thunder, rain, and wind,
Or say with princes if it shall go well
By oft predict that I in heaven find:
But from thine eyes my knowledge I derive,
And, constant stars, in them I read such art
As truth and beauty shall together thrive
If from thy self to store thou wouldst convert:
  Or else of thee this I prognosticate,
  Thy end is truth's and beauty's doom and date.

THE speaker as philosophical mock-astrologer. Dramatically, the first appearance in the *Sonnets* of the linked words *truth and beauty* (a change from the previous pair, *sweets and beauties*). The Platonic triad—the good *(sweet, kind)*, the true, and the beautiful *(fair)*—appears in the *Sonnets* both as a whole (*fair, kind,* and *true*, 76) and in groupings of two of its three qualities. Virtue and beauty can be coupled (*sweets and beauties*, 12) or problematically disjoined (54: *O how much more*). *Sweets* in Shakespeare tend to confer good on others, and (like perfume) to have an extension that survives the bodily extinction of the form in which they originate; *truth* tends to represent for Shakespeare the convergence of inner substance with outer show, and is related to *troth* in personal relation. *Truth* seems to be called into this sonnet by the concept of prognostication; the speaker boasts that he is a seer who can tell the truth about the future. The poem contains a charming inventory of what people in Shakespeare's day, from farmers to princes, wanted from their fortune-tellers; the speaker draws a contrast between those fortune-tellers' local prophetic capacities and his more philosophical ones. Like local astrologers, he "has astronomy" and wishes to predict events; like them, he scans heavenly bodies. But while they search the stars, he gazes at his beloved's eyes; while they foretell particulars, he foretells the metaphysical future of the universe. The poem carefully constructs itself on these parallels and divergences, as shown in the diagram below.

There are, then, two kinds of astrology: from the stars one can read the astrology of specific events (good and evil luck, dearths and plenty, glad and sorry seasons, uncertain weather, princely vicissitudes), and from the beloved's eyes—those mirrors of the soul's beauty—one can read the astrology of the Platonic moral universe. The metaphysical astrology of free will leaves the human subject open to choose: he may choose good ("Truth, Beauty, and thou thyself will thrive in breeding") or evil ("Truth, Beauty, and thou thyself will meet a single doom at the date of your death"). These alternative prognostications, representing two mutually exclusive readings of the beautiful and putatively constant starry eyes, convey for the first time in the sequence the fundamental unreadability of the young man, whose eyes can be seen, but whose heart can only be guessed at. The shaping of this sonnet into impregnable fortunetellingparallels is the formal equivalent of a conviction that inner moral prognostication is an art as secure in its procedures as astrology; in view of Shakespeare's perennial skepticism, we may find the speaker's believability impugned by his very syntactic confidence.

Structure of Sonnet 14

ALL ASTROLOGERS

Ordinary Astrologers	"I": Speaker-Astrologer
Pluck judgment from stars	*derive knowledge from thine eyes (constant stars)*
tell:	*I read such art as*
1. *of good or evil luck* (fortunes told to individuals)	1. *truth and beauty shall together thrive* (if you breed)
2. *of plagues, of dearths, of seasons' quality* (farmers' almanac)	*or else of thee this I prognosticate*
3. *fortune to brief minutes tell, / Pointing to each his thunder, rain, and wind* (weather forecast)	2. *thy end is truth's and beauty's doom and date.*
4. *or say if it shall go well with princess* (court astrologer)	

At least part of the charm of the sonnet lies in Shakespeare's enumeration-by-*praeteritio* of the functions of astrology in his society. Another charm is the run on *p* as the astrologer's letter: *pluck, pointing, predict, prognosticate* (with *plagues* and *princes* thrown in to keep the chain running). Yet another, etymological, charm lies in the change from *con-stant* to *con-vert;* another is the Greek pun ***know**ledge* / *pro**gnostic**ate;* another, the graphic overlaps among ***st**ars*, ***ast**rology*, *con**st**ant*, and ***art.***

Couplet Tie: *Truth* [-'*s*] *and beauty* [-'*s*] (11, 14). The impossibility of dissevering these two Platonic qualities from each other (a fact foregrounded by their twinned repetition), and their association with the Good (implied by the eyes' constancy) puts into relief the anguish of the eventual disjunction of these members of the Platonic triad in later sonnets.

15

WHen I conſider euery thing that growes
Holds in perfection but a little moment.
That this huge ſtage preſenteth nought but ſhowes
Whereon the Stars in ſecret influence comment.
When I perceiue that men as plants increaſe,
Cheared and checkt euen by the ſelfe-ſame skie:
Vaunt in their youthfull ſap,at height decreaſe,
And were their braue ſtate out of memory.
Then the conceit of this inconſtant ſtay,
Sets you moſt rich in youth before my ſight,
Where waſtfull time debateth with decay
To change your day of youth to ſullied night,
And all in war with Time for loue of you.
As he takes from you,I ingraft you new.

When I consider every thing that grows
Holds in perfection but a little moment,
That this huge stage presenteth nought but shows
Whereon the stars in secret influence comment;
When I perceive that men as plants increase,
Cheerèd and checked even by the selfsame sky,
Vaunt in their youthful sap, at height decrease,
And wear their brave state out of memory:
Then the conceit of this inconstant stay
Sets you most rich in youth before my sight,
Where wasteful Time debateth with Decay
To change your day of youth to sullied night,
And all in war with Time for love of you,
As he takes from you, I ingraft you new.

THIS is the first of the *Sonnets* to employ Shakespeare's grand macrocosmic scale, one that is more suited, in common opinion, to philosophical poetry than to the love-sonnet. The *stars* (borrowed perhaps from 14) preside in secret influence over a *huge stage* where everything that lives has its brief day before being destroyed by Time. Even the beloved, alas, will have only that brief day. The subdivisions of the sonnet are themselves wittily introduced. The octave's two introductory verbs, *When I con-sider* [< *sidus*, constellation] and *When I per-ceive*, together give birth (by combination of their respective first and second syllables) to the sestet's hybrid *con-ceit.*

The poem is Shakespeare's self-critique of 13. There, the young man was told that he should *uphold* the beauty and lineage which he *holds* in lease—with the emphasis on *hold* as the verb of sustaining and possessing through time. Here, by contrast, the verb *hold* is despaired of from the beginning: everything that grows *holds* in perfection *but a little moment.* The reassuring feudal *hold*-paradigm of tenancy, possession, and prolongation is replaced by a tragic *hold*-paradigm of rise and fall, proper to everything *sub sidera.* For the first time in the sequence, the speaker here looks on life from the vantage point of the stars above in his con-sideration; yet he sees as well from a helpless human perspective below. Much of the pathos of this and other sonnets derives from the capacity of the philosophical mind to rise to impersonal grandeur or cold self-inspection while the sensual mind remains below, in thrall to passion. The structure of the poem (a structure used again in 25) narrows from the general to the particular. Just as in 25 the speaker descends from the general category *those who are in favour with their stars* to the special category *great princes' favourites* to the particular instance *the painful warrior famousèd for fight* and thence to his own case, so here in 15 he descends from *every thing that grows* to *men and plants* and thence to the young man.

The thesis of 15, in its first voicing, is a broad one describing the rise and momentary stasis that precede tragedy, and almost two lines are devoted to that flourishing time before the fall: *Every thing that grows / Holds in perfection but a little moment.* However, in the thesis' second voicing, the line of rise is immediately accompanied by a fall; and the irony of fate's double-natured agency is emphasized by the ominous alliteration of its participial adjectives, *cheerèd* and *checked:*

I perceive that men as plants increase,
Cheerèd and checked even by the selfsame sky.

In the third voicing of the thesis, the rise is confined to a half-line, and the decline and fall broaden to a line and a half. Men and plants

Vaunt in their youthful sap, at height decrease,
And wear their brave state out of memory.

The decline of the seasons, seen broadly in the octave, is narrowed in the sestet to the short decline of a single day: the young man's day of youth will change (in one line) to sullied night. However, his fate is held suspended while the speaker returns, sublimely, to his sidereal perspective, watching the great emblematic fates, *Time* and *Decay*, as they debate the young man's future end.

The resemblance in structure of 15 to 12 is very striking:

Sonnet 12	*Sonnet 15*
When I do count the clock that tells the time . . .	When I consider everything that grows
When lofty trees I see barren of leaves	When I perceive that men as plants increase
Then of thy beauty do I question make	Then the conceit of this inconstant stay
That thou among the *wastes of Time* must go.	Sets you . . . before my sight, where *wasteful Time*
And nothing 'gainst *Time's* scythe can make *defense*	And all in *war* with *Time*
Save breed . . . when he *takes* thee hence.	As he *takes* from you, I ingraft you new.

We are aided in what it means to "read" a Shakespeare sonnet by the existence of such close pairs as this one and, e.g. 116-117; similarities in structure, language, and thought virtually force us to notice changes in sentiment or manner. What was visually and tenderly suggested in 12 in the emblematic intermixture of violets and curls, sheaves and beard, is in 15 curtly and propositionally asserted: men and plants share the same fate. In a sidereal view there is no pathos available for the individual violet. But the perfect indifference of the sidereal perspective cannot be maintained once the young man comes into focus. If one were to sketch the world of 15, it would narrow down rapidly from the whole universe to the young man.

There is a precious moment in which the young man, at his height of promise, is held in view for a moment; the paradoxical immobilization of temporariness, *the **con**ceit of this in**con**stant stay*, says his lover, *Sets YOU most rich in YOUTH before my sight.* As tru-th is true-ness and streng-th is strong-ness, so you-th is you-ness, in this adoring pun. The young man *(you)* and conceptual *Youth* become indistinguishable; but because this Platonic but unsidereal physical vision in close focus has been summoned by the *CONceit* of this *inCONstant stay*, with its etymological pun on a *stay* (or immobility) which is *incon-stant* [< *stare*, to stand or stay], the speaker immediately conjures up its un-Platonic conceptual opposites, and sees *Time* and *Decay* conspiring to destroy *Youth.* With this move, he regains his sidereal perspective.

In his first position, the speaker had gazed down on earth from the vantage point of the stars; in his second position, he is near enough to the young man to have him *(you/youth)* in close-focus before his sight; in his third position, he is able to watch horizontally, from a celestial position, the cosmic argument between the fates Time and Decay. The last position of the speaker is a vertically Janus-faced one, as he turns sidereally toward Time to engage him in single combat, and turns earthward to the young man to *ingraft him new.* (The meaning of *ingraft*, in the context of plants, seems to mean "to add substance through the gardener's efforts." It has been argued that nothing has yet been said in the sequence about the eternizing power of verse, and that we should read *ingraft* as "urge you to marry." But the proximate reference in 16 to *my barren rhyme* would encourage a retrospective reading of *ingraft* in 15 as "immortalize.")

The sudden leap from the close-focus *you rich in youth* to the macrocosmic wide-focus of Time debating with Decay depends on the words *my sight, / Where*, in which *my sight* works first to mean "my gaze," and second to mean "my thought." Thus do the verb of thought *(consider)* and the verb of sight *(perceive)* come together to generate the single *conceit* (physical and mental at once) of the beautiful beloved, subject to the power of Time and Decay. The concluding use of verbs of active present-tense subtraction and addition *(as he takes from you, I ingraft you new)* comes as a memorable grammatical stroke, since all previous verbs had been phrased in the habitual, not the active, present tense. (Of course, to be precise, it should be said that the whole sonnet is written in the present tense of habit: "*Whenever* I consider this, then this conceit sets you before my sight, and I take the following action." However, the internal closing contrast between a forcible individual action taken—*in war, I ingraft*—and the earlier habitual meditative verbs remains a marked one.)

In offering two models of human sight—the reach of thought and the eye's gaze—Shakespeare reminds us of the inevitable determining of our human perceptions by the focus we adopt. In far-focus, men are simply anonymous *thing[s] that grow* and their individual fates are only one of the *shows* on a *huge stage;* in close-focus, a single life becomes a precious unit of value, worth preserving by constant "ingrafting" effort. At the end of the poem, the speaker sees with binocular vision: he can view the grand celestial colloquy of Time and Decay as well as the endangered single young man whom he engrafts anew. A structure which went from a sidereal view to close-focus *and ended there* would imply that the far-focus was "inhumane" or "careless of human worth," and that only a "humanist" view was worthy of man. A structure which, after descending to the young man, went back up to a "cold," sidereal view would imply that human pathos, while appealing, should be rejected for a sterner sense of universal insignificance. Shakespeare's genius is to participate fully, at the end, in both the pathetic view *and* the sidereal view, and to find a way of fighting to preserve private pathos while maintaining his open-lidded gaze at Fate. The last five lines, sung under the sign of the sullying scythe, remain a hymn to the human love-syllable, *you:* the conceit of impermanence

> Sets YOU most rich in YOUTH before my sight,
> Where wasteful Time debateth with Decay
> To change YOUr day of YOUth to sullied night;
> And all in war with Time for love of YOU,
> As he takes from YOU, I ingraft YOU new.

The couplet rhyme, mimetically and phonetically additive to resemble "ingrafting," is "YOU" / "YOU new."

A few technical matters. The destructive word n-i-g-[h]-t is probably meant to be "vanquished" by the positive word i-n-g-[raf]-t; such letter-by-letter "cancelings" are not rare in the *Sonnets.* Nor are comparable "matchings"; I have no doubt that night (which could be characterized by many possible adjectives of darkness) is ***sull**ied* because the young are *youth**full*** and time is *wast**full*** (in the Quarto spelling, where the old-style *s* of *sull-* even resembles the *f* of *-full*). The sonnet is bound together by one of those alliterative, assonantal, and anagrammatic semantic strings in which Shakespeare delights: On the ***stage*** influenced by ***stars*** is our mortal ***state*** making *incon**stant** **stay**; **waste** **debates** **decay*** to create *ch**ange*** of a ***day***.

KEY WORD: YOU (It could be argued that this word is not present in Q_1, but I suggest it is phonetically hiding in "HUge," chosen precisely for its anticipation of YOU.)

Couplet Tie: *Time* (11, 13). The Quarto capitalization is inconsistent, but since in these two lines Time is humanized (he debates with Decay, he can be warred against), the emblematic figure seems to be intended, and so I give the word an initial capital letter.

you [***you**th*] [***you**thful*] [***hu**ge*] [Foregrounded by couplet rhyme and by collocation of *you/youth*] (3, 7, 10, 10, 12, 13, 14, 14)

16

BVt wherefore do not you a mightier waie
Make warre vppon this bloudie tirant time?
And fortifie your ſelfe in your decay
With meanes more bleſſed then my barren rime?
Now ſtand you on the top of happie houres,
And many maiden gardens yet vnſet,
With vertuous wiſh would beare your liuing flowers,
Much liker then your painted counterfeit:
So ſhould the lines of life that life repaire
Which this (Times penſel or my pupill pen)
Neither in inward worth nor outward faire
Can make you liue your ſelfe in eies of men,
  To giue away your ſelfe, keeps your ſelfe ſtill,
  And you muſt liue drawne by your owne ſweet skill;

But wherefore do not you a mightier way
Make war upon this bloody tyrant Time?
And fortify yourself in your decay
With means more blessèd than my barren rhyme?
Now stand you on the top of happy hours,
And many maiden gardens, yet unset,
With virtuous wish would bear your living flowers,
Much liker than your painted counterfeit:
So should the lines of life that life repair
Which this time's pencil or my pupil pen
Neither in inward worth nor outward fair
Can make you live yourself in eyes of men:
  To give away yourself keeps yourself still,
  And you must live drawn by your own sweet skill.

THE speaker here first explicitly identifies himself as a poet, as he speaks of his *barren rhyme.* The sonnet contrasts, thematically, the superior power of the young man's potential self-representation by biological generation to the inferior representational power of the graphic-artist's pencil or the writer's pen. In addition, in a subcontrast, representation by drawing here enters the *Sonnets* to rival (in truth of depiction) representation by rhyme.

The generating image of the poem seems to be the constrast between *barren* rhyme and fertile bride. The virginal bride as *hortus conclusus,* a *maiden garden,* generates the image of her children as living flowers resembling the young man. It is only a step from the disparaging contrast of barren rhyme with living flowers to the equally disparaging contrast of an imperfect painted resemblance with perfect living flowers. Thence we are led to the rivalry between the ***pain[ting] pencil*** of the artist and the (less powerful?) apprentice ***pen*** of the unhappy poet, whose *barren*ness connects the third quatrain, contrastively, to the putative fertility of the bride-garden. *Living* flowers are contrasted with the failure of poet and painter alike to make the young man *live* as he is today in the eyes of men. The biological *lines of life* (perhaps with a pun on *loins,* probably pronounced as "lines") in sexual conjunction will repair the young man's mortal *life.* The lines of the poet and the artist are, by comparison, failures.

The argument of the sonnet seems at first, and perhaps even at last, oddly conducted. The maiden gardens and lines of life appear insufficient as executors of the forcible martial pressure of the urgent opening couplet:

> But wherefore do not you a mightier way
> Make *war* upon this bloody tyrant Time?

In dramatic plot, this is the last sonnet to argue solely for childbearing alone (17 will reserve that sentiment for its close, and will couple it with an afterlife in rhyme as well). The speaker may feel his biological arguments exhausted, or, as seems more plausible, a personal attachment to the young man may draw him away from these Erasmian adjurations to marry.

The use of the word *drawn* in the speaker's final injunction *(you must live drawn by your own sweet skill)* has been reproved for vagueness. Although the general meaning ("you must do your own self-perpetuating") is clear enough, the *sweet skill* referred to remains unspecified. The sense in which biological reproduction can be termed *drawing* is not entirely apparent, though comparisons of *pen* and *pencil* with "penis" are not lacking (see Booth), and the pun may be intended. Shakespeare is certainly attracted to words because of their capacity to participate in a verbal scheme of some sort. I believe a scheme other than the visual and verbal pun on the penis' putative actual or orthographic resemblance to a *pen* or *pencil* is in play here. The speaker's criticism of rhymer and painter alike says that they cannot immortalize the young man, "Neither in ***inward*** worth nor ***outward*** fair." I think it no accident (given Shakespeare's eye for letters) that ***ward***, read backwards, yields ***draw***, and ***drawn***, backwards, yields most of ***inward***. What artists and poets fail at, outward and inward, the young man successfully can reverse. This is not an especially interesting point, but it at least accounts for the presence of the odd word ***drawn*** for that procreative activity which will reproduce the young man's outward beauty and inward worth. Also, *inward* and *outward* both contain ***war*** (the initial proposed "mightier way" of action), while *drawn*, writes ***war*** in reverse, undoing Time's effect.

The mighty *war* against the bloody ***tirant Time*** (a graphically reduplicative phrase of Time's power in the Quarto spelling) seems to have faded from view by the time we come to the sweet paradoxes of the couplet, unless we remark the anagrammatic strategy *(war, ward, drawn)* which puts the martial in a meaningful relation to the artistic and the biological. We see here too, for the first time, the "phonetic anagram" *time/might*, *tīm/mīt*, used in future sonnets.

Couplet Tie: *live* [*living, life*] (7, 9, 9, 12, 14)

your self (3, 12, 13, 13) Quarto spelling; usually conjoined into *yourself* in modern spelling.

And (if allowed anagrammatically) *war* ***(draw[n]***, ***inward***, ***outward)*** (2, 11, 11, 14), and perhaps even ***flowers*** (7).

17

VVHo will beleeue my verſe in time to come
If it were fild with your moſt high deſerts?
Though yet heauen knowes it is but as a tombe
Which hides your life, and ſhewes not halfe your parts:
If I could write the beauty of your eyes,
And in freſh numbers number all your graces,
The age to come would ſay this Poet lies,
Such heauenly touches nere toucht earthly faces.
So ſhould my papers (yellowed with their age)
Be ſcorn'd,like old men of leſſe truth then tongue,
And your true rights be termd a Poets rage,
And ſtretched miter of an Antique ſong.
But were ſome childe of yours aliue that time,
You ſhould liue twiſe in it,and in my rime.

Who will believe my verse in time to come
If it were filled with your most high deserts?
Though yet heaven knows it is but as a tomb
Which hides your life, and shows not half your parts.
If I could write the beauty of your eyes,
And in fresh numbers number all your graces,
The age to come would say, "This poet lies;
Such heavenly touches ne'er touched earthly faces."
So should my papers (yellowed with their age)
Be scorned, like old men of less truth than tongue,
And your true rights be termed a poet's rage
And stretchèd meter of an ántique song:
But were some child of yours alive that time,
You should live twice, in it and in my rhyme.

SHAKESPEARE now reveals, for the first time in the sequence, how to make the future "come alive" in a poem. He manages a gradual bringing-into-focus of the envisaged future until, in line 9, it brightens into sensuous being as we see *my papers (yellowed with their age).* This visual penetration of the future by the rueful eye of the speaker is far more imaginative than any penetration by thought. And yet one feels, reading the poem, that one has already reached the climax of future verisimilitude in lines 7–8, with the direct quotation from *the age to come.* (The experience of a second, unforeseen, climax in *yellowed* is one of the absolute satisfactions of reading as of music.) The perceived shape has been completed by line 8; and then to perfection is added, in line 9, another completion. It is perhaps the only time when one is justified in saying that something is *more* perfect, because the first climax does not lose the perfection of its own moment by being incorporated into the motion of a second moment—far from it. Here, the first climax *(the age to come)* tallies with the end of the octave, and so is visibly an endpoint; the third quatrain represents both an addition and a subsidence.

The poem is constructed as a series of steps ascending to the future, and then descending from it. The poet first poses a question:

1. *Who will believe my verse in time to come?*

He then represents the sort of escalating praise he wants to put in his verse; he hopes to

fill [it] with your . . . deserts
write the beauty of your eyes
in fresh numbers number all your graces.

2. The age *to come* is heard responding to the poems he will have written if he succeeds in *numbering all your graces.* They will say,

"*This poet lies* [present tense];
Such heavenly touches ne'er touched [past tense] *earthly faces.*"

(The present tense establishes the perpetuation of the living poetic voice in verse; the past tense establishes the irrevocable pastness of the beloved's youth.)

3. The voice from the future falls silent; but the eye of the future reader magically invades the eye of the speaker, who sees his own present sheaf of sonnets instantly yellowed into ancientness; and by inference, himself aged into one of those *old men of less truth than tongue* (a way of denying his own probable death by the time his papers would be *yellowed with their age*). The mention of the *age* to come entails three verbal consequences: the *age* of the paper, the *old* manhood of the poet, and the *antiqu[ity]* of the poet's song. The enthralling reduplicative mimesis aimed at by poetry would succeed if readers believed that *numbers* could magically and mimetically *number* graces; and that such heavenly *touches* had *touched* earthly faces. But when the coming age fails to believe the *truth* of the beloved's *true* rights, mimesis has failed: the verse has become a tomb that, instead of revealing "*high d*eserts," *hides* noble parts. From the direct quotation of future readers, and the visionary and vivid perception of yellowing pages, we descend to indirect quotation *(be scorned, be termed)* as the future becomes less vivid, declining to the colorless phrase, *that time.*

The poem is full of echoes, which enact mimesis empowered and then mimesis undone (even *stretchèd* is the echo-antithesis of *touched*). It is probably not accidental that the denigrating "stretchèd" *miter* (of the Quarto spelling) is triumphantly revealed, in the end-word anagram of the couplet, to contain both *time* and *rime,* and perhaps, graphically, *mīt.*

Couplet Tie: *time* (1, 13)
life [*alive, live*] (4, 13, 14)

18

SHall I compare thee to a Summers day?
Thou art more louely and more temperate:
Rough windes do ſhake the darling buds of Maie,
And Sommers leaſe hath all too ſhort a date:
Sometime too hot the eye of heauen ſhines,
And often is his gold complexion dimm'd,
And euery faire from faire ſome-time declines,
By chance,or natures changing courſe vntrim'd:
But thy eternall Sommer ſhall not fade,
Nor looſe poſſeſſion of that faire thou ow'ſt,
Nor ſhall death brag thou wandr'ſt in his ſhade,
When in eternall lines to time thou grow'ſt,
    So long as men can breath or eyes can ſee,
    So long liues this,and this giues life to thee,

Shall I compare thee to a summer's day?
Thou art more lovely and more temperate:
Rough winds do shake the darling buds of May,
And summer's lease hath all too short a date;
Sometime too hot the eye of heaven shines,
And often is his gold complexion dimmed;
And every fair from fair sometime declines,
By chance or nature's changing course untrimmed:
But thy eternal summer shall not fade,
Nor lose possession of that fair thou ow'st,
Nor shall Death brag thou wand'rest in his shade,
When in eternal lines to time thou grow'st.
    So long as men can breathe or eyes can see,
    So long lives this, and this gives life to thee.

•

TO COME, as a commentator, on this—the most familiar of the poems and the most indisputably Shakespearean, Elizabethan, and sonnetlike—is both a balm and a test: what remains to be said? In its proffering of love and fame, it stands with sonnet 12, free of that fear of the beloved's corruption which enters the sequence at least as early as 24 *(Mine eye hath played the painter).* There are many things to praise here, but I will use this poem as an instance of one of Shakespeare's greatest compositional powers—his capacity to confer greater and greater mental scope on any whim of the imagination, enacting that widening gradually, so that the experience of reading a poem becomes the experience of pushing back the horizons of thought.

Many of Shakespeare's sonnets are constructed, like this one, on a very common cultural contrast (here, the temporality of physical existence and the eternity of verse). But where another poet might begin by showing his hand in a topic sentence, saying, "Things mortal pass away, but rhymes remain," such is not Shakespeare's way. He begins with a trifle—a youth and a day and an apparent whim of the inventive mind:

Shall I compare thee to a summer's day?

It is gentle, light, innocuous, dulcet; and its expansion seems at first dulcet, too: *lovely, temperate*—these are self-reflexive adjectives for a wooing song. Even the *rough winds* leave the *darling buds* on the branches, merely *shake[n],* a danger evaded; and it is only with the *short date* on summer's lease (*Thy end is truth's and beauty's doom and date;* sonnet 14) that a somber quality enters, and we realize that from the lovely day we have come far, to the end of a season. A quick graph of lines 1–12 will show their inexorable widening of scope and deepening of gravity:

thee and a *day* (1–2)
a month *(May)* (3)
end of a season *(summer)* (4)
the eye of heaven (sun, ordainer of seasons) (5)
the weather itself (*hot* or *dimmed*) (6)
the *decline* of *every* beauty (7)
the operations of *chance* (8)

the *changing course* of *nature* (8)
an *eternal summer* (9)
an un*fading fair*[ness] (9–10)
the foiling of *Death* (11)
eternal art (12)

It is a long way from an apparently fanciful natural simile to eternal art, and yet Shakespeare traverses it in twelve lines. Only in the couplet does he concede that art has human perpetuity rather than transcendent eternity.

One can imagine hundreds of ways of proceeding for a poem beginning *Shall I compare thee to X?* One evident structure could be to continue by saying *Or rather should I compare thee to Y? or Z?* with a list of pretty things, a way of proceeding that Shakespeare will satirize in 21 *(So is it not with me)* and 130 *(My mistress' eyes are nothing like the sun)*. It is only when we see that such a list is not forthcoming in 18 that we realize that such a listing *has already taken place.* Shall I compare thee to a rose? Too thorny. To a dawn? Too brief. To a spring day? Too uncertain. What is the most beautiful thing, the *summum bonum,* in an (English) world? A summer's day. And then we see that by taking the pinnacle of perfection as his standard of comparison, the poet/lover, convinced that nothing can outstrip or even equal his beloved, must begin to denigrate his perfect metaphor: ah, but a summer's day could have a wind, could be hot, could be cloudy. Its very inhabitants, the rosebuds and the sun, which reminded him of the beloved in the first place, can be endangered or can play him false; and, once started, the process of impugning the perfect cannot be arrested until it runs the whole gamut of decline. As one uncertainty tumbles into another, and as uncertainty wrecks itself in misfortune, we see Shakespeare's tendency to concatenation (cf. 129) in full spate, mimicked phonemically by ***ch**ance or nature's **ch**anging course.* Other concatenations: *shake, short, shines, complexion, shade; day, darling, dimmed, declines, Death; lovely, lease, lose, lines, long, lives, life.*

Although the ostensible (and perhaps actual) structure of the sonnet is one of contrast (the mutable versus the eternal; *chance or nature's changing course* versus *eternal summer* in *eternal lines*), the principle of expansive claim is as strong, structurally, as the principle of contrast. Such, at least, is the original triumphant tonality of the sestet: *But thy eternal summer shall not fade . . . Nor shall Death brag.* But there is an urbanity, and tempered measure, about the subsequent couplet that makes the end of the poem not so far from the beginning as it would have been had it ended on such a note of apparently pure triumph. Even in Q_3, the triumph is tempered: the eternity of the beloved is paradoxically expressed in intrinsically limited seasonal terms, as an everlasting brevity *(eternal summer)* and the eternal lines grow *to time* (i.e., within duration). The couplet carries the tempering of triumph yet further: the lines last only so long as there exist, among the men who can breathe, eyes that can see this poem. Only *so long* will the putatively eternal lines live in time. The urbanity of the iambic tune of the couplet

So long as men can breathe or eyes can see,
So long lives this, and this gives life to thee

is itself temperate, moderated by the evenness of the clock that tells the time, not driven by the wind of prophecy. Even the prophetic tense—*shall not fade, shall not brag*—gives way to a a possibility *(can)* deceptively expressed in two rhyming present-tense verbs, *lives* and *gives:* this *lives,* this *gives* life. The temperate has proved the temporal, in Shakespeare's (correct) etymology, and to be *more temperate* than natural loveliness one must escape natural chance and the cycle of natural change altogether. It is to Shakespeare's eternal credit that he invented the eternal season growing to time in eternal lines potentiated only by a (finally finite) succession of human readers, thereby entwining, in perpetual paradox, the brevity of love, temporal truth, and the fragile strength of art before its extinction. It is probably needless to praise him again for what has so often been praised, the noticing of the particular (the wind-shaken buds) in such general yet observant terms that they spring to every reader's mind every May in the temperate zones. And it is probably just as unnecessary to remark his ability to step through time:

Sometime too hot the eye of heaven shines,
And *often* is his gold complexion *dimmed,*
And *every* fair from fair *sometime* declines,
By *chance* or nature's *changing course untrimmed.*

From one sun to every fair, from sometimes to often, from dimmed to untrimmed—by one great agency or another, things are undone: it is the pace of Necessity itself.

It should be noticed that in the Quarto spelling, *lines* and *liues* differ only by the turning upside-down of one letter, making a quasi-punning Couplet Tie.

Couplet Tie: *eye* [*-s*] (5, 13) and, phonemically, *I* (1)

19

DEuouring time blunt thou the Lyons pawes,
And make the earth deuoure her owne ſweet brood,
Plucke the keene teeth from the fierce Tygers yawes,
And burne the long liu'd Phænix in her blood,
Make glad and ſorry ſeaſons as thou fleet'ſt,
And do what ere thou wilt ſwift-footed time
To the wide world and all her fading ſweets:
But I forbid thee one moſt hainous crime,
O carue not with thy howers my loues faire brow,
Nor draw noe lines there with thine antique pen,
Him in thy courſe vntainted doe allow,
For beauties patterne to ſucceding men.
  Yet doe thy worſt ould Time diſpight thy wrong,
  My loue ſhall in my verſe euer liue young.

Devouring Time, blunt thou the lion's paws,
And make the earth devour her own sweet brood,
Pluck the keen teeth from the fierce tiger's jaws,
And burn the long-lived phoenix in her blood,
Make glad and sorry seasons as thou fleet'st,
And do whate'er thou wilt, swift-footed Time,
To the wide world and all her fading sweets:
But I forbid thee one most heinous crime,
O carve not with thy hours my love's fair brow,
Nor draw no lines there with thine ántique pen;
Him in thy course untainted do allow
For beauty's pattern to succeeding men.
  Yet do thy worst, old Time: despite thy wrong,
  My love shall in my verse ever live young.

THE disproportionate imaginative efforts in the octave and sestet of this sonnet have been remarked (Kerrigan). It is hard, perhaps, to accept the appearance of wrinkles in a young man's brow as the superlatively *most heinous crime* on the part of Time, occupying the climactic position after a list of Time's potential actions which includes apparently more serious crimes. The murderous vitality of the opening quatrain issues, one might say, from the Shakespeare of the tragedies, while the rest of the poem lies more equably—with its mentions of *swift-footed Time* and the world's *fading sweets*—in the elegiac mode.

It eventually becomes clear that the logical structure of the sonnet runs as follows, as the speaker addresses Time:

Do not carve my love's brow. That is the most heinous crime I can imagine you committing.

What would be the hierarchical order of Time's crimes?

Ordinary crimes of Time's *swift*ness	1. to make sorry seasons (we always want only glad ones) 2. to make the world's sweets fade 3. to erode the world itself

(But these acts are tame, and fall within the laws of nature. We know these crimes. What even *worse* transgressions can we imagine Time undertaking?) Well, Time could act *contra Naturam:* it could *undo* nature's laws:

Crimes contra *Naturam*	1. blunt the lion's paws 2. make the earth devour her own brood 3. defang the tiger 4. kill the phoenix

(But though these are acts directed against the "noblest" species [lion, tiger, phoenix, earth's sweet children], there is a yet nobler creature, the young man, who is a member of no species but rather the Platonic pattern for a species—mankind.)

Crime against form by *Devouring Time*	So the highest crime is pattern-destruction.

In a sense, the speaker has already, in thought, enumerated the ordinary crimes of Time's *swift[ness]* voiced in Q_2 *before* he bursts out with Q_1, which represents the second, worse level of crime, crime *contra Naturam.* "All right—do (besides your ordinary crimes) even crimes *contra Naturam,*" says the speaker, "and of course I know you'll go on doing your ordinary things anyway." Thus, he tucks Q_2 in after the dramatic Q_1. The concessions of the octave—yes, do this or that—prepare for the apparent prohibition of Q_3 *(I forbid thee)* which almost immediately cringes into a prayer. Yet even the *worst* level of crime is reluctantly conceded in the couplet; the young man will be destroyed as an organic form, and the locus of *pattern* must shift from body to *verse.*

Whether or not the poem is fundamentally incoherent, it is interesting in the chaos of its multiple senses of Time's powers. To begin with the proverbial and Ovidian topos of devouring Time is conventional enough, but Time is soon seen doing very odd things. The might of Time is emphasized, but not in the usual way; in other sonnets, Time does what is natural to it (it overthrows monuments, etc.), but here it does, in the first quatrain, exclusively *un*natural things, de-lionizing the lion, de-tigerizing the tiger, de-maternalizing Mother Earth, and de-immortalizing the phoenix. These are *not* devourings—nor are they things that, in the normal course of time, Time does; and *contra Naturam* is one of the most powerful accusations available to Shakespeare's Renaissance speaker.

We must deduce that even Time is not allowed these acts in the ordinary governed course of Nature; a tiger with blunted paws, a devouring Gaia, a toothless tiger, and a mortal phoenix would each be a *lusus Naturae.* Such acts on Time's part would be genuine *crimes* against Nature, as making lions grow old, e.g., would not be. We are to deduce that the young man, as beauty's *pattern,* would in the course of things be naturally exempt, as a Platonic form (a being nobler even than the phoenix), from Time's destruction. Consequently, the *most heinous crime* is not per se the wrinkling of a young man's brow, but the destruction of one of the forms that Nature needs as patterns to create more creatures from: *She carved thee for her seal, and meant thereby / Thou shouldst print more,* said the version putting the responsibility of self-reproduction on the young man (sonnet 11), but here the responsibility for the perpetuation of pattern is shifted to Nature and Time.

The second quatrain attempts to do Shakespearean justice to Time, by admitting that in its *swift[ness]* (the quality dominating Q_2) it makes *glad* as well as sorry *seasons*. But this brief impulse of justice toward the adversary does not extend to indulging the crime of form-destruction. It is because the contemplated crime against the young man is the destruction of form that Time is suddenly transformed into an artist—a sculptor and then a painter, defacing Nature's masterpiece with his *antique pen*. *Untainted*—resembling *antique* in some phonetic respects—also suggests, in the context *pen* and *pattern*, the word *unpainted*, and will in fact seem to "generate" *painted* in sonnet 20. We now see that the Ovidian epithet *devouring* applies properly only to the envisaged disappearance of the beloved.

The couplet (with its implied contrast between corporeal life and life in verse) suggests that physical pattern-destruction is indeed, and always has been, within *old* Time's power. The pattern of beauty may indeed be destroyed in embodied Nature by an unnatural crime committed by a false artist, Time; yet language can preserve the pattern that flesh has forgotten. (It is not necessary to imagine, as Kerrigan does, that time's *worst* is the actual death of the young man; his death would be anticlimactic, since it is his beauty, as pattern, which is the precious form of which the destruction would be time's worst act.)

The almost blustering bravado of uttering, in the face of Time, both positive concessions (*blunt*, *make*, *pluck*, *burn*, etc.) and negative commands *(I forbid thee . . . carve not . . . draw no lines)* must, of course, subside. *Yet do thy worst* ("even if you do the worst you can") allows the transition from the realm of flesh to the realm of art, as defeat conceded in one sphere (the commanding of Time) is avoided by triumph in another (living verse).

The notion that Nature makes a mental pattern and then replicates it in the flesh is fancifully mythologized in the following sonnet, 20. In 19 it is taken for granted rather than made explicit, and the imaginative effort expended on pattern-creation in 20 is here spent on the great hard words, with their frequent trochaic or spondaic emphasis: *blunt*, *paws*, *brood*, *pluck*, *keen*, *teeth*, *tiger's jaws*, *burn*, *blood*. *Dev**our**ing Time . . . the earth dev**our** . . . with thy **hours*** tolls the progression that turns *devouring Time* to *swift-footed* Time and then to *old* Time; by the end all values have been jettisoned except beauty's pattern, *young* in verse.

Couplet Tie: *Time* (1, 6, 13)
love [-'s] (9, 14)

20

A Womans face with natures owne hand painted,
Haſte thou the Maſter Miſtris of my paſſion,
A womans gentle hart but not acquainted
With ſhifting change as is falſe womens faſhion,
An eye more bright then theirs,leſſe falſe in rowling:
Gilding the obiect where-vpon it gazeth,
A man in hew all *Hews* in his controwling,
Which ſteales mens eyes and womens ſoules amaſeth.
And for a woman wert thou firſt created,
Till nature as ſhe wrought thee fell a dotinge,
And by addition me of thee defeated,
By adding one thing to my purpoſe nothing.
　But ſince ſhe prickt thee out for womens pleaſure,
　Mine be thy loue and thy loues vſe their treaſure.

A woman's face with Nature's own hand painted
Hast thou, the master-mistress of my passion;
A woman's gentle heart, but not acquainted
With shifting change, as is false women's fashion;
An eye more bright than theirs, less false in rolling,
Gilding the object whereupon it gazeth;
A man in hue, all hues in his controlling,
Which steals men's eyes and women's souls amazeth.
And for a woman wert thou first created,
Till Nature as she wrought thee fell a-doting,
And by addition me of thee defeated,
By adding one thing to my purpose nothing.
　But since she pricked thee out for women's pleasure,
　Mine be thy love, and thy love's use their treasure.

THIS little myth of origin arises, probably, from the idea (in sonnets 11 and 19) that Nature, as sculptor or artist, conceives a mental pattern from which she then prints or models her creatures. The charming notion that between the moment of pattern-conceiving and the moment of its fleshed accomplishment Nature could change her mind is the idea generating the sestet of the sonnet, which is offered as an explanatory myth to account for the young man's startling simultaneous possession of a man's penis and a woman's face. To the speaker, it is inconceivable that anyone could fail to fall in love with that face, even if the beholder were of the same sex as the face. "If I, a man, could fall in love with that face, even though it belongs to one of my own sex, so could Nature (a woman) also fall in love with it, even though in the original pattern it were a woman's face." By this back-formation of myth, Nature, astonished by her own success in pattern-making, conceives a same-sex attachment, so to speak; but *she* (ah, fortunate Goddess) has the power to make the body attached to the face she falls in love with of the right sex for heterosexual intercourse. "I have fallen a-doting," says Nature, "and must have this creature for my pleasure"; and so she adds, in finishing the embodiment of her best pattern in flesh, a prick for her own use. The speaker who has fallen a-doting on a face of his own sex has, alas, no such divine transformative powers.

The poem is a *jeu d'esprit*, as all such myths of origin are (how the rose became red, etc.), and its lack of inhibition is partly due to its (eventual) lightness of expression in the sestet. However, before its resolution in fancifulness, the poem vents a good deal of aggression.

The *untainted* pattern of sonnet 19 may have provoked the pure (with Nature's own hand *painted*) pattern of the master/mistress. But the octave of this poem is first a denigration of ordinary women, saying that they are, for the most part, false. The *true* pattern of woman can be discerned in the woman's face and woman's gentle heart present in the master/mistress. A hierarchy of aesthetic and moral value is established by the comparatives—*more bright* (outward), *less false* (inward).

There are some difficulties of language, notably the climactic emphasis on *hues* (line 7) and the odd *-eth* endings on verbs *(gaze, amaze)* that could apparently have ended as well in *-es*. Bizarre as it may appear, the poem seems to have been created in such a way as to have the individual letters of the word *h-e-w-s* (the Quarto spelling) or *h-u-e-s* in as many lines as possible (I have not checked all the *Sonnets*, but the random checking of a few has not turned up another sonnet of which a comparable assertion could be made). The list of available letters (not words) in each of the fourteen lines (Quarto spelling) is as follows: hews, hues, hews, hews, hews, hew[z], hews, hews, hews, hews, he[ ], hues, hews, hues (with a phonetic pun on *use*). The *h* needed for *hews* is contributed in line 8 by *amazeth*, thereby perhaps explaining the *-eth* endings. *Hew* is climactic in line 7 because it is the word by which the master/mistress controls almost all the other lines. The high proportion (2.7 percent) of *w*'s in the total of letters in this sonnet is also explicable by the necessity of making *hew* as often as possible. Though neither *hew* nor *hue* can be found complete in line 11, which contains only an *h* and an *e*, there are of course two *hew*'s in line 7, preserving the proportion of one *hew* per line, all *in his controlling*. If this anagrammatic play is in fact intended, the sonnet becomes even more fantastic than its theme suggests.

The speaker's sterile play of the master/mistress against the putative falsity of women can be explained by his anger at women for not being the young man, at the young man for not being a (sexually available) woman. Frustration summons the fantasy of not having to be frustrated, of wielding a power as strong as Nature's—and so the little myth of original tampering by Nature is fantasized into being. Though Galen thought all embryos were originally female (see Evans), it is Shakespeare who creates the causal myth that the change to maleness in this case arises from Nature's falling in love with the projected female, and *therefore* rendering her male. Under all the play, one is only sure that the speaker, too, has fallen a-doting; and the rather bitter wit—on *acquainted* [cunt], "*one* thing" / "*no*-thing," and *prick* (Nature's joke on the speaker)—is the last flicker of the helplessness of one who cannot play fast and loose, as he would like to, with a physical body. The couplet's defiant final scission of love from intercourse will determine a good deal in the later Young Man sonnets. Once one has separated love from the act of sex, love can—indeed must—eventually stand alone, hugely politic, inhabiting the realm of the Forms. It certainly no longer inhabits the realm of the flesh, though it pervades the emotional and erotic *imaginative* life entirely.

The feminine rhymes throughout the sonnet—a unique case—have often been remarked. The Quarto spellings *rowling* and *controwling* help contribute the necessary *w*'s for *hews*.

KEY WORD: WOMAN [WOMEN]

Couplet Tie: *woman* [-*'s*] [*women's*] (1, 3, 4, 8, 9, 13)
hues (use) (7, 7, 14)

21

SO is it not with me as with that Muſe,
Stird by a painted beauty to his verſe,
Who heauen it ſelfe for ornament doth vſe,
And euery faire with his faire doth reherſe,
Making a coopelment of proud compare
With Sunne and Moone, with earth and ſeas rich gems:
With Aprills firſt borne flowers and all things rare,
That heauens ayre in this huge rondure hems,
O let me true in loue but truly write,
And then beleeue me, my loue is as faire,
As any mothers childe, though not ſo bright
As thoſe gould candells fixt in heauens ayer:
   Let them ſay more that like of heare-ſay well,
   I will not prayſe that purpoſe not to ſell.

So is it not with me as with that Muse
Stirred by a painted beauty to his verse,
Who heaven itself for ornament doth use,
And every fair with his fair doth rehearse,
Making a couplement of proud compare
With sun and moon, with earth and sea's rich gems,
With April's first-born flowers, and all things rare
That heaven's air in this huge rondure hems.
O let me true in love but truly write,
And then believe me, my love is as fair
As any mother's child, though not so bright
As those gold candles fixed in heaven's air:
   Let them say more that like of hearsay well,
   I will not praise that purpose not to sell.

THERE are several firsts here: sonnet 21 is the first of the Muse poems (see also 38, 78, 79, 82, 85, 100, 101, 103); the first sonnet offering comparison with rival poets (see also 78–86, except for 81); the first to make the conventional paradoxical announcement that truth in loving leads to a poetics of truth in representation, countering epideictic hyperbole; the first to condemn the hearsay of "heavenly" praises, proposing by contrast to restrict itself to earthly seeing. Since the word *heaven* is repeated in each quatrain (lines 3, 8, 12), I believe one expects *heaven* again in line 13; *Let them say more that like of hea-*, but the expectation is wittily tamed into *hearsay*, which is Shakespeare's final judgment of the tendency of artificial poets to *rehearse* (line 4) (or to *re-hearsay*, so to speak) things heard. It is impossible for me not to find *heare-say* (the Quarto) a derivation from *reherse* (also Quarto spelling), thereby accounting for the rather odd presence of *heare-say* in line 12. The artificial rival poets have been condemned for extravagant hyperbole in the octave, yet not until line 13 do we learn that they have not invented their hyperboles, but have imitated them by saying their piece from *hearsay* (the hyphenated Quarto word *heare-say* emphasizes a listening to the sayings of others). The sestet advocating truth enacts—by repeating in its rhyme-words (*fair* and *air*) rhyme-sounds and rhyme-words from the "artificial" octave *(fair, fair, compare, rare, air)*—what it is to correct falsehood by true writing. (It was forbidden, in Italian poetics, to repeat in the sestet a rhyme-sound or rhyme-word from the octave; Shakespeare's transgression here foregrounds his intent to "correct" his hyperbolic octave-rival.) The rival poet's proud but inane comp*are*, rehearsing his *fair* with every other *fair* and with all things *rare* under heaven's *air*, is replaced by the speaker's calling his love (a) as *fair* as any mother's child (a positive simile), but (b) not so bright as stars in heaven's *air* (a negative simile), thus drawing a distinction between horizontal (human) and vertical (transcendent or "heavenly") "compare." A beloved can properly be called as fair as any one else's beloved (a personal human value), but not so fair as April's flowers, or a pearl, or stars. The latter practice compares things incomparable, setting objectively rare or beautiful objects against the personal value set on a beloved person. Shakespeare is here affecting a pedantry in metaphor that he does not actually practice, but the poetics-by-contrast that structures the sonnet *(So is it not with me; O let me . . . but truly write)* permits him an excess of litotes to counter the rival poet's excess of hyperbole.

The last accusation against false poets (after the accusations that they compare incomparable things, debase heaven to their own uses, and plagiarize from hearsay) is that their tone is that of a pander, who exaggerates praise in order to sell. If one doesn't have selling in mind, there's no need for such hyperbole, says the true poet-lover.

The poetasters have no real sense of *heaven*—for them it is a convenient poetic ornament. The speaker is shocked by this appropriation: to *use heaven itself for ornament* is sacrilege. He himself has two (proper) senses of heaven; one is a cosmic sense that it is the enclosure or hem that surrounds everything in the *huge rondure* of the earth (the *huge stage* of sonnet 15). The other is a visual sense, that heaven is the place where those *gold candles*, the *fixed* stars, shine.

Sonnet 21 is the first sonnet not to suggest by its surroundings the sex of the beloved. In the next fifty sonnets, only 26 *(Lord of my love)*, 33 *(Full many a glorious morning)*, 39 *(O how thy worth)*, 41 *(Those pretty wrongs)*, 42 *(That thou hast her)* 54 *(O how much more)*, 63 *(Against my love)*, 67 *(Ah wherefore)* and 68 *(Thus is his cheek)* have unequivocally male pronouns. However, since no poem has been inserted in the sequence to make a reader think that any of these love poems is directed to a woman, and since the male pronouns regularly recur to keep us in a male frame of reference, and since the tonality and imagery of so many of the sonnets of second-person address match the tonality and imagery of the sonnets using male pronouns, those critics who wish to reserve male reference only to sonnets with visibly male pronouns should bear the burden of any proof that the neutrally pronominal "you" sonnets in 1–126 should not be viewed as addressed to a young man. There are too many verbal and imagistic links in the subsequence of 1–126 for the arrangement to be considered entirely arbitrary or random.

Couplet Tie: This is one of the few sonnets which exhibit no verbal tie between the body of the sonnet and its couplet. If one allows the punning anagrammatic relation (in the Quarto spelling) between *reherse* (4) and *heare-say* (13), then that serves (as I think it does) as the Couplet Tie.

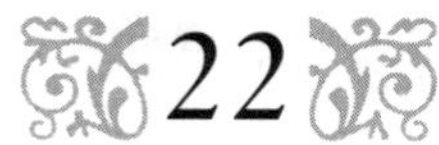

22

MY glaſſe ſhall not perſwade me I am ould,
So long as youth and thou are of one date,
But when in thee times forrwes I behould,
Then look I death my daies ſhould expiate.
For all that beauty that doth couer thee,
Is but the ſeemely rayment of my heart,
Which in thy breſt doth liue, as thine in me,
How can I then be elder then thou art?
O therefore loue be of thy ſelfe ſo wary,
As I not for my ſelfe, but for thee will,
Bearing thy heart which I will keepe ſo chary
As tender nurſe her babe from faring ill,
Preſume not on thy heart when mine is ſlaine,
Thou gau'ſt me thine not to giue backe againe.

My glass shall not persuade me I am old,
So long as youth and thou are of one date,
But when in thee time's furrows I behold,
Then look I death my days should expiate:
For all that beauty that doth cover thee
Is but the seemly raiment of my heart,
Which in thy breast doth live, as thine in me:
How can I then be elder than thou art?
O therefore, love, be of thyself so wary
As I not for myself but for thee will,
Bearing thy heart, which I will keep so chary
As tender nurse her babe from faring ill:
Presume not on thy heart when mine is slain;
Thou gav'st me thine not to give back again.

THE invention in this sonnet is engaged in going backward. Events in time are told in reverse order. In chronological order, they would (properly) go as follows:

1. I gave you my heart [presupposed].
2. You gave me yours, not to be given back again [line 14].
3. I bear your heart tenderly, as nurse to babe, to prevent ill [lines 11–12].
4. Do the same for yourself, bear yourself carefully lest you come to age and harm [lines 9–10].
5. For as long as you preserve your youth and health, my heart in your breast is likewise clothed by that seemly raiment, your body, and is therefore young [lines 5–8].
6. But if you grow old and furrowed by time, I too will think myself old and expect to die [lines 1–4].

What, then, is the formal meaning of this process, which is a whimsical lyric version of Hamlet's mocking words, "You yourself, sir, should be as old as I am if, like a crab, you could go backward"? Backward progresses are usually self-explanatory (cf. sonnet 20, and its backward progress eventually explaining the presence of male genitals on a body with a woman's face and heart). The whole of 22 springs from the fear that the young man is about to *slay* the speaker's heart (a fear not enunciated, of course, until the couplet), and on the conceit that if the young man slays the speaker's heart, which resides in the young man's breast, the young man will become literally (as well as emotionally) heartless, since the speaker will refuse to return, from his own breast, the young man's heart. The mutual exchange of hearts (Q_2) is one of the received Renaissance symbols for reciprocity, but Shakespeare's tendency to literalize conceits, as he investigates their intellectual and expressive potential, leads him to the mannerist visualizing of his literal enclosed heart clothed with someone else's flesh, with interesting consequent possibilities for murder, death, and aging.

The fantasy of mutual care for the other's heart is exploded in the asymmetry of the described caretaking; the young man, bearing the speaker's heart, is to take good care of himself for his own (not the speaker's) sake, while the speaker takes good care of the young man's heart for the young man's sake. Nobody is caring for the speaker's heart for the speaker's sake; indeed, it is in danger of being *slain*. Frightened of this approaching murder-by-violence, the speaker substitutes for it the less imminent aging-and-death-by-attrition with which the sonnet opens. We become able, I think, to see Q_1 as a euphemized defense, and Q_2 as a fantasy, when we become aware of the asymmetrical caretaking in Q_3 and the fear of murder in the couplet (with its implicit threat of a retaliatory retention by the speaker of the young man's heart).

A backward motion that never arrived at an explanation of the obscurantism, fantasy, and self-deception of the first two quatrains would of course be uninteresting. Shakespeare's backward-moving sonnets tend to become (as here and as in 62 [*Sin of self-love*]) exposés of their own false beginnings; or they can offer a gradual revelation of secret desire—as, I think, in 20, the myth of Nature's freedom to turn a young woman into a young man is the revelation, however trifling, of the speaker's wish for the freedom to turn the young man into a young woman, so that intercourse could be accomplished and Platonic "love" between men could add to itself a non-Platonic fleshly form.

Couplet Tie: *heart* (6, 11, 13)
thine (7, 14)

23

AS an vnperfect actor on the ſtage,
Who with his feare is put beſides his part,
Or ſome fierce thing repleat with too much rage,
Whoſe ſtrengths abondance weakens his owne heart;
So I for feare of truſt,forget to ſay,
The perfect ceremony of loues right,
And in mine owne loues ſtrength ſeeme to decay,
Ore-charg'd with burthen of mine owne loues might:
O let my books be then the eloquence,
And domb preſagers of my ſpeaking breſt,
Who pleade for loue,and look for recompence,
More then that tonge that more hath more expreſt.
  O learne to read what ſilent loue hath writ,
  To heare wit eies belongs to loues fine wiht.

As an unperfect actor on the stage,
Who with his fear is put besides his part,
Or some fierce thing replete with too much rage,
Whose strength's abundance weakens his own heart;
So I, for fear of trust, forget to say
The perfect ceremony of love's rite,
And in mine own love's strength seem to decay,
O'ercharged with burthen of mine own love's might:
O let my looks be then the eloquence
And dumb presagers of my speaking breast,
Who plead for love, and look for recompense,
More than that tongue that more hath more expressed.
  O learn to read what silent love hath writ:
  To hear with eyes belongs to love's fine wit.

THIS sonnet is built on one of Shakespeare's impregnable logical structures. (I represent the sonnet with the emended reading *looks* in line 9, following Evans, though plausible arguments have been made for the Quarto's *books.*)

In this sonnet's system of alternatives, the poet, unable to speak (either from fear or surplus emotion), and fearing to be rejected in favor of a rival *tongue that more hath more expressed,* pleads for his preferred form of communication, *looks,* hoping that his beloved will be willing to *read* in lieu of listening. Silent reading carried in Shakespeare's day a powerful reminiscence of oral reading (to oneself or an audience), and the number of auditory puns in the *Sonnets* testifies to Shakespeare's own ever-active ear, trained, of course, by his constant writing for oral delivery on the stage. Given Shakespeare's stage labors, it is even surprising that the *Sonnets* retain so many visual effects (e.g., the anagrams in 7 or the plays on *w* in 9).

And so, dissatisfied with the minimal plea, "O learn to *read* what silent love hath writ," the poet asks for a paradoxical finer competence: "To *hear* with eyes belongs to love's fine wit."

The idea of *hearing with eyes* has been prepared for by the idea of *speaking* in *silen[ce];* the looks, ***plead**ing* and ***look**ing,* are the *dumb presagers* of the lover's *speaking breast:* to speak by heart, not only to hear with eyes, belongs to love's fine wit. (Note the congruence by letters of ***silent love* . . . *writ*** and ***love's fine wit.***)

This elegant mutual solution—the *speaking breast* of *silent love heard with eyes* that *read* what it has *writ*—occupies, however, only the sestet. The octave is about being tongue-tied, and it is one of Shakespeare's most memorable psychological summations: one is tongue-tied when one has either too little or too much to say. The actor who in *fear* forgets his part because the presence of the audience provokes stage fright, and, more curiously, *some fierce thing* with too much *strength's abundance* in his heart for utterance, occupy Q_1. (We can explain the presence of the choked silent beast by the speaker's fear that his tongue-tied lack of language reduces him to a subhuman species.) The actor and beast are summoned only to serve as analogues to Shakespeare's double-edged analytic presentation in Q_2 of human love's agonized lack of words:

So I, for *fear* of trust, forget to say
The perfect ceremony of love's rite,
And in mine own love's *strength* seem to decay,
O'ercharged with burthen of my own love's might.

In a passage such as this, the (inevitable) distance between composing author and fictive speaker narrows to the vanishing point. It is easy to believe that Shakespeare, the master of expression, would tell himself that a *perfect ceremony* for love could be invented, and that he could find it if only he looked long enough; it is equally easy to believe that Shakespeare, the possessor of imagination and language in superabundance, would find himself with too many things to say at once. The double stranglehold—not enough and too much at once—is an extremely interesting case, and only a mentality at home with paradox could recognize and articulate this simultaneity of apparently opposite states.

Though the octave seems to imply that the cause of the tongue-tiedness lies in the psychology of the speaker-poet, citing as analogues the psychological inhibitions of the *actor* and the *fierce thing*, Q_3, in hinting at the beloved's preference for a rival poet, ascribes the tongue-tiedness of the speaker to his new perception of the debased aesthetic judgment exercised by the beloved. At first, *for fear of trust* (line 5) might seem to mean "fearing to trust my own powers," like the frightened actor who *with his fear* can't recite. But when the unnamed rival with the ready tongue is mentioned in line 12, we see the tongue-tiedness rather as a fear of trusting the audience—the potentially faithless beloved. The pathos of the personified looks *who plead for love, and look for recompense* is expressed in the sonnet's rhetorical turn from description *(As an unperfect actor . . . so I . . . forget)* to plea: *O let my looks . . . O learn to read.* At the same time, the stately verbal parallelism of the octave is replaced by a far more irregular line-motion, as agitation, repressed in the (temporary) mastery offered by the first eight lines of explanatory simile-making, returns in full force.

The schematization of the octave appears in the diagram with parallel phases underlined. Two lines for A, two lines for B, two lines for A′, two lines for B′. *Love* is the one word A and B have in common. Careful parallels are drawn between A and A′ by *fear* and *perfect (unperfect)*, between B and B' by *strength* and *own (his/mine).* Whenever Shakespeare sets up Procrustean beds of such exact framing, one knows that something is about to burst loose. Here it is the letters *l* and *o* of the *love* shared by both lack and excess:

Structure of Sonnet 23

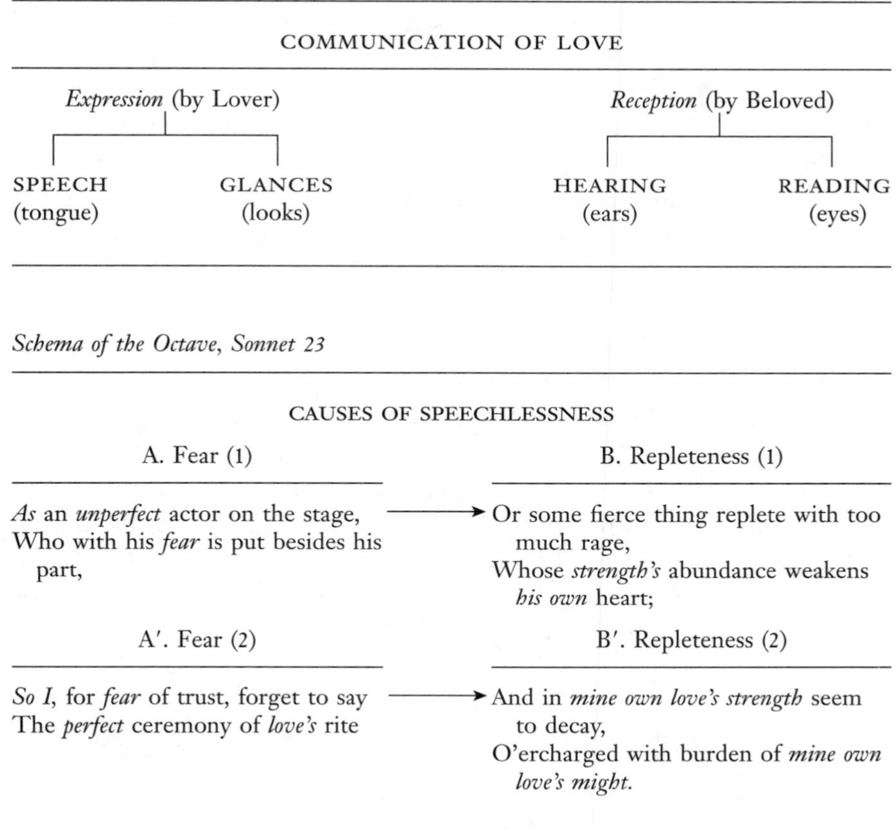
COMMUNICATION OF LOVE
Expression (by Lover)
Reception (by Beloved)
SPEECH (tongue)
GLANCES (looks)
HEARING (ears)
READING (eyes)
Schema of the Octave, Sonnet 23
CAUSES OF SPEECHLESSNESS
A. Fear (1)
B. Repleteness (1)
As an *unperfect* actor on the stage, Who with his *fear* is put besides his part,
Or some fierce thing replete with too much rage, Whose *strength's* abundance weakens *his own* heart;
A′. Fear (2)
B′. Repleteness (2)
So I, for *fear* of trust, forget to say The *perfect* ceremony of *love's* rite
And in *mine own love's strength* seem to decay, O'ercharged with burden of *mine own love's might.*

***O l**et my **lo**oks be then the e**lo**quence*
And dumb presagers of my speaking breast,
*Who p**l**ead for **lo**ve and **lo**ok for recompense,*
. . . . .
***O l**earn to read what si**l**ent **lo**ve hath writ;*
*To hear with eyes be**lo**ngs to **lo**ve's fine wit.*

But there are many other signs of passion in the sestet besides the liquid repeated *l*'s; there is the Latin / Anglo-Saxon pun on *eloquence* and *speaking*, the play on *dumb* and *speak*, the false wisdom-root *sage* in *presagers*, the rhymes of *looks* and *look*, *plead* and *read*, the primary derivation of *wit* from *writ*, the assonance between *eyes* and *fine*, the suggestion of *longs* in *belongs*, and the graphic resonance of *writ* with *rite* (line 6), the latter a homonym of *right.* (I refuse the suggested homonym with *write*, since a verb cannot substitute for a noun.) The frustrating speechlessness of the lover, forced into his plea for "hearing eyes," has suddenly found a way of talking by deviating into the third person in the surprising and beautiful final line: *To hear with eyes belongs to love's fine wit.* This is a new-coined "proverb" invented by the lover, impersonal in its third-person phraseology (unlike the first- and second-person utterance of the rest of the sonnet). Folk genius does not invent generous proverbs like this one ("real" proverbs being characteristically mean-spirited). Receptive love has a sharpened wit: *love's fine wit* must have echoed in George Herbert's mind when he wrote, "And if I please him, I write fine and wittie." The conclusiveness of impersonal epigrammatic utterance has just that happiness of the *trouvaille* that enables the speaker to forget his shyness and cap his plea with his "proverb." The proverb contains a compliment: "*Love's fine wit*—there, that's what you can give me to make up for my inadequacy—and I found a proverb with the words for it!" Joy, pride, power, and an end to the poem. The faulty Quarto spelling in line 14 (*wit* for *with*, and *wiht* for *wit*) suggests that even the compositor's eye was distracted by the play of *with* and *wit* in the one line.

DEFECTIVE KEY WORD: LOVE (absent from the "speechless" Q_1)

Couplet Tie: *love* [-'s] (6, 7, 8, 11, 13, 14)
rite/writ (6, 13)

24

MIne eye hath play'd the painter and hath ſteeld,
Thy beauties forme in table of my heart,
My body is the frame wherein ti's held,
And perſpectiue it is beſt Painters art.
For through the Painter muſt you ſee his skill,
To finde where your true Image pictur'd lies,
Which in my boſomes ſhop is hanging ſtil,
That hath his windowes glazed with thine eyes:
Now ſee what good-turnes eyes for eies haue done,
Mine eyes haue drawne thy ſhape,and thine for me
Are windowes to my breſt, where-through the Sun
Delights to peepe,to gaze therein on thee
  Yet eyes this cunning want to grace their art
  They draw but what they ſee,know not the hart.

Mine eye hath played the painter and hath stelled
Thy beauty's form in table of my heart;
My body is the frame wherein 'tis held,
And pérspective it is best painter's art.
For through the painter must you see his skill
To find where your true image pictured lies,
Which in my bosom's shop is hanging still,
That hath his windows glazèd with thine eyes.
Now see what good turns eyes for eyes have done:
Mine eyes have drawn thy shape, and thine for me
Are windows to my breast, wherethrough the sun
Delights to peep, to gaze therein on thee.
  Yet eyes this cunning want to grace their art,
  They draw but what they see, know not the heart.

THIS sonnet turns on the etymological pun *perspective = see through* [< *per-spicio*]. As the painter-lover must employ *perspective* (his best art), to represent the beloved, so the beloved must employ *per-spective* to *see into* the painter to find his own image engraved on the painter's heart; so also must the sun find his means of "per-spective" to *gaze through* the *windows* of the lover's eyes, glazed with the reflection of the beloved's eyes, to *peep* at the image of the beloved hanging in the *bosom's shop* of the lover. This is all so foreign to a modern reader that the charm of rococo fantasy may be overlooked in a revulsion against seeing a grown man (as cliché would say) writing such "drivel." The poem has its own terrible pathos at its close, however; the painter-lover, though he can employ perspective in his representation, has himself (unlike the beloved or the sun) no capacity for perspective in its etymological sense of *looking-through;* his eyes *draw but what they see, know not the heart.* He cannot look through appearance to reality. In a bitter self-commentary (foregrounded by a transgression of sonnet rules against rhyme-repetition) the couplet repeats, in reverse order, the main rhyme *(heart/art)* of the first quatrain. The boast that *pérspective it is best painter's art*—whether it means that a good painter can paint in perspective, or that looked at perspective-wise the picture is excellent—collapses into the *want of cunning* in the painter-lover, unable to *know the heart* of the enigmatic beloved.

This is one of the many sonnets of asymmetry which stand over against the sonnets of reciprocity, of *mutual render, only me for thee* (125). Although there lurks a possible model here for complementary reciprocity (I paint, you gaze), it becomes asymmetrical in its expansion (I paint you, you gaze at you) and grows finally even more asymmetrical (I paint you, you gaze at you; the sun gazes at you through my eyes glazed with you). The poor painter: no one is installing *his* portrait in a bosom-shop, no one wants to gaze on *him*, neither his beloved nor the sun.

Of course, in the usual epideictic tradition, such objections of asymmetry would not arise, since praise in that genre always originates *de bas en haut.* But the stubborn wish for mutuality in the sonnets will not permit the hierarchical relation (the poet who praises, the lord who is praised) to survive unchallenged. Eventually (123, 124) the putatively inferior poet becomes the only visible object in the world: the pyramids may change, but he does not; *all alone* his absolute love stands *hugely politic.*

The beloved does not even figure in these two "late" poems; and in 126, the adieu, the young man is finally only a plaything of Nature, *a minion* of her *pleasure* (with a backward glance to 20, *she pricked thee out for women's pleasure*). Of all things, only Love is not subject to Nature; *it nor grows with heat, nor drowns with show'rs* (124). This is the final asymmetry to which the early asymmetries, tilted in the other direction (toward the speaker's abjectness and the beloved's perfection), finally, bleakly, tend.

Sonnet 24 is the first extended meditation in the *Sonnets* on representation, and on the curious stratagems to which it is driven. Paradoxically, in representing the beloved, the painter-lover distances him at one remove; it is not thyself, says the painter, but *thy beauty's form*, *your true image pictured*, *thy shape* which I have drawn. These second-order expressions outnumber the single first-order reference: that the sun delights to gaze therein on *thee* (not *thy image*). Representation, though intended as an homage reproducing the whole beloved, turns out to produce, almost unintentionally, a two-dimensional image for public consumption (the sun comes to gaze). The mutual gazing-in-each-other's-eyes in which lovers delight is turned from a "liberal" action (i.e., one with no end in view) to a "practical" action *(Now see what good turns eyes for eyes have done)*. The painter uses his practical skill to draw the young man's shape (doing him a good turn by enabling him to see himself represented) and the young man, by impressing his eye's reflected image on the painter's eyes, has glazed those windows to the painter's bosom with his own overlaid image (presumably beautifying them: *his* good turn). The sun thus apparently sees a double image: first, the young man reflected in the glazing of the painter's cornea, and second, the young man pictured in the heart's painted image. The resemblances among *glaze*, *gaze*, and *grace* remind us that a gaze can lack the grace of cunning (as it does in the pained painter), that a glaze can be a means to a gaze (as it is with the sun). No satisfactory relation is established (in spite of the factitious enthusiasm of *Now see*) among *gaze*, *glaze*, and *grace*. The failure of representation (even while it produces a true image of beauty's external *form*) to produce a true image of beauty's *heart* restricts representation to that *outward fair* (16) belonging to the eye. The collapse of drawing's power creates the pang at the close.

KEY WORD: EYE [-S]

Couplet Tie: *eye* [-*s*] (1, 8, 9, 9, 13)
draw [-*n*] (10, 14)
see (5, 14)
heart (2, 14)
art (4, 13)

LEt thoſe who are in fauor with their ſtars,
Of publike honour and proud titles boſt,
Whilſt I whome fortune of ſuch tryumph bars
Vnlookt for ioy in that I honour moſt;
Great Princes fauorites their faire leaues ſpread,
But as the Marygold at the ſuns eye,
And in them-ſelues their pride lies buried,
For at a frowne they in their glory die.
The painefull warrier famoſed for worth,
After a thouſand victories once foild,
Is from the booke of honour raſed quite,
And all the reſt forgot for which he toild:
  Then happy I that loue and am beloued
  Where I may not remoue,nor be remoued.

Let those who are in favour with their stars
Of public honour and proud titles boast,
Whilst I whom fortune of such triumph bars
Unlooked for joy in that I honour most.
Great princes' favourites their fair leaves spread
But as the marigold at the sun's eye,
And in themselves their pride lies burièd,
For at a frown they in their glory die.
The painful warrior famousèd for fight,
After a thousand victories once foiled,
Is from the book of honour rasèd quite,
And all the rest forgot for which he toiled:
  Then happy I that love and am belovèd
  Where I may not remove, nor be removèd.

LIKE SONNET 15 *(When I consider every thing that grows)*, 25 narrows from a grand conspectus to a single focus, from *those who are in favour with their stars* (*all* of the lucky) to *great princes' favourites* (*some*, a subclass), to *the painful warrior famousèd for fight* (*one*, a single example). (I accept the emendation *fight* for the Quarto *worth*, preferring it to *might* because it joins the alliterative chain in *f* so important to the sonnet.) After Q_1's initial contrast between the boastful lucky people and the quietly content speaker, Q_2 and Q_3 offer exempla of the reversal of fortune when the stars withdraw their favor. In order to differentiate his exempla, Shakespeare writes one in the plural *(favourites)* and one in the singular *(warrior);* he ascribes to favorites an unreal "voluntary" death when they sense their prince's favor withdrawn *(in themselves their pride lies buried, / For at a frown they in their glory die)*, but he also shows the warrior subjected to a violent exterior erasure *(from the book of honour rasèd quite).* The "voluntary" versus involuntary removal is echoed conceptually in the couplet: *I may not remove nor be removèd.* Both the *triumph* of line 3 and the *public honour* of line 2 are rendered hollow, since they can be so easily lost. The lover's *joy in that I honour most* becomes thus the true center of value (not the stars' *favour* nor the *favour* of princes, nor the *famous* history of the warrior in the book of *honour*). The various relations between stars and men, princes and favourites, the public and the warrior—all of them hierarchical relations of power—are rejected in the couplet in favor of perfect reciprocity, that quality beloved of the early sonnets—*I . . . love and am belovèd, / . . . I may not remove nor be removèd.* (These ideas and rhyme-roots [*love, remove*] will recur with especial irony in 116 [*Let me not*]; at this stage in the sequence, they are read innocently, as is the rejection of court intrigue in favor of private mutuality. The rejection of court intrigue in 124 [*If my dear love*] is a far lonelier affair.)

Sonnet 25 ends with a private boast *(Then happy I)*, countering the public boasts of the stars' triumphant favorites. The implicit irony in the fact that the speaker-lover does not expect a reversal of fortune in his own case suggests that he thinks he can hide from the *stars*, which is the most foolish *boast* of all. The complacency of the speaker in boasting of (putative) reciprocal bliss would have been evident to any Renaissance reader, as would the genre of the last two lines—a clear boast rivaling those of the publicly lucky. Yet the wish to make something be so by declaring it to be so lies behind the boastful couplet and gives it pathos; the couplet-sentiment is so far from being harnessed to the determinism of the body of the sonnet that there is no substantive Couplet Tie in this poem at all. The aristocratic words *honour* (2, 4, 11), *pride* [*proud*] (2, 7), and *favour[ites]* (1, 5) form, however, a system of overlapping value-words contrasted with the couplet's reciprocal and private *love/belovèd;* and the body of the sonnet exhibits one of Shakespeare's longest alliterative meaning-chains, the connective tissue of lines 1–12 of the poem, telling its plot in little: *favour, fortune, triumph, favourites, fair, from, painful, famousèd, fight, foiled, forgot.*

Couplet Tie: None

26

LOrd of my loue,to whome in vaſſalage
Thy merrit hath my dutie ſtrongly knit;
To thee I ſend this written ambaſſage
To witneſſe duty, not to ſhew my wit.
Duty ſo great,which wit ſo poore as mine
May make ſeeme bare,in wanting words to ſhew it;
But that I hope ſome good conceipt of thine
In thy ſoules thought(all naked) will beſtow it:
Til whatſoeuer ſtar that guides my mouing,
Points on me gratiouſly with faire aſpect,
And puts apparrell on my tottered louing,
To ſhow me worthy of their ſweet reſpect,
    Then may I dare to boaſt how I doe loue thee,
    Til then,not ſhow my head where thou maiſt proue me

Lord of my love, to whom in vassalage
Thy merit hath my duty strongly knit,
To thee I send this written ambassage
To witness duty, not to show my wit;
Duty so great, which wit so poor as mine
May make seem bare, in wanting words to show it,
But that I hope some good conceit of thine
In thy soul's thought (all naked) will bestow it,
Till whatsoever star that guides my moving
Points on me graciously with fair aspéct,
And puts apparel on my tottered loving,
To show me worthy of thy sweet respect:
    Then may I dare to boast how I do love thee,
    Till then, not show my head where thou mayst prove me.

THE first epistolary sonnet. One of the pieces of wit (in this sonnet professing want of wit) is that although the KEY WORD, appearing in each quatrain and the couplet, is SHOW, its context is always either a personal inability to *show*, or an ascription of *show* to another agency: "[I send this letter] *not to show my wit;* wit *want[s] words to show* [duty]; [I need your aid] Till [my] star . . . puts apparel on my . . . tattered loving / *To show* me worthy; Till then [I dare] *not show* my head."

This showy nonshowing and not-as-yet showing is one example of the many ways in which the sonnets foreground their technical expertise as tours de force, expecting readers to notice the ironic discrepancy (present in all works of art) between expressive immediacy and technical mediation. The careful scheme of a *written ambassage* precludes spontaneity, as the stately measure of this letter bears witness; but the solemn protestations of duty and modest denials of wit conflict with the joyous presence of several forms, hidden and apparent, of the very word *wit:*

[The] ***wri**tten [letter will serve] to* ***wit**ness duty, not to*
show my ***wit**;*
Duty so great, which ***wit*** *so poor as mine*
May make seem bare, in wanting words to show ***it**,*
But that . . . [thy conceit] will bestow ***it*** *. . .*
[Till my star] points on me graciously ***with*** *fair*
aspect . . .
To show me worthy of thy ***sweet*** *respect.*

The closing "boast" of 25 is here rendered more cautiously; the letter writer hopes that he may in the future *dare to boast how I do love thee*, but claims no requited love.

The *bare*, *naked* duty which is all that the writer professes to be able to express will, it is hoped, be clothed by two agents: in the future, the writer's guiding star will, he hopes, *put apparel on* his tattered loving; but for the time being, he implores his lord to bestow on the poet's nakedness *some good conceit of thine / In thy soul's thought.* This saintlike action—"clothing the naked," one of the seven corporal works of mercy—is predicated so equally of the beloved and the guiding star as to make them by succession one.

Structure of Sonnet 26

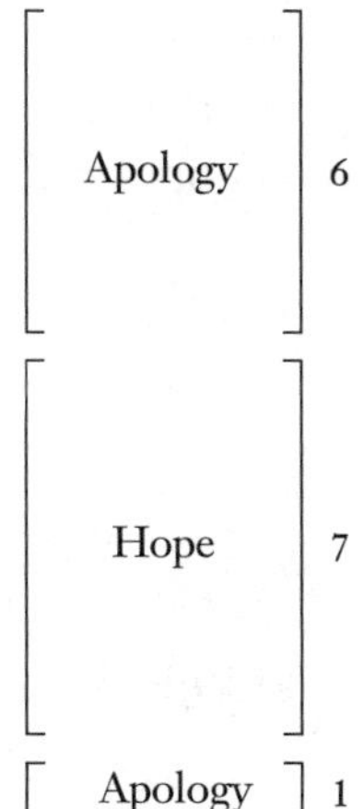

Structurally, the sonnet is divided into apology (lines 1–6), hope (lines 7–13), and a second apology (line 14), as shown in the diagram. This unusual and irregular structural division suggests that an experiment with rhetorical structure is one of the compositional motivations of this sonnet (which is not notable for imagination). The degree to which, in the course of the sequence, Shakespeare engages with play in finding ways around the 4-4-4-2 sonnet structure is very striking. Here, lines 5–6 are connected to Q_1 by the strong verbal parallel *(duty/wit; duty/wit)* linking line 5 to line 4. The lines of hope in Q_2 (7–8) are linked forward to Q_3 by the parallel acts of a patron's *conceit* bestowed on *nakedness* and a star's putting *apparel* on tattered loving. And the single line of hope (13) in the couplet is linked back to the hope in Q_3 by the repetition of *loving* (line 11) in *love* (line 13). These internal semantic and rhetorical connections prevent us from reading the three quatrains and the couplet as separable entities, and encourage us to group lines together, as I have said, in "unorthodox" ways.

Lines 1–6 are conducted in a stilted, rhetorically balanced, and alternately end-stopped way; but the diapason (lines 7–12) beginning with *But that I hope* and swelling to *respect* has recourse to Shakespeare's usual formal equivalent for swelling feeling, enjambment. (See, e.g., similar enjambed moments describing the lark arising in 29 and the mistress' eyes as sun and star in 127.) In one of the ironies already crowding into the sequence, the speaker who predicted that the beloved's youth would become "a *tottered* weed of small *worth* held" (sonnet 2) has now, in the abjectness of love, become ***unworthy*** of respect himself because of his "*tottered* loving," looking to a better fortune to enable him to raise his head. The attempt to suggest that the young man has more wit (good conceits in the thought of his soul) than the writer is one that will not recur; it was perhaps improbable enough to deter its future use even in infatuation. The truest mark of infatuation is the pretense in the couplet that *prove me* rhymes with *love thee.*

KEY WORD: SHOW

Couplet Tie: *love* [-*ing*] (1, 11, 13)
till (9, 14) (foregrounded by repetition of initial line-position)
show (4, 6, 12, 14)

27

WEary with toyle, I hast me to my bed,
The deare repose for lims with trauaill tired,
But then begins a iourny in my head
To worke my mind, when boddies work's expired.
For then my thoughts (from far where I abide)
Intend a zelous pilgrimage to thee,
And keepe my drooping eye-lids open wide,
Looking on darknes which the blind doe see.
Saue that my soules imaginary sight
Presents their shaddoe to my sightles view,
Which like a iewell (hunge in gastly night)
Makes blacke night beautious, and her old face new.
Loe thus by day my lims, by night my mind,
For thee, and for my selfe, noe quiet finde.

Weary with toil, I haste me to my bed,
The dear repose for limbs with travel tired,
But then begins a journey in my head
To work my mind, when body's work's expired;
For then my thoughts (from far where I abide)
Intend a zealous pilgrimage to thee,
And keep my drooping eyelids open wide,
Looking on darkness which the blind do see;
Save that my soul's imaginary sight
Presents thy shadow to my sightless view,
Which like a jewel (hung in ghastly night)
Makes black night beauteous, and her old face new.
Lo thus by day my limbs, by night my mind,
For thee, and for myself, no quiet find.

THE first of the travel sonnets; the first instance of insomnia. The sequence is forever providing these small dramatic incidents as fresh soil for meditation; its drama is not *narrative* so much as *scenic.* Nothing much happens by way of events; but there is an inexhaustible supply of fresh scenes (a characteristic proper to lyric, and visible in sonneteers from Petrarch on, as we see the lover on horseback, or sleepless in bed).

The speaker's night of habitual unrepose is bracketed by brief references to days of equal unrepose, and the summary in the couplet shows that Unrepose *(no quiet)* may be said to be the governing concept for the sonnet:

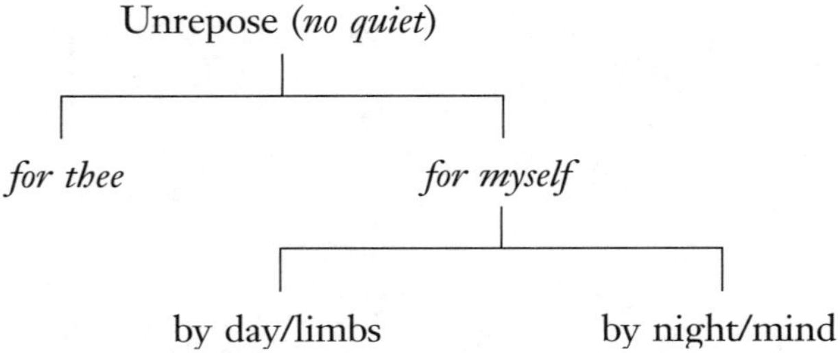

The three parallelisms of the couplet might suggest an even distribution of dramatic interest in (a) *day* and *night;* (b) *limbs* and *mind;* and (c) *thee* and *myself.* In point of fact, no such distribution exists in the body of this splendid nocturne, which is almost exclusively concerned with the night, the mind, and the speaker, rather than the day, the limbs, and the beloved. It is true that the first two lines preserve a chiastic balance—*weary : bed : : repose : tired*—between day and night:

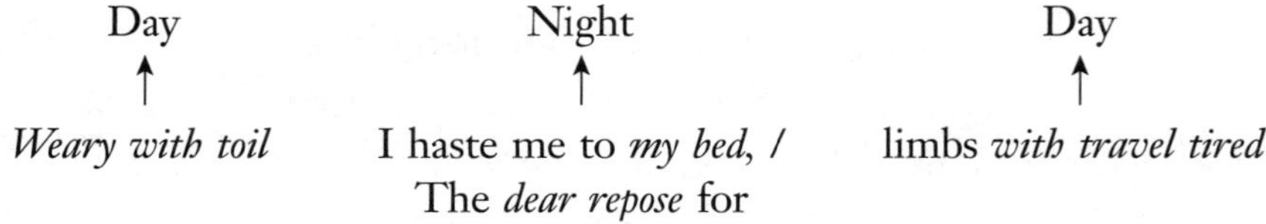

But in the second two lines, the receding day "owns" only two words, *body's work:*

But then begins a journey in my head
To work my mind, when body's work's expired.

From then on, the poem is a pure nocturne, one retelling an increasingly spiritual *work* of the mind replacing the body's *work*. Wittily, the night's work is called a *jour*ney (French: *jour*, day), and the speaker is thus by night a *journeyman* of a different sort from the one his *toil* makes him during the *day*. The mental work begins in the *head*, is internalized to the *mind*, is desubstantialized as *thoughts*, and is spiritualized into a *zealous pilgrimage* resulting in the *soul's . . . sight*.

Invention's task here is to enact both the frustration of insomnia and the creative zeal of the soul's pilgrimage. In its counterpoint of exhaustion against exaltation, the poem is one of the most tonally resonant among the sonnets. The exhaustion is conveyed by the line-by-line *étapes* of the night travail: *But then begins a journey . . . / To work my mind . . . / For then my thoughts . . . / Intend a . . . pilgrimage . . . / And keep my . . . eyelids open . . . / Looking on darkness. . . . / Save that my soul's . . . sight / Presents thy shadow . . . / Lo thus . . . no quiet*. Stage follows stage, with no respite of *dear repose*. On the other hand, the ecstatic paradoxes of erotic vision are reminiscent of those of religious rapture: night, says the speaker, keeps

my . . . eyelids open wide,
Looking on darkness which the blind do see;
Save that my soul's imaginary sight
Presents thy shadow to my sightless view,
Which like a jewel (hung in ghastly night)
Makes black night beauteous, and her old face new.

The words *see, soul, sight, shadow, sightless view* form a minor strain of music in the counterpoint, within which the negatives *shadow* and *sightless* frustrate the full seeing of the soul's *sight*.

The sonnet raises minor questions of word choice that a careful look at Shakespeare's technical work helps to resolve. Why *zealous?* Why *imaginary?* Why *jewel?* Why *ghastly?* Explanations of the presence of these words might differ, but the wish to explain them is provoked by their oddity or by their tendency to suggest shadow-words appropriate to the poem. Behind *zealous* glimmers *jealous;* behind *ghastly, ghostly. Jewel* fits into a phonetic cluster with *view* and *beauteous* (as a replacement-word like *planet* would not). Here, e.g., is a rewriting that does not significantly damage the message, only the poetry:

my thoughts . . .
Intend *an eager* pilgrimage to thee, . . .
Save that my soul *in fair phantasmic* sight
Presents thine *image* to my sightless view,
Which like a *planet* (hung in *hideous* night)
Makes black night *lovely*, and her old face new.

The sentiment—and it is abstracted sentiment which critics have mistakenly persisted in overpraising in Shakespeare—remains relatively undisturbed, I would say, by these substitutions. But we lose phonetic and graphic chains of binding significance *(zealous/eyel**ids**; i**ma**ginary/sh**a**dow; vi**ew**/j**ew**el/b**eau**teous; **s**oul/**s**ight/**s**hadow/**s**ightle**ss**)*. We lose the "double" words like *zealous/jealous* and *ghastly/ghostly;* and we even lose the five scrambled letters-held-in-common *(s,g,h,t,l)* by ***sightl**ess* and ***ghastl**y*.

In another experiment, one could rewrite the sonnet to eliminate jealousy and frustration from the night-vision, and make it purely rapturous:

my thoughts . . .
Intend *an eager* pilgrimage to thee,
And keep my drooping eyelids open wide,
Looking on *images which lovers* see;
Ah then, my soul's *all-visionary* sight
Presents thy *visage* to *enraptured* view,
Which like a jewel (hung in *wakeful* night)
Makes black night beauteous, and her old face new.

Such rewriting makes clear Shakespeare's subversion of the exalted night-vision, a subversion accomplished by *zealous*, *darkness*, *blind*, *imaginary*, *shadow*, *sightless*, and *ghastly*.

The inner evolvings represented by such verbal concatenations keep the night-journey going, and keep it consistent. Without such enactings, the conventional sentiment (insomniac conjuring-up of the beloved's presence) would not make a memorable poem.

One last surprise of pathos and irony has been reserved by Shakespeare for the couplet—the apparently innocuous phrase *for thee*. The beloved is no doubt safely asleep in his bed, *far from where* the speaker *abide[s]*. But the speaker wants to believe that the spirit of the beloved is, at least by his summoning, rendered as full of disquiet as his own insomniac self, and the expression of apparent compunction in *for thee* is in fact a claim. (See 61 for a reworking of this sentiment: *For thee watch I while thou dost wake elsewhere*, which has there degenerated into suspicion of the young man's consorting *with others*.) The notion that the beloved (in his *shadow*-guise) is also engaged in the kind of mind's *work* exhausting the speaker is supported by nothing in the description of the spiritual night-journey, and is therefore convicted, by the poem itself, of being a fantasy. (It is possible I have made too much of *for thee*, and that it should be taken to mean only "on account of thee," but its strict parallel with *for me* authorizes the meaning "for your far-away self.")

Couplet Tie: *limbs* (2, 13)
mind (4, 13)
night (11, 12, 13)

28

HOw can I then returne in happy plight
That am debard the benifit of reſt?
When daies oppreſſion is not eazd by night,
But day by night and night by day opreſt.
And each(though enimes to ethers raigne)
Doe in conſent ſhake hands to torture me,
The one by toyle,the other to complaine
How far I toyle,ſtill farther off from thee.
I tell the Day to pleaſe him thou art bright,
And do'ſt him grace when clouds doe blot the heauen:
So flatter I the ſwart complexiond night,
When ſparkling ſtars twire not thou guil'ſt th' eauen.
  But day doth daily draw my ſorrowes longer,(ſtronger
  And night doth nightly make greefes length ſeeme

How can I then return in happy plight
That am debarred the benefit of rest?
When day's oppression is not eased by night,
But day by night and night by day oppressed;
And each (though enemies to either's reign)
Do in consent shake hands to torture me,
The one by toil, the other to complain
How far I toil, still farther off from thee.
I tell the day to please him thou art bright,
And dost him grace when clouds do blot the heaven;
So flatter I the swart-complexioned night,
When sparkling stars twire not thou gild'st the even:
  But day doth daily draw my sorrows longer,
  And night doth nightly make grief's strength seem stronger.

LIKE SONNET 27, this poem, with its comparably unhappy ending, turns on the indistinguishability of day and night; they were both occasions of *work* in the former poem, but here they are both occasions of *torture*. Day and night are surely natural *enemies*. How can it be that they have now become allies so that they *do in consent shake hands to torture me?* It is because of their *absence* from the beloved that the speaker's personified days and nights are enraged, and wreak their vengeance upon him; he attempts to pacify his torturers by assuring them that they, unlike himself, are in effect in the presence of the beloved. They refuse to believe such sophistry, and their torture goes on.

This exaggerated projection onto cosmic powers (Day and Night) of the tortures of absence suggests that the young man himself is a fellow god of theirs, and that when the sovereigns *Dies* and *Nox* are deprived of his exalted company, they torment the *oppress[ed]* speaker because of their deprivation. The day tortures the speaker by *toil*, the night by making him *complain* of distance from the beloved.

The abject position of the tortured servant-speaker is manifest in his cringing flattery. To the day (to please him and make him stop the torture) the speaker says, "The young man is really with you; when clouds blot the heaven, he shines and does you grace." To the night, the speaker says, "The young man is really with you; when the stars are not visible, he gilds the evening."

The little story of 28 is not told by the speaker about himself in a narration, but rather in a second-person address to the beloved; and so the compelled lies to the torturers are told to the young man as if he were a sympathetic auditor of the speaker's stratagems:

> I tell the day, to please him, that you [the object of the day's love and the absent cause of his rage] are bright and do him grace on cloudy days;
>
> [In the same way] I flatter the swart-complexioned night, saying to him that when the stars are invisible you [the object of the night's love and the absent cause of his rage] gild the evening.

We are to infer that the days are cloudy and the nights starless because sun and stars alike are sulking in their tents, hating their separation from the beloved youth. But all the abjectness does the speaker no good; the torturers resume and intensify their torture, and sorrow and grief expand in suffering. (I accept the emendation of *length* to *strength* in line 14, largely because a *stronger length* seems unidiomatic.)

In its fiction, the poem suggests that the speaker has received a letter from the beloved, saying, "I hope you will return in happy plight." The speaker then bursts out in grievance with his opening reply, which contains an indirect quotation from the beloved's letter:

> How *can* I then return "in happy plight"
> That am debarred the benefit of rest?
> When day's oppression is not eased by night,
> But day by night and night by day oppressed.

The double emphasis on feeling *oppressed* suggests that the speaker in truth feels *oppressed* by the beloved who has sent him away, perhaps, on this errand. But the complaint is deflected (as so often in the *Sonnets*) onto agents who are in fact innocent (here, *day* and *night*), and the words directed at the beloved must be, can only be, words of praise: *thou art bright, and dost* sun-like *grace* to a cloudy day; *thou gild'st the even* in lieu of the stars.

It is a mark of the impossibility of his speaking candidly to the beloved that the speaker has to invent his improbable and contrived fable of placating his torturing oppressors. The degree of contortedness in any given invention always measures its departure from the right angle of truth (see, e.g., 138, *When my love swears*, for a comparable set of contortions). Those who object to sonnets like this as "contrived" or "artificial" cannot see that a "contrived" and "artificial" repression of mutual candid speech is what has engendered such oblique fables, and that what is being enacted is the torment of deflected complaint.

It probably goes without saying that the sonnet first distinguishes Night and Day, the two opposite sovereigns *(enemies to either's reign)*, and then joins them in a plural verb *(shake hands)*, to represent their joint savaging of the speaker. At the end, they are acting once again separately-but-in-conjunction. In the diagram, my medial arrows represent the direction of aggression; the vertical arrows represent the countermovement of the line's progress. The last sentence, though distributive (Day doth; Night doth) makes its two coordinate statements so resemble each other in vocabulary, parallel syntax, and effect that the *shak[ing] hands to torture* is once more enacted in spite of the return from a joint verb *(shake hands)* to separate verbs *(doth draw; doth make)*.

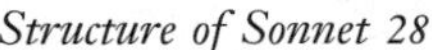

Structure of Sonnet 28

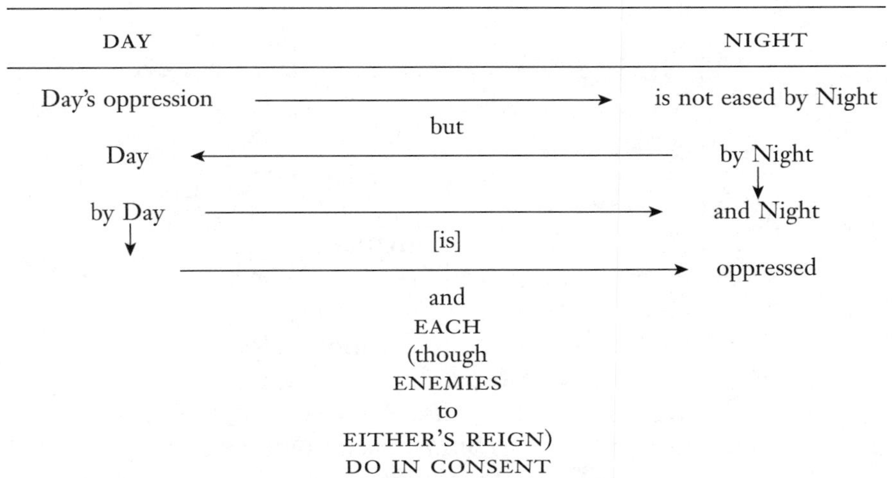

The one by toil, — the other to complain;

I tell the Day; — So flatter I the Night:

but

Day doth daily draw my sorrows longer, — and — Night doth nightly make grief's strength seem stronger.

Such rather formulaic ways of enacting content by form are more typical of the earlier sonnets in the sequence; and though nobody would choose this sonnet (or other such sonnets) as among the best, they are interesting as proving-grounds for Shakespearean convictions about the necessity of poetic enactment. And even the most formulaic sonnets do not lack an imaginative thrust; one does not forget the tortured vassal uttering desperate flattery against the cruelty of overcast days and sullen nights.

Couplet Tie: (as might be expected)
day [*daily*] (3, 4, 4, 9, 13, 13)
night [*nightly*] (3, 4, 4, 11, 14, 14)

29

VVHen in diſgrace with Fortune and mens eyes,
I all alone beweepe my out-caſt ſtate,
And trouble deafe heauen with my bootleſſe cries,
And looke vpon my ſelfe and curſe my fate.
Wiſhing me like to one more rich in hope,
Featur'd like him,like him with friends poſſeſt,
Deſiring this mans art,and that mans skope,
With what I moſt inioy contented leaſt,
Yet in theſe thoughts my ſelfe almoſt deſpiſing,
Haplye I thinke on thee, and then my ſtate,
(Like to the Larke at breake of daye ariſing)
From ſullen earth ſings himns at Heauens gate,
For thy ſweet loue remembred ſuch welth brings,
That then I skorne to change my ſtate with Kings.

When in disgrace with Fortune and men's eyes,
I all alone beweep my outcast state,
And trouble deaf heaven with my bootless cries,
And look upon myself and curse my fate,
Wishing me like to one more rich in hope,
Featured like him, like him with friends possessed,
Desiring this man's art, and that man's scope,
With what I most enjoy contented least;
Yet in these thoughts myself almost despising,
Haply I think on thee, and then my state
(Like to the lark at break of day arising
From sullen earth) sings hymns at heaven's gate,
For thy sweet love rememb'red such wealth brings
That then I scorn to change my state with kings.

THE sonnet begins with a great opening opposition of two models of "reality" (as conceived by the Renaissance), which are summoned by the speaker in order to define his own position: the hierarchical social world and the imitatively hierarchical world of nature. (A third model, in the couplet, will unite nature and society.) A scheme deduced from items in the octave could begin as follows:

I. *Hierarchy of the Social World* (his outcast *state* at bottom)	II. *Hierarchy of the Natural World* (his original implied *state* on sullen earth)
Heaven (here, deaf to cries)	Heaven (the sky, and the four-gated city as well)
↓	↑
Fortuna and her wheel	
↓	
Kings	Lark (in air)
↓	↑
Men in favor	Thee (beloved)
↓	↑
Speaker, outcast and in disgrace	Speaker
	↑
	Sullen earth

The drama of the poem occurs in the speaker's moving himself out of the first (social) world and into the second (natural) one; the puzzle of the poem, solved in the couplet, is how he manages to pull himself up by his own bootstraps, mired as he is in the social world. But he not only moves into and up through the second world, that of nature; he also, by casting retrospective glances back at the social world, relates the two models to each other. The poem consequently ends with an integrated model of the "whole" world, one which reveals itself as a third model by using, as did the other two, the word *state* to place the speaker's relation to the rest of the world:

III. *Hierarchy of the "Whole" World* (where speaker's *state* exceeds that of kings)

Heaven's gate
↑
Speaker (whose newly elevated state sings hymns like lark at dawn)
↑
Kings
↑
Other men

The enjambment of the *lark arising / From sullen earth* has of course been noticed, as has the opposition of the receptive *heaven's gate* to unresponsive *deaf heaven*, and that of *sings* to *bootless cries*. But how are we to account for the (apparently fortuitous) *Haply I think on thee*, on which the whole transformation turns? By means of that thought, the man who once wished to exchange his state with almost anyone *(like to one . . . / like him, like him)* now scorns to exchange even *with kings*. How did the fulcrum-thought arise?

As so often in Shakespeare, the analytic moment (here, line 8) in the sonnet becomes the fulcrum of change. The active narrative in the habitual present tense *(I . . . beweep,* [I] *trouble,* [I] *look . . . and curse, wishing, desiring)* yields to a stunning moment of self-analysis: *With what I most enjoy contented least.* The ostentatious chiastic paradox—*most enjoy contented least*—by foregrounding the two thematic verbals *enjoy* and *contented*, and the two adverbial brackets *most* and *least*—forces us to recognize that this speaker has implicitly done an inner inventory, a triple list: [*what I enjoy; what I more enjoy;*] *what I most enjoy.* He has, however, remained bad-tempered through all his lists of (conventional) good things. It is inconceivable that the speaker's inventory of good things, no matter how glumly conducted, should not end up in the possession of the beloved—and so the *haply* is not so unexpected or fortuitous as it might first seem. Discontent with [*what I enjoy*] has mounted to even less content with [*what I more enjoy*], and has arrived at being *least* content with [*what I (think I) most enjoy*]. But this paradoxical sullenness is broken into by the implied next item on the list: the super-superlative [*what I most most enjoy*]—the beloved (cf. *your most most loving* breast, 110). It is probably not accidental, either, that one of the envious wishes had been to be *possessed of friends*, like someone else. The *haply* is engendered by that train of thought, as well: [Yet I *do* possess a friend!] But the *haply* could not occur without the moment of bitter chiastic self-reflexive self-mockery in line 8's analytic fulcrum. The self-pity of the opening is based on genuine misfortune, if the domestic fiction of the sonnet is to be believed; we do not doubt that the speaker is *outcast, in disgrace* not only vertically with Fortuna but also horizontally with *men's eyes,* the social world. We can well believe, listening to his wishes, that the speaker may be more ill-featured than some men, may lack the art or scope or hope of others, but it is hard to believe that he is utterly destitute. In fact, as he realizes in his self-analytic moment, he is not destitute—he does have things he enjoys; it is just that at this moment he is vexed enough to refuse any enjoyment at all. This childish repudiation is what is analyzed in the chiasmus *most enjoy contented least,* representing a movement up *(most),* a plateau *(enjoy contented),* and a movement down *(least).* This analytic recognition allows true enjoyment to burst forth: "Ah, but I do enjoy something more than 'most'—I think on thee!" In the most joyous play of the poem, the disgruntled present participles—*wishing, desiring,* with their "wrong" arrangement of letters—suddenly give rise to new present participles where the letters are arranged "right": *despi**sing**, ari**sing**,* and then the verb *sing—sing, sing, sing!* The poem fairly carols. Even the first line of the couplet (in ***brings***—"rings!") makes the air resound; but at the end, in the scorned *kings,* the word *sing* lies scrambled again, as it did in *wishing* and *desiring.* As he integrates the world of kings with the world of nature, locates his superlative friend, and, as a lark, finds a listening heaven, the poet rediscovers an integrated mental state.

DEFECTIVE KEY WORD: STATE (missing in Q_2, which describes the state of others, not his own)

Couplet Tie: *state* (2, 10, 14)
sing (-s), [*-sing*] (9, 11, 12)

30

VV Hen to the Seſſions of ſweet ſilent thought,
I ſommon vp remembrance of things paſt,
I ſigh the lacke of many a thing I ſought,
And with old woes new waile my deare times waſte:
Then can I drowne an eye(vn-vſ'd to flow)
For precious friends hid in deaths dateles night,
And weepe a freſh loues long ſince canceld woe,
And mone th'expence of many a vanniſht ſight.
Then can I greeue at greeuances fore-gon,
And heauily from woe to woe tell ore
The ſad account of fore-bemoned mone,
Which I new pay as if not payd before.
But if the while I thinke on thee (deare friend)
All loſſes are reſtord,and ſorrowes end.

When to the sessions of sweet silent thought
I summon up remembrance of things past,
I sigh the lack of many a thing I sought,
And with old woes new wail my dear time's waste;
Then can I drown an eye (unused to flow)
For precious friends hid in death's dateless night,
And weep afresh love's long since cancelled woe,
And moan th'expense of many a vanished sight.
Then can I grieve at grievances foregone,
And heavily from woe to woe tell o'er
The sad account of fore-bemoanèd moan,
Which I new pay as if not paid before.
But if the while I think on thee (dear friend)
All losses are restored, and sorrows end.

SHAKESPEARE here, as in many other sonnets, takes pains to construct a speaker possessing a multilayered self, receding through panels of time. We might give such temporal panels the names "now," "recently," "before that," "yet farther back," "in the remote past." It is hard to construct a credible present-tense self in the short space of fourteen lines; to construct a richly historical present-and-preterite-and-pluperfect-self in such a space is a tour de force. The speaker of sonnet 30 is (he tells us) a person who has long been stoic, whose tears have for a long time been *unused to flow*. In the situation sketched in the poem, he begins by deliberately and habitually making these tears flow again; he willingly—for the sake of an enlivened emotional selfhood—calls up the griefs of the past. In receding order, before the weeping "now" (T_5, where T = Time), there was the "recent" dry-eyed stoicism (T_4); "before that," the frequent *be-moanèd moan* (T_3) of repeated grief; "further back in the past," the original loss (T_2) so often mourned; and "in the remote past" (T_1), a time of achieved happiness, or at least neutrality, before the loss. These panels of time are laid out with respect to various lacks, grievances, and costs, as we track the emotional history of the speaker's responses to *losses* and *sorrows* (the two summarizing categories of line 14).

The initial, habitual "now" of weeping, T_5, is at the end surprisingly transformed into a final, actual "now" T_5, which resembles T_2—that remote happy past when one had love, precious friends, and the full enjoyment of those vanished sights, before sorrow entered, extended itself in mourning moans (T_3), and (even worse) hardened the soul into stoicism (T_4). The act described in the sonnet—a deliberate, willed, and *habitual* turn from the stoic T_4 back to T_3 (mourning)—is the only way the speaker has found to reconstitute the pre-stoical feeling self. However, this technique turns out to be a dangerous one. In line 12, we see the speaker not self-consciously remourning a woe that he knows to be an old one, but pitched, beyond his original intention, into a grief that no longer is aestheticized, but rather seems rawly new, original, horrible: "I new pay *as if not paid before*." The *pay / not paid* locution cancels out the previous locutions in which the second use of a verb or noun positively intensifies the first one, as in "*grieve* at *grievances*" or "fore-be*moan*ed *moan*." It is

Structure of Sonnet 30

NOW	THEN			
T_5 *Habitual present*	T_4 *Time of stoicism*	T_3 *Times of loss*	T_2 *Happy time*	T_1 *Neutral Time*
I summon remembrance		things past		
I sigh		lack of things sought	things sought and found	pre-seeking
new wail		old woes / waste		pre-woe
can drown eye	unused to flow	dead friends	friends	pre-friends
weep afresh	cancelled love-woe	love's woe	love	pre-love
moan		vanished sight	sights present	pre-sight
grieve	grievances foregone	grievances	happiness	pre-happiness
tell o'er account		bemoanèd moan	wealth	pre-debt
new pay		[debt] paid	possession	
as if		not paid		
		BUT		
			if [among things summoned to thought]	
I think on			thee (dear friend)	
		ALL LOSSES (lack of things sought) (dead friends) (vanished sights) (accounts payable)		
ARE RESTORED				
		AND SORROWS (old woes) (love's woe) (grievances) (moanings)		
END				

this wholly unexpected result—as an aestheticized, voluntarily summoned memory of "paid" grief turns into real "not paid" grief—that pitches *thought* into "I *think*." The speaker calls a halt, even if in supposition, to the "sessions of *sweet* silent thought" because they have grown suddenly painful.

The intricacy of the temporal scheme is pointed out by the sonnet itself, in its ostentatiously repetitious Q_3 *(grieve at grievances foregone . . . fore-bemoanèd moan . . . pay as if not paid)*. The overlap of successive thoughts is also emphasized by various phonetic concentrations of "thought-strings," of which I list the chief ones:

sessions	remembran-ce	woes	flow	drown	lack	precious
sweet	sin-ce	wail	friends	death's	love's	a-fresh
silent	can-ce-lled	waste			long	
summon	expen-se	woe			losses	
sigh	grievan-ce-s	woe				
sought		woe				
sight		sorr-ow				
since						
sad						

One could say (especially given the Renaissance confusion of *sigh* and *sight*, recalled by Kerrigan) that Shakespeare is here inventing a new verb: *sigh, sight, sought*. A sigh is the eventual result of a sight sought.

The ingenuity of this sonnet has not prevented generations of readers from being drawn into its vortex. The increasing psychological involvement, as the quatrains proceed—*I summon up . . . Then can I . . . Then can I*—acts as a present vertical emotional intensification balancing the horizontally broadening panorama stretching into further panels of the past. To be able to find pleasure in resummoning griefs that were once anguishing indicates, in itself a loss of perceptual freshness. This is, however, balanced by the genuine pathos of the elegiac recollection *(precious friends)*. The hardness of long-maintained stoicism *(foregone, cancelled, unused)* threatens the capacity both to mourn the past and (most especially) to love afresh. Altogether, 30 is not only one of the richest sonnets of the sequence, but also one of the most searching, in its analysis of inevitable emotional phases, and of the dangerous delectation (whether morose or not) of reexperienced grief. In the exactness of Shakespeare's psychological portraiture, the roaming generalities of Q_1 (*things* past . . . many a *thing* . . .old *woes*) yield to the greater specificities of Q_2 *(friends, love, vanished sight[s])*, which yield in their turn to the accelerating intensifications of Q_3 *(grieve-grievances, woe-to-woe, fore-bemoanèd-moan, pay-paid)*.

And yet the successive phases of feeling (so well enacted by the general, the particular, and the rapidly intensified) seem to melt into one another because of the resemblance of their syntactic structures, as if they were all one long process, each generating the next. Shakespeare respects the *fluidity* of mental processes (exemplified in lexical and syntactic concatenation) as much as the *division* of those processes (for analytic purposes) into phases reaching from a present into four layers of the past.

The credibility of the couplet depends on the probability that once the things summoned up in *thought* become rawly painful, the speaker will in reaction turn to the (recent) friendship with the young man ("I *think* on thee"), at which event the unexpected renewed pain of the speaker can be consoled. It is important that the consolation itself is expressed in the passive voice in one verb and intransitively in the other: "If I think on thee, losses *are restored* and sorrows *end*." No agency is ascribed to the young man. Not "You restore all losses; you end my sorrows." The speaker does not dare to claim any active participation by the young man in the restoration of happiness.

It is in such simultaneous marshaling of temporal continuity, logical discreteness, and psychological modeling that Shakespeare's *Sonnets* surpass those of other sonneteers. His enormous power to order intellectually recalcitrant material into lyrically convincing schemes is nowhere more visible than in this example.

KEY WORD: WOE [-S] (the last is a pun: sor-WOES)

Couplet Tie: *thought/think* (1, 13)
friend [-*s*] (6, 13)
woe [-*s*] (4, 7, 10, 10, 14)

31

Thy bofome is indeared with all hearts,
Which I by lacking haue fuppofed dead,
And there raignes Loue and all Loues louing parts,
And all thofe friends which I thought buried.
How many a holy and obfequious teare
Hath deare religious loue ftolne from mine eye,
As intereft of the dead, which now appeare,
But things remou'd that hidden in there lie.
Thou art the graue where buried loue doth liue,
Hung with the tropheis of my louers gon,
Who all their parts of me to thee did giue,
That due of many, now is thine alone.
  Their images I lou'd, I view in thee,
  And thou (all they) haft all the all of me.

Thy bosom is endearèd with all hearts
Which I by lacking have supposèd dead,
And there reigns love and all love's loving parts,
And all those friends which I thought burièd.
How many a holy and obsequious tear
Hath dear religious love stol'n from mine eye,
As interest of the dead, which now appear
But things removed that hidden in thee lie.
Thou art the grave where buried love doth live,
Hung with the trophies of my lovers gone,
Who all their parts of me to thee did give;
That due of many now is thine alone.
  Their images I loved I view in thee,
  And thou (all they) hast all the all of me.

THE *precious friends hid in death's dateless night* of 30 are resurrected, so to speak, in this sonnet. The sonnet turns on the substitution of the resurrective claim *buried love doth live* (in the solemn vocative of line 9) for the expected phrase "love doth lie" (the word lie being already present in line 8, *which hidden in thee lie*). Line 9 hails the beloved:

Thou art the grave where buried love doth live.

The astonishing joy, as the probable *grave . . . buried love . . . lie* is replaced by *love doth live* [*love* + *lie* = *live*], lasts only briefly. Keats remembered *Thou art the grave where buried love doth live / Hung with the trophies of my lovers gone* as a piece of somber coloring:

His soul shall taste the sadness of her might,
And be among her cloudy trophies hung.
("Ode on Melancholy")

And in fact the somber quality of this sonnet never entirely vanishes: even in the couplet, the mournful phrase *Their images I loved* weighs down, in its elegiac gravity, the phrase *I view in thee*, its resurrective counterpart.

The reassembling of parts into wholes (bones into bodies) at the general resurrection is the conceit *(parts / all the all)* on which the poem is founded, as the resurrection of Christ is the doctrine on which, in Christian literature, resurrection in any other form is based. These two theological doctrines (of general and personal resurrection) are so weighty that it is only with difficulty that they can be coerced into the form of a love-compliment. Inside this complimentary sonnet lies a powerful metaphysical one (on the order, perhaps, of *Not mine own fears,* [107], or *Poor soul* [146]) trying to get out. Shakespeare's philosophical sonnets, one feels, came later in the sequence of composition than the complimentary ones. The visible wrestling of two genres here lends 31 an especial interest. It becomes as much a *Liebestod* as a love-poem.

This sonnet depends on a claim of double restitution. It is asserted that the present beloved contains all previous *lovers;* and that he also contains all the *parts* of the *speaker* ("love's loving *parts . . . parts* of *me*") previously vowed to former lovers. These restitutive assertions first occur in lines 1–4 and 7b–8.

The lines (5–7a) occurring between the two restitutions contain the small narrative of the grieving past, the interim of weeping before the advent of the present beloved. That time of loss, paid for with tears as *interest of the dead*, is *buried*, literally, in the middle of the poem; but it should be noticed that the elegiac tone of the whole sonnet stems from the presence of a burial in each of its three quatrains: Q_1—*dead, buried;* Q_2—*dead, things removed, lie;* Q_3—*grave, buried love, lovers gone.* The poem thus enacts its statement that the beloved (as figured in each of the three descriptive quatrains) is the *grave* of *buried love.*

The poem also enacts one of the forms of apparent "reciprocity" in which the *Sonnets* abound. There are two sets of directed-vector actions: the speaker views the hearts and images of former lovers in the beloved; dead lovers give their trophies of the speaker to the beloved. The couplet-summarizing of the actions, if it were to agree with the actions as hitherto described, "ought" to go as follows: [*I view their images in you; they give you me.*] But instead, a different form of reciprocity is put in the couplet:

> *I view* [in thee] their images;
> *Thou hast* all the all of me.

On the one hand, we find *I view*, and, on the other, *thou hast*, linked by the *and* of parallelism and inner symmetry. The true former parallelism—*I view* [hearts]; *they* [former lovers] *give* [parts]—has vanished in favor of an appearance of the speaker's desired reciprocity between himself and the beloved. *They* (former lovers) have been demoted to a passive position as viewed images, no longer as active *giv[ers].* Often, the sonnets propose by grammar the appearance of reciprocity, as in this couplet, without any real reciprocity being present. Here, the beloved gives nothing, but receives everything.

KEY WORD:	LOVE [-'S] [-RS] [-D]
DEFECTIVE KEY WORD:	ALL (missing in Q_2, which concerns absence and removal, rather than presence)
Couplet Tie:	*love* [-'*s*] [-*ers*] [-*d*] (3, 3, 6, 9, 10, 13) *all* (1, 3, 4, 11, 14, 14, 14)

32

IF thou ſuruiue my well contented daie,
When that churle death my bones with duſt ſhall couer
And ſhalt by fortune once more re-ſuruay:
Theſe poore rude lines of thy deceaſed Louer:
Compare them with the bett'ring of the time,
And though they be out-ſtript by euery pen,
Reſerue them for my loue, not for their rime,
Exceeded by the hight of happier men.
Oh then voutſafe me but this louing thought,
Had my friends Muſe growne with this growing age,
A dearer birth then this his loue had brought
To march in ranckes of better equipage:
But ſince he died and Poets better proue,
Theirs for their ſtile ile read, his for his loue.

If thou survive my well-contented day,
When that churl Death my bones with dust shall cover,
And shalt by fortune once more re-survey
These poor rude lines of thy deceasèd lover,
Compare them with the bett'ring of the time,
And though they be outstripped by every pen,
Reserve them for my love, not for their rhyme,
Exceeded by the height of happier men.
O then vouchsafe me but this loving thought:
"Had my friend's Muse grown with this growing age,
A dearer birth than this his love had brought
To march in ranks of better equipage:
But since he died and poets better prove,
Theirs for their style I'll read, his for his love."

THE speaker of 29 had fretted that he was *least contented* with what he most enjoyed; but having in his inventory of enjoyments arrived at his beloved (that which he super-superlatively most most enjoys), he was supremely contented, no longer in disgrace with Fortune. In 32, he can therefore speak of his "well-contented day" of death, regretting only that he may not, by that day, have perfected his verse, and that Fortune (chance), causing his beloved to reread his lines, may once again disgrace him.

This is the first sonnet to envisage the speaker's own death (elided in 17 in favor of his *papers yellowed with their age*). The invention of future events (whether of a putative child of the young man, or of *yellowed papers*, or of a future reading of *these lines*) is so frequent an event in the *Sonnets* as to rival the creation (as in 30) of a multilayered past. Shakespeare often enacts the future as having happened, rather than leaving it solely as a prediction or a wish, where it would remain an uncertainty. He does this here, as in 17, by putting words in future mouths. In 17, future readers of his lines said, *This poet lies.* Here in 32, the beloved says, reading the poet's lines after his death, "Had he lived, he would have done better than this; but although he died inferior to our present poets, I'll read their poems for their style, his for his love." Now this *loving thought* in the act of reading this very sonnet (wishing for "a dearer birth than *this* very poem") is exactly what the poet had earlier recommended in his hypothetical conjecture: "If thou shalt resurvey *these* lines, compare them with the bett'ring of the time, and though they be outstripped by every pen, reserve them for my love, not for their rhyme." The exact match created between events as foreseen by the poet (his death, the increasing poetic sophistication of the age and consequently of the beloved's taste) and the beloved's conjectured thought as he rereads the poet's verse makes intelligible Shakespeare's choice of a structure of superposition (in which lines 9–14 [beloved's thought] repeat lines 3–8 [speaker's wish]). A diagram shows the double-exposure parallel formulations of present wish and future "event":

Wish	*"Event" of speech-act*
If thou resurvey *these* lines	A dearer birth than *this*
of thy *deceasèd lover*	since he *died* . . . his *love*
the *bett'ring* of the *time*	poets *better* prove . . . this growing *age*
reserve them for *my love*	his for *his love*

The fact that Shakespeare closes his poem with the (fancied) quoted thought of the beloved means that we end in the future. There is no return to a closing statement by the poet in the present, e.g. (with my apologies): "If thou wilt read me thus, I'll not repine, / For all I think and all I write is thine." No: we end in the future; the poet is long dead, already dust, and his friend (we hear his internal voice) is speaking, saying in thought (ah, with what judgment and love combined!) *exactly* what the poet asked him to say, years before, when he wrote this sonnet. Such symmetry of wish and event is another token of the longed-for reciprocity that animates many of these "early" sonnets. Of course, since the future "event" is grammatically contained within the sentence of wish—*O then vouchsafe me but this loving thought: / "Had my friend's Muse . . . love."*—the superposition is actually that of fantasy on fantasy, but it simulates the superposition of later fulfillment on earlier prophecy, in the classic enacting power of the word. However, the baleful separation of *style (rhyme)* from content *(love)* in the modesty topos cannot be long sustained in any serious way by Shakespeare.

(There are minor gestures enacting the persistent comparative thrust of the sonnet: we see graphic and thematic comparative "increase" in the alliterative ***h**eight of **h**appi**er**; grown . . . growing; dear**er**; bett'ring, better, better;* and in the punning production of the written page in *equi**page**.*)

KEY WORD: LOVE [-R] [LOVING]

Couplet Tie: *love* [*-r*] [*-ing*] (4, 7, 9, 11, 14)
better [*bett'ring*] (5, 12, 13)
Death [*died*] (2, 13)

33

FVll many a glorious morning haue I ſeene,
Flatter the mountaine tops with ſoueraine eie,
Kiſſing with golden face the meddowes greene;
Guilding pale ſtreames with heauenly alcumy:
Anon permit the baſeſt cloudes to ride,
With ougly rack on his celeſtiall face,
And from the for-lorne world his viſage hide
Stealing vnſeene to weſt with this diſgrace:
Euen ſo my Sunne one early morne did ſhine,
With all triumphant ſplendor on my brow,
But out alack,he was but one houre mine,
The region cloude hath mask'd him from me now.
Yet him for this,my loue no whit diſdaineth,
Suns of the world may ſtaine,whẽ heauens ſun ſtainteh.

Full many a glorious morning have I seen
Flatter the mountain tops with sovereign eye,
Kissing with golden face the meadows green,
Gilding pale streams with heavenly alchemy;
Anon permit the basest clouds to ride
With ugly rack on his celestial face,
And from the fórlorn world his visage hide,
Stealing unseen to west with this disgrace:
Even so my sun one early morn did shine
With all triumphant splendour on my brow;
But out alack, he was but one hour mine,
The region cloud hath masked him from me now.
Yet him for this my love no whit disdaineth,
Suns of the world may stain, when heaven's sun staineth.

LIKE SONNET 32, this poem depends on a structure of superposition. This time, however, it is not a superposition of future event on present wish, as it was in 32. Here, a single marked preterite event *(my sun one early morn did shine . . . but . . . the region cloud hath masked him)* is superimposed on a frequent habitual happening *(Full many a glorious morning have I seen flatter . . . anon permit the basest clouds to ride. . . disgrace).*

Now, the "normal" lyric way of presenting such an analogy is to give the literal version ("He has forsaken me") followed by the metaphorical version that one conjures up to clarify the literal one ("as the sun forsakes the world"). There is even a "normal" way of reversing the "normal" presentation, one which "telegraphs" the arrival of the metaphorical by the simile-signal "just as": "Just as the sun sometimes forsakes the world, so he has forsaken me." However, by suppressing the analogical signal "just as," or "as," at the opening of the poem, Shakespeare lets us see the octave as a "pure" and literal landscape. Its figurative language *(glorious, flatter, sovereign, kissing, heavenly, alchemy, permit, basest, celestial face, visage, hide, stealing, disgrace)* thus remains putatively innocent, a form of poetic license in natural description.

With *Even so,* the poem formally becomes analogical and formally announces the coming superposition. The superposition, considering that it retells a bitter experience of human disappointment, is curiously bare, in three of its four lines, of ornament; most of its words are ethically neutral:

Even so my sun one early morn did shine
. . . on my brow;
But out alack, he was but one hour mine,
The region cloud hath masked him from me now.

The single moment of ornament in Q_3—*with all triumphant splendor*—enlarges, in a burst of glory, on the recent past; but the rest is colorlessly said. We notice that the blame is here placed solely on the cloud: *sun did shine : cloud hath masked him.* Of course, the effect of the superposition means that the initial octave "landscape" has taught us how to read the actual Q_3 "story," and that in the bare narrative of Q_3 we are meant to insert the vocabulary already made available in the octave:

> Even so my sun *(glorious, golden, sovereign)* one early morn did shine *(flattering, kissing, alchemizing)* with all-triumphant splendor on my *(pale)* brow; but out alack, he was but one hour mine, the *(basest)* region cloud *(permitted by him to ride with ugly rack on his celestial face)* hath masked him (hiding *his visage*) from *(forlorn)* me now (as he *steals in disgrace* away).

This accusatory version is a conflation of the superposed opening—an ethically "neutral" habitual landscape—and the professedly nonaccusatory event-narrative (which accuses only the cloud, not the sun).

It is of course always possible to draw a necessitarian parallel between a social phenomenon (a friend gone) and a natural phenomenon (the obscuring of sun by clouds). The event happens in nature; therefore, why not in social relations? It is to this deterministic position that the sonnet gradually retreats (or advances) in the couplet:

1. Totally anthropomorphized parallel (Q_1, Q_2);
2. Partially anthropomorphized parallel (Q_3);
3. Deanthropomorphized parallel (C).

The anthropomorphizing words (from *eye* and *face* to *kissing* and *basest*) of the octave are very visible; in Q_3 the sun/friend, though still literally spoken of as a sun, is called "*my* sun," and the obscuring cloud is given active power (not *he is masked by the cloud* but *the cloud hath masked him*). By the last line, however, we have abandoned both anthropomorphized landscape and human narrative for the realm of proverb (cf. what *the world well knows,* 129); and the choice of the verb *stain* (meaning *take a stain*) is, in this passive sense, ethically blameless: *Suns of the world may stain, when heaven's sun staineth.* Here, the parallel of social phenomenon to natural phenomenon appears in pure form, its purity evidenced by word-identity and positional analogy among the deanthropomorphized words, all putatively "neutral": *sun, world, stain; heaven, sun, staineth.* (There is no justification for invoking, as Kerrigan does, the meaning "diminish by its brightness all other light" for the word *stain.* "Be obscured" is the only meaning of *stain* that fits the octave's pictorial narrative and the sestet's moral application of that meaning as "basely obscured.")

This sonnet displays a progressive acceleration of its narrative from eight lines to four lines to one line, as the accompanying diagram makes clear. By the end we are down to half-line eclipses, whereas the first narrative of eclipse had taken eight lines, the second four. Love and its eclipse will soon, we feel (extrapolating from the hastened trajectory of the poem) accelerate from "one hour" to the wink of an eye.

Acceleration of the Narrative in Sonnet 33

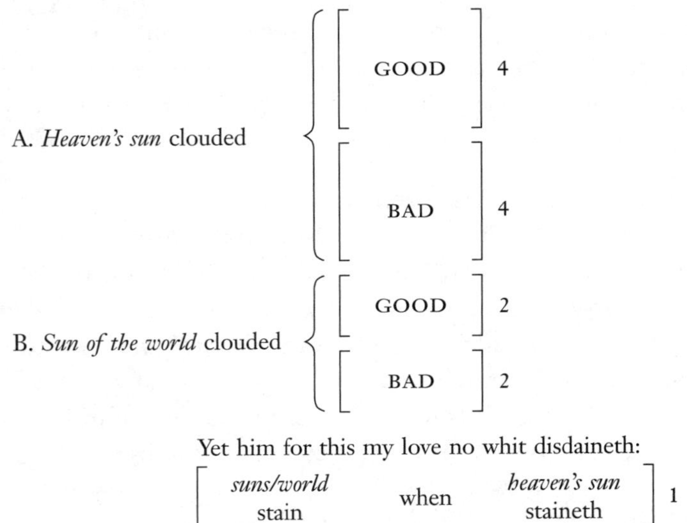

The chiastic structure of the whole poem (heaven's sun : sun of world :: sun of world : heaven's sun), with its great disproportion of attributed lines (8 : 4 :: ½ : ½) accounts for the unease we feel when given the neat "proverb" of line 14 as a theoretically satisfactory wrapping-up of the case presented. The explanatory insufficiency of pat analogy (as in the closing proverb) demonstrates the real rhetorical usefulness of the narrative of analogy as a form of implicit accusation. The archness of the proverb, and its removal from the world of feeling fully represented in the octave (and briefly in the splendor of Q_3) serves, in one possible reading, as an urbane self-removal from the anguish of the octave. In another, and more probable, reading, the proverb can be seen as a self-reproach: what all the world well knows should have been foreseen by the naively unwary lover of the recent past, who felt *all triumphant* once, and felt *forlorn* later. Is irony, lover of proverbs, a better state than hopeful attachment and anguished loss? The poem has the power to present irony as its last resort, without impugning the felt reality—still felt—of either glory or anger. Dramatically, this is the first sonnet to remark a true flaw in the friend. Even so, it is stated as a flaw by omission *(permit)* rather than a flaw by commission.

Couplet Tie: *heaven* [*-ly*] [*-'s*] (4, 14)
sun [*-s*] (9, 14, 14)
world (7, 14)

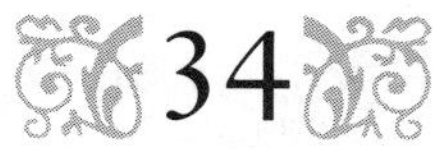

34

VV Hy didſt thou promiſe ſuch a beautious day,
And make me trauaile forth without my cloake,
To let bace cloudes ore-take me in my way,
Hiding thy brau'ry in their rotten ſmoke.
Tis not enough that through the cloude thou breake,
To dry the raine on my ſtorme-beaten face,
For no man well of ſuch a ſalue can ſpeake,
That heales the wound, and cures not the diſgrace:
Nor can thy ſhame giue phiſicke to my griefe,
Though thou repent , yet I haue ſtill the loſſe,
Th' offenders ſorrow lends but weake reliefe
To him that beares the ſtrong offenſes loſſe.
  Ah but thoſe teares are pearle which thy loue ſheeds,
  And they are ritch,and ranſome all ill deeds.

Why didst thou promise such a beauteous day,
And make me travel forth without my cloak,
To let base clouds o'ertake me in my way,
Hiding thy brav'ry in their rotten smoke?
'Tis not enough that through the cloud thou break,
To dry the rain on my storm-beaten face,
For no man well of such a salve can speak,
That heals the wound, and cures not the disgrace:
Nor can thy shame give physic to my grief;
Though thou repent, yet I have still the loss:
Th'offender's sorrow lends but weak relief
To him that bears the strong offence's cross.
  Ah, but those tears are pearl which thy love sheeds,
  And they are rich, and ransom all ill deeds.

FOR six lines sonnet 34 continues 33. The *basest clouds* of 33 reappear as *base clouds* causing a rainstorm through which the beloved, as sun, breaks; and the use of the metaphorical-as-literal which we remarked in 33 *(Even so my sun . . . did shine)* is replayed here in the second person *('Tis not enough that through the cloud thou break)*. However, after the sixth line, the meteorological metaphor disappears, and the metaphorical appeal undergoes startling changes, as follows:

A. Medicine *(salve, heals, wound, cures, physic);*
B. Pain, both social and emotional *(disgrace, shame, grief, loss, sorrow, relief, bear[ing] [a] cross);*
C. Religion *(repent, cross, ransom);*
D. Sin, meaning ethical offense *(offender, strong offence, ill deeds);*
E. Wealth *(pearl, rich, ransom);*
F. Love.

Though these categories roughly follow one another, each begins in a line where the former is still present, or recurs after another has begun, as the diagram of lines 7–14 shows. Roughly speaking, A (Medicine) precedes B, which precedes C, and so on; but during B's reign of pain (lines 8–9) there appears "belatedly" an element of A *(physic);* during C's religious reign one element of B *(loss)*, during D's sinful reign (lines 10–12) several elements of B (*sorrow*, *relief*, *bear[ing] [a] cross*, and *tears*) and one of C *(cross)*, and during F's reign of love (lines 13–14), elements of C *(ransom)*, D *(ill deeds)*, and E *(rich)*. Shakespeare's strategy here thus affords us a map of a mind resorting over time from one of its compartments to another in order to find adequate metaphorical expression for a shocking experience. The success of the sonnets in constructing a credible "self" lies as much in this portrait of a mind plunging among its categories to find resemblances as it does in the creation of multiple temporal phases (as in 30). The speaker constructs the relationship differently with each metaphor.

We have still to ask why it is these particular categories that appear, and why the remarkable breaks in metaphorical consistency occur, as well as the reason for the interconcatenation diagrammed here (in which Medicine and Emotional Pain have been dropped by the sestet, to be re-

Structure of Sonnet 34, Lines 7–14

Metaphor	Line							
	7	8	9	10	11	12	13	14
A. Medicine	salve	heals wound cures	physic					
B. Emotional pain		disgrace	grief	loss	relief	bears	tears	
C. Religion			shame	repent	sorrow	cross		ransom
D. Sin / Ethical offence					offender's	offences		ill deeds
E. Wealth							pearl	rich
F. Love							love	

placed by Religion, Sin, Wealth, and Love).* The repeated shocks of metaphorical change force us to invent a putative motive for each shift in the metaphorical register. I suggest that the shifts in the speaker's metaphors respond to the implied words and actions of the friend. I put these implied words and actions to the left in the following diagram, which reconstitutes (from the evidence of the sonnet alone) the temporal sequence of interchanges visible "beneath the surface" of the poem.

Intervention 1 by the friend, then, takes place between lines 4 and 5; intervention 2 between lines 8 and 9; intervention 3 between lines 12 and 13. These implied interventions thus motivate the striking changes of metaphor in Q_2, Q_3, and the couplet. By implying that things happen offstage between and within lines, Shakespeare drives the action of the poem invisibly forward. In drama, speeches change their color in response to the imagined or real interventions of another character in the play, and a speech thus becomes a *reply* rather than merely a soliloquy. Many of the sonnets, too, are replies, and declare their reply-nature unequivocally

*Kerrigan suggests that, since the Elizabethans thought the dust of ground pearl medicinal, *pearl* ought probably to be taken to mean "curative" as well as "precious." On the principle that whole pearls (*tears*) are not ground pearl, and that the only context Shakespeare offers is one of *rich ransom,* I would continue to argue that the later complex of Religion, Sin, Wealth and Love has replaced (not been added to) the complex of Medicine and Pain.

Temporal Sequence of Interchanges in Sonnet 34

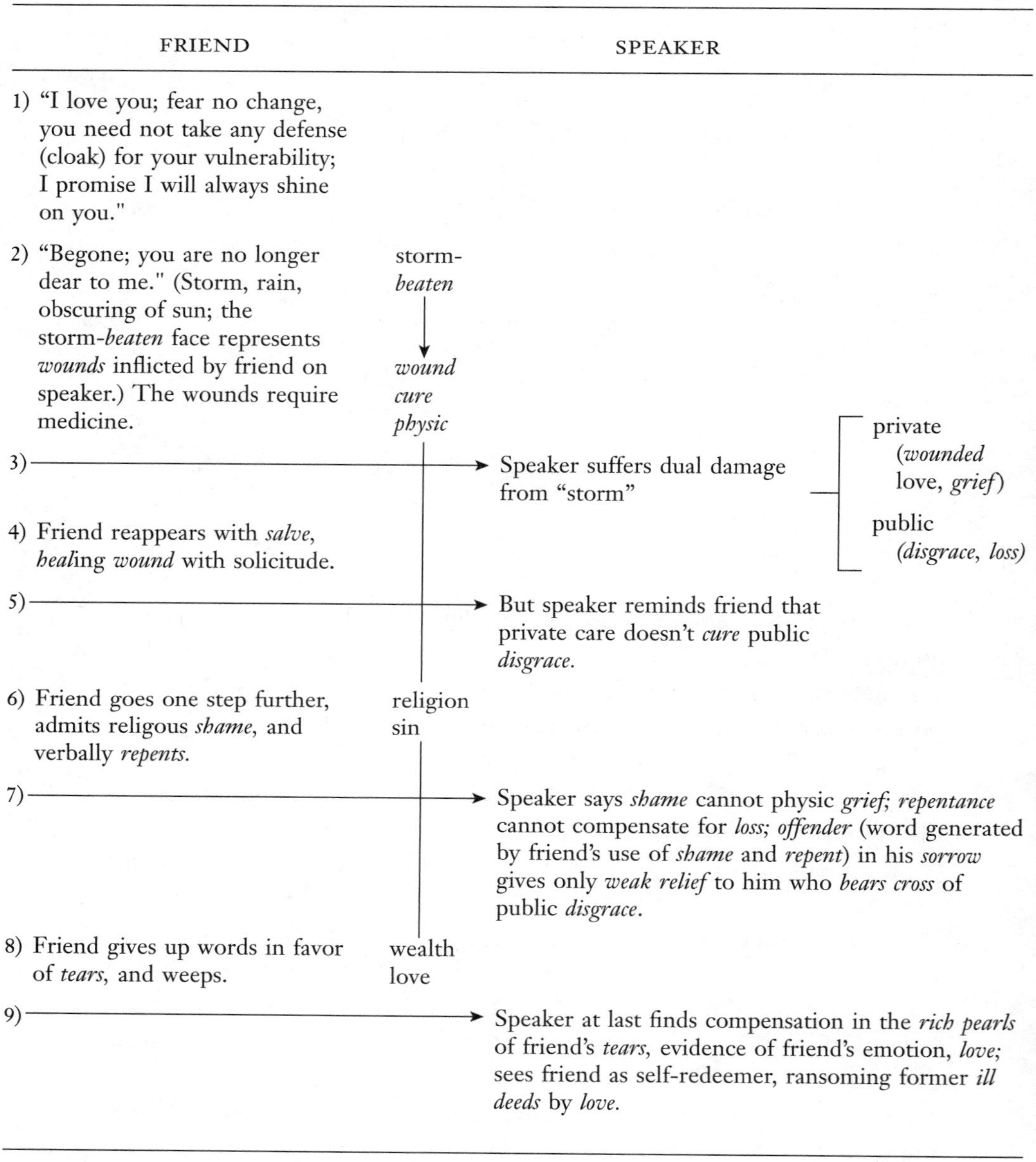

FRIEND		SPEAKER	
1) "I love you; fear no change, you need not take any defense (cloak) for your vulnerability; I promise I will always shine on you."			
2) "Begone; you are no longer dear to me." (Storm, rain, obscuring of sun; the storm-*beaten* face represents *wounds* inflicted by friend on speaker.) The wounds require medicine.	storm-*beaten* ↓ *wound* *cure* *physic*		
3) ——→		Speaker suffers dual damage from "storm"	private (*wounded* love, *grief*); public (*disgrace, loss*)
4) Friend reappears with *salve*, *heal*ing *wound* with solicitude.			
5) ——→		But speaker reminds friend that private care doesn't *cure* public *disgrace*.	
6) Friend goes one step further, admits religous *shame*, and verbally *repents*.	religion sin		
7) ——→		Speaker says *shame* cannot physic *grief; repentance* cannot compensate for *loss; offender* (word generated by friend's use of *shame* and *repent*) in his *sorrow* gives only *weak relief* to him who *bears cross* of public *disgrace*.	
8) Friend gives up words in favor of *tears*, and weeps.	wealth love		
9) ——→		Speaker at last finds compensation in the *rich pearls* of friend's *tears*, evidence of friend's emotion, *love;* sees friend as self-redeemer, ransoming former *ill deeds* by *love.*	

(see, e.g., 117, which begins by indirectly quoting the friend: *Accuse me thus* . . . etc.). Others, by various conspicuous strategies (such as the startling change of metaphors here) imply that the speaker is replying either to a changing exterior demeanor (as here, the friend's progress from wordless medical solicitude to verbal repentance to weeping), or to a previous utterance (as in 116, by the deployment of rhetorical devices intrinsic to rebuttal, e.g., "O no!").

Because the friend's interventions are themselves *replies* to what the speaker has just said, and the speaker's remarks are *replies* to the friend's interventions, we can see why the concatenation of categories is necessary. As the *salve* (Medicine) is offered, the speaker counters with his continuing *disgrace* (Pain); the word *disgrace* engenders in the friend *shame* and *repentance* (Religion), which themselves engender in the speaker *offence* (Ethics) and *cross* (Religion). Diction is borrowed freely, from one (implied) interlocutor to the other, so that it is evident that a colloquy is going on, back and forth.

Logically speaking, the rain has come from the clouds, but pictorially a *rain-beaten face* is one covered with tears; and the eventual tears of the young man are felt, pictorially, to be a just amends because they make *his* suffering visually parallel to that undergone by the speaker—tears for tears, another example of the reciprocity desired by the early sonnets.

Although the originating metaphor of the sun (borrowed from 33) still exempts the friend from direct blame (he "let" the clouds appear to do *their* evil work), the friend's guilty *shame* and *repentance* in lines 9ff. warrant the speaker's subsequent assignment of direct ethical blame in lines 11–14, with a vocabulary of *offence* and *ill deeds*. The final line, with its introduction of *deeds*, begins the sequence's condemnation of the friend's sins of commission, opposed memorably in 94 to nonaction:

> For sweetest things turn sourest by their *deeds;*
> Lilies that fester smell far worse than weeds.

The turn in the *Sonnets* from sins of omission to sins of commission happens visibly here, in 34, and is continued in 35.

Couplet Tie: none (though *ill* [14] echoes *still* [10])

Logically, it is proper that there should be no Couplet Tie, since the narrative of the sonnet divides the couplet powerfully from the accusatory body of the poem:

1–4: Offense described
5–8: Medicine is not enough *(salve)*
9–12: Remorse is not enough *(shame, repentance)*
13–14: Ah, but this amends *(tears) is* enough.

35

NO more bee greeu'd at that which thou haſt done,
Roſes haue thornes,and ſiluer fountaines mud,
Cloudes and eclipſes ſtaine both Moone and Sunne,
And loathſome canker liues in ſweeteſt bud.
All men make faults,and euen I in this,
Authorizing thy treſpas with compare,
My ſelfe corrupting ſaluing thy amiſſe,
Excuſing their ſins more then their ſins are:
For to thy ſenſuall fault I bring in ſence,
Thy aduerſe party is thy Aduocate,
And gainſt my ſelfe a lawfull plea commence,
Such ciuill war is in my loue and hate,
  That I an acceſſary needs muſt be,
  To that ſweet theefe which ſourely robs from me,

No more be grieved at that which thou hast done:
Roses have thorns, and silver fountains mud,
Clouds and eclipses stain both moon and sun,
And loathsome canker lives in sweetest bud.
All men make faults, and even I in this,
Authórising thy trespass with compare,
My self corrupting salving thy amiss,
Excusing thy sins more than their sins are;
For to thy sensual fault I bring in sense—
Thy adverse party is thy advocate—
And 'gainst myself a lawful plea commence:
Such civil war is in my love and hate
  That I an áccessary needs must be
  To that sweet thief which sourly robs from me.

IN THE drama of the sequence, the speaker now recognizes his own corruption. By his sophistry of excuse exerted on behalf of the young man, he becomes an accomplice (his word is *áccessary*) in the friend's sin. *Myself corrupting salving thy amiss* is the line of the poem that reaches deepest, poetically as well as morally, and we must ask why.

This sonnet wonderfully employs self-quotation. The first four lines are an antechamber containing past remarks by the self, quoted by the present self who speaks from line 5 onward in mordant self-analysis. "I have excused your sensual fault to yourself and to myself in various ingenious metaphorical ways, and I remember all of them, from the most trusting to the most sophisticated":

1. *Roses have thorns* (even the most beautiful things in nature have intrinsic defects, inseparable from their being);
2. *Silver fountains [have] mud* (every beautiful earthly thing has a gross base from which it springs);
3. *Clouds and eclipses stain both moon and sun* (even superlunary heavenly bodies are not exempt from momentary stains of necessary physical motions);
4. *And loathsome canker lives in sweetest bud* (the powers of ill have—as even the common wisdom tells us in proverbs of this sort—a particular wish to corrupt the beautiful and good. *Sweet* = good or virtuous, as 54 makes evident).

Thus—*authórising . . . trespass with compare* (to solace the friend's apparent grief at what he has done)—has the speaker reasoned in the past, when confronted with the friend's *sensual fault.* The bitter disjunction between present speech and past speech means that we should mentally put in quotation marks the first four patently unconvincing arguments (they are unconvincing now, to the speaker's self-lacerating eye of *hate,* but they were convincing in the past, to the eye of *love*):

> "No more be grieved at that which thou hast done:
> Roses have thorns, and silver fountains mud,
> Clouds and eclipses stain both moon and sun,
> And loathsome canker lives in sweetest bud."

> All men make faults, and even I in this,
> Authórising thy trespass with compare,
> *My self* corrupting salving thy amiss,
> Excusing thy sins more than their sins are.

(I accept the emendation of the first *their* to *thy* in line 8, considering *their* to have as antecedent *all men.*)

The *dédoublement* by which the speaker now bitterly scrutinizes his past exculpatory commonplaces (roses with thorns, fountains with mud, suns with eclipses, cankers in buds) is visible chiefly in the violent departure from those Q_1 commonplaces in the knotted language of Q_2. The "same person" cannot speak both the first quatrain and the second: the speaker of the first was misguided, and even corrupt, according to the speaker of the second. Therefore, the speaker resorts to the subsequent analytic metaphor of civil war: the first quatrain was spoken (according to subsequent analysis) by *love* (not besottedness or moral fatuity) and the second by *hate* (a far cry from clear moral logic). But although the closing judgment will name Q_1 *love* and Q_2 *hate*, as we actually encounter the poem we hear the sentences of Q_1 *as quoted* by the present speaker of Q_2; the sentences are therefore given in a foolish, flat, and debased form, which would not convince a flea, and which in fact amount (so cunningly is *hate* arranging them) to a progressive indictment of the friend ("You are a rose with thorns, you are a fountain with mud, you are a stained sun, you have a loathsome worm living in you"). One imagines that when these excuses were made in the true voice of love (rather than the voice of love summarized by hate), they sounded passionate and convinced.

The octave, then, belongs to *hate*, who scornfully summarizes his own former excusings of the friend, and savagely exposes his own fault in so doing. *Hate* goes in two directions—toward the friend and his loathsome canker and toward the self and its self-corruption—but the latter is the stronger.

The rhetoric of self-hate anticipates that of 129 *(Th'expense of spirit)* in affecting an apparently sober response:

> *All men make faults, and even I in this,*
> *Authórising thy trespass with compare.*

This sobriety may be compared to the formal equilibrium at the opening of 129:

> *Th'expense of spirit in a waste of shame*
> *Is lust in action, and till action, lust . . .*

In both cases, the next lines exhibit *débordement*, as the words run off on a headlong emotional course represented by a repeated grammatical form (here in 35, present participles; in 129, adjectives) from which the poem cannot detach itself for some time. In 129, we see the overmastering emotion in adjectival fixation on the social trespasses of lust, as it

Is perjured, murd'rous, bloody, full of blame,
Savage, extreme, rude, cruel, not to trust.

In 35, we see the overmastering emotion in the participial fixation on personal fault:

authórising	*thy trespass* with compare
corrupting	*my self*
salving	*thy amiss*
excusing	*thy sins*

The odd man out among the speaker's participial phrases is of course *my self corrupting*, in which the direct object is the reflexive *my self*, whereas in the other phrases the direct object is *thy* (offense), in which the offense remains unspecified, described only in general terms as a *trespass*, an *amiss*, and some *sins*. Because of the asymmetry of *my self corrupting* in the series, and because of the absence of a comma following *corrupting*, the series may more logically be seen:

	authórising / thy trespass
my self corrupting {	*salving / thy amiss*
	excusing / thy sins

In this case, *my self corrupting* serves as a sort of "floating modifier," logically modifying all three actions—*authórising*, *salving*, and *excusing*.

I believe that the correct reading of line 8 is *Excusing thy sins more than their sins are*, in which *their sins* refers to the *faults* of *all men*, which were used to introduce this quatrain. The speaker's reasoning would then run: "All men make faults, and I [sin] in this, corrupting my self by salving thy amiss, excusing thy sins more than their sins are [by me excused]." This is no more tortured than other readings of the emended line.

The powerful aesthetic effect of line 7—*My self corrupting salving thy amiss*—can thus be seen to originate in part from the slight shock of the nonsymmetry of *my self corrupting* with the other participial phrases as well as the notice of intensity it conveys by continuing, as if by emotional fixation, the participial lead of *authórising*. Line 7 also doubles the pace of sin (with two participles per line—*corrupting*, *salving*—instead of one, as in the lines preceding and following). The iron grasp of line 7's chiasmus *(my : -ing :: -ing : thy)* shows us a character trapped by relationship into a doubly sinful action.

It is impossible not to see that by the couplet the speaker has achieved a *love-hate* voice in speaking of the *sweet thief that sourly robs* (the metaphor recurs in sonnet 40). Sober fact, we might say, lies in the grammatical kernel: *thief robs*. Feeling lies in the adjective and adverb: *sweet/sourly*.

As usual in the sonnets, the tertium quid of the couplet becomes possible as a result of an analytic process applied to the experiential narrative, and the usual place for the analytic process is in Q_3 (see, e.g., the analytic Q_3 of 73, *That time of year*). The signs of analytic expression are, in 35 as often elsewhere, analytic metaphors summing up the situation (here, a *law*suit and *civil war*) and epigrammatic, often punning, verbal summary (here, *sensual* and *sense*).* When Shakespeare uses two successive metaphors, he usually adds the second because the first omits some aspect which demands recognition (see, again, 73 for its successive tries at an encompassing true metaphor, finding a truth in the metaphysical self-consuming fire that it was not able to find in the visual figure of autumn and the emblematic figure of twilight).

Here, immediately after the opposition of the greater sin of reason *(sense)* to the lesser sin of the flesh *(sensual fault)*, with the usual theological implication of the greater seriousness of the sins of the mind, Shakespeare introduces the metaphor of the lawsuit. In the first instance, this would seem to be a suit in which the friend is the defendant (charged with erotic thievery) and the speaker is the plaintiff, who has been robbed. The judge is presumably God, judging the *sensual fault*. But the plaintiff, *thy adverse party*, suddenly turns *advocate* for the friend.

Then a second lawsuit supervenes on the first. In the second, the speaker is both defendant (guilty of self-corruption) and plaintiff: *[I] 'gainst myself a lawful plea commence*. This is *a lawful plea* because the speaker is in fact guilty of this sin (as he has admitted); and after all, is not this self-prosecution for a spiritual sin more to the point (the beam in his own eye) than the prosecution of the thief for a sensual fault (the mote in another's eye)?

The speaker wishes to make, then, three pleas:

a. the prosecution argument made by *hate* as *adverse party* against the young man;

**Incense*—a pun suggested by some readers—is a substance not found in law courts.

b. the defense argument made by *love* as *advocate* for the young man;
c. the self-prosecution argument against the defending self, in *self-hate*.

These conflicting pleas cause the metaphor of *civil war* to be invoked. All *pleas* then disappear, and the speaker returns to complicity in *fault*, acquiescence in the status quo, self-definition as *áccessary* with open eyes. Anger (which has been implied by all the metaphors of lawsuits of one sort or another) has subsided through analysis to a recognition of a bittersweet (here, *sweet-sour*) relation with a beloved deceiver. *Needs must* is the language of involuntary necessity, not of *fault*, whether of sense or sensuality. The *facts* of thievery and robbery are inarguable, as is the *fact* of accessory status; but the relation between them is no longer *theologically* governed. Rather, it is governed by the image of civil strife, the division of selfhood in two, *love* and *hate*, each with a valid voice.

"I have corrupted myself" is a statement that presupposes a *true* "higher" self which has, by a "lower" self, been corrupted, and which should once again take control. Even the metaphor of lawsuits implies that one side, in each suit, is "lawful" and should win. In the close, *love* and *hate* have equal civil voices, and the robbed plaintiff (feeling *hate*) is at the same time the willing criminal accessory (feeling *love*). Though this expressed dualism cannot be called self-integration, it is an epistemological advance over the attempt by the voice of *hate* to suppress, in lines 1–8, the voice of *love* (which, so long as it speaks from a feeling that still exists, cannot in poetry be suppressed without formal crime).

The difficulty of maintaining love for an unpredictably unfaithful beloved will henceforth preoccupy the sonnets to the friend. The speaker's final solution will be, in 124, to separate completely the act of love from its object, and to make it absolute in its own grandeur, without respect to the worth of the beloved. It is a drastic but sublime (and also tragic) solution.

Couplet Tie: *sweet* [*-est*] (4, 14)

36

LEt me confeſſe that we two muſt be twaine,
Although our vndeuided loues are one:
So ſhall thoſe blots that do with me remaine,
Without thy helpe, by me be borne alone.
In our two loues there is but one reſpect,
Though in our liues a ſeperable ſpight,
Which though it alter not loues ſole effect,
Yet doth it ſteale ſweet houres from loues delight,
I may not euer-more acknowledge thee,
Leaſt my bewailed guilt ſhould do thee ſhame,
Nor thou with publike kindneſſe honour me,
Vnleſſe thou take that honour from thy name:
  But doe not ſo, I loue thee in ſuch ſort,
  As thou being mine, mine is thy good report.

Let me confess that we two must be twain,
Although our undivided loves are one:
So shall those blots that do with me remain,
Without thy help, by me be borne alone.
In our two loves there is but one respect,
Though in our lives a separable spite,
Which though it alter not love's sole effect,
Yet doth it steal sweet hours from love's delight.
I may not evermore acknowledge thee,
Lest my bewailèd guilt should do thee shame,
Nor thou with public kindness honour me,
Unless thou take that honour from thy name:
  But do not so; I love thee in such sort,
  As thou being mine, mine is thy good report.

THIS sonnet is painfully linked to 39, with which it shares three sets of rhyme-words: *me/thee*, *one/alone*, and *twain/remain;* both also use the word *[un]divided.* (The intervening 37 and 38, with their mutual use of *ten times*, represent material much more closely linked to sonnet 6, with its triple use of *ten times*, than to their neighbors 36 and 39.) Though some sonnets which seem to create "breaks" in the sequence do prove, on inspection, to have real verbal or thematic links with their neighbors, such is not the case with 37; and 38, though it is has some matter (and the words *worth* and *praise*) in common with 39, bears no thematic trace of the separation of lovers which is the common content of 36 and 39. It seems to me that a "break" such as this one lends credence to the argument (a sensible one in any case) that in arranging his sequence Shakespeare (or another editor) made room for some earlier and less practiced sonnets among the ones more clearly written in close temporal sequence. The relation of father to son, taken on by the poet with respect to the young man in 37 *(As a decrepit father)*, may have been more natural in one of the earlier advice-giving moments than in later poems; see my discussion of 37. The tetrameter sonnet 145, *Those lips*, is the always-cited instance of an "interpolated" sonnet.

Sonnet 36 offers a difficulty, since it closes with the couplet used also to close 96 *(Some say thy fault is youth)*. The couplet "fits" here both logically and syntactically ("You cannot honor me except by depriving yourself of honor; but do not so," etc.), and is acceptable in all respects as the end of the poem. For its more problematic location in 96, see my commentary on that poem.

Sonnet 36 represents, in the ongoing drama of the sequence, the first acceptance by the speaker of permanent division from the beloved. The division is enacted by the way in which the first-person plural which dominates in the octave *(we, our)* is replaced by the first- and second-person singular *(I, thou)* which dominate in the sestet; this contrast sets up an Italianate two-part form. In the diagram, I chart the couple's unity (past and present) against their divided future, calling attention to the climactic pun, *hours* ("ours"), in line 8. The "we" of the past *hours* ("ours") turns before our very eyes into the *I* and *thou* of the cruel future.

Unity of the Couple in Sonnet 36

(Together) *Past and Present*	(Divided) *Future and Evermore*
we two	must be *twain*
our undivided loves are *one*	so blots [remaining] with *me* shall be borne by *me alone* without *thy* help
our two loves . . . but *one* respect *our* lives	a separable spite
love's *sole effect* sweet *hours* ["*ours*"] love's delight	steal from
	I . . . thee; my guilt do *thee* shame, nor *thou . . . me* unless *thou* take from *thy* name. Do not [*thou*] so; *I* love *thee . . . thou* being *mine*, *mine thy* report.

Though such is the apparent poem—with its apparent speech-acts of acceptance *(Let me confess)* and self-blame *(my bewailèd guilt)*—one deduces that its putative moment—the last moment in which one can possibly say the blessèd word *ours*—has already passed. A more accurate rendition of the speaker's plight would be one that said, [*We are now twain, and I am bearing alone, without thy help, the blots that do with me remain*]. The terrible division has already happened (occasioning the poem), but love's nostalgia prolongs the mutual past into the separating spite of the present, and projects the actual hideous present into a threatened envisaged future. The poem proceeds by an almost invisible alteration of tenses and moods—from the modal necessitarian future *must be* to the indicative future *shall be* to the indicative present *doth it steal* to the modal present *I may not acknowledge thee . . . nor [mayst] thou honour me*. Thus the present "real" separation which the speaker suffers and the reader intuits is viewed in a continuum with a rhetorically envisaged future separation, causing the poem's intrinsic pathos. The casuistry of expression—between unified *two*ness and divided *twain*ness, between an inseparable *one respect* and a *separable spite*, between an inalterable *effect of love* and stealable *[h]ours* of love—reinforces the pathos by which one's already having been repudiated is wishfully described as present unity.

The asymmetry by which *I love thee* appears unaccompanied by anything resembling "thou lovest me" is reinforced by the phrase *thou being mine* appearing unmatched by anything from the beloved resembling "I being thine." *I love thee; thou [art] mine; thy good report is mine* are all one-sided declarations, exhibiting no real confidence that the corresponding declarations from the beloved will be forthcoming. Thus, the discourses of reciprocity (the first-person plural *we*, followed by the symmetry of *I may not / nor [mayst] thou*) collapse into the isolation of the repudiated lover. The beloved's act of repudiation is motivated, according to the speaker, solely by what used to be called "respect of others" and what we would now call concern for one's reputation. The beloved might draw *shame* on himself and *take honour* from his own *name*, might damage his *good report*, in associating with the speaker. It should be noticed that the *blots* may well be mutual ones, but that in dissociating himself from the speaker's company, the young man lets the blots *remain* with the speaker alone, who must bear them with no *help.* If speaker and beloved were to remain a couple, the *guilt* ascribed to himself by the speaker might well become the *shame* projected by others on the beloved—a slippage suggesting mutual anterior complicity in the *blots.* The suggestion of injustice in *without thy help . . . borne alone* is hard to ignore.

DEFECTIVE KEY WORD: LOVE [-S] (missing in Q_3)

Couplet Tie: *love* [*-s*] (2, 5, 7, 8, 13). It is not accidental that the word love is "suppressed" from Q_3, in which the absence of love *(I may not acknowledge thee, nor thou honour me)* is demonstrated. Mutual *loves* are present in Q_1 and Q_2, one-sided *love (I love thee)* in C; in between, there is lovelessness.

37

AS a decrepit father takes delight,
To ſee his actiue childe do deeds of youth,
So I, made lame by Fortunes deareſt ſpight
Take all my comfort of thy worth and truth.
For whether beauty, birth, or wealth, or wit,
Or any of theſe all, or all, or more
Intitled in their parts, do crowned ſit,
I make my loue ingrafted to this ſtore:
So then I am not lame, poore, nor diſpiſ'd,
Whilſt that this ſhadow doth ſuch ſubſtance giue,
That I in thy abundance am ſuffic'd,
And by a part of all thy glory liue:
Looke what is beſt, that beſt I wiſh in thee,
This wiſh I haue, then ten times happy me.

As a decrepit father takes delight
To see his active child do deeds of youth,
So I, made lame by Fortune's dearest spite,
Take all my comfort of thy worth and truth;
For whether beauty, birth, or wealth, or wit,
Or any of these all, or all, or more,
Intitled in thy parts, do crownèd sit,
I make my love ingrafted to this store:
So then I am not lame, poor, nor despised,
Whilst that this shadow doth such substance give
That I in thy abundance am sufficed,
And by a part of all thy glory live:
Look what is best, that best I wish in thee;
This wish I have, then ten times happy me.

WE FIND in sonnet 37 more *th*'s than chance would usually allow. You*th*, wor*th*, tru*th*, bir*th*, and weal*th* introduce the poem, as though the talismanic *thy* (*thy* worth, *thy* parts, *thy* abundance, *thy* glory) began to reproduce itself—and not only in the nouns ending in *th* but also in many other words: fa*th*er, whe*th*er, *th*ese, *th*is, *th*en, *th*at, *th*is, do*th*, *th*at, *th*at, *th*ee, *th*is, *th*en. It is hard to know just what Shakespeare's principle of composition is; here as in 77 *(Thy glass will show thee)*, he appears compelled to exhibit at least one *th* per line. Every line in 37 except the third displays at least one *th*, and several display more than one; this happens so flagrantly that one cannot miss the graphic repetition. Line 3, the exception, takes on in the Quarto the form of a joke: it possesses a *th*, indeed, but reversed to *ht* in spig*ht*. The opening quatrain, in the Quarto spelling, rhymes *ht*, *th*, *ht*, and *th*, rendering any reader more conscious of the odd prevalence of these letters.

I think anagrammatic and graphic games of this sort (remarked already in sonnets 7 and 9 and appearing elsewhere, as in 77) were attractive to Shakespeare as hurdles to jump and tests to set himself; they are far more common in the earlier sonnets to the young man than in the later ones (which deal more in puns and conceits than in letter games). The fancifulness of 37, with its "naive" boast, *So then I am not lame* etc., and its even more "naive" conclusion, *then ten times happy me*, demonstrates desperate argument in the service of sophistry. The vacuity of some lines *(Or any of these all, or all, or more; Look what is best, that best I wish in thee; / This wish I have)*, together with the repetitiveness of argument, makes this a sonnet hard to explain except as an early, unengaged effort or one constructed on the basis of a game I have not succeeded in finding.

It introduces, nonetheless, the ultimately fascinating play, for Shakespeare, of *shadow* against *substance*, in which instead of *substance* casting a *shadow*, a *shadow* casts *substance*. (See 53, *What is your substance*, for the development of this conceit.) The plays by which *thy parts* (I accept the emendation from *their* to *thy* in line 7) confer *a part of all thy glory*, and by which *abund-ance* confers a *subst-ance*, are typical examples of Shakespeare's early wordplay. The first is semantic *(parts/part)*, the second etymological (since the *-ance* in *abund-ance* and the one in *subst-ance* are not etymologically parallel). The play on tenfoldness, originating in sonnet 6 *(Then let not winter's)* and present in 38 as well as 37, seems a cliché of hyperbole, while the argument—that the decrepit, fortune-lamed speaker is *not lame, poor, nor despised*—is hardly credible, and stems only from desire: *that best I wish . . . / This wish I have, then ten times happy me.* The promptness with which Shakespeare drops the initiating metaphor of father and child may be contrasted to the fullness of comic development of the analogous metaphor (with roles reversed, the speaker being the child) in 143 *(Lo, as a careful huswife).*

Couplet Tie: None. Such is the force of the graphic liaisons in *th* that no verbal liaison is needed.

38

HOw can my Muſe want ſubiect to inuent
While thou doſt breath that poor'ſt into my verſe,
Thine owne ſweet argument,to excellent,
For euery vulgar paper to rehearſe:
Oh giue thy ſelfe the thankes if ought in me,
Worthy peruſal ſtand againſt thy ſight,
For who's ſo dumbe that cannot write to thee,
When thou thy ſelfe doſt giue inuention light?
Be thou the tenth Muſe,ten times more in worth
Then thoſe old nine which rimers inuocate,
And he that calls on thee,let him bring forth
Eternal numbers to out-liue long date.
  If my ſlight Muſe doe pleaſe theſe curious daies,
  The paine be mine,but thine ſhal be the praiſe.

How can my Muse want subject to invent
While thou dost breathe, that pour'st into my verse
Thine own sweet argument, too excellent
For every vulgar paper to rehearse?
O give thyself the thanks if aught in me
Worthy perusal stand against thy sight,
For who's so dumb that cannot write to thee,
When thou thyself dost give invention light?
Be thou the tenth Muse, ten times more in worth
Than those old nine which rhymers invocate,
And he that calls on thee, let him bring forth
Eternal numbers to outlive long date.
  If my slight Muse do please these curious days,
  The pain be mine, but thine shall be the praise.

THE mythological Muse appears *in propria persona* for the first time (sonnet 21 had called another poet a Muse). The concept is immediately made problematic by being doubled: "*my* Muse," "be *thou* the Muse." The classicizing figure of the Muse will vanish eventually from the sequence after appearing in some sonnets of the "rival poet" group—78, 79, 82, and 85. The fact that the Muse appears chiefly in the context of poetic rivalry suggests that it is the use of this figure by other poets which occasions its appearance in Shakespeare. On his own, Shakespeare is in the *Sonnets* an astonishingly nonclassical poet. The gods and goddesses who populated many continental sonnets play almost no part in his sequence (though he briefly mentions Adonis, Saturn, and Mars, and uses a myth of Cupid at the Anacreontic close). The impression of naked and immediate speech conveyed by Shakespeare's sequence is due in great part to the absence of the stately and playful distance conferred by classical reference. Shakespeare's declassicizing of lyric seemed to Keats to make poetry "northern" rather than "southern" (Mediterranean, Latin, classical); and in refusing classical reference—to Apollo, Demeter, Pluto, and Proserpine—in his ode "To Autumn," Keats hoped to attain a "northern" quality of the sort he had found in these sonnets. *The teeming autumn big with rich increase* (97) is Demeter made "northern." The Greek Muses—*those old nine which rhymers invocate*—are dismissed here as conventional and no more.

As Booth has pointed out, one of the fanciful principles of invention here is the little test "Let us have the sound ***to*** in every line in the first quatrain": ***to*** *invent*, ***into*** *my verse*, ***too*** *excellent*, ***to*** *rehearse*. (The pattern continues in ***to*** *thee* and ***to*** *outlive* in lines 7 and 12.) There is a similar pattern in ***in****:* ***in****vent*, ***in****to*, ***in*** *me*, ***in****vention*, ***in*** *worth*, ***in****vocate; invent/invention* brackets the octave.

These fundamentally uninteresting aural doodles, together with the *ten times* repeated from sonnets 6 and 37, betray a fanciful rather than an imaginative state in writing, reflected, e.g. in the way a *slight* Muse (line 13) contains the *light* (line 8) given by invention; in the way that *invocate* (line 10) is "Englished" by *call on* (line 11); and in the way that better *numbers* can be brought forth by a higher-numbered Muse (the *tenth*) than by the *old nine*. The structure of the first thirteen lines of the poem is ostentatiously chiastic: *My Muse : Give thyself :: Be thou : My Muse*. And this chiastic structure is mimicked in the fourteenth line: *pain : mine :: thine: praise*.

It seems to me that Shakespeare uses a fanciful poem like this not for a "serious" purpose but in order to play with complicated syntax, especially in the opening quatrain, which in lines 2–4 "decorates" the elements of its opening line in a series of Chinese boxes: "How can (while thou [that pour'st thy argument {too excellent}] dost breathe) my Muse want subject to invent?" This is of course only the syntactic skeleton; *argument* is further modified by *sweet*, and *excellent* by the *rehearsal* of the *vulgar*.

Shakespeare's powerful invention of subordinate phrases and clauses, as in this first sentence of 38, suggests a mind which has already seen clearly the mutual hierarchical relations of its concerns:

1. Thyself breathing and thy sweet argument [are from on high] poured into ↓
2. my Muse and my verse and its invented subject [yourself, who are] too excellent for ↓
3. the vulgar papers and their rehearsals.

The sonnet here suggests, perhaps, a too-facile separation of writing and its content—between the poet's *argument* and its *thou*, between the poet's *Muse* and its *subject*, between another's *paper* and what it *rehearses*. (Even here, the slipperiness of the distinctions predicts future reflection in the area of form and matter, culminating in 86, *Was it the proud full sail*).

This sonnet is conscious of the relation between *rehearsal* (by the poet) and *perusal* (by others). It emphasizes the process from *invention* to *rehearsal* (with only a casual mention of *perusal* in line 6) until it reaches its moment of closure in the couplet, which glances at the public turning of invention and rehearsal to *please these curious days* and by those *pains* to garner *praise*. The imagining of someone (the beloved as future reader) surveying the *Sonnets* is never far from Shakespeare's mind, and is one of the means by which a turn from the expressive-mimetic mode to the analytic mode can be produced.

"My Muse" is a phrase normally taken to mean "the spirit of inspiration within me," personified, depending on the genre produced, as Clio, Calliope, Erato, etc., *those old nine*. But when the Muse is externalized and named as the friend, an unnerving literalizing of allegory has been permitted, and the descriptive *object* of the poem—the friend—alienates the faculty of inspiration from the poet to itself. Is poetry inspired by the swelling heart of the poet or by the excellent object to which the poet responds? In this early confrontation between aesthetic response and aesthetic object, Shakespeare's vote, via his speaker, goes toward locating aesthetic worth, *and* poetic essence, in the object itself rather than in the poet's inner "inspiration." The final mention of the poet's Muse treats it dismissively—"my *slight* Muse."

Couplet Tie: *Muse* (1, 9, 13)

39

OH how thy worth with manners may I ſinge,
When thou art all the better part of me?
What can mine owne praiſe to mine owne ſelfe bring;
And what is't but mine owne when I praiſe thee,
Euen for this,let vs deuided liue,
And our deare loue looſe name of ſingle one,
That by this ſeperation I may giue:
That due to thee which thou deſeru'ſt alone:
Oh abſence what a torment wouldſt thou proue,
Were it not thy ſoure leiſure gaue ſweet leaue,
To entertaine the time with thoughts of loue,
VVhich time and thoughts ſo ſweetly doſt deceiue.
  And that thou teacheſt how to make one twaine,
  By praiſing him here who doth hence remaine.

O how thy worth with manners may I sing,
When thou art all the better part of me?
What can mine own praise to mine own self bring,
And what is't but mine own when I praise thee?
Even for this, let us divided live,
And our dear love lose name of single one,
That by this separation I may give
That due to thee which thou deserv'st alone.
O absence, what a torment wouldst thou prove,
Were it not thy sour leisure gave sweet leave
To entertain the time with thoughts of love,
Which time and thoughts so sweetly doth deceive;
  And that thou teachest how to make one twain,
  By praising him here who doth hence remain.

IN SONNET 9, there was a grammatical change of person, from second-person address to the friend in the octave *(Is it for fear to wet a widow's eye / That thou consum'st thyself in single life?)* to third-person description of the friend in the sestet *(No love toward others in that bosom sits / That on himself such murd'rous shame commits).* Sonnet 39 changes in a comparable way from octave to sestet, while retaining throughout second-person address. It turns in line 9 from addressing the beloved *(O how thy worth with manners may I sing)* to addressing Absence itself: *O absence, what a torment wouldst thou prove,* etc. Since any abstraction, once addressed in the second person, is thereby made into a personage (and usually a governing personage), Absence becomes the tutelary deity of the sestet, instructing the dutiful poet in a better way of writing, thus fulfilling the poet's original wish: to sing with manners the beloved's worth without any of the praise accruing to himself. The elevation ("O altitudo") accompanying the "O Absentia!" and the paradox of fortunate absence are marked by a madrigalesque "turn" in the prosody of the sonnet, in which two metrically irregular lines (9–10) yield to a lulling regular music in 11–12.

9. *O absence // what a / torment / wouldst thou / prove,*
10. *Were it not / thy sour / leisure / gave sweet / leave*
11. *To en / tertain / the time / with thoughts / of love,*
12. *Which time / and thoughts / so sweet / ly doth / deceive.*

In whatever way one may scan lines 9–10, the change from them to the perfectly regular lines 11–12 marks the "mending" of the poet's style into one which, with perfect *manners,* entertains the time. (I accept the emendation in line 12 by which love [not absence] *doth* [not *dost*] sweetly deceive time and thoughts.)

This enactive metrical "turn" to untroubled musicality, paradoxically afforded by the thoughts of love possible in absence, is one way in which this poem guarantees its assertions. Another is the way in which the plot of its final written form reverses the "experiential" temporal sequence which can be inferred from its narration. In the "real life" narrated by implication in the sonnet, the speaker's psychology is represented in four sequential temporal stages:

a. I am in torment because of this absence of my beloved and our consequent separation.
b. But his absence gives me leisure to praise him as he remains hence.
c. Therefore, separation—since it gives leisure to praise not him-as-joined-to-me but rather him-as-himself (a more convincing because less self-serving praise)—is good.
d. Therefore, togetherness is bad, since the praise it utters is contaminated by self-interest.

If I reduce this to its plot elements, it reads:

a. Separation = torment; but
b. Separation = leisure to sing; and
c. Separation = praise of him alone; therefore
d. Togetherness = suspect praise.

The written poem as we have it, however, reverses this "experiential" sequence. The poem says, in its turn:

a. How can I properly praise you, since we are so close that praise of you seems to be praise of myself?
b. Therefore let us live divided, so I can give you your due.
c. O Absence, what a torment would I find you, were it not for the leisure you afford for thoughts of love,
d. And you teach me how to offer mannerly praise by praising him alone, dividing him from me, painful though the division is.

Reduced, this reads as a near-perfect reversal of the "lived" plot above:

a. Togetherness = suspect praise;
b. Separation = praise of him alone;
c. Separation = torment except for leisure to sing;
d. Separation = mannerly praise.

The poem as we have it starts where it wants to finish, pretending that its "experiential" rationalization of the torments of absence ("I can praise him more properly") is in fact an *answer* to a constructed pseudo-question: "How can I praise him in a way that does not seem to reflect praise on myself?" This "question" never did exist in the inferred experiential order, which began not in such speculation but in the raw torment of absence. Thus, torment, by the invention of the pseudo-question, which for its answer *necessitates* absence as an aesthetic and moral *a priori*, is sublimated into the suffering necessary for sweet entertainment and mannerly praise.

This poem, then, contains behind it a shadow-poem or ghost-poem—the "experiential" lyric it could have been: "I hate our separation; can I see any good in it? Well, I can praise him more properly when we seem less close; good, I endorse absence on that account." Such an "experiential" narrative would produce a poem remaining on the single level of personal meditation. The implied reworking of such a "first model" accounts for three aspects of the poem: (1) the invention of the pseudo-problem ("How can I properly praise you who are the better part of me?"); (2) the decision for the lovers to separate being ascribed not to the beloved (who *doth hence* remain and has, in logic, therefore, been the one to bring about the separation and its continuance) but to the poet *(that I may give / That due to thee)*; and (3) the small ode of gratitude to Absence, the divinity who has happily "solved," for the poet, his aesthetic problem of mannerly praise.

In the little lyric playlet enacted in the sonnet, the perplexed poet, dissatisfied with his aesthetic production, banishes the beloved *(Even for this, let us divided live)* in order to praise him better, and finds with joy that his strategy works (*O absence, . . . thou* [giv'st] *sweet leave*, etc.) This playlet is a motivated pseudo-dramatic structure, with its little question *(O how)*, its resolutely "plucky" decision *(let us divided live)*, its thanks to its tutelary divinity Absence, and its final pose of humble instruction-taking. Such a long tradition of love-plaints-in-absence lies behind it, however, that we know we are to "hear" the "experiential" drama behind the constructed rationalizing poem. It is in such shadow play between written lyric and inner implied experience that much of the psychological richness of the *Sonnets* lies; we hear the pain of the betrayed voice behind the re-formed and rationalized whimsicality of the written praise.

Such sonnets correspond to paintings which contain a mirror reflecting a part of the painting, or which show an easel on which a painting of the "real" subject is displayed. The distortion of the "actual" in the mirror or on the easel is the measure of artifice, of which we are thus made particularly conscious. A poet uses the conventionally expected (here, the love-plaint in absence) as the "real"; and the measure of artifice becomes the degree of stylized departure from it (here, the congratulation of Absence as an aid to aesthetic propriety).

The "conjugation" *live, love, leave* (lines 5, 6, 10) "invented" here will reappear as *leaves, love, leave* (2, 14, 14) in sonnet 73.

Couplet tie: *praise* [-*ing*] (3, 4, 14)
one [al*one*] (6, 8, 13)

As I mentioned in commenting on 36, sonnet 39 repeats three rhyme-pairs from 36 (*me/thee*, *one/alone*, and *twain/remain*), two of them in the same order, with one *(me/thee)* reversed. That two sonnets on the same subject, sharing three of their seven rhymes, should belong together is given more credence by the chiastic arrangement of the coupled rhymes when 36/39 is printed as a double sonnet:

Sonnet 36:	Q_1	twain remain
	Q_2	one alone
	Q_3	thee me
Sonnet 39:	Q_1	me thee
	Q_2	one alone
	C	twain remain

This mirror-resemblance between 36 and 39, suggesting that they may have been conceived as a double sonnet like 98/99, confirms one's sense of 37 and 38 as an interruption in the sequence.

40

TAke all my loues,my loue,yea take them all,
What haſt thou then more then thou hadſt before?
No loue,my loue,that thou maiſt true loue call,
All mine was thine,before thou hadſt this more:
Then if for my loue,thou my loue receiueſt,
I cannot blame thee,for my loue thou vſeſt,
But yet be blam'd,if thou this ſelfe deceaueſt
By wilfull taſte of what thy ſelfe refuſeſt.
I doe forgiue thy robb'rie gentle theefe
Although thou ſteale thee all my pouerty:
And yet loue knowes it is a greater griefe
To beare loues wrong,then hates knowne iniury.
  Laſciuious grace,in whom all il wel ſhowes,
  Kill me with ſpights yet we muſt not be foes.

Take all my loves, my love, yea take them all;
What hast thou then more than thou hadst before?
No love, my love, that thou mayst true love call,
All mine was thine, before thou hadst this more.
Then if for my love thou my love receivest,
I cannot blame thee, for my love thou usest;
But yet be blamed, if thou this self deceivest
By wilful taste of what thy self refusest.
I do forgive thy robb'ry, gentle thief,
Although thou steal thee all my poverty;
And yet love knows it is a greater grief
To bear love's wrong than hate's known injury.
  Lascivious grace, in whom all ill well shows,
  Kill me with spites yet we must not be foes.

THE masochism of abjectness in love here reaches its first peak: *Kill me with spites yet we must not be foes.* This poem offers also one of those striking phrases with which the *Sonnets* are sprinkled, phrases which have a greater aesthetic effect than can, at first, be accounted for: here, the phrase is the fascinating *lascivious grace.* The phrase skirts blasphemy, since the moral import of the immediately following *ill* and *well* immediately brings religious *grace* into earshot; and the fallen state of the infatuated speaker (by comparison to his better state when he called the youth a *gentle thief*) is shown by his now making the positive word *(grace)* of the characterizing phrase the noun (the part of speech which conveys essence) with the condemnatory word *(lascivious)* becoming only a modifying adjective. Though he adds that all *ill* (substance) *shows* (appears) *well* in the beloved, this concession does not mitigate the positive force of the defining noun, *grace.* "Graceful lasciviousness" would show a speaker properly defining the relation between graceful show and lascivious substance; *lascivious grace* shows a speaker helplessly enthralled by beauty, for whom the aesthetic is the central necessary essence and substance of anything, and for whom other qualities, even deadly sins, are only contingent and adjectival. *All ill well shows / Kill* stammers the couplet. And yet, even with all this said, one does not at first know why *lascivious* falls on the ear with such absolute rightness. It is conspicuous, of course, by being the only "sophisticated" polysyllable in a couplet of monosyllables:

> *Lascivious* grace, in whom all ill well shows,
> Kill me with spites yet we must not be foes.

But why does *lascivious* fall on the ear like something *expected?* We can account for that, I think, only by its echo of the trisyllables of evildoing that make up the amphibrachic (˘ ´ ˘) rhyme words *(receivest, deceivest)* of the second quatrain:

*re**ceiv**e**s**t*	[*seev-s*]
thou usest	
*de**ceiv**e**s**t*	[*seev-s*]
refusest	
*las**civ**iou**s***	[*siv-s*]

It is by such confirmatory coffin nails that binding correspondences are hammered home; and, of course, the evil *grace* has some hooks of its own, not only its initial consonants and vowels which remind us of the ***greater grief*** (line 11) that that ***grace*** (line 13) has caused, but also its possession of the same satanic hiss that exists in *receivest*, *usest*, *deceivest*, *refusest*, and—of course—*lascivious*. *Lascivious grace:* the phrase, gathering up so many foregoing sounds and the damning amphibrachic foot, is like a Hopkinsian inscape. It serves (like *gentle thief*, which anticipates it) as a vocative *[O] lascivious grace, [thou] in whom all ill well shows, kill me!* The phrase is like a stunning discovery, as though the speaker were for the first time seeing that there exists a form of highest beauty *(grace)* intimately incorporating the corrupt. For someone whose ultimate value is the aesthetic, this is the worst possible recognition. (It was present in incipient form in sonnet 35, which shares the words *thief* and *rob* with 40.)

The structure of 40 changes at the "turn" to forgiveness. In the octave, left and right half-lines (loosely defined) match each other verbally and syntactically. Sometimes they do this laterally, sometimes vertically, as shown in the diagram. The poem, in short, encourages us to read by half-lines, both "across":

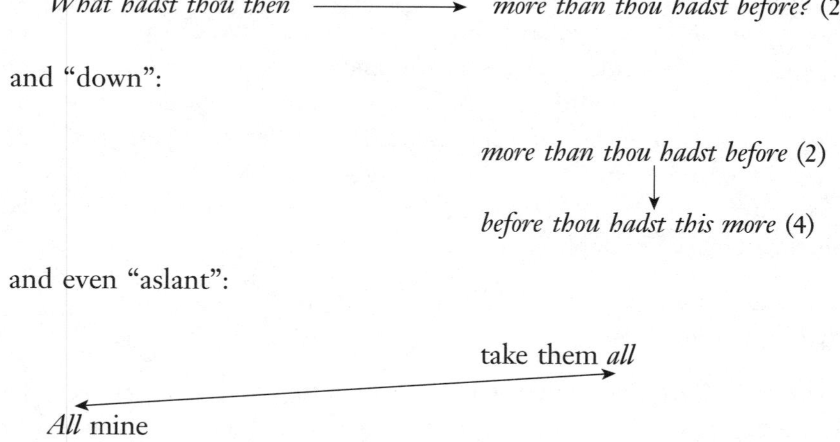

What hadst thou then
more than thou hadst before? (2)
and "down":
more than thou hadst before (2)
before thou hadst this more (4)
and even "aslant":
take them all
All mine

I think the half-line effects must strike anyone reading the sonnet. It is an interesting invention to compose a sonnet by half-lines, so to speak; it really creates a little twenty-eight-line poem:

Take all my loves, my love,
Yea take them all:

What hast thou then
More than thou hadst before?
No love, my love,
That thou mayst true love call,
All mine was thine
Before thou hadst this more.
Then if for my love
Thou my love receivest,
I cannot blame thee
For my love thou usest;
But yet be blamed
If thou this self deceivest
By wilful taste
Of what thy self refusest.
I do forgive thy robb'ry,
Gentle thief,
Although thou steal thee
All my poverty;
And yet love knows
It is a greater grief
To bear love's wrong
Than hate's known injury.
Lascivious grace,
In whom all ill well shows,
Kill me with spites,
Yet we must not be foes.

Of course, there are many half-lines in other sonnets that bear parallel and antithetical relations to each other, and there are both "lateral" and "vertical" relations of this kind elsewhere. But the half-line organization elsewhere is fairly often interrupted by whole-line organization, and is maintained less strictly, and with less repeated lateral and vertical foregrounding, than in this case. Here, the half-line organization breaks down for a while in the sestet, where the whole-line utterance is "stronger" than the vestiges of lateral and vertical parallelism, which nonetheless are maintained:

I do forgive thy *robb'ry*, gentle *thief* (lateral connection)
Although thou *steal* thee all my poverty. (vertical connection)

Structure of Sonnet 40

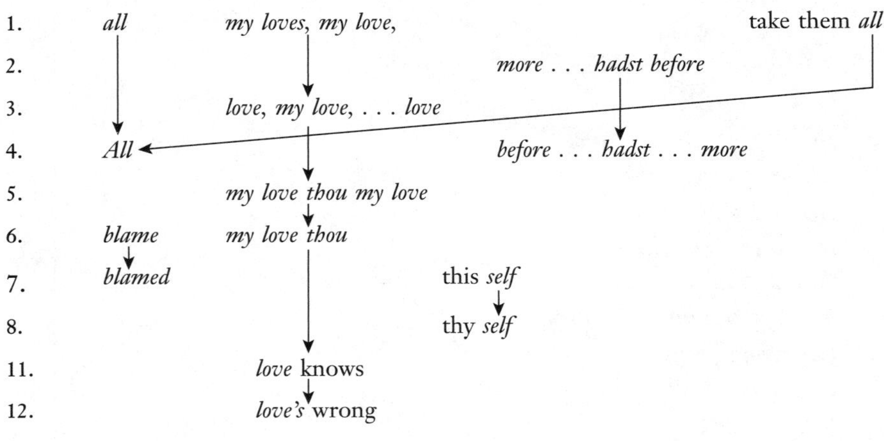

I believe that the zigzag half-line motion of this sonnet (perhaps influenced by the Anglo-Saxon / medieval alliterative verse line, with its strong medial caesura) formally enacts the speaker's vacillation between blame and excuse, and that this yes/no motion ensures the "rightness" of *lascivious grace* when it erupts as the helpless unifying summary of all the divisions preceding it.

Lines 5–8 with their long chiasmus *(if : blame :: blamed : if)* are the "knot"—a Gordian knot—which the speaker must attempt to untie:

Then

If for my love you receive my love, I cannot *blame* you that
you use my love.

But yet

If you deceive this self by willful taste of what you refuse,
be *blamed.*

The Gordian knot is the quatrain in which the speaker asks, "Why did he deceive me by a relation with my mistress?" and its contortions show the impossibility of both conjectures: "He did it because, loving me, he wants to have the same mistress as I do; he did it because he wanted a taste of what he had always repudiated (to me) as distasteful." The sonnet eventually gives up on both conjectures. "Never mind why; what am I to do about it?" the speaker asks himself, and answers in the sestet, "I do forgive." The blame persists in the putatively impersonal form of a proverb: "Love's wrong's a greater grief than hate's known injury"—its epigrammatic form marking its proverbial origin. When the speaker of a sonnet gives up on personal utterance and resorts to proverbial form, we have generally reached a situation that will not yield itself up to the forces of rational analysis (as the tortures of the present Gordian knot show). A hapless resort to forgiveness and proverb here takes the place of analytic resolution.

Such as it is, the truncated "analytic" resolution of 40 is the acceptance of the aesthetic paradox of *lascivious grace;* one is still in love with beauty, even after seeing not only its infidelity but the corrupted form that that beauty's infidelity has assumed—infidelity undertaken, as it was, for *wilful taste* rather than for infatuation or love. That is why the speaker admits that *all* ill shows well in the young man—coldblooded ill as well as hot-blooded, *spites* as well as *wrong.* "Though he slay me, yet will I trust in him" (Job) is the utterance of the saints, blasphemed here in *Kill me with spites yet we must not be foes.* It is a terrifying end. The "song" of *Take all my loves, my love . . . no love, my love* has degenerated to *Kill . . . spites . . . foes.*

Couplet Tie: *all* (1, 4, 10, 13)
The striking absence from the couplet of the word *love* [*-s*] (which is lavishly used ten times in the body of the sonnet) is necessarily remarked.

41

THose pretty wrongs that liberty commits,
When I am ſome-time abſent from thy heart,
Thy beautie,and thy yeares full well befits,
For ſtill temptation followes where thou art.
Gentle thou art,and therefore to be wonne,
Beautious thou art,therefore to be aſſailed.
And when a woman woes,what womans ſonne,
Will ſourely leaue her till he haue preuailed.
Aye me,but yet thou mighſt my ſeate forbeare,
And chide thy beauty,and thy ſtraying youth,
Who lead thee in their ryot euen there
Where thou art forſt to breake a two-fold truth:
  Hers by thy beauty tempting her to thee,
  Thine by thy beautie beeing falſe to me.

Those pretty wrongs that liberty commits
When I am sometime absent from thy heart,
Thy beauty, and thy years, full well befits,
For still temptation follows where thou art.
Gentle thou art, and therefore to be won,
Beauteous thou art, therefore to be assailed;
And when a woman woos, what woman's son
Will sourly leave her till she have prevailed?
Ay me, but yet thou mightst my seat forbear,
And chide thy beauty, and thy straying youth,
Who lead thee in their riot even there
Where thou art forced to break a twofold truth:
  Hers, by thy beauty tempting her to thee,
  Thine, by thy beauty being false to me.

THE extraordinary aesthetic emphasis of sonnet 40, focusing on a *lascivious grace* irresistible because beautiful in its essence, continues in 41, which begins by blaming two causes for the young man's lapses: his *beauty* and his tender *years*. It then personifies both causes—his *beauty* and *straying youth*—which become the bad companions *lead[ing]* him in *their riot* into *temptation* (which contradictorily *follows* where he is). But the couplet, strikingly, drops all mention of *tender years* and *straying youth*. The young man's *beauty* alone reigns in full aesthetic domination, as he is *forced* to break a *twofold truth:*

> Hers, by *thy beauty* tempting her to thee,
> Thine, by *thy beauty* being false to me.

The young man's beauty here seems a magnetic energy separate from himself; and "forced" suggests that he has no free will. Yet we must ascribe free will to the young man rather than seeing him as the innocent dupe of bad companions. We have been led to believe that the young man does have free will by the speaker's single exception in finding excuses for the young man's *pretty wrongs: Ay me, but yet thou mightst my seat forbear.* This protest certainly ascribes free will to the young man, who should assume control (as the speaker deems possible) over his bad companions. He should *chide* his *beauty and* his *straying youth*. To forbear and to chide are just what the young man has not done, but what he could have done, and could still do. Therefore, the subsequent statement *thou art forced to break a twofold truth*, and the ascription of independent agency to *beauty* (as earlier to *liberty*), ring not as facts but as reiterated excuses.

"And lead us not into temptation" is what Michael Riffaterre might call the hypogram underlying this sonnet, as we can see (a) from the witty verbal reversal of *lead* to *follow* in the octave, *For still temptation follows where thou art*, and (b) from the reversion to the biblical norm in the sestet: "[they] *lead* thee in their riot . . . *tempting* her." Temptation followed by wrongdoing is the chronological dramatic scenario of the sonnet, but it is first played out in *reverse* chronological order in two scenes of "excuse," the first general, the second specific:

wrongs commit[ted] (line 1) ⟵ *temptation* (line 4)

won (line 5) ⟵ *assailed* (line 6)

The third scene of excuse, however, is played out in "correct" chronological order:

woo (line 7) ⟶ *prevail* (line 8)

So is the subsequent chronologically-ordered long reproach:

forbear ⟶ *lead* ⟶ *riot* ⟶ *[broken] truth.*

The sonnet therefore may be divided into two phases, one (lines 1–6) which goes "backward" from ill-doing to temptation, and a second (lines 7–12) which goes "forward" from temptation to ill-doing. The first phase is a twice-reiterated process of ascribing blame for wrongs committed; the second is a twice-reiterated re-creation of the act from start *(and when a woman woos . . . thou mightst forbear)* to finish *(prevailed . . . break truth).* The first phase is retrospectively analytic, the second phase chronologically dramatic. The couplet's dry and bitter ascription of the young man's twofold truth-breaking to the invincible power of beauty alone shows the speaker capitulating on the question of free will, excusing the young man entirely.

This sonnet is perhaps a good place to glance at the way Shakespeare contrives the effect of what Frost, in "Birches," would call "truth [breaking] in." In the midst of all the sophistry of infatuation (and Blackmur's phrase about the *Sonnets*, "the *poetics* of infatuation," has never been bettered), a note is struck of what, in the dramatic sense, one must call "sincerity." "Sincerity" and "insincerity" are mutually self-defining in any given sonnet, and often the "sincere" outburst comes at the turn in line 9. Whatever has preceded tends to seem like irony, ingenuity, or sophistry by contrast to the "sincere" language that follows. Notable examples of "truth breaking in" include:

Ay me, but yet thou mightst my seat forbear (sonnet 41)
O no, thy love though much, is not so great (61)
But when my glass shows me myself indeed (62)
But wherefore says she not she is unjust? (138)

It is therefore worth looking briefly at what precedes and follows the fulcrum of "sincerity" in 41, while remembering that it is in the "sincere" outburst *(Ay me)* that the young man's free will is assumed, and that the outcry therefore serves not only as an emotional or psychological or linguistic fulcrum (as it does) but as a moral fulcrum as well.

The first quatrain excuses the friend by the speaker's assuming on his own part a light, libertine, and "worldly" attitude toward *pretty wrongs*, ascribing them to an apparently desirable *liberty*, and minimizing their frequency *(sometime);* the "enthusiastic" concurrence in *full well* ("boys will be boys") and the lurking presence of libertine companions *(temptation follows where thou art)* serve as excuses as well. The young man walks in a generalized atmosphere of youth, beauty, liberty, and temptations, and it is "only natural" that he will fall into pretty wrongs.

This first excuse is almost wholly incompatible with the second, which displaces all blame onto the woman, who *assail[s]*, *woos*, and *prevail[s]*. (I believe that the Quarto *he* should be emended to *she*, though the wooing woman would remain the principal agent of sin even if *he* is retained as the prevailer.) The gentle and beauteous youth must acquiesce if only for good manners' sake; he cannot *sourly leave* her. It is probably the strain in maintaining a falsely logical note *(and therefore . . . therefore . . . and)* as much as the incompatibility of the second excuse with the first that makes the irruption *Ay me* seem inevitable as a corrective to the preceding "libertine" sophistry and the repetition of the oldest excuse in myth, "The woman tempted [him]."

The fulcrum of "sincerity" lasts for just two lines, and then we revert to excuse. At first (line 10), beauty and youth are rebel powers to be chided, but one line later they *lead thee in their riot* to the forbidden, but not forborne, *seat.*

Metaphor is present, but in the phrase *forbear[ing a] seat* we are still at the realistic level of diction, not the allegorical, When we then pass into the allegory of *[tempters] who lead thee*, this change is a sign of renewed estrangement from "sincerity." The couplet, verbally, has it both ways. An "insincere" version blames the tempter *(beauty)* and excuses the young man, by construing *tempting* as predicated of the rioter *beauty:* "thy beauty's tempting [of] her." A "sincere" version would blame the young man himself, and would construe *tempting* as modifying *thou:* "thou tempting her by thy beauty." The speaker adroitly maintains himself as both excuser and potential blamer; but the reader, having once heard the "sincere" voice of pain and betrayed love, sides with that implied voice over the voice of "pretty" libertine excuse and accusation of the wooing woman.

Couplet Tie: [tempt] [*-ation*] [*-ing*] (4, 13)
thy beauty (10, 13, 14)

42

THat thou haſt her it is not all my griefe,
And yet it may be ſaid I lou'd her deerely,
That ſhe hath thee is of my wayling cheefe,
A loſſe in loue that touches me more neerely.
Louing offendors thus I will excuſe yee,
Thou dooſt loue her,becauſe thou knowſt I loue her,
And for my ſake euen ſo doth ſhe abuſe me,
Suffring my friend for my ſake to approoue her,
If I looſe thee,my loſſe is my loues gaine,
And looſing her,my friend hath found that loſſe,
Both finde each other,and I looſe both twaine,
And both for my ſake lay on me this croſſe,
But here's the ioy,my friend and I are one,
Sweete flattery,then ſhe loues but me alone.

That thou hast her, it is not all my grief,
And yet it may be said I loved her dearly;
That she hath thee is of my wailing chief,
A loss in love that touches me more nearly.
Loving offenders, thus I will excuse ye:
Thou dost love her because thou know'st I love her,
And for my sake even so doth she abuse me,
Suff'ring my friend for my sake to approve her.
If I lose thee, my loss is my love's gain,
And losing her, my friend hath found that loss,
Both find each other, and I lose both twain,
And both for my sake lay on me this cross.
But here's the joy, my friend and I are one:
Sweet flattery! then she loves but me alone.

THESE early betrayal sonnets (40, 41, 42) are usually, and probably correctly, read against their supposedly "corresponding" sonnets in the second half of the sequence (133, 134, 135, 136, 144, 152, etc.) and an intertextual force-field is thereby created, directing in part how the reader transfers meaning from one (*twice forsworn . . . thy bed-vow broke*, 152) to another (*break a twofold truth*, 41). The advantage in writing a sequence arises from the creation of this energetic force-field, in which not only individual sonnets, but individual quatrains and couplets, and even individual lines, float free, collide, combine with, or repel each other. One can even mentally "create" entire false combinatory octaves or sestets which sometimes seem almost as real as the true ones.

In 42, after line 9, the young man is no longer addressed in the second person, but rather referred to in the third person (this is the reference used throughout 42 for the mistress). By this midway change of address, the speaker demonstrates that he is no longer in a "thou" relation to the young man. The speaker is excluded from the relation between friend and mistress; they become *my friend* and *she*, not *thou* and *she*. The sonnet has first attempted to draw the mistress into the "thou" mode reserved for the young man by attempting a second-person plural—*Loving offenders, thus I will excuse ye*—but the attempt to magnetize her into the circle of the speaker's affection fails. She entered the poem conspicuously referred to in the third person ("That *thou* hast *her*"), and after the brief ingathering into *ye* she falls back into the third person—"even so doth *she* abuse me"—but, disastrously, she takes the young man away with her, into her third-person sphere.

In a final desperate attempt not to lose the young man, the speaker moves him from the third person into the first person, arguing that he is implicitly gathered into the accusative *me*, since the speaker and friend are one: "My friend and *I* are one . . . then *she* loves but *me* alone." The mistress remains outside, ungathered, in her third-person *she*. The young man and the speaker together are supposedly caught up into the *I* of the poem.

The distribution of persons in love is brought out by the distribution of the lurking word *love* itself. As the accompanying diagram reveals, the word *love* is distributed across the same frequency, so to speak, as the word *lose;* and the distribution of clauses (where I capitalize forms of *love* and *lose*) exhibits the sophistry of rationalization. I use S to represent the speaker, M to represent the mistress, and YM to represent the young man, as they regroup themselves during the progress of the sonnet. While the left column gathers together the moments when the young man is said to possess the mistress, and the right column the moments when the speaker comments on his own position, the middle column documents the mistress' moments of possession as the speaker continually rephrases them. It will be noticed that the first reference to the young man in the third person (not *thee* but *my friend*) is made from the point of view of the mistress as she "suffer(s) *my friend* for my sake to approve her." Immediately after this, the speaker lays claim, for the last time in the poem, to

Distribution of Love *and* Lose *in Sonnet 42*

YM in Possession of M	M in Possession of YM	S in (Non)-Possession
That *thou hast her*	That *she hath thee*	*I* LOVED *her* A LOSS in LOVE that touches *me*
	M and YM in Possession of Each Other	
	LOVING offenders, thus *I* will excuse *ye:*	
Thou dost LOVE *her* because *I* LOVE *her*	*she* doth abuse *me* for *my* sake suff'ring *my friend* for *my* sake to approve *her*	
		If *I* LOSE *thee*, *my* LOSS
	is *my LOVE'S* gain	
		and [*I*] LOSING *her*
my friend hath found that LOSS		
	Both find *each other*	and *I* LOSE *both twain*
	M in Possession of YM and S	
my friend		and *I*
are one:		
	she LOVES but *me* alone.	

his former second-person address: "If I lose *thee*," he says, envisaging his worst fear. Thenceforth the mistress' view dominates, and the young man remains *my friend*, not *thee*, even during the final desperate move of ingathering him from his third-person status to first-person identity (a move Shakespeare characterizes as self-deceiving—*sweet flattery*—even as it is being made).

The third quatrain is where the feared loss occurs in actual fact, since after its first foreboding words—*If I lose thee*—the second person disappears, and in place of the domination of *love* (three times in Q_2) we find the domination of *lose* (*loss*, etc.), which I here capitalize—five times in Q_3, against one occurrence of *love* (there are no occurrences of *lose* at all in Q_2):

Q_1: *loved*, LOSS, *love*
Q_2: *loving*, *love*, *love*
Q_3: LOSE, LOSS, *love*, LOSING, LOSS, LOSE
C : *love*

Shakespeare offers four models to describe the relations between the three persons in the triangle. The models become increasingly tortured, as the speaker tries to find a way to include himself in the relationship of the young man to the mistress. The first model (Q_1) is the apparently true one. The young man (YM) and the mistress (M) are together in a relation that excludes the speaker (S), who has formerly been in a relation of love to both of them:

S: YM has M
M has YM

In the second model (Q_2), their previous relationship of love with the speaker is the cause and very means by which the young man and mistress have fallen into their present affair *(because, for my sake, for my sake):*

YM—via S—M
M—via S—YM

In the third model (Q_3) their relation is the speaker's fault: he has somehow lost them both, because they have sought out each other—doing so even *for [his] sake*, presumably to solidify their relation with him:

S → loses YM
S → loses M
} they find each other

In the last model (C), the speaker has absorbed the young man into himself, and the relationship therefore becomes one between himself and the mistress, eliding the young man altogether *(she loves me):*

S = YM;
M loves S (YM).

By inserting himself somehow as cause or agent of the relation between the young man and the mistress, the speaker preserves a connection with the young man which (as the last fantasy of ingestion of the young man reveals) is the overriding motive of this poem. It is the psychological ingenuity of the models of possible connection—where, as Q_1 admits, no such fantastic connection exists—that here controls the deployment of *love* and *lose.* But the aesthetic pathos of the poem arises from the loss of the power to say *thee* any longer. "*Thou* and I are one" is the pathetic second-person shadow-statement, unsayable, behind the third-person fantasy-statement, "*My friend* and I are one." The loss in love that touches the speaker most nearly is the loss of the *thou* of affection. In the Couplet Tie, where we expect to find a surviving *lose* [*loss*] we find only a pathetic *love.*

KEY WORD: LOVE

Couplet Tie: *my friend* (8, 10, 13)
love [*-d*] [*-ing*] [*-s*] (2, 4, 5, 6, 6, 9, 14)

43

WHen moſt I winke then doe mine eyes beſt ſee,
For all the day they view things vnreſpected,
But when I ſleepe,in dreames they looke on thee,
And darkely bright,are bright in darke directed.
Then thou whoſe ſhaddow ſhaddowes doth make bright,
How would thy ſhadowes forme,forme happy ſhow,
To the cleere day with thy much cleerer light,
When to vn-ſeeing eyes thy ſhade ſhines ſo?
How would (I ſay)mine eyes be bleſſed made,
By looking on thee in the liuing day?
When in dead night their faire imperfect ſhade,
Through heauy ſleepe on ſightleſſe eyes doth ſtay?
  All dayes are nights to ſee till I ſee thee,
  And nights bright daies when dreams do ſhew thee me.

When most I wink then do mine eyes best see,
For all the day they view things unrespected,
But when I sleep, in dreams they look on thee,
And darkly bright, are bright in dark directed.
Then thou, whose shadow shadows doth make bright,
How would thy shadow's form form happy show
To the clear day with thy much clearer light,
When to unseeing eyes thy shade shines so!
How would (I say) mine eyes be blessèd made,
By looking on thee in the living day,
When in dead night thy fair imperfect shade
Through heavy sleep on sightless eyes doth stay!
  All days are nights to see till I see thee,
  And nights bright days when dreams do show thee me.

NORMALLY, one to three significant words used in the body of a sonnet reappear in the couplet, forming what I term the Couplet Tie—a locking device without which the couplet would, so to speak, fall off. In 43 Shakespeare experiments with a substantial amount of couplet glue: seven words used in the body of the poem (besides forms of *I* and *thou*) reappear in the couplet. These—*all*, *day*, *night*, *see*, *bright*, *dreams*, and *show*—make up, with repeats, one-half of the couplet's words. In fact, there are *no* words in the couplet except *till* which are *not* repeated from the body of the poem (*me* is only a variant form of the repeated *I/my/mine*). Redundancy is the experiment of the whole poem, perhaps best seen in the play on three sounds, *sh*, *d*, and *b*, represented by the following lists:

shadow	day	best
shadows	dreams	bright
shadow's	darkly	bright
show	dark	bright
shade	directed	blessèd
shines	doth	bright
shade	day	
show	day	
	dead	
	doth	
	days	
	days	
	dreams	
	do	

These lists of alliterating words are the "constants" with respect to which the other words, changing as the sonnet progresses, are the variables.

Sonnet 43 looks like a poem which makes the "same" statement, more or less, four times, a statement announced by the first line ("My eyes see best when I am asleep") and reiterated through the quatrains to the couplet ("When dreams show you to me, nights are bright days"). This absence-poem would prefer the beloved's presence, but lacking that presence, will make do with dreams in which the beloved object can be seen. For all the lexical constancy evidenced by the redundancy in the word lists and the Couplet Tie, the slippage in the phrasing of this central statement, as the sonnet evolves, is extraordinary.

The slippage can be shown by isolating some main clauses about the night seeing. I rearrange some words to display their syntactic parallelism with other phrases:

when most I wink	*mine eyes best see*
when I sleep	*in dreams they look on thee*
	to unseeing eyes thy shade shines
	on sightless eyes thy imperfect shade doth stay
	dreams do show thee

The phrasing passes from active supercompetent eyes that *best see*, that *look* on the object; to *unseeing eyes* passively illuminated by a *shade* that *shines;* to *sightless eyes* on which rests an *imperfect shade*. The poem, in short, gets darker as the *seeing* eyes become *unseeing* and then *sightless*, and as the shade darkens from *shin[ing]* brightness to *imperfect[ion]*. Finally, the eyes disappear; *dreams* are the active agents which *show*.

Such slippage in the *Sonnets* invariably betrays an original self-deception. The confident paradox *When most I wink, then do mine eyes best see*, invented by the speaker to cheer himself up ("Oh well, even in absence I can see you in my dreams"), is sabotaged on all sides. A crude sketch of the relations of *day* and *night* in the poem reveals that we are talking about a *real* day (in which the beloved is absent and there is nothing worth looking at), versus a hypothetical *ideal* day (in which the beloved would be present in the flesh), versus a *real* night (in which the beloved is present only in dreams). Compared with the empty real day, the real night of vivid dreams is desirable. But compared with the plenitude of the hypothetical ideal *living day*, the real night, even with its dreams, is dead and undesirable. As the real night is first favorably compared to the real day and then unfavorably to the better *living day*, it slides downward in esteem; as the vacant real day is hypothesized into the Living Day, day mounts upward in estimation; as the Real Presence arises in the hypothesis of the *living day*, the dream presence fades into imperfection and loses its brilliance. All of these slippages happen in the body of the sonnet, and the place where they "bottom out" is the last two lines of the body:

. . . in *dead* night thy fair *imperfect* shade
Through heavy sleep on *sightless eyes* doth *stay!*

The power of dream is still affirmed, but its radical imperfection as a substitute for real presence is admitted. Absence is still the fact, during the day and even during the night. What then can the couplet now say? The couplet offers a frank longing for presence: "All days are nights to see *till I see thee.*" *I see thee* is the kernel sentence for presence. It has hitherto been ingeniously repressed by the displacement of agency from the personal pronoun onto the speaker's eyes: "Mine *eyes* best see; *they* view; *they* look on thee; [*they*] are directed; thy shade shines to *eyes;* mine *eyes* would be made blessèd by looking on thee; thy shade doth stay on sightless *eyes.*" The second line of the couplet finally admits the lack of all agency in the self, including its (putatively hitherto active) eyes: "And nights [are] bright days when *dreams do show* thee me." Truth has arrived with a vengeance: "*I* do not see thee, not yet; *my eyes* do not see thee either; I am dependent on *dreams* to show you to me."

The psychological interest of the poem lies in its portrayal of the slippage from compensatory sparkle to abject admission. The aesthetic interest, however, is concentrated in the fancy footwork of lines 3–8, in which the friend's true form (which can be seen when he is present) is contrasted in its illuminatory power with his shadow-image, which is seen in dreams when he is absent. A fundamentally disappointing "night" baseline *(night/dreams . . . shade/shadow/shines)* is repeatedly drawn in lines 1–5 in the present tense, and then is exceeded in lines 6–10 by a hypothetical better comparative "daylight" line drawn in some form of the conditional.

The two *How would* conditional clauses (Q_2 and Q_3) destroy the "cheerful" paradox of *darkly bright . . . bright in dark* of Q_1, first by denigrating the quality of its shadowy dream-brightness in comparison to the *much clearer* light of the true daylight form, and second by pointing out the *imperfect[ion]* of the shadow itself and by calling night *dead.* The logical force of these two "destructive" quatrains is, however, overmastered by their forceful summarizing of authentic presence in lines 3–10 by what I can only call a staircase technique of directed aimed-and-climbing vision, which begins in line 3 (see diagram).

All these lines are "bright-directed": they all brighten as they end. They are directed, in their closing words, to look on thee, to be bright, make bright, form happy show to the clear day with clearer light, shine so, be made blessèd, look on love in the living day. This is a brightening-till-line-end pattern we can see as well in the first line of the sonnet and in both lines of the couplet. This driven vector-shape is contradicted, in fact, by only two lines in the body of the poem, the relatively undeluded lines 11–12:

Staircase Structure of Sonnet 43

on thee
they look
in dreams
When I sleep

directed.
(in dark)
are bright
And darkly bright,

shadows doth make bright
Then thou whose shadow

with thy much clearer light
To the clear day
happy show /
How would thy shadow's form form

shines so!
When to unseeing eyes thy shade

in the living day
thee
By looking on
blessèd made /
[M]ine eyes [would be]

When in dead night
thy fair imperfect shade /
Through heavy sleep
on sightless eyes
doth stay!

As we might by now expect, desire and frustration both appear in the couplet: the down-drive of depression is followed by the up-driven push of desire. First, line 13:

All days till I see thee.
are nights to see

The complex last line of the couplet triumphantly includes motions of frustration, desire, and a truthful end in self-perception:

[are] bright days show thee
And nights when dreams do me.

The continual upward push of the ends of most lines in 43 is the clearest enactment in the sonnets of the vector of desire pressing for presence. The stammering directive of desire, its way of trying to impose its will on recalcitrant reality, generates the "unreadability" or "unintelligibility" of desire's best lines: *Then thou, whose shadow shadows doth make bright, / How would thy shadow's form form happy show*, etc.

show
py
hap-
form
form
dow's
shad-
thy
would
How

One is pressed to read the lines in this way because the monosyllabic words *how* and *show* attract the matching monosyllabic phoneme *-dow*, and the monosyllabic word *thy* attracts the matching monosyllable *-py*, while the closing *d* of the monosyllabic word *would* attracts the matching *shad-*. The line becomes a staircase of ascending phonetic monosyllables (resembling *When I sleep in dreams they look on thee*) of which *form form* is the model and nucleus. The absurdity of such formations is the very absurdity of desire itself fantasizing its wishes into a slippery hypothetical existence.

This sonnet is unusual in possessing two KEY WORDS.

KEY WORDS: DAY [-S]
SEE [unSEEing] [SIGHT]

Couplet Tie: *day* [*-s*] (2, 7, 10, 13, 14)
night [*-s*] (11, 13, 14)
see [*unseeing, sight*] (1, 8, 12, 13, 13)
bright (4, 4, 5, 14)
dreams (3, 14)
show (6, 14)

44

IF the dull ſubſtance of my fleſh were thought,
Iniurious diſtance ſhould not ſtop my way,
For then diſpight of ſpace I would be brought,
From limits farre remote, where thou dooſt ſtay,
No matter then although my foote did ſtand
Vpon the fartheſt earth remoou'd from thee,
For nimble thought can iumpe both ſea and land,
As ſoone as thinke the place where he would be.
But ah, thought kills me that I am not thought
To leape large lengths of miles when thou art gone,
But that ſo much of earth and water wrought,
I muſt attend, times leaſure with my mone.
　Receiuing naughts by elements ſo ſloe,
　But heauie teares, badges of eithers woe.

If the dull substance of my flesh were thought,
Injurious distance should not stop my way,
For then despite of space I would be brought,
From limits far remote, where thou dost stay.
No matter then although my foot did stand
Upon the farthest earth removed from thee,
For nimble thought can jump both sea and land
As soon as think the place where he would be.
But ah, thought kills me that I am not thought,
To leap large lengths of miles when thou art gone,
But that, so much of earth and water wrought,
I must attend time's leisure with my moan,
　Receiving naught by elements so slow
　But heavy tears, badges of either's woe.

IN SONNET 27, the speaker had said his *thoughts . . . intend a zealous pilgrimage to thee*, but the sad pilgrim *badges* in 44 mark the insufficency of such an incorporeal pilgrimage. The obstacles of *space* (line 3) and *time* (line 12) generate the speaker's wish in the octave to be pure mind, not flesh; and the descent in the sestet from the octave's fantasy (of being composed not of flesh but of thought) closes with the solid *earth[ly]* flesh melting and resolving itself in part into the *water* of tears. The twin sonnet that follows (45) compares thought and desire to *air* and *fire*, thereby making up the tally of the four elements necessary to a complete human being. Flesh, tears, thought, desire = earth, water, air, fire. Sonnet 44 is a poem spoken by flesh secreting tears: flesh furious at space, flesh wishing to be pure thought.

Space is obtruded in phrases (in uppercase, below) that put distance between speaker *(I)* and object *(thou, thee)*, both in the octave-hypothesis *(If . . . my flesh were thought)* and in the sestet's admission of fact *(I am not thought):*

If the dull substance of *my flesh* were thought,
INJURIOUS DISTANCE should not stop MY WAY,
For then DESPITE OF SPACE *I* would be brought,
From LIMITS FAR REMOTE, where *thou* dost stay.
No matter then although *my foot* did stand
Upon THE FARTHEST EARTH REMOVED from *thee*,
For nimble thought can jump BOTH SEA AND LAND
As soon as think THE PLACE where he would be.
But ah, thought kills me that *I* am not thought,
To leap LARGE LENGTHS OF MILES when *thou* art gone.

The obstructive presence of physical places, physical distances, or adverbs of remoteness in all but two of the first ten lines suggests that the wishful hypothesis of translation in space is being destroyed even as it is being fabricated. The fiction of spatial instantaneity is ruthlessly succeeded by the fact of time, that ruler whose leisure the speaker must attend (cf. 58, where the speaker calls himself *your vassal bound to stay your leisure*).

The substitution in line 12 of time for space entails the speaker's reentry into earth and water, those heavy elements which confer on their unwilling subject their badge of heavy tears. Sea and land, water and earth, are "slow" elements, in that traversing them in bodily form is a slow process. As thought returns home from its rapid journey of desire, it marks its homeward return by tears, badges testifying to the pilgrim-thought's successful journey to his absent shrine. These are badges of woe by earth, woe by water—the speaker's return to either element is sorrowful. The *moan* of the poem echoes its cause, the word *remote*, subsequently translated for emphasis into *removed.* If it were not for *sub-stance*, *di-stance* would not be troublesome; and if it were not for one's killing *thought* (in the sense of "reflection") one could pretend to be pure *thought* (in the sense of "spirit").

The poem resorts to self-splitting in the usual Platonic/Christian dualism, contrasting *my flesh* with *thought*—significantly not "*my* thought," but "*nimble* thought," referred to as *he* (a third-person self-distancing which hopes to defeat the heavy flesh, but impotent against the ascription of *my* to both *flesh* and *foot*). *I* is used to refer to the heavy thing that needs to be passively *brought* to the beloved's presence. The dualism becomes most acute in the paradoxical line embodying the two senses of *thought:*

thought [reflection] kills *me* (the body who wishes to be thought)
that
I am not thought [spirit]

As soon as this self-reminding takes place, the surmounting of space by thought is made ridiculous: *to leap large lengths of miles* sounds hare-like. And this deflation causes the subsidence into the heavily inorganic *(earth, water)* badged with tears. The dropping of slow tears, as in a clepsydra, marks time's leisure.

Injurious distance has mutated into injurious time, and the *dj*-sound first manifested depressively in *injurious* and later happily revised in *jump* returns to its original lugubrious import in the *badges* of tears.

Couplet Tie: None. The couplet indeed verbally "falls off," via the consciousness of temporality expressed in line 12's *time* and line 13's *slow*, by contrast with the first eleven lines concerned with *space.* The antonymic conceptual relation of *slow* to *as soon as* and *heavy* to *nimble* is of course a thematic contrastive Couplet Tie, serving in lieu of the more usual repetitions of words.

45

THe other two,ſlight ayre,and purging fire,
Are both with thee,where euer I abide,
The firſt my thought,the other my deſire,
Theſe preſent abſent with ſwift motion ſlide.
For when theſe quicker Elements are gone
In tender Embaſſie of loue to thee,
My life being made of foure,with two alone,
Sinkes downe to death,oppreſt with melancholie.
Vntill liues compoſition be recured,
By thoſe ſwift meſſengers return'd from thee,
Who euen but now come back againe aſſured,
Of their faire health,recounting it to me.
This told,I ioy,but then no longer glad,
I ſend them back againe and ſtraight grow ſad.

The other two, slight air and purging fire,
Are both with thee, wherever I abide;
The first my thought, the other my desire,
These present-absent with swift motion slide.
For when these quicker elements are gone
In tender embassy of love to thee,
My life, being made of four, with two alone
Sinks down to death, oppressed with melancholy,
Until life's composition be recured
By those swift messengers returned from thee,
Who even but now come back again assured
Of thy fair health, recounting it to me.
This told, I joy, but then no longer glad,
I send them back again and straight grow sad.

THIS twin of its two-element predecessor-sonnet commits sleight-of-hand with tenses, notably the habitual present and the actual present:

The other two *are* [always] with thee These present-absent [always] *slide* For when [now or whenever] these *are gone*	Habitual present
My life *sinks* [now or whenever] down to death	Habitual or actual present
Until life's composition *be recured* by messengers	Subjunctive future
Who even but now *come* [at this very moment] back, recounting thy health; this told, I [now] *joy*	Actual present
But then I *send* them *back* [as usual] and grow [as usual] sad.	Habitual present

The object of this play with the two uses of the present tense is to mimic the present-absent slide of the *swift motion* of the *swift messengers* air and fire, thought and desire, now here, now there. The recursive motion is reinforced by the three *re-* words *(recured, returned, recounting)* in Q_3, as well as by the Couplet Tie *back again.*

The circuit is enacted three times, first (as Booth points out) as a "false" circuit, in which air and fire, thought and desire, are always with the beloved object, no matter where the speaker is; but we may perhaps take this as the remark of the earth-and-water self who closes the previous poem and presumably opens this one. A more truthful picture of the circuit is given in line 4, in the present-absent slide of thought and desire. The next repetition of the circuit suggests that the lighter elements go off of their own volition, impoverishing the self: "When these *are gone*, my life being made of four, with two alone sinks down to death." Purging fire and slight air then return, dispersing melancholy by their arrival; the friend's fair health restores life's composition. This third rehearsal of the circuit is the most detailed and complete, becomes a present-tense fact *(now)* and in fact spills over into the couplet: *This told, I joy.* In the fourth and final picture of the circuit, personal agency is at last avowed: *I send them back again.* Thought and desire, no longer seemingly independent agents, are ambassadors of the active self, who fantasizes that they are also messengers from the friend, messengers who *come back again* with news of the friend's fair health, in reciprocity for the speaker's earlier *tender embassy of love.*

Come back again (line 11) is matched with *send back again* (line 14), as if those who come must have been sent. We now see the reason for ascribing independent agency to the messengers. As long as the speaker imagines they do their flitting by themselves, he can beg the question whether his own embassies of love are being returned by the friend. The fatal absence of a counteragent to the closing *I* suggests that the assumed (and desired) reciprocity is fantasized, not real. *Returned from thee* is not the same as "sent back by thee." But the swift motion has been believably represented. Both 44 and 45 "illegally" repeat a rhyme-word (*thought* in Q_1 and Q_3 of 44, *thee* in Q_2 and Q_3 of 45). They share rhyme-words as well: *thee* and *gone.* These devices, as well as their logical connections, bind the two sonnets to each other.

Couplet Tie: *back again* (11, 14)

46

MIne eye and heart are at a mortall warre,
How to deuide the conqueſt of thy ſight,
Mine eye,my heart their pictures ſight would barre,
My heart,mine eye the freeedome of that right,
My heart doth plead that thou in him dooſt lye,
(A cloſet neuer pearſt with chriſtall eyes)
But the defendant doth that plea deny,
And ſayes in him their faire appearance lyes.
To ſide this title is impannelled
A queſt of thoughts,all tennants to the heart,
And by their verdict is determined
The cleere eyes moyitie,and the deare hearts part.
As thus,mine eyes due is their outward part,
And my hearts right,their inward loue of heart.

Mine eye and heart are at a mortal war,
How to divide the conquest of thy sight:
Mine eye my heart thy picture's sight would bar,
My heart mine eye the freedom of that right.
My heart doth plead that thou in him dost lie
(A closet never pierced with crystal eyes),
But the defendant doth that plea deny,
And says in him thy fair appearance lies.
To 'cide this title is impanellèd
A quest of thoughts, all tenants to the heart,
And by their verdict is determinèd
The clear eye's moiety and the dear heart's part,
As thus: mine eye's due is thy outward part,
And my heart's right thy inward love of heart.

THIS sonnet and its sequel form a double poem just as 44 and 45 do. Sonnet 46 playfully presents a *mortal war* between the eye and the heart which is solved by a jury; 47 presents an equally lightly sketched league of mutual benefit undertaken by the former enemies, eye and heart. The conceit of eye and heart, outer and inner, is a traditional one, and the distributive solution also is traditional (the speaker's heart owns the beloved's inward heart, the speaker's eye the beloved's outward part), thus reaffirming the dualism of "inner essence" and "outward show" so often invoked by the *Sonnets.* None of this conceptual apparatus reveals Shakespeare's method, however, which is, as usual, to create a flurry of entities to describe the object of the dispute between his eye and his heart. What is it eye and heart seek possession of? *Thy sight? Thy picture's sight? Thou? Thy fair appearance?* The different names given to the desired object suggest the obscurity of the proceeding, and explain why a *quest of thoughts* has to be summoned to sort out the emotional confusion. The jury is predisposed (since *all* the thoughts are *tenants to the heart*) to see the heart satisfied; and in fact eye and heart are in the end both pacified, in a Couplet Tie joining *eye, heart, part* and *right.* A simple distributive division into *inward* and *outward* seems to do the trick, producing the symmetries of the couplet-verdict. If we look back to the pleas of the contestants, we can now see that each is in the right. The eye's assertion is true:

> Mine eye would bar the sight of thy picture from my heart;
> [Mine eye] says thy fair appearance lies in him.

Fair enough: to the eye belong picture and appearance. The heart-plaintiff, wishing to forbid the eye its freedom to bar the heart from its right, pleads that the beloved *(thou)* lies in him, a windowless chamber. This claim also proves to be true, since it seems the beloved can actually lie in one place, while his appearance is kept separately in another.

What do these sophistries add up to? In effect, the interior quarrel represented here is Shakespeare's recurrent one between the aesthetic and the affective. Do I love with my eyes (and does the beloved therefore belong to them)? Or do I love with my heart (and is the beloved's appearance therefore irrelevant)? (Cf. *In faith I do not love thee with mine eyes,* 141.)

Since the speaker knows he loves, his thoughts accept that fact as a given, and then reasonably enough decide, as a jury, that the eye, like the heart, plays a part in love. We recall *The Merchant of Venice,* which at one point ascribes all love exclusively to the eye, denying heart and head any part at all in love:

Tell me where is fancy bred,
Or in the heart or in the head?
How begot, how nourishèd? . . .
It is engend'red in the eyes,
With gazing fed, and fancy dies
In the cradle where it lies.

The aesthetic strategy of 46 might be called "dividing up." After the declaration of pretty hostilities *(Mine eyes and heart are at a mortal war),* there come in Q_1 two moments of enacted direct clash:

Mine eye my heart
My heart mine eye

(These are the only two possible permutations of head-on clash—ab : ba. The figures represent two separate versions of clash, not primarily, as Booth thinks, chiasmus.)

Subsequently, in Q_2, a fuller (two-line) plea by the heart-plaintiff and a fuller (two-line) denial by the eye-defendant represent a turning away from *mortal war* to pacific legal means. A six-line jury trial (the impaneling and verdict-determining take four lines, the rendered verdict two) opens out yet further into distributive justice. We sense a rabbit-out-of-the-hat preciosity in the last three lines, when they are read as legal verdict, as a solution on the verbal level. But like most of Shakespeare's lines in the *Sonnets,* they can also be read as self-discovery: the eye is as clear as the heart is dear, and as *heart* and *part* rhyme in Q_3, *part* and *heart,* in an "illegal" couplet repetition of the same rhyme, seal the chiastic pact. The defensible wish to deny that the eye plays any part in love, to assert that love is entirely the heart's doing, is set gently aside: the heart must be satisfied that it can claim a part, but only a part, in love. The eye owns beauty. The heart owns reciprocity.

The fact that this sonnet, like its sequel, is addressed to the beloved, means that its narrative conceals a veiled plea for love. In purporting *to di-*

vide the conquest of thy sight, it in fact requests the bestowal of that precious sight, with its attendant beauty of countenance and warmth of love. The poem is a bagatelle to amuse, with its toy *mortal war*, but also an invitation, a beckoning, a claim of *Hertzrecht*.

A few technical points. Sonnets 46 and 47 share three rhyme-words: *sight*, *part*, and *heart*, and share *eye* and *heart* in their respective Couplet Ties, reinforcing their conceptual connections.

I do not believe that the phrases *thou in him dost lie* and *thy fair appearance lies* (46, lines 5, 8) contain a pun (*lie* = "prevaricate"). The poem makes no sense as a whole when "prevaricate" is substituted in these lines. I believe puns need to be able to be inserted intelligibly in *the meaning of the whole poem* to be credible. This poem presumes the knowability and reliability of the *inward love of heart*, and does not raise the question of the visage's potential falsity. I think 46 and 47 are both early sonnets, perhaps even antedating the acquaintance with the young man. They would do as pretty compliments composed by any young versifier. This sonnet naturally possesses two KEY WORDS.

KEY WORDS: EYE [-S] [-'S]
HEART

Couplet Tie: *eye* [-*s*] [-'*s*] (1, 3, 4, 6, 12, 13)
heart (1, 3, 4, 5, 10, 12, 14, 14)
part (12, 13)
right (4, 14)

47

Betwixt mine eye and heart a league is tooke,
And each doth good turnes now vnto the other,
When that mine eye is famisht for a looke,
Or heart in loue with sighes himselfe doth smother;
With my loues picture then my eye doth feast,
And to the painted banquet bids my heart:
An other time mine eye is my hearts guest,
And in his thoughts of loue doth share a part.
So either by thy picture or my loue,
Thy seife away, are present still with me,
For thou nor farther then my thoughts canst moue,
And I am still with them, and they with thee.
Or if they sleepe, thy picture in my sight
Awakes my heart, to hearts and eyes delight.

Betwixt mine eye and heart a league is took,
And each doth good turns now unto the other:
When that mine eye is famished for a look,
Or heart in love with sighs himself doth smother,
With my love's picture then my eye doth feast,
And to the painted banquet bids my heart;
Another time mine eye is my heart's guest,
And in his thoughts of love doth share a part.
So either by thy picture or my love,
Thyself, away, are present still with me,
For thou not farther than my thoughts canst move,
And I am still with them, and they with thee;
Or if they sleep, thy picture in my sight
Awakes my heart to heart's and eye's delight.

THE Couplet Tie in 47 is threefold, and tells of the *league* between the formerly warring parties: *heart, eye, picture.* As the enacting of reciprocal *good turns* between eye and heart takes place, a species of cross-minuet of mutual courtesies is danced:

	WHEN	
eye is famished (line 3)	or	heart smothers self in sighs (line 4)
	THEN [GOOD TURNS]	
BY EYE		BY HEART
eye feasts and bids heart to picture-banquet (lines 5–6)	or	eye is heart's guest and shares his thoughts of love (lines 7–8)

The recitation of alternating *good turns* has obscured the fact that this is actually a second-person, not a third-person, poem. The octave-minuet is actually a claim on the absent beloved. The league betwixt eye and heart is, it seems, a league to capture the beloved in perpetuity, even in his absence. In Q_3, a second minuet, by which either eye or heart always has the beloved in view, succeeds the first:

	SO	
	either by	
(EYE) thy picture	or	(HEART) my love
	thyself away art present thou canst not move farther than	
		my thoughts (I with them, they with thee)

The air of triumphant success in maintaining possession of the beloved, directly attributable to the minuet of courtesy between eye and heart, is a mask for the desolation of absence. The eye is famished for a look; the abandoned heart is smothering himself in sighs. Starvation and asphyxia are the diagnosis: the starving, asphyxiated speaker is offering himself a painted banquet. The enameled Midas-replica of true possession offered by the *painted banquet,* repeated in the couplet's *picture,* haunts the pretended double delight of the close.

The anomalous structural division (2-6-4-2) "frames" the two minuets fore and aft. The absence of both *eye* and *heart* in Q_3, given their insistent presence in the other three parts of the sonnet, is arresting, as the speaker attempts to reintegrate his hitherto separate faculties of seeing and loving into a single self *(me, I)*, and to reintegrate the fragmented beloved, too, into a single manifestation *(thyself, thou, thee)*. This hope for a true reciprocity *(I, thou)* disappears as the couplet once again stylizes the beloved as *thy picture*, and divides the speaker again into his aspects *(my sight, my heart)*, relinquishing the personal pronoun.

DEFECTIVE KEY WORDS: HEART (missing in Q_3)
EYE (missing in Q_3)

Couplet Tie: *heart* (1, 4, 6, 7, 14, 14)
eye (1, 3, 5, 7, 14)
picture (5, 9, 13)

48

HOw carefull was I when I tooke my way,
Each trifle vnder trueſt barres to thruſt,
That to my vſe it might vn-vſed ſtay
From hands of falſehood,in ſure wards of truſt?
But thou,to whom my iewels trifles are,
Moſt worthy comfort,now my greateſt griefe,
Thou beſt of deereſt,and mine onely care,
Art left the prey of euery vulgar theefe.
Thee haue I not lockt vp in any cheſt,
Saue where thou art not,though I feele thou art,
Within the gentle cloſure of my breſt,
From whence at pleaſure thou maiſt come and part,
And euen thence thou wilt be ſtolne I feare,
For truth prooues theeuiſh for a prize ſo deare.

How careful was I, when I took my way,
Each trifle under truest bars to thrust,
That to my use it might unusèd stay
From hands of falsehood, in sure wards of trust!
But thou, to whom my jewels trifles are,
Most worthy comfort, now my greatest grief,
Thou best of dearest, and mine only care,
Art left the prey of every vulgar thief.
Thee have I not locked up in any chest,
Save where thou art not, though I feel thou art,
Within the gentle closure of my breast,
From whence at pleasure thou mayst come and part;
And even thence thou wilt be stol'n, I fear,
For truth proves thievish for a prize so dear.

To a modern reader following Shakespeare's sequence, the comparatively direct utterance of sonnet 48 perhaps comes as a relief after the elaborate court-conceits of 46 and 47. The initial conceit of 48—about keeping the beloved from being stolen—is reconceptualized at the close, and thereby put into question. The opening conceit says, "The world is full of thieves with hands of falsehood, and therefore when a person goes away he must lock up his valuables. I did lock up my goods, including even my trifles. But I did not lock up thee, my treasure, except in the open closure of my breast, where thou art free to come and go. I am therefore afraid some thief will steal thee." But the couplet opens a new abysmal possibility. Ordinary thieves are not the only danger; every passerby, no matter how honest, turns thief for a prize as valuable as the beloved. When truth's very self turns thievish, the whole world becomes corrupt. The first conceit—fear that the beloved will prove unfaithful—has been displaced by the more acceptable fear that the beloved will be stolen, if not by a "vulgar thief" then by an honest-man-turned-thief-by-desire.

As shown in the diagram, the poem is organized as a small hierarchical comparative narrative with two pasts (one referring to jewels, one to the beloved), two presents (with the same reference), and three envisaged futures. The paradox by which less valuable things are locked up, while the most valuable possession is left unguarded, and may or may not continue to reside within the breast's closure, seems at first the motivating drama of the poem. Will the unfettered beloved *come* or *part?* This question seems to offer anxiety enough. But then, the couplet's yawning possibility of absolutely universal crime casts the previous restricted fear of *hands of falsehood* and *vulgar thie[ves]* into a totalizing fear of every passerby, no matter how upright. The *truest* bars themselves are untrustworthy when truth proves thievish. It is no accident that the Couplet Tie consists of *dear*, *true*, and *thief.* The confusions of the present-tense moment—*now* my greatest grief; *thou art left; thou art not; thou art*—give plausibility to the reluctant prophecy, *thou wilt be stol'n.*

Structure of Sonnet 48

Past	*Present*
I locked up my valuables in a chest (lines 1–4)	My valuables are safe from false hands (line 4)
I did not lock up my best jewel (lines 5–8)	You are prey of every vulgar thief (line 8)
I "locked" you safe in my breast (line 11)	You may come and part thence (line 12)

Future
Valuables will stay unused for my use (line 3)
You may come and part (line 12)
You will be stolen by corrupted truth (lines 13-14)

The specter of the beloved's infidelity is so inadmissible that the speaker would rather believe all the honest people of the world to be thieves rather than believe the beloved capable of parting from him. Anxiety permeates the self-reproachful lines, *How careful was I; But thou . . . art left the prey; And even thence thou wilt be stol'n.*

The rhythmic motion of lines 11–12 (representing the beloved in the breast's closure) is more equable than the motion of the other lines. Lines 11–12 are true undisturbed pentameters, and resemble each other rhythmically except for the penultimate foot:

Within	the gentle	closure	of my	breast
From whence	at pleasure	thou mayst	come and	part

The simple rocking heartbeat of these lines—portraying an ideal and unpossessive love-relation—stands in sharp contrast to the more agitated and caesura-split rhythms preceding and following. The confident semantic antithesis, "*From* hands of *false*hood / *in* sure wards of *trust*," is destroyed by the closing adage, as *truth* puns on the past *truest* and on *trust:* "For *truth* proves *thievish* for a prize so dear." (Cf. *Venus and Adonis*, line

724: "Rich preys make true-men thieves.") Phonetically speaking, the sonnet is bound together by all the words closing in *st: truest, thrust, trust, most, greatest, best, dearest, chest, breast, mayst.* And, in a chain of significant words, we find *truest* → *thrust* → *trust* → *truth*, rising to the final dismantling, in line 14, of the concept of anything lastingly true.

Couplet Tie: *dear* [-*est*] (8, 14)
true [-*st*], *trust, truth* (2, 4, 14)
thief [*thievish*] (8, 14)

49

AGainſt that time (if euer that time come)
When I ſhall ſee thee frowne on my defects,
When as thy loue hath caſt his vtmoſt ſumme,
Cauld to that audite by aduiſ'd reſpects,
Againſt that time when thou ſhalt ſtrangely paſſe,
And ſcarcely greete me with that ſunne thine eye,
When loue conuerted from the thing it was
Shall reaſons finde of ſetled grauitie.
Againſt that time do I inſconce me here
Within the knowledge of mine owne deſart,
And this my hand, againſt my ſelfe vpreare,
To guard the lawfull reaſons on thy part,
To leaue poore me, thou haſt the ſtrength of lawes,
Since why to loue, I can alledge no cauſe.

Against that time (if ever that time come)
When I shall see thee frown on my deféct,
Whenas thy love hath cast his utmost sum,
Called to that audit by advised respects;
Against that time when thou shalt strangely pass,
And scarcely greet me with that sun thine eye,
When love converted from the thing it was
Shall reasons find of settled gravity:
Against that time do I insconce me here
Within the knowledge of mine own desert,
And this my hand against myself uprear,
To guard the lawful reasons on thy part:
To leave poor me thou hast the strength of laws,
Since why to love I can allege no cause.

HERE we find a series of delaying protases:

Q_1: *Against that time*
(if ever that time come)
when I shall see thee frown
whenas thy love has cast . . . sum

Q_2: *Against that time* *when thou shalt strangely pass*
and
scarcely greet me
when love . . . shall reasons find

Q_3: *Against that time* *do I insconce me here*
and uprear this my hand against myself.

This entire picture—"I here and now uprear my hand against myself (become my own enemy, taking your part), endorsing your right to leave me whenever you cease to love me"—is an apotropaic charm, meant, by mentioning the unspeakable, to prevent it from happening. But the speaker's expert delineation of the phases of potential repudiation—the beloved's frown, the withdrawal of credit, the taking stock, the cold greeting, the phlegmatic indifference—suggests that repudiation has already been fearfully observed. The hypothetical *against* and *if ever* are ways of avoiding saying that the dreaded time has already come; but we read behind the words to the existence of the cold distance already noticed. Cordelia's "no cause" is anticipated in the close, but in the sonnet it is abject rather than noble. The Couplet Tie opposes *love* to *law* [*-s*] [*-ful*], including the pun in *allege.*

The beloved's former *love* has decomposed verbally into *leave* and *laws;* and we witness the awful descent from *love* through the declension *frown, cast . . . utmost sum, audit, strangely pass, scarcely greet me,* and *shall reasons find of . . . gravity,* all the way to *leave. Leave* has an odd plausibility as an imagined past tense of *love,* as if by a spiritual vowel-shift (cf. also 73 and 87). The commercial and legal vocabularies here, as elsewhere, have always been noticed, and serve as implicit reproach, despite the exonerating rhetoric of *no cause.*

The moments of greatest pathos occur in lines 6–7, as we notice that the formulation is not the one which would give primacy to fact—[*greet me with thine eye (that sun)*]—but rather one giving primacy to feeling: *greet me with that sun (thine eye).* We also remark in the octave the most conspicuous figure in all of Shakespeare's repertoire—the figure of "words fail me," a symptom of overmastering emotion: *when love, converted from* ——— *?* In place of the dash, the speaker helplessly inserts a place-marker for ineffability, *the thing it was.*

Couplet Tie: *law* [*-s*] [*-ful*] [*al-*]*lege* (12, 13, 14)
love (3, 7, 14)

50

HOw heauie doe I iourney on the way,
When what I ſeeke (my wearie trauels end)
Doth teach that eaſe and that repoſe to ſay
Thus farre the miles are meaſurde from thy friend.
The beaſt that beares me,tired with my woe,
Plods duly on,to beare that waight in me,
As if by ſome inſtinct the wretch did know
His rider lou'd not ſpeed being made from thee:
The bloody ſpurre cannot prouoke him on,
That ſome-times anger thruſts into his hide,
Which heauily he anſwers with a grone,
More ſharpe to me then ſpurring to his ſide,
For that ſame grone doth put this in my mind,
My greefe lies onward and my ioy behind.

How heavy do I journey on the way,
When what I seek (my weary travel's end)
Doth teach that ease and that repose to say,
"Thus far the miles are measured from thy friend."
The beast that bears me, tirèd with my woe,
Plods dully on, to bear that weight in me,
As if by some instínct the wretch did know
His rider loved not speed being made from thee:
The bloody spur cannot provoke him on,
That sometimes anger thrusts into his hide,
Which heavily he answers with a groan,
More sharp to me than spurring to his side;
For that same groan doth put this in my mind:
My grief lies onward and my joy behind.

ANOTHER set (like 44–45, 46–47) of paired sonnets, 50–51 are about the speaker on horseback. In the first, the speaker is carried away from the beloved; in the second, he envisages his return. Sonnet 50 is one of those organized by a KEY WORD—here, the emblematically suitable word of forward progress, ON. The Couplet Tie is *groan.* "Onward with a groan" sums up the poem, and the horse's *groan* reminds Shakespeare that ***grief*** lies ***onward:***

> How heavy do I journey *on* . . . .
> The beast plods dully *on* . . . .
> The spur cannot provoke him *on,*
> My grief lies *on*ward.

Horse and master are twinned:

> I journey *heavy*
> he answers *heavily*
>
> [his] groan is more sharp *to me*
> than [my] spurring is *to his side*
>
> [my] *weary* travel
> the beast, *tirèd*

A weary quatrain for the rider; a weary quatrain for the horse (I accept the emendation of *duly* to *dully,* making a connection to the *dull bearer* of 51); and a third quatrain divided between the speaker's attack on his horse and the horse's replying groan of pain. The speaker's suppressed anger at his banishment from the beloved's presence breaks forth in a cruel angry spurring of the steed. Even the horse's pathetic groan cannot dislodge the rider's obsession; the horse's quasi-human groan from his bloodied side reminds the speaker not of the animal's pain nor of his own cruelty, but only, yet once again, of his distance from the beloved. The depression of the journey is relieved only by the anger released against the horse, but it soon relapses, via the horse's groan, into the same dull plodding onward.

The repetitive phonemes—*miles/measured*, *beast/bears*, *woe/weight*, *speed/spur*, *anger/answers*, *groan/grief*—register the "sheer plod" (Hopkins) of the lines. Nowhere is the obsessiveness of love better exemplified in the *Sonnets* than in the speaker's response to his bloodied horse's groan. He feels a sharp pang, but not for the horse; all that the horse's pain means to him is a reminder that further pain is in store for himself. We are meant, I think, to wince at this tenacity in private grief in the presence of the horse's pain.

KEY WORD: ON

Couplet Tie: *groan* (11, 13)
on (1, 6, 9, 14)

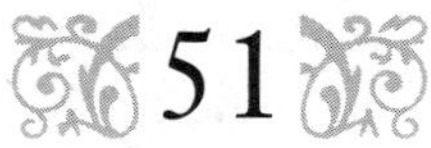

51

THus can my loue excuſe the ſlow offence,
Of my dull bearer,when from thee I ſpeed,
From where thou art,why ſhoulld I haſt me thence,
Till I returne of poſting is noe need.
O what excuſe will my poore beaſt then find,
When ſwift extremity can ſeeme but ſlow,
Then ſhould I ſpurre though mounted on the wind,
In winged ſpeed no motion ſhall I know,
Then can no horſe with my deſire keepe pace,
Therefore deſire(of perfects loue being made)
Shall naigh noe dull fleſh in his fiery race,
But loue,for loue,thus ſhall excuſe my iade,
    Since from thee going,he went wilfull ſlow,
    Towards thee ile run,and giue him leaue to goe.

Thus can my love excuse the slow offence
Of my dull bearer, when from thee I speed:
From where thou art, why should I haste me thence?
Till I return, of posting is no need.
O what excuse will my poor beast then find,
When swift extremity can seem but slow?
Then should I spur though mounted on the wind,
In wingèd speed no motion shall I know:
Then can no horse with my desire keep pace;
Therefore desire (of perfects love being made)
Shall weigh no dull flesh in his fiery race,
But love, for love, thus shall excuse my jade:
    Since from thee going he went wilful slow,
    Towards thee I'll run, and give him leave to go.

SONNET 51 is sometimes emended in line 10 from *perfects* to *perfect'st*, and in line 11 from *neigh* (printed *naigh* in the 1609 quarto) to *weigh* or *rein*. The difficulty in conjecturing the second emendation arises from the only vaguely specified relations between the speaker, his erotic desire, a wingèd Pegasus-steed, and love. I do not accept the emendation to *perfect'st* (see below). The second crux may be insoluble, but I prefer *weigh*, since I believe the import of the inserted word should be "employ"; the rider needs to mount no dull horseflesh, since his desire alone will convey him more rapidly. Compare the use of *weight* in 50.

The sonnet shares a number of words with its preceding brother, 50: *speed*, *dull* (providing one accepts, as I do, the emendation in 50 of *duly* to *dully*), *bear*, *spur*, *beast*, and *weigh/weight*, if one emends *naigh* to *weigh*. And it uses as its Couplet Tie two markers reminiscent of the previous poem: *from thee* and *slow*. I think Shakespeare in fact intends 51 to have SLOW as its KEY WORD: *slow* appears as itself in Q_1, Q_2, and C, and appears (in the Quarto spelling) in abbreviated nonphonetic form in Q_3 as "perfectS LOve" (this graphic appearance of "slo" provides my argument for not emending line 10). SLO in line 10, as KEY WORD, is reminiscent of LIV in "obLIVious" as KEY WORD in 55 *(Not marble)*. See Evans for examples of "perfectest" spelled "perfects."

The conceptual pretext for sonnet 51 is that the *slow pace* of the rider's horse requires *excuse*—forgiveness or apology (the word *excuse* appears in each of the three quatrains). The performative act of excusing (releasing) a horse from performing a service appears conceptually in the couplet, making this an example of a sonnet organized around a DEFECTIVE KEY WORD *(excuse)* which in the couplet eliminates itself in favor of a synonymous performative act—verbally the horse will be *given leave to go*, or "excused" in another, punning sense. The horse is relieved of the obligation to serve, since his master has chosen to run instead of ride. There is a peculiar insistence on the word and phoneme *no*, as well; it appears in *no need, no motion, I [k]no[w], no horse, no dull flesh;* this may have given credence among editors to the suitability of *neigh* (nay), another play (like *know*) on the negative. The long *o* of *no* is reiterated in the triple use of *slow*, twice in the rhyme position, the second time "illegally" *(slow, know, slow, go)*, and in the presence of *motion* and *going*.

There is in the couplet an air of speciously triumphant demonstration, as though the speaker has (eureka!) solved the initial problem of "excusing" the jade. This air derives from the chain of logical and temporal signifiers—*thus, when, then, when, then, then, therefore, but, thus, since*—surrounding the narrative. In fact, the whole "problem" of how to excuse the horse is of course a pretext for the central demonstration of passionate desire to see the beloved again—a desire to which a slow jade is impossibly inadequate. Even the wind itself is too slow a horse for this rider ("then should I *spur though mounted on the wind*"), and Pegasus himself in full flight would seem immobile *([even] in wingèd speed no motion shall I know).* Since even the best horse, the *swift extremity* of the wind, or Pegasus' self *can seem but slow* matched with the desiring speed of thought, the speaker's love will dispense with any mount whatsoever, and haste to the beloved via the speedy foot of internal desire. By choosing to *run* toward the beloved, the speaker can dismiss (or "excuse") the horse—can give him *leave to go.* (The horse presumably learned his willful slowness in his former reluctant departure from the beloved.)

The poem is divided into two phases—going *from* thee and returning *to* thee:

From thee (four lines)	*To thee* (ten lines)
from thee } lines 1–3	return } lines 4–12
from thee } line 13	towards thee } line 14

A map of this sort reveals how much the poem is focused on the *To thee* moment of return. The whole is an elaborate compliment, which emphasizes the speaker's fiery desire to return by remarking that even the horse was reluctant to depart from the beloved and by noting its obvious inadequacy to the speed of desire. Since even the wind, even Pegasus, would be an inadequate steed, the poor ordinary *jade* can be excused or dismissed with good will. He is given leave to go with a humorous compliment on his previous sympathetic enactment, at the time of the original departure, of his master's unwillingness to depart. The speed of *desire's* fiery race (the word *race* meaning "movement," not "lineage") makes it practical in "perfectest love" to run rather than to ride. The amusement of writing the poem, for a poet, lies in drawing the comic disproportion between the impetus of desire and any and all physical means to its accomplishment. Even magical means (riding wingèd Pegasus, using the wind as a mount) would seem slow to desire. The foil-vehicle for the hyperbolic valuation of desire is the inept jade, and the comic strategies include the joke on the (absent) fourth *excuse* (*leave* is substituted), the joke on the (present) fourth *slow (slo)*, and the jokes on *know* (and perhaps *neigh* if the word is not emended) as "synonyms" for the repeated word *no.*

I find *neigh* unconvincing not only because of the appalling sound made in reading it aloud by those who have recorded the *Sonnets,* but because the analogue that some editors offer from *Venus and Adonis* has to do, after all, with a stallion's mounting a mare, and not with "perfectest love," a Platonic phrase. Desire, by definition here, is bodiless fire (sonnet 45), and a bodiless quality cannot "neigh," a severely flesh-bound verb.

KEY WORD:	SLOW [SLO]
DEFECTIVE KEY WORD:	EXCUSE (missing in C, except conceptually as *leave to go*)
Couplet Tie:	*slow* [*slo*] (1, 6, 10, 13) *from thee* (2, 13)

52

So am I as the rich whose blessed key,
Can bring him to his sweet vp-locked treasure,
The which he will not eu'ry hower suruay,
For blunting the fine point of seldome pleasure.
Therefore are feasts so sollemne and so rare,
Since sildom comming in the long yeare set,
Like stones of worth they thinly placed are,
Or captaine Iewells in the carconet.
So is the time that keepes you as my chest,
Or as the ward-robe which the robe doth hide,
To make some speciall instant speciall blest,
By new vnfoulding his imprison'd pride.
   Blessed are you whose worthinesse giues skope,
   Being had to tryumph, being lackt to hope.

So am I as the rich whose blessèd key
Can bring him to his sweet up-lockèd treasure,
The which he will not ev'ry hour survey,
For blunting the fine point of seldom pleasure.
Therefore are feasts so solemn and so rare,
Since, seldom coming, in the long year set,
Like stones of worth they thinly placèd are,
Or captain jewels in the carcanet.
So is the time that keeps you as my chest,
Or as the ward-robe which the robe doth hide,
To make some special instant special blest,
By new unfolding his imprisoned pride.
   Blessèd are you whose worthiness gives scope,
   Being had to triumph, being lacked to hope.

AFTER the high artifice of the horse sonnets (comparable to the high artifice of the eye/heart sonnets), a moment of plain speaking is as welcome in 52 as it was in 48. It appears to me that this is one of the sonnets (like 51, with the joke on *slo[w]*, or 55, with the joke on ***live*** in ***oblivi****ous*) having a KEY WORD which is obvious in three units of the poem, but is "hiding out" in the fourth. That word in 52 is *blessèd* (Q_1, Q_3 [*blest*], and C), replaced by its near homophone *placèd* in Q_2. The line in which *placèd* appears could as easily have rhymed, "like stones of worth they thinly do appear" (for example), but the presence of the inverted verb *placèd are* suggests an intended phonetic correspondence with *blessèd.* There is in 52 another visible play on words: the speaker refers to *the ward-robe which the robe doth hide*—the word *robe* is literally hidden inside the word *ward-robe* (Q spelling).

This poem is a rationalization for the all-too-rare meetings between the speaker and the beloved. We suspect—and our suspicion is confirmed by the end of the poem—that the speaker can do nothing but helplessly wait for these occasions of joy, granted only rarely by the beloved.

The sonnet exposes its truth gradually, through its similes. In the first, the speaker compares himself to a rich man who deliberately rations his glimpses of his treasure, so as not to blunt *the fine point of seldom pleasure.* This aesthetic refinement and voluntary control animate, too, a simile in the second quatrain: a jeweler, the speaker explains, places his stones of worth or *captain jewels* at some distance from each other in the carcanet, so that each may be separately prized. However, this simile is attached to another analogy, that of the feasts of the liturgical or civic year. The feasts come *seldom* (an adverb harking back to the earlier adjectival "*seldom* pleasure"). They arrive predictably but cannot be commanded at will; in this they are unlike the rich man's viewings of his treasure. On the other hand, feasts are also said to be *set* and *placèd* in the year, in the same way that jewels are distributed in the carcanet. This suggests that someone once had voluntary control over their original placement, but it is certainly not their present celebrants, who rather must await (at Christmas, at Easter) their coming. Rich man and jeweler are in control; the celebrant of the occasional feast in the *long* year is not. In the third quatrain, this uncertainty between predictable awaiting and complete controlling is tilted in favor of helpless and unpredictable waiting. Time is the chest that keeps the jewel, or the wardrobe (room, "garderobe") that conceals the robe: only at Time's pleasure is the *imprisoned pride* revealed. The *sweet up-lockèd treasure* is indeed under lock and key; yet it is not the speaker who owns the key, as we thought in Q_1, but rather Time, *the time that keeps you.* The last line swiftly sums up the only two possibilities—possession or lack. *Treasure* causes *triumph;* lack gives *scope* only to *hope.*

The gradual fading of the original rush of joy—*So am I as the rich*—is enacted in the increasing verbal distance to be covered before one attains the desired object: we go, in fact, from possession to lack, from—in the last line—triumph to (forlorn) hope. The Couplet Tie, reflecting that hope, consists of *blessèd* [*placèd*] and *worth* [*-iness*]. The bifurcated couplet shifts emphasis away from concentration on the speaker's feelings to the *blessèd* worth of the person (anticipated by *treasure, feasts, stones of worth, jewels, robe*). One may see this swerve from speaker to object as a defense against naming the unnameable possibility of total loss—a fourth possibility never named in the poem but easily extrapolated from the increasingly fearful possibilities that *are* given:

1. Seeing at will: rich man's key; treasure and triumph
2. Seeing on schedule: (predictable) feasts; joy
3. Seeing at whim of time: luck, hope
4. ?

The missing fourth possibility is "Never seeing again at all." The shift of agency from *I*—*So am I as the rich*—to *you*—*Blessèd are you*—leaves open item 4, total separation, as a "ghost" behind the couplet officially endorsing hope.

KEY WORD: BLESSÈD [BLEST] [PLACÈD]

Couplet Tie: *blessèd* [*blest*] [*placèd*] (1, 7, 11, 13)
worth [*-iness*] (7, 13)

53

VV Hat is your ſubſtance, whereof are you made,
That millions of ſtrange ſhaddowes on you tend?
Since euery one, hath euery one, one ſhade,
And you but one, can euery ſhaddow lend:
Deſcribe *Adonis* and the counterfet,
Is poorely immitated after you,
On *Hellens* cheeke all art of beautie ſet,
And you in *Grecian* tires are painted new:
Speake of the ſpring, and foyzon of the yeare,
The one doth ſhaddow of your beautie ſhow,
The other as your bountie doth appeare,
And you in euery bleſſed ſhape we know.
In all externall grace you haue ſome part,
But you like none, none you for conſtant heart.

What is your substance, whereof are you made,
That millions of strange shadows on you tend?
Since every one hath, every one, one shade,
And you, but one, can every shadow lend:
Describe Adonis, and the counterfeit
Is poorly imitated after you;
On Helen's cheek all art of beauty set,
And you in Grecian tires are painted new;
Speak of the spring and foison of the year:
The one doth shadow of your beauty show,
The other as your bounty doth appear,
And you in every blessèd shape we know.
In all external grace you have some part,
But you like none, none you, for constant heart.

THERE seems an arbitrary pattern in vowel/diphthong plus *n*—an/en/on/oun (eighteen such phonemes)—running through the poem, perhaps as a reflection of the *millions* of strange shadows cast by the object:

1. *-st**an**ce*
2. *-ions, on*
3. *one, one, one*
4. *one, l**en**d*
5. *-on-, -oun-*
7. *On Hel**en**'s*
9. *-on*
10. *one*
11. *-oun-*
14. *-one, -one, -onst**an**t*

The philosophical basis of the sonnet is drawn from the Platonic contrast between substance and appearance. Substance was conventionally considered to be simple and indivisible, a problem when appearance is multiple and contradictory. ("Or maybe substance can be composite," says Yeats in "A Bronze Head"; "Profound McTaggart thought so." Yeats's poem asks 53's question again, this time concerning Maud Gonne: "Which of her forms has shown her substance right?") What sort of substance can it be that can manifest itself in so many shapes? (According to Aristotle, substance confers form on matter.) The final quatrain-claim of 53, "You in *every* blessèd shape we know," allows for no exceptions, and this hyperbole is reiterated in the couplet opening: "In *all* external grace you have some part." This explains why the Couplet Tie should be the two words *you* and *all:* they sum up the claim.

The question of the first line—"What is your *sub-stance?*"—is answered in the last line: a "*con-stant* heart." This illogical paradox—"Though you cast millions of shadows, you do so because you have a faithful heart"—is the "scientific" explanation for the anomalous powers possessed by the beloved. The punning on *-stant* enables the passage from *substance* to *constant*, making the philosophical suggestion that ethics, rather than metaphysics, is the guarantee of formal stability.

On the other hand, although the poem appears at first to be about those anomalous powers, it turns out in fact to be about the perceiver of those powers. That is, the poem is about the speaker more than about the beloved. Although the poem first gives active agency to the young man—"you can lend every shadow"—it passes to a generalized mental hypothesis—[Let anyone] *Describe Adonis, and the counterfeit / Is poorly imitated after you*—and ends with the active agency of the perceiver—"We know you in every blessèd shape." And the very last statement is a remark by the speaker about how he perceives other people: "none [are] like you for constant heart."

Probably the easiest way to perceive the motive underlying this structure is to track the implied state of the speaker. As I see it, the closing line is propitiatory—the speaker hopes, by uttering praise of a putative "constant heart," to bring about the very fidelity he praises but which he fears is not to be found in the young man. The captivating variety in the appearances of the beloved suggests that millions of adorers may hover about him together with his millions of seductive shadows. The beloved has an androgynous beauty that is as suitable to a portrait of Helen as to a portrait of Adonis, thus doubling the potential number of his admirers.

In the series of neutral hypotheses of representation—*describe* Adonis, *set* out on Helen's cheek, *speak* of spring and harvest—we recognize things that Shakespeare (or Marlowe) has already done. The writer-in-love writes a poem about Adonis, and behold, the fictive Adonis turns out to look exactly like the actual beloved; the playwright adorns his portrait of Helen, and behold, Helen uncannily resembles the beloved; the speaker looks at spring flowers and will say to his beloved, *They were but sweet, but figures of delight, / Drawn after you, you pattern of all those* (98); he speaks of harvest, and it becomes the beloved's bounty (cf. *Antony*). In short, in every act of literary representation—mythical (Adonis), literary-historical (Helen), or natural (spring and harvest)—one has ended up, willy-nilly, representing the single beloved.

The experimental interest of this poem lies in part in its structure (which is repeated, more or less, in the following sonnet 54). Between the introduction (Q_1) detailing both the centripetal attraction *(tend)* and the centrifugal powers *(lend)* of the beloved, and the closing couplet explaining those powers, Shakespeare places the eight lines concerning representation *(describe, set, speak)*. This conceptual structure (4-8-2) is one of the more unusual ones in the *Sonnets*, violating as it does both the Italian structure (8–6) and the English structure (4-4-4-2). The central eight-line passage on representation has a nicely intricate bifurcation-structure of its own:

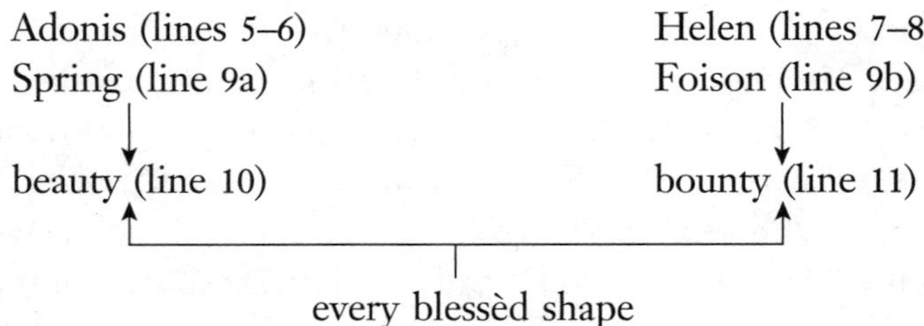

On the left we have Adonis, on the right we have Helen; on the left we have spring, on the right, autumn. Left, beauty; right, bounty: *every*where we recognize you. This is a structure that confers an appropriate left-right gestural omnipresence, rather than an unfolding narrative temporality, on the philosophical question of multiple appearance.

KEY WORD: If one is prepared to find it orthographically hiding, as well as phonetically present, ONE [ON]: milliONs (2), ONE (4), AdONis (5), ON (7), foisON (9), ONE (10), nONE (14), cONstant (14).

Couplet Tie: *all* (7, 13)
one (3, 3, 3, 4, 10), ***none*** (14, 14)
art (7), *heart* (14)

54

OH how much more doth beautie beautious ſeeme,
By that ſweet ornament which truth doth giue,
The Roſe lookes faire, but fairer we it deeme
For that ſweet odor, which doth in it liue:
The Canker bloomes haue full as deepe a die,
As the perfumed tincture of the Roſes,
Hang on ſuch thornes, and play as wantonly,
When ſommers breath their masked buds diſcloſes:
But for their virtue only is their ſhow,
They liue vnwoo'd, and vnreſpected fade,
Die to themſelues. Sweet Roſes doe not ſo,
Of their ſweet deathes, are ſweeteſt odors made:
  And ſo of you, beautious and louely youth,
  When that ſhall vade, by verſe diſtils your truth.

O how much more doth beauty beauteous seem
By that sweet ornament which truth doth give!
The rose looks fair, but fairer we it deem
For that sweet odour which doth in it live.
The canker blooms have full as deep a dye
As the perfumèd tincture of the roses,
Hang on such thorns, and play as wantonly,
When summer's breath their maskèd buds discloses;
But for their virtue only is their show,
They live unwooed, and unrespected fade,
Die to themselves. Sweet roses do not so,
Of their sweet deaths are sweetest odours made:
  And so of you, beauteous and lovely youth,
  When that shall vade, my verse distils your truth.

BEAUTY has been a major component in the sequence beginning with the first sonnet, where we desire that *beauty's rose might never die. Beauty* has been thematized together with *truth* before (see sonnet 41), but in 41 *truth* means *troth*, and in (for example) 21, the truth in question *(true, truly)* belongs both to the writer's fidelity and to his veracity. In 41, *truth* and *beauty* were unproblematically linked as clear attributes of the beloved, just as *sweets and beauties* are linked as things of comparable worth in 12. Sonnet 54, however, is a dark reprise of sonnet 5, in which the distillation of perfume, used as a metaphor for reproduction, was predicated of all flowers:

> *. . . flowers distilled, though they with winter meet,*
> *Leese but their show; their substance still lives sweet.*

Shakespeare now divides the universal *flowers* of 5 into two subspecies: true *roses* (with odor) and *canker* roses (without), the first a source of distilled perfume, the second not. By a further symbolic elaboration, hue is equated with merely outward beauty, and organic *odour* (sweetness) with inner truth and substance. The Couplet Tie, naturally, consists of *beauty* and *truth.*

Truth here is not propositional truth, but rather what we would call virtue. Once truth and beauty have been conceptually separated, the possibility of representational falsity—the flower that looks like a real rose but isn't—enters the sequence, and will lead to other poems about deceived husbands, perjured eyes, and so on.

This sonnet sets the erotics of the eye against the erotics of the heart; and the deceiving eye is helplessly given the ravishing poetry. Before our eyes we see emblem-poetry metamorphosing into "naturalistic" poetry, as lines 1–4 (with their moralizing adage-plus-exemplum) yield to the astonishing eroticism of the wanton beauty of deep-dyed blooms. The identity-in-all-but-odor of the canker blooms with real roses means that the only words in Q_2 *not* belonging to both categories of roses are *canker, perfumèd*, and *tincture.* The effect of the passage with its "excessive" feminine rhyme is heady and disturbing, as it defends the swoon of the eye before the visual seduction of the canker blooms. The rather prim correction that follows in lines 9–10 suggests repression: it certainly has *not* occurred up till now in the poem that the canker blooms live unwooed. On the contrary, they have seduced the sight with their wanton play and deep-dyed hue. With *summer's breath* standing in, so to speak, for the missing odor, one could certainly woo and even succumb to the canker blooms.

After the sensuality of Q_2 the poem resumes its allegorical mode, enacting in verbals the logical downward slide of unreformed sinners:

> But for their virtue only is their show,
> they *live unwooed,*
> and *unrespected*
> *fade,*
> *Die.*

The contrast to this richly various "harlot's progress" of verbals is the adjectival but invariant endurance of *sweet roses* via the *sweetest odours* made from their *sweet deaths;* the adjectival repetition mimics the increasing concentration of distillation. (Cf. 67–69 for related themes of substance and show.)

It is the undeniability of visual beauty that gives it its aesthetic force. Shakespeare never even hints that the beauty of the beloved might not be universally acknowledged: on the contrary. There is no allowance for an alternate ideal of beauty, or, later, for a dissent from the speaker's condemnatory verdict. As roses are universally admired, so, says Shakespeare, is human beauty; it is instantly recognizable and without exception powerful. The canker bloom is, however, not precisely analogous to human corruption, in that the roses' lack of odor immediately betrays that their "show" is all they have to offer. Sight confronted by roses may be briefly misled—and how seductively that brief misleading moment is described!—but the distinction between canker blooms and "real" roses is not only soon perceived, it is already known, horticulturally speaking. However, no such anterior scientific knowledge or immediate sense-perception warns those who approach a beautiful (but faithless) human being; and the rage of the deceived lover breaks out in many later sonnets, especially in those closing the Dark Lady sequence (e.g., 147):

> *For I have sworn thee fair, and thought thee bright,*
> *Who art as black as hell, as dark as night.*

The major theme of the sonnets, more powerful even than the themes of friendship, love, death, and time, is the deception purveyed by appearance. The Elizabethan consciousness of appearance (supported by sumptuary laws, patronage, attendants, ritual, glorification of power by commissioned artworks, etc.) entails an equal consciousness of dis-appearance, as in Lear's disrobings, but also entails an especially acute consciousness of appearance as dis-guise. The parable of the wolf in sheep's clothing (the folk allegory of false guise) will appear in sonnet 96; and it is here, in the canker blooms of sonnet 54, that this rich vein of the imagery of deception is fully opened. Later in the sequence, the images will become more galled, acerbic, hard-edged; but here the senses still swoon under the lavish spell of the canker blooms, even emerging briefly to defend their charm: the canker blooms, after all, *have full as deep a dye as . . . roses, hang on such thorns,* and *play as wantonly.* Who could be blamed for yielding to them? The touch of genius comes in the brief ascription to the canker blooms of a borrowed sweet odor: *[they] play as wantonly / When summer's breath their maskèd buds discloses.* Summer's "honey" breath (as it is called in 65) momentarily sweetens the canker blooms by borrowing for its lines the very sound of the rose's perfume (the *k*-sound of the preceding *tincture*) in *maskèd* and *discloses.* Early on, the poem had represented its own confusion between canker roses and real roses by melding their naming sounds:

the ***canker blooms***	***perfum****èd* ***ti****n****ct****ū****re***
k nker b oom	*er ūm nk ūr*

Now, as the summer's breath does duty for the (missing) perfumèd tincture, the shared *canker/tincture k*-sound reappears in *discloses* and *maskèd,* with overtones of *damasked* (used of "real" roses in 130).

If we return to the compositional problem of the sonnet—how to use the "drier" language of moral discourse against the sheer onslaught of sensual seduction—we see that the sensual language of the canker blooms' appeal is allowed to return, but in a morally directed way, in the appeal to distillation with its triple *sweet.* Real roses are sweet in life, sweet in death, and sweetest in their posthumous existence as perfume. However, this moral sweetness of odor has absolutely no visual appeal, and we lose the deep dye, the wanton play, the disclosèd buds of visuality. Can ravishing beauty be well-lost for invisible odor? Is virtue as appealing as—more appealing than—heartstopping beauty?

The poem reaches its honesty about distilled odor-sans-beauty gradually. The speaker first envisages truth/odor as something added to beauty, an *ornament* which confers a *more,* a comparative degree, on beauty in the positive degree, the addition being enacted by the doubling of the word *beauty:* "O how much *more* doth *beauty beauteous* seem!"

We proceed with "that sweet *ornament* which truth doth give": truth is an ornamental addition. Next, to the visual fairness of the rose is added (by the second comparative, *fair . . . fairer*) the increment of *sweet odour;* odor is here a contributor to superior fairness, and the speaker proposes that moral goodness is itself an aesthetic intensifier:

The rose looks fair, but *fairer* we it deem
For that *sweet odour* which doth in it live.

The small life history of the canker rose, ending in its unrespected death, is given in the six and a half lines following. (This non-Italian, non-English structure—in which the most interesting part of the sonnet is a large central block flanked fore and aft by its preparatory and concluding material, will recall the structure of the preceding sonnet 53.) By introducing the fact of death in the emphatic reversed initial foot of line 11 *(Die to themselves),* the poem wipes out its entire initial comparative conceits, by which truth is something superadded to beauty, or a contributor toward it. When the positive degree of the canker rose, *(beauty, fair)* vanishes, the comparative degree *(more beauteous, fairer)* must vanish along with it.

The conceit must then be adjusted, and truth can no longer be seen as an *additive* to beauty. Instead, it is the constitutive *essence* of the (real) rose, whose visual beauty is now shown to be (in philosophical terms) mere accident rather than substance, *show,* not essence. Both beauty and odor are, in the language of the poem, *virtue* (i.e., power or strength); but the virtue of *show* is temporary, while the virtue of *substance* is permanent. The comparative degree of the earlier, erroneously predicated relation between beauty and truth—that truth is the comparative form of beauty, *more beauteous, fairer*—is replaced by the superlative degree in *sweetest:* odor-bearing roses are *sweet* (positive degree); their *sweet* deaths (playing a quasi-comparative transitional role) certainly yield *sweetest* odors, pure substance, all virtue—but can yield no visual pleasure. Truth, now, is definitively separable from the beauty of appearance, but not from a different, still aesthetic, gratification, that which is provided by a sweet (and lasting) odor. Shakespeare will not admit an unaesthetic "truth"; truth itself is always aesthetic.

We may expect this poem to end with an admonition to the beauteous youth: Live in such a manner that you may die a real rose and not a canker bloom. Instead, *truth* is predicated as already extant in the youth, and he is said to be already lovable ("beauteous *and lovely*": see OED definition 2). The canker roses, unlovable, are neither wooed, nor respected, nor partnered. The *lovely* young man is unlike them. The speaker relies on verse—which must, unlike painting, work with the invisible—to distill the *truth* of the young man when his *beauty* shall *vade* (a pun on the canker rose's *fade*). And yet, by splitting the youth's qualities into the two separable aspects, show and substance (*beauteous* and *lovely*), the poem, though preserving in him something distillable after beauty goes, endorses the essential separability of sensual eroticism from the devotion of true love, and maintains the perplexity with which it began. By rhyming *youth* and *truth*, the couplet attempts to affirm the identity of the two nouns—but the two separable adjectives *beauteous* and *lovely* impugn the effort. The major aesthetic effect of the sonnet is the reluctant relinquishing of the spectacularly visual language of aesthetic resonance in Q_2 in favor of the redundant and aesthetically inward language of invisible "sweetness." The language of moral virtue, in what we might call the Cordelia effect, renounces external aesthetic and linguistic *(sweet . . . sweet . . . sweetest)* variety.

I adopt *my* (in lieu of Q's *by*) in line 14 because outside agency is presumed in the distillation of line 12. (*By* implies that the young man's truth distills itself.)

Couplet Tie: *beauty* [*beauteous*] (1, 1, 13)
truth (2, 14)
fade [*vade*] (10, 14)

55

NOt marble, nor the guilded monument,
Of Princes ſhall out-liue this powrefull rime,
But you ſhall ſhine more bright in theſe contents
Then vnſwept ſtone, beſmeer'd with ſluttiſh time.
When waſtefull warre ſhall *Statues* ouer-turne,
And broiles roote out the worke of maſonry,
Nor *Mars* his ſword, nor warres quick fire ſhall burne:
The liuing record of your memory.
Gainſt death, and all obliuious emnity
Shall you pace forth, your praiſe ſhall ſtil finde roome,
Euen in the eyes of all poſterity
That weare this world out to the ending doome.
So til the iudgement that your ſelfe ariſe,
You liue in this, and dwell in louers eies.

Not marble nor the gilded monuments
Of princes shall outlive this pow'rful rhyme,
But you shall shine more bright in these conténts
Than unswept stone, besmeared with sluttish time.
When wasteful war shall statues overturn,
And broils root out the work of masonry,
Nor Mars his sword nor war's quick fire shall burn
The living record of your memory.
'Gainst death and all oblivious enmity
Shall you pace forth; your praise shall still find room
Even in the eyes of all posterity
That wear this world out to the ending doom.
So, till the Judgement that your self arise,
You live in this, and dwell in lovers' eyes.

ONE chief ingenuity of 55 lies in its bestowing grandeur on entities when they are connected to the beloved, but bestowing squalor on the very same entities when they are mentioned in connection with ordinary objects. Thus, in Q_1, memorial edifices are grand *marble* or *gilded monuments* when they are compared to the verse immortalizing the beloved, but when they are connected to *sluttish time* the very same splendid monuments become *unswept stone besmeared.* In Q_2 the same technique reappears: When battle occurs against the mortal monuments of princes, the conflict is represented as a vulgar one between low objects: *wasteful war* overturns (unelaborated) *statues; broils* root out the (laborer's) *work of masonry.* But when battle occurs against the young man's immortal verse-memorial, the foes are immediately ennobled and the memorial preserved: the earlier *wasteful war* becomes *war's quick fire* and the earlier *broils* become *Mars his sword,* while the verse becomes the sacred *living record of your memory.* The youth's nobility ennobles his contexts, by a beneficent moral contagion. The palpable scorn of the speaker in calling memorial monuments *unswept stone besmeared with sluttish time* and calling the agents destroying such monuments *wasteful war* and *root[ing] broils* raises by contrast the tone of adoration of the attempt to perpetuate the being of the young man, and even the tone of destructive conflict when it touches the young man.

The other chief ingenuity of the sonnet is the gradual transformation of a memorializing and commemorative impulse into a resurrective one. Does one perpetuate a memory, an image, or a person? Is it the record that lives, or the dead beloved *in propria persona?* It is no accident (this poem being about a record which will be read) that the Couplet Tie consists of *live* and *eyes.* This is, I believe, one of the sonnets composed around a KEY WORD, though at first the word—LIVE—seems absent in Q_3. It is visibly present in Q_1 ("outLIVE)," Q_2 ("LIVing") and C (LIVE); but it is not until we search Q_3, alerted by these precedents, that we find it hiding in "obLIVious"—one of Shakespeare's ingenious jokes. How does *liv*ing outwit ob*liv*ion? We can see a tension in Q_1 and Q_2 in the two formulations of the young man's survival: "*You shall shine in these conténts* more brightly"; "war shall not burn *the living record of your memory.*" These two formulations ask: Does the person [*you*] remain alive in the contents, or does only a record [*of your memory*] remain?

Q_3 offers a second set of formulations, revealing the same tension but in an acute fashion. No longer confined to *shin[ing] in these conténts*, the beloved—especially in the conspicuous enjambments—lives and moves:

> *'Gainst death and all oblivious enmity*
> *Shall you pace forth.*

On the other hand, posterity reads a written record: *Your praise shall . . . find room . . . in the eyes of all posterity.*

The couplet solves the tension by assigning "real" living to the day of the Last Judgment, when indeed all shall be raised incorruptible:

> So, till the Judgement that *your self arise*,
> You *live in this*, and *dwell* in lovers' eyes.

The inertness of *your memory* and *your praise* have both fallen away as modes of phrasing in favor of three active verbs: *till your self arise, you live, [you] dwell.* The intensive your *self* of the Last Judgment—your very self, your physical self—allows the subsequent *you/[you]* to take on various meanings: your mortal self, spiritual self, inscriptive self, verbal self. The hyperbolic claim of *pace forth* has been deferred to the *aris[ing]* of Judgment Day: even the somewhat less hyperbolic *shine bright* has been reduced to the more natural *live* and *dwell.* The hyperbolic audience of *all posterity* has been reduced to the more probable audience for sonnets, *lovers.* And the truth-claims for where the beloved will live are believable ones—*in* the rhyme, *in* the eyes of those reading it, *in* this, *in* lovers' eyes. Even the shades of final meaning are delicately drawn: you *live* (i.e., "are immortalized") in this, and *dwell* (i.e., "have a habitation," however temporary) in lovers' eyes. Whenever a Shakespearean hyperbole is allowed to dwindle down to a more modest formulation which counters the poet's compelling drive to contest time's power with emotional lies *('Gainst death . . . shall you pace forth)*, we are brought to admire the way in which a middle terrain is found that both emotionality and accuracy can inhabit.

The chiastic structure of the octave—noble contest : base contest :: base contest : noble contest—shows the initial wish for a noble lie against time, reasserted in the excesses of Q_3 with its *pace forth* and *all posterity.* It is not till the happy "solution" of the Last Judgment ("I don't have to keep him alive; God will do that for me") that the poet can temper his language to the level of modest truth.

KEY WORD: LIVE [outLIVE] [LIVING] [obLIVious]

Couplet Tie: *live* (2, 8, 9, 14)
eyes (11, 14)

56

Sweet loue renew thy force , be it not ſaid
Thy edge ſhould blunter be then apetite,
Which but too daie by feeding is alaied,
To morrow ſharpned in his former might.
So loue be thou,although too daie thou fill
Thy hungrie eies,euen till they winck with fulneſſe,
Too morrow ſee againe,and doe not kill
The ſpirit of Loue,with a perpetual dulneſſe:
Let this ſad *Intrim* like the Ocean be
Which parts the ſhore,where two contracted new,
Come daily to the banckes,that when they ſee:
Returne of loue,more bleſt may be the view.
  As cal it Winter,which being ful of care,
  Makes Sōmers welcome,thrice more wiſh'd,more rare:

Sweet love, renew thy force, be it not said
Thy edge should blunter be than appetite,
Which but today by feeding is allayed,
Tomorrow sharp'ned in his former might.
So, love, be thou: although today thou fill
Thy hungry eyes even till they wink with fullness,
Tomorrow see again, and do not kill
The spirit of love with a perpetual dullness:
Let this sad int'rim like the ocean be
Which parts the shore, where two contracted new
Come daily to the banks, that when they see
Return of love, more blest may be the view;
  As call it winter, which being full of care,
  Makes summer's welcome, thrice more wished, more rare.

WITH respect to the *sad int'rim* represented here, the octave stands for time *(today, tomorrow)*, and the third quatrain stands for space *(the ocean . . . which parts the shore)*. The couplet offers a mediating *tertium quid:* not the impossible succession of reassuringly identical days of love—*today, tomorrow*—prayed for in the octave, nor the desolate *daily* vacancy of the ocean endured in Q_3, but rather the succession of spacious contrasting seasons (*winter* followed by *summer*). The Couplet Tie is hopefully constituted of *fill* [*full, full*ness], *come* [wel*come*], and *more:* there is also a persistent repetition throughout the sonnet of the words *be* (*being* in the couplet) and *love*. "*Come, being, fill love* with *more*," is the message of the words reiterated in the couplet, reinforcing by repetition the import of the body of the sonnet. One can see BE as a KEY WORD.

The cause of the *sad int'rim* separating the lovers is not specified, but its result is a fear that love may have lost its force. This fear is (somewhat unbelievably) displaced from suspicion of the waning affection of the other onto the fidelity of the self. If physical appetite needs daily food, should love be any the less desirous? How can love lose its appetite? Can love-hunger become a *blunted edge?* (This odd connection—through the idea of *sharp[ness]*—of love-appetite to a knife with a potentially blunted edge turns up more mysteriously in 95.) These questions are those one asks when one has been deserted; they are asked normally of the absent other, not of the self. In addressing his own power to love as *sweet love*, the speaker can indirectly address the beloved in a concealed plea.

The shift from time (Q_1 and Q_2) to space (Q_3) tracks the modulation from physical *appetite* allayed by *feeding* to hungry *eyes* assuaged by *see[ing]*, a change which responds to an adjustment of argument from physically *appetit[ive]* corporeal *force*, to *contract[ual]* (personal, marital, legal) *love*. In this manner the speaker shifts from a model of lust to one of love.

When one metaphor (*two* lovers *contracted new* who come *daily* hoping to see each other) displaces another (love needing to *fill* its appetite every *day*) it is because something in the first metaphor seems inadequate in descriptive amplitude or accuracy—notably, here, its emphasis on physical appetite alone. When the second (more satisfactory because personal) metaphor (the daily looks of betrothed lovers on opposite banks of the ocean) is itself newly displaced by a third metaphor (summer after winter), we have to ask what has been unsatisfactory about the second.

We discover that the second, spatial metaphor is unsatisfactory because it, like the first, temporal one, cannot guarantee the return of love. The fear in the octave has been that of a "*perpetual* dullness," in which the appetite for love would never reappear. The metaphor of Q_3 has spoken, more favorably, of a sad *int'rim* between presence and return of presence, but the interim has been of an unspecified duration. The final couplet-metaphor here (like that of the *seldom coming*, but nonetheless joyfully predictable *feasts* of the *year* in 52) is that of a foreseeable return at a confidently known seasonal time—the return of summer after winter.

The *full[ness]* of *care* in winter makes one long even more for eyes *fill[ed]* with *fullness* of seeing. The eye as a vessel that can be filled till it *winks with fullness* (cf. 114), brimming with tears of joy, may have suggested the waters of the separating ocean. The gluttony of physical appetite has been chastened, by the end, into a legitimized happiness at the re-fruition of the earth at a seasonable time after the deprivation—*care*—of winter.

The only guarantee that the force connecting two persons is that of settled love, not temporary lust, is the willingness to enter into a contract to marry and to remain together in perpetuity, ensuring by legal means that tomorrow will resemble today—or, at the least, that return of presence will arrive as predictably and joyfully as summer follows winter. The yearning of a heterodox form of attachment to be a socially sanctioned one is visible here, as elsewhere in the sequence (e.g., 116).

KEY WORD: BE [-ING] (Normally, a word as common as *be* is not sufficiently foregrounded by the poem to take on salience in the reader's mind. In this sonnet, however, it is initially foregrounded by a trochaic rhythm—*Sweet love, renew thy force, bé it not said*—and later by alliteration: *blunter be, blest may be.* It is also used as the rhyme-word in line 9.

Couplet Tie: *fill* [*full*-ness, *full*] (5, 6, 13)
come [wel-*come*] (11, 14)
more (12, 14)
be [*-ing*] (1, 2, 5, 9, 12, 13)

57

Being your slaue what should I doe but tend,
Vpon the houres, and times of your desire?
I haue no precious time at al to spend;
Nor seruices to doe til you require.
Nor dare I chide the world without end houre,
Whilst I (my soueraine) watch the clock for you,
Nor thinke the bitternesse of absence sowre,
VVhen you haue bid your seruant once adieue.
Nor dare I question with my iealous thought,
VVhere you may be, or your affaires suppose,
But like a sad slaue stay and thinke of nought
Saue where you are, how happy you make those.
So true a foole is loue, that in your Will,
(Though you doe any thing) he thinkes no ill.

Being your slave, what should I do but tend
Upon the hours and times of your desire?
I have no precious time at all to spend,
Nor services to do till you require.
Nor dare I chide the world-without-end hour
Whilst I (my sovereign) watch the clock for you,
Nor think the bitterness of absence sour
When you have bid your servant once adieu.
Nor dare I question with my jealous thought
Where you may be, or your affairs suppose,
But like a sad slave stay and think of nought
Save where you are how happy you make those.
So true a fool is love that in your will
(Though you do any thing) he thinks no ill.

DO AND *THINK* AND *NO:* You do as you please; what should I do while you do that? Should I think no ill about you as you do it? The Couplet Tie *do* and *think* and *no* summarizes the sonnet: "in your will, / (Though you *do* any thing) he *thinks no* ill," says the couplet, punning, like several other sonnets (58, 89, 135, 136, 143), on the writer's name. But this *servant*, this *slave* (as he is misleadingly called in 58 as well), *sad* while watching through an absence like the *sad int'rim* of the preceding poem, reproaches his "sovereign" even as he affects a tone of servile abjectness.

The anaphora in *nor* constructs a set of alternatives to the present enslaved attendance on the hours and times of the sovereign's desire. In fact, the writer is neither servant nor slave: *being your slave* modulates into the more accurate *like a sad slave*, which in itself yields to the better representation of the speaker as a *true fool* in *love*. The alternative forms of behavior, detached from their anaphoric *nor*'s, show what the speaker should, as a free man, be doing with his time: he should

spend [his] precious time;
do [other] services;
chide the world-without-end hour of clock-watching;
think the bitterness of absence sour;
question with his jealous thought the place or affairs of the "friend";
depart (implied by his choice to *stay*).

The inner dismissal of all these free alternatives is the speaker's act of self-enslavement, and his appropriation of the term *slave* leads us less to pity him than to resist his equation between real slavery and his own infatuation. In lieu of independent action, the speaker passively *stay[s]*, and thinks of nothing except how happy the beloved, wherever he is, must be making other people. (What is the beloved doing to make them so happy? A curtain is drawn over the speculation.) The love-besotted speaker says he is determined to think no ill. But because the strategy of the sonnet is to show the speaker meaning the opposite of what he says, we take it that the speaker is in fact thinking nothing but ill.

Several of the sonnets construct ironic shadow-poems (here, one of reproach and suspicion) lying behind their actual statements ("I do not chide," "I think no ill"). The speaker's slippage into the vocabulary of the truth of his situation *(world-without-end hour, my jealous thought)* gives us permission to read the shadow jealousy-poem behind the abjuring-of-rights poem. The two remain equally present, and the end result is a double hologram-image, winking on and off as we tilt it in one direction (toward suspicion) or the other (toward abjectness). Above all, one hears the suppression of impulse as the psychological beat of the poem: *no, nor, nor, nor, nor, [n]or, nought, no.* Against all this negation in the speaker appears the licentious contrastive phrase of line 14: *any thing*. It belongs, of course, to the doings of the absent sovereign.

Couplet Tie: *do* (1, 4, 14)
think [*thought*] (7, 9, 11, 14)
no (3, 14)

58

THat God forbid, that made me firſt your ſlaue,
I ſhould in thought controule your times of pleaſure,
Or at your hand th' account of houres to craue,
Being your vaſſail bound to ſtaie your leiſure.
Oh let me ſuffer(being at your beck)
Th' impriſon'd abſence of your libertie,
And patience tame, to ſufferance bide each check,
Without accuſing you of iniury.
Be where you liſt, your charter is ſo ſtrong,
That you your ſelfe may priuiledge your time
To what you will, to you it doth belong,
Your ſelfe to pardon of ſelfe-doing crime.
I am to waite, though waiting ſo be hell,
Not blame your pleaſure be it ill or well.

That god forbid, that made me first your slave,
I should in thought control your times of pleasure,
Or at your hand th'account of hours to crave,
Being your vassal bound to stay your leisure.
O let me suffer (being at your beck)
Th'imprisoned absence of your liberty,
And patience, tame to sufferance, bide each check,
Without accusing you of injury.
Be where you list, your charter is so strong
That you yourself may privilege your time
To what you will; to you it doth belong
Yourself to pardon of self-doing crime.
I am to wait, though waiting so be hell,
Not blame your pleasure, be it ill or well.

THE *slave* of 57 reappears, rhyming for his couplet *hell* and *well* instead of their cousins *will* and *ill* of 57. The *hell/well* rhyme will return in the couplet of 129, and the *will/ill* of 57 has already been introduced into the sequence by 12 and 22. The complex *will/ill/hell/well* shared by 57/58 seems to have a life of its own, as its components add to themselves other conceptually related words: in 40, we find *ill/will/kill;* in 89, *ill/will;* in 112, *ill/well;* in 119, *ill/evil;* in 121, *vile/will/evil;* in 144, *ill/evil/devil/hell.* In 121 Shakespeare clearly recognizes that *evil* (so spelled in the Quarto version of 119, though not in that of 121) is an anagram of *vile;* and in the quarto spelling of 121 and 144 *evill* contains *ill,* while *devil (divel),* contains—depending on the spelling—a direct or an anagrammatic form of *evil.*

Sonnet 58 is a sardonic fantasia on the words *you* and *your,* with seventeen instances in fourteen lines. "Only *you* are in control. *I* am not allowed to control, to crave, to accuse, to blame: *I* am to stay, to suffer, to bide, to wait." The verb chains, negative and positive, of the forbidden and the exhorted connect the parts of the poem to each other. In effect, 58 is a topsy-turvy revision, in literary terms, of the *explicit* patience and *implicit* accusation of 57; here, the accusation has come into the open, as though the "sovereign" had read 57, and objected to its implicit blame. Sonnet 58 has the air of a response to an anterior utterance. The anterior utterance by the young man seems to have been on the order of: "You have no right to ask me why I was away so long, or what I was doing, or to blame me for finding pleasure elsewhere." "Oh yes," says the speaker, "God forbid that *you* should have to account for *your* doings, or that *I* should blame *your* pleasure." The bitter intonation on the speaker's part—not employable, needless to say, by any genuine slave—is conveyed chiefly by the reiterated *your* and *you;* and the substance of the reproach is carried by the Couplet Tie *pleasure* (2, 14), as well as by the word *time[s]* (2, 10), which connects Q_1 to Q_3. If the young man, as has been suggested by Booth, has been spending his time with women (*hours*/whores), we may read a pun on *cunt* in *cont-rol* and *ac-count.*

Whereas Q_1, Q_2, and C are concerned with the behavior of the vassal-slave-attendant, Q_3 is the speaker's resentful picture of the absolute sovereignty of the feudal lord. *He* is self-licensing, self-privileging, self-doing. The vocabulary approaches the theological: words like "self-begotten" and "self-sustaining," used of God, come to mind. But the godlike self-referring words in the poem are tainted by the addition of two denigrating words: *crime* and self-*pardon*. This sovereign is godlike only in the scope of his power, not in the substance of what he does.

The vassal's two *be* phrases—*being your vassal, being at your beck*—are contrasted to the reflexive *be* phrase of the sovereign: *Be where you list* (an echo of divinity once more: "The spirit bloweth *where it listeth*"). Q_1 is about the slave's duty, but Q_2, the place where interesting writing occurs, concerns the slave's suffering. *Patience* is derived from *patior* ("I suffer"), and is the doublet of *suffer/sufferance*. (Shakespeare puns macaronically on *patior/suffer* not only here but also in *Troilus and Cressida* I, i, 27–28.) The two phrases that most attract commentary are *suffer . . . th'imprisoned absence of your liberty* and *patience, tame to sufferance, bide each check*. Booth has rung the changes on possible meanings, but what is striking in the phrases is the necessity to condense so much in so little. What drives this compression?

The phrases of the speaker's possible revenge, of actions-that-might-be-taken—*[to crave] th' account of hours, [to] blame your pleasure*—show no such condensation-fusions at work. It is, then, not anger but suffering that causes the verbal meltdown: the representation of the inner chaos of suffering cannot offer a clear logical outline. The repetition of *suffer/patience/sufferance* shows clearly enough what is at issue, conceptually speaking; but what does it feel like? It feels the way these bizarre accusatory phrases feel. *Your liberty*—Yes, he has a right to go and come at will, he's free. *Imprisoned*—Well, if I too am theoretically a free agent, why do I feel bound hand and foot? *Absence*—Why, if he is away, do I interpret it, bitterly, as *absence*, referring it to *my* own location rather than as *liberty*, referring it to *his* location? (*Absence* is the grammatical object of *suffer*.) The suffer*ing* turns into suffer*ance* (endurance) after a series of repeated insults. The point of words like *patience*, *tame*, *sufferance*, *bide*, and *each* is to enact the slow and horrible passage of time, and make a single neglect, at first considered a nonce "check," mount up into a series of inflicted injuries. *Being, bound, bide, blame:* the conjugation of the verb of suffering. The helpless submission of the speaker to the principle of absolute feudal sovereignty—still a political and theological reality in the sixteenth century—is at least as strong as his wounded accusation of his beloved's behavior. *Charter, privilege, pardon, crime* are words from the legal system, and the speaker resorts to public discourse both to excuse and to indict his beloved, unsure where his own rights lie.

Since the *god . . . that made me first your slave* is Eros, the arbitrariness and cruelty conventionally ascribed to Eros are easily transferred to the sovereign. The closing distinguishing of *ill* from *well*—"Your pleasure, be it *ill* or *well*"—has become a distinction without a difference, as it had in 40: "Lascivious grace, in whom *all ill well* shows, / *Kill* me."

Couplet Tie: *pleasure* (2, 14)

IF their bee nothing new,but that which is,
Hath beene before , how are our braines beguild,
Which laboring for inuention beare amiſſe
The ſecond burthen of a former child ?
Oh that record could with a back-ward looke,
Euen of fiue hundreth courſes of the Sunne,
Show me your image in ſome antique booke,
Since minde at firſt in carrecter was done.
That I might ſee what the old world could ſay,
To this composed wonder of your frame,
Whether we are mended,or where better they,
Or whether reuolution be the ſame.
Oh ſure I am the wits of former daies,
To ſubiects worſe haue giuen admiring praiſe.

If there be nothing new, but that which is
Hath been before, how are our brains beguiled,
Which, labouring for invention, bear amiss
The second burthen of a former child!
O that recórd could with a backward look,
Even of five hundred courses of the sun,
Show me your image in some ántique book,
Since mind at first in character was done,
That I might see what the old world could say
To this composèd wonder of your frame:
Whether we are mended, or whe'er better they,
Or whether revolution be the same.
O sure I am the wits of former days
To subjects worse have given admiring praise.

FORMER is the Couplet Tie of 59, promising a backward-looking scan. The artificial pretext for the scan is literary economy: *If* someone like the beloved *did* exist in the past, and had been described by a wit of former days in some antique book, then the poet's work has already been done for him, and he need not (punningly) *labor* for invention, since he would simply, in producing a description of the beloved, be bearing, to no purpose, *the second burden of a former child*—repeating a previous, historically successful, labor and delivery. This playful pretext in Q_1 gives a plausible practical motive for the actual desire and practice of the poet-lover—to read, habitually, his predecessor-poets in their acts of praising, and see his present beloved continually exceeding their former ones. (A rewriting of this sonnet is presented in 106, which repeats the couplet rhyme *days/praise* used here.)

This is a poem embodying the old quarrel between the Ancients and the Moderns: it concerns written representation, past and present. It exhibits some uncertainty as to what representation represents: Is it the subject's *image?* or *mind?* or *frame?* Is it the visual, intellectual, or corporeal self? It is in fact all three: representation aims, as the couplet says, at the portrayal of the whole *subject.*

The speaker's desire for a backward look at the actual (now dead) subjects of representation is frustrated, and the writer must go on bearing his burden of invention. He cannot know what the old world would have said of the present beloved, whether our writing is better or whether they excelled us, or whether each age expresses *wonder* at the same level of excellence in its subjects of representation. Since we cannot see former beauties, we have to think up a probable answer to our unanswerable speculations. The couplet asserts that (as the poet knows from his reading) there was plenty of *admiring praise* written in former days, but it was all, he contends, lavished on *worse subjects.* No age could have contained a paragon equal to ours; consequently no former praise—no matter how admiring—could equal ours, since earlier writers had not the subject, or the image, or the mind, or—most excellent of all, and surely unique—the *composèd wonder of your frame.* The elaborateness of this phrase proves that this eighth wonder of the world is chiefly a corporeal presence, rather than a visual or a mental one. The wit of the poem lies in the elaboration both of the speculation and of the defensive answer-on-no-evidence, justifying the continuing production, by the poet-speaker, of admiring praise for his historically unparalleled subject.

The "backward look" of fantasy occupies lines 5–10; and though it is motivated by erotic response to beauty, it stimulates the poet-speaker to the larger speculations of lines 11–12, on the shape of the history of literature: whether it is a history of progress, or of decline, or of a steady-state of perennial sameness. The two quatrains concerning literary production, Q_1 and Q_3, both conclude by suspecting that the true account is the steady-state one—a fearful conclusion for the speaker, who wants to believe that his love, and consequently his own literary production, are unique. Therefore the speaker defends his own necessity of writing by an over-assertion of the inferiority of the past, "O *sure* I am," in the couplet. Both Q_1 and lines 11–12 are phrased in the first-person plural—"*our* brains," "whether *we* are mended." These are the steady-state intellectual portions. The first-person portion is not intellectual, however, but infatuated, refusing to credit the steady-state conclusion to which reason has led the poet when he considers himself as one of a transhistorical band of writers. Speaking as *we*, he is a mind; speaking as *I*, he is a lover. These pronominal shifts account in part for the odd structure of the sonnet: 4-6-2-2, where the longest portion is the erotic backward look in the first person, in which the tone of wonder prevails; this tone contrasts sharply with the tone of the first-person couplet, where the focus has shifted, almost petulantly, to the *subjects worse*, ranked dismissively lower than the young man. The desperate uncertainty underlying *O sure I am* is pitted against the intellectual juggernaut of recurring sameness.

Behind this sonnet lie two conceptions of history: the classical, which believes that there is nothing new, and that all returns in cycles of time; and the Christian, which believes that there was once a unique intervention in history, the Incarnation of Christ, preventing all mere recurrence. In positing the young man's uniqueness, and denying that historical revolution is the same, the speaker is offering a (blasphemous) analogy to the Christian paradigm. I think we are expected to perceive the analogy.

Couplet Tie: *former* (4, 13)

60

Like as the waues make towards the pibled ſhore,
So do our minuites haſten to their end,
Each changing place with that which goes before,
In ſequent toile all forwards do contend.
Natiuity once in the maine of light,
Crawles to maturity, wherewith being crown'd,
Crooked eclipſes gainſt his glory fight,
And time that gaue, doth now his gift confound.
Time doth tranſfixe the floriſh ſet on youth,
And delues the paralels in beauties brow,
Feedes on the rarities of natures truth,
And nothing ſtands but for his ſieth to mow.
And yet to times in hope, my verſe ſhall ſtand
Praiſing thy worth, diſpight his cruell hand.

Like as the waves make towards the pebbled shore,
So do our minutes hasten to their end,
Each changing place with that which goes before,
In sequent toil all forwards do contend.
Nativity, once in the main of light,
Crawls to maturity, wherewith being crowned,
Crookèd eclipses 'gainst his glory fight,
And Time that gave doth now his gift confound.
Time doth transfix the flourish set on youth,
And delves the parallels in beauty's brow,
Feeds on the rarities of nature's truth,
And nothing stands but for his scythe to mow.
And yet to times in hope my verse shall stand
Praising thy worth, despite his cruel hand.

LIKE 73, sonnet 60 is one of the "perfect" examples of the 4-4-4-2 Shakespearean sonnet form. Each quatrain introduces a new and important modification in concept and tone, while the couplet—here a "reversing" couplet contradicting the body of the sonnet—adds yet a fourth dimension. One member of the Couplet Tie is the enemy, *time* [*-s*]. The other is the word on which the reversal pivots: *stand* [*-s*].

> And nothing *stands* but for his scythe to mow.
> And yet to times in hope my verse shall *stand.*

Stand is the one thing that the three quatrain models—waves, light/life, and the vegetation of the earth—cannot do: waves hasten to their end, light/life is undone by crooked eclipses, and vegetation is scythed down. The way in which verse *stands* (with its feet, perhaps?) is different from the way material things *stand* only to be mowed down.

Three models of what life is like are offered in the three quatrains. Q_1, derived from Ovid, could be spoken by a preacher: his model of steady-state change is orderly, horizontal, *sequent.* Life is divided into equal temporal segments, *minutes,* each knowing his expected *toil* and his *place* within it. Above all, according to the preacher, the motion of our life is natural and is voluntary *(hasten);* it is as physical and predictable as the waves, as orderly as a choreographed dance in which each partner changes place *with that which goes before.* We associate this model with ritual and with repetitive narrative.

The second model is the one we associate with tragedy: the fall of princes. We have in Q_2 a single changing protagonist, nativity-becoming-maturity. The narrative of his rise and fall is tracked by the paradigm *crawls/crowned/crookèd/confound.* The apogee and eclipse occur at the very same moment in the immediate affronting of *crowned* by *crookèd,* and of *gift* by *confound.* In this model, existential change is unnatural (*eclipse,* not sunset), involuntary, and destructive; it is ascribed to an agent, Time, who is at first generous *(gave)* and, at the end, malign *(confound).*

In the third model, Time is exclusively malign, and existential disaster is, temporally speaking, incessant. Time is now unrelentingly rapid in its destructiveness. Whereas the waves took a full quatrain to change places, and nativity took three lines to be confounded, the catastrophic events in Q_3 take place one per line. Time *doth transfix*, *delves*, *feeds on*, and will *mow*. If the first model was sequential and narrative, and the second dramatic and tragic, this third model is exclamatory and almost cartoonlike, the carnage speeded up until it begins to lack the human dignity so visible in Q_2. In Q_3, to summarize it crudely, *youth* is transfixed, *beauty* is delved, *truth* is eaten, and *nothing* stands but to be mown. A death per line is the norm.

If youth, beauty, and truth are extirpated, what can stand? The answer (as in 54) is that only *worth* can survive to be praised by *verse*. *Time* the destroyer is replaced by *times in hope*, the future.

Nonetheless, although the intent of the couplet is certainly one of reversal (*nothing stands . . . And yet . . . verse shall stand)*, a couplet in which the optimistic reversal were formally *enacted* as well as semantically asserted would read in "upbeat" fashion:

> [And yet to times in hope standing 'gainst dearth,
> My verse, despite old Time, shall praise thy worth.]

The "bad" would be tucked somewhere in the middle ("despite old Time"), and the couplet would close with a resounding positive value. In the sonnet as we have it, the triumphant *my verse shall stand, / Praising thy worth* is followed by the deflating admission of Time's *cruel hand*, with *cruel* being the last echo of the destructive *cr-* words (*crookèd*, etc.) of the tragic paradigm.

The interesting writing in Q_3 needs some commentary. I said "to summarize it crudely" earlier because time's actions—*transfix*ing, *delv*ing, and *feed*ing *on*—do not have the simple direct objects I originally gave them. Time transfixes not *youth* but *the flourish* [which has been] *set on youth;* it *delves* not *beauty* but *the parallels in the brow* [belonging to] *beauty*, it *feeds* not on *truth* but on *the rarities of the truth* [present in] *nature*. What can these nested structures mean? They enact, I think, the gradualness and selectivity of *tempus edax* even in the rapidity, unpredictability, and cruelty of its assaults. Time begins its attack on youth by piercing its decorative accessories, its *flourish;* it begins its attack on beauty at one localized site of loveliness, the brow; it begins its attack on nature at the most distinctive and rare representations of nature's genius. Instead of watching single waves in motion or a single heavenly body in its rise and eclipse, as in Q_1 and Q_2, we see many valuable things being directly and destructively, if selectively and stealthily, attacked.

It is also worth noting that Shakespeare's first three formulations in Q_3, unlike those in Q_1 and Q_2, put the destructive action (*transfix*, etc.) *before* the thing destroyed, so that we are not allowed to see youth healthfully flourishing before it is transpierced. We see the waves *mak[ing] towards* the shore before they end, and we see nativity *in the main of light* before catastrophe occurs. If Q_3 maintained this former vectored "beauty-then-destruction" model, it would have to read something like this:

[We know one flourish, and our youth's deflowered;
And beauty's brow is delved with wrinkles slow;
The rarest truths of nature are devoured,
And nothing stands but for Time's scythe to mow.]

By reversing in lines 9, 10, and 11 this chronological model to a post hoc model, where, horribly, *transfix* actually precedes *flourish*, Shakespeare gives us his own analytic and philosophical model in place of the victim's own chronological one. We read our own lives chronologically, but the philosopher reads them analytically, perceiving the undeflectable end even in the flourishing beginning. The ensuing philosophical despair ("and *nothing* stands except to be mowed down") is consequently believably motivated, and the suggestion of malign destiny ("nothing stands *but for* his scythe to mow") is made plausible.

The several reversed initial feet *(Like as, So do, Crawls to, Crookèd, Time doth, Feeds on, Praising)* draw attention to the hastening of the waves, the attacks by eclipses and by Time, and the countervailing praising by verse.

Couplet Tie: *stand* [*-s*] (12, 13)
Time [*-s*] (8, 9, 13)

61

IS it thy wil,thy Image ſhould keepe open
My heauy eielids to the weary night?
Doſt thou deſire my ſlumbers ſhould be broken,
While ſhadowes like to thee do mocke my ſight?
Is it thy ſpirit that thou ſend'ſt from thee
So farre from home into my deeds to prye,
To find out ſhames and idle houres in me,
The skope and tenure of thy Ielouſie?
O no,thy loue though much,is not ſo great,
It is my loue that keepes mine eie awake,
Mine owne true loue that doth my reſt defeat,
To plaie the watch-man euer for thy ſake.
  For thee watch I,whilſt thou doſt wake elſewhere,
  From me farre of, with others all to neere.

Is it thy will thy image should keep open
My heavy eyelids to the weary night?
Dost thou desire my slumbers should be broken,
While shadows like to thee do mock my sight?
Is it thy spirit that thou send'st from thee
So far from home into my deeds to pry,
To find out shames and idle hours in me,
The scope and tenure of thy jealousy?
O no, thy love, though much, is not so great;
It is my love that keeps mine eye awake,
Mine own true love that doth my rest defeat,
To play the watchman ever for thy sake.
  For thee watch I, whilst thou dost wake elsewhere,
  From me far off, with others all too near.

AN "Italian" structure of question-octave / answer-sestet organizes the speaker's insomnia in the beloved's absence; the theme is summarized in the Couplet Tie: *watch*, *wake*, *far*. The couplet itself emphasizes nonreciprocity between speaker and beloved: the speaker *watches* (keeps vigil) while the beloved *wakes* (carouses)—far off from the speaker, but all too near others. The beloved *wakes;* the speaker is *awake.*

If it were not for the scorpion's sting in its tail—*with others all too near*—we could read this sonnet innocently as one in which the speaker conceived his *beloved's* imagined jealousy as the cause of his *own* insomnia. A first reading of the sonnet follows the author's lead in construing the poem along those lines, at least until the last five words of the couplet reveal the speaker's own torments of jealousy. A second, parallel reading then construes (and "rewrites") the octave as a projection of the speaker's own agony; Q_2 would then say:

> [It is *my* spirit that I send from me
> So far from home into *thy* deeds to pry,
> To find out shames and idle hours in *thee*,
> The scope and tenure of *my* jealousy.]

Only such an implicit undersong justifies the apparently otiose repetition of two nearly synonymous questions in the first quatrain, and the sinister elaboration that takes place in the second quatrain under the guise of a further question:

1. Is it thy will	thy image	should keep open my *eye*lids?
2. Dost thou desire	shadows like to thee	to mock my *sight?*
3. Send'st thou	thy spirit	to pry into my *deeds* and find out *shames* in me?

Question 2 is almost synonymous with question 1; but question 3 makes the spirit-envoy an active spy rather than a mere eidetic image. The expansion of question 3 beyond two lines (the length of questions 1 and 2) to a prying four lines marks the intrusion of the speaker's own projected jealous agitation.

Just as behind the second interrogative quatrain, putatively about the *beloved's* jealousy, we read a declarative ghost-quatrain actually about the *speaker's* jealousy, so, behind the speaker's declaration of love in Q_3, we can, on a second reading, hear a ghost declaration of jealousy rather than love:

> [It is my *fear* that keeps mine eye awake,
> Mine own *dark fear* that doth my rest defeat,
> To play the watchman ever for thy sake.]

Finally, the assertion *Thou dost wake . . . with others* is framed neither as fear nor as suspicion, but as fact.

Often, in scanning the sonnets, one feels one is reading two poems at once: the actual poem, and the ghost-poem behind it. The actual poem is the sayable one: the ghost-poem is for various reasons indecorous, shaming, or accusatory. Nonetheless, we are almost invariably given enough information to construe the ghost-poem from the actual one. Here, the assertion of the beloved's night-carouse with others gives us license to read the speaker's jealousy and fear in the ghost-poem ("the scope and tenure of [my] jealousy"; "[fear] . . . keeps mine eye awake"). The beloved waking-with-others is not likely to have undertaken any of the haunting and spirit-prying of the octave, which we conclude, on second reading, to be entirely a projection on the part of the speaker.

In this light, the most pathetic phrase in the poem is the concessive which opens the sestet: *O no, thy love, though much, is not so great.* Since "great love" is in the sonnet a synonym for imputed jealousy and fear—neither of which is exhibited by the beloved—the quality of the beloved's putative *much* love for the speaker is left entirely undescribed, and is in fact vitiated.

The chief aesthetic effect in the poem is the illustration of slow "unconscious" slippage of expression in the apparent synonymy of lines 1–8. *Dost thou desire* would normally be taken as synonymous with *Is it thy will*, just as *shadows like to thee* would seem synonymous with *thy image*, and so on. But the gradual increase in purposiveness from *Is it thy will* to *Dost thou desire* to *Is it thy spirit that thou send'st from thee* alerts us to the comparable differences between an "image that keeps eyelids open" to "shadows that mock sight" to a "spirit sent to pry to find out." As pieces from question 1 are putatively reinforced by pieces of questions 2 and 3, we may note at first the reinforcement rather than the distinctions. But the third question has moved away from the insomniac *broken slumbers* and *mock[ing] shadows* which disturb the speaker, to center on the (putative) prying and jealousy on the part of the beloved. The poem is no longer at all synonymously explaining first-person insomnia, but has slipped into a whole other realm, one investigating second-person motivation. By comparable incremental slippages and creepings, the words *will* and *desire* and *jealousy* turn into the second-person word *love* in line 9, consequently infecting the subsequent first-person uses of *love* in lines 10–11.

It is worth remarking the structure of 61, since it demonstrates Shakespeare's spatial sense of sonnet writing. The initial questions are sequentially answered below:

1. Is it thy will thy image should *keep my eyelids open?* (1–2)	O no . . . it is my love that keeps *mine eye awake.* (8–9)
2. Dost thou desire *my slumbers should be broken?* (3–4)	Mine own true love that does *my rest defeat* . . . sake. (10–12)
3. Is it thy spirit . . . *far from home* to pry? (5–8)	For thee watch I, whilst thou dost wake . . . *far off.* (13–14)

This structure—A, B, C : A′, B′, C′—will also appear in 146, where the latter part of the sonnet is spatially "arrayed" as a set of "right-hand" replies to a set of "left-hand" questions.

Couplet Tie: *watch* [*watch*-man] (12, 13)
far (6, 14)
[a-]*wake* (10, 13)

62

Sinne of ſelfe-loue poſſeſſeth al mine eie,
And all my ſoule,and al my euery part;.
And for this ſinne there is no remedie,
It is ſo grounded inward in my heart.
Me thinkes no face ſo gratious is as mine,
No ſhape ſo true,no truth of ſuch account,
And for my ſelfe mine owne worth do define,
As I all other in all worths ſurmount.
But when my glaſſe ſhewes me my ſelfe indeed
Beated and chopt with tand antiquitie,
Mine owne ſelfe loue quite contrary I read
Selfe,ſo ſelfe louing were iniquity,
  T'is thee(my ſelfe)that for my ſelfe I praiſe,
  Painting my age with beauty of thy daies,

Sin of self-love possesseth all mine eye,
And all my soul, and all my every part;
And for this sin there is no remedy,
It is so grounded inward in my heart.
Methinks no face so gracious is as mine,
No shape so true, no truth of such account,
And for myself mine own worth do define,
As I all other in all worths surmount.
But when my glass shows me myself indeed,
Beated and chopped with tanned antiquity,
Mine own self-love quite contrary I read;
Self so self-loving were iniquity.
  'Tis thee (my self) that for myself I praise,
  Painting my age with beauty of thy days.

THE dramatic scenario which sonnet 62, by its oddity, encourages us to reconstruct has consisted, we deduce, of four chronological phases:

1. The speaker (flattered by being loved by the young man) has engaged in physical, intellectual, and moral vanity and complacency, forgetting his true age, looks, and inadequacy;
2. He then looked in the mirror and, seeing how greatly his outward looks belied his inner complacencies, felt himself a fool;
3. Seeking an explanation for his former fatuousness, he realizes he has so identified with the beloved as to have formed a delusory inner self (a self as young and beautiful and worthy as the young man is) in order to believe in the young man's affection for him;
4. Upon the controverting of this fantasized narcissistic self-image by the mirror-image, he is disgusted with himself, and condemns himself for the sin of pride and self-love.

The poem, for reasons we must examine, rearranges these chronological steps: $Q_1 = 4$; $Q_2 = 1$; $Q_3 = 2$; $C = 3$. But Shakespeare's strategy is not simply one of rearrangement; he represents the early narcissistic phase through the lens of later judgment, deliberately making it absurd. In the octave of the poem, the speaker judges the psychology of his self-flattering Phase 1 with the mortified hindsight of Phase 4, calling Phase 1 "sin" but leaving its inner fatuity mimetically visible in Q_2. Since in Phase 1 (in "real" time) the speaker is still engaged in his own preening, to conflate the later with the earlier phase as Shakespeare does causes a cognitive dissonance in the reader. The poem (in chronological logic) should present the unjudged (deluded) self-love first:

Methinks no face so gracious is as mine.

This should be followed by the disillusioning glance in the mirror:

But when my glass shows me myself indeed;

and that should be followed by the conviction of sin:

Sin of self-love possesseth all mine eye.

But by the time the poem begins, this whole process has *already* taken place, and yet the vanity and complacency that we see mimetically represented in Q_1 and Q_2 seem to be continuing unabated.

What is being presented, then, is what the moralists call habitual sin. The speaker admits as much in saying (blasphemously) that this sin is so much a part of his identity that there is no remedy for it. (Kerrigan cites the Prayer Book "grafted inwardly in our hearts.") Two blasphemies are evident here: one says, without exception, "I surmount all other in all worths;" the other alludes in lines 1–2 to the commandment, "Thou shalt love the Lord thy God with all thy heart, and with all thy soul, and with all thy mind" [Matthew 22:37].

By allowing an unrepentant confession of sin (Q_1) to *precede* both an enacting of the sin (Q_2) and a revelation of the nature of the sin (Q_3) Shakespeare enters the cycle of habitual sin at the endpoint (self-judgment), which nonetheless (cf. the couplet of 129) precedes a new beginning of the vicious circle. The inner identification of the *beated and chopped* speaker with the youthful *beauty* of the young man is reenacted in the infatuated *thee (myself)* of the couplet, and in the KEY WORD "SELF."

To love and be loved by the young man to the point of identity makes one feel, indeed, superior to everyone else—in looks, in form, in character, in worth. But the self-justification is here phrased in comparative terms, in a comic mounting concatenation: "Compared with others, there is *no* face so gracious, *no* shape so true, *no* truth of such account, as mine." To this comic self-exaltation, the mirror comes as an astringent corrective. And at the end, the speaker's identification with the young man is recognized as superficial *maquillage*—the speaker's true *age* is said to be *painted* over with the *beauty* of youth's young *days.*

It is not only by logic that the three quatrains (acceptance of habitual sin, sinning by vanity, renewed judgment of sinfulness) are distinguished. Each has its own chief register(s) of diction: Q_1, theological; Q_2, aesthetic/intellectual/moral; Q_3, naturalistic. The arrangement of Q_2 is cunning, borrowing the members of the Platonic triad—the Beautiful *(gracious face)*, the True *(true shape, truth of such account)*, and the Good *(worth)*—and arranging them in a hierarchy of total vanity.

The collapse into reality here *(But when my glass shows me myself indeed)* links this sonnet to 138, which, as we will see, exhibits a similar collapse:

But wherefore says she not she is unjust?
And wherefore say not I that I am old?

Like 62 (and 129), 138 exhibits a state of habitual sin, and its octave is structured to present the same cognitive dissonance as that of 62, for the same reason: both speakers knowingly practice, again and again, a self-deceptive illusion, compulsively complying with it rather than giving it up.

The couplet of 62 presents, as Booth suggests, an alternative reading of the "sin" of Q_2. It is not really himself the speaker has been earlier praising, but rather the young-man-in-himself, a cosmeticized inner self, painted with the young man's beauty. Perhaps the speaker is not iniquitous after all: he loves not himself but the friend. Yes, *self so self-loving were [would be] iniquity*—but the alternative proffered in the couplet allows the "virtue" of love of the friend to supplant the vice of self-love. In this way, the dramatic scenario is further complicated, making this sonnet that of a man vacillating between two readings of his (former and habitual) self-love as he stands before his mirror. Reading 1 is that of Q_1: he is guilty of the (habitual) iniquity of self-love. Reading 2 is *quite contrary:* he is consumed not with love of self but with praise of the young man, whose semblance he has assumed inwardly through love. The "contrary readings"—backward to vice, forward to virtue—make this sonnet an exemplary instance of Shakespeare's recognition that it was possible to write two poems in one by—in this instance—rearranging the chronological ordering of experience. Yet he does not show merely the repentant sinner; he shows the complacent habitual sinner in full erotic illusion (Q_2) as well.

KEY WORD: SELF (1, 7, 9, 11, 12, 12, 13, 13) (The Quarto prints *self-love* as one hyphenated word, but *my self* and *self loving* as two words. Following Evans, I retain the two word *my self* only in line 13.)

Couplet Tie: (because of thematic emphasis) *myself* (7, 9, 13)

63

AGainſt my loue ſhall be as I am now
With times iniurious hand chruſht and ore-worne,
When houres haue dreind his blood and fild his brow
With lines and wrincles,when his youthfull morne
Hath trauaild on to Ages ſteepie night,
And all thoſe beauties whereof now he's King
Are vaniſhing,or vaniſht out of ſight,
Stealing away the treaſure of his Spring.
For ſuch a time do I now fortifie
Againſt confounding Ages cruell knife,
That he ſhall neuer cut from memory
My ſweet loues beauty,though my louers life.
His beautie ſhall in theſe blacke lines be ſeene,
And they ſhall liue , and he in them ſtill greene.

Against my love shall be as I am now,
With Time's injurious hand crushed and o'erworn;
When hours have drained his blood and filled his brow
With lines and wrinkles, when his youthful morn
Hath travelled on to Age's steepy night,
And all those beauties whereof now he's king
Are vanishing, or vanished out of sight,
Stealing away the treasure of his spring:
For such a time do I now fortify
Against confounding Age's cruel knife,
That he shall never cut from memory
My sweet love's beauty, though my lover's life.
His beauty shall in these black lines be seen,
And they shall live, and he in them still green.

ONE who has been crushed by *time's injurious hand* speaks the poem, looking at the way individual *beauties* vanish as youth fades, and asking how *beauty* can be preserved. The poem, recalling the ruined self-image of 62, rewrites 60 in first-person form. The two poems share the words *confound* and *cruel, Time* and *hand, brow, beauty,* and *youth;* and they share as well the image of a youthful man traveling on to age. In 63, Time's hand holds not a reaping *scythe* as in 60, but a *cruel knife* (the word *cruel,* with its etymological meaning of "bloody," is retrieved from Time's *cruel hand* in 60). It is now *Age,* rather than *Time,* that *confounds.* It is typical of Shakespeare's capacity to change his mind that he could, in 60, think of Time as *delving* parallels in beauty's brow (harrowing a blank field), and in 63 speak of Time as *filling* the brow with lines and wrinkles. Time is writing on a blank page—the metaphor finds the phoneme "ink" in the Quarto's *wrincles,* and prepares us for the "*black* lines" of the couplet.

The savage imagining in Q_1 of the young man's eventual destruction by Time is framed in a deliberate incoherence of metaphor, as all the lovingly invented metaphors for the young man's state—his morn of youth, his royalty, his resemblance to treasure, his springtime, his summer's greenness—are obliterated in one rout and ruin. He (like the speaker) is at once *crushed* (as by violence) and *o'erworn* (as by attrition); and he is at once *drained* and *filled.* (I read the Quarto *fild* as "filled," not as "(de)filed," largely because of the antithetical play with *drained.*)

The metaphors pass from the inorganic to the organic. The drainings and fillings speak of mechanical work; the travel of *morn* to *night* speaks of astronomy; *beauties of which he is king* speaks of feudal hierarchy; *treasure* speaks of wealth; but *spring* is ostentatiously organic. Though *life* can be cut down by Time's knife, *beauty* can be preserved in black lines. Though the lines are inorganic in their color—the color of Age's *steepy night*—their continued life, though an inorganic life, paradoxically preserves in memory the organic *green* of *spring.*

The avoidance of end-stops mimics the unstoppable advance of time, as does the self-correcting variation *are vanishing, or vanished* (Kerrigan). The unusual distribution of clauses over lines disturbs the equilibrium we are used to in the line-management of the Sonnets: in the octave, the clauses occupy, respectively, 2, 1½, 1½, and 3 lines, resulting in a very rocky rhythm mimicking the disturbance of the natural order. And the use of enjambment to represent never-resting time (resembling its use in sonnet 5: *For never-resting time leads summer on / To hideous winter and confounds him there*) is repeated here often enough (lines 3, 4, 6, 9, 11) so that it becomes, together with the irregular length of the clauses, symbolic of the rapid and unpredictable pace of aging:

Clause 1: *When hours have drained his blood and filled his brow / With lines and wrinkles,*

Clause 2: *when his youthful morn / Hath travelled on to Age's steepy night,*

Clause 3: *And all those beauties whereof now he's king / Are vanishing, or vanished out of sight, / Stealing away the treasure of his spring.*

In the context of the extreme orderliness of some series that appear in the *Sonnets* (see, e.g., 66), a series such as this—which ranges in length from a line and a half *(When hours have drained his blood . . . wrinkles)* to three full lines (the last item)—is meant to be taken, representing Time's ravages, as expressing Pelion piled on Ossa.

Though the octave is concerned with gradual decline and entropy, the sestet is concerned with the speaker's concession to his lover's eventual death at the hand of *Age* and his *cruel knife*, its steel adumbrated in *stealing*. This distinction of emphasis between octave and sestet accounts for the double personification employed by the poem: personified *Time* stands for gradual destructive motion, while personified *Age* stands for instant and total cessation. These two personifications (for both of which I retain the Quarto's initial capitalization) animate the octave and the third quatrain respectively. Once both these enemies are worsted, the poem can move on to its resurrective couplet.

The very deft couplet resurrects the young man by incremental stages. *His beauty* shall be seen (by readers) in Shakespeare's printed *lines;* and the *lines* shall *live;* and *he [shall live] still green* in them. To find a way from the initial part *(his beauty)* to the final whole *(he . . . still green)* the path must go through the *living lines*. These are regarded as the deposit of, and stimulus to, memory, the only final repository of beauty. I suspect Shakespeare felt the need to rewrite 60 because he realized that in its couplet the sentiment *(my verse shall stand, / Praising thy worth)* was subverted by the closing phrase, *his cruel hand*, which leaves us with Time's cruelty as the last poetic image. In 63, by contrast, the last image—*he in them still green*—enacts, in its positive organic image, the resurrective assertion of the couplet. (Or, if we disregard the order of the *Sonnets*, we can see 60 as a pessimistic revision of 63.)

The words of the Couplet Tie—representing the things that survive the physical wreck of both lover and beloved—are *lines*, *beauty*, and *life* [*live*]—all transgeneric concepts (the first punningly) which are used equally of physical and literary entities.

Couplet Tie: *lines* (4, 13)
beauty [*beauties*] (6, 12, 13)
life [*live*] (12,14)

64

VV Hen I haue ſeene by times fell hand defaced
The rich proud coſt of outworne buried age,
When ſometime loftie towers I ſee downe raſed,
And braſſe eternall ſlaue to mortall rage.
When I haue ſeene the hungry Ocean gaine
Aduantage on the Kingdome of the ſhoare,
And the firme ſoile win of the watry maine,
Increaſing ſtore with loſſe, and loſſe with ſtore.
When I haue ſeene ſuch interchange of ſtate,
Or ſtate it ſelfe confounded, to decay,
Ruine hath taught me thus to ruminate
That Time will come and take my loue away.
  This thought is as a death which cannot chooſe
  But weepe to haue, that which it feares to looſe.

When I have seen by Time's fell hand defaced
The rich proud cost of outworn buried age,
When sometime lofty towers I see down razed,
And brass eternal slave to mortal rage;
When I have seen the hungry ocean gain
Advantage on the kingdom of the shore,
And the firm soil win of the wat'ry main,
Increasing store with loss, and loss with store;
When I have seen such interchange of state,
Or state itself confounded to decay,
Ruin hath taught me thus to ruminate:
That Time will come and take my love away.
  This thought is as a death which cannot choose
  But weep to have that which it fears to lose.

LIKE 60, 64 works the form of the Shakespearean sonnet to great advantage. Ruin, it says, takes place in two ways; and this sonnet, progressing inductively, acts out the two forms of ruin—later summarized as *state confounded to decay* (Q_1) and *interchange of state* (Q_2)—before arriving, by way of *ruminate* (a word of Latinate grandeur), at the naked childlikeness of *Time will come and take my love away.*

The writing throughout is exceptionally interesting, both locally and structurally. Locally, *Time's hand* and *confounded* link this sonnet to 60 and 63, and the *ocean* and *main* connect to the *waves* and *main* of 60 as well. To 60's three clear models of life-process (narrative, tragic, and prophetically cartoonlike, as I have called them), this sonnet opposes its own two equally clear models of change (which is now unequivocally called *ruin*). The first model, later generalized as *state . . . confounded to decay,* is shown in Q_1 by a series of visually appropriate diagrams of either (a) architectural construction followed by destruction, or (b) destruction actually preceding, syntactically (as in *defaced*), the construction it presupposes (as in Q_3 of 60):

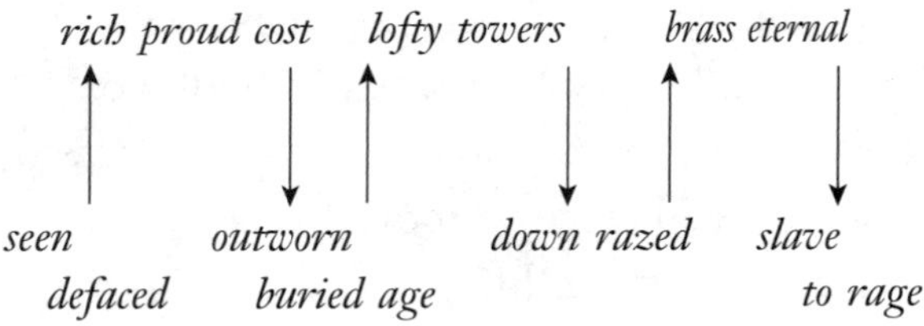

When lofty trees I see barren of leaves, Shakespeare wrote in sonnet 12, instantly despoiling the trees he had lifted aloft; here, in *When sometime lofty towers I see down razed,* he tears down the towers he has just erected. These are examples of what Q_3 will call *state confounded to decay.*

What disturbs Shakespeare even more than these enumerated jolts of cultural decline and mortal destruction is the suspicion that Fate makes these changes without purpose or end. (Even a destructive purpose would be philosophically preferable to change with no purpose at all.) Purely meaningless change is what the speaker perceives in that horizontal phenomenon he calls the *interchange of state* between natural entities (ocean and shore), in their endless physical battle of tidal ebb and flow, with now the *ocean gain[ing] advantage*, now the *firm soil win[ning]*. The speaker manifests his horror at this purposeless exchange of terrain by his unparaphrasable summary line, *Increasing store with loss, and loss with store*. Loss is added to store; and loss is increased by store. Loss wins in both cases. It is of course impossible to increase abundance with loss, and equally impossible to increase loss by adding abundance to it. Behind such a line—store with loss, loss with store—one sees Time's purposeless playing at ruin: and by our almost instinctive deletion of *m*, *ruminate* comes to contain *ruinate*, in the last philosophical observation of the body of the poem:

> *Ruin hath taught me thus to ruminate,*
> That Time will come and take my love away.

The collapse into (often monosyllabic) truth—one of the salient features of the *Sonnets*—usually follows earlier (often polysyllabic) protestations and ruminations, which are often revealed as defense-reactions by their complications of language. After the philosophical Latinity of *Ruin hath taught me thus to ruminate*, we expect something equally Latinate, like [*Corruption and mortality prevail*]. Instead, we see the naked primary defenselessness of Shakespeare's helpless monosyllables: *Time will come and take my love away*. In its collapse, its unprotected vulnerability, and its dismayed adolescent simplicity of rhythm, this line feels like a death.

The Couplet Ties are, wittily enough, *have* and *lose* [*loss*], and HAVE, the ironic KEY WORD, is used punningly. After all the auxiliary *have*s (*when I have seen*, thrice repeated), the nonauxiliary use, *weep to have*, comes as a shock. The ruminative *When I have* is answered by the declarative *weep to have:* you have not, even as you think you have.

The *ruin* of the three quatrains pertains to the inanimate world; the couplet departs from this to the true concern of the speaker: the *death* of his living beloved. In retrospect, we can see the first twelve lines as a long defense—by thinking about the end of inanimate things—against thinking about the death of a living person.

It has always been noticed that the generalizations stand in a chiastic relation to their *exempla*. State confounded (Q_1) : interchange of state (Q_2) :: *interchange of state* (line 9) : *state confounded* (line 10). This arrangement has the rhetorical advantage of putting the initial generalization of line 9 directly after its ocean/shore exemplum of interchange in Q_2—and indeed immediately following the line 8 summary of that exemplum *(store with loss and loss with store)*, which itself exhibits chiasmus, always an analytic trope. It is also true that any chiastic structure exerts a visual "wrap-up" effect, rounding on itself—as *decay* at the end of the chiasmus (line 10) echoes *defaced* at the end of line 1, where the chiasmus began.

Within the larger conceptual pattern of the twelve-line body of the sonnet (decay : interchange :: interchange : decay), there are other patterns of conceptual, verbal, and phonetic chiasmus. The inner chiastic pattern noticed in Q_1—*defaced : cost :: towers : razed*—is repeated in both Q_2 and Q_3: *ocean : shore :: soil : wat'ry main* is followed by *store : loss :: loss : store*, followed in its turn by *interchange : state :: state : decay*. This chiastic pattern represents resolved thought, thought which has already come to its conclusions, which has imposed its conceptual organization on linear or fluctuating nature.

But this chiastic pattern of wrapped-up conclusions has been accompanied here by a different pattern, the linear pattern representing entropy: *towers* become *down razed; brass* becomes *slave*. In the last three lines, this "natural" pattern of unreversed ruin "defeats" the intellectual mastery-by-chiasmus, as the concept of gradual leakage comes to represent personal loss. Time takes love away, a thought is like a death, one weeps to have what one fears to lose. In fact, the striking parallelism of the last line—*weep to have . . . fears to lose*—is the direct syntactic antithesis of chiasmus. *Hav[ing]* while *fear[ing] to lose* is already a form of losing, imaginatively speaking, and the "leakage" represented by the several instances of unmastered linearity in the couplet—where nothing curls, gathers in, or rounds off—shows Shakespeare's choice of a rhetorical figure of decline for apprehensive and doomed possession, which even a "philosophical" view cannot succeed in defeating.

KEY WORD: HAVE (because of pun on auxiliary and full use)

Couplet Tie: *have* (1, 5, 9, 14)
lose [*loss*] (9, 9, 4)

65

SInce braſſe,nor ſtone,nor earth,nor boundleſſe ſea,
But ſad mortallity ore-ſwaies their power,
How with this rage ſhall beautie hold a plea,
Whoſe action is no ſtronger then a flower?
O how ſhall ſummers hunny breath hold out,
Againſt the wrackfull ſiedge of battring dayes,
When rocks impregnable are not ſo ſtoute,
Nor gates of ſteele ſo ſtrong but time decayes?
O fearefull meditation, where alack,
Shall times beſt Iewell from times cheſt lie hid?
Or what ſtrong hand can hold his ſwift foote back,
Or who his ſpoile or beautie can forbid?
  O none,vnleſſe this miracle haue might,
  That in black inck my loue may ſtill ſhine bright.

Since brass, nor stone, nor earth, nor boundless sea,
But sad mortality o'ersways their power,
How with this rage shall beauty hold a plea,
Whose action is no stronger than a flower?
O how shall summer's honey breath hold out
Against the wrackful siege of batt'ring days,
When rocks impregnable are not so stout,
Nor gates of steel so strong, but Time decays?
O fearful meditation: Where, alack,
Shall Time's best jewel from Time's chest lie hid?
Or what strong hand can hold his swift foot back,
Or who his spoil of beauty can forbid?
  O none, unless this miracle have might,
  That in black ink my love may still shine bright.

SONNET 65 reconsiders decay, and admits, with regret but with stoicism as well, that in order to combat decay the poem must leave the natural order altogether. The body of 65 demands some form of *hold[ing]* in the contest that it imagines beauty will have to wage against Time. How shall beauty *hold a plea* (Q_1), how shall summer's breath *hold out* (Q_2), what swift hand can *hold back* Time (Q_3); the rage, the siege, the spoil must in some way be contested. Some sort of holding action by some *strong hand* is in order. We might expect to find the couplet playing on *hold*, too, somewhat as the couplet of 60 plays on *stand*. But the couplet abandons the physical means of holding called for by the body of the sonnet, realizing that in the natural order there is no hope for winning that future battle. Instead, the couplet departs from the natural order altogether, putting its hope in *miracle*. I call this sort of arrangement that of a DEFECTIVE KEY WORD, since Shakespeare has trained us, through his repeated construction of KEY WORD sonnets, to expect *hold* in C once we have found it in Q_1, Q_2, and Q_3. (The same is true, e.g., for *excuse* in 51.) We are then forced to ask what, in the member missing the KEY WORD, takes the KEY WORD's place. Here it is *miracle;* (in 51 it is *leave to go*).

There is a second DEFECTIVE KEY WORD in this sonnet: it is STRONG[-ER]. Like HOLD, STRONG is absent in C, because it too belongs to the (mistaken) hope that Time's depredations can be prevented by opposing to them some contrary strength that exists in the inorganic or organic order. When this hope of physical survival is abandoned in favor of the virtual order of *miracle*, the STRONG HOLD of physical force disappears as well.

After the powerlessness of organic nature has been acknowledged, the beloved cannot be said to *live . . . still green* organically in black lines (63); but if one leaves the realm of nature for the supernatural realm of *miracle* (etymologically, "that which is to be wondered at"), the beloved may *still shine bright in black ink*, inorganically, as a jewel or star might. The *might* of the auxiliary *may* can be said to be the generative pun of the couplet (noted by Booth). It is not until we notice the sounds and letters held in common by ***miracle*** and ***black inck*** (Quarto spelling) that the conjunction of *miracle* and *black in[c]k* makes poetic sense.

When we look at the view of the natural order that precedes the couplet's trust in *miracle*, we find that Time, like Proteus, has more than one form: there are two enemies to permanence. The first is *sad mortality*, or entropy, which is more powerful than all those inorganic forms previously named in sonnet 64, even the most architecturally enduring *(brass, stone)* and the most extended *(earth, boundless sea)*. The second enemy to permanence is *rage*, which seems to be (as in 64) the martial version of natural destructiveness. This *rage*, once named, is presented again in the periphrasis *the wrackful siege of batt'ring days* (the word *rage* may be said to be the portmanteau version of *wra[ckful sie]ge*). *Rocks* and *gates of steel* are as unable to resist wrathful Time as *stone* and *brass* were unable to outface *sad mortality*. It will be observed that Time's combats with brass, stone, earth, boundless sea, rocks, and gates of steel have already happened: Time's combats with the organic flower and its honey breath are yet to come *(shall)*, and their outcome is feared by the speaker, given Time's success against stronger opponents. The organic order, summoned up in the octave, is the chief casualty of the sestet, which must reenvisage beauty in inorganic terms, as a *jewel* which can shine in black ink. This sonnet abandons, with the poignant valedictory allusion to *summer's honey breath*, any hope of an organically analogous *eternal summer* (sonnet 18).

Though Time was first entropic *mortality*, then martial *rage*, it soon becomes a force that *decays;* and finally it is feared as a possible de[*spoil*]er of *beauty* whose *swift foot* eludes restraint. When we attempt to account for these changes of metaphor, we see that Protean Time seems to change his ways depending on his opponent, using mortality, battering, or decay as he sees fit; but there is something disproportionate about imagining his heavy artillery being expended (as the speaker fears it will be) against the delicate and the evanescent. Precisely this disproportion causes the pathos of the envisaged ill-matched contests of Time with flowerlike beauty and summer's sweet fragrance in Q_1 and Q_2. In Q_3, by contrast, in the wake of beauty's transformation into an inorganic jewel, Time suddenly becomes a majestic victor claiming the spoils of war—an opponent worthy of his envisaged prize (not, interestingly, the "vulgar thief" feared in sonnet 48).

In the major aesthetic internal rearrangement of the poem, the speaker's hopes have shifted from the organic to the inorganic: although a flowerlike beauty may not endure the envisaged future contest with time, he hopes that a diamondlike beauty-as-*jewel* may; and in a coordinate change, *beauty* (whose action is no stronger than a flower) need no longer be its own defender, but gains a champion who will dispute Time on beauty's behalf. This champion will have to be the poet, who is at first awed by his own venture: *O fearful meditation: Where? . . . What hand? . . . Who? . . . O none, unless—.*

The final change in tone from the lament for organic fragile beauty and evanescent fragrance to the strong hope for inorganic miracle is a marked one. It entails abandoning the three organic uses of *hold*, one per quatrain: that flowerlike beauty *hold a plea* (impossible); that fragrance *hold out* (impossible); that a hand *hold back* (impossible for an organic hand; possible only if the strong *hand* found to work the miracle is a punningly inorganic one). The *mira* of *miracle* may have appealed to Shakespeare as an anagram of *rima* (rhyme), as he decided to assert that human literary powers could *o'ersway* sad mortality, martial rage, and Time's swift foot. What is preserved in black ink is not solely the quality of beauty, however, but the poet's entire beloved—in his carbonized allomorph as jewel. The changing of beauty from organic to inorganic form enables Shakespeare to "save" the beloved, but at the cost of admitting as well the inorganic nature of writing (*hand* as "handwriting") and what is preserved in it. The contrast of the chiastic order of the octave (strong things : beauty :: beauty : strong things) with the linearity of the sestet once again (as in 64) exhibits the "collectedness" of chiastic philosophical meditation compared to the linearity of "presentness" in thinking. It should be noticed that of the three questions—*Where? What hand? Who?*—the author modestly answers only the first, but by his answer—*in black ink*—implies the answers to the other two: "*my* hand," "*I.*"

The break between octave and Q_3 here is marked by the ejaculation *O*, but the break does not disturb the twelve-line pattern of interrogatives constructing the body of the poem: *how* (twice), *where*, *what*, and finally *who*. The chiastic *Since : how :: how : when* of the octave again serves to define it as a philosophical construct against the immediacy of Q_3; but the increasingly shorter line-lengths of the questions (4-4-2-1-1) join the octave to Q_3 in an *accelerando*.

The effects of sound in the poem are notable—*rage/wrackful/siege/battering/rocks impregnable*, ***steel** so **strong***, etc.—especially when contrasted with the innocent hum of *summer's honey breath*. The prosody too claims attention, especially in the retarding spondees of the monosyllabic *Or what strong hand can hold his swift foot back*. (I accept the emendation "spoil *of* beauty".)

DEFECTIVE KEY WORDS: HOLD (missing in C)
STRONG[-ER] (missing in C)

Couplet Tie: *steel, still* (8, 14).
Also, if one accepts phonetically anagrammatic Couplet Ties, *Time, might* [tīm, mīt] (8, 13). In this phonetic case, the two possessive *Time's* do not enter into the Couplet Tie.

66

TYr'd with all theſe for reſtfull death I cry,
As to behold deſert a begger borne,
And needie Nothing trimd in iollitie,
And pureſt faith vnhappily forſworne,
And gilded honor ſhamefully miſplaſt,
And maiden vertue rudely ſtrumpeted,
And right perfection wrongfully diſgrac'd,
And ſtrength by limping ſway diſabled,
And arte made tung-tide by authoritie,
And Folly (Doctor-like) controuling skill,
And ſimple-Truth miſcalde Simplicitie,
And captiue-good attending Captaine ill.
Tyr'd with all theſe, from theſe would I be gone,
Saue that to dye, I leaue my loue alone.

Tired with all these, for restful death I cry:
As to behold desert a beggar born,
And needy nothing trimmed in jollity,
And purest faith unhappily forsworn,
And gilded honour shamefully misplaced,
And maiden virtue rudely strumpeted,
And right perfection wrongfully disgraced,
And strength by limping sway disablèd,
And art made tongue-tied by authority,
And folly (doctor-like) controlling skill,
And simple truth miscalled simplicity,
And captive good attending captain ill.
Tired with all these, from these would I be gone,
Save that to die, I leave my love alone.

TIRED WITH ALL THESE—with what? The poem answers with a masquelike procession of ill-doing which contains sixteen people (more or less, depending on how one sees certain lines). The figures pass before the speaker, and he describes them for us. Halfway through the procession, the look of the masque changes: the figures begin to pass by in twos—master and slave—instead of by ones. What does this mean?

"A couplet preceded by its expansion" might be the most accurate structural description of 66. Here is its couplet-summary:

> Tired with *all these* (i.e., lines 2–12) from these would I be gone,
> Save that to die, I leave my love alone.

By the pre-positioning of the deictic *these* in the first line of the poem, before its referents have been named, Shakespeare makes his speaker one who is summing up a list of anterior experiences which, as we are to learn, have exhausted his faith in justice and his hope for a better society. Suicide would be his choice except that to leave his love the prey of others in such a savage social world would be a betrayal of his sole anchor of value, fidelity in love. The burden thereby placed on that value is evident.

Although the eleven-line procession of social crimes (one per line) at first appears random, it is not. As I have said, in the major modulation of the poem, which occurs at line 8, the nature of the one-by-one processional masque of victims and profiteers changes: now the victim at last begins to be accompanied by the victimizer. We no longer see *maiden virtue rudely strumpeted* without being told who was responsible: instead we see *strength disablèd* accompanied by the person, *limping sway*, who did the disabling, and so on. Who makes art tongue-tied? *Authority.* Who controls skill? *Folly.* Who is in charge of limping sway, censor-authority, and doctorlike folly? *Captain ill.* Whereas the first half of the sonnet engaged only in lament, the second half, naming the criminals, says "*J'accuse.*" With respect to its speech-acts—lament followed by resolve—this poem resembles its predecessor, 65.

The organizing grammatical figures of the poem are the past participle and the present participle: the speaker, powerless to intervene, can only behold what has already happened and what is happening before him.

In a "neater" version of this poem, the octave would show only unaccompanied persons, and the third quatrain would show victims-plus-victimizers. Instead we see the coupled victim-plus-victimizer entering one line too early (in the last line of the octave), and the third quatrain making up for this proleptic insertion by possessing a strayed "victim-only" line (line 11). So too, in a neater version, the past participle would "own" the octave, the present participle the third quatrain. Instead, the past participle "spills over" into the sestet, in a Shakespearean example of the *volta*, a characteristic figure for feeling overflowing its banks. It is as though the speaker in line 8 "accelerates" by anticipation his saved-up *J'accuse* (in showing the victimizer with the victim), and in line 11 "overspills" his original single-figure procession of victims into his later coupled one. Also, a "neater" version would have populated the octave with victims alone, whereas Shakespeare shows us people unjustly raised up *(needy nothing . . . gilded honour)* as well as those unjustly cast down. He thus shows himself to be concerned with two kinds of injustice, in which elevation of the undeserving is as reprehensible as the victimizing of the innocent.

Past and present participles come attended (lines 4–7) by adverbs of indictment—*unhappily*, *shamefully*, *rudely*, *wrongfully*—which suggest that, to the speaker's mind, there does exist a real social alternative: the happy alternative to the unhappy, the pure alternative to the shameful, the courteous to the rude, the right to the wrong—an alternative by which faith could be honored, honor justly bestowed, virtue preserved, and perfection exalted. The corrupt society is being measured against an independent morality firmly held to be self-evident. The many prefixes of undoing suggest a perversion in the social order: *un-happily*, *for-sworn*, *mis-placed*, *dis-graced*, *dis-ablèd*, *mis-called.*

The overwhelming cry—*How? Why? By Whom?*—is at first repressed as the allegorical procession of social crimes begins to pass by us. Worth *(desert)* files by in beggar's robes; he is followed, in contrast, by (as the context makes clear) a worthless person dressed in fine clothes; next comes *faith*, betrayed; next a courtier who does not deserve the *gilded honour* awarded him; next a prostituted girl once a virgin; next a virtuous person now wrongfully disgraced. None of this is explained. Finally the *cui bono* bursts out: *Sway* limps, and would be worsted by *strength* unless it took pains to disable that strength; *authority* is false, and its falsity would be exposed by *art*'s disclosure, except that art has had its tongue tied (in a spondee) by that very authority; *skill* would excel except that the *docti*, or learned *fools*, control it institutionally; simple *truth* would prevail were it not labeled (by those same *docti*, no doubt) "naiveté"; and *good* would exert its power were it not held captive by the evil *(ill)* who is everywhere the prince of this world. The diabolic is here naturalized and secularized as *captain* (i.e., chief) *ill*. It is implied that any deserving, rightly perfect, good, virtuous, faithful, honorable, strong, skillful, and truthful person will soon find himself caught by one of the victimizers. And who, under such conditions, could justify leaving his love—somewhere in the procession—alone?

As the poem progresses, passing in its paratactic *and . . . and . . . and* from social, moral, and political wrongs to aesthetic, cognitive, and linguistic evils, we see that the speaker has a hierarchy of social abuses in mind. These roughly parallel the Christian hierarchy of sins, in which sins of the flesh are ranked as less serious than sins of the will and the intellect. For Shakespeare (the artist in language) *miscall[ing]* is the greatest sin, and is therefore placed in the climactic position, closely preceded by the pretense of learning *(doctor-like folly)* and censorship of art.

If indeed art has been rendered tongue-tied, the poem cannot afford to appear "eloquent." What would a tongue-tied art sound like? It would sound (to use a modern simile) like a needle stuck in a groove, which is precisely what this wearily reiterative and syntactically poverty-stricken *and . . . and* sonnet offers as utterance. It is so tired, and so tongue-tied, that it sounds repetitive and anticlimatic: the Couplet Tie is *tired with all these* and *death* [*die*]. Even its generalizing lack of specificity is tongue-tied; and the un-Shakespearean tri- and quadrisyllabic rhymes *(jollity, strumpeted, disablèd, authority, simplicity)* make lines end weakly. The sonnet "comes alive" only if readers "animate" it by reflecting, as each character in the masque passes by, on the contemporary face they would attach to each personage. The poem then becomes acute, relevant, and painful.

Since this is the most visible instance of Shakespeare's use of one-line units in the sonnets, I should perhaps say that his more usual strategy is to use one-line units to precede two-line and/or three- or four-line ones. See, e.g., 130 *(My mistress' eyes are nothing like the sun)*, which allots one line to eyes, lips, breasts, and hair; then two lines apiece to cheeks, breath, voice, and gait. The putatively early tetrameter "Hathaway" sonnet (145) is partitioned into units as follows: 3,4; 1; 4,2, where the one-line unit represents the mistress' change from *I hate* to *I hate not you:* the free-standing line says the mistress *taught [her tongue] thus anew to greet.* Point-making of this sort is the usual dramatic function of one-line units: *Music to hear, why hear'st thou music sadly?* (sonnet 8), *O change thy thought, that I may change my mind!* (sonnet 10) Since one is accustomed to the innate drama of the one-line unit by the time one arrives, in reading the sequence, at 66, its one-line units seem designedly pointed, and, by their superfluity of presence, designedly exhausted.

Couplet Tie: *Tired with all these* (1, 13)
death [*die*] (1, 14)

67

AH wherefore with infection ſhould he liue,
And with his preſence grace impietie,
That ſinne by him aduantage ſhould atchiue,
And lace it ſelfe with his ſocietie ?
Why ſhould falſe painting immitate his cheeke,
And ſteale dead ſeeing of his liuing hew?
Why ſhould poore beautie indirectly ſeeke,
Roſes of ſhaddow, ſince his Roſe is true?
Why ſhould he liue, now nature banckrout is,
Beggerd of blood to bluſh through liuely vaines,
For ſhe hath no exchecker now but his,
And proud of many, liues vpon his gaines?
  O him ſhe ſtores, to ſhow what welth ſhe had,
  In daies long ſince, before theſe laſt ſo bad.

Ah wherefore with infection should he live,
And with his presence grace impiety,
That sin by him advantage should achieve,
And lace itself with his society?
Why should false painting imitate his cheek,
And steal dead seeming of his living hue?
Why should poor beauty indirectly seek
Roses of shadow, since his rose is true?
Why should he live, now Nature bankrout is,
Beggared of blood to blush through lively veins,
For she hath no exchequer now but his,
And 'priv'd of many, lives upon his gains?
  O him she stores, to show what wealth she had,
  In days long since, before these last so bad.

SONNETS 67 and 68 are in some sense the "same" poem, bearing the "same" couplet:

O him she stores, to show what wealth she had,
And him as for a map doth Nature store
In days long since, before these last so bad.
To show false Art what beauty was of yore.

The beloved has outlived the Golden Age, his era; he is a museum piece, a living relic, maintained alive by Nature as her exhibit of what beauty and truth once were, when they were conjoined in one person. It is that paradisal conjunction of beauty-and-truth which is the governing idea of both 67 and 68, as of 54 (roses against canker blooms) and 14 *(Thy end is truth's and beauty's doom and date).* Various metaphors about the decay of nature are loosely (and perhaps incoherently) associated in 67: health has yielded to *infection*, piety to *impiety*, *grace* to *sin*, the *true* to the *false*, substance to *shadow*, *living hue* to *dead* art, creation to *imitat[ion]*, directness to *indirect[ness]*, *gains* to *beggar[y]*, use to usury *(gains)*. The chief incoherence seems to lie in the abrupt change from the moral (Q_1) and aesthetic (Q_2) contexts of the young man's life to the financial and mythological contexts of the sestet (associated with *bankrout Nature*). I am not entirely sure of the aesthetic motivation for this change. It certainly serves to defuse (through mythological play in the personification of Nature) the indignant horror of the first quatrain, which betrays, by its inner and outer rhymes and its repetition of *with*, the false young man's collusion with sin:

He [does] *live with* infection and *grace impiety;*
Sin [does] *achieve* advantage and *lace* itself *with* his *society.*

The rhyme of *impiety* with *his society* suggests that they resemble each other, and the end rhyme of *he live / sin atchive* (Quarto spelling) reinforces the association of the young man with sin.

The pained outcry against the young man's habits of evil company is rapidly deflected onto the acts of his bad coevals *false painting* and *poor [imperfect] beauty*, who use cosmetics to acquire the beauty which in him is natural. *Wherefore should he live with infection?* finally modulates into *Why should he live?* as the disturbed question of Q_1 becomes mock-aggression. The Latinate eloquence of *infection* and *impiety* declines into the bald statement *these bad days*. The sestet's Euphuism—*bankrout, beggared, blood, blush*—suggests a deflection of the poem into fancifulness, away from intensity.

The rhetorical structure—four questions plus a couplet-answer—piles up rhetorical suspense, or would do so if the poem did not appear, after Q_1, to be toying with its own queries. The proportioning of the questions (4-2-2-4) exhibits a chiastic symmetry that ultimately "calms down" the genuine agitation of Q_1.

Though there is no unmistakable Couplet Tie, there are several aspects linking the couplet to the body of the poem. One link is a phonetic one, *sin*, present in line 3 and hidden in line 14's *since*. The use of *stores* in line 13 is, as Booth notes, "not idiomatic"; I suspect that here, as elsewhere in the sonnets, *store* is used because it is a word that contains within itself the letters of *rose*. (*Roses of shadow, since his rose is true* [line 8] rather drags the rose in where it is not expected.)

DEFECTIVE KEY WORD: LIVE [-S] [-ing] (missing in C). This is a DEFECTIVE KEY WORD sonnet, since we expect, after seeing *live* [*-ing*] [*-s*] in Q_1, Q_2, and Q_3, to find some variant of *live* in C. We discover, by its absence in C, that the young man does not really "live" in the present, rather, he is a preserved relic of the past. Nature is now bankrupt, and would not now be able to produce another such as the young man; so she "stores" him, whom she created long ago, as an exemplum of her past wealth. The "deletion" of *live* from the couplet makes us realize, as nothing else could, the museum-piece nature of the young man. "Why should he live with infection? Why should he live?" Answer: "He does not *live;* he is *store[d].*"

68

THus is his cheeke the map of daies out-worne,
When beauty liu'd and dy'ed as flowers do now,
Before these bastard signes of faire were borne,
Or durst inhabit on a liuing brow:
Before the goulden tresses of the dead,
The right of sepulchers, were shorne away,
To liue a scond life on second head,
Ere beauties dead fleece made another gay:
In him those holy antique howers are seene,
Without all ornament, it selfe and true,
Making no summer of an others greene,
Robbing no ould to dresse his beauty new,
And him as for a map doth Nature store,
To shew faulse Art what beauty was of yore.

Thus is his cheek the map of days outworn,
When beauty lived and died as flowers do now,
Before these bastard signs of fair were borne,
Or durst inhabit on a living brow;
Before the golden tresses of the dead,
The right of sepulchres, were shorn away,
To live a second life on second head;
Ere beauty's dead fleece made another gay:
In him those holy ántique hours are seen,
Without all ornament, itself and true,
Making no summer of another's green,
Robbing no old to dress his beauty new;
And him as for a map doth Nature store,
To show false Art what beauty was of yore.

STORE (repeated from 67) may be employed, as I have said, because it contains the letters making up *rose.* Four other words in this sonnet (in the Quarto spelling) also contain the letters for *rose: shorne*, *flowers*, *howers*, and *others*. These, with *store*, compose a bouquet of five invisible roses—in fact, one might say, *roses of shadow* (67). Sonnet 68 may be taken as an expansion of Q_2 of 67.

The ostensible plan of 68 is to praise the young man as a living example of the Golden Age. This praise is the way the octave begins; this praise (after the "derailing" in lines 3–8 of the octave's original intent) also marks the fresh start undertaken in the sestet. But the sestet too is "derailed" away from praise, and into satire of the present, even faster than the octave was.

The octave begins with two lines comparing the natural flourishing of beauty in the Golden Age to the life and death of flowers in the present; but this positive aspect of the present is replaced by a series of contrasts which denigrate the present. In these, the poem ceases to be a praise of the young man and becomes instead "a satire to decay" (100). The critique of the present progresses from the vague *(these bastard signs of fair)* to the specific *(the golden tresses of the dead . . . on second head)*, reintroducing the *poor beauty* of 67 which has to rely on stealing adornment for itself.

The octave, concerned with the extinction of living beauty in the criminal present age, plays repeatedly on the words *live* and *die*, both in its initial statement and in the three *Before*, *Before*, *Ere* clauses that follow:

"when beauty *lived and died*"	(the natural paradigm)
"bastard signs *borne* . . . inhabit on a *living* brow"	(contamination)
"tresses of *dead* shorn away"	(violation of corpse)
"to *live* a second *life*"	(violation of natural order)
"beauty's *dead* fleece . . . another gay"	(profit from grave-robbery)

The three "before" clauses might seem merely a bizarre excursus into the evils of wig-making were it not for lines 5–6, with their expression of the felt physical pang of *the golden tresses of the dead*, felt even more in the parallel passage from *The Merchant of Venice* III, ii, 72–101. This speech of Bassanio's follows the song "Tell me where is fancy bred," which imputes all phases both of passion and of the extinction of passion to the eye alone. Bassanio, before repudiating the golden casket, discourses on the horrifying noncoincidence of appearance with reality; one of his examples is fair (but false) hair worn by a deceiving woman:

> So are those crispèd snaky golden locks,
> Which make such wanton gambols with the wind
> Upon supposèd fairness, often known
> To be the dowry of a second head,
> The skull that bred them in the sepulchre.

But it is not only the sensuous actuality of the reminiscence embodied in *the golden tresses of the dead* that gives 68 seriousness; a different sort of gravity underlies the phrase *the right of sepulchres.* This phrase summons up the demarcation of sacred ritual space: it is not only robbery to steal the tresses of the dead—it is profaneness (< *pro-fanum,* outside the shrine).

Once the octave's deviation into indictment of the present as a grisly grave-robber has been completed, it would seem that the speaker should be able to resume, in the sestet, his original intent—to praise his friend. But once again the nostalgically positive beginning *(holy ántique hours)* yields to a reference to contemporary *ornament,* contrasting a garishly bedecked present to the unadorned past. Finally, another accusation of *robbing* recurs, as Q_3 veers to accusation of present thieves who rob the *old* and dress themselves in others' *green.*

Even Nature (as we see from the couplet) is not immune from contamination by the present. She keeps the young man, not, as in 20, for her own doting, but rather for defensive and public purposes of bitter contrast—*To show false Art what beauty was of yore.*

In its repeated fall, in both octave and Q_3, from positive praise into satiric contrast, the poem enacts the present impossibility of lasting Edenic beauty. The peculiarly reductive comparison of the young man's cheek (line 1) and then the young man himself (line 13) to a *map* (rather than to, say, a statue) suggests that the whole rich three-dimensional being of *days outworn* can be stored in him only in a schematic and flat way. Therefore, praise cannot be "rounded," but continually skids off into satiric contrast.

KEY WORD: BEAUTY [-'S]

Couplet Tie: *map* (1, 13)
beauty [-'*s*] (2, 8, 12, 14)

69

THose parts of thee that the worlds eye doth view,
Want nothing that the thought of hearts can mend:
All toungs(the voice of soules)giue thee that end,
Vttring bare truth,euen so as foes Commend.
Their outward thus with outward praise is crownd,
But those same toungs that giue thee so thine owne,
In other accents doe this praise confound
By seeing farther then the eye hath showne.
They looke into the beauty of thy mind,
And that in guesse they measure by thy deeds,
Then churls their thoughts(although their eies were kind)
To thy faire flower ad the rancke smell of weeds,
  But why thy odor matcheth not thy show,
  The solye is this,that thou doest common grow.

Those parts of thee that the world's eye doth view
Want nothing that the thought of hearts can mend;
All tongues (the voice of souls) give thee that due,
Utt'ring bare truth, even so as foes commend.
Thy outward thus with outward praise is crowned;
But those same tongues that give thee so thine own,
In other accents do this praise confound
By seeing farther than the eye hath shown.
They look into the beauty of thy mind,
And that in guess they measure by thy deeds;
Then, churls, their thoughts (although their eyes were kind)
To thy fair flower add the rank smell of weeds:
  But why thy odour matcheth not thy show,
  The soil is this, that thou dost common grow.

WE encounter here the conventional Renaissance inherited lists, physiological and psychological, of the parts of the human form. We hear in Q_1 of *eyes, thoughts, hearts, tongues, souls;* and in Q_3 these aspects are further complicated by the introduction of *beauty, mind,* and *deeds.* These terms exist not in isolation, but rather in intense social and psychological interaction. *Hearts* produce loving *thoughts,* which normally attempt to *mend* the lacks perceived in the looks of ordinary beloveds. (Only in the young man's exterior do they find nothing to mend.) But certain *souls,* though they use *tongues* to praise the young man's beauty, do so unwillingly and scantily *(even so as foes commend),* because they see into the young man's nature, as the more distant *world's eye* cannot.

If most of the octave is devoted to the (indubitable presence of) external beauty in the friend, Q_3 (really beginning with the *But* of line 6) is devoted to a measurement (necessarily indirect) of his interior *mind.* Its state—is it beautiful? is it ugly?—can be measured only by the external evidence of the young man's *deeds;* and though the *eyes* of others are still delighted by his beauty, the *thoughts* of others ascribe to him the *rank smell of weeds.* The couplet affects to explain (*solye*—the Quarto spelling—is a crux) the disparity between the praise recorded in the octave and the dispraise of Q_3, between *show* and substance *(odour),* blaming the production of *weed-deeds* on the *commonness* (perhaps the infected and impious society of 67) in the young man's growth (a pun on "common soil," terrain held in common, may be suggested if one interprets *solye* as *soil*).

Shakespeare's representations of both the viewers and the young man can be schematized as a set of concentric circles, as shown in the diagram. The synecdochic *eyes* and *tongues* of the viewers organize the poem, both of them commending the young man's outward *beauty,* but the tongues finding they must, at least in their *hearts' thought,* condemn the young man's *mind.* The sonnet's play on a mismatch between substance and appearance, *odour* and *show,* looks to 54 and to 94: the canker rose, the festering lily, the flower in the bed of weeds, belong to the same image-cluster.

The Couplet Tie, emphasizing the deceptiveness of appearance, is *show* [*-n*]. The very proportions of the sonnet betray the governing power of judgmental *soul-tongues* over the power of the visible *parts,* how-

Structure of Sonnet 69

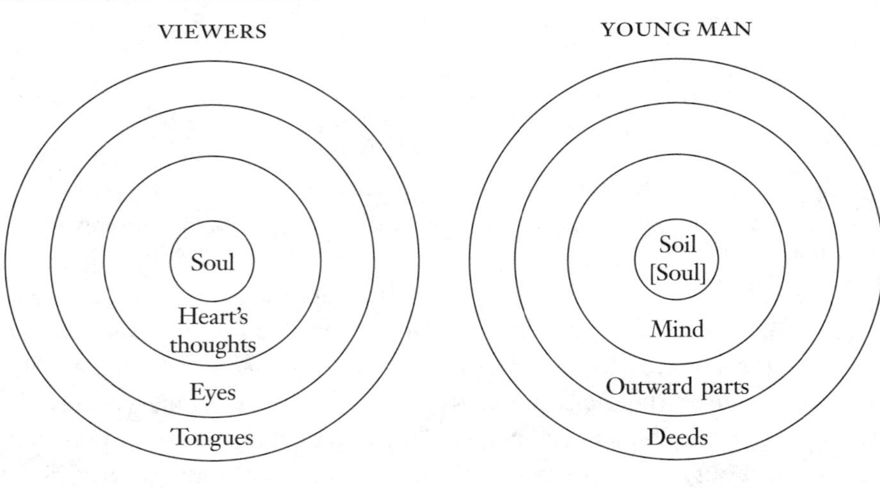

ever beautiful, of the young man. The young man's outward *parts* govern the first two lines; the charily praising *tongues* the next two. *Thy outward* (crowned with *outward* praise) governs line 5, but condemning *tongues-thoughts* govern lines 6–12, clearly tipping the scale of proportion increasingly in favor of moral condemnation.

The naked confrontation here between the Platonic conviction that a beautiful body necessarily betokens a beautiful mind, and the Christian conviction that solely by a man's deeds may his inner beauty be measured, is only feebly resolved by ascribing the young man's defects of mind to his environment (as he grows *common*) rather than to himself. The careful avoidance of the word *soul* ("essential form"), after its first occurrence in line 3, suggests that the speaker flinches from the ascription of the young man's evil *deeds* to a corrupt soul within. It is less damning to ascribe them to an [un]beauti[ful] *mind*. But the repressed word *soul* arrives, perhaps, in the *solye* (variously emended) of the close. (Shakespeare's early editor, George Steevens, chose *sole* as his emendation, perceiving perhaps how the word *mind* has repressed the expected *soul* in line 9. Shakespeare puns on soul/sole in *Merchant of Venice*, IV, i, 123, and in *Romeo and Juliet*, I, iv, 15. The consensus of editors has been that the printer incorrectly set *soyle;* but even that word harks back to the *souls* of line 3. I adopt *soil*, though I think Steevens' *sole* is also persuasive.)

This poem exhibits the word *eye(s)* in each member except the couplet, making this a DEFECTIVE KEY WORD poem. One must ask why *eye*, present in Q_1, Q_2, and Q_3, should be omitted from C, and what replaces it. The sonnet concerns the puzzle to perception set by the dissonance between the young man's looks and his deeds. All would-be judgments of his corruption are baffled by the eye's involuntary capitulation to his beauty. As long as the eye is in the picture, the judgment remains ambiguous. Even the churls can only *guess* the nature of the young man's mind. But, alas, by the time of the couplet no ambiguity remains: the speaker bluntly concedes that *thy odour matcheth not thy show*. This moral verdict is made without the distraction of the eye; it is made by the cognitive mind, judging virtue *(odour)*. The eye is shut, and vanishes from C.

DEFECTIVE KEY WORD: EYE [-S] (missing in C)

Couplet Tie: *show* [-*n*] (8, 13)
eye [-*s*] (1, 8, 11, 14)

70

THat thou are blam'd ſhall not be thy defect,
For ſlanders marke was euer yet the faire,
The ornament of beauty is ſuſpect,
A Crow that flies in heauens ſweeteſt ayre.
So thou be good,ſlander doth but approue,
Their worth the greater beeing woo'd of time,
For Canker vice the ſweeteſt buds doth loue,
And thou preſent'ſt a pure vnſtayined prime.
Thou haſt paſt by the ambuſh of young daies,
Either not aſſayld,or victor beeing charg'd,
Yet this thy praiſe cannot be ſoe thy praiſe,
To tye vp enuy,euermore inlarged,
  If ſome ſuſpect of ill maskt not thy ſhow,
  Then thou alone kingdomes of hearts ſhouldſt owe.

That thou are blamed shall not be thy defect,
For slander's mark was ever yet the fair;
The ornament of beauty is suspéct,
A crow that flies in heaven's sweetest air.
So thou be good, slander doth but approve
Thy worth the greater, being wooed of time,
For canker vice the sweetest buds doth love,
And thou present'st a pure unstainèd prime.
Thou hast passed by the ambush of young days,
Either not assailed, or victor being charged,
Yet this thy praise cannot be so thy praise
To tie up envy, evermore enlarged:
  If some suspéct of ill masked not thy show,
  Then thou alone kingdoms of hearts shouldst owe.

THE Couplet Tie here is *suspéct* (a noun meaning "suspicion"). This reinforces the theme of ill-doing, which the speaker does his best to dismiss by a succession of sophistries addressed to the young man: The fair, like you, are always blamed; Slander, seen to be false, will improve your reputation; Even if ambushed by vice, you have emerged victorious; and so on. Though one might expect some warning (as in sonnet 94) to the young man to mend his ways so as not to give occasion for slander, no such advice is offered. Instead, the poem ends in a final economic sophistry, saying that the young man would exert a monopoly over all hearts, more or less (whole *kingdoms of hearts*), leaving few hearts available for others, were it not that some people are deterred from loving him by the *suspéct of ill* detracting from his appeal.

The aesthetic dynamic here is based on a mock battle of words. As soon as a "bad" word enters, a "good" one springs up to refute it. A fusillade begins the poem: *blamed, defect, slander. Fair, ornament,* and *beauty* leap to the defense. *Suspéct* and *crow* are countered by *heaven's sweetest air. Slander* (in its reappearance) is bracketed by *good* on the left, *worth* and *wooed* on the right; *canker vice* is followed by *sweetest buds* and *pure unstainèd prime. Passed by* precancels *ambush,* which is further canceled on the right by *not assailed* and *victor being charged.* The doubled *praise* (line 11) struggles hard, but loses to its wonderfully onomatopoetic "bad" foe, *envy, evermore inlarged* (Quarto spelling), which enacts the ever-widening crescendo of "slander." This envisaged defeat of ever-redoubled praise by the chorus of "envious" tongues poisons, by retroactive implication, the whole anterior part of the poem. The fair will continue to be branded by suspéct and slander, heaven's sweetest air will contain more and more cawing and obscuring crows, canker vice will eat away more and more of the sweet buds. Less and less will one hear of the young man's victories over ambush, more and more will one hear reports that stain his prime. *Suspéct of ill* is permanent. It masks not his true substance, as we would expect his defender to assert, but his *show*—a curious evasion of a discussion of his inner merit. The evasion is particularly telling since the poem has progressed to questions of virtue in Q_2 *(good, worth, pure, unstained)* after having dwelt on questions of appearance *(fair, beauty)* in Q_1, with *sweetest* the adjective ambiguously shared—since it can mean aesthetically "loveliest" as well as virtuously "best"—by both quatrains. By resolving itself only on the aesthetic side ("Your beauty would win you all hearts were it not for the suspicion of evil masking your appearance"), the poem betrays its speaker's terror of investigating too closely the moral purity of his beloved. The *mark* of line 2 becomes the *mask* of line 13, a near Couplet Tie. *Masked* shares the *kt* end-sound with *defect* and *suspéct*, a "suspicious" sound when compared to the open, "candid" vowel sounds found in words like *pure* and *fair.*

The organization of 70 in two-line units represents another of Shakespeare's structural experiments. Though two-line units occur very often in the *Sonnets,* only a limited number of the poems have as their logical construction seven two-line units; usually at least one of the quatrains spreads itself, logically, over four lines. Among those constructed in two-line units (e.g., 4, 36, 75, 133, and perhaps 148), it is here in 70 and in 75 that Shakespeare most exploits the potential of two-line units for antithesis, using them to represent the back-and-forth of inner division. In 75, for instance, we see in two two-line units, the miser uncertain, from line to line, whether to enjoy his wealth or fear its loss, whether to remain alone with it or show it off:

Now proud as a enjoyer, and anon
Doubting the filching age will steal his treasure;
Now counting best to be with you alone,
Then bettered that the world may see my pleasure.

The zigzag from line to line visible in 75 is complicated here in 70 by the wish to refute the slanderers in their own coin—the coin of "everybody says." To this end Shakespeare resorts to proverbs. We might repoint the sonnet thus, as Shakespeare thinks of old saws to quote back to the slanderers (and to his own suspicions):

[That thou art blamed shall not be thy defect,
For "slander's mark was ever yet the fair";
"The ornament of beauty is suspéct"
(A crow that flies in heaven's sweetest air).
So thou be good, slander doth but approve
Thy worth the greater, being wooed of time;
For "canker vice the sweetest buds doth love,"
And thou present'st a pure unstainèd prime.]

The line-by-line back-and-forth movement of these two-line octave-units and those of the sestet (except for the enjambed lines 11–12) make the distinct "evermore enlarged" crescendo pattern of lines 11–12 doubly foreboding by contrast. The rationalizing couplet may obscure, but not obliterate, the conclusion that praise, however prolonged, cannot restrain the malice of "slandering" tongues. The speaker's equivocation in line 9—has the young man been assailed or not?—suggests that he has a less-than-perfect knowledge of the young man's past, and therefore an insecure base for his praise.

Couplet Tie: *suspéct* (3, 13)

71

NOe Longer mourne for me when I am dead,
Then you ſhall heare the ſurly ſullen bell
Giue warning to the world that I am fled
From this vile world with vildeſt wormes to dwell:
Nay if you read this line, remember not,
The hand that writ it, for I loue you ſo,
That I in your ſweet thoughts would be forgot,
If thinking on me then ſhould make you woe.
O if (I ſay) you looke vpon this verſe,
When I (perhaps) compounded am with clay,
Do not ſo much as my poore name reherſe;
But let your loue euen with my life decay.
  Leaſt the wiſe world ſhould looke into your mone,
  And mocke you with me after I am gon.

No longer mourn for me when I am dead
Than you shall hear the surly sullen bell
Give warning to the world that I am fled
From this vile world with vildest worms to dwell;
Nay, if you read this line, remember not
The hand that writ it, for I love you so,
That I in your sweet thoughts would be forgot,
If thinking on me then should make you woe.
O if (I say) you look upon this verse,
When I (perhaps) compounded am with clay,
Do not so much as my poor name rehearse,
But let your love even with my life decay,
  Lest the wise world should look into your moan,
  And mock you with me after I am gone.

THE double sonnet 71–72 rehearses reasons it would be better for the beloved to forget the speaker after the speaker's death.

C. L. Barber's discussion (in his edition of the *Sonnets*) of Shakespeare's capacity for selflessness is to the point in considering these poems, more to the point than Booth's finding "narcissistic smugness" and "a cosmic caricature of a revenging lover," or Kerrigan's suggestions of "arm-twisting." The hyperboles of love say something to us about passion itself; and critics' uneasiness with (overmastering) passion means an uneasiness with Shakespeare's *Sonnets* themselves. It is true that there is irony in the *Sonnets*—both irony openly voiced by the speaker himself (as in 138) and authorial irony suggested at the expense of the (deceived) speaker (as in 67). But there are also, I believe, sonnets of hapless love—intended as such by the author, expressed as such by the speaker. Shakespeare does not encourage us, in such cases, to second-guess the speaker (as he does, for instance, by the "rhyming" of the young man's action [*live*] with the actions of sin [*atchive*] in 67). Judging the presence or absence of authorial irony is a matter of poetic tact in reading. Thematic irony (by contrast to the necessary temporal irony implicit in the formal written representation of anterior experience) does not always improve a poem; on the contrary, if present, it would vitiate any poem dealing with capitulatory love, where the author's aesthetic aim is the reader's sympathy with the speaker, not an adverse or ironic judgment on him.

A separate question, often confused with the former, is the presence of self-consciousness (not to be thought always identical with thematic irony) in every poetic text. Every poetic text has an object of representation, which it is concerned to represent, and which it takes enormous pains to represent accurately and interestingly. Self-abnegation in love to a hyperbolic degree can of course be represented either sympathetically or satirically. Ideally, the author should control the context sufficiently to direct readers to the desired stance: on the evidence of Booth's and Kerrigan's readings, either sufficient controls are not present here to guarantee a "sympathetic" reading, or Booth and Kerrigan are inexplicably immune to controls which have worked, in the past, well enough to generate the (historically) sympathetic response to these poems by expert readers like Barber.

The Couplet Tie sums up the poem: *look*, *mourn* [*moan*], *world* (also, perhaps, *you* and *I* [*me*] foregrounded by repetitive pairing). I hear, behind the successive posthumous scenarios of the speaker's quatrains, an imagined desired dialogue: this dialogue (as reconstructed below) begins with the poet's threat of suicide, and continues with a series of follow-up questions:

Poet: I am going to flee this vile world, preferring a dwelling with vilest worms to any further existence here. What will you do after my death?

Beloved: I will mourn *you* forever.

Poet: No, mourn for me no longer than it takes to toll my passing bell.

Beloved: Well, then I will read *your lines*, and grieve while reading them.

Poet: Nay, if you read this line, remember not the hand that wrote it, if that memory would cause you grief.

Beloved: Then I will, from love, mention *your name* to others.

Poet: No, do not rehearse my name, but let your love for me cease when my life does.

Beloved: Why do you forbid me to remember you, grieve for you, read you, name you?

Poet: Because the world, which has so mocked me, will then associate you with me, and you will find yourself mocked by association. [This reading of *mock you with me* seems to me more probable than "taunt you by mentioning me."]

The bitterness of the speaker against the vile *wise* world and its mockery is not to be doubted, and can be compared to his outcries in other sonnets against his disgrace in men's eyes (29), and his branded name (111). The personified *surly sullen bell*, ungenerous to its parishioner even in the hour of his death, epitomizes the reach of social disapproval. If, when the speaker dies, even the church's charity is compromised into sullenness, the beloved cannot expect, once linked to the speaker, to be gently treated by society. The speaker's fears for the beloved's future do not seem chimerical, given his own implied social suffering. And since being mourned by the survivor can be of no personal benefit to one who is dwelling with worms and compounded with clay, the only object of the poet's concern must be the beloved's own future.

It may seem unnecessary to rehearse such obvious thematic content, but the speaker's forgoing of the only kind of posthumous life he envisages in the *Sonnets*—the record of memory—is the ultimate self-sacrifice, and presented as such: *I love you so [much] that I . . . would be forgot.*

An important consideration in reading such a poem ought to be its management of tone. What is most noticeable in the posthumous hypotheses offered by the quatrains is the increasing self-consciousness of utterance. Q_1 presses on (when punctuated logically, rather than with the rhetorical comma of the Quarto after line 1) without hesitation through to its end. Q_2 narrows the question from general mourning over the poet to mourning over the *hand* that wrote a line. Q_3 narrows from the hand to the mere *name*—as if to render the mourning ever more tenuous, while having the beloved still enact the putatively wished-for behavior. The negatives *(no longer mourn, remember not, do not . . . rehearse)* presuppose the beloved's positive impulses to mourn and moan; the speaker then forbids those impulses (as my imaginary dialogue proposes).

It is of course possible, and even likely, that the cold-hearted beloved will have no impulse to mourn at all, and it is equally likely that the speaker knows and fears this. We may read this poem, then, in a second, and truer, way—as a defensive construct hoping to awaken in the shallow young man the very depths of mourning that it affects to prohibit. This in fact seems to me the most probable reading, and one in which the pathos of the unloved speaker is most nakedly exposed. As the poet reduces his requests for mourning—"Mourn *me;* or at least mourn my poet's *hand;* or at least say my *name* once more"—we see how little he dares ask for, even as he declares he does not ask it. The "thinning down" of request is the principal aesthetic dynamic of the poem, and its principal result in us is sympathy for the lover who must ask less and less, lest he find his least request callously refused. The secondary dynamic is the speaker's increasingly distanced view of himself and his utterance, foregrounded by the self-reflexive, parenthetical *I say* and *perhaps* of Q_3, and aided by the progressive "deadness" of the speaker. In Q_1, he is so recently dead that his death knell is still sounding; in Q_2, the detached *hand that writ it* seems long dead, but still an integral body part. But by Q_3, the speaker is wholly *compounded . . . with clay,* dissolved into dust. In C, he is *gone,* no longer corporeal at all.

Couplet Tie: *world* (3, 4, 13)
mourn [*moan*] (1, 13)
look (9, 13)
and perhaps, because foregrounded by repetitive pairing
you and *I* [*me*] (passim)

72

O Leaſt the world ſhould taske you to recite,
What merit liu'd in me that you ſhould loue
After my death(deare loue)for get me quite,
For you in me can nothing worthy proue.
Vnleſſe you would deuiſe ſome vertuous lye,
To doe more for me then mine owne deſert,
And hang more praiſe vpon deceaſed I,
Then nigard truth would willingly impart.
O leaſt your true loue may ſeeme falce in this,
That you for loue ſpeake well of me vntrue,
My name be buried where my body is,
And liue no more to ſhame nor me,nor you.
  For I am ſhamd by that which I bring forth,
  And ſo ſhould you,to loue things nothing worth.

O lest the world should task you to recite
What merit lived in me that you should love,
After my death (dear love) forget me quite,
For you in me can nothing worthy prove;
Unless you would devise some virtuous lie
To do more for me than mine own desert,
And hang more praise upon deceasèd I
Than niggard truth would willingly impart:
O lest your true love may seem false in this,
That you for love speak well of me untrue,
My name be buried where my body is,
And live no more to shame nor me nor you:
  For I am shamed by that which I bring forth,
  And so should you, to love things nothing worth.

THE mockery of the beloved by the vile world, feared by the speaker in sonnet 71, is here permitted to occur on the stage of his imagination before he begins to speak sonnet 72. I offer this imaginary scenario:

The world to the beloved: "What merit lived in your dead poet that you should still love him?"

The beloved offers a virtuous lie, an exaggerated—even untrue—set of praises, beyond the poet's desert.

The world: "These are lies. Your love was based on nothing, if these asserted virtues were its base, since your friend did not possess them. It was a false, not a true, love."

Stipulating that the works he *bring[s] forth* are *things nothing worth*, the poet denies his own merit as a beloved, as though he and his works were the same thing. The poem modulates stealthily from "You *in me* can *nothing worthy* prove" to "You should be shamed to love *things nothing worth*." The forsaking of the last shred of corporeality in 71 animates 72: the poet hopes that the beloved will remember him, and that after the poet's death, he will want to recite, even to exaggerate, the poet's merits to an unfeeling world. But whereas the successive hopes in 71 become increasingly attenuated—from mourning the poet himself, to remembering his hand, to rehearsing his name—72 has turned away from the wan and slim hopes of 71 to a strong hope for posthumous aggressive defense by the beloved of his worth—even to the point of exaggeration. Real love, the poet has come to think, would not only mourn for him but would rise to his active defense. The absolute unlikelihood of the faithless beloved's doing any such thing causes the (necessary) defensive excuse that any such recitation of praise is impossible, given the absolute unworthiness of the poet and his creations. The extent of doubt about the beloved's fidelity creates the proportional degree of abjectness in the speaker, as the degree of failed hope creates the degree of deployed fantasy. In both directions, 72 is an exaggeration of 71, displaying the usual Shakespearean tendency to pursue any thought to its logical end.

By contrast to the long, temporally linear chains of hypotheses that compose 71, with its speculations on future exercises of grief, the body of

72 has the chiastic structure characteristic of a thought-through conclusiveness. The two parallel injunctions—*O lest the world should task you . . . forget me*, and *O lest your true love may seem false, [let] my name be buried*—bracket the inner speculations about virtuous lies and excessive praise, showing the thought to be chiastically complete even before the poem is begun. In Shakespeare, as I have said, the chiastic version of a poem is always a thought-through after-image of the linear version.

This may be a DEFECTIVE KEY WORD poem: LOVE is missing from Q_2, perhaps to represent the speaker's fear that he will *not* be loved after his death.

DEFECTIVE KEY WORD: LOVE (missing in Q_2)

Couplet Tie: *love* (2, 3, 9, 10, 14)
shame [-*d*] (12, 13)
nothing (4, 14)
worth [-*y*] (4, 14)

73

THat time of yeeare thou maiſt in me behold,
When yellow leaues,or none,or few doe hange
Vpon thoſe boughes which ſhake againſt the could,
Bare rn'wd quiers,where late the ſweet birds ſang.
In me thou ſeeſt the twi-light of ſuch day,
As after Sun-ſet fadeth in the Weſt,
Which by and by blacke night doth take away,
Deaths ſecond ſelfe that ſeals vp all in reſt.
In me thou ſeeſt the glowing of ſuch fire,
That on the aſhes of his youth doth lye,
As the death bed,whereon it muſt expire,
Conſum'd with that which it was nurriſht by.
This thou perceu'ſt,which makes thy loue more ſtrong,
To loue that well,which thou muſt leaue ere long.

That time of year thou mayst in me behold
When yellow leaves, or none, or few, do hang
Upon those boughs which shake against the cold,
Bare ruined choirs, where late the sweet birds sang.
In me thou seest the twilight of such day
As after sunset fadeth in the west,
Which by and by black night doth take away,
Death's second self that seals up all in rest.
In me thou seest the glowing of such fire
That on the ashes of his youth doth lie,
As the death-bed whereon it must expire,
Consumed with that which it was nourished by.
This thou perceiv'st, which makes thy love more strong,
To love that well which thou must leave ere long.

THE *self-substantial fuel* of the first poem of the *Sonnets* reappears as the self-nourished, self-consuming fire of 73. *Thou . . . feed'st thy light's flame with self-substantial fuel* is a reproach to the young man's refusal of generative power in sonnet 1, but, since the question of breeding is now a dead issue, self-nourishment and self-consumption can be regarded as the very description of life itself.

After Q_1 and Q_2, Q_3 of 73 represents a change of mind; and 73 can stand as an example of the sonnet of self-correction. Many sonnets offer several modelings of their theme in sucessive lines or quatrains. In some, the successive modelings reinforce each other: e.g., in sonnet 12, the models of vanished day, faded violets, and silvered hair reinforce each other as images of decline. But in other sonnets, a later modeling corrects earlier ones, and this kind of correction can be illustrated by 73 (as well as by 60).

Three models of life are proffered by the speaker: although he displaces them into perceptions he ascribes to the addressee *(thou mayst in me behold; in me thou seest; this thou perceiv'st)*, they are really self-created perceptions. I will return to the problem of ascribed perceptions and ascribed sentiments *(This . . . makes thy love more strong)*, but for the moment I want to sketch the three models: a season, a day, a fire. It has been noticed that the third differs from the first two, but an accommodated criticism has generally slighted the difference in favor of the similarities among the models. All are models of aging, but the structuring of each is meaningfully different from that of its predecessor.

The first two models are linear ones—spring, summer, autumn, winter; morning, noon, afternoon, sunset, twilight, night. (A poet can invoke these models either with emphasis on potential cyclicity—"And though the last lights off the black west went, / O morning at the brown brink eastward springs" (Hopkins, "God's Grandeur")—or with emphasis on their terminal force: "All life death does end, and each day dies with sleep" (Hopkins, "No worst, there is none"). We are not, I think, justified in invoking cyclicity when *the poem itself* does not. Shakespeare, since he is allegorizing human life, does not say, "But the tree will have new green leaves in the spring," and we are not at liberty to invoke here the cyclicity of days or seasons.)

In the first model, the speaker has placed himself, in the time-line of the year, at autumn. We notice that the moment in the time-span where the speaker places himself advances in the second model: twilight is later in the course of the day than autumn is in the course of the seasons. Nor does the speaker look so far back in the second model as he had done in the first; Q_1's glance back to spring, suffused with nostalgia, is not paralleled in Q_2 by a yearning glance back to the dawn, or even to noon. Instead, there is a short glance back to sunset, and a willing look forward to a future *rest* (where the first model could implicitly envisage in the future only increasing palsy and cold). In spite of these advances in Q_2 toward a less wrenching nostalgia and a calm resignation, these two time-line quatrains resemble each other more than they differ from each other.

This cannot be said of the third quatrain, which abandons the linearity—early to late—of its predecessors in favor of a stratified verticality. A glowing fire lies on top of *(upon)* the ashes of youth, its eventual deathbed. In the earlier models, the speaker's present self-image *(bare ruined choirs, twilight)* has been constructed by contrast to an earlier state (*lea[fy] boughs . . . where . . . sweet birds sang*, a *day* and its *sunset*). In the third quatrain, the speaker has redefined his self-image: by a radical reversal, he defines himself not by contrast but by continuity with his earlier state. He is the *glowing*—a positive word, unlike *ruin* or *fade*—of a *fire*. He is not the ashes of a fire, or the embers of a fire—he is no longer (as he was in the first two quatrains) a noun, but rather a verbal, an action, a *glowing* (not a dying).

How did this change of mind take place—the discovery of an *élan vital* within the ruin, of a steady heat in the twilight? It came about, I believe, by the speaker's gradual withdrawal from the idealization of his own youth. The nostalgic glance backward in Q_1 is almost forgone (except for *sunset*) in Q_2; and by Q_3 *youth* is viewed not as the phase of sweet birds singing—its past reality—but in its present reality, which is *ashes*. Once it is admitted that youth wanes, it is clear that the only locus of true life is the present, which can now truthfully be called by a positive name, *glowing*.

The first two quatrains fancifully posit a villain who robs the speaker of life: if the *cold* did not make the boughs shake, the leaves would not have fallen, the choirs would be entire, and the birds would still be singing. In the second quatrain, the day would still be here if *black night* did not gradually *take away* the light and *seal all up*. But the third quatrain, released from a self-image as victim, can see, accurately, that there is no villain to be blamed: one dies simply of having lived, as the fire is *consumed with that [heat] which it was nourished by*.

I return to the ascribing of various perceptions and sentiments to the beloved. The speaker's appeal to the love of the beloved is at first an appeal of physical pathos *(ruin)*, and next an appeal of mental decline (*fad[ing]* light). The speaker has read the text of his own aging physical body and has seen a *ruin[ed]* organic object (a tree, resembling the body in its trunk and limbs); he has gauged the emblematic mental light of his life-span, and has seen a *fad[ing] twilight*. He has ascribed these readings to the beloved to represent the beloved as a mirror perfectly reflecting the speaker's own self-image. But when the speaker reads the erotic text of his emotional life, he sees a *glowing*. It is certainly easier to ask someone to love a *glowing* rather than a *ruin* or a *fad[ing]*, and the *more strong* love ascribed to the beloved is believable chiefly because the speaker has changed his own mind about his proffered selfhood.

It has often been remarked that "lose" would make better sense in the couplet than *leave;* but because everything, love included, is consumed by that which it was nourished by, Shakespeare enacts his analytic "law of nourishment and consumption" by reconjugating the verb "to love" so that it reads "loving, leaving, leafless." The Couplet Tie reenacts the pun.

Couplet Tie: *leave* [-*s*] (2, 14)

74

BVt be contented when that fell areſt,
With out all bayle ſhall carry me away,
My life hath in this line ſome intereſt,
Which for memoriall ſtill with thee ſhall ſtay.
When thou reueweſt this,thou doeſt reuew,
The very part was conſecrate to thee,
The earth can haue but earth,which is his due,
My ſpirit is thine the better part of me,
So then thou haſt but loſt the dregs of life,
The pray of wormes,my body being dead,
The coward conqueſt of a wretches knife,
To baſe of thee to be remembred,
  The worth of that,is that which it containes,
  And that is this, and this with thee remaines.

But be contented when that fell arrest
Without all bail shall carry me away,
My life hath in this line some interest,
Which for memorial still with thee shall stay.
When thou reviewest this, thou dost review
The very part was consecrate to thee:
The earth can have but earth, which is his due;
My spirit is thine, the better part of me.
So then thou hast but lost the dregs of life,
The prey of worms, my body being dead,
The coward conquest of a wretch's knife,
Too base of thee to be rememberèd:
  The worth of that is that which it contains,
  And that is this, and this with thee remains.

THE key word here might more properly be seen as a key phrase: WITH THEE, TO THEE, OF THEE, WITH THEE. What is being referred to is the poet's spirit, present in his verse, in the very line now being *review[ed]*. The deictic of proximal presence, *this* (used in adjectival and pronominal ways four times in the poem) is at first contrasted with *that*, the deictic of distance, used initially with regard to death ("*that* fell arrest") and subsequently for the speaker's physical body ("the worth of *that*"). But by a sleight-of-hand in the couplet, turning on the relative pronoun *that which*, body is sublimed to spirit:

> The worth of *that* [body] is *that which* it contains [the spirit],
> And *that* [spirit] is *this* [this line] and *this* [the poet's spirit
> embodied in verse] with thee remains.

The paradox of presence distilled from absence, as *that* becomes *this*, is reinforced by the rhyme of *away* with *stay* in Q_1.

Like 71 and 72, which imagine the beloved rereading the poet's lines, 74 implies a hope, on the poet's part, that the young man's love will survive the poet's death, and that the beloved will want to review his lines. The view of death here resembles that in 146, in which the body is also the prey of *worms;* no mention is made of the Christian resurrected body. The disparaging of the body is done, of course, in the service of ascribing greater value to the spirit, and the deictics at first act out the total disjunction between the two entities. Why, then, the eventual merger of *that* and *this* in the couplet?

It is necessitated, I think, by the material and mediating function of verse. The *line* is a physical container of *spirit*, just as the body is, and to kill the body entirely is to render the line imaginatively dispensable too. The *line* is originally presented solely as a *memorial;* in Q_2 it becomes *the very part was consecrate to thee, my spirit, the better part of me.* A certain surprise, almost, on the speaker's part is betrayed by that *very;* he finds that the material line contains his devoted spirit. But the equation of *line* with *spirit* will not satisfy Shakespeare. After the speaker's exaggerated denigration of the body as *the dregs of life, the prey of worms, the coward conquest of a wretch's [Time's] knife*, the body's *worth* is suddenly affirmed via its contents, by which the young man is to be *content[ed]*. The *line* is then prized as the container of what was contained by the body (if only by the slippage between *that* and *this* at the close).

The pun that leads from the wished-for *rest* of 73 to the *fell arrest* of 74 enacts the turn from death-resignation to life-affirmation. But life is chiefly affirmed not of the body, but (as in the *glowing* of 73) of the spirit. The pun on the Latin meaning of *interest* ("joint being") points out the fact that *line* and *life* share interbeing, one disturbed only by a variation in their intervocalic consonant. Evans' suggested emendation of the Quarto's *reuew* to *renew* is, though plausible, not finally preferable, I think, to *reviewest . . . review*, used for intensification.

KEY WORD: Here, more properly, a KEY PHRASE, for which the formula is "preposition-plus-*thee*":

with
to
of
with } THEE (4, 6, 12, 14)

Couplet Tie: *with thee* (4, 14)

75

SO are you to my thoughts as ſood to liſe,
Or as ſweet ſeaſon'd ſhewers are to the ground;
And for the peace of you I hold ſuch ſtriſe,
As twixt a miſer and his wealth is found.
Now proud as an inioyer,and anon
Doubting the filching age will ſteale his treaſure,
Now counting beſt to be with you alone,
Then betterd that the world may ſee my pleaſure,
Some-time all ful with feaſting on your ſight,
And by and by cleane ſtarued for a looke,
Poſſeſſing or purſuing no delight
Saue what is had,or muſt from you be tooke.
Thus do I pine and ſurfet day by day,
Or gluttoning on all,or all away,

So are you to my thoughts as food to life,
Or as sweet seasoned showers are to the ground;
And for the peace of you I hold such strife
As 'twixt a miser and his wealth is found:
Now proud as an enjoyer, and anon
Doubting the filching age will steal his treasure;
Now counting best to be with you alone,
Then bettered that the world may see my pleasure:
Sometime all full with feasting on your sight,
And by and by clean starvèd for a look;
Possessing or pursuing no delight
Save what is had, or must from you be took.
Thus do I pine and surfeit day by day,
Or gluttoning on all, or all away.

IN USING the *strife . . . 'twixt a miser and his wealth* to illustrate his speaker's erotic uncertainties, Shakespeare inserts a six-line block of contrastive pairs between his four-line introduction and his four-line summary, one of his several reformulations of sonnet structure. Although many of the sonnets exhibit a logical structure parallel to the rhyme-pattern, many (e.g., 76) borrow their logical structure fom the Italian model, and exhibit a well-defined octave. (I read 73 as such a poem, because the third quatrain departs so radically in its modeling from its predecessors.) Yet in spite of the domination of the series by the patterns 4-4-4-2 or 8-4-2, almost every conceivable restructuring possible within fourteen lines is invented by Shakespeare in the course of the sequence. The 4-6-4 structure here, the 1-11-2 structure of 66 *(Tired with all these)*, the 8-4-1-1 structure of 94 *(They that have pow'r to hurt)*, the 4-10 structure of 98 *(From you have I been absent in the spring)*, the 7-7 structure of 111 *(O for my sake do you with Fortune chide)*, the 12-2 structure of 117 *(Accuse me thus)*, are examples of this variety. Sometimes, when a sonnet seems otherwise unremarkable, as in the present case of 75, we may suspect that Shakespeare's interest lay less in the theme than in structural invention.

All is the Couplet Tie, and the alternatives the speaker recounts, as he enacts the ups and downs of possession, are characteristically all or nothing, as the couplet declares. The couplet itself is an experiment in acceleration, summing up very quickly *(pine/surfeit; gluttoning on all / all away)* what had earlier been spun out at more leisure, one line per alternative. The *Now . . . anon, Now . . . then, Sometime . . . by and by* of the more leisurely changes speed up to a *day by day* change in the couplet, with an up-down alternative crammed into each of the closing lines.

The poem begins in the joy of the beloved's return to the starved, parched speaker. The wish to see the beloved as an originary force, rather than a derivative one, accounts for the revision of the initial simile of food to the one of *sweet seasoned showers*, which are the necessary condition before *food* can even grow. (The two similes also serve to provide food *and* drink.) The confusion of reference between organic *food* and inorganic *wealth* is resolved in favor of food, through the final sestet-metaphor of surfeit and gluttony. This metaphor changes the capital sin described here from the mental sin of avarice (the miser's gaze) to the fleshly sin of gluttony, a "truth-correction" admitting the sensual base of the attachment, originally said to be one of "thoughts" (line 1) rather than of the body.

It is surprising that the innocent and beautiful two-line beginning of 75 should be followed by allusions to these two of the seven "deadly" sins, avarice and gluttony. The speaker, frightened by his own joy and gratitude on receiving erotic *food* and drink, resorts to extremes in describing his moral behavior. His "sins" are explained only in lines 9–10, which suggest that the speaker is not entirely in control, as he has seemed hitherto to be, of the occasions of "consumption." He is *clean starvèd for a look*, and this situation seems not to be of his own contriving. It is suggested that the beloved gives and witholds himself at pleasure, and that the pattern he has adopted toward the speaker—feasting and starving him—has now become habitual to the speaker himself. *Pin[ing]* when *all* is *away*, he is forced into *gluttoning* while he can. The displacing of the beloved's (voluntary) absence into a suspicion in Q_2 of a theft by *the filching age* shows the paranoia of the miser, but also the speaker's suspicion that his beloved is unfaithful. The speaker's pretense that he has *possession*, implicit in the Q_1 figure of the miser poring over his (secured) wealth, is exposed as a falsehood in the naked substitution of *pursuing* for *possessing* in line 11, which we must read, "Possessing (or, rather, more truly) pursuing . . . you." The beloved does not bestow; in another self-correction by the speaker, the beloved's love is not exactly had; it must *from [him] be took*. Such a relation is indeed a pursuing, not a possession.

The chiastic structure of the couplet *(pine : surfeit :: gluttoning : all away)* both begins and ends with the speaker *clean starvèd*, thus correcting the apparent grateful plenty of Q_1.

Couplet Tie: *all* (9, 14, 14)

76

VV Hy is my verſe ſo barren of new pride?
So far from variation or quicke change?
Why with the time do I not glance aſide
To new found methods,and to compounds ſtrange?
Why write I ſtill all one,euer the ſame,
And keepe inuention in a noted weed,
That euery word doth almoſt fel my name,
Shewing their birth,and where they did proceed?
O know ſweet loue I alwaies write of you,
And you and loue are ſtill my argument:
So all my beſt is dreſſing old words new,
Spending againe what is already ſpent:
For as the Sun is daily new and old,
So is my loue ſtill telling what is told,

Why is my verse so barren of new pride?
So far from variation or quick change?
Why with the time do I not glance aside
To new-found methods and to compounds strange?
Why write I still all one, ever the same,
And keep invention in a noted weed,
That every word doth almost tell my name,
Showing their birth, and where they did proceed?
O know, sweet love, I always write of you,
And you and love are still my argument;
So all my best is dressing old words new,
Spending again what is already spent:
For as the sun is daily new and old,
So is my love still telling what is told.

LIKE 116, SONNET 76 has been misunderstood because its form of speech-act has not been accurately described. It is not an apology (Kerrigan) but an *apologia*, a reply in self-defense, responding to a complaint by the bored young man against the "monotony" of his receiving "old-fashioned" poems that are so tediously constant in form that anyone can identify them as Shakespeare's. Shakespeare repeats the charges of reproach:

> *Why [you ask me] is my verse so barren of new pride?*
> *So far from variation or quick change?*

We hear behind these and subsequent lines (as we do in 116) the very accents of the fashionable young man: "Why do you always write the *same* sort of poems, why don't you ever say anything *new*, why don't you *vary* your style, why don't you try something modern, why do you stick to your old-fashioned sonnets?" Of all the indictments that could be made against these astonishingly inventive poems, monotony is the furthest off the mark. Yet Shakespeare (in the person of his speaker) must endure this criticism and somehow reply to it. The octave represents his oblique but incredulous rephrasing of the young man's obtuse questions, and the sestet represents his pained and gently reproachful answer: If my sonnets are "monotonous," it is the "monotony" of fidelity:

> *O know, sweet love, I always write of you,*
> *And you and love are still my argument.*

So much for the thematic "monotony," *all one, ever the same.* What of the stylistic "monotony"? Here Shakespeare's self-defense is triply formulated as *dressing old words new, spending again what is already spent,* and *telling what is told.* The Couplet Ties are unusually numerous in this sonnet (*new, old, tell* [*-ing*] [*told*], *love, still,* and *so*), and they clearly sum up the poet's self-defense. No Couplet Tie echoes the fickle young man's (false) values—he likes everything exhibiting *new pride, variation, quick change, new-found methods,* and *compounds* (*strange* I take to be an editorializing insertion by Shakespeare, though it may be meant as *étrange,* "foreign," the young man's "continental" desire).

The young man is a reader who reads only for theme; and the poet freely admits the monotony of his theme *(you and love)*. But Shakespeare is a writer whose eye is on style. The verbal lexicon of any language is finite, as is the generic lexicon of any poetic: there *are* no words but old words. Style is dressing them new (chiefly in the sense of the French *dresser:* "to erect, to build"). Every word in the language has already been coined; but money *spent* never buys the same thing twice, being a neutral medium of exchange. In his final self-defense, Shakespeare bifurcates the significance of the sun, and bifurcates as well his own activity:

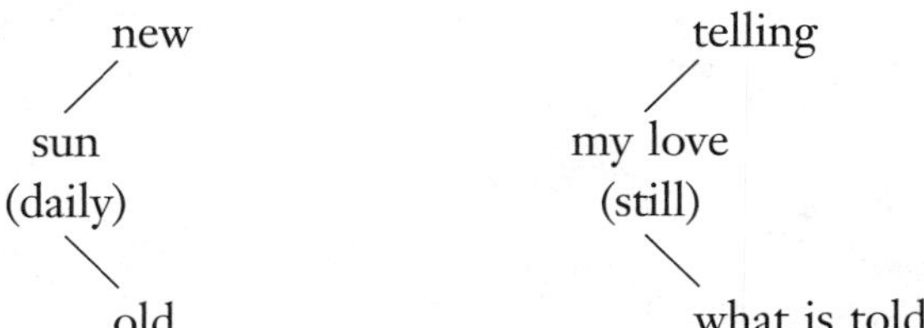

What is *told* (love) is *old* (*old* is encapsulated in the very word *told* itself, demonstrating the invariance of the love-genre and of its theme), but the *telling* (style) is *new* (as in words dressed *new*). The sun enters the poem as the proverbial example of the ever-new, ever-old, which everyone is glad to see every morning, no matter how often it has been seen before. (Cf. Wallace Stevens, in "An Ordinary Evening in New Haven," XVI: "The oldest-newest day is the newest alone.") The extreme simplicity of Shakespeare's defense of *style* as the *true* measure of novelty marks his refusal to concede to the young man's standard of ever-changing fashionable elaboration as the *stylistic* test of literary value (he has already refused the young man's standard of variety of subject as the *thematic* test of value).

The aesthetic dynamic of the sonnet takes off, of course, from the "artless" repetition by Shakespeare of the young man's complaining questions, which condemn the young man out of his own mouth, and explain the deliberate contrastive plainness of the sestet. There are two DEFECTIVE KEY WORDS. (1) NEW: it is missing in Q_2, where the poet defends its absence (in the young man's sense) in his verse. In Q_3, the poet redefines *new* as "newly" saying something with *old words* (the young man likes *compounds strange*); and in C he re-defines *new* as "freshly wondrous," but, like the sun, familiar. (2) STILL: it is missing in Q_1 which repeats the young man's criteria of ever-changingness. It appears in the other three units of the poem as the word symbolic of fidelity.

SONNET 76

DEFECTIVE KEY WORDS:	NEW (missing in Q_2) STILL (missing in Q_1)
Couplet Tie:	*new* (1, 4, 11, 13) *old* (11, 13) *tell* [*-ing*] [*told*] (7, 14, 14) *love* (9, 10, 14) *still* (5, 10, 14) *so* (1, 2, 11, 14)

77

THy glaſſe will ſhew thee how thy beauties were,
Thy dyall how thy pretious mynuits waſte,
The vacant leaues thy mindes imprint will beare,
And of this booke,this learning maiſt thou taſte.
The wrinckles which thy glaſſe will truly ſhow,
Of mouthed graues will giue thee memorie,
Thou by thy dyals ſhady ſtealth maiſt know,
Times theeuiſh progreſſe to eternitie.
Looke what thy memorie cannot containe,
Commit to theſe waſte blacks,and thou ſhalt finde
Thoſe children nurſt,deliuerd from thy braine,
To take a new acquaintance of thy minde.
These offices,ſo oft as thou wilt looke,
Shall profit thee,and much inrich thy booke.

Thy glass will show thee how thy beauties wear,
Thy dial how thy precious minutes waste;
The vacant leaves thy mind's imprint will bear,
And of this book, this learning mayst thou taste:
The wrinkles which thy glass will truly show
Of mouthèd graves will give thee memory,
Thou by thy dial's shady stealth mayst know
Time's thievish progress to eternity.
Look what thy memory cannot contain
Commit to these waste blanks, and thou shalt find
Those children nursed, delivered from thy brain,
To take a new acquaintance of thy mind.
These offices, so oft as thou wilt look,
Shall profit thee, and much enrich thy book.

LIKE SONNETS 10, 36, 37 (if we allow for the playful reversal in spig*ht*), 54, 69, 128, and 131, sonnet 77 registers a *th* in every line. The reiteration may be unintentional in some sonnets of this group, given the natural recurrence in the *Sonnets* of *thee* and *thou* (and their variants), *there*, the deictics *this* and *that* (with their plurals), and such common words as *the*, *with*, *death*, *breath*, *thought*, *truth*, *thus*, *doth*, and *though*. Still, in 77 the compulsion to mark each line with one or more words including *th* becomes evident through such odd expressions as "*mouthèd* graves," "thy dial's shady *stealth*," and "time's *thievish* progress." The repetition of the single sound *th* (principally through deictics and possessives) seems to me one of Shakespeare's arbitrary self-testing games, but here it also reflects the sonnet's principal aesthetic figure, which is incremental repetition.

The poem concerns three objects—a mirror *(glass)*, a sundial *(dial)*, and a blank notebook *(vacant leaves)*—the latter a gift from the speaker, with the sonnet as accompaniment. The mirror and sundial are already, it seems, in the possession of the young man, and are always referred to by the possessive adjective: *thy* glass, *thy* dial. The notebook, on the other hand, is referred to by proximal deictics: *this* book, *these* waste blanks. (*The* vacant leaves are attached proleptically to the deictic—*the* leaves of *this* book—until the last line, when the gift has become *thy* book.) Gradually, each object receives more structural space:

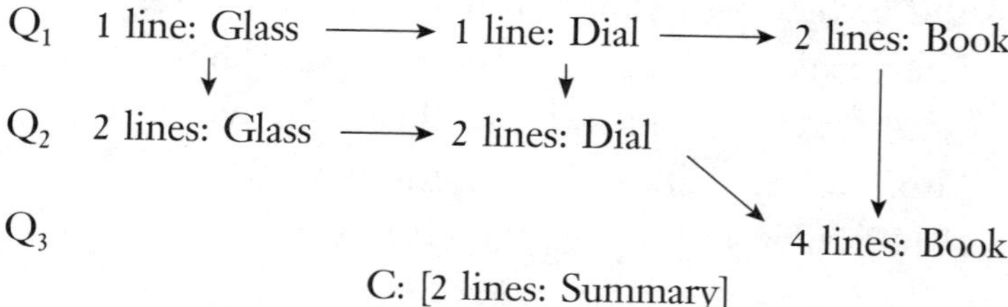

Whereas the glass or dial can serve only as a gloomy *memento mori*—calling up *wrinkles*, day's *shady stealth*, and the thievishness of *time*—the gift-book promises (it is a blank book offered by a poet, who has himself no doubt used such a book to write in) procreation of thought and literary enrichment. The notebook enriches itself, as the thoughts inscribed in it breed new thoughts. The phrase ***much enrich*** by its vowel and consonant-rhymes with ***children***, bears out the speaker's assertion (from his own experience) of intellectual procreative profit, now preferred to the biological children of the early sonnets. Though there is certainly a growth in knowledge enabled by the glass and the dial (as the enlarging incremental repetition of the poem shows, and as words like *memory* and *know* assert), the notebook offers even "more" growth—eventually occupying four lines to the dial's and glass's two, just as it had occupied two lines to their earlier respective one. The profit to the young man in knowledge, and the enrichment of his book, are comparatively valued by their enacted relative proportions in the poem. The ***offices oft*** done will ***profit*** the young man—another concatenation of sounds "acting out" the link between symbolic possessions, contemplations of their significance, and incremental spiritual growth.

Couplet Tie: *book* (4, 14)
look (9, 13)

These two elements of the Couplet Tie are foregrounded by being linked to the most important of the three proposed spiritual "offices," and by being the rhyme-words of the couplet itself.

78

SO oft haue I inuok'd thee for my Muſe,
And found ſuch faire aſſiſtance in my verſe,
As euery *Alien* pen hath got my vſe,
And vnder thee their poeſie diſperſe.
Thine eyes, that taught the dumbe on high to ſing,
And heauie ignorance aloft to flie,
Haue added fethers to the learneds wing,
And giuen grace a double Maieſtie.
Yet be moſt proud of that which I compile,
Whoſe influence is thine,and borne of thee,
In others workes thou dooſt but mend the ſtile,
And Arts with thy ſweete graces graced be.
  But thou art all my art,and dooſt aduance
  As high as learning,my rude ignorance.

So oft have I invoked thee for my Muse,
And found such fair assistance in my verse,
As every alien pen hath got my use,
And under thee their poesy disperse.
Thine eyes, that taught the dumb on high to sing,
And heavy ignorance aloft to fly,
Have added feathers to the learnèd's wing,
And given grace a double majesty.
Yet be most proud of that which I compile,
Whose influence is thine, and born of thee:
In others' works thou dost but mend the style,
And arts with thy sweet graces gracèd be;
  But thou art all my art, and dost advance
  As high as learning my rude ignorance.

SHAKESPEARE excels in a form of verbal emphasis pointing up the conceptual oppositions of his verse. His mind operates consistently on the basis of antithesis, and the antitheses are carried by paired, pointedly antithetical words as well as by paired concepts. (His love of antithesis is so great that he employs it even within analogy. "You are like the best thing I can think of, a summer day," he muses, on beginning 18, and immediately is compelled to create an antithesis between the young man and the day, the very terms of his original comparison: "Thou art *more* lovely, *more* temperate," etc.).

In this first poem of the "rival-poet" group, a firm antithesis is drawn between the putatively *rude* speaker and the other poets clustered round the young man. They are all *learnèd*, practicing both *style* and *art*, while the poor speaker's *ignorance* is twice insisted on, as is his muteness (he was *dumb*) before he saw the young man. The mock-*débat* of the sonnet is: Should the young man be prouder of Shakespeare's poems compiled out of *rude ignorance*, or of those of his more learnèd admirers?

The mock-answer is that the young man should be prouder of having taught a hitherto *dumb* admirer to *sing*, and of having advanced *ignorance* as high as *learning*, because these achievements on his part testify more impressively to his originary power than his (slighter) accomplishments with respect to his learnèd poets—he but *mends* their style and *graces* their arts. This debate is presented in a Petrarchan logical structure, with a clearly demarcated octave and sestet.

The dramatization of the *débat*—with the young man in the middle between *ignorant* Shakespeare and the *learnèd* rival poets—is carried by an antithetical verbal pointing so heavy—as *my* is contrasted to *their*, *ignorance* (twice) to *learnèd/learning*, *I* to *others*, *assistance* to *dispersal*, *my art* to [*their*] *arts*, and so on—that the rivalry is unmistakably enacted by these persistent antitheses. That is, the poem gives us directions as to how we should read it, which words we should emphasize.

The words of the Couplet Tie—*art*, *high*, *learning* [*learnèd*], *ignorance*—repeat in little the topics under dispute. For the poem to be credible, Shakespeare has to exhibit his present art as at least equal to that of his rivals, and he does this first by resorting to a country-bumpkin, fairy-tale idiot-son role, presenting himself as a Cinderella, so to speak, raised from the cinders to the skies. The rival poets' improvements are minimal compared to his: they already had grace and style and art, and though their graces have been doubled (a fact stated in line 8, enacted in line 12) and their style mended, these additions hardly testify to the young man's full power, which seems almost miraculous insofar as it has advanced the bumpkin *as high as learning*. Nor has it helped the learnèd to come under the young man's aegis: they *disperse* their poetry, while the speaker *compiles* his.

In fact, the additions that the learnèd have assumed seem impediments as much as improvements. Does the learnèd's wing need *added feathers?* Coming after the first soaring of the speaker, the heavy *added feathers* and *given grace* seem phonetically leaden, while later the line *arts with thy sweet graces gracèd be* suggests that the learnèd verse has become surfeited with elaboration. The phonetically and grammatically tautological pun—"Thou *art* all my *art*"—which conflates the copula and its predicate noun, enacts that plain *mutual render, only me for thee* (125) aspired to by the *Sonnets*, and enacts as well the poet's simplicity contrasted with the affectations of the learnèd.

The most interesting grammatical move in the poem is the use in Q_2 of aspectual description: not "thou hast" as we would expect—to parallel the later "thou dost" and "thou art"—but *thine eyes . . . have.* The eyes govern the only four-line syntactic span (the rest of the poem is written in two-line units). We are made to pause for a two-line relative clause between *thine eyes* and its verb, *have;* in between subject and predicate we find, within the compound relative clause, the poet twice arising, once to sing, once to fly:

> Thine eyes, *that taught the dumb on high to sing,*
> *And heavy ignorance aloft to fly,*
> Have added . . .

The syntactic "lift" here (in one of Shakespeare's few self-repetitions in the Sonnets) parallels the one used in 29, where we also are lifted up, this time in a prepositional phrase, between subject and verb:

> . . . and then my state,
> *(Like to the lark at break of day arising*
> *From sullen earth)* sings hymns.

The speaker's yearning aspectual praise of the young man's eyes is comparable to his praise of the mistress' eyes in 132 *(Thine eyes I love).* The delicate difference between direct second-person pronominal address to the beloved and third-person aspectual description of one of the beloved's attributes is exploited here and in 132.

Couplet Tie: *high* (5, 14)
ignorance (6, 14)
[learn] [*-èd's*] [*-ing*] (7, 14)
art [*-s*] (12, 13, 13)

79

WHilſt I alone did call vpon thy ayde,
  My verſe alone had all thy gentle grace,
But now my gracious numbers are decayde,
And my ſick Muſe doth giue an other place.
I grant (ſweet loue)thy louely argument
Deſerues the trauaile of a worthier pen,
Yet what of thee thy Poet doth inuent,
He robs thee of,and payes it thee againe,
He lends thee vertue,and he ſtole that word,
From thy behauiour,beautie doth he giue
And found it in thy cheeke: he can affoord
No praiſe to thee,but what in thee doth liue.
  Then thanke him not for that which he doth ſay,
  Since what he owes thee,thou thy ſelfe dooſt pay,

Whilst I alone did call upon thy aid,
My verse alone had all thy gentle grace,
But now my gracious numbers are decayed,
And my sick Muse doth give another place.
I grant (sweet love) thy lovely argument
Deserves the travail of a worthier pen,
Yet what of thee thy poet doth invent
He robs thee of, and pays it thee again:
He lends thee virtue, and he stole that word
From thy behaviour; beauty doth he give,
And found it in thy cheek; he can afford
No praise to thee but what in thee doth live.
  Then thank him not for that which he doth say,
  Since what he owes thee, thou thyself dost pay.

IN THIS rewriting of 78, the favor of the young man granted to a (putatively) more gifted poet causes at first a crisis of confidence in the speaker. He counters by asserting that the rival poet deserves no thanks for his work, since his invention is all borrowed (or stolen) from the attributes of the beloved. There can be, in Platonic fact, no one pen *worthier* than another, since all written value flows solely from the beloved.

After its brief initial narrative and disclaimer of personal worth, the poem finds its verve in acting out its imaginative premise of robbery-and-restitution on the part of the rival poet. Enjambments illustrate the circuit of lendings and stealings; syntactic parallelism and unclear synonymy and antonymy (*rob-steal-find* versus *pay-lend-give*) reinforce the repetitiveness and confusion of the rival poet's depredations and returns. But the chief tactic of the poem renders Shakespeare's own outraged mimicking of the rival's work. We always see first the written line, and then its living source, whence it was "plagiarized." In the diagram, my arrows represent Shakespeare's repeated glances back and forth from the rival poet's verse to its original source in the young man. By inserting, into the phrases in the left column, the telltale sign *thee (of thee, to thee)*, Shakespeare shows the encapsulation betraying the plagiarism.

Structure of Sonnet 79

Other's Verse	*Source* (*thee*)
What of thee thy poet doth invent ←	he robs thee of
and pays *it* thee again.	
He lends thee *virtue*	and he stole
that word from ←	thy behavior.
Beauty doth he give	and found
it ←	in thy cheek.
He can *afford* no praise to thee but *what* ←	in thee doth lie

The chiastic structure of lines 7–11 *(what : virtue :: beauty : what)* reveals totalizing generalizations including the two Platonic essentials, *virtue* and *beauty*. This arrangement reveals how carefully the poet-speaker has framed his accusation of his rival. The motion of the poem enacts the very compulsion of "truth" itself, as it hisses, so to speak, its *sotto voce* enjambed commentary on the apparent bestowings (in reality, thefts) of the rival poet:

Yet what of thee thy poet doth invent ⟶
He (robs thee of and) pays it thee (again).
He lends thee virtue (and he stole that word ⟶
From thy behaviour); beauty doth he give ⟶
(And found it in thy cheek); he can afford ⟶
No praise to thee but (what in thee doth live).

The implied comparison with the (legitimate) circulation of money from *lender* to borrower, and its *repayment* by the borrower to the lender, shows by contrast the illegitimate "lending" of *stolen* goods, payment in *robbed* currency, and so on, at work in the rival poet's economy.

The apparent bestower-role of the rival poet as *payer*, *giver*, *lender*, *sayer* is reversed in the couplet, where the young man is at last restored to his rightful subject-position as the patron who *pays*, and the rival poet is demoted to the position of one who *owes*. The Couplet Tie is *pay*, significantly used of the rival poet in its first occurrence (line 8) and "correctly" ascribed to the young man in its reappearance in line 14. But the poet-speaker, by contrast, has never pretended to confer *(give, lend, pay)* anything, and he would never expect or accept *thanks* for his own verses. *Because* the rival poet accepts thanks, he becomes guilty of treating as his own largesse what in fact he only borrowed or stole, and never owned at all.

Structurally, the sonnet falls into a 6-6-2 division, with the illegal traffic in "invention" occupying the second block of six lines. Since this traffic, deduced from its written result, is the chief interest of the poem, it is worth noting that what the speaker says of his rival's invention is (he answers) equally true of his own practice—whatever he writes, he derives from the beloved's *gentle grace*.

Couplet Tie: *pay* [*-s*] (8, 14)

O How I faint when I of you do write,
Knowing a better ſpirit doth vſe your name,
And in the praiſe thereof ſpends all his might,
To make me toung-tide ſpeaking of your fame.
But ſince your worth (wide as the Ocean is)
The humble as the proudeſt ſaile doth beare,
My ſawſie barke (inferior farre to his)
On your broad maine doth wilfully appeare.
Your ſhalloweſt helpe will hold me vp a floate,
Whilſt he vpon your ſoundleſſe deepe doth ride,
Or (being wrackt) I am a worthleſſe bote,
He of tall building, and of goodly pride.
Then If he thriue and I be caſt away,
The worſt was this, my loue was my decay.

O how I faint when I of you do write,
Knowing a better spirit doth use your name,
And in the praise thereof spends all his might,
To make me tongue-tied speaking of your fame.
But since your worth (wide as the ocean is)
The humble as the proudest sail doth bear,
My saucy bark (inferior far to his)
On your broad main doth wilfully appear.
Your shallowest help will hold me up afloat,
Whilst he upon your soundless deep doth ride,
Or (being wracked) I am a worthless boat,
He of tall building and of goodly pride.
Then if he thrive and I be cast away,
The worst was this: my love was my decay.

ONCE again, a vigorous antithesis of contested ground between the speaker and a rival poet (expressed by the use of *I*, *he*, and their derivatives) organizes this poem. I count pronouns here (as I usually do not) as visible components of the Couplet Tie *(he, I)* precisely because of their being set in such emphatic contrast; they are therefore mnemonically and structurally foregrounded. The unusual logical structure (4-8-2) is caused by the obtrusive figure of the ocean (the beloved) bearing both a *saucy bark* (the speaker's verse) and a *proudest sail* (the verse of the rival poet). The *proud full sail* of the rival poet's verse reappears in sonnet 86, but the young man has there been metamorphosed into the galleon's *prize*. Later, the dark lady will be represented as the ocean (in 135 and 137).

The fear expressed in 79 ("My gracious numbers *are decayed*") seems to generate the fear of repudiation at the close of 80, as "If . . . I b*e* *c*ast aw*ay*" shrinks to its rhyme word "*decay*." The anticipation of repudiation arises when the speaker concedes (apparently genuinely) that the rival poet (far from being the dishonest thief of 79) is in fact a *better spirit* than the speaker himself. The rival's power renders the poet *tongue-tied* (cf. 66, "art made *tongue-tied* by authority," and 85, "my *tongue-tied* Muse"); it makes him *faint*. (This conclusion will be disputed in 86, when the speaker realizes that it was not the various powers of the rival poet, but rather the defection of the beloved, that enfeebled his own creation.) Once it has been conceded that the beloved now sponsors a poet of greater distinction, the only question is whether the patron will be willing to welcome two poets in lieu of one, in an artistic *ménage à trois*. If not, when the patron casts the speaker away, whose fault will the separation be? To this there can be only one answer: the poet would prefer to abase himself, as he does in the last four lines, rather than criticize the young man. (It is hard to doubt, in the light of the "Will" sonnets, that a pun is intended in line 8 on *wilfully*.)

The motive for the invention of the ocean metaphor is not clear. Many other metaphors of joint-habitation in the patron's worth could have been found. The boat metaphor is absent in the four-line exposition, as well as in the two-line conclusion (a castaway is a person, not a boat), and the eight-line ocean/boat passage seems almost to have wandered in from a different poem. Nor does the last line seem to cohere with the rest of the sonnet. I confess that I am somewhat at a loss here to explain what Shakespeare had in mind. I can only conjecture that since the first, expository quatrain suggests a power struggle of the rival poet against the writer (he "spends all his might in praising your name to make me tongue-tied"), Shakespeare, knowing that his speaker cannot demand the expulsion of his rival, seeks a figure in which the two poets would not directly lock horns. Ships side by side on the sea afford such a figure; the sea has *shallows* for the little boat, *deeps* for the big one, so they are not rivals in the same space; and they are not engaged in personal combat. If the little boat is wrecked, it will be defeated by its own frailty, not by the proud ship. This scenario at least removes the hazards of battle between unequally matched powers. The last line remains disconnected, however; and though it is probable that *my love* means "my affection" rather than "my beloved" (making the line mean, "The worst aspect of my wreck was that I, by loving, and venturing in my small craft out into ocean seas, was the agent of my own destruction"), nobody seems to know whether *the worst was this* means "the worst thing about it was" or (as Kerrigan suggests) "at worst, I will be suffering at the hands of my beloved." Why, one wonders, except by a holdover from 79's *decayed*, does Shakespeare use a rather unidiomatic word like *decay* for shipwreck and being cast *away*, when *-ay* is a sound easy to find rhymes for?

Couplet Tie: *worth, worthless, worst* (5, 11, 14), a species of punning Couplet Tie

I [*me, my*]
he [*his*] } foregrounded throughout

81

OR I ſhall liue your Epitaph to make,
Or you ſuruiue when I in earth am rotten,
From hence your memory death cannot take,
Although in me each part will be forgotten.
Your name from hence immortall life ſhall haue,
Though I (once gone) to all, the world muſt dye,
The ea'th can yeeld me but a common graue,
When you intombed in mens eyes ſhall lye,
Your monument ſhall be my gentle verſe,
Which eyes not yet created ſhall ore-read,
And toungs to be, your beeing ſhall rehearſe,
When all the breathers of this world are dead,
You ſtill ſhall liue (ſuch vertue hath my Pen)
Where breath moſt breaths, euen in the mouths of men.

Or I shall live your epitaph to make,
Or you survive when I in earth am rotten,
From hence your memory death cannot take,
Although in me each part will be forgotten.
Your name from hence immortal life shall have,
Though I (once gone) to all the world must die;
The earth can yield me but a common grave,
When you intombèd in men's eyes shall lie:
Your monument shall be my gentle verse,
Which eyes not yet created shall o'er-read,
And tongues to be your being shall rehearse,
When all the breathers of this world are dead;
You still shall live (such virtue hath my pen)
Where breath most breathes, even in the mouths of men.

INVESTIGATING 81, we discover that a play on *death* [*die, dead*] in the octave, countered by living *breath* [*breathes*] in the sestet, is the principle of construction underlying the whole. A subsidiary game is being played which redefines Shakespeare's verse from its printed form (lines 8, 10, *you intombèd in men's eyes . . . eyes . . . shall o'er-read*) to its oral recitation (lines 11, 12, 14, *tongues . . . rehearse . . . breathers . . . breath . . . breathes . . . mouths*). Yet a third game, I believe, toys anagrammatically with words-inside-words: *created* contains *read*, *breathers* conceals "hearers," and *earth* and *rehearse* contain "hear." Of their respectively eight and nine letters, *rehearse* and *breathers* have seven in common.

These words all act out, *mutatis mutandis*, the central paradox that two such opposed words as *death* and *breath* differ only by their initial consonants; that is, they share more than they realize, and only the poet, who rhymes them, knows in his bones the "binding secret" (Seamus Heaney's words) between them. Language, and especially self-conscious rhyme, is thus seen as an access route to paradoxical but true relations among entities. Shakespeare has already (in 21, 38, and 71) employed the rhyme *verse/rehearse* which he revives here; and in 21 he has put into relief the letters shared by *rehearse/hearsay*—letters 3, 4, 5, 6, 7 of *rehearse* are letters 1, 2, 3, 4, 5 of *hearsay*. Here in 81, he simply does a comparable literal punning with several words at once.

The augmentative structure of 81 begins with the concept that there are only two kinds of existence: biological *(you survive)* and memorial *(epitaph, memory, intombèd in men's eyes)*. At first it seems as though the beloved, through his own life and his potential Shakespearean epitaph (if he is survived by the poet) will have had both personal *surviv[al]* during life, and memorial proper-name existence after death—(a living *name*, even if self-*intombèd*). But in the sestet, two more sorts of existence rise into view: the young man gains personal literary existence in physical perpetuity (*you* shall live, not solely your *name*), and the poet gains permanent authorial existence himself: ("*You* still shall live—such virtue hath *my* pen"). A further bifurcation asserts that one form of memorial existence for the young man depends on the *eyes* of others, eyes which will read the *gentle verse* of the sonnets and the (potential) epitaph, but this silent reading can only *intomb* the young man in print. A more actual living existence for him comes about through sound, as the poem is uttered aloud and heard by an audience: "Tongues to *be* your *be*ing shall re*hear*se." (The young man's present existence is identical to his future embodiment in the tongues of posterity, as we are told by the coincidence of his future *being* with their "tongues to *be.*")

Central words in the poem are phonemically or graphically linked: the *monument* is an *immortal* and *gentle* one in which *memory* is *intombèd*, rehearsed by *men's mouths*. By such linkages are the poet's sentiments made to seem almost neurologically conclusive. In this sequence, all the *m/o/n/u/m/e/n/t* responses, phonemic and graphic, are made to fire repeatedly (by my count, m = 8, o = 5, n = 4, u = 2, e = 7, t = 5). I sometimes suspect that the persistent appeal to poets of stanzas from six to sixteen lines in length is that in such lengths the brain can accumulate, by the end, a decent amount of memory pile-up, retaining what has resonated before. *Memory* (line 3) can resonate all the way down to *mouths of men* (line 14), because it is helped by the other *m/e* links along the way. Could the resonance survive through, say, twenty-five lines? I suspect not, even if a reader had undergone the intensive ear training (now vanished in the West) of the Renaissance poet. (The period of memorial sound retention may be longer in the case of oral literature strung on a narrative plot or on formulaic expression.)

The original pathos of the sonnet lies in the repeated (and now ironic) assertion by the poet of his own ignominy and anonymity after death: *When I in earth am rotten . . . in me each part will be forgotten . . . I (once gone) to all the world must die . . . The earth can yield me but a common grave.* There is an interesting formal distinction in this respect, however, as the octave progresses. The little "plot" of lines 1–2 offers alternative life-lines: Or *I* shall survive *you*, or *you* will survive *me*. In both cases, *I* and *you* are linked in reciprocal regard in *each* line. The next four lines set up a parallel alternation of *you* (one line) and *I* (one line):

YOU	*I*
From hence death cannot take *your* memory	Although *in me* each part will be forgotten
Your name from hence immortal life shall have	Though *I*, once gone, to all the world must die

We then expect:

When *you* intombèd in men's eyes shall lie	The earth can yield *me* but a common grave

But we get the reversal:

I	*YOU*
The earth can yield *me* but a common grave	When *you* intombèd in men's eyes shall lie.

Formally speaking, we notice that this makes Q_2 repeat in reverse *(Your name : I :: me : you)* Shakespeare's initial chiasmus in Q_1 *(I : your :: you : I)*. In Q_1, the speaker "embraces" the young man; in Q_2, the young man "embraces" the speaker. Their mutual intertwining as poet and that which is "poeticized" is thus enacted.

The introduction of posterity, the *tertium quid*, in line 8 gives the sestet three entities, rather than two, to handle. Still, the intertwined you-and-I-in-one-line of lines 1–2 reappears in lines 9 and 13: "*Your* monument shall be *my* gentle verse"; "*You* still shall live—such virtue hath *my* pen." The theme of the poet's disappearance—so firmly emphasized in the octave—vanishes utterly in the sestet, where, by the invention of memorial *utterance* as well as memorial *reading*, the poet and the young man together are given perpetual spoken life by posterity until the end of time. Booth notes at the opening of the sestet the coincidence for the first time of a common destiny for *your* and *my—Your monument shall be my gentle verse*—after the repeated antitheses of the destiny of the two persons in the octave.

The opening of this sonnet has been criticized for its putative banality. Of course it is self-evidently true that of any two people, one will survive the other. But to assert this obvious proposition is not the intent of lines 1–2. Rather, the sentiment arises from the poet-lover's meditation, "Perhaps one day I will have to write my beloved's epitaph" (a normal fear in Shakespeare's era, when life-expectancy was short). The writer then thinks, "Or perhaps it will be the other way around, and he'll outlive me." This prospect inspires fear: will the young man then lack, his poet being dead, a fitting epitaph? No; because the poet's sonnets exist, the beloved already has a monument. The poet's wish to furnish an epitaph, his realization that he may not live to do it, and his further recognition that he has already provided a monument in his sonnets, are all, to my mind, genuine and nonbanal psychological motions.

Couplet Tie: *live* [*life*] (1, 5, 13)
men [-*'s*] (8, 14) and perhaps [monu-*men*-t] (9)
breath [-*es*] [-*ers*] (12, 14, 14)

82

I Grant thou wert not married to my Muſe,
And therefore maieſt without attaint ore-looke
The dedicated words which writers vſe
Of their faire ſubiect,bleſſing euery booke.
Thou art as faire in knowledge as in hew,
Finding thy worth a limmit paſt my praiſe,
And therefore art inforc'd to ſeeke anew,
Some freſher ſtampe of the time bettering dayes.
And do ſo loue,yet when they haue deuiſde,
What ſtrained touches Rhethorick can lend,
Thou truly faire,wert truly ſimpathizde,
In true plaine words,by thy true telling friend.
  And their groſſe painting might be better vſ'd,
  Where cheekes need blood,in thee it is abuſ'd.

I grant thou wert not married to my Muse,
And therefore mayst without attaint o'erlook
The dedicated words which writers use
Of their fair subject, blessing every book.
Thou art as fair in knowledge as in hue,
Finding thy worth a limit past my praise,
And therefore art inforced to seek anew
Some fresher stamp of the time-bettering days.
And do so, love; yet when they have devised
What strainèd touches rhetoric can lend,
Thou, truly fair, wert truly sympathised
In true plain words by thy true-telling friend;
  And their gross painting might be better used
  Where cheeks need blood; in thee it is abused.

LIKE 116, with which it shares the metaphor of marriage, this poem is a reply to an anterior utterance by the patron, which itself is a reply to an anterior utterance by the speaker. The antecedent scenario implied by the sonnet is this:

The poet-speaker, who has seen a new book of verse by another poet dedicated (with the patron's permission) to the young man/patron, expresses his wounded sense of having been cast aside: "You have moved into loving association with another Muse!" The young man, to the implied reproach of infidelity, replies, "I'm my own master. After all, I'm not *married* to *your* Muse; you're acting as though *I've* committed adultery." The poet replies, "I grant that you were *not married* to my Muse"—and the poem begins.

The sonnet opens with an apparent exculpation of the young man, who, since he is *not* "married," may without offense read *(o'erlook)* other authorial dedications to himself and commend *(bless)* a new book (or several or indeed *every* one). The second quatrain offers a further exculpation of the patron: the young man is *forced* to seek a better poet who can do justice to his worth and knowledge as well as to his beauty *(hue)*. In the sestet, exculpation yields to apparent outright permission: *And do so, love*—but the speaker's anger against rival poets (to whose work he hitherto granted apparent respect as a *fresher stamp of the time-bettering days*) bursts out in the abusive term *their gross painting*.

The pathos of the wish to excuse the straying of the unfaithful young man reaches its most abject note in the *volta—And do so, love*—producing, by reaction to that abjectness, the same kind of self-asserting rebound that appears in 121 *('Tis better to be vile than vile esteemed): No, I am that I am*. The role played there by the repetition of the divine *I am* is enacted here in 82 by the fourfold repetition of the word *true*, used to stand for the identity, at once, of the *truly* fair youth, the *truly* sympathizing poet, the *true words* of the poet's verse, and the *tru[th]* contained as their matter or "argument." Matter, verse, poet, youth—the four points of the poetic world-compass—are here united in a poetics of truth, which is opposed to one of servility, exaggeration, devices of rhetoric, and hypocritical strain. The "dispassionateness" of lines 9–12 after the pitiful concessive *volta* reveals a shift from the young man as an active subject of verbs *(may'st . . . o'erlook)* or as the passive subject of them *(art enforced to seek)* to the young man as passive subject of a purely passive verb *(wert sympathised)*, putting the poet in the logically "active" role. We expect, from the prior sentences, something like [*thou . . . wert truly pleased to hear*] after the previous pattern of active verbs. Instead we find *wert sympathised*, as the young man is caught up, in lines 11–12, in an ever-expanding and enjambed protest of troth/truth (in every sense) on the poet's part. The Couplet Tie, emphasizing the contrast in poetics between the true poet and the rival poets, is *use* [M-*use*] [ab-*use*-d] (1, 3, 13, 14). The phonetic connection between *attaint* and *painting* connects the young man to the corrupt court-poets even while seemingly excusing him.

In a move unusual for the *Sonnets*, the young man is here praised for his *knowledge*—though that knowledge is seen as another aesthetic accoutrement rather than as an intellectual virtue: "Thou art *as fair* in knowledge as in hue." Knowledge has appeared in the sonnet because the young man has been representing himself as a literary connoisseur, seeking new and *fresher* books and commending *(blessing)* them, if (as the speaker implies with *every*) too promiscuously. Since the young man is interested in literature only insofar as it engages in better praise of him than the speaker has been able to provide, his *knowledge* is undermined by his taste (at last revealed) for *strainèd touches* and *gross painting*.

The passage from *books* (literal) to *painting* (figurative) in the couplet suggests that false representation is more palpable in visual form than in verbal form, since the eye can make a direct comparison between the living model and the painted portrait. If the young man cannot perceive—in fact takes pleasure in—the flattering hyperbole in verbal portraits, perhaps he can be reminded of truth by a mention of the well-known, and ridiculous, flattery of their subjects practiced by portrait-painters to the rich. The apparently modest self-dismissal as the speaker admits that *finding [the young man's] worth [is] a limit past my praise* seems to justify the efforts of more ambitious others; but such an admission properly licenses greater artists, not *gross* ones. The use of the word *hue* here (cf. sonnet 20) suggests once again that it may bear some occult reference (now lost) to the young man's name.

Couplet Tie: *use* [-*d*] [ab-*use*-d] [M-*use*] (1, 3, 13, 14)

83

I Neuer ſaw that you did painting need,
And therefore to your faire no painting ſet,
I found (or thought I found) you did exceed,
The barren tender of a Poets debt:
And therefore haue I ſlept in your report,
That you your ſelfe being extant well might ſhow,
How farre a moderne quill doth come to ſhort,
Speaking of worth, what worth in you doth grow,
This ſilence for my ſinne you did impute,
Which ſhall be moſt my glory being dombe,'
For I impaire not beautie being mute,
When óthers would giue life, and bring a tombe.
There liues more life in one of your faire eyes,
Then both your Poets can in praiſe deuiſe.

I never saw that you did painting need,
And therefore to your fair no painting set;
I found (or thought I found) you did exceed
The barren tender of a poet's debt:
And therefore have I slept in your report,
That you yourself, being extant, well might show
How far a modern quill doth come too short,
Speaking of worth, what worth in you doth grow.
This silence for my sin you did impute,
Which shall be most my glory, being dumb;
For I impair not beauty, being mute,
When others would give life, and bring a tomb.
There lives more life in one of your fair eyes
Than both your poets can in praise devise.

A continuation of the self-defense in 82. Again, this is a reply-sonnet implying a whole antecedent scenario (as do 82, 110, 116, 117, 125, and 130, among others). The preceding events might be conceived as follows:

Convinced of the beloved's self-sufficient beauty, and of his own modesty of powers, Shakespeare has not recently written poems about the young man. The young man complains, noticing Shakespeare's muteness, "Why don't *you* write me any more poems? I haven't heard a word out of *you.* While my other poet has written poems praising me, you have slept in my report, and that is a sin for a poet." Shakespeare replies: "I find you ascribe to me not imputed grace or glory, but imputed sin. But let me defend myself: *I never saw that you needed to be decorated with praise*"—and thus the poem begins.

The sonnet's past-tense narration is shaken by the present need for self-defense: "*I found—or thought I found*—that you did not require praise, being so wealthy in worth that any praise could add nothing, would be only a *barren tender.*" The facts are therefore not in dispute between the young man and his poet; the poet *has* been *silen[t], mute, dumb.* The only question between them is whether the accusation "You have slept in my report" is the right description of the poet's *silence,* and whether *sin* is the correct judgment of that act of omission. In one concession, the poet decides to let the description pass—I *have,* he agrees, "slept in your report," but he refuses the judgment: not *sin,* he counters, but *glory.* The salvific Christian resonance here is deliberate. The chiasmus *silence : sin :: glory : dumb* "jams up" *sin* against *glory* for greater shock. A phrasing in parallel construction—"This silence you imputed as my sin, / But being dumb shall rather be my glory"—would have lost the direct retort-force of *glory* against *sin.* Similarly "You *impute;* I *impair* not" perhaps suggests, by a back-formation, *you impair;* and the internal rhyme between *beauty* and *mute* in line 11 suggests they "belong together" (at least for the purposes of this poem), especially since those who are not *mute* are succeeding only in burying the young man in the *tomb* of their leaden verse instead of immortalizing him.

Of the significant words shared by sonnets 82 and 83 (*painting, find, fair*, *worth*, and *devise*) *devise* is contaminated by its association in 82 with the *strainèd touches* of rhetoric. The bizarre hyperbolical isolating of *one of your fair eyes* (since nobody ever wrote an ode to the beloved's left eye) suggests that "devisèd" (i.e., ingeniously rhetorical) praise by any poet (or even two together, Shakespeare and one of those leaden *others*) will originate in a desire to shine technically, rather than to represent accurately. The Couplet Tie—*fair*, *poet's* [*poets*], *life*—resumes the question of the contest: Which life—your natural one or a rhetorically *poetic* one—best exhibits your *fair* self? The "painting" done by the "colors of rhetoric" in *praise* loses the contest. Booth points out the play by which the syntax of line 8 "comes too short" to quite make sense, bearing out the insufficiency of the modern quill.

Couplet Tie: *fair* (2, 13)
[poet] [-*'s*] [-*s*] (4, 14)
life [*lives*] (12, 13, 13)

84

WHo is it that ſayes moſt, which can ſay more,
Then this rich praiſe, that you alone, are you,
In whoſe confine immured is the ſtore,
Which ſhould example where your equall grew,
Leane penurie within that Pen doth dwell,
That to his ſubiect lends not ſome ſmall glory,
But he that writes of you, if he can tell,
That you are you, ſo dignifies his ſtory.
Let him but coppy what in you is writ,
Not making worſe what nature made ſo cleere.
And ſuch a counter-part ſhall fame his wit,
Making his ſtile admired euery where.
You to your beautious bleſſings adde a curſe,
Being fond on praiſe, which makes your praiſes worſe.

Who is it that says most which can say more
Than this rich praise – that you alone are you,
In whose confine immurèd is the store
Which should example where your equal grew.
Lean penury within that pen doth dwell
That to his subject lends not some small glory,
But he that writes of you, if he can tell
That you are you, so dignifies his story:
Let him but copy what in you is writ,
Not making worse what nature made so clear,
And such a counterpart shall fame his wit,
Making his style admirèd every where.
You to your beauteous blessings add a curse,
Being fond on praise, which makes your praises worse.

THE speaker has conjectured an explanation of the young man's willingness (82) to let many poets dedicate their work to him, of his *blessing every book:* the young man wants to see *who can say most.* But nothing, says the speaker, that even the one who *says most* can say can exceed the *rich praise that you alone are you.* Therefore, by initiating the competition for praise outbidding praise, the young man has, far from *blessing* every book, added a *curse* to them, since each is aesthetically more deplorable in hyperbole *(worse)* than its predecessors.

Like 82 and 83, sonnet 84 opposes rival poets, but suggests that there is a unique poetics appropriate only to the young man. The rival poets, who follow epideictic convention, believe that their pen should *lend glory* to their subject, otherwise their *pen* would betray *penury* of means. But the young man, like God, cannot have qualities added to his (already unique and superlative) glory: *You alone are you.* (We would nowadays say, "Only you are you.") This exhibits the *tu solus* frequent in the liturgy ("Tu solus sanctus, tu solus dominus," etc.); and the tautology of *you are you* (like the *I am that I am* of 121) suggests a uniqueness normally reserved to the Deity. The emphasis on unique personal identity in both the poet (in 121) and the young man (here in 84) dominates the *Sonnets*' investigations of subjectivity. The young man is incomparable: no one can *example where [his] equal grew,* since in himself is *immurèd* the whole stock from which someone like him could grow (a conclusive statement giving up on the hope of children expressed in the "breeding" sonnets). The new poetics then, will not be one depending on contrastive comparison, that resource of all epideictic verse ("*I* sing of a maiden / That is makeles"; "O *my* love's like a red, red rose"). Elsewhere, Shakespeare reproves "*false* compare" (130), but here he reproves "compare" of any sort. The new poetics is a poetics of identity: *copy, counterpart.* Still, in the pun on *copia* (left over from the "breeding" sonnet 11, line 14) we see that in *copying* the young man's *store,* we are *rich* in praise already.

The difficulty of the poetics of pure description, deprived of simile and metaphor, is acknowledged in the *if* and *can* of line 7: "*If* he *can* tell / That you are you." The duty of the copyist is to reproduce the writing of nature. The young man, as anterior text (what in you is *writ*), must be copied without error. Since he cannot be bettered by the copyist-scribe, he resembles the archetype of such sacred texts, the word of God, faithfully recopied in scriptoria before the advent of printing. In appropriating a pre-Gutenberg scribal process as the appropriate one for the transmission of the sacred text of the young man, Shakespeare suggests (as he has elsewhere) that the young man is a precious and not-to-be-altered relic of a former age.

The danger for the poet of this "new poetics" of copying is that his paltry descriptive powers, deprived of the rhetorical resources he might normally fall back on, will mar, *make worse,* their high subject. Since the matter of the new poetics is invariant *(you alone are you)*, its only resources are those of sedulous fidelity, which will be esteemed as *style* and *wit,* upon which the future *fame* and *admiration* given to the poet must rest. Polonius' "More matter with less wit" is exaggerated here into a poetics of "pure matter with no wit," a Shakespearean reproach to the flattery of commendatory verse.

The interesting word *dignifies* enters 84 as a Latin pun on the repeated English root *worth* in 83. The word *worth* could not enter 84 since it would clash graphically with the emphatic use of *make worse* (which, together with *praise,* is the significant Couplet Tie). The *glory* here desired by epideictic poets and their greedy subjects had been rejected for the *glory* of *silence* in 83; but the new poetics fortunately allows one step up from *silence:* not *glory,* but the *dignifie[d] story* of the perfect *copy.* The possibility of a perfect copy is not yet brought in question: as soon as the new poetics extends its ambition to copying the (hidden) inward moral nature of the young man, its hope for an exact descriptive poetics will collapse.

Couplet Tie: *praise* [*-s*] (2, 14, 14)
make [*-s*] [*-ing*] *worse* (10, 14)

85

MY toung-tide Muſe in manners holds her ſtill,
While comments of your praiſe richly compil'd,
Reſerue their Character with goulden quill,
And precious phraſe by all the Muſes fil'd.
I thinke good thoughts, whilſt other write good wordes,
And like vnlettered clarke ſtill crie Amen,
To euery Himne that able ſpirit affords,
In poliſht for ne of well refined pen.
Hearing you praiſd, I ſay 'tis ſo, 'tis true,
And to the moſt of praiſe adde ſome-thing more,
But that is in my thought, whoſe loue to you
(Though words come hind-moſt) holds his ranke before,
Then others, for the breath of words reſpect,
Me for my dombe thoughts, ſpeaking in effect.

My tongue-tied Muse in manners holds her still,
While comments of your praise, richly compiled,
Reserve their character with golden quill
And precious phrase by all the Muses filed.
I think good thoughts, whilst other write good words,
And like unlettered clerk still cry "Amen"
To every hymn that able spirit affords
In polished form of well-refinèd pen.
Hearing you praised, I say, "'Tis so, 'tis true,"
And to the most of praise add something more;
But that is in my thought, whose love to you
(Though words come hindmost) holds his rank before.
Then others for the breath of words respect,
Me for my dumb thoughts, speaking in effect.

AGAINST the inkhorn style of *precious phrase* the poet reverts, as in 83 and 84, to silence, but here it is a silence broken by a serio-comic scene of ratification, as the speaker repeatedly assents to the praise offered the young man by others *(Amen, 'Tis so, 'tis true)*, like an ignorant listener in church assenting to the splendid phrases of the prayers or sermon. Each quatrain juxtaposes the style of the poor *unlettered* poet's *dumb thoughts* to the style of the rival poets' *precious phrase.*

But—in the subversive wit of the structure—the space occupied by the aureate style dwindles with each successive quatrain: that inflated style occupies the last three lines of Q_1, the last two lines of Q_2, and only a tautological two phrases *(praised, the most of praise)* in Q_3. Q_1 contains ornate diction, literally *rich* and *golden* and *precious;* Q_2 offers only *good words, able, polished form,* and *well-refinèd* (qualities which seem accomplished rather than truly valuable); and Q_3 offers only *praised,* and *the most of praise.* In the couplet, aureate diction is no longer even honored as *good words,* and has become simply *the breath of words.* Love in the speaker will always precede his inadequate words; these latter will come (in a splendid pun on serflike praise) *hind-most* (Quarto spelling).

Frequently, when quatrains seem to repeat the same sentiment, one of the thematic constants (here, aureate diction) turns into a linguistic variable before our very eyes, dwindling into moral insignificance while retaining its position as a thematic and structural anchor. The comic image of *all the [other] Muses* busy filing (polishing) precious phrases, while the poet's poor *Muse* is tongue-tied, allows the poet's thoughts no dramatic vehicle of action; and so, to find such a vehicle, in Q_2 the original construction of antithetical competing Muses gives way to that of the unlettered clerk and his inadequate phrases of assent to the words of others. But just as the aureate diction becomes a variable that declines, so the whole structure with respect to the speaker is subtly incremental, as a *tongue-tied* holding-still is joined by *good thoughts,* which are amplified by the ratifying speech-act verbs *cry, say,* and *add.* Finally, the *hold[ing]-still* of the speaker's beginning is replaced by the *hold[ing of love's] rank before* all words. In the wit of Q_3, the apparent superlative *most of praise* turns out to be bettered by the comparative *more* of the speaker. As aureate diction declines, the speaker rises in our esteem. His thoughts speak *in effect*, in the *ex-facio* of sincerity.

The Couplet Tie—[*other*] [*-s*], *words*, and *thoughts*—encapsulates, as so often, the thematic material. The DEFECTIVE KEY WORDS, by their absence in Q_1, enact the poet's silence.

DEFECTIVE KEY WORDS:	WORDS, THOUGHT [-S] [THINK] (missing in Q_1, the quatrain representing the poet's Muse's *tongue-tied still[ness]* while listening to others' comments)
Couplet Tie:	*other* [*-s*] (5, 13) *words* (5, 12, 13) *thought* [*-s*] [*think*] (5, 5, 11, 14)

86

VVAs it the proud full ſaile of his great verſe,
Bound for the prize of (all to precious) you,
That did my ripe thoughts in my braine inhearce,
Making their tombe the wombe wherein they grew?
Was it his ſpirit, by ſpirits taught to write,
Aboue a mortall pitch, that ſtruck me dead?
No, neither he, nor his compiers by night
Giuing him ayde, my verſe aſtoniſhed.
He nor that affable familiar ghoſt
Which nightly gulls him with intelligence,
As victors of my ſilence cannot boaſt,
I was not ſick of any feare from thence.
But when your countinance fild vp his line,
Then lackt I matter, that infeebled mine.

Was it the proud full sail of his great verse,
Bound for the prize of (all too precious) you,
That did my ripe thoughts in my brain inhearse,
Making their tomb the womb wherein they grew?
Was it his spirit, by spirits taught to write
Above a mortal pitch, that struck me dead?
No, neither he, nor his compeers by night
Giving him aid, my verse astonishèd.
He, nor that affable familiar ghost
Which nightly gulls him with intelligence,
As victors, of my silence cannot boast;
I was not sick of any fear from thence.
But when your countenance filled up his line,
Then lacked I matter, that enfeebled mine.

THIS, the most famous of the "rival-poet" group, probably derives its popularity from its great rhetorical sweep attempting to account for the poet-speaker's silence:

Q_1: Was it X (the rival poet's verse)?
Q_2: Was it Y (his spirit-taught spirit)? No, neither
X (he), nor Y (his compeers);
Q_3: Nor X (he), nor Y (ghost)—No.
C: But it was *your* infidelity with him.

The individual items in this sequence are all constructed with the poet's silence as their climax:

Was it his verse that *struck me dead?*
No, neither he nor his compeers *my verse astonishèd.*
Nor he, nor his familiar ghost *of my silence* cannot boast:
But your presence in *his* verse *enfeebled mine.*

This remarkable degree of parallelism both in content (as the answers in lines 7–12 to the two opening questions repeat the content of the questions) and in form (as the periodic questions and sentences conclude each time in the poet's silence or enfeeblement) ensures the memorable quality of the sonnet, as do the dramatic enjambments of lines 5, 7, and 9, enacting the demonic energy contributed to the rival writer by his ghostly collaborating compeers. The turbulence of this poem springs largely from the way the speaker's original involuntary admiration for the *proud full sail* of the rival's *great verse* modulates into scorn for a writer who profits from, and is gulled by, the nightly intelligence of an *affable familiar* (and corrupting) *ghost* (perhaps the ghost of Homer, with whom Chapman had claimed to converse, as commentators have remarked).

There is an inverse relation between the state of the rival poet and the state of the speaker. As the presence of the rival poet dwindles linguistically in power and force (from a splendid galleon to a writer dependent on compeers to the gull of a ghost), the condition of the poet himself also varies. First, his brain is a chiastically enclosed *hearse* and *tomb* for potentially *ripe* thoughts that remain unborn in the *womb;* next, in the most serious result, he himself is *struck dead;* but a partial recovery then begins to take place: his verse is *astonishèd* (thunderstruck), he is *silent*, he is *sick*, and finally his line is *enfeebled* from lack of matter. There is clearly a direct proportion (which Shakespeare must have enjoyed devising) between awe of the rival and extinction of self; and as awe of the rival declines, the self proportionally recovers—if not to health, then certainly to something better than a corpse. Although the poet's *line* is enfeebled, he is, by the end, alive and even an active writer, though of "enfeebled" verse. Since the poem is written in the past tense, the poet's *silence* may be thought to have ended.

The long twelve-line suspense as to the cause of the writer's ills gives the couplet a greater prominence here, and emphasizes the unusualness of the 12-2 logical construction (used again in another effect-to-cause sonnet, 147, in which the speaker's long description of his sickness—*My love is as a fever*—finally closes with an explanation of his madness: *For I have sworn thee fair, and thought thee bright, / Who art as black as hell, as dark as night*).

Sonnet 86, in attempting to account for the power of the rival poet's verse, ascribes it at first to almost any quality in him of internal manner or external motive: pride, expansiveness, covetousness, inspiration by spirits, help by compeers, illegal "intelligence." The one explanation that is successfully fended off for twelve lines is the question of the rival poet's *matter.* When, after all the flurry of alternative explanations, the dread question of *matter* raises its head, the poet is defeated: the rival poet was not only *bound for* the young man—he has him. The sinister echo of the "*full* sail" in the "*filled-up* line" clinches the couplet. Even though the rival poet has been scornfully reduced to a spy's gull, the speaker's line cannot regain its full strength, since its *matter* is gone. The young man is conceived of here as a quantitatively limited substance who cannot bilocate; to the extent that he is absorbed by the rival, he is lost to the speaker. *Countenance* also implies "favor"; and the emphatic pronouns—"when *your* countenance filled up *his* line"—convey the poet's incredulity. The world is out of joint: wombs are tombs, mortals write above a mortal pitch, ghosts gull human beings; but of all these signs and wonders, the most untoward is that *your* countenance should appear in *his* line. *His* line, *filled* with you, was able to swell to a *full* sail: mine, matterless, grew *enfeebled. Full*-ness and *feeble*-ness arise in the two poets in inverse proportion relative to their possession of the young man; *he* was the missing link in the whole rivalry of inverse proportion that occupied the body of the poem. The spirits, compeers, and ghosts vanish—seen as the rigged defenses they were—

once the new inverse proportion, dependent on the young man's "countenance" (in both senses), is admitted. Once upon a time the speaker's verse, too, was full; but we see in the declension *full*, *filled*, *enfeebled* the trajectory of his decline. The resemblance in sound between *affable* (< *fari*, "to speak") and *enfeebled* offers a second Couplet Tie.

Couplet Tie: *full* [*filled*] (1, 13)
and perhaps
af-*fable* [en-*feeble*-d] (9, 14)

87

FArewell thou art too deare for my poſſeſſing,
And like enough thou knowſt thy eſtimate,
The Charter of thy worth giues thee releaſing:
My bonds in thee are all determinate.
For how do I hold thee but by thy granting,
And for that ritches where is my deſeruing?
The cauſe of this faire guiſt in me is wanting,
And ſo my pattent back againe is ſweruing.
Thy ſelfe thou gau'ſt,thy owne worth then not knowing,
Or mee to whom thou gau'ſt it,elſe miſtaking,
So thy great guiſt vpon miſpriſion growing,
Comes home againe,on better iudgement making.
  Thus haue I had thee as a dreame doth flatter,
  In ſleepe a King,but waking no ſuch matter.

Farewell, thou art too dear for my possessing,
And like enough thou know'st thy estimate;
The charter of thy worth gives thee releasing:
My bonds in thee are all determinate.
For how do I hold thee but by thy granting,
And for that riches where is my deserving?
The cause of this fair gift in me is wanting,
And so my patent back again is swerving.
Thy self thou gav'st, thy own worth then not knowing,
Or me, to whom thou gav'st it, else mistaking;
So thy great gift, upon misprision growing,
Comes home again, on better judgement making.
  Thus have I had thee as a dream doth flatter,
  In sleep a king, but waking no such matter.

BESIDES the master-mistress sonnet (20), 87 is Shakespeare's chief experiment in feminine endings (though in this poem, two of the rhymes are masculine—*estimate* and *determinate*). (Booth mistakenly says that 87 uses "feminine rhymes throughout," but Kerrigan gets it right.) In 20, the feminine rhymes enact the originally intended feminine sex in Nature's creation of the young man. Here, as in 126, where they appear strikingly though intermittently, feminine endings enact the poet's unwillingness to let the young man go, a lingering farewell to his pliant self.

The deposed-by-daylight *king* of the last line generates the several puns of the closing: *mist-a-king*, *m-a-king*, *w-a-king*, the "nutshells" hiding the nut, *a king*, which is, phonetically speaking, close to "aching." Ten of the fourteen rhyme-words end in *-ing*, so that the rhyme internally present in *a king* and *waking* (the only internal words in the poem ending in *-ing*) is therefore necessarily foregrounded, rendering the pun noticeable—though it does not seem, for all its flagrantness, ever to have been noticed. *A king* is the single Couplet Tie (a phonetic, not semantic one), which foregrounds it all the more.

This sonnet imitates (if one imagines it as a current coursing back and forth between two poles labeled "speaker" and "young man") the giving-and-recalling, or *swerving*, of what was (or seemed to be) a *gift*. The melancholy repetition of forms of that word *(give* [*-s*], *gift*, *gav'st)* five times in fourteen lines is countered by the hard legal imagery of financial transactions—*estimate*, *charter*, *bonds*, *determinate* (i.e. "short-term"), *riches*, *patent*—and of course *dear* and *worth* in their financial senses. The diagram shows the back-and-forth movement between the two poles, after *Farewell* sets the occasion.

"Back again swerving" is the name of the imitative aesthetic of this sonnet. What is carefully avoided in every line is the explicit form of accusation [*You took back your gift*]. In order to avoid the (true) implication of direct action on the part of the young man, inanimate things take on life: a *charter . . . gives*, a *patent . . . is swerving*, a *gift . . . comes home*, a *dream . . . flatter[s]*. Shakespeare is so expert at representing mental defenses that we cannot suppose him unconscious of his own cunning. The stratagems of the mind's excuses are one of the great themes of the *Sonnets*, as are—in the best sense—the stratagems of intense speculative thought (as in 73 or 129).

Structure of Sonnet 87

Young Man		*Speaker*
Farewell,		
thou art too dear for	→	*my* possessing,
And like enough *thou* know'st *thy* estimate;		
The charter of *thy* worth gives *thee*	→	releasing [from me];
in *thee*	←	*My* bonds
	→	are all determinate.
thy granting?	←	For how do *I* hold thee but by
And for that riches	→	where is *my* deserving?
this fair gift	←	The cause of
	→	in *me* is wanting,
back again is swerving.	←	And so *my* patent
Thyself thou	→	gav'st [to me],
thine own worth then not knowing,	←	
	→	Or *me* to whom
thou	→	gav'st it else mistaking;
So *thy* great gift	→	[to me]
upon misprision growing,	→	[of me]
Comes home again,	←	
on better judgement making.		
Thus		have *I* had thee
as a dream doth flatter,		
		In sleep a king,
but waking no such matter.		

The fantasia in this poem on the "meanings" that *-ing* can possess is a measure of Shakespeare's persistent meditation on linguistic structures. Here is a rough sketch of these "meanings" of *-ing:*

possess*ing*	noun: *a state of* possession
releas*ing*	noun: *potential* of being released
grant*ing*	noun: *act of* gift
deserv*ing*	noun: *capacity for* inner desert

want*ing*	adjective: *state of* lack
swerv*ing*	verb: *action of* turning
know*ing*	adjective: *habit of* knowledge
mistak*ing*	adjective: *attribute of* mistake in other
grow*ing*	adjective: *action of* enlargement
mak*ing*	noun: *action*
k*ing*	noun: *person*
wak*ing*	adverb: *at the time* of the end of sleep.

The phoneme *-ing* can participate in all these parts of speech—noun, verb, adjective, adverb—and its unstable linguistic shifting acts out, perhaps, the unpredictability of the young man's impermanent *gift.*

Because no gift of love can entail guaranteed permanence, the withdrawal of a beloved's affection is something everyone has feared or felt. The universal appeal of this much-anthologized sonnet springs from its very lack of particular detail: there are no sexually precise pronouns, no references to a new sexual or affectional or poetic rival, and (because of the modern persistence of most of its legal vocabulary) no estranging historical allusions. The chief metaphorical range remains accessible to the modern reader, who feels competent (even if mistakenly so) when encountering *estimate*, *charter*, *bonds*, and *patent.* The idealization consequent to love has made every lover feel the beloved is *too dear for . . . possessing.* This sonnet fulfills the apprehension of separation in 49 *(Against that time)*, and through its legal imagery and sense of fate bears out the couplet of 49: "To leave poor me thou hast the strength of *laws* / Since why to love I can *allege* no cause."

The sobriety of the legal excuses for the young man's actions is broken, to great effect, four times in the sonnet, when the speaker's emotions of loss "show through" his bare and precise language: *that riches*, *this fair gift*, *thy great gift*, and *a king.* We are encouraged, in reading the poem, to think that GIFTand its variants [GIVES] [GAV'ST] will be a KEY WORD since it appears in each successive quatrain (3, 7, 9, 10, 11). Its conspicuous *absence* in the couplet, making it a DEFECTIVE KEY WORD, speaks silently of the gift withdrawn.

DEFECTIVE KEY WORD:	GIFT [GIVES] [GAV'ST] (missing in C)
Couplet Tie:	*a king* [mist-*aking*] [m-*aking*] [w-*aking*] (10, 12, 14, 14) (a phonetic, not semantic, Couplet Tie)

88

VVHen thou ſhalt be diſpode to ſet me light,
And place my merrit in the eie of skorne,
Vpon thy ſide,againſt my ſelfe ile fight,
And proue thee virtuous,though thou art forſworne:
With mine owne weakeneſſe being beſt acquainted,
Vpon thy part I can ſet downe a ſtory
Of faults conceald,wherein I am attainted :
That thou in looſing me,ſhall win much glory:
And I by this wil be a gainer too,
For bending all my louing thoughts on thee,
The iniuries that to my ſelfe I doe,
Doing thee vantage,duble vantage me.
Such is my loue,to thee I ſo belong,
That for thy right,my ſelfe will beare all wrong.

When thou shalt be disposed to set me light,
And place my merit in the eye of scorn,
Upon thy side, against myself, I'll fight,
And prove thee virtuous, though thou art forsworn:
With mine own weakness being best acquainted,
Upon thy part I can set down a story
Of faults concealed wherein I am attainted,
That thou in losing me shall win much glory;
And I by this will be a gainer too,
For, bending all my loving thoughts on thee,
The injuries that to myself I do,
Doing thee vantage, double vantage me.
Such is my love, to thee I so belong,
That for thy right myself will bear all wrong.

AS IN 49 and 87, the speaker in sonnet 88 has already decided that his own *desert* (49) / *deserving* (87) is so minimal that he cannot protest when he is deserted. But this sonnet goes beyond not only the apparent acquiescence of 87 but even the defense of the young man's position in 49, where the speaker *uprears his hand* against himself to *guard the lawful reasons* on the young man's part. Whereas 49 ended with the aggression of the self against the self, 88 restricts this act, as a major theme, to the octave, and surpasses 49 in asserting in the octave that, far from losing by this self-injuring act, the speaker is *double vantage[d]*, made a *gainer.*

Sonnet 88 is rather flatly said, and flatness of expression is usually, in the *Sonnets,* a warning that emotional expressiveness is not the aim a particular poem has in mind. What, then, is governing the choice of words, if not expressiveness?

The "doubling" vantage that is the theme of the sestet of 88 helps to organize the whole sonnet. Booth notes the play of *set* (1, 6) *place,* and *disposed* (< *ponere,* "to place") but does not associate it with the wish to enact doubling. *Set* (1, 6) is repeated in identical form; *pose/place* is an etymological doubling; *upon thy side* is repeated by *upon thy part* (a doubling with variation); *eye/I* is a phonetic doubling; *though thou* (echoed by *thoughts*) is a stuttering repetition as is *loving/love;* ***b****eing* ***b****est* is a frustrated repetition; *will/will* is an identical repetition like *set/set* and *all/all; to/too/to* returns on itself; *thee/The* bridges a line break, as does *do/Doing.* ***Do****/****do****ing/****du****ble* (Quarto spelling) is the most attention-getting self-repetition, with the double repetition of *vantage* setting it off: I ***do****/****Do****ing thee vantage,* ***du****ble-vantage me.* *Such/so* is perhaps another instance, as is *against* and *a gainer.* All of these doubles add up to the *all wrong* borne by the speaker, so that the young man can possess the *right.*

The crucial phrase of the whole poem is, of course, the quiet bombshell in line 4—*though thou art forsworn.* This can be taken as fact, in the reading of a certain future: "When, in the future, you scorn my merit, I'll fight on your side and prove you virtuous, even though in fact you are forsworn." But it can also be taken as the reading of a hypothetical situation: "Whenever, if ever, you scorn my merit, I'll nevertheless prove you virtuous, even in the extreme case of your being forsworn." The second reading is the more likely, perhaps; but the startling *thou art forsworn* takes on the force of a factual accusation, justifying the speaker's *merit*, so scorned by the young man.

The masochism which the speaker exhibits as he fights against himself, sets down the story of his own hidden faults, and does himself numerous injuries, bearing all wrong, is offered as a proof of love *(Such is my love)*, but also as a claim of *belong[ing]*. The propitiatory octave is "balanced" by the witty arithmetic of triumph in *double vantage*, but ensconced in the arithmetic is an abdication of personal subjectivity on the part of the speaker. Since *all [his] loving thoughts* are bent on the beloved, that which benefits the beloved accrues by an automatic spiritual osmosis to the spirit of the speaker, whose injured *self* has now been completely split off from his loving *thoughts*. The depersonalization of the speaker, his thoughts on the young man's *right*, his self bearing all *wrong*, is, as the last line shows, now complete.

Couplet Tie: *love* [-*ing*] (10, 13)

89

SAy that thou didſt forſake mee for ſome falt,
And I will comment vpon that offence,
Speake of my lameneſſe, and I ſtraight will halt:
Againſt thy reaſons making no defence.
Thou canſt not(loue)diſgrace me halfe ſo ill,
To ſet a forme vpon deſired change,
As ile my ſelfe diſgrace,knowing thy wil,
I will acquaintance ſtrangle and looke ſtrange:
Be abſent from thy walkes and in my tongue,
Thy ſweet beloued name no more ſhall dwell,
Leaſt I(too much prophane)ſhould do it wronge:
And haplie of our old acquaintance tell.
   For thee,againſt my ſelfe ile vow debate,
   For I muſt nere loue him whom thou doſt hate.

Say that thou didst forsake me for some fault,
And I will comment upon that offence;
Speak of my lameness, and I straight will halt,
Against thy reasons making no defence.
Thou canst not (love) disgrace me half so ill,
To set a form upon desirèd change,
As I'll myself disgrace; knowing thy will,
I will acquaintance strangle and look strange,
Be absent from thy walks, and in my tongue
Thy sweet belovèd name no more shall dwell,
Lest I (too much profane) should do it wrong,
And haply of our old acquaintance tell.
   For thee, against myself I'll vow debate,
   For I must ne'er love him whom thou dost hate.

THE doubling of 88 is continued in 89, with several words carried over from 88 *(fault, against, love, will, acquaint, wrong).* Other forms of doubling also occur (I include antonyms): *fault/offense, lame/halt, lame/straight, disgrace/disgrace, thy will/I will, acquaintance/acquaintance, strangle/strange, halt/walk[s], wrong/hap, for thee/against myself, love/hate.*

Sonnet 88 had found a way to keep utterance afloat: the speaker will at least be able to *set down a story* by echoing—and in fact inflating—the vicious story the young man is telling about him. (The rhyme *story/glory* was ironically repeated from 84.) Sonnet 89 begins with the same wish to prolong utterance by repeating the young man's story: "'*Say*' thus and so, and I will '*comment.*'" But after these two transitional lines, the speaker seems to accept a silence foretold by the phrase *no defense. Strangle* is strangulated into *strange*, and it is asserted that *in my tongue thy . . . name no more shall dwell.* As Kerrigan points out, *vow debate* can be nonverbal, and here probably is.

The structure of 89 exhibits an unusual enjambment between Q_2 and Q_3, when the speaker, seeing that his beloved wishes to disgrace him, vows he will outdo his beloved in self-disgracing: "Knowing *thy* will, / *I* will . . . look strange, / Be absent," etc. The enumeration that begins here halfway through line 7 occupies (in my pointing) 5½ lines, and swells to an increased resolve. The distinct enjambment of Q_2 with Q_3 effectively makes them, together, an "octave," and we could say that this structure, 4-8-2, represents Shakespeare's experiment with an octave of silence bracketed, fore and aft, with the separated parts of a "sestet" of external and internal speech *(comment, debate).*

The pathos of the speaker's remarks springs from his successive fall-back positions in the face of the young man's unexplained withdrawal. *Say, speak of, [reveal] thy reasons,* he pleads. The silence continues. He then indirectly implores to *know* the *will* of the young man, what changed *form* he envisages for their relationship, vowing that once he knows the young man's will, he will disgrace himself more effectively than the young man could disgrace him. Silence still greets him. He goes his past offer one better: he will abolish (not simply *change*) the relationship, a form of self-murder, as he will *strangle acquaintance* and *be absent.* More silence. He offers up all he has left, his memories; he will not even tell of that *old acquaintance* before it was strangled. More silence. He now realizes the depth of the young man's animus: the young man must *hate* him. What has the speaker left to offer by way of love except a congruent self-hate, euphemized as *ne'er love*. The coercive power of the young man's continued silence motivates all the desperate stratagems of the speaker. The mimetic object of the sonnet is propitiatory speech as it becomes more and more abject.

The Couplet Tie of both 88 and 89 is *love*, but the speaker finally in 89 admits—after the euphemisms of 88 *(set me light, attainted of faults)*—that what the young man feels for him is *hate*. This word, *hate*, ushers in the last of this group of attainder poems, 90.

Couplet Tie: *love* [*belovèd*] (5, 10, 14)

90

THen hate me when thou wilt, if euer,now,
Now while the world is bent my deeds to croſſe,
Ioyne with the ſpight of fortune,make me bow,
And doe not drop in for an after loſſe:
Ah doe not,when my heart hath ſcapte this ſorrow,
Come in the rereward of a conquerd woe,
Giue not a windy night a rainie morrow,
To linger out a purpoſd ouer-throw.
If thou wilt leaue me, do not leaue me laſt,
When other pettie griefes haue done their ſpight,
But in the onſet come,ſo ſtall I taſte
At firſt the very worſt of fortunes might.
    And other ſtraines of woe, which now ſeeme woe,
    Compar'd with loſſe of thee,will not ſeeme ſo.

Then hate me when thou wilt, if ever, now,
Now while the world is bent my deeds to cross,
Join with the spite of Fortune, make me bow,
And do not drop in for an after-loss.
Ah do not, when my heart hath scaped this sorrow,
Come in the rearward of a conquered woe;
Give not a windy night a rainy morrow,
To linger out a purposed overthrow.
If thou wilt leave me, do not leave me last,
When other petty griefs have done their spite,
But in the onset come; so shall I taste
At first the very worst of Fortune's might;
    And other strains of woe, which now seem woe,
    Compared with loss of thee will not seem so.

SONNETS 87–90 make up a small group which turn on the young man's repudiation of the speaker. The true organizer of 90 is the word *woe.* Its essential graphic components, in both true and reversed order *(wo, ow),* are sprinkled eleven times through the poem: ***now***, *now*, ***world***, ***bow***, *sorrow*, ***woe***, *morrow*, *overthrow*, ***worst***, ***woe***, ***woe***. Seven of the eleven instances appear in the rhyme position, in both phonemic possibilities, "oh" and "ow," and the usage is thereby conspicuously foregrounded.

When Shakespeare, later in the sequence, wants to refer to the young man's "unkindness" related in sonnet 90, he repeats his "woe" rhymes. (Sonnet 120 repeats exactly, in the same position, the Q_1 rhyme ***now/bow***, of 90; it also repeats *woe* and *sorrow* (twice), and adds ***wounded.***) The Couplet Tie of 90 is *woe* and *loss*, both of them rhyme-words in the poem.

The sonnet is logically organized, it would seem, into octave and sestet (an 8-6 structure) by its two "if" hypotheses: *If ever, now* (line 1) and *If thou wilt leave me* (line 9). On the other hand, it is also rhetorically organized by its "[do] not" sequence: *do not drop in, do not . . . come, give not, do not.* A set of negative injunctions (lines 4–10) is bracketed on either side by positive injunctions: *hate me, join, make me* on the left, and *come* on the right, suggesting a 4-6-4 structure. From another point of view, though, the *do not . . . come in the rearward* of line 6 matches the *in the onset come* of line 11, the climax of the poem; this suggests a 6-6-2 structure rather than an octave/sestet structure.

However, the single most powerful organizing force in the sonnet is the account of the wrongs suffered by the speaker up to the present. These are "compulsively" repeated and rephrased, a sign of the speaker's wounded response to the earlier indignities he has suffered from the world. The aesthetic intent in piling up these world-inflicted indignities is ultimately to diminish them, as the diagram demonstrates. The tiny phrase *loss of thee,* when placed on the scale, so outweighs all the *might* and *spite* on the other side, that the former indignities now not only seem *petty griefs* (as they began to seem when the desertion of the young man grew more fully imagined), but they are even denied the name of *woe.* There really are not any *strains of woe* other than the loss of the beloved; there is only real erotic *woe*, alone and huge.

Structure of Sonnet 90

Seeming Woe (Now)	*Real Woe (To Come)*
world, bent to cross deeds	hate
the spite of fortune	
[loss]	after-loss
sorrow	
a conquered woe	rearward [woe]
windy night	rainy morrow
	purposed overthrow
petty griefs	last [worst] [grief]
spite	
[fortune's might (bad)]	very worst of fortune's might
strains of woe	
seem[ing woe]	
[no woe]	loss of thee

The odd move, in this socially phrased poem, is the resort to a natural proverb: *Give not a windy night a rainy morrow.* This plea to the young man seems irrelevant: What difference does it make whether his desertion comes first or last? The justification for the plea, summed up in *taste/worst/first,* is explained as being a Mithridates-prophylactic against all other sufferings, and therefore as an effective obliteration of that heap of present *strains of woe.* This poem is—or wishes to be—a self-destroying artifact, in which seeming woe no longer seems so, overborne as it will be by real woe.

The psychological effect hoped for is pity: Could anyone—the young man especially—bear to add to the strains of woe so enumerated? The move from reality *(other strains of woe)* to appearance *(which now seem woe)* is followed by a move to the abolition of reality by change of appearance: woes *will not seem so* (will not appear as woe), and therefore will not *be* woe. The restriction of the meaning of the word *woe* to mean *loss of thee* leaves those other *strains of woe* insusceptible to a category name, even one so apologetic as *petty griefs.* The draining of meaning from the (usual) appearances of the word *woe* is enacted in the deletion of "woe-ness" phrase by phrase in the couplet.

Couplet Tie: *other* (10,13)
woe [6, 13, 13] In the form of [*wo-*][*-ow*]—an orthographic tie—see also (1, 2, 3, 5, 7, 8, 12)

91

Some glory in their birth,ſome in their skill,
Some in their wealth, ſome in their bodies force,
Some in their garments though new-fangled ill:
Some in their Hawkes and Hounds,ſome in their Horſe.
And euery humor hath his adiunct pleaſure,
Wherein it findes a ioy aboue the reſt,
But theſe perticulers are not my meaſure,
All theſe I better in one generall beſt.
Thy loue is bitter then high birth to me,
Richer then wealth,prouder then garments coſt,
Of more delight then Hawkes or Horſes bee:
And hauing thee,of all mens pride I boaſt.
  Wretched in this alone,that thou maiſt take,
  All this away,and me moſt wretched make.

Some glory in their birth, some in their skill,
Some in their wealth, some in their body's force,
Some in their garments, though newfangled ill,
Some in their hawks and hounds, some in their horse;
And every humour hath his adjunct pleasure,
Wherein it finds a joy above the rest;
But these particulars are not my measure:
All these I better in one general best.
Thy love is better than high birth to me,
Richer than wealth, prouder than garments' cost,
Of more delight than hawks or horses be;
And having thee, of all men's pride I boast:
  Wretched in this alone, that thou mayst take
  All this away, and me most wretched make.

CURLING round on its punning fulcrum *better* (verb) / *best* (noun) / *better* (adjective) in lines 8–9, this sonnet lets Q_3 ostentatiously repeat Q_1 as *particular* pleasures are resumed in one *general best:*

some in Q_1: *birth; wealth; garments; hawks; horse*
I in Q_3: high *birth; wealth; garments'* cost; *hawks; horses*

The positive, comparative, and superlative degrees of comparison organize this witty sonnet: the pride of other men represents the positive degree; the surpassing of them by the speaker's possession of the young man's particular qualities represents the comparative degree *(better);* and the young man's love, in itself absolute, is the *general best,* the superlative degree. But there is another set of positive and superlative degrees: the speaker is *wretched* now in the fear of loss, and lives in anticipation of the superlative *most wretched* if love is withdrawn. The phonetic play between *richer* (line 10) and *wretched* (lines 13–14) links the two degrees of comparison, positive and negative, in an alarming and foreboding way.

The Couplet Tie—*all these* and *all this*—links the positive of others and the superlative of the speaker. From the proverbial vocabulary of consumer relish *(every humour hath his adjunct pleasure),* the poem has passed to its own mounting triad *cost, boast, most.* But instead of the climactic *most* attaching itself, as we would expect, to the superlative degree of the positive pride of *cost,* attended by its comparative (above the lot of others) *boast, most* turns out to be—horribly—the superlative culmination of *wretched* [*more wretched*].

The amused social observations of the speaker about the different *humour[s]* of human beings and his repudiation of them in favor of love is reminiscent of the Platonic choice of the spiritual over the material; but in choosing the erotic rather than the spiritual, the speaker leaves open the possibility that he too has merely put on *garments newfangled ill* rather than a lasting vesture. His scorn for the weakness of others in their temporary "adjunct pleasures" suddenly rebounds against himself as he imagines himself stripped of *all this* and newly wretched.

The assertion—in Elizabethan society—that *thy love is better than high birth to me* presages the fall in the couplet. High birth cannot be taken away, but love can be. As soon as the speaker prefers the ephemeral *(love)* to the inalienable *(high birth)*, he begins to weep to have that which he fears to lose. It is tempting to think that the *lapsus linguae* in the Quarto—*thy love is bitter*—was a Freudian slip of Shakespeare's own.

DEFECTIVE KEY WORD: ALL (missing in Q_1, the account of *some*)

Couplet Tie: *richer* [*wretched*] (10, 13, 14)
all these [*all this*] (8, 14)
all (8, 12, 14)

92

BVt doe thy worſt to ſteale thy ſelfe away,
For tearme of life thou art aſſured mine,
And life no longer then thy loue will ſtay,
For it depends vpon that loue of thine.
Then need I not to feare the worſt of wrongs,
When in the leaſt of them my life hath end,
I ſee, a better ſtate to me belongs
Then that, which on thy humor doth depend.
Thou canſt not vex me with inconſtant minde,
Since that my life on thy reuolt doth lie,
Oh what a happy title do I finde,
Happy to haue thy loue, happy to die!
  But whats ſo bleſſed faire that feares no blot,
  Thou maiſt be falce, and yet I know it not.

But do thy worst to steal thyself away,
For term of life thou art assurèd mine,
And life no longer than thy love will stay,
For it depends upon that love of thine.
Then need I not to fear the worst of wrongs,
When in the least of them my life hath end;
I see a better state to me belongs
Than that which on thy humour doth depend.
Thou canst not vex me with inconstant mind,
Since that my life on thy revolt doth lie:
O what a happy title do I find,
Happy to have thy love, happy to die!
  But what's so blessèd-fair that fears no blot?
  Thou mayst be false, and yet I know it not.

THE threat of 91—that the young man will withdraw his love, making the speaker *most wretched*—is now, by one of the most extravagant *volte-faces* in the *Sonnets*, rendered impotent by the declaration that the speaker will die at the instant of the lessening of love. *Fear/fair*—the Couplet Tie—summarizes the flaw in the possession of any beauty. This flaw is revealed only in the couplet (and expanded on in 93).

The word *humour*, repeated from 91 but here applied to the young man, reveals him as one of the *inconstant* minds which tend towards *revolts* rather than fidelities. And the superlative *worst* (twice used), matching *most wretched* in 91, reveals that we are approaching not the *general best* of possession, but the *worst of wrongs*, total withdrawal of *love*. Even the *least* blot on the relation—foretelling its imminent end—will, the speaker declares, end his life. The superlatives here—*worst*, *least*—betray the hysteria of the speaker faced with the young man's infidelity.

The speaker's threat of suicide (if that is what it is) is a form of emotional blackmail. If it is a statement of believed physical fact ("I shall die on the spot if you begin to love me less"), it will still serve as emotional blackmail if it is addressed to the young man. On the other hand, many of the sonnets of apparent direct address may be read as internal meditations silently directed toward the image of the young man. In that case, we read the sonnet differently, not as emotional blackmail but as a form of defensive and sophistical self-persuasion. Of course, this delusion of control-by-dying-on-the-spot collapses in the couplet, which introduces the idea of an infidelity that is not suspected.

What causes the collapse of the "happy" delusion that the end of love will be the end of life? It is the subterranean logical progress from *the worst of wrongs* to *the least of [wrongs]* to the implied missing third term [*no wrongs*]. But there is no human being who never commits wrongs, so presumably the young man has already committed wrongs. The perfect *better/blessèd state* with *no blot* is—on theological grounds, even on moral ones—unattainable.

The concatenation by which the futile self-persuasion here proceeds is as follows: "Thou art mine for *life*, because *life depends upon thy love;* in the *least of wrongs* (from you) my *life ends*. A state in me that *depends on* thy humor is replaced by a better state in me which does not *depend on* another's *inconstant mind;* rather, my new state is one in which my *life lies on thy revolt,* and death, once that *revolt* occurs, will occur instantaneously." The speaker's specious "happy" alternatives—a life of untroubled possessiveness of a blameless lover or a death at the instant of the least of wrongs—are the content of the body of the poem, lines 2–12. The exclamatory climax in the three uses of *happy—O what a happy title, happy to have, happy to die!*—is linked by its use of infinitives, even if unwittingly, to the only preceding infinitive in the poem: *to fear.* In this interesting revelation of the persistence of memory traces in the speaker's mind—as the use of an infinitive brings an earlier infinitive use (line 5) to mind—we see why *fear* rises to the surface in line 13. It collects around itself the two alliterating adjectives *fair* and *false.* These connections give the couplet its telling and convincing power to bring down the previous defensive house of cards.

Since 92 is one of the sonnets in which the couplet is opposed to the body of the poem (a 1-11-2) structure, it is important that the couplet be able to bear the stress of "outweighing" something almost six times its size. The strong religious overtones (noted by Booth) surrounding *a better state, happy, blessèd,* and *fair* suggest that the speaker is already viewing himself from a posthumous perspective. This perspective gives lines 11–12 their air of unreality, a willed complacency instantly undermined. The synonymy in the couplet between *blot* and *false* probably proceeds by way of the invisible middle term between them, *fault[s].* Similarly, the word *lie* is a telling reduction of *life,* just when *love* and *life* try to become interchangeable. Even the phonetic pun in "*know* [no] it *not*" suggests the slipperiness of reasoning underlying all these slippages of language.

One would expect, finding LIFE present in Q_1, Q_2, and Q_3, to find it in the couplet. Its absence in lines 13–14, after its appearance in lines 2, 3, 6, and 10, means that with the suppression of *love* (present three times in the body of the poem, in lines 3, 4, and 12) comes the instant death prophesied in the sonnet. Therefore, the absence of LIFE is foregrounded in the couplet, which consequently shows the speaker to be erotically "dead."

DEFECTIVE KEY WORD: LIFE (missing in C)

Couplet Tie: *fear* [*fair*] (5, 13, 13)

93

SO ſhall I liue,ſuppoſing thou art true,
Like a deceiued husband ſo loues face,
May ſtill ſeeme loue to me,though alter'd new:
Thy lookes with me,thy heart in other place.
For their can liue no hatred in thine eye,
Therefore in that I cannot know thy change,
In manies lookes,the falce hearts hiſtory
Is writ in moods and frounes and wrinckles ſtrange.
But heauen in thy creation did decree,
That in thy face ſweet loue ſhould euer dwell,
What ere thy thoughts, or thy hearts workings be,
Thy lookes ſhould nothing thence, but ſweetneſſe tell,.
   How like *Eaues* apple doth thy beauty grow,
   If thy ſweet vertue anſwere not thy ſhow.

So shall I live, supposing thou art true,
Like a deceivèd husband; so love's face
May still seem love to me, though altered new:
Thy looks with me, thy heart in other place.
For there can live no hatred in thine eye,
Therefore in that I cannot know thy change;
In many's looks, the false heart's history
Is writ in moods and frowns and wrinkles strange,
But heaven in thy creation did decree
That in thy face sweet love should ever dwell;
What e'er thy thoughts or thy heart's workings be,
Thy looks should nothing thence but sweetness tell.
   How like Eve's apple doth thy beauty grow,
   If thy sweet virtue answer not thy show!

THE speaker's play on appearance and reality recalls 54 *(O how much more doth beauty beauteous seem)*, but we find *Eve's apple* (with its implied serpent) substituted for the deceptive *canker blooms*, perhaps by transit through the canker worm. The Couplet Tie is both the phonetic *-eive/Eve* [dec*eiv*èd, *Eve*'s] and the semantic *sweet* [*sweetness*]. The play on *Eave* (Quarto spelling) is reinforced by the presence of the same letters in h*eave*n. The *hate* of 89 and 90 reappears here as *hatred;* the *false* of 92 recurs in 93; and the play on *live* and *love* is like that on *life* and *love* in 92. The appearance of Eve may have been caused by the *eave* in h*eav*en, or by the thought of the tree of *know*ledge, itself suggested by the repetition with reversal of *no/know* from 92, and by the Edenic suggestion of *no blot* (< Latin *macula*, spot: "immaculate" = sinless, without blot).

The categories organizing the sonnet are external qualities like *face, looks, eye, beauty, show* on the one hand, and internal qualities like *heart, thoughts, virtue, true* on the other. *Sweet love* (line 10) is the ambiguous essence yet to be assigned to one side or the other. Of these words, *beauty, true (truth), sweet, virtue, show*, and *love* (as *love*ly) appear also in 54, reinforcing the connection between the two poems and perhaps anticipating the recurrence of *canker* and *rose* in 95. But whereas 54 presented itself as a parable about true and false roses, with a final analogizing moral drawn between the true rose and the "virtuous" young man, this sonnet has abandoned the flower-parable. Here, the "true" are, paradoxically, those whose *heart's history* (whether virtuous or immoral) manifests itself on their faces. The "false" are those whose faces always look sweet, but whose *show* does not correspond to their *hearts.* The word *alter*—to become so important in 116—appears here in conjunction with the startling simile of cuckoldry, *like a deceivèd husband.*

In deciding to live in pretense, *like a deceivèd husband*, the speaker consents in Q_1 to a permanent disjunction between *looks* and *heart.* Quatrains 2 and 3 utter a heartbroken hymn to the surpassing beauty of the young man, which can survive even the depredations of inner falsehood. *Thine* eye, *thy* creation, *thy* face are stressed contrastively against the behavior of those ordinary *many* who evince their hearts' falsity by *moods and frowns and wrinkles strange.* In this sonnet, one of those structured with an "octave" in the middle (4-8-2), the deceived husband plays the role of Adam, reaching toward a beautiful apple (a descendant of the canker bloom), while suspecting that its *show* covers not *sweet virtue*, but rather its opposite. The word *hatred* conceals the word *heart;* or we could say the *heart* has added a new ingredient, *d*, changing itself to *hatred.* Because no *h-a-t-r-e-d* can live in the young man's eye, his *h-e-a-r-t* cannot live in his eye either.

The oddity of phrasing in line 14 of the couplet needs remarking. A more logical way of putting it would be, "If *a* sweet virtue" or "If *some* sweet virtue." The predication "*thy* sweet virtue" is a tenuous remnant of the asseveration in the couplet of 54 that the youth is *beauteous and lovely*, possessed of *truth.*

The speaker's acceptance here of the habit of suffering—after the specious declaration in 92 that life would end on the spot once falsehood was suspected—is the most painful aspect of the poem. The prediction *So shall I live, supposing* and the habitual present tense of "how . . . *doth* thy beauty *grow*" consort with the hymn to the young man's face as proof that the speaker is still caught in the toils of a beauty so powerful that alone it creates love.

The aesthetic disgust exhibited in the phrase *moods and frowns and wrinkles strange* partially explains the love-stricken tone of the hymn to the young man's face, a face which tells, always, only, *nothing* . . . *but sweetness*, making it the idol of every lover of beauty.

Since the original organization of the poem operated from a single disjunction, that between the young man's *looks* (appearance) and his *heart* (feelings), the late introduction of the young man's mind ("thy *thoughts*") needs some explanation. With the introduction of *thoughts*, a more considered realm is brought into play. Since sins of the intellect are ranked by moralists as more serious than sins of the flesh, the young man's vices are—being lodged in his *thoughts* and not only in his *heart*—shown to be habitual and conscious rather than impulsive and fleeting.

The rhyme *change* and *strange* is repeated from 89, the sonnet of the young man's *hate.* This poem offers another case of foregrounded absence, another DEFECTIVE KEY WORD set, LOOKS/HEART. This pair, present as the violated ideal in Q_1, Q_2, and Q_3, disappear when the speaker gives up, in the couplet, the hope that LOOKS and HEART will match.

DEFECTIVE KEY WORDS: LOOKS, HEART (missing in C)

Couplet Tie: *sweet* (10, 12, 14)
dec-*eiv*-èd [*Eve*] (2, 13)
and perhaps an orthographic tie,
[h]*eave*[n] *Eave* (Quarto spelling) (9, 13)

94

THey that haue powre to hurt,and will doe none,
That doe not do the thing,they moſt do ſhowe,
Who mouing others,are themſelues as ſtone,
Vnmooued,could,and to temptation ſlow:
They rightly do inherrit heauens graces,
And husband natures ritches from expence,
They are the Lords and owners of their faces,
Others,but ſtewards of their excellence:
The ſommers flowre is to the ſommer ſweet,
Though to it ſelfe,it onely liue and die,
But if that flowre with baſe infection meete,
The baſeſt weed out-braues his dignity:
For ſweeteſt things turne ſowreſt by their deedes,
Lillies that feſter, ſmell far worſe then weeds.

They that have pow'r to hurt, and will do none,
That do not do the thing they most do show,
Who, moving others, are themselves as stone,
Unmovèd, cold, and to temptation slow—
They rightly do inherit heaven's graces,
And husband nature's riches from expense;
They are the lords and owners of their faces,
Others but stewards of their excellence.
The summer's flow'r is to the summer sweet,
Though to itself it only live and die,
But if that flow'r with base infection meet,
The basest weed outbraves his dignity:
For sweetest things turn sourest by their deeds;
Lilies that fester smell far worse than weeds.

THIS powerful and much-commented-upon poem, turning oddly from *pow'r* to *flow'r* (lines 1, 9), is remarkable for its structural experiment, by which Shakespeare "splits" the couplet into two separate lines, each of which gives closure to a different segment of the poem. Line 13 sums up the human octave of *pow'r*, which turns on the word *do* and its derivative *deeds;* line 14 sums up the following vegetative quatrain of *flow'r*, which turns on a botanical hierarchy of *weeds* and their vegetative superiors (in general, *flowers*, specifically *lilies*). The sonnet thus contains two mini-poems, represented by the several elements of the Couplet Tie: *do [deeds]* and *thing* [*-s*] for the first, human mini-poem; *weed* [*-s*] for the second, vegetative one; and *sweet*[*-est*] as the ambiguous Couplet Tie belonging to both mini-poems, linking people and flowers.

Octave: Social Realm *(pow'r)*

line 1: *pow'r, do*
line 2: *do, do, thing, do*
line 5: *do*

↓

½ Couplet: Social Realm

line 13: *sweetest things* turn sourest by their *deeds*

Q_3: Vegetable Kingdom *(flow'r)*

line 9: *flow'r, sweet*
line 11: *flow'r*
line 12: *weed*

↓

½ Couplet: Vegetable Kingdom

line 14: *lilies* that fester smell far worse than *weeds*

This is, so far as I can tell, the only experiment with a split couplet in the sequence. It will be seen that *sweet* [*sweetest*] is the only word that "crosses" from the "flower side" (right, line 9) to the "power side" (left, line 13), though *things* is so vague it too belongs implicitly to both.

The split couplet, and the remarkable and unforeseen substitution in Q_3 of the vegetable kingdom for the social realm described in the octave, suggest something intractable and insoluble about the argument as it is first formulated. Although the ideal of mutuality is the one that informs the sonnets, *mutual render, only me for thee* (125), an aristocratic social order is based not upon mutuality but upon a system of asymmetrical relations. If one expects *mutual render* from an aristocrat, one will be disappointed. An aristocrat takes, but does not give. Should we resent this? After all, the speaker muses, there are many things in the *natural* order from which we expect no consideration of our wishes or needs—e.g., a flower. We benefit from the summer flower's mere existence, and we do not reproach it for its self-directed life. Perhaps (the speaker thinks) that is how he should regard the aristocratic young man: as a beautiful object, indifferent to others, in whose presence the lover should bask without any expectation of its paying attention to him.

Some such train of "logic" lies behind the poem, which is, like 129, an impersonal sonnet. The mask of impersonality is always assumed for a reason—at least in a sequence so determined to use personal pronouns throughout. Because the young man's ill *deeds* are as yet concealed (they will erupt as *vices* in 95), he seems on the surface irreproachable. Therefore, the first generalized description of people resembling him can offer only the reproach of the asymmetrical absence of mutuality: moving others, they are themselves unmoved; they are lords, others but stewards. The description can also point out a discrepancy between appearance and action: they *do not do* the *thing* they *most do show*. Linked to 93 by *face* and *show* and *sweet*, *heaven*, *husband*, and *live*, 94 puts these words into question afresh.

The reproach implicit in the simile of *stone* and the adjective *cold* yields to the kinder metaphor of the *flow'r* by a process of thought in the speaker not overtly revealed. The suspicion of vice in the young man by others, who to his *fair flower add the rank smell of weeds* (69), recurs here, but the metaphor of the flower is put to different use. The rhyme *deeds/weeds* has been revived from 69, but is here more deliberately organized. The rapid degeneracy of *flow'r*, *fester*, *smell*, and *weeds* proves that the qualification *to temptation slow* is disbelieved even as it is uttered.

The mixed feelings toward the unnamed powerful *they* that have power to hurt press for resolution. Are they good (they are apparently favored by heaven and responsible to nature, as well as sparing of their power) or are they bad (in their deceptive appearance, their coldness, and their immobility)? Balked on this level, the speaker attempts to shift the venue of description, and brings forward a new hypothesis: How would I feel (speculates the speaker) if he really *were* (as I have already named him in 69) a *flower?* By this move, the speaker makes a bid to take metaphor as the literal truth. If the young man *is* a flower, then how would one feel about his indifference?

Most of the putatively admirable qualities mentioned in the octave—discretion in the exercise of power, resistance to temptation, frugality in the expenditure of nature's riches—drop away, in Q_3, as irrelevant. The only qualities persisting into the quatrain of the flower are heaven's graces and self-possession, proving those to be the crucial qualities the speaker cannot bear to be without. The flower, wholly the owner of its face, living and dying only to itself, is nonetheless a balm to those moved *others* (here generalized into the season, the *summer*) surrounding it.

The speaker's powerful set of mixed responses to the beautiful but indifferent young man has led to a self-protective retreat from the social to the vegetative realm—to the invention of the flower and its adoring summer. But contaminating that idyllic scene—drawn from the lilies of the field of Jesus' parable—is the repressed suspicion of 93, that the infection of the flower has already taken place. By phrasing this intuition as a hypothesis ("But *if* that flow'r"), the speaker attempts to preserve his sweet flower, and to blame, in the event his suspicions prove true, the flower's corruption on a meeting with *base infection,* the villain of the piece. The speaker admits that he himself is a *base weed* by comparison to his aloof *flow'r;* but even if he should be the *basest* weed, he would be higher in the order of vegetation than an *infected* flower. There is a retort to the young man here embedded in the word *outbraves:* "You have in the past scorned me (perhaps defensibly); but if you have now sinned, your sweetness is lost, and I outrank you in dignity." The double superlatives predicated of *things (sweetest, sourest)* act out the proverbial corruption of the best into the worst, and connect semantically and phonetically the *sour* (formerly *sweet) flow'r* to the *pow'r* of the octave. The concluding proverb reveal-ingly leaves out any mention at all of *base infection:* lilies can *fester* (in the sense of "decay") all by themselves. The retaliatory overturning of normal vegetative hierarchy in the last line is connected to *outbraves* in Q_3, while the lingering look at *deeds* in the penultimate line connects its *sweetest things*—a last nostalgia—to the undone "shown" *thing* which now—unspecified—must have been *done.* (Cf. *Othello,* to "do the deed of darkness.")

The shift from *pow'r* to the alternate venue of flower-metaphor has been proved unavailing: both "lines of thought," the social one and the flower one, have ended up in the same place, a place where no excuses for the young man persist. By *deeds, things* have become *sour,* and festering flowers *smell worse* than the weeds around them. With the failure of 94's hopeful diversion into organic metaphor, the accusations suppressed in 93 and 94 can burst out in full cry in 95: *O what a mansion have those vices got / Which for their habitation chose out thee!* The fiction of the external villain that *chose out* and corrupted the young man is hard to maintain, but still clings in 95. The sternness of tone in 94—a tone not of infatuation but of social reproof and moral authority—grows in the sequence from its origins in such poems as 66 through its exertions in 94 on to such famous sonnets as 116, 124, and 129.

DEFECTIVE KEY WORD: DO [DEEDS] (missing in Q_3, the flower quatrain)

Couplet Tie: *do* [*deeds*] (1, 2, 2, 2, 5, 13)
thing [*-s*] (2, 13)
sweet [*-est*] (9, 13)
weed [*-s*] (12, 14)

95

HOw ſweet and louely doſt thou make the ſhame,
Which like a canker in the fragrant Roſe,
Doth ſpot the beautie of thy budding name?
Oh in what ſweets doeſt thou thy ſinnes incloſe!
That tongue that tells the ſtory of thy daies,
(Making laſciuious comments on thy ſport)
Cannot diſpraiſe,but in a kinde of praiſe,
Naming thy name, bleſſes an ill report.
Oh what a manſion haue thoſe vices got,
Which for their habitation choſe out thee,
Where beauties vaile doth couer euery blot,
And all things turnes to faire,that eies can ſee!
Take heed(deare heart)of this large priuiledge,
The hardeſt knife ill vſ'd doth looſe his edge.

How sweet and lovely dost thou make the shame
Which, like a canker in the fragrant rose,
Doth spot the beauty of thy budding name!
O in what sweets dost thou thy sins inclose!
That tongue that tells the story of thy days
(Making lascivious comments on thy sport)
Cannot dispraise but in a kind of praise;
Naming thy name blesses an ill report.
O what a mansion have those vices got
Which for their habitation chose out thee,
Where beauty's veil doth cover every blot,
And all things turns to fair that eyes can see!
Take heed (dear heart) of this large privilege:
The hardest knife ill used doth lose his edge.

HIDDEN *evils*, full or partial, here carry out the theme of concealed vices. The two graphemes of *evil*—the *ev* (Eve) part and the *il* (ill) part—keep cropping up, as do its four component letters: ***lovely***, ***lascivious***, ***ill***, ***vices***, ***vaile*** (Quarto spelling), *cover*, ***every***, ***privilege***, ***ill***, (and perhaps ***knife ill***). In the couplet of 40, *lascivious* was paired with *ill* and *kill*, and prefaced by *receivest* and *deceivest*, keeping "evil" sounds in view. The same sort of play on *evil* will also occur in 121 *('Tis better to be vile than vile esteemed)* where the words in question embodying either the *il* or the *ev* motif, or both, include the *evil-vile* anagram, *receive*, *sportive*, *level*, *bevel*, *ill*, *wills*, *frailties*, and *frailer*.

The imaginative strategy of 95, often recommended in sermons—to hate the sin and love the sinner—is here extended to a blasphemous eroticism and aestheticism. The disharmony between show and substance is complete, and in the several exclamations of dismay within the poem, various displacements of guilt from the young man to something else—to a shame, a canker, a spot, a blot, a set of vices—are brought forward in company with the more directly accusatory *thy sins* and *thy sport*.

The octave concerns the young man's *name* (the word is thrice repeated), while Q_3 emphasizes his physical beauty. Q_1 and Q_3 are helplessly exclamatory: *How sweet and lovely! O in what sweets! O what a mansion!* The problem of this sonnet resides in the couplet. It is clear that ***privilege*** appears in the couplet as the overlapping embodiment of [*ivil*] [*vile*], and that *ill* reinforces the letters shared by *evil* and *vile*. And the juxtaposition of *heart* and *hard[est]* concocts perhaps the underlying phrase *hard-hearted*. The identical spelling of knife ***edge*** and ***priviledge*** in the Quarto suggests that a privy edge, as well as a private law, privy-lege *(lex, legis)*, is in question (Booth, quoting Lanchy, notes the phallic implication of the knife).

The theme of 95 is the hiddenness of vice: the canker in the rose, the spot in the bud, the sins in the sweets, the vices in the mansion, the blot in the beauty. The Couplet Tie *ill* (and *lose* if one counts the *lose* in ***inclose***) points out one (or two) hidden syllables to look for, to which I have added *ev/iv*. Vices in a *mansion* may call up vices in a *man*, and the *habitation*, as Booth notes, can enclose a *habit*; *edge* is enclosed in *priviledge* (Quarto spelling), *praise* in *dispraise*, and *name* in *naming*. *In* is even redundantly present: "O *in* what sweets dost thou thy sins *in*close!" This habit of enclosure suggests that an outer skin, peeled off, shows something underneath; when *priviledge* loses his *edge*, what is left is no longer private, or privy, but seen. Blots and spots will show; with sweets stripped away, sins show through.

What is interesting about the structure of the poem is the interruption of the speaker's helpless exclamations of wonder and dismay in Q_1 and Q_3 with the small narrative of Q_2, which concerns the gossip about the young man's *sport*. This narrative clarifies words that precede and follow it like *shame* and *eyes*, revealing that the speaker's final warning concerns not only the young man's vices, but also the public knowledge of them. The paradox by which an *ill* report is *blessed* if it contains the young man's name, and *dispraise* is covered by *praise*, duplicates the young man's eerie power to veil every *blot* (resurrected from 92) with *beauty*. The continual tropes of enclosure—orthographic and metaphorical and epideictic—act out the persistent theme of cover-up.

Line 12 reads oddly until one realizes that the subject of *turns* (singular) is *beauty's veil*; "properly" rearranged, lines 11–12 would say:

> [*Where beauty's veil doth cover every blot,*
> *And turns all things to fair that eyes can see!*]

The awkward (and misleading) pre-positioning of the direct object *all things* has been done, we realize with hindsight, in order to make this two-line summary a chiastic one:

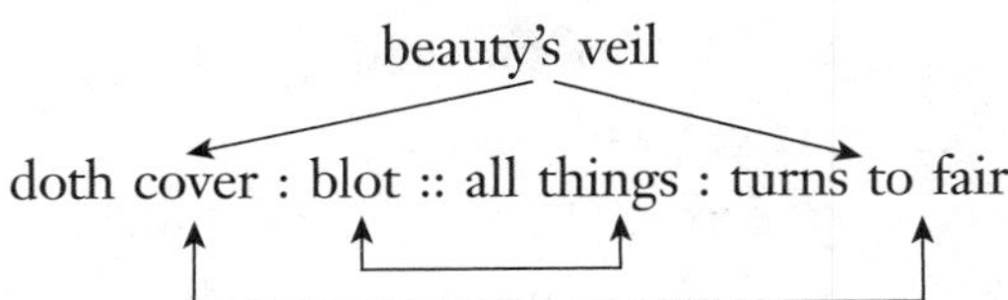

To achieve chiasmus—the signal that the speaker has passed from narration to analysis—Shakespeare is even willing to subvert "readable" syntax.

Couplet Tie: *lose* [inc-*lose*] (4, 14)
ill (8, 14), and perhaps *priv-il-ege* (13)

96

SOme ſay thy fault is youth,ſome wantoneſſe,
Some ſay thy grace is youth and gentle ſport,
Both grace and faults are lou'd of more and leſſe:
Thou makſt faults graces,that to thee reſort:
As on the finger of a throned Queene,
The baſeſt Iewell wil be well eſteem'd:
So are thoſe errors that in thee are ſeene,
To truths tranſlated,and for true things deem'd.
How many Lambs might the ſterne Wolfe betray,
If like a Lambe he could his lookes tranſlate.
How many gazers mighſt thou lead away,
If thou wouldſt vſe the ſtrength of all thy ſtate?
  But doe not ſo,I loue thee in ſuch ſort,
  As thou being mine,mine is thy good report.

Some say thy fault is youth, some wantonness,
Some say thy grace is youth and gentle sport;
Both grace and faults are loved of more and less:
Thou mak'st faults graces that to thee resort.
As on the finger of a thronèd queen
The basest jewel will be well esteemed,
So are those errors that in thee are seen
To truths translated, and for true things deemed.
How many lambs might the stern wolf betray,
If like a lamb he could his looks translate!
How many gazers mightst thou lead away,
If thou wouldst use the strength of all thy state!
  But do not so; I love thee in such sort,
  As thou being mine, mine is thy good report.

THE couplet which 96 shares with 36 seems in 36 to follow logically from the body of the sonnet. It fits 96 less well, especially since it repeats the rhyme in *-ort* used in Q_1 of 96. (Kerrigan points out that 36 and 96 both close groups critical of the young man, and that the couplet-repetition might therefore be meaningful.) The gossip about the young man's faults mentioned in 95 is here inquired into not from the point of view of the young man's reputation, but from the point of view of the *lambs* who admire this *wolf*. The comparisons appearing in Q_2 and Q_3 epitomize the speaker's own conflict about the young man: Is he a thronèd queen or a stern wolf? Is his baseness an extrinsic addition, like a queen's ring, or an intrinsic viciousness, like that of the wolf in lamb's clothing? The verbal link between these two comparisons—queen and wolf—is the word *translate* (lines 8, 10), a Latin version *(trans-ferre)* of the Greek *metapherein*, to carry across, whence translation = metaphor. We need to relate these quatrains to each other and to the one which introduces them, as well as to see what Shakespeare may be implying about metaphor itself.

The first quatrain, using the sleight-of-hand by which two things equal to the same thing are equal to each other, makes (by the middle term *youth*) *faults* into *graces*, as their gradual physical *rapprochement* in the quatrain makes clear. Line 1 contains *fault* and *youth*, line 2 *grace* and *youth*, line 3 *grace and faults*, and line 4 *faults graces*. Shakespeare's punning ("Thou mak'st *false* [those] graces that to thee resort") suggests the evaporation of (true) graces in the presence of such *faults*. Because all classes *(more and less)* love the young man, line 4 might insinuate not only that he turns faults in himself into graces, but also that all those graces (in others) that resort to him are thereby converted into faults.

In Q_1, the errors of those who (like the speaker in line 4) interpret faults as graces are merely indulgent social and aesthetic mistakes. But in Q_2 the errors concerning the base *jewel* take on a more intellectual tinge within the word cluster *esteemed, errors, truths, true, translate,* and *deemed.* Then in Q_3 we pass from the intellectual to the moral, in the context of *betray* and *lead away;* the errors of the lambs become mortally dangerous to them. In the back-and-forth between reference to others and address to the young man—*some say* and *thou mak'st* (Q_1), the *queen* and *errors . . . in thee* (Q_2), the *wolf* and *mightst thou* (Q_3)—one can perceive an instructional aim, in which the speaker, warning the young man, thrice illuminates text by gloss. Yet the "instructor" has not admitted his own complicity-by-obfuscation in the young man's deception: the curious predominance of the passive voice—*are loved, will be well esteemed, are seen, [are] translated, [are] deemed*—suggests that a euphemizing vagueness is covering the speaker's participation in these errors of perception and judgment. (Later, in 114, a truer outburst suggests that the young man is a poisoned cup, and the active voice will be used by the speaker, indicting aspects of himself: "If it be poisoned, 'tis the lesser sin / That *mine eye loves it* and *doth* first *begin.*")

It is the discrepancy in 96 between the speaker's wish to impart moral instruction by exempla and his refusal to repudiate the company of the sinner that causes the uneasiness of the exhortations. The Couplet Tie, *love* and *sort* [*re-sort*] is for once uninformative, except that it calls attention to the unusual repetition of a Q_1 rhyme-sound in the couplet. One should notice how an emphasis on seeing (the vehicle of aesthetic deception), in the words *seen, looks,* and *gazers,* unites the affective, aesthetic, intellectual, and moral errors of the body of the poem.

The concern with metaphor in the sonnet is evoked by the initial bewilderment of the speaker with respect to substance and accident. A *fault* is a rift in substance; a *grace* (as used here) is an ornament of the surface. The buzz of social commentary about the young man centers first on what is wrong with him: some say he is simply immature, some say he is wanton. If the first judgment is correct, the *fault* is temporary and reparable; but if the second is correct, the *fault* is dangerous. The second camp of gossipers say the young man's impulsiveness is charming and his actions playful; they speak of appearance *(grace)* rather than substance. It is left to the speaker to decide whether the qualities visible in the overlapping category *(youth)* are substantial or accidental, charming or degenerate. So far, the question raised is a logical one of the proper ascription of qualities to essence; but the case is immediately complicated by the introduction of emotion. We suspect that the love streaming toward the young man from all is an illusion projected, by the speaker, from his own hapless infatuation. *Because* love enters the equation, substance and accident begin to be indistinguishable, but only in one direction: the young man makes (substantial) *faults* into (superficial) *graces.* The converse—that he makes graces into faults, which may be only too true—is carefully not said.

The odd and unexpected introduction of the ornamental queen reverses the speaker's suspicion that the young man's substance is *fault*, ornamented with *graces*. The queen is a respectable queen, whose essence is unimpugnable; but her ornament is contemptible, both in itself and in its effect. One might say that analogically the queen represents estimable matter adorned with debased tropes. The underlying question is why the queen would lend herself to such a hoodwinking of her subjects, who think her ring valuable only because it is on her finger. If metaphor is the *dulce* to the *utile*, why should the *utile* need it at all, especially if its effect is a contemptible one?

The wolf examines, analogically, a second possibility of style. The matter may be base, and capable of betraying the innocent: Is the use of metaphor to gild, say, sexual seduction any recommendation for metaphor? Are in fact tropes—adornments, garments, things transferred onto an underlying body (of fact or of idea)—necessary at all? If bad, like the queen's ring, they may degrade virtue; if attractive, they may adorn vice. The speaker offers no counterexamples—of good tropes exalting virtue (the true ring on a true sovereign), of good tropes exposing vice (the child exposing the emperor's new clothes). It is preferable, according to this speaker, that the queen be ringless and the wolf naked. In pleading with the young man *not* to use *the strength of all [his] state*, the narrator equates the *errors . . . seen* in the young man with the later-mentioned lamblike *looks*, confusing once again *faults* and *graces*, and making them both into forms of *strength* over others.

Transparent selfhood—in which the queen displays nothing unsuited to her dignity, and the wolf is always visibly a wolf—is both a utopian moral wish and an indictment of rhetoric, especially of tropes. It is not a position that Shakespeare can defend for long, and the awkwardness of the two metaphors for the young man—queen and wolf—reveals the speaker's unease. The nontroped account of the young man attempted in 84—*You alone are you*—coupled with a nonrhetorical poetics of praise, led to the necessity of silence on the poet's part in 85, broken by the reproaches of betrayal in subsequent sonnets. If unitary selfhood cannot be predicated of another, Shakespeare reflects, it can perhaps be predicated of oneself. The defense of a unitary and non-aspectual and non-troped selfhood is carried to its utmost extreme in 121 *('Tis better to be vile than vile esteemed)*, which, like 96, concentrates on the estimation of others. *No, I am that I am* is the speaker's defiant response there; but that response necessitates the withdrawal from the social world of estimation and suspéct (70) into the solitude of 123 and 124, together with the scornful dismissal of that last estimator, the *suborned informer* of 125. In the solitary unity of the speaker, he is transparent to himself, and can go ringless and garmentless; but the social world generates ornamental rhetoric and tropes embroidering suspicion as readily as it generates rings on queens and sheep's clothing on wolves.

Couplet Tie: *love* [*-d*], 3, 13
sort [*re-sort*], 4, 13 [cf. *sport/resort* (Q_1) with *sort/resort* (C)]

97

HOw like a Winter hath my abſence beene
From thee,the pleaſure of the fleeting yeare?
What freezings haue I felt,what darke daies ſeene?
What old Decembers bareneſſe euery where?
And yet this time remou'd was ſommers time,
The teeming Autumne big with ritch increaſe,
Bearing the wanton burthen of the prime,
Like widdowed wombes after their Lords deceaſe:
Yet this aboundant iſſue ſeem'd to me,
But hope of Orphans,and vn-fathered fruite,
For Sommer and his pleaſures waite on thee,
And thou away,the very birds are mute.
Or if they ſing,tis with ſo dull a cheere,
That leaues looke pale,dreading the Winters neere.

How like a winter hath my absence been
From thee, the pleasure of the fleeting year!
What freezings have I felt, what dark days seen!
What old December's bareness every where!
And yet this time removed was summer's time,
The teeming autumn big with rich increase,
Bearing the wanton burthen of the prime,
Like widowed wombs after their lords' decease:
Yet this abundant issue seem'd to me
But hope of orphans, and unfathered fruit,
For summer and his pleasures wait on thee,
And thou away, the very birds are mute;
Or if they sing, 'tis with so dull a cheer
That leaves look pale, dreading the winter's near.

KEATS remembered 97 so well that he transmuted it into his ode "To Autumn." Its intransigent modeling of the relation between imagined/perceived reality and factual reality has made it famous. A factually "normal" rendition of its content would read, "I was absent from you in the summer; yet it seemed like winter." In fact, such a model of factual reality followed by imagined reality is indeed offered by Q_2. But the model offered by Q_1 privileges imaginative reality, which precedes, in the unrolling of the poem, factual reality—a topsy-turvy beginning. Q_2, therefore, with its corrective "and yet" plays the pivotal role between two models of reality construction—an earlier one (Q_1) in which imagination thrusts itself forward first and governs perception; and a later one (Q_3) in which imagination rises, in a second correction, to correct the previously asserted reality of Q_2. This accounts for the two adversative *yet*'s (lines 5 and 9), the first "correcting" Q_1, the second "correcting" the corrective Q_2. The mind of the speaker is thus shown by Q_3 to be dissatisfied with both earlier models of "reality," the "imagined" one of Q_1 and the "factual" one of Q_2. The Couplet Tie *winter* exhibits this nakedly: in its first appearance (line 1) the word refers to "imagined winter," but in line 14 it refers to "factual winter."

Within these quatrains, the references to reality and appearance are willfully confused. The sentence "What *freezings* have I *felt*, what *dark days seen!*" though factually phrased, refers only to imagined reality. And the most reliably factual statement is itself doubly referent to two seasons at once: *this time . . . was summer's time, / the teeming autumn.* In no time, this "fact" embroiders itself into the fantastic simile making autumn into a widow bearing posthumous children to a dead father. (Shakespeare is drawing on the old generation-myth of "mother earth" impregnated by the sun, her "paramour," as Milton will say in the Nativity Ode.)

The statement about mute birds, too, presents itself as bare fact: *thou away, the very birds are mute.* But by now, the mind of the speaker is suspicious of what it perceives as "reality"—and the "reality" of *mute* birds (which we know to be factually false in summertime) is corrected by a "truer reality," the factual *dull cheer* of the birds, which is itself immediately sicklied o'er by the imagined reality of a sudden ghastly pallor in the leaves. The sonnet's instabilities of reference, meaning, perception, and factuality are put into relief by the phonetic pun on *bare/bear*, which is used to mean both the barren (*bareness*, line 4) and the fruitful (*bearing*, line 7). The phrase *bareness every where* is repeated from sonnet 5, just as the phrase *widowed wombs after their lords' decease* harks back to sonnet 9: *Every private widow well may keep, / By children's eyes, her husband's shape in mind.*

Because one rhyme-sound of Q_1 *(year/where)* is repeated in the couplet *(cheer/near)*, and because the *winter* of line 1 is repeated in line 14, the sonnet seems to come full circle: the cycle whereby imagined appearance replaces evidential reality is ready to begin once again. Shakespeare's discovery that the mind can entertain mutually incompatible models—"It is winter, yet it is summer"; "It is summer, yet it is autumn" (or "I am a ruin; I am a glowing" in 73)—is his richest invention with respect to the construction of subjectivity. And the rapidity of these changes—"the very birds *are mute*, / Or *if they sing*"—argues for the mind as a place of rapid vacillation, oscillation, and self-correction.

The repeated subversion of any pleasure—as *teeming* and *rich* yield to *widowed wombs* and *decease*, as *abundant issue* becomes *orphans* and *unfathered fruit*, as *singing* turns to *dull cheer*—suggests the final power of the imagination over what might be called objective reality. The power of feeling over perception also puts the very notion of "objective reality" into question, since what the speaker (in reality) feels *is* freezings, what he (in reality) sees *are* dark days. In spite of his attempt to be factual in resorting to phrases such as *like* or *seemed to me*, a moment later the birds *are* mute, and the leaves *look pale*. The final perceived reality is a *dull cheer* which, though asserted as true, immediately provokes the little playlet of imaginative pathos as the leaves grow pale with dread. The tautology by which "summer and *his pleasures* wait on thee, . . . the *pleasure* of the . . . year" shows the impossibility of escaping from the cycle of perception-controlled-by-imagination into the cycle of seasonal factuality.

Though there have been earlier sonnets (e.g., 73) where a later quatrain corrected an earlier one, this is the first in which Shakespeare attempts double corrections, as Q_2 corrects Q_1, and Q_3 corrects Q_2, returning us to the stance of Q_1 again. Such cycles demonstrate that for the mind there is no eventual point of rest, since mental frames, driven by feeling, are engaged in continual corrective replacement of each other. This replacement can be cyclical (as suggested here and in 129, where by the end a given process is about to repeat itself) or linear (as in 73, where a final emotionally satisfying resting-place is achieved).

Couplet Tie: *winter* ['-*s*] (1, 14)

98

FRom you haue I beene abſent in the ſpring,
When proud pide Aprill (dreſt in all his trim)
Hath put a ſpirit of youth in euery thing:
That heauie *Saturne* laught and leapt with him.
Yet nor the laies of birds, nor the ſweet ſmell
Of different flowers in odor and in hew,
Could make me any ſummers ſtory tell:
Or from their proud lap pluck them where they grew:
Nor did I wonder at the Lillies white,
Nor praiſe the deepe vermillion in the Roſe,
They weare but ſweet, but figures of delight:
Drawne after you, you patterne of all thoſe.
Yet ſeem'd it Winter ſtill, and you away,
As with your ſhaddow I with theſe did play.

From you have I been absent in the spring,
When proud-pied April (dressed in all his trim)
Hath put a spirit of youth in every thing,
That heavy Saturn laughed and leapt with him.
Yet nor the lays of birds, nor the sweet smell
Of different flowers in odour and in hue,
Could make me any summer's story tell,
Or from their proud lap pluck them where they grew:
Nor did I wonder at the lily's white,
Nor praise the deep vermilion in the rose;
They were but sweet, but figures of delight,
Drawn after you, you pattern of all those.
Yet seemed it winter still, and, you away,
As with your shadow I with these did play.

THIS seems a simpler version of 97, exhibiting the same *summer, seemed, winter,* and *away*, and exhibiting as well two comparable adversative *yet*'s, one at the beginning of Q_2, the other at the beginning of the couplet. It is tempting to think that 98—with only one self-reversal, despite its two adversatives—was written first, and that 97 represents a more complicated evolution of the theme. The *proud lap* of 98 represents an earlier stage of the *widowed wombs*, and the undifferentiated *lays of birds* seem a simpler version of the *mute / sing / dull cheer* of 97.

Though even *heavy Saturn* has been persuaded by April to laugh and leap, the gloomy speaker has not; and the persuasions of *birds* and *flowers* in Q_2 are no more successful than those of *proud-pied April* in Q_1. As C. L. Barber remarks in his edition of the *Sonnets*, it is implied in Q_3 that the speaker's normal response would have been to *wonder at the lily's white*, to *praise . . . the rose;* therefore we conclude that his faculty of admiration has been drawn away from shows and *figures* to be absorbed by the true *pattern* of delight, the young man. In spite of the preceding refusals to be attentive enough to birds and flowers to *laugh* or *leap* or *wonder* or *praise*, the speaker concedes that he did *play* with all these flowers, as representations *(shadows)* of the young man. We are not told here of what the *play* consisted, but we are about to see an example of it in 99. What we do know is that *p-lay* is a compound by which the *lay* of a bird has been prefaced by the consonant *(p)* associated throughout the sonnet with the young man and the season, and visible in ***p**roud-**p**ied, A**p**ril, s**p**irit, lea**p**t, **p**roud la**p** **p**luck, **p**raise, dee**p**, **p**attern,* and ***p**lay.* (This erotic use of *p* will reach its phallic apogee in 151, where it mutates into cynicism.)

Shakespeare has tended to ban mythology from his *Sonnets;* in fact, his avoidance of myth is one of his chief corrections of the continental sonnet. The rarity of an appearance of a mythological or astronomical figure suggests we should take Saturn within the context of psychology, as representing the heavy Saturnine temperament. *Lap, play,* and *leapt* were probably generated from *April.* The pattern by which the mind is led from the opposed genii of the place (April and Saturn) to earth (*birds* and *flowers*) and thence to a focus on two single flowers *(lily, rose)* represents Shakespeare's frequent narrowing and focusing of the poetic gaze. The

KEY WORD and Couplet Tie is *you* [*youth*] [*hue*], emphasized by the repetition in *you, you* (line 12) and by the pattern *from you . . . after you . . . you away.*

Structurally 98 (showing a 4-6-2-2 pattern) suggests that Shakespeare is trying out a double-couplet structure. The poem could in fact end, logically, with its coupletlike summing up in lines 11–12. Instead, it tacks on a "second" couplet, lines 13–14, introducing the perceptual contradiction *summer/winter* of which 97 makes so much. The couplet, however, surprises us by negating all the former negations: the speaker *did* in fact "play" with all of spring's manifestations. We "believe" the couplet because we *have* seen the speaker betrayed into a moment of sensual delight; even as he declares he did not praise *the deep vermilion* in the rose, he is noticing it with relish.

KEY WORD: YOU [YOUTH] (Q_1); HUE (Q_2); YOU (Q_3, C)

Couplet Tie: *you* [*youth*] [*hue*] (1, 3, 6, 12, 12, 13)

99

THe forward violet thus did I chide,
Sweet theefe whence didſt thou ſteale thy ſweet that
If not from my loues breath,the purple pride, (ſmels
Which on thy ſoft cheeke for complexion dwells?
In my loues veines thou haſt too grofely died,
The Lillie I condemned for thy hand,
And buds of marierom had ſtolne thy haire,
The Roſes fearefully on thornes did ſtand,
Our bluſhing ſhame,an other white diſpaire:
A third nor red,nor white,had ſtolne of both,
And to his robbry had annext thy breath,
But for his theft in pride of all his growth
A vengfull canker eate him vp to death.
More flowers I noted,yet I none could ſee,
But ſweet,or culler it had ſtolne from thee.

The forward violet thus did I chide:
"Sweet thief, whence didst thou steal thy sweet that smells,
If not from my love's breath? The purple pride
Which on thy soft cheek for complexion dwells
In my love's veins thou hast too grossly dyed."
The lily I condemnèd for thy hand,
And buds of marjoram had stol'n thy hair;
The roses fearfully on thorns did stand,
One blushing shame, another white despair;
A third, nor red nor white, had stol'n of both,
And to his robb'ry had annexed thy breath,
But for his theft, in pride of all his growth
A vengeful canker eat him up to death.
More flowers I noted, yet I none could see
But sweet or colour it had stol'n from thee.

THE first "quatrain" of 99 has five lines, rhyming *ababa.* The first line serves as an introduction to both (a) the directly quoted chiding (lines 2–5) administered to the precocious violet; and (b) to the indirectly reported subsequent chiding (lines 6–7) of the lily and marjoram, introducing Q_2. The second chiding reveals to us that the poem, rather than being solely the narrative it first appeared to be as it referred to the beloved in the third person *(my love's breath),* is in fact an address to the beloved *(thy hand . . . thy hair).* At the same time, the narrative component is maintained even in the second-person address as a concatenation of several myths of origin (comparable to that in 20 explaining the paradoxically androgynous nature of the young man).

The several myths of origin here are partly grouped around two questions: How did certain plants get their *sweet* odor? How did certain flowers get their *colour?* The couplet summarizes the results of the mock-investigation: all the flowers stole their attributes, "*sweet* or *colour,*" from some aspect of the beloved. The chiastic treatment in 99 of "different flowers in *odour* and in *hue*" (as 98 had called them) makes clear that the relation of *buds of marjoram* to the beloved's *hair* (debated by various editors, cf. the *Variorum* and Kerrigan) is exclusively one of *odour* (not, as Kerrigan suggests, one of "fairness" and "thickness of growth"). A neatly symmetrical chiasmus occupies lines 2–7:

A. ODOR: violet's *sweet . . . that smells* ←——— *love's [sweet] breath*
B. HUE: violet's *purple . . . complexion* ←——— *love's veins*
B. HUE: lily's [white] ←——————————— *[love's] hand*
A. ODOR: marjoram's [fragrance] ←———— *[love's] hair*

After this six-line odor-plus-hue chiasmus on the violet, the lily, and marjoram, Shakespeare writes a six-line excursus on the hue of roses, containing two myths of explanation: How did the roses acquire their separate colors (red, white, or particolored)? And why has the particolored rose alone died? The speaker tells the young man that the roses standing fearfully on their thorns have taken on their color either from *shame (red)* or *despair (white)*—with an extended courtesy-meaning of *blushing* to cover all acquisitions of emotional color. The shame and despair, if we follow the logic of the poem, arise in the roses because they fear to be condemned as thieves by the speaker, since they, like the lily, have stolen their *colour* from the young man's red and white.

It is at this point, where Shakespeare has apparently abandoned *odour* in favor of *hue*, that *odour* returns with a vengeance. The wicked particolored rose had not only stolen both *red* and *white*, combining them, but had also, like the forward violet, stolen a sweet odor from the *breath* of the young man. The lily and marjoram have committed only *one* robbery, either of color (lily) *or* of fragrance (marjoram), and the violet has stolen only a single color *(purple)* and a single odor *(sweet that smells.)* But the particolored rose, the chief villain, has stolen one odor and *two* colors. His *pride* (line 12) in his threefold theft, verbally linked to the purple *pride* (line 3) of the violet drawn from the young man's veins, has caused the particolored rose, unlike the other lesser criminals, to be *eat[en] up to death* by the worm. (I retain the Quarto spelling *eat* for "ate" because of its graphic overlay with *death.*) This warning to the young man—that the pride gained by means of greed and thievery leads to fear, shame, and despair, and ultimately to death by worms—presages 146:

> Why so large cost, having so short a lease,
> Dost thou upon thy fading mansion spend?
> Shall *worms*, inheritors of this excess,
> *Eat up* thy charge? Is this thy body's end?

In spite of these warning undertones, 99 returns demurely to the conventions of compliment in its close. It touches, however, a series of explosive feelings, expressed by *too grossly* of Q_1, by *condemnèd* of Q_2, by the *pride* of Q_1 and Q_3, by the chiding of thieves, and by the myths of stealing and vengeful death. The robbery and stealing are shared with 79 *(he robs thee of . . . he stole that word)*, and perhaps the flowers here resemble the poems (poetry/poesy/posy) of the rival poet, ornamented with rhetorical colors not their own. The short life of the mixed two-color sweet-smelling particolored rose is summed up by the allegorizing end-words of its quatrain: *both, breath, growth, death;* and seeing this, we may be encouraged to read a punning sense as well into the end-words of the violet's quatrain: *smells, pride, dwells, died* (Quarto spelling). There is reason for the roses to stand *fearfully*, given nature's vengeance on theft.

However, as the pervasive KEY WORD (STEAL/STOL'N) suggests, there are no noncriminals in the world of 99, and so the couplet serves as a general exoneration: since all are guilty, none is. The implied beauty and virtue of the beloved are acted out in terms of the beauty and fragrance of flowers, but as the playful speech-acts of chiding and condemning give way to the terminated life of the unhappy triply-thievish rose, a sinister suggestion of thieves stealing too many of the young man's beauties creeps in, not to be entirely dismissed by the placating couplet. From now on in the sequence, Shakespeare writes a narrative of self-blame rather than blame of the beloved. The experiment with a sonnet of fifteen lines is not repeated.

KEY WORD: STEAL [STOL'N]

Couplet Tie: *sweet* (2, 15)
steal [*stol'n*] (2, 7, 10, 15)

100

VV Here art thou Muſe that thou forgetſt ſo long,
To ſpeake of that which giues thee all thy might?
Spendſt thou thy furie on ſome worthleſſe ſonge,
Darkning thy powre to lend baſe ſubiects light.
Returne forgetfull Muſe,and ſtraight redeeme,
In gentle numbers time ſo idely ſpent,
Sing to the eare that doth thy laies eſteeme,
And giues thy pen both skill and argument.
Riſe reſty Muſe,my loues ſweet face ſuruay,
If time haue any wrincle grauen there,
If any,be a *Satire* to decay,
And make times ſpoiles diſpiſed euery where.
Giue my loue fame faſter then time waſts life,
So thou preuenſt his ſieth,and crooked knife.

Where art thou, Muse, that thou forget'st so long
To speak of that which gives thee all thy might?
Spend'st thou thy fury on some worthless song,
Dark'ning thy pow'r to lend base subjects light?
Return, forgetful Muse, and straight redeem
In gentle numbers time so idly spent;
Sing to the ear that doth thy lays esteem,
And gives thy pen both skill and argument.
Rise, resty Muse, my love's sweet face survey,
If Time have any wrinkle graven there;
If any, be a satire to decay,
And make Time's spoils despisèd every where.
Give my love fame faster than Time wastes life;
So thou prevent'st his scythe and crookèd knife.

THE Muse of 79 reappears here in a group of sonnets—100, 101, 103; her sins increase as the poems succeed each other. In 100, she is addressed as the forgetful Muse; in 101 as the truant, neglectful, and silent Muse; and in 103 as an impoverished and marring Muse. However, at first her case is not hopeless: she is adjured in the first two sonnets to improve her performance. The third sonnet, by contrast, is addressed to the friend, and apparently gives up on versing altogether. All of these sonnets represent the displacement of the poet's anxiety of performance onto his surrogate the Muse.

Sonnet 100 is organized by the various capacities of the Muse: she can *speak of* a subject; *sing to* an audience; *survey* a visual object; *be a satire to* a disagreeable event; and *give fame.* Sonnet 100 is almost a paradigmatic case of the poem produced by schematic "invention," itself stimulated by going through the familar logical "places" of *speak:* to whom, of what, in what manner, to what end, etc. The poem (after the opening reproachful question of Q_1) is one long series of adjurations (*return, redeem, sing, rise, survey, be, make,* and *give*) followed by a result-clause concluding not in the optative or the future but in the congratulatory present tense of narration: *So thou prevent'st his scythe and crookèd knife.*

The concatenation of words in which the sonnet abounds suggests a firmly back-stitching logic; *forget'st, forgetful; spend'st, spent; song, sing; gives, give; time, Time, Time's, Time; my love's, my love; Muse, Muse, Muse; any, any.* There is an unusual amount of graphic and phonemic repetition of all sorts here as well, down to such "hidden" effects as *gra**ven*** and *pre**vent**'st,* ***spoil**s* (pronounced ***spile**s*) and *de**spis**èd,* and *fa**ste**r* and ***waste**s.*

The two aspects of the Muse's work emphasized here are her *skill* and her *argument*—her technical resources and her theme, as we might today call them. Both are dependent on the friend's esteeming ear, since as long as he is favorably disposed, the Muse has a worthy incentive to excellence and a worthy subject. The young man, the Muse's true *argument/subject,* can inhabit two possible states: he can be young and beautiful, or else he may already be undergoing the process of decay. In the first instance, the Muse's *skill* will be employed on praise (envisaged in the *gentle numbers* of the octave, stimulated by the *sweet face* of line 9); but in the second instance *(wrinkles)*, the Muse's skill will be spent on *satire* and commination. The aggressive *might*, *fury*, and *power* ascribed to the Muse when she is introduced in Q_1 seem somewhat inexplicable there, even though she is said to be expending them perhaps on unworthy subjects. The *gentle numbers* of Q_2 seems a more probable epithet for composition even on base subjects when lending them the light of praise.

We understand the early emphasis on *might*, *fury*, and *power* only when we come to Q_3, and its appalled supposition that the young man already exhibits decay. Since that is so, the (dormant) fury *(furor poeticus)* of the Muse, latent while she was singing in gentle numbers, can believably lash out in satire and despising. After that exercise of her *might* in aggression against *Time* (that phonetic reversal mīt/tīm which appears so often in the *Sonnets*), she can exercise the splendidly invented third skill-mode (neither gentle nor satiric) of the couplet: a competitive mode, in which—as Time entropically wastes life—the Muse energetically gives fame, faster. (I accept the emendation of *prevenst* to *prevent'st*.) The Muse's victory is enacted by the accretive *v/f* schema, ***give***, ***love***, ***fame***, ***faster***, by contrast to the relatively weak, because phonetically almost unreinforced, *Time wastes life;* but there is also a suggestion of perpetual standoff in the equal length of *f-**aste**-r* and *w-**aste**-s.*

Why, one wonders, has the Muse so long forgotten the friend? The only answer suggested by the sonnet is that the friend has begun to age; a wrinkle has been graven on his sweet face. Other, perhaps unwrinkled faces—base subjects—seem recently to have had a greater appeal to the speaker's Muse. If she is to return to her "worthy" subject, the young man, she will have to turn herself from a Muse of epideictic poetry into a Muse of satiric poetry, reproaching Time. The "reversion" to fame-giving in the couplet is pointedly not a reversion to praise of the young man's sweet face as such. Instead, the couplet proposes a species of alchemical transmutation of elements in the young man, so that by the time the scythe and knife reach any part of him, it will already be all fame and no flesh. It seems that the loving *gentle numbers* of the idyllic first phase of unravaged beauty can really never return, as they are commanded to do in Q_2. Instead, the competitive and public "third skill" of eternizing—which draws on power and might more than on gentleness—will replace both private lyric (sung to the esteeming ear of the friend) and public satire of decay.

Time appears in Q_2, Q_3, and C, but not as such in Q_1. However, if one wants to consider *might* (mīt) a phonetic anagram of *time* (tīm), as I think Shakespeare does, then one could say that TIME/MIGHT is the KEY WORD of the poem.

SONNET 100

POSSIBLE (ANAGRAMMATIC) KEY WORD: TIME/MIGHT

DEFECTIVE KEY WORD: TIME [-'S] (missing in Q_1)

Couplet Tie: *give* (8, 13)
my love (9, 13)
Time [-'s] (6, 10, 12, 13)

101

O H truant Muſe what ſhalbe thy amends,
For thy neglect of truth in beauty di'd?
Bo:h truth and beauty on my loue depends:
So doſt thou too, and t:erein dignifi'd:
Make anſwere Muſe, wilt thou not haply ſaie,
Truth needs no collour with his collour fixt,
Beautie no penſell, beauties truth to lay:
But beſt is beſt, if neuer intermixt.
Becauſe he needs no praiſe, wilt thou be dumb?
Excuſe not ſilence ſo, for't lies in thee,
To make him much out-liue a gilded tombe:
And to be praiſd of ages yet to be.
Then do thy office Muſe, I teach thee how,
To make him ſeeme long hence, as he ſhowes now.

O truant Muse, what shall be thy amends
For thy neglect of truth in beauty dyed?
Both truth and beauty on my love depends;
So dost thou too, and therein dignified.
Make answer, Muse; wilt thou not haply say,
"Truth needs no colour with his colour fixed,
Beauty no pencil, beauty's truth to lay;
But best is best, if never intermixed"?
Because he needs no praise, wilt thou be dumb?
Excuse not silence so, for 't lies in thee
To make him much outlive a gilded tomb,
And to be praised of ages yet to be.
Then do thy office, Muse; I teach thee how
To make him seem long hence as he shows now.

THOUGH the actual presence of the beloved in the world may be entirely sufficient for the moment, the world needs art to keep his appearance alive in the future, after his death. The Muse errs, says the speaker-poet, by forgetting her future usefulness. There is, however, no real need for her in the present, according to this poem. Eternizing becomes here the *sole* function of art; the other three functions named in the poem (mimetic representation, adornment, and praise) have no present use, since, with respect to the first, the world can behold the beloved (and needs no substitute image of him); and with respect to the others, the beloved is too beautiful to need adorning or praise.

Shakespeare invents a colloquy to constitute the poem:

Poet: O truant Muse, what will you say to explain your neglect and silence? You exist only to attend him.

Muse: But he doesn't need ornament, he doesn't need an image of himself; he is self-sufficient.

Poet: a. It's not a question of *need;* of course, he doesn't *need* our praise, but we should still respond with outbreaks of grateful commendation; and

b. You can make him eternal; you can guarantee that his praises will continue after he is dead, so

c. Your duty is to make such a good image of him that it can serve, in the future, as a stand-in for the presence we now enjoy.

The two reasons for the Muse to speak—to utter praise and to construct an icon—are both borrowed from the motives given for religious art: to praise God (who, in Milton's words, "doth not need / Either man's work or his own gifts") and to perpetuate visually the presence of Jesus and the saints after their departure from this earth. To the extent that these are recognized by the reader as reasons transferred from theological discourse, they will appear (designedly) blasphemous.

Aesthetically, the interesting doctrine of the poem appears in lines 6–8, where the Muse's discourse is imagined. She sums up the Platonic triad in three epigrams—one about truth, one about beauty, and one about "the best," or "the good" (as we call it in the positive degree). The Muse emphasizes the self-sufficiency of each member of the Platonic triad (invoked again in, e.g., 105):

1. *Truth needs no colour with his colour fixed.* This is a repudiation of the "colors" of rhetoric when applied to a true proposition.
2. *Beauty [needs] no pencil to lay beauty's truth.* This second use of the word *truth* means "representationally exact image." The speaker declares the origin's independence of the icon. The icon may be absolutely accurate—the pencil does not lay "beauty's shadow" or even "beauty's image," but rather "beauty's truth," an absolute and faultless delineation—but nothing in the self-sufficient original presence requires that it be aesthetically reproduced for present consumption.
3. *Best is best, if never intermixed.* Value (which here includes beauty and truth, since this epigram also serves as a summary of the two preceding ones as well as a remark about "the good") is diminished, rather than augmented, by aesthetic interference. The dangers of contamination, pollution, and adulteration of "the best" are all suggested by the word *intermixed,* and the Muse rightly quails before the idea that her earthly intermixing could be salutary to the Platonic absolutes.

The poet grants the truth of all that the Muse says, and consequently founds his argument on (a) the Muse's obligation in gratitude to praise, and (b) the future usefulness of mimesis. Ultimately, the Muse's argument is Plato's (as the play on *truant* and *truth* might suggest), denouncing art as the copy of a copy, inevitably debasing the original Form. By refuting what he "knows" the Muse will say, the poet shows himself a revisionist anti-Platonist, urging mimesis as the way to satisfy the legitimate desire of times to come to see vanished beauty.

The beloved is described from the outset as the locus of value: *truth and beauty depend* on him for their existence (as sonnet 14 had said), and the Muse (whose dignity depends on having a worthy, not a debased, object) should make a song that would be, like the young man, *truth in beauty dyed*—mimetic accuracy steeped in eloquence. Interestingly, the anxiety of the poet—"Can I rise to such a task?"—is displaced onto the severity of repudiation by the Muse-Oracle: "Truth needs no orator-Muse; Beauty needs no artist-Muse; Best never should have intermixture." Where does the poet find strength to repudiate these austere refusals? He finds it in a turn away from the self-sufficiency of the supreme Platonic

Form to the choral duty of acolyte-subordinates, a duty required not only now but in the future. The poet, by "demoting" his Muse from goddess or oracle to feudal subordinate, gives her the incentive to praise and thereby make possible the praises of future generations. The Muse must "do her office"—behave as a good functionary—instructed by that other (superior) functionary, the poet, who will *teach [her] how*. The young man's present *show* will become his future *seeming:* here, *show* is reality, while *seem* is mimesis.

There is an internal joke on *a-**mend**-s* and *make*. To *make* is the office of creation; to *mend* what is marred is a lesser act (cf. 103). The Muse will *amend* her neglect by *making* (line 11) the beloved outlive death and *making* (line 14) him appear in the future as he now looks.

The aesthetic mainspring of the poem is the invention of the Platonic epigrams for the Muse; everything else leads up to, or away from, them.

DEFECTIVE KEY WORD: MUSE (missing in Q_3). Q_1, Q_2, and C all contain the word *Muse*, which is missing in Q_3, the "dumb," "silent" quatrain. But there we find a ghost of her in her silent form: *exc**use***.

Couplet Tie: *Muse* (1, 5, 13)
make (5, 11, 14)

102

MY loue is ſtrengthned though more weake in ſee-
I loue not leſſe, thogh leſſe the ſhow appeare, (ming
That loue is marchandiz'd, whoſe ritch eſteeming,
The owners tongue doth publiſh euery where.
Our loue was new, and then but in the ſpring,
When I was wont to greet it with my laies,
As *Philomell* in ſummers front doth ſinge,
And ſtops his pipe in growth of riper daies:
Not that the ſummer is leſſe pleaſant now
Then when her mournefull himns did huſh the night,
But that wild muſick burthens euery bow,
And ſweets growne common looſe their deare delight.
  Therefore like her, I ſome-time hold my tongue:
  Becauſe I would not dull you with my ſonge.

My love is strengthened, though more weak in seeming;
I love not less, though less the show appear:
That love is merchandised whose rich esteeming
The owner's tongue doth publish every where.
Our love was new, and then but in the spring,
When I was wont to greet it with my lays,
As Philomel in summer's front doth sing,
And stops her pipe in growth of riper days:
Not that the summer is less pleasant now
Than when her mournful hymns did hush the night,
But that wild music burthens every bough,
And sweets grown common lose their dear delight.
  Therefore like her, I sometime hold my tongue,
  Because I would not dull you with my song.

IN THIS, one of the rare sonnets obliquely invoking myth, the poet likens himself to the classical Philomel (< Greek, "lover of sweetness"), voicer of mellifluous *mournful [summer] hymns [that] hush the night*, while the rival poets are the subsequent singers of a harsh song, introduced in a phrase full of stops and clashing sounds—*But that wild music.*

Philomel, however, appears only in line 7. The poem begins and ends in a self-justification on the literal level, which replies to an implied accusation by the beloved: "You love me less, your love has weakened, I haven't had any poems from you lately. Has my attractiveness diminished? Why do you hold your tongue?" The concessions *(though . . . though)* in the sonnet are the poet's way of remaining polite while defending himself, and he engages in both positive *(strengthened)* and negative *(not less)* refutation of the antecedent accusations:

> My love is *strengthened*, though [I grant you] more weak in
> seeming;
> I love *not less*, though [I grant you] less the show appear:
> . . . . .
> *Therefore* . . . I sometime hold my tongue,
> *Because* I would not dull you with my song.

This clear skeleton of refutation or rebuttal (cf. 76, 116, 117, etc.) is anchored by the exemplum of Philomel, who is said to sing only in the early summer, ceasing to sing in *riper days.* Strictly speaking, the analogy alone should suffice as explanation, since Philomel is the archetype of Voice, and what she does any lesser voice is justified in doing.

Q_3, however, invents a *motivation* for Philomel. *Why* does Philomel sing in early summer and fall silent in riper days? Not, certainly, because of any diminished beauty or pleasantness in the summer itself; no, it is the cacophonous chorus of the other birds which leads her to withdraw. The *rara avis* will not descend to join the common flock, since (proverbially) *sweets grown common lose their dear delight.*

The genre we originally ascribe to the poem—a self-defense for silence—thus changes (by this ascription of scornful motivation to Philomel) into a rebuke of rival poets. It fades back into self-defense in the couplet, using for its diction not the public diction of Q_1 *(seeming, show, merchandised, esteeming, owner, publish)* but rather the private *I-you* joined by *song,* the latter phrased as dull anticlimax because it is here mimetic of silence. The private *I-you* couplet is not, however, intimate, because it represents a falling-off (in its splitting into *I* and *you*) from the ecstatic moment of "we-ness" represented nostalgically in lines 5–6:

> *Our* love was new, and then but in the spring,
> When I was wont to greet it with my lays.

The lays have ceased because the intimacy represented by *our love* has been intruded on by the rival flock of poets burdening every bough. As the young man has moved into their company, *we* has given way to a new grouping:

> (you + they) (I)

and the myth of Philomel is introduced to explain the new configuration to one who can scarcely be unaware of the change in his company, and whose initial reproach—"Why don't I hear any singing from you lately?"—is thereby shown to be disingenuous.

The three competing discourses in which the poet speaks are of interest: one is the discourse of reminiscent nostalgia *(Our love . . . Philomel . . . summer . . . mournful hymns did hush . . . night);* another, the discourse of self-defending logic *(strengthened, though; not less, though; Not that . . . but; Therefore . . . because);* and the third, and most revealing, is the discourse of proverb, when the poet steps out of both his elegiac love-narrative recalling the beloved's former affection *and* his defense of the logic of his own present silence to appeal to the *consensus gentium* by way of his two warning "proverbs": "Published love is merchandised love," and *Sweets grown common lose their dear delight.* Both of these appeals to proverbial wisdom come as "clinchers" to their respective arguments—the argument *in propria persona* (lines 1-4) and the argument as Philomel (lines 6–12). By positioning these proverbs as the most persuasive of his reasons (the most persuasive reason always being placed at the climax of the argument), the poet suggests that they are the sort of argument the beloved is likely to find most convincing (cf. *Lilies that fester smell far worse than weeds,* 94). The person who finds proverbs (which are usually a minatory form) more convincing than a personal plea is a person whose eyes are on his audience. "You wouldn't want to seem covetous and vulgar in being fond of overt praise, would you?" the poet implies by his first proverb about merchandised and published love; and "You wouldn't want to join the common crowd (by being the topic of a lot of common singers), would you?" he implies by the second proverb about *sweets* grown *common.* The young man's character is frequently revealed in the speaker's use of just those rhetorical strategies which are most likely to convince him. The "impersonal" effect as the poet turns to his proverbs—saying, in effect, "In guiding your conduct, believe, prudentially, in the shrewd and undeceived wisdom of that *consensus gentium* you care so much about, even if you won't believe in or act on the pleas of your friend"—is one of the more chilling effects produced, frequently and resignedly, by the speaker of the *Sonnets.*

The resort to both proverbs and exemplum (Philomel) shows how much the intimate discourse of colloquy *(I-you)* needs now to explain and defend itself by auxiliary discourses. Even these auxiliary discourses can show inner proliferation: for instance, the Philomel-discourse appears first as a natural seasonal phenomenon (she sings, then stops); second as an externally motivated voluntary cessation (as she disdains to join the cacophonous chorus of the common flock); and third as an inner-directed active holding-of-the-tongue to protect the young man (which turns Philomel into what Keats called "a tongueless nightingale" ["Eve of St. Agnes"]), thereby increasing the pathos of the poet's silence. Punningly, the innocent agricultural discourse of the "*growth* of riper days" is replaced by the debased social fact of "sweets *grown* common," just as, alliteratively, what can privately give ***dear delight*** can, in a debased social system, ***dull*** its object. As Shakespeare's lines slide from one discourse to another, from one form of *growth* to another, even from one *dl* to another, the poem achieves its definition. Of course the norm to which all the other discourses are referred is set by the elegiac onomatopoetic hum of Philomel's lost summer. (I accept, for consistency, the emendation of *his* to *her* in line 8.)

Couplet Tie: *tongue* (4, 13) and *sing/song* (7, 14), showing the extent to which Philomel is the structural base of the poem.

103

ALack what pouerty my Muſe brings forth,
That hauing ſuch a skope to ſhow her pride,
The argument all bare is of more worth
Then when it hath my added praiſe beſide.
Oh blame me not if I no more can write!
Looke in your glaſſe and there appeares a face,
That ouer-goes my blunt inuention quite,
Dulling my lines,and doing me diſgrace.
Were it not ſinfull then ſtriuing to mend,
To marre the ſubiect that before was well,
For to no other paſſe my verſes tend,
Then of your graces and your gifts to tell.
  And more,much more then in my verſe can ſit,
  Your owne glaſſe ſhowes you,when you looke in it.

Alack, what poverty my Muse brings forth,
That, having such a scope to show her pride,
The argument all bare is of more worth
Than when it hath my added praise beside.
O blame me not if I no more can write!
Look in your glass, and there appears a face
That overgoes my blunt invention quite,
Dulling my lines, and doing me disgrace.
Were it not sinful then, striving to mend,
To mar the subject that before was well?
For to no other pass my verses tend
Than of your graces and your gifts to tell;
  And more, much more than in my verse can sit,
  Your own glass shows you, when you look in it.

ONCE again, in this poem referring to but not addressing the Muse, the poet reveals that the beloved has been reproaching him for his silence, and he bursts out, in the exclamation-fulcrum (line 5) that spills over the quatrain limits:

O blame me not if I no more can write!

Because the poem re-begins after this outburst, and re-begins as self-defense (after originally beginning—*Alack*—in lament), the sonnet exhibits an anomalous structural division: 5 + 7 + 2.

The lament says, establishing a hierarchy of value:

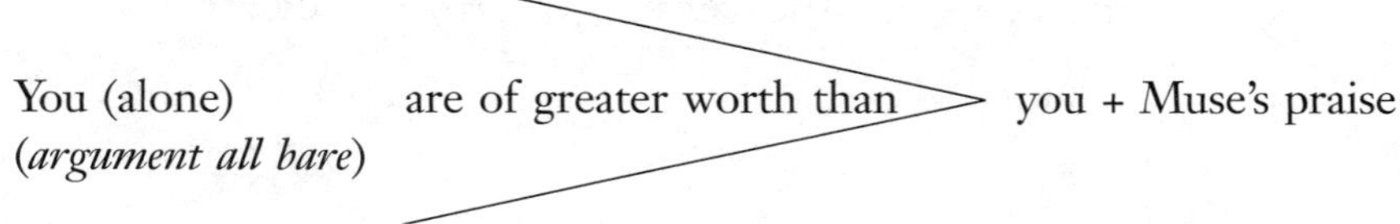

The subsequent self-justification continues the hierarchizing impulse in such phrases as *[your imaged] face . . . overgoes my blunt invention*, and *[your glass shows you] more, much more than in my verse can sit.*

We see, then, that this is a sonnet of competing representations, but not the simple one "*yourself* versus *my verse.*" No: it is "*your imaged self* versus *my verse.*" The beloved is placed before a mirror, so that he can gaze on two representations of himself—one in the mirror, one in the poet's verse—and judge which is superior. In this Judgment of Paris between Mirror Image and Invented Image, the Mirror Image (which may, here, be taken to stand for a perfect mimesis) succeeds where the image which is dependent (even in part) on invention must fail. The lover watching the beloved regarding her/his face in the glass had been used before, notably by Sidney in *Certain Sonnets.* It is not a new motif. What does Shakespeare do with it?

The Couplet Tie in 103 is unusually full—and I include in it the two pronominal adjectives *your* and *my*, since they are present in contrastively accentuated positions—"*my* verse," "*your* glass"—which transforms the feet in which these words appear from iambs to spondees:

And more, much more than in my verse can sit,
Your own glass shows you when you look in it.

The dialectic organizing the poem (stressed in the couplet) is that between *my verse* and *your glass*, both of them instruments of representation, but the second (mimesis by reflection) putatively exceeding the first (mimesis by invention). The beloved stands behind both, as *a face* to the mirrored mimesis, *the argument* to the poetic invention, *the subject* to the *mending*, the *graces and . . . gifts* to the *tell[ing]*.

The poet's self-condemnation for the inadequacy of verse is made most damningly in the only two "impersonal" lines in the sonnet:

Were it not sinful then, striving to mend,
To mar the subject that before was well?

The proverbial and theological base of this question means that the conventional triad *make/mar/mend* (drawn on, e.g., by George Herbert in "Love (III)" and elsewhere) is in question; and since its ultimate referent is the Fall of Man, the word *sinful* (inappropriate in the epideictic register) slips in without difficulty. In referring to invention as the effort to *mend*, rather than to *make*, the poet gives priority to God's *making* (of the face, the argument, the graces, and the gifts). In this view, lowly verse is a mere *addition* of praise, a *mending* of what, since it does not need mending, is therefore more marred than mended or made by verse. Verse is a *more;* and the pun on *more* as additive *(more worth)*, and *more* as "longer" *(I no more can write)* sees the impossibility of addition as the cause of the impossibility of creative prolongation. The added pun on the near-homophone *mar* means that the *more* of verse is actually harmful. And the ***p**overty* of the Muse seems to generate a string of *p*-words to accompany itself: *pride, praise, pass.*

The attempt to blame the Muse (a screen, a displacement of culpability) occupies the first quatrain, and makes the poet able to join with the beloved in lamenting the absence of new poems. The daunting scope of the beloved's *gifts* turns the Muse's potential *pride* to *poverty*, just as the beloved's *graces dis-grace* the poet.

The series of "greater than" and "less than" assertions organizes the sonnet both when the poet hides behind his Muse and when he subsequently (line 5) takes personal responsibility (after which the Muse vanishes from the poem). The reiteration of the substantial inferiority of praise, invention, lines, and verse reaches its keenest point in the paradox by which the *grace* of the beloved does *disgrace* to the poet. The actual phrase is not "doing my verse disgrace" but rather "doing *me* disgrace"; and the substitution of the poet's self for his art (which occupies the inferior position in all the other hierarchical comparisons) is placed in the sensitive climactic moment of the octave. The personal fall from grace—as the poet is *dis-graced*—generates the parallel to Adam's fall from grace, and introduces the theological analogy.

The narcissistic chiastic circle in the couplet—*glass : you :: you : it*—leaves the beloved in a self-contemplating closed circuit, in which neither the excluded poet nor his excluded verse can find a point of entrance. Although the poem has begun with what the Muse brings forth, it slides to the face of the beloved and to its image in the glass as principal subject. Its arch argument—"I would sin before heaven and thee to attempt to mend (only to mar) what God hath made"—is of course one of the sophistries of the *Sonnets*, used to imply that the divinely created beloved needs no reflection other than the one in the mirror.

But the theory of art here expressed—that art is entirely ancillary rather than constitutive, that it becomes even destructive in its attempts to be constructive—will change entirely by sonnets 124–125.

KEY WORD: MORE/MAR (if the near-homophone is allowed)

Couplet Tie: *more* (3, 5, 13, 13, with a near-homophone in *mar*, 10)
verse [-*s*] (11, 13)
glass (6, 14)
show [-*s*] (2, 14)
look (6, 14)
your (6, 12, 12, 14) } foregrounded by contrast
my (1, 4, 7, 8, 11, 13) }

104

TO me faire friend you neuer can be old,
For as you were when firſt your eye I eyde,
Such ſeemes your beautie ſtill:Three Winters colde,
Haue from the forreſts ſhooke three ſummers pride,
Three beautious ſprings to yellow *Autumne* turn'd,
In proceſſe of the ſeaſons haue I ſeene,
Three Aprill perfumes in three hot Iunes burn'd,
Since firſt I ſaw you freſh which yet are greene.
Ah yet doth beauty like a Dyall hand,
Steale from his figure,and no pace perceiu'd,
So your ſweete hew,which me thinkes ſtill doth ſtand
Hath motion,and mine eye may be deceaued.
For feare of which,heare this thou age vnbred,
Ere you were borne was beauties ſummer dead.

To me, fair friend, you never can be old,
For as you were when first your eye I eyed,
Such seems your beauty still. Three winters cold
Have from the forests shook three summers' pride;
Three beauteous springs to yellow autumn turned
In process of the seasons have I seen;
Three April perfumes in three hot Junes burned,
Since first I saw you fresh, which yet are green.
Ah yet doth beauty, like a dial hand,
Steal from his figure, and no pace perceived;
So your sweet hue, which methinks still doth stand,
Hath motion, and mine eye may be deceived;
For fear of which, hear this, thou age unbred:
Ere you were born was beauty's summer dead.

The acceleration in the pace of transience is enacted in the three transformations narrated:

1. *spring summer autumn winter*
   (*winter* shakes summer's pride
   from forest) (endpoint at end of year)
2. *spring summer autumn winter*
   spring turned to yellow *autumn* (endpoint earlier in year)
3. *April May June . . .* [*December*]
   June burns April perfumes (endpoint yet earlier)

The first change mentioned is a gross change: the trees lose their leaves. The second is still a visible one: the leaves turn yellow. The third is an invisible but perceivable one; in June one can no longer smell the perfume of April flowers. Because the series is an increasingly accelerating one, one can extrapolate to the next events in it: first, some loss that would take place between April and May—say, the disappearance of primroses; and next, some vanishing between April 1 and April 15—say, the fading of violets; and eventually something that would disappear between April 1 and April 2—if only April 1 itself.

Booth, commenting on 128, calls 104's repetition *eye I eyed* a "self-conscious rhetorical gimcrack." But in Laurence Olivier's recitation of this poem to Katharine Hepburn (in the movie *Love among the Ruins*), these (apparently) awkward repetitions in line 2 were revealed as the stammering of a lovestruck boy, astonished at his first glimpse of the potential intercourse of love:

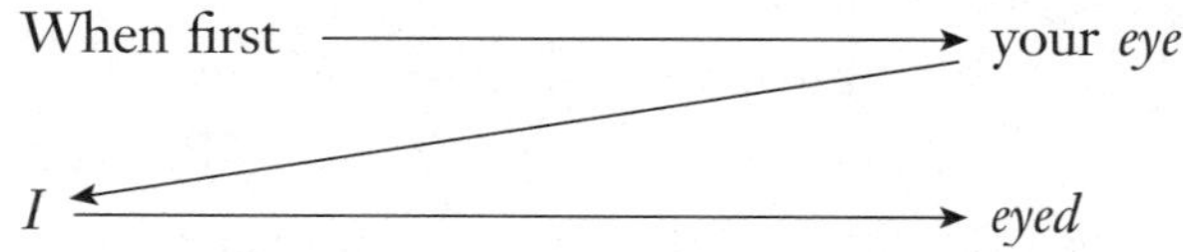

In its serving as the resonant Couplet Tie, *summer* (4, 14)—that season which the speaker would like to believe eternal—is in the end shown to be transient. *Process* and *pace* are put in tension with *perceiv*[ing], and Q_3 is organized around the contradictions among (acknowledged) seasonal fact, (limited) sensory perception, and (desire-driven) conclusions, as shown in the diagram.

Structure of Sonnet 104, Quatrain 3

	beauty doth steal from his figure (fact)	
	no pace [is] perceived (perception)	
Your sweet hue	(as object of mistaken conclusion)	*doth stand* (methinks)
	(as subject)	*hath motion*
	and	
	mine eye may be deceived (speculation)	

After this statement—that appearances may be wrong—the poem can no longer address the "eternally young" friend, who has in effect died as soon as his beauty is seen to have *motion.* The maw of accelerative process has engulfed him (its pace quickening from line 7 onward), and his summer, as soon as it is perceived to be seasonal, is in fact dead. The stunning "turn" by which the young man "dies" in the space between Q_3 and C is in fact the major aesthetic achievement (along with the speed-up of change which caused it) of the poem.

The couplet thus, in the lyric "now" of the poem, has to call out to the age about to be conceived; before the nine months of its gestation are accomplished, the young man's summer flourishing will be dead. (The rapid succession of *unbred, born, dead* perhaps taught Yeats, in "Sailing to Byzantium," to denominate the age unbred as "Whatever is *begotten, born,* and *dies.*") The cruel undoing of a generation in three words enacts, in 104, the theme of the transience of mortal forms.

Couplet Tie: *summer* (4, 14)

105

LEt not my loue be cal'd Idolatrie,
Nor my beloued as an Idoll ſhow,
Since all alike my ſongs and praiſes be
To one,of one,ſtill ſuch,and euer ſo.
Kinde is my loue to day,to morrow kinde,
Still conſtant in a wondrous excellence,
Therefore my verſe to conſtancie confin'de,
One thing expreſſing,leaues out difference.
Faire,kinde,and true,is all my argument,
Faire,kinde and true,varrying to other words,
And in this change is my inuencion ſpent,
Three theams in one,which wondrous ſcope affords.
  Faire,kinde,and true,haue often liu'd alone.
  Which three till now,neuer kept ſeate in one.

Let not my love be called idolatry,
Nor my belovèd as an idol show,
Since all alike my songs and praises be
To one, of one, still such, and ever so.
Kind is my love today, tomorrow kind,
Still constant in a wondrous excellence;
Therefore my verse, to constancy confined,
One thing expressing, leaves out difference.
"Fair, kind, and true" is all my argument,
"Fair, kind, and true" varying to other words,
And in this change is my invention spent,
Three themes in one, which wondrous scope affords.
  "Fair," "kind," and "true" have often lived alone,
  Which three till now never kept seat in one.

THE Couplet Tie—*fair, kind, true, one (al**one**, **won**drous), three*—sums up the whole argument about unity and Trinity enunciated and enacted in the poem. Because of its absence of metaphor, the sonnet has been called "dull" and "tautologous" by several of its critics (Weiner, Vickers, and Kerrigan among them) who prefer a visibly imagistic poetics to a poetics of wit. Of the early editors, only Wyndham (1898) saw its Platonic implications.

The poet here rebuts an antecedent reproach from a putatively Christian onlooker: "Your love seems to me idolatry, a religion worshiping a competing and different divinity." The poet's refutation depends on our perceiving that the accuser is a Christian who worships one God in three persons and who recites, in church, the doxology, "Glory be to the Father, and to the Son, and to the Holy Spirit; as it was in the beginning, is now and ever shall be, world without end, Amen." The poet responds to his accuser, "No, mine is not a different religion, it's *just like yours.* My songs are directed to one divine being, who is ever the same, just as your Divine Being is; and my object of worship is also triune (fair, kind, and true) as your Trinity is; and in fact my trinitarian doctrine (three qualities in one person, hitherto never seen together) is very much like yours, in which three persons keep seat in one God."

This witty refutation—"The object, structural form, and ritual words of my religion are indistinguishable from yours, and therefore you can't call my practice 'idolatry'"—depends first of all on the reader's recognizing the speaker's inventive transmutation of Christian Trinitarian theology and of the doxology. But this substantial piece of cleverness is accompanied by others. First of all, by identifying his beloved's qualities *(fair, kind, and true)* as those of the Platonic Triad (the Beautiful, the Good, the True), the poet opposes to his accuser's Christian Trinity an equally powerful, but classical, cultural totem as an emblem of the divine. The early Christianizing of the Platonic Triad had somewhat muted the contrast between classical and Christian values, but Shakespeare here restores them to full opposition. He points up the opposition by having his poet-speaker change his original order of value. At first (in the octave), he gives precedence to the Goodness of the beloved:

> *Kind* is my love today, tomorrow *kind*,
> Still constant in a wondrous excellence.

But in the sestet, the poet-speaker reverses his order of precedence, placing the Beautiful three times above the Good:

> "*Fair*, kind, and true" is all my argument,
> "*Fair*, kind, and true" varying to other words,
> . . . . .
> "*Fair*," "kind," and "true," have often lived alone . . .

Whereas the Good is the highest value in Christian practice, Shakespeare decides to make the Beautiful the highest value in his formulation of the Platonic Triad. (A counterargument proposing that *Fair, kind, and true* represents a climactic order privileging *true* seems to me implausible in face of both the poem's earlier privileging of *kind*, and the emphasis throughout the *Sonnets* on the physical beauty of the friend.) Shakespeare thus produces a clear cultural opposition of the (Christian) priority of the Good to the (aesthetic) priority of the Beautiful, and lets his speaker (as he enunciates his parodic version of accepted belief) expose the tension between two sovereign cultural systems, a tension often obscured in Christianized neo-Platonism. (Cf. also the confrontation of the Petrarchan with the Pauline in 116.)

The wit of the sonnet further resides in devoting one segment of the poem to each part of the total trinitarian concept. The octave is concerned with one-ness; Q_3, in its first three lines, is concerned with threeness; and line 12 and the couplet are concerned with three-in-one-ness. The sonnet consequently is what it describes: a combination of *one* and *three* to make up *three-in-one*.

Moreover, this is a sonnet—the only one of its kind—in which Shakespeare *doubly* repeats a KEY WORD in each of the four units of the sonnet. Here the KEY WORD (ONE) appears graphically or phonetically *twice* in each member:

> Q_1: to *one*, of *one*
> Q_2: *won*drous, *one* thing
> Q_3: in *one*, *won*drous scope
> C: al*one*, in *one*.

It is of course a joke that in a poem about *three* and *one*, the word *one* should be repeated *two* times in each segment. The clause "My verse, . . . /

One thing expressing, leaves out difference" thus becomes a joke not only with respect to the gross differences among octave, Q_3, and couplet (one, three, three-in-one), but also with respect to the concealed presence of "two" in a four-times-repeated twice-ness. Since the two members of the "couple" represented by the *one/won*-pair cannot be distinguished from each other, this may be a same-sex couple.

Of course, explaining these charming changes in this heavy-footed way robs them of the *esprit* they display as they succeed each other on the page. The poem is one of Shakespeare's many witty defenses of the (apparently) invariant matter and form of the *Sonnets*, warning his readers that if they are to find the poetry within his sequence, they will not find it either in "tautologous" subject matter *(love; belovèd; to one; of one; still such; ever so; kind today; tomorrow kind; constant; wondrous; constancy confined; one; fair, kind, and true; fair, kind, and true; three; one; wondrous; fair, kind, and true; alone; three; one)* nor in the Shakespearean sonnet "form" as such (the formal segmentation, the invariant rhyme scheme). Invention in this sequence lies deeper; and the strategies of this sonnet—its reprise of the cultural oppositions between Christianity and an aesthetic Platonism, between the Good and the Beautiful; its clever invention of an erotic religion structurally and ritually indistinguishable from Trinitarian Christianity; its enacting of trinitarian relations in its triune segmentation of octave, Q_3, and couplet; and its playful insertion of the KEY WORD "ONE" in groups of *two*—show us what Shakespearean invention is.

KEY WORD: ONE [alONE] [WONdrous]

Couplet Tie: *fair* (9, 10, 13)
kind (5, 5, 9, 10, 13)
true (9, 10, 13)
one [al-]*one*, *won*[-drous] (4, 4, 6, 8, 12, 12, 13, 14)
three (12, 14)

106

WHen in the Chronicle of wasted time,
I see discriptions of the fairest wights,
And beautie making beautifull old rime,
In praise of Ladies dead, and louely Knights,
Then in the blazon of sweet beauties best,
Of hand, of foote, of lip, of eye, of brow,
I see their antique Pen would haue exprest,
Euen such a beauty as you maister now.
So all their praises are but prophesies
Of this our time, all you prefiguring,
And for they look'd but with deuining eyes,
They had not still enough your worth to sing:
For we which now behold these present dayes,
Haue eyes to wonder, but lack toungs to praise.

When in the chronicle of wasted time
I see descriptions of the fairest wights,
And beauty making beautiful old rhyme
In praise of ladies dead and lovely knights,
Then in the blazon of sweet beauty's best,
Of hand, of foot, of lip, of eye, of brow,
I see their ántique pen would have expressed
Even such a beauty as you master now.
So all their praises are but prophecies
Of this our time, all you prefiguring,
And for they looked but with divining eyes,
They had not skill enough your worth to sing:
For we, which now behold these present days,
Have eyes to wonder, but lack tongues to praise.

As commentators have long noted, the basic conceit here is that of typology. Just as certain characters or events in the Old Testament truly foretell by anticipation events in the life of Christ (as the sacrifice of Isaac is a type of Christ's sacrifice, or the regurgitation of Jonah by the whale a type of Christ's resurrection), so certain beautiful men and women described in ancient chronicles are types, or authentic preimages, of the beloved.

There is an interpretative crux in lines 11–12. The ancient chroniclers are said to have looked with *divining eyes.* This, to my view, likens them to the ancient Hebrew prophets who were, before the appearance of Christ *in propria persona,* able to typify and describe him truly because they were divinely inspired. Accepting the emendation of *still* to *skill,* I therefore believe that, of the two competing readings of these lines—

A. And had they not been possessed of (authentically) divining eyes,
they would not have had the skill to sing your (present) worth;
B. And, because they looked only with guessing eyes,
they had not skill enough to sing your eventual worth;

—A is to be preferred, as keeping the analogy between the verse-chroniclers and the divinely inspired and visionary prophets who had the skill to sing—as, say, Isaiah did—of the worth of Jesus before his Incarnation. *Prophecy* and *prefiguration* are serious and validating words. God is *visible* in prophecies and prefigurings. The old verse-chroniclers, too, saw, divined, and sang. They sang the Platonic absolutes: *fairest, best.* In the reading which denigrates the precursors—"they did not have skill enough to sing your worth"—the analogy of types and figures has no point, and the sacrilegious wit of the sonnet is lost.

The linkages between typology and poetry are made by a semantic series: *praise, ex**press**ed, praises, prophecies, prefiguring, present, praise.* If one chooses, one can see *praise(s)* as the KEY WORD. Here *praise* is "concealed" in Q_2 in *expressed:*

Q_1: *praise*
Q_2: [*ex*]*press*[*ed*]

Q_3: *praises*
C: *praise*

"Seeing" and "singing" organize this poem: to be a poet it is necessary to *see* (as the speaker does in the main verb of Q_1 and Q_2) but it is also necessary (Q_3) to *sing* (as the apologetic speaker cannot, but as the ancient chroniclers, in their *beautiful old rhyme*, did).

This is a poem—one of countless in the lyric tradition—saying "I cannot write a poem." Commentators sometimes find this paradoxical; but we are always entitled to separate the narrative fiction of a poem from the existence of the artwork itself. Otherwise we could not have the fiction, common in lyric, that a dead person is speaking. Here, a "dumb" or "mute" person is speaking, one who deplores the fact that although he sees supreme beauty he cannot praise it in song; he and his contemporaries lack the tongues of the old minnesingers and trouvères. The word *beauty* (3, 3, 5, 8) and its synonyms, *fairest* (2), *lovely* (4), and *best* (5), proliferate in lines 1–7; they are "replaced" in lines 8–12 by *you* (8, 10) and *your worth* (12); but they are desolately absent from the couplet, which lacks both *you* and value. We may behold the young man and his worth, but we cannot enunciate or enact them, tongueless as we are.

There are incidental felicities and inventions here. Time has a ***chron**icle* (Greek *kronos*); time is *wasted*, but you *master*. When we ask why, after the phrase *fairest wights*, the phrase that occurs is not the parallel one "ladies *sweet* and lovely knights," but rather the unsettling *ladies dead*, we see that ***ladies*** generated *dead; wasted time* is set against *our time;* the mutation from the private *I see* to the plural *we behold* occurs in order to form a contemporary plural complement *(we)* to the ancient chroniclers *(they)*. The chronicle insensibly is personified (via "*their* ántique pen") into chroniclers, as the present mute poet summons up his singing ancestors as exemplars.

In this meditation on tradition, the central assertion is that beauty in its object makes rhyme beautiful—in other words, that content has something to do with aesthetic worth, that *descriptions of the fairest wights* are something to which the beauty-seeking eye of a latter-day reader might be drawn. At the same time, description alone does not suffice; the old poems were also *praises*—that is, examples of a rhetorical genre. By insisting on the contribution of not only *content* and *rhetoric* but also poetic *sound* (this is, after all, "old *rime*" made to *sing* the subject's worth) Shakespeare suggests that what is degenerate now is both contemporary rhetoric and contemporary rhyme; singing praise cannot be found, though the object (the friend as *fairest wight*) is certainly present, and beheld.

Structure of Sonnet 106

Type		*Antitype*
When *I see* descriptions and beauty . . . rhyme *in praise of* ladies and knights Then *in the blazon of* beauty's best *I see* . . . pen would have expressed such beauty	as →	*you* master *now*
So All their *praises* are prophecies of	→	*this our time*
All prefiguring	→	*you*
And [unless] they had looked with [truly] divining *eyes*, they would not have had the skill to sing	→	*your* worth
For although we behold	→	*these days*
and have *eyes* to wonder, we lack tongues to *praise*.		

As shown in the diagram, the structure of 106 is organized, by its typological analogy, into "Type (Then)" and "Antitype (Now)," and the entire octave is devoted to a huge chiasmus [*I see : in praise :: in blazon : I see*] building up to the eventual Messiah-like incarnation of the Antitype—*You*—as he bursts on the scene—*now,* in *this our time.* The anticlimax of the couplet (lacking, as I have said, *you* and any noun associated with the friend) is all the more shaming, given the actual glory of the young man's presence in the *now* and his typologically prefigured beauty in the *then.* Without the typological splendor climaxing in line 8, and the contrasting diminished couplet, the sonnet would not have enacted its own impoverishment. Shakespeare's blasphemy in secularizing Messianic prophecy would have been clear, of course, to any contemporary reader.

KEY WORD: PRAISE [-S] [exPRESS'd]

Couplet Tie: *now* (8, 13)
eye [*-s*] (6, 11, 14)
praise [*-s*] [*ex*]*press*[*'d*] (4, 7, 9, 14)

107

NOt mine owne feares,nor the prophetick ſoule,
Of the wide world,dreaming on things to come,
Can yet the leaſe of my true loue controule,
Suppoſde as forfeit to a confin'd doome.
The mortall Moone hath her eclipſe indur'de,
And the ſad Augurs mock their owne preſage,
Incertenties now crowne them-ſelues aſſur'de,
And peace proclaimes Oliues of endleſſe age.
Now with the drops of this moſt balmie time,
My loue lookes freſh,and death to me ſubſcribes,
Since ſpight of him Ile liue in this poore rime,
While he inſults ore dull and ſpeachleſſe tribes.
　And thou in this ſhalt finde thy monument,
　When tyrants creſts and tombs of braſſe are ſpent.

Not mine own fears, nor the prophetic soul
Of the wide world, dreaming on things to come,
Can yet the lease of my true love control,
Supposed as forfeit to a cónfined doom.
The mortal moon hath her eclipse endured,
And the sad augurs mock their own preságe,
Incertainties now crown themselves assured,
And peace proclaims olives of endless age.
Now with the drops of this most balmy time
My love looks fresh, and Death to me subscribes,
Since spite of him I'll live in this poor rhyme,
While he insults o'er dull and speechless tribes.
　And thou in this shalt find thy monument,
　When tyrants' crests and tombs of brass are spent.

IN THE second quatrain of 107, the sound of satisfaction, as Booth notes, governs four neat assertions, themselves grouped in two two-line accounts of event and adjunctive speech-act:

EVENT		*SPEECH-ACT*
The mortal moon *has endured* her eclipse;	AND	the augurs *mock* their own presage.
Incertainties *crown* themselves assured;	AND	peace *proclaims* olives.

The event *and* the speech-act immediately reporting it are cast in the same general syntactic pattern: three of these subject-predicate groups in Q_2 append a direct object; one *(incertainties . . . crown themselves)* also appends a predicate adjective. Because of these similarities, we feel that speech-acts advance *pari passu* with events. The duration allotted for each speech-act (one line) is exactly the same as the duration allotted to its predecessor-event. These complacent symmetries appropriately "stand for" the moment when the in-*certain* becomes the *sure*.

This moment of certitude in Q_2 is flanked by Q_1 and Q_3, each considerably more complex syntactically. The single complex sentence composing Q_1 has a compound subject (*fears* and *soul*) with a single verb *(can control)*; by contrast, the single compound-complex sentence of Q_3 has a double subject/predicate, event/speech-act, kernel:

My love looks fresh, AND *Death to me subscribes.*

We notice that this kernel repeats the Q_2 structure by which speech-act follows event (moon has endured AND augurs mock, etc.), and so we are justified in taking death's subscribing as another verbal event following a "real" event; the pun on "scribe" assures this interpretation. *Death* in Q_3 is the word which clarifies all the vague foreboding words of Q_1: *fears, things to come, a cónfined doom.* With this in view, we can see that the quatrains make up a small poem in themselves, in which the real conflict is that between life and death, between the author living in love-rhyme, and the alternate powerful scriptor, Death. The external victories (the moon, the assured events, whatever they may refer to) "guarantee" the poetic victory of the author: "*Death* to me subscribes, / Since spite of him I'll *live* in this poor rhyme." There is even an echo of the assured ***incertainties*** in the triumphant ***since*** and the ***insults*** of death, just as *I'll live* echoes the peace-proclaimed *olives*, and *now* (line 9) repeats the *now* (line 7) of Q_2.

In this view, the couplet then apparently becomes an afterthought, almost a footnote. For the first time, the friend is mentioned. If verse is for the author a vehicle of immortality *(I'll live)*, it is for the friend (who will be dead) at least a *monument* more lasting than the crests and tombs of tyrants. The two immediately evident structures of the sonnet, then, look something like I and II in the diagram. There is yet a *third structure* (III in the diagram)—already mentioned, but at first almost invisible—in which, following the introductory quatrain, events are followed by speech-acts, always introduced by *and.* There are four *and*s in the sonnet, each of which introduces a speech-act. This structure (4-10) makes the couplet not an afterthought, but an integral part of the whole. The partitionings 12-2, 10-4, and 4-10 are thus the three main overlapping structures of 107. The first is a pronominal structure of love-colloquy (I/thou), so frequent in the *Sonnets;* the second a conceptual structure (love/verse) setting feeling/content next to rhyme/form; and the third (after the introduction) a grammatical structure (*x* AND *y*, in which *x* is always an event, *y* a speech-act), representing the way words comment on history. Such overlapping structures on different planes of thought and feeling are one of the great strengths of the *Sonnets* as poems.

Within these overlapping structures, Q_2 plays the normative syntactic role:

Event Report
Event Report.

Q_2 is offered as a series of "proofs" to support the boast in Q_1 of the superiority of love's fate over the ill-wishing of its inner and outer enemies. The boast ("Neither my own fears nor the world's soul can control my love's duration") turns, by Q_3, into fact: "My love looks fresh." This in turn "guarantees" the triumphant prophecy "I'll live." The expected co-prophecy "You'll live," last pronounced in 81, is no longer viable, because verse itself has begun to take priority over mimetic reproduction. (By 121, the *Sonnets* use, instead of *live*, its anagrams *vile* and *evil.*)

Structures of Sonnet 107

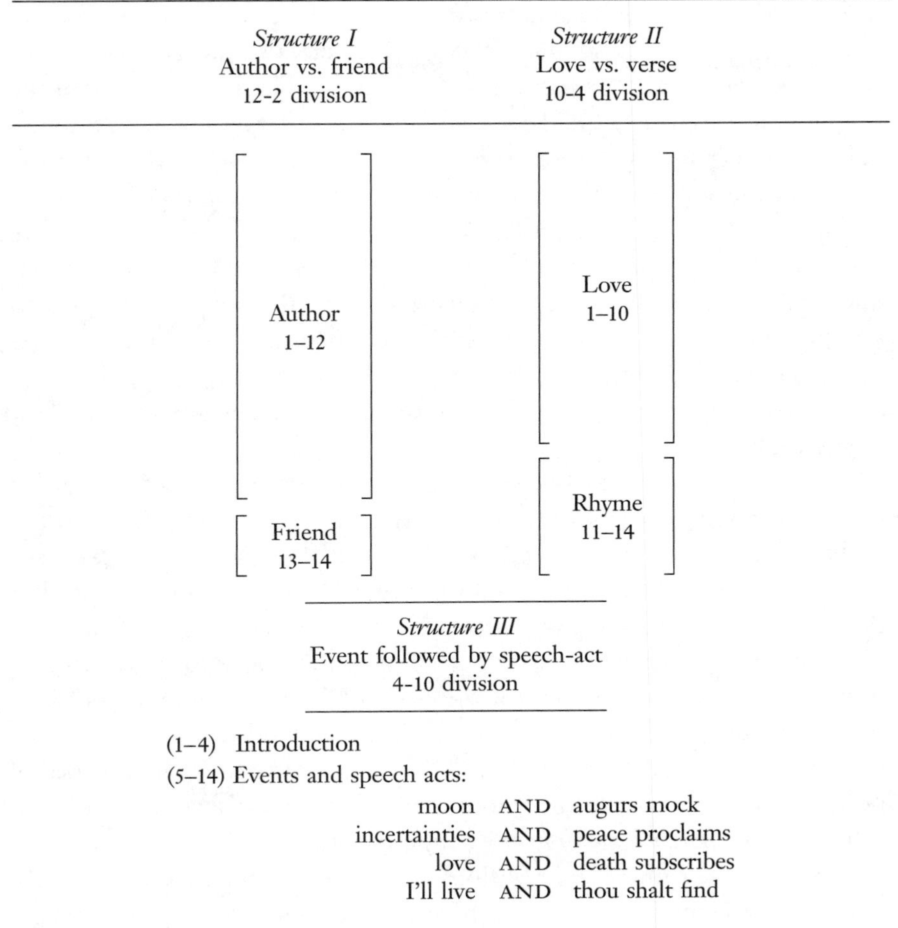

Opposed, conceptually, to the *dull and speechless tribes* whom death *insults* (another speech-act) are all the "speakers" of this sonnet: the *prophetic* soul of the world, the *presag[ing]* augurs, the peace which *proclaims*, and the *rhym[ing]* author. "As I am superior to (mortal) speechless tribes, so your verse-monument is superior to the (mortal) crests and tombs of tyrants." The ***tyrants*** are wonderfully reduced, by their association with the ***tribes*** with which they alliterate and assonate, to inferior species.

The lexicon of this sonnet is extremely ornate and Latinate. There are of course many Anglo-Saxon derivatives too, but the presence of the augurs gives prominence to the classic (Latin or Greek) and French-derived words. These include *prophetic, control, supposed, forfeit, cónfined, mortal, eclipse, endured, augurs, mock, presage, incertainties, crown, assured, peace, proclaims, olives, age, balmy, time, fresh, subscribes, spite, poor, rhyme, insults, tribes, monument, tyrants, crests, tombs, spent.* The Latinate ring of the sonnet seems to be its chief lexical strategy, coordinating with its impulse toward a macrocosmic scale by which to measure the survival of love, verse, and the author. The microcosmic personae are *I, mine own fears, my true love, this poor rhyme, tribes,* and *thou.* The macrocosmic personae are *the prophetic soul of the wide world, the mortal moon, incertainties, peace, this balmy time, Death,* and (at first sight) *tyrants.* In the couplet, micro- and macrocosmic words change places: the microcosmic *this poor rhyme* becomes the macrocosmic *thy monument,* while the (formerly) macrocosmic *tyrants* see their *crests* and *tombs of brass* now *spent* and microcosmically negligible.

The necessity of the opening complex syntax can now be seen: it serves to "zoom up" from the microcosmic scale *(mine own fears)* to the highly expanded macrocosm *(the prophetic soul of the wide world, dreaming on things to come.)* The large arc of Q_1 is never repeated in the poem, but the cumulative macrocosmic "proofs" of Q_2 become the guarantors of the microcosmic *my love looks fresh.* The greatest topsy-turvy reversal of micro- and macrocosmic occurs when Death—one of the macrocosmic personae—doffs his hat, so to speak, to the simple poet and his "poor" rhyme. Death usually *insults o'er,* and does not *subscribe to.* The reversal of power decisively reverses the importance of the *poor rhyme,* so that it can justifiably be called a *monument* of superior survival value.

Shakespeare cannot resist various "puns" between and among words. *__Pro__phetic* and *__pro__claim* use two different *pro*'s: the first means "earlier" in Greek and the second is a Latin intensifier. *__Sup__posed* presages *__sub__scribes.* *__Con__trol* prefaces *__cón__fined.* *Presage* (which calls out to *__pro__phetic* and *__pro__claim*) contains within itself not only the sages (augurs) but also its sonnet rhyme-word *age.* *Con__fin'd__* (Quarto spelling) yields its nonetymologically related homophone *find* (the Couplet Tie) and its graphically related *__ind__ured,* while etymologically it generates *__end__less.* *Incertain__ties__* generates *a__ssured__;* and *__cr__own, __cr__ests.* *Olives* creates *I'll live,* and *__in__cer__tain__ties* creates *__since__* and *__ins__ults.* *Rime* even contains *me,* visually, so that "*I*'ll live in this poor ri*me*" becomes a self-guaranteeing statement. It is easy to see that some of these jokes are semantic *(__cónfined__/__end__less);* some etymological—both false (*__pro__phetic* and *__pro__claim*) and true (*__sup__posed* and *__sub__scribes*); some are visual *(o__lives__, r__ime__);* some alliterative *(__dr__eaming, __dr__ops; __cr__own, __cr__ests);* some assonantal *and* alliterative *(__t__r__i__bes/__ty__rants);* some more generally phonetic *(ince-*, *since*, *ins-)*, some portmanteau-ish *(pre**sage**/**age**)*. (Portmanteau tricks are most interesting when the smaller word is etymologically unrelated to the larger one; *sage* and *age* are not etymological cousins, but *expressed* and *pressed* are, and would not make such an interesting portmanteau rhyme as *expressed* and *rest* would.)

There are of course other words which call out to each other in the poem. The words with prefixes and suffixes make an audible polysyllabic and usually classical under-song: *pro-phetic*, *con-trol*, *sup-posed*, *for-feit*, *cón-fined*, *ec-lipse*, *en-dured*, *au-gur (avis + gerere)*, *pre-sage*, *in-certainties*, *as-sured*, *pro-claims*, *end-less*, *sub-scribes*, *in-sults*, *speech-less*. The largely monosyllabic couplet distinguishes itself from the body of the poem by having no such prefixes or suffixes attached to its words, I suppose because monuments are fixed, and prefixes and suffixes generally denote some dynamism of more and less, upper and under, earlier or later.

Couplet Tie: [cón]*fin*[e]*d*, *find* (4, 13)

Note: Booth says one can't assure incertainties, that to say that *incertainties* are assured is to assert there is nothing sure. But of course the inserted "now" makes the line mean "[Former] incertainties are *now* assured things." The outcome of a war was an uncertainty yesterday, but now that the war is over, victory is an assured fact. Shakespeare's meaning need not be tortured to make a poem interesting.

108

VVHat's in the braine that Inck may character,
Which hath not figur'd to thee my true ſpirit,
What's new to ſpeake,what now to regiſter,
That may expreſſe my loue,or thy deare merit?
Nothing ſweet boy,but yet like prayers diuine,
I muſt each day ſay ore the very ſame,
Counting no old thing old,thou mine,I thine,
Euen as when firſt I hallowed thy faire name.
So that eternall loue in loues freſh caſe,
Waighes not the duſt and iniury of age,
Nor giues to neceſſary wrinckles place,
But makes antiquitie for aye his page,
    Finding the firſt conceit of loue there bred,
    Where time and outward forme would ſhew it dead,

What's in the brain that ink may character
Which hath not figured to thee my true spirit?
What's new to speak, what now to register,
That may express my love, or thy dear merit?
Nothing, sweet boy; but yet, like prayers divine,
I must each day say o'er the very same,
Counting no old thing old, thou mine, I thine,
Even as when first I hallowèd thy fair name.
So that eternal love in love's fresh case
Weighs not the dust and injury of age,
Nor gives to necessary wrinkles place,
But makes antiquity for aye his page,
    Finding the first conceit of love there bred,
    Where time and outward form would show it dead.

THE aural pun on *wrinkles* and *ink* (like *wrinkles* and *writ* in 93 and the conceptual puns on *wrinkle* and *pen* and *graven* in 100); the pun on *writ* in ***spirit*** and ***merit***; and the fact that *bred* includes *read* (preterite) suggest the anxieties of writing aroused by the *sweet boy* who wants novelty from his poet. The Couplet Tie is *first* and *love*, and the poem argues that all love is first love, that love never ages. The *bred/dead* rhyme occurs as well in 104 and 112, with the same paradoxical chime, and, coming after the book-word *page*, the *read* in *bred* may make itself felt. The *k*-sound in *ink, character, speak, counting, case, wrinkles, antiquity*, and *conceit* serves to join these words together so that we can see that in a loose way they all suggest inscription.

The question of Q_1—"What's new to think, write, speak, register?"—which we understand as one originally posed by the *sweet boy* but echoed in verse by the poet, receives first a tentative (but eventually mistaken) answer in Q_2. "I cannot say anything *new;* I can only say the same *old* things." Q_3 finds a better way of formulating the problem: it refuses to accept the young man's enslavement to novelty (and thus to temporality); and, against both *new* and *old*, it introduces the concept of the *eternal.* Under the rubric of the eternal, the old *(age, wrinkles, antiquity)* is no different from the new *(love's fresh case)*, and the couplet consequently announces the logical identity of ancient *conceit[s] of love* (which judged by time and outward form appear *dead*) with the poet's own fresh verses.

How is this plotted out poetically? We first notice the enslavement of the whole poem to repetition, both semantic and syntactic, posing the critical question: What does it mean to repeat? So much of art is repetition—of themes, conventions, motifs, rhyme schemes—that the sulky weariness of the young man ("What, *another* sonnet?") mirrors the jadedness, in all ages, of the novelty-seeking public itself. Therefore, to argue for his own poetics, the poet exaggerates his compulsion to repeat, positionally as well as semantically, syntactically, and phonetically. There are successive overlaps, as shown in the diagram.

Overlaps in Sonnet 108

{ *What's in the brain* / *What's new to speak* } { *my true spirit?* / *thy dear merit?* / *thy fair name* }

{ *What's new to speak* / *What now to register* }

may, may, prayers, day, say, name, case, weighs, age, place, page

count, no, old, thou

thou mine, I thine

eternal love, love's fresh case

age, page

first, first

The couplet tie is *first* and *love*, as I have said, but this is also a sonnet with a KEY WORD, "LOVE," which appears in all four members (4, 8, 9, 9, 13). LOVE "hides" in Q_2 in the form of ***hallowèd***, where the presence of an "extra" *v* in the *w* would not have lessened Shakespeare's joke, any more than the absent *e* in ***oblivious*** did in 55.

The force of the poet's rebuttal to the young man's implied reproach, "Don't you have anything *new* to show me?" is felt in the *not* of the opening question of the sonnet: "What *hasn't* my brain used to explain myself?" The subsequent abjectness of *Nothing, sweet boy* is only apparent (as it turns out), but it is dramatically real when it appears, as the poet seems to abjure invention altogether. After the rhythmic abruptness of the first 4½ lines, the monotony early established in Q_2 is striking:

bŭt yét, lĭke práyers dĭvíne,
Ĭ múst ĕach dáy săy o'ér thĕ véry̆ sáme.

The poet's inner "rebellion" against acquiescence in the young man's judgment of monotony is first felt in the initial trochees of lines 7 and 8, repeated in lines 9 and 13. Yet the singsong of traditional repetition—*nŏ óld thĭng óld, thŏu míne, Ĭ thíne*—resumes its counterpoint, as it will throughout.

The quatrain of eternity, Q_3, requires something different from either the abrupt demands for novelty in Q_1 or the monotone of liturgy in Q_2. How will Q_3 enact eternity? First of all, it assures us of the persistence of repetition: this is the only quatrain in which *love* appears twice, the first time in the form *-al love (eternal love)* to make us notice, if we haven't already, the play on ***hallowèd*** that preceded it. Also, this quatrain plays on a variety of words meaning both temporality and lack of temporality, but which are all etymologically related: *eternal*, *age*, and *aye* are all derivatives of *aevum* and *aeon*.

The meaning of Q_3 has seemed obscure to commentators. Both Kerrigan and Booth follow previous editors in interpreting *page* as "servant boy," and *antiquity* as "old age." As I understand it, the word *page* here means not "a serving boy" but rather the page one reads; and "to make *antiquity* one's page" is to choose to read love poems by early authors, as in *When in the chronicle of wasted time* (106) just preceding, which mentions the *ántique pen* of earlier writers. Poring over the pages of antiquity, one finds ladies who are, though *dead* (106, 108) in terms of time and outward form, still visible *in the blazon of sweet beauty's best* (106).

The *first* conception of love is to be found in the pages of old authors, and one can do no better in affirming the eternal nature of true love, as it appears in a *fresh* instance, than to see how accurate to one's own feelings (no matter how old one's beloved is, how wrinkled, how injured by age; and no matter how overlaid with dust old books may be) are the love-encomia found in antiquity's pages. That is, literary convention is the true repository of the eternal, since the persistence of convention makes antiquity's page understandable to, and moving to, the modern reader.

I take Q_3 as in part an admonition to the *sweet boy* so that he will love his aging poet as well as prize the (apparent) repetitiveness of the poet's sonnets. "Eternal love, when it arises in a new instantiation, does not take into account age and wrinkles, but instead sees how analogous the eternal youthfulness of personal feeling is to the paradoxical freshness of feeling encoded in old books by and about people long dead." The interesting phrase *necessary wrinkles* not only represents Shakespeare's liking for putting a grandly Latinate adjective with an Anglo-Saxon noun, but may also recall the Renaissance meaning of *necessary* as "fated." (See the etymological relation between *necesse* and the Greek *ananke* [Necessity, Fate] in *The Oxford Latin Dictionary, s.v. necesse.)*

The syntactic grandeur of the single long sentence comprising Q_3 and C contrasts with the fretful echoed questions of Q_1 and the repetitive saying and counting of Q_2. The interminableness of this sentence, with its triple main verb *(weighs not, nor gives place to, but makes)*, and its long subordinate participial phrase (*finding*, etc.), itself containing an adverbial clause *(there . . . where)*, which itself contains a double subject *(time, form)*, is as good an enactment of "eternity" as one could make. It ends only with the ending of the poem. Once again, as in 105 and 106, sonnet 108, in its "hallowing the name" of the young man instead of the name of the Deity, finds its wit in blasphemy.

KEY WORD: LOVE [-'S] [halLOWÈd]

Couplet Tie: *first* (8, 13)
love [-'s] hal[-*lowè*-]d (4, 8, 9, 9, 13)

109

O Neuer ſay that I was falſe of heart,
Though abſence ſeem'd my flame to quallifie,
As eaſie might I from my ſelfe depart,
As from my ſoule which in thy breſt doth lye:
That is my home of loue, if I haue rang'd,
Like him that trauels I returne againe;
Iuſt to the time, not with the time exchang'd,
So that my ſelfe bring water for my ſtaine,
Neuer beleeue though in my nature raign'd,
All frailties that beſiege all kindes of blood,
That it could ſo preposterouſlie be ſtain'd,
To leaue for nothing all thy ſumme of good:
For nothing this wide Vniuerſe I call,
Saue thou my Roſe, in it thou art my all.

O never say that I was false of heart,
Though absence seemed my flame to qualify;
As easy might I from my self depart
As from my soul, which in thy breast doth lie:
That is my home of love; if I have ranged,
Like him that travels I return again,
Just to the time, not with the time exchanged,
So that myself bring water for my stain.
Never believe, though in my nature reigned
All frailties that besiege all kinds of blood,
That it could so preposterously be stained
To leave for nothing all thy sum of good:
For nothing this wide universe I call,
Save thou, my rose; in it thou art my all.

THIS, like the preceding and following sonnets, is a rebuttal to an implied antecedent utterance by the young man. The young man has said to the speaker, "You are false of heart; you have ranged; you have left me." The speaker replies, *O never say that I was false of heart,* etc., and repeats the same syntactic form of injunction in Q_3, *Never believe,* etc. The Couplet Tie is *for nothing* (12, 13) and *all* (which occurs not only as itself in lines 10, 10, 12, 14, but also, in hidden guise, in ***false***, ***qualify***, and ***call***). The opposition in *nothing* and *all* is one concept governing the sonnet, while another is the climactic word *stain* (line 8; appearing in line 11 as *stained*) which, as it also governs phonetically, generates the peculiar series of six end-rhymes in ā*n* or ā*n[g]ed: ranged, again, exchanged, stain, reigned, stained.* The vowel sound "ā" is kept alive, so to speak, by its running appearance in *say, flame,* and *frailties,* as well as in the rhymes. Only in the couplet is the "stain" of *ā*—rising in Q_1, dominating Q_2, and present in Q_3—wholly absent, suggesting that it has been removed by love, that the *water* brought to the poem by return and repentance has made the *stain* disappear.

Sonnet 109 and the following 110 both refer to the *breast* of the beloved as the home to which the speaker returns. In 109, *ranging* is expunged by *returning;* to return on time *is* to be faithful. This "solution" is possible because the speaker admits to no sin *except* that of absence. The beloved has suggested by his accusation of *fals[ity] of heart* that the speaker's absence was caused by the wish to join another lover, but the speaker denies the inference. The only *stain* in the octave is that of absence, remedied by his return when promised, *just to the time.*

However, Q_3 introduces ideas of sin, a fall from grace, bodily frailty, the unruliness of the beloved, etc. When *blood* and *stained* are juxtaposed as end-words, falseness is not far away. The most conspicuous word in Q_3 is *preposterously,* which matches in its *prepost-* the *nothing all* of the following line. There is a strange current running through the sonnet—*my flame, my self* (the Quarto reading), *my soul, my home, my self* (Quarto), *my stain, my nature, my rose, my all*—emphasizing the fluent and changing import of the first-person possessive adjective. Is *my stain* mine in the same way as *my self* or *my nature* is? Does *my all* subsume *my home* and *my soul?*

What the sonnet presents us with, by means of all the nouns preceded by *my*, is the picture of a speaker ringed round with qualities:

my flame
my self
my soul
my home
my self
my stain
my nature
my rose
my all

These qualities suggest a plethora of self-definitions: I am a lover *(my flame);* I am a self; I am a soul; I am a home-dweller; I am a stained person; I am a natural being; I am the possessor of a rose; I am the estimator of value *(my all)*. One of the reasons we "believe in" Shakespeare's speaker is that his "I" is so variously defined.

The *reign* of *frailties* here will return in 121. The pun on *love* and *leave* in 73 recurs here (lines 5, 12). There is a pun on "*no*-thing" and "*uni*[one]-*verse*," and it is hard to believe that Shakespeare would not have intended a pun on *uni-verse* (Latin: *one turn*) with respect to both the turn in *pre-post-erously* (back to front) and with respect to *verse.*

The conceptual wit in the sonnet depends on the fallen nature of man. The speaker represents himself as the weakest in virtue of all men, willing to grant that in his nature reign *all* frailties that besiege *all* kinds of blood. Yet though all men (theologically speaking) are sinners, forsaking the *summum bonum (sum of good)* through frailty, this frailest of all will never disobey the evidence of Reason and forsake his All for nothing. This protest virtually exempts the speaker from the fallen state he has conceded is his. In short he has it both ways—"Yes, I am the sinner to outdo all sinners; but *this* sin of falsity I haven't let my nature be stained by." This paradox is reflected in the admission of (a minor) *stain* (line 8) while denying a *stained* (line 10) nature.

Couplet Tie: *all* (10, 10, 12, 14), as well as ***false*** (1), ***qualify*** (2), and ***call*** (13)
for nothing (12, 13)

110

ALas 'tis true,I haue gone here and there,
And made my ſelfe a motley to the view,
Gor'd mine own thoughts, ſold cheap what is moſt deare,
Made old offences of affections new.
Moſt true it is,that I haue lookt on truth
Aſconce and ſtrangely: But by all aboue,
Theſe blenches gaue my heart an other youth,
And worſe eſſaies prou'd thee my beſt of loue,
Now all is done,haue what ſhall haue no end,
Mine appetite I neuer more will grin'de
On newer proofe,to trie an older friend,
A God in loue,to whom I am confin'd.
  Then giue me welcome,next my heauen the beſt,
  Euen to thy pure and moſt moſt louing breſt.

Alas 'tis true, I have gone here and there,
And made myself a motley to the view,
Gored mine own thoughts, sold cheap what is most dear,
Made old offences of affections new.
Most true it is that I have looked on truth
Askance and strangely; but, by all above,
These blenches gave my heart another youth,
And worse essays proved thee my best of love.
Now all is done, have what shall have no end:
Mine appetite I never more will grind
On newer proof, to try an older friend,
A god in love, to whom I am confined.
  Then give me welcome, next my heaven the best,
  Even to thy pure and most most loving breast.

PROBABLY related (by its nature as a reply to accusation and by the mention of *breast*) to 109, this sonnet is organized not only by tense changes—present perfect (lines l-6), preterite (lines 7–8), present (line 9), future (lines 10–12), all in the indicative—but also by mood changes from the indicative to the imperative (*have*, line 9; *give*, line 13).

The couplet tie—*best* (8, 13), *most* (3, 5, 14, 14), *love* [*loving*] (8, 12, 14), and *give* [*gave*] (7, 13)—is a complex one, and suggests, in its superlatives *best* and *most*, the strenuous efforts of the speaker to reduce experience into the simple categories that pervade the sonnet: *here* and *there*, *cheap* and *dear*, *old* and *new*, *worse* and *best*, *newer* and *older*, *best* and *most most*. The assertive comparisons (ranging from positive to comparative to superlative to super-superlative) enact the self-in-repentance protesting that he has repossessed the one, true (and simple) value system, and knows each of its hierarchical levels. This simplification of experience betrays itself as the desperate remedy that it is by putting the friend, momentarily, in the position of the Deity with power to set the limits of the moral universe: he is a god in love *to whom I am confined*. The unwilling word *confined* arises from the speaker's overly simple polarities for moral experience. The *no end* of return is also a *con-fine-ment*, a Latin pun on *finis*, "end." The blasphemy *a god in love* is rapidly withdrawn as the friend is denominated next best to the speaker's personal salvation *(my heaven);* but the super-superlative *most most* once again replaces the friend in a quasi-divine position above all human beings, even the *most loving*. Within *breast* is contained the *rest* the speaker seeks after going here and there; in his looking on truth *st-range-ly* is contained his *rang-ing* described in 109.

Sonnet 110, by admitting infidelity (evaded in 109), becomes a stronger outburst than its predecessor. Among the speaker's concessions, only lines 1–2 seem to repeat an accusation made by the young man—"You've ranged all over and made a fool of yourself." One senses from subsequent lines that the speaker has been reviling himself inwardly with accusations quite different from the one of self-exposure voiced by the young man. The self-reviling inner accusations are: "I have gored my own thoughts, I have sold my dearest things for a farthing, I have taken up new affections, and the truest accusation of all is that I have avoided telling the truth." These inward-looking thoughts are brought outward again as the speaker spends the rest of the poem reiterating the increased love that his offense has awakened in him, bringing the poem back from moral to emotional concerns.

Underneath the admitted actions of the octave lies the motive for them, unrevealed until line 10: the sharpening of the speaker's appetite on *worse essays.* Until then, the offenses seem aimless and unconnected—going here and there, goring his thoughts, selling dear things cheap, acquiring new affections, looking askance on truth. These actions are called *blenches* (blinks) and *essays*—trivial categories. It is only with the vow of repentance—"I never more will grind my appetite on newer proof *to try* an older friend"—that we learn that the motive was "sadistic" appetite, and that the *essays* were really (punningly) ***trials*** aggressing against the friend. The *__ap__petite* is shown to be the cause of the new *__aff__ections,* and the demands of *appetite* (< *petere,* "to ask for") cause the eventual "all is *done*" of the *affections* (< *facere,* "to do").

The saccharine quality of the couplet arises from the extirpation of all complex value in favor of the highly oversimplified value of repentance. Repentance rises to its peak in the exaggerations of 111, where every penance is redoubled.

Couplet Tie: *best* (8, 13)
love [*-ing*] (8, 12, 14)
most (3, 5, 14, 14)
give [*gave*] (7, 13)

111

O For my ſake doe you wiſh fortune chide,
The guiltie goddeſſe of my harmfull deeds,
That did not better for my life prouide,
Then publick meanes which publick manners breeds.
Thence comes it that my name receiues a brand,
And almoſt thence my nature is ſubdu'd
To what it workes in, like the Dyers hand,
Pitty me then, and wiſh I were renu'de,
Whilſt like a willing pacient I will drinke,
Potions of Eyſell gainſt my ſtrong infection,
No bitterneſſe that I will bitter thinke,
Nor double pennance to correct correction.
Pittie me then deare friend, and I aſſure yee,
Euen that your pittie is enough to cure mee.

O for my sake do you with Fortune chide,
The guilty goddess of my harmful deeds,
That did not better for my life provide
Than public means which public manners breeds.
Thence comes it that my name receives a brand,
And almost thence my nature is subdued
To what it works in, like the dyer's hand.
Pity me then, and wish I were renewed,
Whilst like a willing patient I will drink
Potions of eisel 'gainst my strong infection;
No bitterness that I will bitter think,
Nor double penance to correct correction.
Pity me then, dear friend, and I assure ye
Even that your pity is enough to cure me.

"DO NOT chide *me* (as you have done, making me respond with 109 and 110); rather chide Fortune, who made me as I am. *She* is the guilty one, not I." That is the octave; the sestet changes the imperative from an upward-directed one ("chide the goddess") to a downward-directed one ("pity me"), twice repeated. (I accept the emendation of *wish* to *with* in line 1.)

The cure for the speaker's state seems at first to lie in a hope that Fortuna will reverse for him the motion of her wheel. He himself has had no luck in chiding Fortune; perhaps the friend will encounter better success, and relent from chiding the speaker in favor of chiding Fortune.

What causes the speaker, then, to change his mind until he sees not Fortuna but the friend as the agent of his potential cure? The speaker's metaphorical criminality *(harmful deeds)* in the octave is exchanged for his (guiltless) *infection* in the sestet, and, by this change in self-representation, the poet's disorder has become humanly curable, not requiring divine intervention. Geoffrey Hill's etymological reminder that *infection* derives from *inficere*, to dye [*The Lords of Limit*, p. 153], shows that the Anglo-Latin "macaronic" pun *dye/infection* makes possible the change in self-representation.

The metaphor of infixing or dyeing or double-dipping till the color "takes" produces the many doublings in the sonnet (some of them noted by Booth, but without causal explanation). A list follows, using Quarto spelling:

th: — *the, that, than, thence, that, thence, the, then, that, think, then, that*

Double letters: — *goddesse, harmfull, deeds, better, manners, breeds, pitty, willing, eysell, bitternesse, bitter, pennance, correct, correction, pittie, assure, yee, pittie, mee*

Chiastic arrangements of letters *(abba):* — *goddesse, deeds, better, willing, bitternesse, pittie, pittie*

Word repetitions, exact and inexact:

for . . . , *for*tune . . . , *for my life;*
my sake . . . *my* . . . deeds . . . *my life* . . . *my* name . . . *my* nature . . . *my* . . . infection;
better . . . ***bitter**ness* . . . *bitter*
public . . . *public*
means . . . ***manners***
pity . . . *pity* . . . *pity*
*will*ing . . . *will* . . . *will*
***patien**t* . . . ***potion**s*
correct . . . ***correct**ion*

And then there are the many alliterations, including such an unusual one as *for**tu**ne/**ch**ide/na**tu**re*. There are also "visual alliterations" like the repeated initial *w*'s in *with*, *which*, *what*, *works*, *wish*, *whilst*, *will*, *will*. And there is the play on Shakespeare's "branded" name, *willing*, *will*, *will*. These indelible "dyes"—persisting down to the couplet with its two appearances of *pittie*, not to speak of the couplet-rhyme *yee* and *mee*—suggest that no cure is to be found for this plague, which, unlike the "real" plague, will not yield to medicinal eisel.

Couplet Tie: *pity me then* (5, 13), [*pity*] (14)

112

Your loue and pittie doth th'impreſſion fill,
Which vulgar ſcandall ſtampt vpon my brow,
For what care I who calles me well or ill,
So you ore-greene my bad,my good alow?
You are my All the world,and I muſt ſtriue,
To know my ſhames and praiſes from your tounge,
None elſe to me,nor I to none aliue,
That my ſteel'd ſence or changes right or wrong,
In ſo profound *Abiſme* I throw all care
Of others voyces,that my Adders ſence,
To cryttick and to flatterer ſtopped are:
Marke how with my neglect I doe diſpence.
  You are ſo ſtrongly in my purpoſe bred,
  That all the world beſides me thinkes y'are dead.

Your love and pity doth th'impression fill
Which vulgar scandal stamped upon my brow,
For what care I who calls me well or ill,
So you o'er-green my bad, my good allow?
You are my all the world, and I must strive
To know my shames and praises from your tongue;
None else to me, nor I to none alive,
That my steeled sense or changes right or wrong.
In so profound abysm I throw all care
Of others' voices, that my adder's sense
To critic and to flatterer stoppèd are.
Mark how with my neglect I do dispense:
  You are so strongly in my purpose bred
  That all the world besides methinks th'are dead.

THE difficulties caused by both line 8 and line 14, and the arguments for and against the emendation of line 14, are well laid out by Booth, though I cannot agree with his retention of *y'are;* I have adopted Evans' *th'are* ("they are"). Booth has also written illuminatingly on the sonnet's various schemes of antithetical words *(love/pity, well/ill, bad/good, shames/praises, right/wrong, critic/flatterer, alive/dead).* The central word linking octave and sestet is *sense*, which in its first appearance is general in meaning (Steevens in 1780 translated *steeled sense* as "stubborn resolution," as Booth notes), but in its second appearance denotes the single sense of hearing, predicated of the adder which could stop its ears at will. Though Booth suggests possible puns on *world*/word, *sense*/sins, and *voices*/vices, such hovering puns, if they exist, do not help to explain the presence in the poem of such strange words as *steeled, abysm, adder's, dispense,* and so on.

It may be the speaker's self-representation as a deaf adder that introduces these words, with their persistent use of *s* and its compounds, as an onomatopoetic suggestion of a snake's hiss: *impression, scandal, stamped, calls, so, must, strive, shames, praises, else, steeled, sense, changes, so, abysm, others' voices, adders, sense, stopped, dispense, so, strongly, purpose, besides, methinks.* There are other sonnets with equal numbers of *s*'s and *sh*'s, of course, but the sounds are perhaps more audibly foregrounded here by such unusual words as *abysm* and *adder's sense*, and by the visible chain of initial *st* words *(stamped, strive, steeled, stoppèd, strongly).*

The antitheses scattered through the sonnet are placed both within and outside the speaker, and their equivocal locations seem to populate the world with either/or choices. Only the beloved seems at first to reconcile these antitheses, expressing both love (for the good in the speaker) and pity (for the speaker's "brand"), overgreening the speaker's bad and allowing his good.

Yet soon the beloved, too, joins in the either/or world, uttering mixed *shames* and *praises* to which the speaker must attend by responding with changes in his otherwise "steeled" sense. In this uncertain world (the poem suggests), one never knows, even with one's beloved, whether one will hear shames or praises, criticism or flattery. A later sonnet (121) will reply to worldly criticism, *No, I am that I am,* and will not resort, as this one does, to sequestering the self privately with the beloved. If 112 did not include *shames*, the sonnet could have preserved a safe place to hide within the dyad of lover/beloved. While the beloved was content to *o'er-green* the bad, instead of blaming it, the speaker was safe; but surely to know one's *shames* from another's tongue is to hear blame expressed by that tongue.

The reiterative nature of the sestet—it reinscribes Q_2's *you are* and *all the world,* and repeats Q_1's *what care I* as *I throw all care;* it repeats Q_2's *steeled sense* as *adder's sense*—suggests that something vital has not yet been said in Q_1 and Q_2. The octave had carefully distinguished between the beloved and everyone else, asserting that the speaker would attend *only* to the beloved. Q_3, on the other hand, with its image of the totally deaf adder, suggests that the speaker refuses to hear any voice at all. Perhaps this change occurs because the speaker has realized he will have to hear *shames* as well as *praises* from the beloved. In any case, while in the octave the speaker was exclusively listening to the beloved, he now seems to be neglecting the beloved's voice (whether it appears as critic or flatterer, shaming or praising) along with all the others.

This necessitates the apology in lines 12–14. How do I explain my neglect of you as well as of everyone else? I do it thus: you are already within me, not outside me. The two phrases *you are* and *all the world* were conjoined in the octave: *you are my all the world.* Yet in the couplet, they have been disjoined, with *you are* in line 13 and *all the world* in line 14, where *all the world* now excludes the beloved. Earlier, the speaker had said "I am alive to none except you." Now he is saying, "No one is alive to me but you, because you are within me."

It is a backhanded way to make the beloved be the speaker's all-the-world. The dyad now, on both sides, excludes everyone else; and the speaker lays entire claim to the beloved. *Bred/dead* has occurred as a couplet rhyme before, in 104 and 108, and the paradoxical conjunction of origin and end clearly appealed to Shakespeare.

To make *You are so strongly in my purpose bred* mean "You are so strongly incorporated in myself" is probably no more tortured than other readings of the couplet. After all, the young man has been busy with love and pity, filling in the brand of scandal, "o'ergreening" the speaker's faults. He has shown himself (except when recalling *shames*) to be strongly bred in the purpose of the speaker. As for the speaker's explanation in the couplet, it is difficult to see why the speaker should have to excuse himself to the beloved for "neglect" if he has been neglecting only *other* people. *All the world . . . methinks th'are dead* is another way of saying line 7, *None else to me, nor I to none alive*, preserving the dyad. If everyone else is dead, *shames* are no longer relevant.

The attempt to reduce the world to the I-you dyad tries to salvage some remnant of society for the speaker. The living couple in the dead world is a prize requiring a self-mutilation and species-reduction on the part of the speaker, as he demeans himself by resigning his sense of hearing and turning himself emblematically into an adder, deaf to the social world. For a writer (especially a dramatist) to stop listening to the world is to dry up a vital source of language. If he were merely adopting an attitude of indifference *(what care I who calls me well or ill)*, he would hear voices and disregard them. But the intensification of *what care I* into "In so profound abysm I *throw all care*" entails the willed deafness which replaces indifference. Thus is constructed the paradox *you are my all the world* ending *all the world besides . . . th'are dead. All the world* is mightily shrunken; and it will eventually shrink to a world of the speaker alone in sonnet 124, though the dyad returns almost hopelessly in 125.

Couplet Tie: *all the world* (5, 14)
you are (5, 13)

113

Since I left you,mine eye is in my minde,
And that which gouernes me to goe about,
Doth part his function,and is partly blind,
Seemes seeing,but effectually is out:
For it no forme deliuers to the heart
Of bird,of flowre,or shape which it doth lack,
Of his quick obiects hath the minde no part,
Nor his owne vision houlds what it doth catch:
For if it see the rud'st or gentlest sight,
The most sweet-fauor or deformedst creature,
The mountaine,or the sea,the day,or night:
The Croe,or Doue,it shapes them to your feature.
Incapable of more repleat,with you,
My most true minde thus maketh mine vntrue.

Since I left you, mine eye is in my mind,
And that which governs me to go about
Doth part his function, and is partly blind,
Seems seeing, but effectually is out;
For it no form delivers to the heart
Of bird, of flow'r, or shape which it doth latch;
Of his quick objects hath the mind no part;
Nor his own vision holds what it doth catch:
For if it see the rud'st or gentlest sight,
The most sweet-favoured or deformèd'st creature,
The mountain, or the sea, the day, or night,
The crow, or dove, it shapes them to your feature.
Incapable of more, replete with you,
My most true mind thus maketh mine eye untrue.

THE aesthetic effect here arises from the contrast between octave and sestet. In the octave, the speaker, away from the beloved, is simply incapable of registering the outside world at all. Not only does the eye not deliver to the *heart* or the *mind* the *quick objects* of its sight, but it cannot hold onto those objects even for its *own vision*, so preoccupied is the speaker with his inner sight of the beloved.

The sestet explains why the sight itself does not properly retain its objects: it transforms every object, however unlikely, into something resembling the beloved. The faithful mind, filled to repletion by the image of the beloved, can hold nothing else. (I accept the usual emendation, in line 14, of *mine* to *mine eye;* and the emendation of *sweet-favour* to *sweet-favoured*, for parallelism with *deformèd'st creature*.)

By calling the transformative eye *untrue* at the end, the speaker labels metaphor a falsification. As the eye lights on a dove, it says, "In this way the dove resembles my beloved"; it no longer *sees*, but *sees as*. The objects named in the octave are common, natural, agreeable objects of metaphor, to which Shakespeare has himself often resorted. One can accept the generalization of such gentle and sweet-favored *form[s]* as *bird* or *flower* as metaphors for the beloved, but it is harder to imagine (and the next sonnet immediately raises the question) how *rude* or *de**form**ed* creatures, introduced in the sestet, can serve the metaphorical purpose of assimilating all that is seen to some version of that Platonic form, the friend.

Blindness to *form* organizes the octave, whereas distortion of form *(de**form**ation)* organizes the sestet. The inner disturbance aroused by the recognition of distortion ("untruth") causes the sestet to instance the *rud'st* sight first, thus setting the chiastic pattern noted by Booth *(rud'st, gentlest, sweet-favoured, deformèd'st; day, night, crow, dove)*, in which the second chiasmus reverses the bad/good order of the first, making the transformations even more unsettling. As Booth notes, there is a speed-up in the instances of transformable sights in the sestet, and this too suggests the lightning sleight-of-hand by which every perception is reshaped into a simulacrum of the friend. The octave, by contrast, is concerned exclusively with lack expressed in negatives: sight delivers *no form* to the heart; mind has *no part* in sight's objects; *nor* does the eye's *own vision* hold onto what it catches.

This lack is, in effect, blindness; but blindness is perhaps preferable to the dizzy prestidigitations of Q_3. The word linking the octave and Q_3 is *shape[s];* it is a stable noun in the octave, but an active verb in the disturbing Q_3. The couplet sums up the octave by another lack-word: the mind is *in-capable* (< *capere*, "to catch") *of more* (sights). It sums up Q_3 by a fullness-word, *replete* (< *replere*, "fill up"). *You* in line 13 now means "you in all the metaphorical shapes I have cast you in, using every perception of the world that my eye has taken in since I left you." The eye, no longer objectively seeing the world, is now *untrue*, as by a pathetic fallacy it shapes its every sight to one feature.

There is a complacency in the final paradox which will not be allowed to persist. (Sonnet 114 will disengage the sense of madness which distorted vision brings with it, and will question further the veracity of metaphor.) In structure, 113 uses a shape like that of 66, a vastly unsymmetrical proportion of 1-11-2. The last line (as emended) arrives at a near-chiastic symmetry: *true, mind, mine eye, untrue*. After the initial statement of visual dislocation *(eye in mind)*, the poem devotes itself to the consequent irregularities of perception. The last line does not dispute the vagaries of visual response (it concedes that *mine eye* is *untrue*) but the epigrammatic complacency of l. 14 suggests that this is no longer matter for anxiety, as it was earlier. The speaker is reassured by realizing that his mind is still *most true*, and that it is in fact the troth of the mind that is responsible for the *untru*[th] of perception. These concerns will be raised, far more darkly, in 114, 148, and 152.

Couplet Tie: *eye* (1, 14)
mind (1, 7, 14)
you [*your*] (1, 12, 13)

The symmetry of this Couplet Tie supports the emendation *eye* in line 14.

114

OR whether doth my minde being crown'd with you
Drinke vp the monarks plague this flattery?
Or whether ſhall I ſay mine eie ſaith true,
And that your loue taught it this *Alcumie?*
To make of monſters,and things indigeſt,
Such cherubines as your ſweet ſelfe reſemble,
Creating euery bad a perfect beſt
As faſt as obiects to his beames aſſemble:
Oh tis the firſt, tis flatry in my ſeeing,
And my great minde moſt kingly drinkes it vp,
Mine eie well knowes what with his guſt is greeing,
And to his pallat doth prepare the cup.
  If it be poiſon'd, tis the leſſer ſinne,
  That mine eye loues it and doth firſt beginne.

Or whether doth my mind, being crowned with you,
Drink up the monarch's plague, this flattery?
Or whether shall I say mine eye saith true,
And that your love taught it this alchemy,
To make of monsters, and things indigest,
Such cherubins as your sweet self resemble,
Creating every bad a perfect best
As fast as objects to his beams assemble?
O 'tis the first, 'tis flatt'ry in my seeing,
And my great mind most kingly drinks it up;
Mine eye well knows what with his gust is 'greeing,
And to his palate doth prepare the cup.
  If it be poisoned, 'tis the lesser sin
  That mine eye loves it and doth first begin.

THE too easy explanation in 113 of visual falsification—"My eye, while you're away, shapes everything to your feature and reports a world identical to you"—is here replaced by a tenacious fear of being given, by the eye, a permanently false view of the objective world. This fear is no longer visual, however, but moral. Has moral sight been deceived by visual sight? To transform a "rude creature" like a crow into one's beloved ("The glossy wing of the crow is his raven hair") has no ethical import. But what if one's eye deliberately misrepresents the moral *monsters and things indigest* of the world as harmless or beautiful so as to make them agreeable to the obsessed mind? This *alchemy* is dangerous, even poisonous.

The interesting asymmetrical structure of the sonnet, 2-2-4-6, displays its logical alternatives, as shown in the diagram.

Structure of Sonnet 114

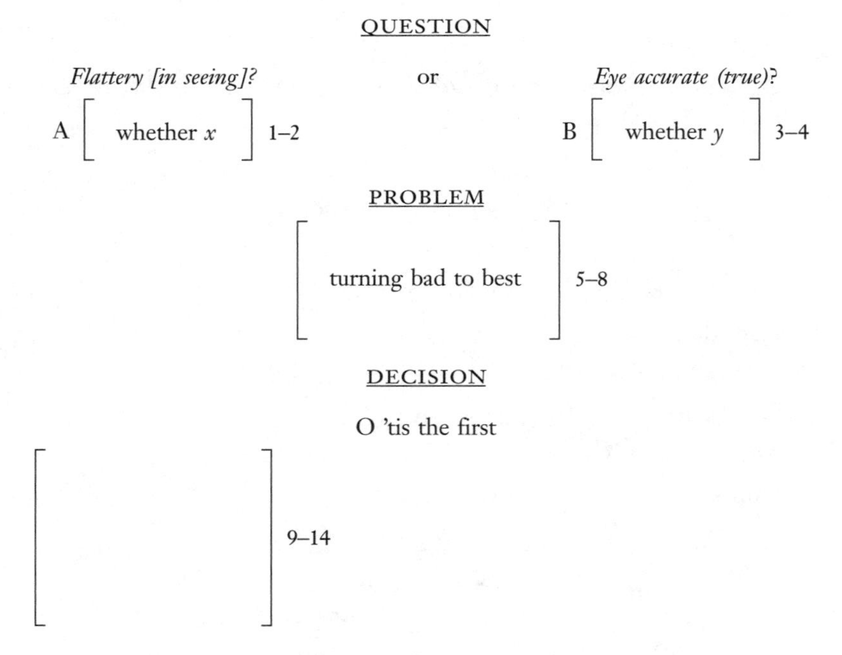

The eye, a servile courtier, serves up to the mind what will please, what the mind demands. The mind has become a monarch to whom the truth is never disclosed; the monarch is told only what he wants to hear, shown what he wants to see. Here, he drinks the cup prepared to his liking by the servile eye. (The phrase *drink up*—phonetically incorporating *cup* in line 2, though not in line 10, where it appears as *drink it up*—and the words *flattery*, *mind*, and *eye* link the octave and Q_3.)

His in lines 11–12 refers to the mind; the eye, knowing the taste *(gust)* of the mind, prepares the cup to suit the mind's palate. But the couplet adds the sinister fact that the corrupt servitor has even preceded his master in relishing the poisoned cup. The complex Couplet Tie (*'tis*, 9, 9, 13; *mine eye*, 3, 11, 14; *love* [*-s*] 4, 14; *first*, 9, 14) in effect emphasizes the conclusion "'Tis mine eye loves first." The anterior corruption of the eye is suggested by the rhymes of Q_2, *resemble* and *assemble*, both incorporating the French root *sembler*, meaning "to seem"; and the apparently perfect graphic congruence between the endings of *re-semble* and *as-semble* dissimulates their different etymological provenances (the first from *similis*, "similar," the second from *simul*, "together"). The sound pattern in unvoiced and voiced *k/g* (suggested perhaps by the word *king*) may help to explain some of the odder word choices: *crowned*, *drink*, *plague*, *alchemy*, *creating*, *objects*, *great*, *kingly*, *drinks*, *gust*, *greeing*, *cup*.

The moral inquiry of the poem, as the speaker catches himself creating *perfect best* from *every bad*, ends in a moral suicide; the mind knowingly drinks the poisoned cup, calling that moral monster, the young man, a cherub (the cherubim are the most exalted of the nine orders of angels). Such, at least, is the speaker's underlying fear, though the poem still strives, by separating the idea "I transform monsters into cherubim" from the idea "cherubim resemble you," to separate monsterhood from the young man.

The strategy of separating the ego into *mind* and *eye* (successful in 113, where the only appearance of the undivided ego occurs in the first line, *Since I left you*) cannot be sustained in 114, where the integrated ego tries to decide between the alternatives offered in Q_1. This dilemma of the disintegrating ego is emphasized by the pun which distinguishes-while-identifying mental and visual activity *(I say/eye saith):* "Or whether shall *I say* mine *eye saith* true." The "I" must, it thinks, decide between truth and falsity, and its intolerable alchemical attempts at turning "lead" monsters into "gold" cherubim, *bad* into *best*, must be brought to an end. The speaker's decision that his eye does not see true, that he will continue to accept *flattery*, is thus justly seen as suicidal *(poison)* to the would-be integrated ego. The speaker abandons his original reputation-saving division between mind and eye, as both are now seen to be corrupt. Originally, the eye was thought to be a passive learner from love: *your love* (with the usual ambiguity—"my love of you," "your love of me") *taught it* (mine eye) *this alchemy*—but now the eye itself is seen to be the agent of appetite *(mine eye loves it)*. The moral outrage of being taken in by *monsters and things indigest*, which has briefly appeared in Q_2, is stifled in the cup of continued and acquiescent erotic self-deception, guided by slavish visual worship, the eye's initial capitulation to the physical beauty—resembling that of the cherubim—of the young man. Infatuation is preferred to moral acuity, and by the end, self-loathing for immoral complicity has replaced the original moral loathing of *monsters* like the young man.

Though the speaker still proposes the flattering unction that sins of the flesh (here, the eye) are *lesser* than sins of the mind, the cup of flattery has been prepared by the eye to accord with the *palate* of the (sardonically described) *great mind;* and so we may deduce that the mind has become as corrupt as the eye. The sonnet exposes a sin of the spirit as much as of the flesh, and the couplet's excuse has been vitiated by the picture of the actively cooperating mind in Q_3. (Booth is surely wrong to call this anguished and self-lacerating poem an "inevitably barren, self-consciously cute, basically frivolous exercise in intellectual ingenuity.")

Couplet Tie: *mine eye* (3, 11, 14)
love [-*s*] (4, 14)
'tis (9, 9, 13)
first (9, 14)

115

Those lines that I before haue writ doe lie,
Euen those that said I could not loue you deerer,
Yet then my iudgement knew no reason why,
My most full flame should afterwards burne cleerer.
But reckening time, whose milliond accidents
Creepe in twixt vowes, and change decrees of Kings,
Tan sacred beautie, blunt the sharp'st intents,
Diuert strong mindes to th' course of altring things:
Alas why fearing of times tiranie,
Might I not then say now I loue you best,
When I was certaine ore in-certainty,
Crowning the present, doubting of the rest:
  Loue is a Babe, then might I not say so
  To giue full growth to that which still doth grow.

Those lines that I before have writ do lie,
Even those that said I could not love you dearer;
Yet then my judgement knew no reason why
My most full flame should afterwards burn clearer.
But reckoning Time, whose millioned accidents
Creep in 'twixt vows, and change decrees of kings,
Tan sacred beauty, blunt the sharp'st intents,
Divert strong minds to th'course of alt'ring things—
Alas, why, fearing of Time's tyranny,
Might I not then say "Now I love you best,"
When I was certain o'er incertainty,
Crowning the present, doubting of the rest?
  Love is a babe: then might I not say so,
  To give full growth to that which still doth grow.

THE major aesthetic strategy in 115 is the change in love-analogy between the body of the sonnet and its couplet. The body of the poem resorts to standard metaphorical descriptions of love (a burning *flame*, lovers' *vows*), while the couplet resorts to the mythological image of Cupid *(love is a babe)* in order to solve its mock-dilemma, "Why was it illegitimate of me in the past to write *'Now I love you best'?*" The poem is also structured by the speaker's mock-search for an appropriate *verb* for "love." He tries *burn* (attended by Shakespeare's usual formula for amplitude, a comparative—*clearer*—tacked amendingly onto a superlative—*most full*), and he makes various hyperbolic declarations—"*I could not love you dearer*" and "*Now I love you best*"—but finally settles on a verb of progressive action, *grow. To grow* (like *to brighten, to wane*, etc.) is a word-in-motion with a potentially infinite extent: one cannot give "full growth" to *grow*. Whereas the body of the poem attempts to fix love in temporality, in a "now," the couplet offers it an open-ended perpetual crescendo.

The problem is phrased as a problem first of writing *(writ)* and then of saying *(said)*; the implied fixity of writing is rejected in favor of the provisionality of saying. One can perhaps see SAY as a KEY WORD, appearing thrice as itself *(said, say, say)* and once, in Q_2, in covert form within ***sa**cred* (cf. *ob**liv**ion* in 55).

Everyone has remarked the ungrammaticality of Q_2, unanchored as it is to the rest of the poem. It is worth saying that the sense of the poem is entirely complete without Q_2, and that we cannot explain its presence in terms of logic alone. Q_2 is one of the quatrains which immensely enlarge the scope of the poems in which they occur, like Q_1 of 19, *Devouring Time*. Here, Q_2 brings in monarchic authority, religious images, and intellectual power, all powerless against the effects of *reckoning Time*.

Judgement, knew, reason: these three judicious words bound the rational world, but Time's calendrical *reckoning* is of a different order of reason entirely. Logically speaking, the poem is torn between its intuitions about Time (which run to destructiveness) and its surprise that Time has for once acted creatively, causing love to grow. The lover's wish to fix the day of greatest happiness before time's accidents *creep in 'twixt vows* has made him write a false poem, saying, "I could not love you dearer," the cause of his *Alas*. The undisturbed growth of love, however, simply means that it has so far escaped an encounter with one of Time's *millioned accidents*, its *tyranny*. The *factual* growth of love has absolutely no stabilizing effect on the speaker's metaphysical knowledge of Time's destructive potential, and so the unsettling effect of the poem remains in place, with fact *(growth)* and possibility *(accidents)* in perpetually unstable relation to each other.

One can't doubt that the "best writing" in the poem comes in the rapid and savage inventory of Q_2, with its successive verbs and verbally derived words. These words are so metaphorically incoherent that they forbid all attempts at intelligible reconstruction. On the one hand, time *reckons*, a word suggesting intelligibility; but on the other hand, its occurrences are *accidents* (< *ad* + *cadere*, "how things fall out"), and these accidents, in a wonderful series of catachreses, variously *creep*, *change*, *tan*, *blunt*, and *divert*. Because there are *million[s]* of these accidents, we are to understand that the list of catachrestic verbs could be infinitely extended.

The millioned *accidents* in Q_2 are played off first against Q_1's emotional stasis. That stasis was expressed by the denial of comparative increase to the lover's superlatives (the *most full* flame could not burn *clearer*, he could not love him *dearer*). *Accidents* are also played off against C's predictable-in-a-babe *physical growth*, which is far more stable than love's possible growth. In short, the incompatibilities of the poem arise from a confusion of categories. Emotion is made by Q_2 into simply another vulnerable temporal event, but made by C into a knowable biological development. The underlying question, then, is "Under which categorical rubric is 'Love' best placed?" The lover has been thinking of it as a temporal event, like vows, subject to Time's tyranny; now he learns he is to think of it in mythological terms, and consider it a biologically growing infant in mythological (Cupid) guise. He neglects to say whether mythology is subject to Time's tyranny, however, and the couplet seems a forced compliment rather than a satisfactory ending.

As we read Q_3, it sounds like (and is, in part) a reprise of Q_1. However, if we fit an overlay of Q_3 on Q_1, we see that a new ingredient—present at the time of Q_1 but omitted (repressed?) in the formulation of Q_1—has been added. This new element is represented by the words *fearing of Time's tyranny*, *incertainty*, and *doubting of the rest*. In short, as we hear Q_1, it tells of a lover who, knowing no reason why his love should ever be stronger, celebrates that climactic moment in a jubilant verse. As we read Q_3, it tells of a lover who, fearing that his love can only go downhill from its present strength, commemorates the peak moment elegiacally. The chaotic set of fears expressed in Q_2 thus can be seen as the real motive for Q_1; repressed in Q_1, fear bursts out in the ungrammatical and unanchored *But* of Q_2.

The encouraging and complimentary emphasis of Q_1, then, must turn mournful and foreboding in its reprise in Q_3. C returns to the *judgement* and its *reasons:* "Now I know a reason my love can burn clearer as time goes on: because it's governed by a waxing verb, *grow*, rather than by a steady-state verb, *burn*. Back then, *my judgement knew no reason why.*" The "reason" is given by the perhaps proverbial *Love is a babe*, triumphantly "quoted" as if now a sufficient "reason" has been found never again to write, *either* jubilantly *or* elegiacally, "*Now* I love you best."

DEFECTIVE KEY WORDS: THEN, LOVE (both missing in Q_2, the quatrain interrupting the narrative of *love* as it was *then*)

KEY WORD (perhaps): SAY [SAID] [SAcred]

Couplet Tie: *then* (3, 10, 13) (listed because emphasized)
love (2, 10, 13)
say [*said*] (2, 10, 13) and possibly
***sa**cred (7)*
full (4, 14)

116

Let me not to the marriage of true mindes
Admit impediments,loue is not loue
Which alters when it alteration findes,
Or bends with the remouer to remoue.
O no,it is an euer fixed marke
That lookes on tempests and is neuer shaken;
It is the star to euery wandring barke,
Whose worths vnknowne,although his higth be taken.
Lou's not Times foole,though rosie lips and cheeks
Within his bending sickles compasse come,
Loue alters not with his breefe houres and weekes,
But beares it out euen to the edge of doome:
If this be error and vpon me proued,
I neuer writ,nor no man euer loued.

Let me not to the marriage of true minds
Admit impediments; love is not love
Which alters when it alteration finds,
Or bends with the remover to remove.
O no, it is an ever-fixèd mark
That looks on tempests and is never shaken;
It is the star to every wand'ring bark,
Whose worth's unknown, although his heighth be taken.
Love's not Time's fool, though rosy lips and cheeks
Within his bending sickle's compass come;
Love alters not with his brief hours and weeks,
But bears it out even to the edge of doom.
If this be error and upon me proved,
I never writ, nor no man ever loved.

THIS famous almost "impersonal" sonnet on the marriage of true minds has usually been read as a definition of true love. That is, most readers decide to see the poem (guided by its beginning) as an example of the genre of definition, and this initial genre-decision generates their interpretation. Let me begin by saying that I read this poem as an example not of definition but of dramatic refutation or rebuttal.

The aesthetic motivation governing 116 springs (as I hope to show) from the fiction of an anterior utterance by another which the sonnet is concerned to repudiate. My interpretation—suggesting that the usual interpretation is untrue, and not simply incomplete—springs from reading along a line of difference: the quatrains differ powerfully from one another. Also, there are too many *no*'s and *nor*'s, *never*'s and *not*'s in this poem—one *nor*, two *no*'s, two *never*'s, and four *not*'s—for it to seem a serene one. The prevalence of negation suggests that this poem is not a definition, but rather a rebuttal—and all rebuttals encapsulate the argument they refute. As we can deduce the prior utterance being rebutted (one made, it seems reasonable to assert, by the young man), it has gone roughly as follows:

> "You would like the marriage of minds to have the same permanence as the sacramental marriage of bodies. But this is unreasonable—there are impediments to such constancy. After all, persons alter; and when one finds alteration, one is himself bound to alter as well; and also, people (or some qualities in them) leave, and one's love is bound to remove itself when the qualities of one's lovers remove. I did love you once; but you have altered, and so there is a natural alteration in me."

It is the iambic prosody that first brings the pressure of rhetorical refutation into Shakespeare's line: "Let *me* not to the marriage of true minds / Admit impediments." The speaker says these lines schematically, mimicking, as in reported discourse, his interlocutor's original iron laws of expediency in human intercourse: "To find alteration is to alter; to see a removal is to remove." (This law is, on the part of the young man, a self-exculpating move; we see in it a grim parody of the laws of true reciprocity proposed throughout the *Sonnets.*) And yet we are struck by the dreadful plausibility of the young man's laws: they read like laws of mathematics. Alter the left side of the equation, and you will alter the right; remove X from the left, and of course something must vanish from the right. Alteration causes altering; removers cause removing.

On the other hand, it is not very clear what the young man has had in mind in framing his laws. What is all this vague talk of altering and removing? Of course one who argues as the young man does has something specific in mind (usually a new erotic attachment), but prefers to cloud it under large self-excusing generalizations. And the one who disingenuously argues for "impediments" must have some of his own in mental reserve.

The speaker's first technique has been to replicate the dishonest discourse of his interlocutor by mimicking it, even quoting it:

> Let *me* not to the marriage of true minds
> Admit "impediments": love is *not* love
> Which "alters when it alteration finds,"
> Or "bends with the remover to remove,"
> O *no!*

However, the speaker's own denial, using the given schematic terms of his opponent, is unsatisfactory, because it simply accepts the terms ("altering," "removing") already established by another, giving them the lie direct. Shakespeare therefore makes his speaker move (in obedience to well-known oratorical principles) away from the negative refutation of his opponent to a positive refutation couched in new terms, apparently his own—"O no, it is [rather] X." The speaker leaves behind the as-yet-unclarified abstractions of vague "alterations" and "removers" in favor of his own emblematic North Star, a navigational *fixèd mark.* (I see no reason to interpret *mark* as "lighthouse"; when Shakespeare means "lighthouse" he says *sea-mark.*) We can see, however, that even that star-symbol has itself been conjured up by his opponent's terms. *Alteration* has engendered *ever-fixèd* (used proleptically of the fixed North Star); and against the linear *remove,* the speaker sets a circular *wandering* that may err but cannot, thanks to the star, ever be permanently lost. Love, in terms of this positive refutation, is said to be able to look unshaken not only on those vaguely euphemized "alterations" and "removes" but on very tempests. And love does not fall within those grimly calculable materialist laws invoked by the young man: though it is describable, it is inestimable.

We now come, pursuing a reading for difference, to a reinscription in the poem of a previous pattern: the third quatrain repeats, in briefer form, the pattern of negative refutation followed by positive assertion which the preceding two quatrains had initiated. In this way, as reinscription, this quatrain initiates our sense of the poem as repetitive—as something that is reinscribing a structure which it has already used once. The poem says yet again, "Love is not X, but rather Y."

But the third quatrain is not simply a rhetorical restating of those two threatening words *alter* and *bend* (so undefined in the young man's utilitarian rhetoric). The two words are now unpacked in their full significance as they are reinscribed in the poem. The *remover* who *bends* turns out to be the grim reaper, Time, with his *bending* sickle. What *alters* are Time's *brief hours and weeks.* (The indignant speaker will not dignify time with seasons and years, not to speak of epochs and ages; time, so important to the young man, is to be denigrated, to be denied all majesty and power.) Only the Day of Judgment (invoked from the sacramental liturgy of marriage) is the proper measure of love's time. The speaker calls on Saint Paul as witness that love bears all things (the Geneva Bible had "endureth"; the Authorized Version only later [1611] substituted "bears"). What then is this talk of removal?

Q_3 departs from its function as reinscription of Q_2 in considering the merit of the young man's view. It begins by keeping up the vehemence of refutation, remaining within the debater's genre; but suddenly, a new concessive appears as one had earlier—in line 8's *although his heighth be taken.* The young man is granted another point. Something in fact, it is true, *is* removed; something, it is granted, comes into the bending compass of the sickle. The thing that the young man values, that he has in mind with his occluded talk of "alteration" and "removes," turns out to be physical beauty, *rosy lips and cheeks,* which, it is conceded, fall to Time's sickle. The speaker cannot deny the actual truth of those removals, but the concession is a painful one. The young man, even though concealing his motives behind his euphemizing vagueness, has been exposed (by this unpacking-by-reiteration of his very words *alters* and *bends*) as a man in thrall to the sensual bloom of youth; when he sees the sickle bend, he must, he has said, bend with it, remove himself when he sees beauty removed, and find another as-yet-unreaped beauty. (The speaker's tenderness toward the young man forbids his showing narratively, or in prophecy, the destruction of sensual beauty in the young man; he admits here only the general law, that within the compass of the sickle all sensual beauty falls.)

Once the speaker has admitted the tragic law of the destruction of physical beauty, he cannot forget it. Love can now no longer be the superlunary fixed star contemplating from above even tempests unmoved; it becomes instead, in the second positive refutation, the human endurer, bearing it out, in the same horizontal plane in which life is lived, even to the edge of doom. In changing its mind about the proper description of love, this sonnet of reinscription (wherein the early impediments cited by the vague young man are resummoned and made explicit in their specific reference to time and physical aging) also exhibits an authorial pentimento, by which a love first described in transcendent vertical terms as a secular Petrarchan fixed star subsequently takes on the immanent horizontal Christian Pauline form of stoic fidelity in endurance.

The couplet of this sonnet is at once a legal challenge in equity and a last refutation (and implicit condemnation) of the position of the young man. The young man has, after all, said, "I did love you once, but now impediments have arisen through alterations and removes." The speaker argues by means of the couplet that the performative speech-act of Platonic fidelity in quasi-marital mental love cannot be qualified; if it is qualified, it does not represent love. Therefore, if he himself is in error on the subject of what true love is, then no man has ever loved; certainly the young man (it is implied) has not loved, if he has not loved after the steady fashion urged by the speaker, without alteration, removals, or impediments. The poem entertains, in the couplet, the deconstructive notion of its own self-dissolution; the impossibility of error is proved by the contrary-to-fact hypothesis, *I never writ.* The triple negative here *(never, nor, no)* is the last signal of the refutational rhetoric or the poem, linking the couplet to all the *O no*'s, *never*'s, and *not*'s that precede it.

I think it important that we see the speaker savagely clarifying, with his rephrasing into the visibly pictorial emblematic form of Time, the vague "alter" and "bend" of the disingenuous young man. But of course the hyperbolic, transcendent, and paradigmatic star is the casualty of the refutational reinscription contained in the third quatrain. The vertically conceived star cannot be reinscribed in the matrix of the metonymic hours and weeks of linear sublunary mortality. Stars are not present at the edge of doom; the burdened pilgrimage to that utmost verge is human, stoic, and linear. The star lingers, semi-effaced, a rejected model.

Without the differential model of refutation, reinscription, and authorial rethinking, the poem is imperfectly seen; we cannot judge its representational aim. No reader, to my knowledge, has seen *Let me not to the marriage of true minds* as a coherent refutation of the extended implied argument of an opponent, and this represents an astonishing history of critical oversight, a paradigmatic case of how reading a poem as though it were an essay, governed by an initial topic sentence, can miss its entire aesthetic dynamic. Because many readers still seek, in the anxiety of reading, a reassuring similarity of patterning among quatrains rather than a perplexing difference, and prefer to think of the *Sonnets* as discursive propositional statements rather than as situationally motivated speech-acts, we remain condemned to a static view of any given sonnet. It is as useful to ask of each sonnet what form of speech-act it performs as to ask what aesthetic problems generated the poem as their exfoliated display; but these are not the same question, though they are often related. Here, the speech-act we call refutation could equally well, for instance, have been carried out entirely in the first person, as it is in the following sonnet *(Accuse me thus)*. To discuss the aesthetic problems set by Shakespeare in writing the sonnet, we must ask first the reason in decorum for the use of the impersonal definition-form governing the middle ten lines; next the reason for the necessity of doubling the definition-form, so as to offer negative definitions as well as positive ones; and third, why the negative-positive arrangement had to be done *twice*, so as to make two negative and two positive refutations in lieu of one of each. There are various answers to these problems; I am concerned only that they should be named as problems. We can perhaps see the indecorum of insisting entirely in the first-person singular on the exclusive worth of one's own fashion of loving (though the speaker resorts to that move in the couplet); but the problem of the two refutations doubled is a more interesting one, as is the necessity for the reinscription (as I have called it) of the young man's vague words *(alter; bend)* in the full clarity of their exposure as they are given, in the person of the grim reaper, emblematic form.

The chilling impersonality of the hideous implied "law of alteration and removal" gives a clue to the sort of language used by the young man which is here being refuted, just as the speaker's first refutational metaphor, the metaphor of transcendent worth, establishes another form of diction wholly opposed to the young man's sordid algebraic diction of proportional alteration. The second refutational passage, in the third quatrain, proposes indirectly a valuable alternative law, one approved by the poet-speaker, which we may label "the law of inverse constancy": the more inconstant are time's alterations (one an hour, one a week), the more constant is love's endurance, even to the edge of doom. The impersonal phraseology of law, at first the young man's euphemistic screen for his own infidelity, is triumphantly but tragically modified by the speaker into the law of constancy in trial. That is, the reinscription (using *alters* and *bending*, adapted from *alters*, *alteration*, and *bends*), not only brings out the latent significance of these euphemistically disguising words, but also (by proposing a different "universal" law) reinscribes with new significance the very structural form (an invariant law) of the young man's objections. The model which I call "reinscription," then, consists here of a first message about alteration and bending inscribed in the implied form of a self-serving law, and a second message about alteration and bending inscribed in the form of a constancy-law. We can now see why the transcendent metaphorical star alone could not refute the young man: he had to be refuted in his own temporal and metonymic terms, as the identical form (a "law" of physical necessity) of the reinscribed message indicates.

The young man, by his mentioning of "impediments," has announced the waning of his own attachment to the speaker, dissolving the "marriage of true minds." It is not surprising to see, in the following sonnets, the young man's attempts to project the blame for his own faithlessness on the speaker (117), and the speaker, taking his cue, acting out his own infidelities (118).

DEFECTIVE KEY WORD: LOVE [-D] (missing in Q_2) (Since I can see no cause for its absence in Q_2, I conclude this effect may be accidental. On the other hand, a portmanteau *lover* may have been expanded in Q_2 into ***look never***.)

Couplet Tie: *love* [*-d*] (2, 2, 9, 11, 14)
no (5, 14)
never (6, 14)
ever (5, 14)

117

ACcuſe me thus,that I haue ſcanted all,
Wherein I ſhould your great deſerts repay,
Forgot vpon your deareſt loue to call,
Whereto al bonds do tie me day by day,
That I haue frequent binne with vnknown mindes,
And giuen to time your owne deare purchaſ'd right,
That I haue hoyſted ſaile to al the windes
Which ſhould tranſport me fartheſt from your ſight.
Booke both my wilfulneſſe and errors downe,
And on iuſt proofe ſurmiſe,accumilate,
Bring me within the leuel of your frowne,
But ſhoote not at me in your wakened hate:
Since my appeale ſaies I did ſtriue to prooue
The conſtancy and virtue of your loue

Accuse me thus: that I have scanted all
Wherein I should your great deserts repay,
Forgot upon your dearest love to call,
Whereto all bonds do tie me day by day;
That I have frequent been with unknown minds,
And given to time your own dear-purchased right;
That I have hoisted sail to all the winds
Which should transport me farthest from your sight.
Book both my wilfulness and errors down,
And on just proof surmise accumulate;
Bring me within the level of your frown,
But shoot not at me in your wakened hate:
Since my appeal says I did strive to prove
The constancy and virtue of your love.

SONNET 117 offers, like 116, a rebuttal of an anterior discourse by the young man, who has said, in rather artificially equalized two-line indictments:

> "You have scanted all wherein you should repay my great deserts. You have forgotten to call upon my dearest love, to which all bonds tie you day by day. You have been on familiar terms with unknown minds, and given to time the hours which are my dearly purchased right. You have hoisted sail to all the winds which would transport you farthest from my sight."

The sonnet spends its whole octave quoting the reported discourse of the accusatory young man, in another of Shakespeare's wonderfully devised strategies of having him condemn himself through his own mean-spiritedness. It is only after the octave that the speaker's voice proper, heard up to now only in the first three words of the poem, enters in summarizing fashion, continuing the series of concessive verbs that began with *Accuse*, saying,

> "Yes, [accuse me in all these ways,] do an inventory of my willfulness and errors, heap up suspicion on the basis of what you've found, frown on me, but don't shoot at me in hate. My defense is that I did what I did as a test of the constancy and virtue of your love."

The overlap between 117 and 116 in topics, diction, and imagery, noted by Booth, is used by Booth to comment that "in 116 the speaker is grand, noble, general, and beyond logic; in 117 he is petty, particular, and narrowly logical." To my mind, neither characterization is true. Sonnet 117, like 116, is an exposure of the young man's ignoble nature. The speaker never quite admits guilt. His appeal asserts only that he strove to prove the young man virtuous and constant, but he gives no particulars of his own actions. He invites the young man to accumulate *surmise* (conjectural inferences), but only upon *just proof.* No *just proof* has been proffered as yet by the young man, at least not in the discourse we have heard reported. The young man has accused the speaker of insufficient attendance upon him, of spending hours away from him (perhaps with others, but the young man seems unable to name them), of engaging in undertakings that have distanced him from the young man. None of this "proves" anything about the speaker's previous whereabouts and company; it suggests only that the young man is feeling insufficiently courted. Both the vehemence of the young man's apparently groundless accusations (since absence does not necessarily denote either lustful *wilfulness* nor moral *errors*) and the extent of his own self-regard ("You have scanted my great deserts," etc.) lead us to question his position. He is an accuser uttering without proof his bill of attainder; he is full of suspicion (accumulating surmises); he is setting himself up as a judge *(frown; appeal);* he even sets himself up as a potential executioner, ready to *shoot* with *hate.* He may even have employed spies ("You have been frequent with unknown minds," says he; how does he know?).

The young man has invited no explanation from the speaker, has proffered in friendship no plausible excuses for him, has not tendered forgiveness. He has, in short, shown no signs of past, present, or future love for the speaker. Instead, he has shown fury *(hate)*, suspicion, jealousy, and wounded self-esteem.

In his sestet of response, the speaker recalls to the young man his (previous) oaths of constancy to the speaker and virtue in love. The speaker thus utters the only rebuke possible to his superior's *great deserts.* To be upbraided in this fashion by a superior, and to be unable to defend oneself (except by the quiet insertion of *just* and *proof* into this atmosphere of vague hyperbolic accusation) is to find no solution except to call upon the strength of the beloved's past vows of constancy. (I take "accumulate surmise on just proof" to mean "on just proof, *if you have it.*")

Even if one adopts an alternative explanation—that the speaker is guilty as charged, and is blaming himself, and that such words as *great deserts* and *dearest love* are editorial interpolations by the speaker into the young man's reported discourse, still the young man's accusations come thick and fast, with not a mention of excuse, forgiveness, love, or welcome.

The speaker's eleven-line string of apparent abject concessions, positively phrased *(accuse, book, accumulate, bring)* is counterweighted, before the couplet, with one closing negative plea *(shoot not)*, so that the rhetorical structure of the sonnet becomes 11-1-2.

The Couplet Tie is *love* (3, 14) and *prove* [*proof*] (10, 13), suggesting the quarrel between the young man's absence of *proof* and the speaker's appeal to some proof of *love.* It is the vulgarity of the young man's diction that chiefly condemns him. (He sounds like an irate parent, quoting proverbs, "You've hoisted sail to all the winds," and haranguing, "God knows with whom you've been spending your time," and "Is this what I deserve from you?" etc.) By contrast, the dignity of the language of the speaker—"I strove to prove your constancy and virtue"—while it may represent a specious excuse, still appeals to a side of the young man that his hectoring accusations have not revealed.

Couplet Tie: *love* (3, 14)
prove [*proof*] (10, 13)

118

LIke as to make our appetites more keene
With eager compounds we our pallat vrge,
As to preuent our malladies vnſeene,
We ſicken to ſhun ſickneſſe when we purge.
Euen ſo being full of your nere cloying ſweetneſſe,
To bitter ſawces did I frame my feeding;
And ſicke of wel-fare found a kind of meetneſſe,
To be diſeaſ'd ere that there was true needing.
Thus pollicie in loue t'anticipate
The ills that were,not grew to faults aſſured,
And brought to medicine a healthfull ſtate
Which rancke of goodneſſe would by ill be cured.
  But thence I learne and find the leſſon true,
  Drugs poyſon him that ſo fell ſicke of you.

Like as to make our appetites more keen
With eager compounds we our palate urge,
As to prevent our maladies unseen
We sicken to shun sickness when we purge:
Even so, being full of your ne'er–cloying sweetness,
To bitter sauces did I frame my feeding,
And, sick of welfare, found a kind of meetness
To be diseased ere that there was true needing.
Thus policy in love, t'anticipate
The ills that were not, grew to faults assured,
And brought to medicine a healthful state
Which, rank of goodness, would by ill be cured.
  But thence I learn, and find the lesson true,
  Drugs poison him that so fell sick of you.

THE specious argumentation of 118 is a form of apology for infidelity. Its strategy for excusing the taking of malign *drugs*, or sampling other loves, is based on its alternation of various "non-I's" with the "I." Q_1 refers to what *we* normally do to aid health in the habitual present, and Q_2 follows this with what *I* did of that sort, but smoothly translated to the emotional realm, as though such a translation (highly dubious) went without saying. Q_3 then says what *policy in love* did (phrasing it in the past tense so that we assimilate Q_3 with the past-tense Q_2, even though Q_3 has abandoned the first person of Q_2). Finally, C returns in line 13 to the first person, as the *I* affirms the lesson learned; and then the lesson is summed up in line 14 in a third-person "objective" form.

The aesthetic problem posed by such a structure is that of the anomaly of Q_3. The "normal" structure of such a poem of self-defense would be "Just as 'we' do this in ingestion, so '*I*' did it in love; but *I* have learned it doesn't work in love as it does in ingestion." A reader is thrown off stride by the departure of Q_3 from the first person, and further disturbed by the strange interpenetration in Q_3 of metaphorical and literal elements, preventing a distinct picture of the two analogized units, ingestion and love.

The confusion arises in part because the generalized "ingestion of drugs," a supercategory, is never mentioned at the start. Rather, two of its subcategories are invoked as if in improvisational fashion, an excuse "making itself up as it goes along." The speaker first mentions the ingestion of an appetite stimulant (an *eager compound*) and next, the ingestion of a laxative (a *purge*). The structure imposed by this imagery is as follows:

Ingestion of Drugs

Appetite Stimulant		*Laxative*
1–2 (eager compounds)	⟶	3–4 (purge)
Love Stimulant		*Disease*
5–6 (bitter sauces)	⟶	7–8 (diseased)

So far, the analogies between ingestion and misbehavior have, with some strain, been maintained: the *bitter sauces* resemble the *eager compounds*, and *diseased ere . . . needing* matches *sicken to shun sickness.* However, Q_3 moves away from the vocabulary of appetite and sickness into a more complex vocabulary mixing cunning *(policy)*, moral evaluation *(faults, goodness)*, medicine *(medicine, healthful, cured)*, and the grandly applicable-to-all-realms *ill(s).*

At this nexus, the carefully drawn *like as . . . even so* pretense that digestion and sexual morality are separable realms which can be made analogous to each other breaks down. The genre of homily demands exempla, of which lines 1–8 offer a fair sample; but poetry prefers the undifferentiated—and therefore mentally stimulating—chaos of the mixed metaphor, found in the nexus of Q_3. Though C returns to an apparently tame "lesson" couched in the single compartment of medicinal terms (*drugs, poison,* and *sick*), abandoning the decompartmentalizing of Q_3, the sting in its tail is the word *poison,* pointing to a degree of "ill" not previously envisaged. If not dying, the speaker is at least poisoned; the word *poison* generates its etymological source-word, *potion,* in the next sonnet.

The analytic mode adopted by 118 mimics, in genre, the explanation of a penitent who has "learned his lesson." It therefore follows various exculpatory defensive moves:

1. My sexual peccadillo is really as minor as what we all do in drinking an apéritif or taking a preventive laxative;
2. After all, you *can* metaphorize infidelities as "feeding on different sauces" or "preventive purges";
3. I thought infidelity was a "medicine" I was taking, and I thought if I took up other attachments it would either help our love toward keener appetite or prevent our becoming too "involved."

Casting these arguments in the "we" or "policy in love" or "he" form, in lieu of the "I" form, makes them of course both slippery and self-serving; and we can scarcely trust the tortured logic that produces phrases like *full of your nere* [Quarto spelling] *cloying sweetness* (which must be transcribed *ne'er* but may allow for the pun on *near*), *sick of welfare,* and *rank of goodness.* The speaker's real motives for the new attachments (sexual pleasure? boredom? a desire for variety? self-advantage?) cannot be admitted to the patron, ever, and so various transparently false motives are adduced, bringing with them their contorted analogies to palate-stimulations and preventive purgings.

Various plays on words link the parts of the sonnet. The word ***mal**adies* contains etymologically the French version *mal* of the words most repeated in the poem: *sick* [*-en*] [*-ness*] and *ill(s). True needing* and *les-*

son true have their antonym in *faults* (a homonym of *false*); *full* is echoed in *health**ful***, and *welfare* contains *well* within it. Q_3 conspicuously does not exhibit the word *sick* so prominent in Q_1, Q_2, and C; but it seems haunted by the phoneme [si], unable to attach [k] to its several appearances in *poli**cy***, *anti**ci**pate*, and *medi**ci**ne*, but letting [k] erupt in the violently unexpected word *rank*.

The phrases *sick of welfare* and *rank of goodness* sum up the psychological knot confronted by the poem. How can one tire of well-being and goodness? How can one turn against them and seek out "diseased" loves? The psychological mastery of the sonnet lies in its seeing one's ennui with *welfare* as itself a sickness, like loss of appetite or indigestion. When putative *health* is a *sick*ness, and *cures* are *disease[s]*, there is scant hope for a better future state. And indeed, all hope of the future, after the chaos of Q_3, is given up in the couplet, where the anterior lovesickness, bad enough in itself, has led to the drugs by which the speaker announces that he has been *poison[ed]*—apparently a terminal state, since no prospect of cure is announced. This confession of infidelity forbodes the end of the Young Man sonnets.

DEFECTIVE KEY WORD: SICK [-EN] [-NESS] (missing in Q_3, the quatrain describing the state anterior to the ingestion of the sickness-producing drugs)

Couplet Tie: *sick* [-*en*], [-*ness*] (4, 4, 7, 14)
true (8, 13)

119

WHat potions haue I drunke of *Syren* teares
Diſtil'd from Lymbecks foule as hell within,
Applying feares to hopes,and hopes to feares,
Still looſing when I ſaw my ſelfe to win?
What wretched errors hath my heart committed,
Whilſt it hath thought it ſelfe ſo bleſſed neuer?
How haue mine eies out of their Spheares bene fitted
In the diſtraction of this madding feuer?
O benefit of ill, now I find true
That better is, by euil ſtill made better.
And ruin'd loue when it is built anew
Growes fairer then at firſt,more ſtrong,far greater.
So I returne rebukt to my content,
And gaine by ills thriſe more then I haue ſpent.

What potions have I drunk of Siren tears
Distilled from limbecks foul as hell within,
Applying fears to hopes, and hopes to fears,
Still losing when I saw myself to win!
What wretched errors hath my heart committed,
Whilst it hath thought itself so blessèd never!
How have mine eyes out of their spheres been fitted
In the distraction of this madding fever!
O benefit of ill: now I find true
That better is by evil still made better,
And ruined love when it is built anew
Grows fairer than at first, more strong, far greater.
So I return rebuked to my content,
And gain by ills thrice more than I have spent.

IN SONNET 119, the speaker's use of the present perfect *(have drunk, hath committed, have been fitted)* in the "sinning" octave "sets up" the enlightened *now* of the sestet. This is, then, a post-facto description of infatuations which have led one away from true love and have even *ruined* true love in the process. Before this poem of retrospect begins, however, the *ruined* love (according to the speaker) has been *built anew*, and has improved its former status (fair, strong, great) to an increasingly superior present condition *(fairer, more strong, far greater)*. There is something *voulu* about this assertion.

The triple gain ("gain *thrice* more") mentioned in the couplet is generated not only by the triple comparatives, just mentioned, of line 12, but also by the triple "evils" of the octave: (1) drinking potions, (2) committing errors, (3) allowing one's eyes to be distracted (< *dis-trahere*, "to drag"). A large amount of self-exculpation enters into this confession of "evil": the *Siren tears* had presumably the power of magic over the helpless speaker, the imbibing heart was deceived (thinking itself *blessèd*), and a *madding fever* was the infectious agent of the eyes' (involuntary) distraction from their spheres.

Sonnet 119 is one of those poems which, like 30, set up a many-paneled past. Here, reading backward from a "now" established in the first line of the sestet, is an analysis of the successive time-frames of the poem:

T5	T4	T3	T2	T1
Now	*Rebuilding Phase*	*Phase of Ruin*	*Phase of Ruining*	*Intact Love*
love fairer more strong far greater	love built anew	ruined love	tears, errors, fever	love fair strong great

The multiple temporal phases are kept in play all through the sonnet; even the couplet moves from the present tense *return* to a backward glance—via the last verb, the present perfect *have spent*—at the present perfects of the beginning *(have drunk, hath committed)*.

Booth gives a convincing account of the multiple puns in *benefit*, *bene fitted* (Quarto spelling), and *made better*; and of the play on *hell/ill/evil*. It remains to be added that *ill* seems to govern the running choice of many words: *dis**till**ed*, *hell*, *st**ill***, *wh**il**st*, *ill*, *ev**il***, *st**ill***, *bu**il**t*, *ills*.

On the octave's temporal structure of multiple phases of past time is superimposed another structure, this time the structure of illusion versus reality:

	Q_1	Q_2 *(lines 5–6)*	Q_2 *(lines 7–8)*
Illusion:	seeing oneself winning	thinking self blessèd	["love"]
Reality:	losing	committing wretched errors	eyes out of spheres by fever

It will be seen by the bracketed word ["love"] under "Illusion" in Q_2 that by the time of the third stage of "evil," there is no illusion left: the speaker does not say, "How have mine eyes been fitted out of their spheres by this fever [*while all the time I thought I was seeing heavenly sights*]." The interesting use of the present perfect (*have drunk*, etc.) instead of the possible preterite ["What potions *did I drink;* what errors *did I commit;* how *were* my eyes *fitted*"] puts the sonnet into the "waking-up" phase, where one is within a durational moment that contains past action as still included within present contemplation.

In terms of syntactic structure, three sentences compose the octave, each ending with a question mark in the Quarto (lines 4, 6, 8), but now conventionally given an exclamation point. (One might prefer to retain the question mark, if one wants to read this, as the present perfect suggests, as a waking-up poem, asking "What have I done?") Each of the three exclamations describes one of the "evils" committed by the speaker, and they chart, taken together, the coming-to-consciousness of the speaker—who may remind us of the implied speaker of 129. Because 119, like 129, opens in self-disgust, Q_1 gives most of its lines, in general, to self-rebuke, and the *bliss* and *joy* that 129 will recall as authentic parts of lust creep here into Q_1 only in the brief close *I saw myself to win*. Q_2 begins with rebuke but immediately adds deluded nostalgic reminiscence, *While it hath thought itself so blessèd never!* One might expect by sequential extrapolation that lines 7–8 would be all nostalgic reminiscence, but instead they are all rebuke, with no recollection at all of the rewarding illusions (winning, blessedness) of the *madding fever.* In short, the delights of infatuation (including those *hopes* that alternated with fears) are tucked away in the middle of the octave, and the octave as a whole is framed by repentance. The early frenzied alternation of infatuation and withdrawal is mimicked by the poultice-like circular act of *Applying fears to hopes, and hopes to fears.* This gives way to the simultaneous overlay of (a) illusory conviction ("I *saw myself* to win") on fact *(losing);* and (b) illusory estimation ("my heart *thought itself* blessèd") on fact *(errors).* These in turn are followed by the suppression of *any* mention of internal illusion at all in lines 7–8.

This gradual waking-up to the utter disappearance of illusion, enacted by the theatrical octave, prepares the way for the sobriety of the sestet, which presents the simple word *ill* (line 9) as the true name for all the previous melodramatic words: *potions . . . of Siren tears, wretched errors, madding fever.* The anterior appearances (chiefly in *distilled* and *still*) of *ill* have prepared us for the word *ill* in line 9, and account for the conclusive sound of the word *ill* when it first falls on our ears.

When we compare the exclamatory, theatrical, self-dramatizing octave to the sober, "adult," proverbial sestet, we see that the person speaking has not integrated the two selves represented by the two halves of the poem. The sober, rebuked, bettered self hardly knows, any more, the earlier deluded, thrashing, fevered self. Self 2 simply abjures self 1. In 129, the structure of the ego is far more complexly presented, and the putative speaker knows all the sides of himself equally—retrospectively, chronologically, and ironically.

The speaker resorts to the proverbial to exemplify the repentant self in the sestet of 119 (see Evans, and cf. Herbert, "Fractures well cured make us more strong"). And the tone of the proverbial is very strongly conveyed by the gnomic formulation of line 10—*better is by evil still made better*—for which, though no one among sonnet editors has found such a proverb, one can imagine various proverbial forms ("Better is bettered by evil"; "Evil makes better better," etc.). The introduction to line 10, *Now I find true,* alleges that this is an old saw which has *now* been proved true upon the pulse of experience. The closing line, "[I] gain by ills *thrice more* than I have spent," also has, with its fairy-tale *thrice,* a folk-wisdom ring. Use of the proverbial about himself by a speaker is always a sign of his rejoining common wisdom, of leaving the error of his former ways (as a rolling stone or a too-early counter of eggs), of acquiescing in the conventional. No irony is here attached, I think, to this acquiescence. But the strain of abjuring the former self pictured in the octave "shows through" in the two too-brief "proverbs" of the sestet.

If we attempt to distinguish among the three "proverbial" moments of the sestet, those threefold gains of the repentant lover, we can see that the first and third are the more "proverbially phrased"—epigrammatic, balanced, shrewd. But the second is descriptive, eloquent, and fresh—what Herbert would call "new, tender, quick":

And ruined love when it is built anew
Grows fairer than at first, more strong, far greater.

Shakespeare takes advantage here of the progressive sense of *grow* as he had used it in 115 *(that which still doth grow)* and adds to it the persistent comparatives *(fairer, more strong)*, ending in an intensified comparative, ***far*** *greater*. When he made up his own "new" proverbs (lines 10, 14), Shakespeare made them rhetorically "proverbial"; but when he took an old proverb, he vivified it into a growing beauty of love, as each phrase enacts the continued development not only of grandeur (from *fair* to *strong* to *great*) but also of intensity of growth (*-er, more, far -er*). If it were not for this enactment of hope, one would scarcely credit the economy of better made better by ill.

KEY WORD: ILL (if one accepts its "hidden" forms below)

Couplet Tie: *ill* [*-s*] (9, 14); see also *distilled* (2), *hell* (2), *still* (4, 10), *whilst* (6), *evil* (10), *built* (11)
have I [*I have*] (1, 14)

120

THat you were once vnkind be-friends mee now,
And for that ſorrow , which I then didde feele,
Needes muſt I vnder my tranſgreſſion bow,
Vnleſſe my Nerues were braſſe or hammerèd ſteele.
For if you were by my vnkindneſſe ſhaken
As I by yours , y'haue paſt a hell of Time,
And I a tyrant haue no leaſure taken
To waigh how once I ſuffered in your crime.
O that our night of wo might haue remembred
My deepeſt ſence,how hard true ſorrow hits,
And ſoone to you,as you to me then tendred
The humble ſalue,which wounded boſomes fits!
But that your treſpaſſe now becomes a fee,
Mine ranſoms yours,and yours muſt ranſome mee.

That you were once unkind befriends me now,
And for that sorrow which I then did feel
Needs must I under my transgression bow,
Unless my nerves were brass or hammerèd steel.
For if you were by my unkindness shaken
As I by yours, y'have passed a hell of time,
And I, a tyrant, have no leisure taken
To weigh how once I suffered in your crime.
O that our night of woe might have rememb'red
My deepest sense, how hard true sorrow hits,
And soon to you, as you to me then tend'red
The humble salve which wounded bosoms fits!
But that your trespass now becomes a fee;
Mine ransoms yours, and yours must ransom me.

LIKE 90, this is a fantasia on *wo[e]* (line 9), adding to it ***now***, *sorrow*, ***bow***, *how*, *sorrow*, ***wounded***, *now*. The imaginative fiction is a parodic rendition of *mutual render* (125) in which what is here rendered is trespass for trespass, transgression for transgression, as the past unkindness of the friend is recalled to excuse the recent unkindness of the speaker. Yet even in this episode of specious reciprocity, trading wrong for wrong, we find a modulation in Q_3 toward mutuality, in the brief pang of recourse to the first-person plural, *our*, which intimates a juncture between lovers rather than the distributive I-you pattern which rules the rest of the poem. If we ask why the moment of juncture, of "we-ness," can arrive only in Q_3, we immediately see that what distinguishes Q_3 from the other parts of the sonnet is its absence of blame. Phrases elsewhere—*You were unkind, my transgression* (Q_1); *my unkindness, I a tyrant, your crime* (Q_2); *your trespass, mine* (C)—imply legal, religious, and social sanctions which have been violated. But Q_3 refers—in *our night of woe, true sorrow, humble salve, wounded bosoms*—only to the realm of feeling, in which regret for causing emotional sorrow overpowers all ideas of what is owed or due by religious, legal, or social standards.

This isolation of pure *woe* in Q_3, once we have noted it, puts into retrospective relief the anticipatory verbal presence of forms of woe in the earlier "offense" quatrains of the poem—in Q_1, the references to *unkind[ness], sorrow*, and *nerves;* in Q_2, mention of *unkindness* and *suffer[ing]*. C, however, is ruled by "offense" and its cancellation *(trespass, fee, ransom)*, suppressing emotional "woe" in favor of legal, economic, and social reference. This, then, is the "partitive" conceptual structure of the sonnet:

Q_1: woe/offense
Q_2: woe/offense
Q_3: woe
C: offense/cancellation of offense

What this "gross structure" omits is the appearance, in Q_3, of the "solution" to offense, which is the *humble salve* of sympathy. The friend had *tend'red* (the pun is deliberate) this sympathy to the speaker in the past, but the speaker has so far omitted to soothe with that salve his transgression against the friend. The contrary-to-fact framing of Q_3 ("O that our night of woe *might have remembered . . . and . . . tend'red*") means that the opportunity of *mutual render* on the level of "we-ness" has been missed. The couplet therefore must return to the I-you pattern, dropping all mention of salve, and simply urging that comparable trespasses must be allowed to cancel each other out. The *must* is a plea, not a necessity, unlike the earlier *must* (line 3).

The arrangement of the poem interweaves two situations: (A) *your* (past) *trespass;* and (B) *my* (recent) *transgression.* (A) took place *then;* (B) has recently taken place; and the time of the poem is (T) *now.* In the diagram, I have placed the implied within brackets, and the hypothetical and optative in italics.

Structure of Sonnet 120

(A) "YOUR TRESPASS"	(B) "MY TRANSGRESSION"	(T) NOW
You were once unkind		befriends me now
I did feel sorrow	my transgression	I must bow
I was shaken by yours [I passed a hell of time]	*If you were shaken by my unkindness y'have passed a hell of time*	
I suffered in your crime	[. . . how you have suffered in my crime]	I, tyrant, have taken no leisure to weigh . . .
You to me tendered salve	*O that our night of woe might have remembered my deepest sense, how hard true sorrow hits, and tendered salve*	
your trespass ——————→	——————→	becomes fee
yours ←(ransoms)——	mine	
yours —(must ransom)→	me	

The poem is a deliberately confusing one. It shuttles to and fro among its three time zones, (A), (B), and (T); and also shuttles, rhetorically, among the narrated, the implied, the contrary-to-fact, the hypothetical, and the optative. It also shuttles between *I/you* and *our.* It connects abuse (***h**am-merèd*, ***h**ell*, ***h**ard*) with remedy (***h**umble*). And even in its final mutuality-of-offense-and-ransom, it confuses by its pronominal asymmetry. The couplet "should" read in one of two ways:

> [Mine ransoms yours, and yours must ransom mine.]
> *or*
> [Mine ransoms you, and yours must ransom me.]

Instead, it puts the whole selfhood of the speaker *en jeu:* "Yours [*your trespass*] must ransom *me.*" The final *me* looks back to the initial *befriend[ed], me;* the speaker realizes that he needs not only to be *befriended* but also to be *ransomed.* The friend needs only to have his offense ransomed, but the speaker needs to be ransomed in his entire self, bought back into the current of love.

Commentators have sometimes seen a Christian allusion in *ransom;* its derivation from *redemption* ("buy back") suggests the self-sacrifice that the offended and unsalved friend must make to let the memory of his own former trespass persuade him to restore the speaker to his *wounded bosom.* In that sense, there is a play on the economic and religious meanings of *ransom:*

> [My trespass] "buys back" yours,
> *and*
> [Your memory of your trespass] must "forgive/save" me.

The mixture of self-accusation (*my transgression*) and accusation (*your crime*) in the octave contributes to the mixed tonality of the poem, which breaks out of its neat antitheses of *then* and *now*, *mine* and *yours*, with startling and "excessive" phrases:

nerves [of] brass or hammerèd steel
by my unkindness shaken
a hell of time
I, a tyrant
your crime
how hard true sorrow hits

The resulting aesthetic effect is one of schematic rationalization achieved over a distraught undertone. The surprise of finding *weigh how once I suffered* where one expects "weigh how you must be suffering" reinforces the illogical logic of repentance, accusation, plea, and self-reproach all combined, retained even in the unsettling asymmetry of the apparently "pat" couplet. The *must* of the couplet, though deceptively phrased like the *must* of *must bow* in line 3, is in fact quite different: the first *must* is one of necessity *(needs must)* while the second, as I have said, is an implicit plea for a future pardon. Shakespeare puns even on auxiliary verbs.

Couplet Tie: *now* (1, 13)
must (3, 14)
It might be proper to add, since they here bear emphatic weight:
you [-*r*] [-*s*] (2, 5, 6, 8, 11, 11, 13, 14, 14)
I [*me*] [*my*] [*mine*] (1, 2, 3, 3, 4, 5, 6, 7, 8, 10, 11, 14, 14)

121

TIS better to be vile then vile eſteemed,
When not to be,receiues reproach of being,
And the iuſt pleaſure loſt,which is ſo deemed,
Not by our feeling,but by others ſeeing.
For why ſhould others falſe adulterat eyes
Giue ſalutation to my ſportiue blood?
Or on my frailties why are frailer ſpies;
Which in their wils count bad what I think good?
Noe, I am that I am,and they that leuell
At my abuſes,reckon vp their owne,
I may be ſtraight though they them-ſelues be beuel
By their rancke thoughtes,my deedes muſt not be ſhown
  Vnleſſe this generall euill they maintaine,
  All men are bad and in their badneſſe raigne.

'Tis better to be vile than vile esteemed,
When not to be receives reproach of being,
And the just pleasure lost, which is so deemed
Not by our feeling but by others' seeing.
For why should others' false adulterate eyes
Give salutation to my sportive blood?
Or on my frailties why are frailer spies,
Which in their wills count bad what I think good?
No, I am that I am, and they that level
At my abuses reckon up their own;
I may be straight though they themselves be bevel;
By their rank thoughts my deeds must not be shown,
  Unless this general evil they maintain:
  All men are bad, and in their badness reign.

THE tissue of language in 121 is more than usually complex. In the Quarto spelling we see (a) a gradual play on the word *vile*, (b) a chain of *r*'s and *b*'s, and (c) a scrambling of the elements of *raigne*, the closing word.

vile	*__rece__ives*	better	*st__raig__ht* [r-a-i-g]
vile	*__re__proach*	be	***generall*** [r-a-g-n-e]
rece__ive__s	*__reck__on*	be	***raigne*** [r-a-i-g-n-e]
spor__tive__	*__ranck__e*	being	
fra__il__ties	*__rai__gne*	by	
fra__iler__		by	
wils		blood	
levell		bad	
selves		be	
bevel		be	
evill		bevel	
		by	
		be	
		bad	
		badness	
		a-buses	

Live hovers unseen, I believe, under *vile*, and the concealed KEY WORD "IL[L]" plays hide-and-seek throughout the poem. Even the *-ign* of *raigne* is only the transposal of the *-ing* in *being, seeing, feeling*. Against these orthographic intricacies the opening of the sestet—*No, I am that I am*—rings out with all the force of its stark biblical language. (It does not, I think, benefit from Booth's suggestion of the pun "I AM WILL I AM"; this is too stark a moment for concealed levity. There may, however, be a pun in the preceding line: "Which in their *wills* count bad what I [*Will*] think good.")

The sonnet revolves around statements of what is *count*[*ed*] bad versus what *is* bad ("All men *are* bad"), around perceived ill-doing *(vile esteemed)* and true ill-being *(be[ing] vile)*. Appearance and reality, old themes in the *Sonnets*, but earlier expressed in metaphors like *show* versus *odour* or *shadow* versus *form*, are now thrust nakedly and literally on the page. The speaker's defiant urge to bareness of expression *(I am that I am)* reduces even the loftily literary *evil* to the low vernacular *bad* at the end. But against these very plain moments ("be *vile . . . vile* esteemed"; "*not to be . . . being*"; "[they] count *bad* what I think *good*") are set the arabesques of contrasts, relative valuations, distinctions, questions, subordinate clauses, compound verbs, etc. It is an amazing counterdance, which sets the semantic simplicity of the counters *(bad, good; being, esteeming; being, not being; feeling, seeing; straight, bevel; thoughts, deeds)* against the paradoxical propositions made with them (lines 1–2, 9–12).

The personal relations between others *(they)* and the speaker *(I)* revealed in Q_2 have, it appears, stimulated the impersonal bitter generalizing of Q_1. This back-to-front arrangement, whereby judgment (Q_1) precedes motivation (Q_2), keeps the "mystery" of the assertions in Q_1 afloat through the two questions of Q_2. However, there is a discrepancy between the situation described in Q_1 and that in Q_2: in Q_1 the *others* seem morally neutral, merely onlookers who are esteeming the speaker to be vile. In Q_2, the speaker asserts that it is *they* who are vile, with their *false adulterate eyes*, and their constitutions *frailer* than his own. He offers, of course, no proof for this assertion; it is projected from his anger at their estimate of him. So far, the sonnet consists of accusation and counter-accusation, both unsupported.

Q_3 introduces a cleverer account of the situation: "By accusing me, they indict themselves." The opening choice—"'Tis better *to be vile* than vile esteemed"—is forsaken in favor of the choice to be one's moral self (*sport**ive***, perhaps; with *fra**ilties***, perhaps; but not *vile*, escaping vileness always by a significant graphic fraction). *I am that I am* is indisputable; *I may be straight* is also indisputable unless the axiom "All men are bad"—the implicit motto of the calumniators—is true. The couplet would therefore read:

> Unless this general evil they (of the *rank thoughts*) maintain:
> "All men are bad," and in their badness reign.

The sonnet is overwhelmingly concerned with valuation: its verbs of choice are *esteem, reproach, deem, spy on, count bad, think good, reckon up*, and *show*. "Their estimate of me," "My estimate of them"—how are these related, and by what standard can that relation itself be judged? *The just pleasure* we receive from being judged correctly by others is useless as a moral confirmation of our own worth, since we may well never receive it.

If moral beauty lies in the eye of the beholder, then it will never be found by these calumniators, who project their own *rank thoughts* on what the speaker *think[s] good.* The persistent sestet association of *evil*—and its anagrams and analogues—with those "others" (in *level*, *-selves*, *bevel*, and *evil*) exonerates the speaker from connection with the bad, rendering the calumniators' motto untrue (since the four total letters of "evil" are never associated with the speaker).

Booth thinks that *I am that I am* makes "the speaker sound smug, presumptuous, and stupid." I cannot agree: to me the speaker sounds as if he is getting a third wind. The first "wind" was, "I'd rather *be* vile"; the second was the semi-apologetic "*I* may be sportive and possess frailties, but *they* are adulterate and false and frailer"; the third jettisons both (1) having the game if you have the name, and (2) admitting to minor degrees of "vileness," in favor of (3) pure recognition of independent moral self-identity. I take *abuses* to be set in the quotation marks of indirect reported discourse: "They that level at my [so-called] 'abuses' [really] reckon up their own."

The anger in 121, marked by its bitter paradoxical opening, its indignant questions in Q_2, and its resolute declarations in Q_3, is converted to a sardonic irony in the strange and unexpected couplet, which in effect adopts satirically the motto of the calumniators, *All men are bad*, and makes the whole world subject to the evil others, *they.* There are two ways of reading line 14, depending on what you think the *others*' motto is: *either* they maintain that "All men are bad and in their badness reign" *or* they maintain that "All men are bad" and therefore the speaker concludes that they (the *others*) are the sovereigns of this kingdom of bad men, in which (by definition via their motto) both they themselves and the speaker are included. I am inclined, in spite of the absence of medial line-punctuation in the Quarto, to the second reading because of the speaker's former *Unless;* he would not necessarily be convicted of evil if the others simply uttered line 14 as their motto; but if they *both* utter the short motto *All men are evil* and *also* reign in their badness, then they win and the speaker loses. The Couplet Tie *their* (8, 12, 14) and *bad* [*-ness*] (8, 14, 14) emphasizes the link between *badness* and "them," acting as a sly ratification of the innocence of the *I.*

The moral desperation driving the first line of the sonnet—"'*Tis better to be vile* than vile esteemed"—shows extreme vulnerability to the judgment of others, one which reveals itself again in the phrase *my frailties* and the sentence *I may be straight* (in place of [*I am straight*]). I think that somewhere behind this sonnet lies the parable of the woman taken in adultery, and Jesus' adjuration, "Let him who is without sin cast the first stone." The closing motto of the evil men here says, "Anyone may cast a stone at the sins of others, because no one is virtuous; all are bad." One can read the couplet as the speaker's own suspicion that in fact no one, including himself, is innocent; after all, the *others* have not enunciated their own motto—he has invented it for them. In that case, his initial despair at being judged evil, and even his defense of a transparent selfhood *(I am that I am)*, are undermined.

Couplet Tie: *their* (8, 12, 14) (because of emphasis)
bad [*-ness*] (8, 14, 14)

122

T Thy guiſt,,thy tables,are within my braine
Full characterd with laſting memory,
Which ſhall aboue that idle rancke remaine
Beyond all date euen to eternity.
Or at the leaſt,ſo long as braine and heart
Haue facultie by nature to ſubſiſt,
Til each to raz'd obliuion yeeld his part
Of thee,thy record neuer can be miſt:
That poore retention could not ſo much hold,
Nor need I tallies thy deare loue to skore,
Therefore to giue them from me was I bold,
To truſt thoſe tables that receaue thee more,
To keepe an adiunckt to remember thee,
Were to import forgetfulneſſe in mee.

Thy gift, thy tables, are within my brain
Full charactered with lasting memory,
Which shall above that idle rank remain
Beyond all date, even to eternity;
Or, at the least, so long as brain and heart
Have faculty by nature to subsist;
Till each to razed oblivion yield his part
Of thee, thy record never can be missed.
That poor retention could not so much hold,
Nor need I tallies thy dear love to score;
Therefore to give them from me was I bold,
To trust those tables that receive thee more:
To keep an adjunct to remember thee
Were to import forgetfulness in me.

THE word *rank*, appearing with different meanings in 118 and 121, makes a third appearance (in a new meaning) here, confirming the way in which Shakespeare's mind dwelt on the potential semantic riches in a single word.

The speaker apologizes for having given away *thy gift, thy tables*, and offers two (ingenious and perhaps specious) reasons for his "offense": (1) his memory can store more than the tables' *poor retention;* (2) he could be accused of indifference to the young man—a willingness to forget him—if he needed to keep his tables to remember him by. Booth comments on the reversal of normal order by which one has to wait until line 11 to discover that the speaker has given away the young man's gift, and comments, too, on the deflation which occurs between lines 4 and 8, wherein the original claim—that memory will last *beyond all date, even to eternity*—declines into the claim that memory will, *at the least*, last as long as *brain* and *heart* have not yielded memory and affection to *razed oblivion.* But Booth does not comment on the cause for such deflation, nor on its connection with other oddities in the poem.

The poem is constructed around what is today called an absent center. The (legitimate) question of the young man, "Why did you give away my gift to you?" expects a factual and circumstantial answer; but of course no circumstantial answer—"I forgot they were a gift"; "They were useless to me"; "Someone asked me for them"—could be other than insulting. And so the circumstantial true answer is never given, and remains absent, stimulating substitutes for itself. Q_1, for instance, acts as a deflecting gesture into the rhetoric of "eternizing poesy," ending in an adjectival and adverbial crescendo which begins with *lasting*, moves into *beyond all date*, and climaxes with *to eternity*. As an answer to "Where are the tables I gave you?" this reply hovers at a plane far above that of the question.

The interrogator, with his factual question, no doubt responds with a lifted eyebrow to the hyperboles of Q_1, prompting the decline into the somewhat chastened "realism" of Q_2—"Well yes, I know, my brain and heart are only mortal, and so my record of you *isn't* of course eternal." From *lasting* to *at the least* is the measure of collapse here; and the poetic Latinate diapason of *Full charactered with lasting memory* subsides into the scholastic Latin tedium of *Have faculty by nature to subsist.*

Anticlimax is the trope of Q_2; the enjambments lead to collapses. We can see this best if we fill in what an "eternizing" diction (in square brackets) *might* have said in Q_2 versus what actually *is* said:

So long as brain and heart	[love on as strongly as they now do]
	have faculty in nature to subsist
Till each to razed oblivion	[yields, but with defiance and resistance]
	yield his part of thee
Thy record	[will endure forever]
	never can be missed

The denigration of the young man's gift in lines 3 and 9 *(that idle rank, that poor retention)* is not exactly a winning stroke in explaining the absence of the tables. Q_3 eventually departs from its disparagement of the gift—by which the *tables* were, by comparison to the brain, denigrated ("*poor* retention")—and moves to a rephrasing by which, in the sestet, the gift-tables come to occupy a neutral plane *(tallies, them, an adjunct)* while the brain-tables come to occupy a comparative plane of advantage: they *receive thee more.* The gift is thereby rescued from depreciation as such, and regarded as simply a mnemonic superfluity. In its final phase, the sonnet invents a playful compliment: "How could I ever forget you? To keep tables on which to tally your dear love would be to assume I need reminders of you—a clearly inconceivable situation."

These shifts by the speaker from strategy to strategy are Shakespeare's way of mimicking social unease, an unease prompted by the unanswerability (in factual terms) of "Why did you give away my gift?" As though to insist, over and over, that memory constantly renews the image of the young man, the poem emphasizes the particle *-**re**-*, present in ***re**main*, ***re**cord*, ***re**tention*, ***re**ceive*, ***re**member*, *sco**re***, *the**re**fo**re***, *mo**re***, and *we**re***.

A larger import hovers behind the specific question of the given-and-regiven tables. The *Sonnets* have consistently linked love to various material signifiers—the song of birds, the odor and hue of flowers, the distilled perfume of roses, the beauty of the Young Man's face, even the yellowed pages of the poet's verse in times to come. The end of the young man sequence, however, engages in a divestment of love from all such signifiers, as it rises above Time and its records (123), and all alone stands hugely politic (124). Eventually (126) it divests itself even of the young man in the two "missing" lines of the envoy. There is literally no more to be said after the young man himself is "rendered" by Nature to Time. The tablets may simply have been the first divestment, ending all materiality as a means of significance in order to pass to a nonmaterial and virtual realm *builded far from accident* (124). One could hardly explain such a motive to the young man.

Couplet Tie: *re-* (passim, because of emphasis)
memory [*remember*] (2, 13)

123

NO! Time, thou ſhalt not boſt that I doe change,
Thy pyramyds buylt vp with newer might
To me are nothing nouell,nothing ſtrange,
They are but dreſſings of a former ſight:
Our dates are breefe,and therefor we admire,
What thou doſt foyſt vpon vs that is ould,
And rather make them borne to our deſire,
Then thinke that we before haue heard them tould:
Thy regiſters and thee I both defie,
Not wondring at the preſent,nor the paſt,
For thy records,and what we ſee doth lye,
Made more or les by thy continuall haſt:
  This I doe vow and this ſhall euer be,
  I will be true diſpight thy ſyeth and thee.

No! Time, thou shalt not boast that I do change:
Thy pyramids built up with newer might
To me are nothing novel, nothing strange;
They are but dressings of a former sight.
Our dates are brief, and therefore we admire
What thou dost foist upon us that is old,
And rather make them born to our desire
Than think that we before have heard them told.
Thy registers and thee I both defy,
Not wond'ring at the present, nor the past,
For thy recórds, and what we see, doth lie,
Made more or less by thy continual haste.
  This I do vow and this shall ever be:
  I will be true despite thy scythe and thee.

THE zigzagging changes of person here from singular to plural are very visible, and establish the poem at once on two planes:

I		*we*
1–4	⟶	5–8
9–10	⟶	11–12
13–14		

What does the plane of common wisdom *(we)* have here to do with the plane of personal resolve *(I)?* Usually in poetry, and even in these *Sonnets*, the plane of common wisdom reinforces (by aphorism, apothegm, epigram, proverb, or ethical reflection) the "message" of the poem. Here, however, the *I* finally separates himself from the *we* of the common herd; the latter are deceived by "novelty," and do not realize there is nothing that history has not seen before. This would be clearer in the poem if the Q_1 statement *Thy pyramids . . . / To me are nothing novel* were followed by a third-person contrastive statement, saying [*The fools of Time are those who do admire / What thou dost foist upon them that is old.*] Instead, the speaker includes himself among those who are deceived by Time: *Our dates are brief, and therefore we admire / What thou dost foist upon us that is old.* In short, he is telling us of his own past: [*I have admired*] / *What thou [hast foisted on me] that is old, / And rather made [it] born to [my] desire / Than think that [I] before have heard [it] told.* But this newly wise speaker has lived through one cycle of "novelty," and so can, in the disabused Q_1, call the new pyramids *but dressings of a former sight.* In the past, the speaker has been impressed, but no longer; he asserts a superior view—that there is nothing new under the sun.

In his second (Q_2) invoking of the first-person plural, the *we* represents the (visually) deceived but mentally undeceived: *What we see doth lie.* Although the poem represents our deception as one arising from *both* sight and hearing *(we before have heard them told)*, sight plays a larger part than hearing, a part reinforced by the persistence of rhymes in *ī: might, sight; admire, desire; defy, lie.* These make the final standoff—*I . . . despite . . . thy scythe*—the more salient.

The sonnet is organized by rapidly altering temporal perspectives, as shown in the diagram.

Structure of Sonnet 123

Past	*Present*	*Future*
		shalt not boast I do [in future] change
	pyramids are nothing novel are dressings	
former sight	are / admire / foist	
what is old	make / think	
before heard told		
thy registers		
	defy / not wondering at present	
nor past		
thy recórds	what we see / doth lie	
made more or less		
	do vow	
		shall ever be I will be true

The constant perceptual shuttling between present and past that orders the main body of the poem is contained by firm future brackets, fore (line 1) and aft (lines 13–14), encapsulating Time's boast of the speaker's potential infidelity and the speaker's present vow which binds his personal future. *I do change* is punningly repudiated in *I do vow*, where the tense of *do* has changed from its implied future in *I do change* (since *do* is governed by *shall not*) to a present in *I do vow.*

Similarly, the comparative in *newer*, reinforced by the graphically parallel (noncomparative in meaning but "comparative" by the *-er* of its orthographic form) *former*, is canceled out by the denial of all meaningfulness to degrees of comparison in line 12: things and records are not really *more* or *less*, but are only made to appear so by the repetitive cycles of time foisted on human beings of such *brief dates.*

The Anglo-Latin pun *we admire / Not wond'ring* is appropriate to this sonnet of *nil admirari*, as are the comparable pairings *newer/novel* and *built up / dressings* (< French *dresser*, "to erect"). Time always brings out the

Latin side of Shakespeare, as his mind instinctively goes to Ovid, but then his English begins to confront it. Time's attributes are, in sequence, *thy pyramids*, *thy registers*, *thy recórds*, and *thy continual haste*—and though *haste* is Germanic, the others are suitably Egyptian and Latin. It is *Tempus* we meet in these attributes; but when we come to the last attribute, *thy scythe*, we meet the Anglo-Saxon *Time*.

The poem is a contest to decide which speech-act will win—Time's *boast* that the speaker, like everything else in Time's registers, undergoes change, or the speaker's *vow* not to change. Since Time's ultimate law is that of *change*, and since the speaker *will* change physically (he is subject to Time's scythe, like everything in Time's registers), his only available resistance is the verbal one symbolized by the performative *vow*, which as a speech-act and promise, inhabits that virtual realm where the scythe of material ruin has no power. The *vow*, or *votum*, is Latin; *true*, its content, is English.

Because lines 1–7 are concerned with monuments, the appearance in lines 8 and 10 of *registers* and *recórds* is at first puzzling. Registers and records are the apparatus of human chronicling, of history, rather than of Time per se. It is easy to say that because of the brevity of our temporal existence *(dates)*, we don't recognize that this is not the first time pyramids have been erected. As long as sight alone is in question, we can be deceived. But do not registers and records exist precisely to inform us that nothing is really new? It is as though the significant rhyme ***old/told*** in line 8 has summoned up—through the *old* in *told*, and through the faculty of listening-to-chronicles *(heard)* rather than seeing-sights—the question of the contents of registers and records. The first explanation of our credulity given by Q_2 is our *brief dates;* but I suggest that Q_3 elaborates the second explanation (given in the latter two lines of Q_2) that even when we hear it *told* by chroniclers that there have been, e.g., former instances of pyramids, we would rather believe that we were the first ever to see pyramids. Like the speaker, we therefore *defy* registers, and decide that *recórds lie*, because that is the way we would prefer to have things. The scorpion sting in Q_3 is the joining of both these *lies:* the lie that there *are* new things (the lie offered by *what we see*) and the self-deceiving belief that the *recórds lie* (because we want to be the first to see pyramids). The mixed true-and-self-deceiving state of mind with which the speaker utters the summary crucial line, *For thy recórds, and what we see, doth lie*, is the aesthetic triumph of the sonnet. *What we see* is *made more*, magnified by our willed ignorance that Time has actually done this pyramid trick before; *thy recórds* are *made less* by our wish to believe ourselves the first to see pyramids.

The *continual haste* of time both obliterates *former sight[s]* and allows the compiling of chronicles, which are repellent to our desire to inhabit first-ness, not to be belated. At the same time, the chronicles *lie* because they record nothing but change, and the speaker is proposing that there are some things, like his *vow*, that do not obey the "universal" law of change.

At first, the speaker seems to be adopting the distanced perspective of Time itself, to whom *nothing* is *novel, nothing strange.* The conspectus of all history seems to lie before the speaker's eyes. And yet, by Q_3, we see that Time's *haste*, its *continual* change of things to *more* themselves or *less* themselves, makes historiography the most unreliable of witnesses, as unreliable as our brief view of things during our lifetime. The speaker posits a perspective, finally, outside both that of Time itself and that of Time's chronicles: this is the virtual perspective of the immobility of the devoted will, which admits of no haste, no changing. This perspective is indeed *born to [his] desire*, a phrase implicitly redefined (by the couplet) from a state of self-deception to a state of "resolvèd will. " "I *will* be true; this I do *vow.*" When *desire* becomes *will*, when *vow[ing]* replaces yearning, then one has entered a nonmaterial realm of fidelity independent of mutability.

Couplet Tie: *I do* (1, 13)
Insofar as antonyms form a conceptual Couplet Tie, *lie* (11) and *true* (14) should be noticed here.

124

YF my deare loue were but the childe of ſtate,
It might for fortunes baſterd be vnfathered,
As ſubiect to times loue, or to times hate,
Weeds among weeds, or flowers with flowers gatherd.
No it was buylded far from accident,
It ſuffers not in ſmilinge pomp, nor falls
Vnder the blow of thralled diſcontent,
Whereto th'inuiting time our faſhion calls:
It feares not policy that *Heriticke*,
Which workes on leaſes of ſhort numbred howers,
But all alone ſtands hugely pollitick,
That it nor growes with heat, nor drownes with ſhowres.
  To this I witnes call the foles of time,
  Which die for goodnes, who haue liu'd for crime.

If my dear love were but the child of state,
It might for Fortune's bastard be unfathered,
As subject to Time's love, or to Time's hate,
Weeds among weeds, or flowers with flowers gathered.
No, it was builded far from accident;
It suffers not in smiling pomp, nor falls
Under the blow of thrallèd discontent,
Whereto th'inviting time our fashion calls.
It fears not Policy, that heretic,
Which works on leases of short-numb'red hours,
But all alone stands hugely politic,
That it nor grows with heat, nor drowns with show'rs.
  To this I witness call the fools of Time,
  Which die for goodness, who have lived for crime.

THE diction in the refutational middle of 124 (lines 5–12) is imitation-biblical, as the speaker says of his immutable love:

No, it was builded far from accident
it suffers not
nor falls
it fears not
But . . . stands hugely politic
That it nor grows nor drowns.

The two positive claims *(it was builded, [it] stands)* enclose the three negative claims *(suffers not, nor falls, fears not)* in what would be a satisfactory quasi-chiastic pattern, were it not for the "dangling" "extra" dependent clause of line 12 concerning growing and drowning. This latter clause oddly reverts from the architectural solidity of lines 5–11 to the vegetative realm of line 4. Such an unexpected reversion requires explanation.

In small, this "extra" clause in line 12 shows us the superabundance here of "change passages"—those which present seesaw effects. Theoretically, the seesaw unreliability of state status, Fortune's favor, and Time's love has been covered (and denied) by the contrary-to-fact supposition of Q_1, which precedes the refutational body of the poem. Someone has (presumably) said, "Well, love is uncertain; it changes with changes in status, in fortune, and in time," to which the speaker replies, with an emphasis on *were*, "If my love *were* the offspring of state or fortune or Time, yes, it might be changeable, [but it is not]; No, it was builded far, etc." The refutational energy in 124, as in 116, is marked by all the negatives: one *no*, two *not*'s, three *nor*'s. But whereas the doubled structure of 116 tended to shore up a negative refutation with a subsequent positive one, here the sturdy positive refutations *(builded far . . . stands)* alternate (with no climactic place-holding) with the negative ones, which keep reminding us of the alterability of other "loves." We amass many remarks about these more ordinary "loves," which form a shadow-poem behind the present one:

False "loves":

they are children of "state";
they are likely, given a change of Fortune, to be repudiated as illegitimate;
they are as subject to Time's hate as to its love;
they can be categorized as weeds one day, flowers the next;
they are built subject to accident;
they endure smiling pomp one day, fall under the blow of discontent the next;
they fear the pressure of Policy;
they grow with heat and drown with showers;
they are the fools of time;
they live for one thing [*crime*], die for another [*goodness*].

There may well have been some (lost) proverb—about people living for crime and dying for goodness—which symbolized all those—"Time's fools"—whose values change with the weather. This seems to me at least as likely as the long-continued scholarly hunt for historical personages (Jesuits et al.) who could be said to satisfy the conditions sketched in the couplet. The paradox of the intermingling of *goodness* and *crime* appealed to Shakespeare: Cf. *All's Well*, IV, iii, 71 ff.: "The web of our life is of a mingled yarn, *good* and ill together: our virtues would be proud, if our faults whipt them not, and our *crimes* would despair, if they were not cherish'd by our virtues." Cf. also *Henry V*, IV, i, 4–5, 11–12: "There is some soul of *goodness* in things *evil* would men observingly distil it out . . . Thus may we *gather honey from the weed*, and make a *moral* of the *devil* himself." The fools of time, who have lived for crime (expedient inconstancy in love) may serve one good purpose, if by their deaths they bear witness to the folly and criminality of infidelity and inconstancy. They die for the good (to us) of being exempla here of crime. (Booth, without drawing this inference from it, notes the closing congruence of *wit**ness*** and *good**ness***.) They die for the goodness of witnessing to their own criminality. They (at least) die to some moral purpose, having wasted their lives on crime. (The air of differentiation created by *which /who* instead of *who /who* in line 14 may bear out this reading.)

The speaker's fascination with the seesaw of mortal behavior *(love/hate, weeds/flowers, smiling pomp / thralled discontent, grow/drown, heat/showers)*, summed up in the word *fashion*, is rebuked, I think, by the "good distilled out of evil" in the couplet. Here alone, the appearance of seesaw *(goodness/crime)* does not represent the repetitive cyclicity of Fortune's wheel, state's caprices, or Time's fickleness. Instead it represents a providential finality: even though Time's fools have lived for crime, their deaths serve goodness. Cf. the proverbs "Fools live poor to die rich" [*Oxford Dictionary of Proverbs*, *s.v.* "die"] and "They live well that die well" [ibid., *s.v.* "Die well"].

The curious anticlimactic quality by which the fourth line in each quatrain of 124 is logically unnecessary is "repudiated," I believe, by the couplet, in which the last phrase is logically indispensable. One might call the structure of the quatrains, in which line 4 of each quatrain reechoes the seesaw motif, the structure of temporality, contingency, policy, and heresy; then the structure of the couplet, in which witness and goodness are distilled, in the end, out of crime, is the structure of eternity, necessity, constancy, and revealed truth. The price of this stability is of course the forsaking of the pathos of the organic in favor of the asceticism of the architectural: true love is *builded* and *stands hugely politic.* It has therefore removed itself utterly from the biological *(flowers, weeds, children, what grows)* and from the expedient *(policy, that heretic)* and has constructed itself as a Platonic form, virtual, biologically uninhabitable, and aloof, *all alone.*

DEFECTIVE KEY WORD: TIME (missing in the "immutable" Q_3)

Couplet Tie: *Time* (3, 3, 8, 13) [*might*, (2)]. If one wishes, given the constant proximity of the words *time* and *might* in Shakespeare, to see them as phonetic reversals or anagrams of each other [tīm; mīt], one can add line 2 to this Couplet Tie list.
call [*-s*] (8, 13)

125

VVEr't ought to me I bore the canopy,
With my extern the outward honoring,
Or layd great bafes for eternity,
Which proues more fhort then waft or ruining?
Haue I not feene dwellers on forme and fauor
Lofe all,and more by paying too much rent
For compound fweet;Forgoing fimple fauor,
Pittifull thriuors in their gazing fpent.
Noe,let me be obfequious in thy heart,
And take thou my oblacion,poore but free,
Which is not mixt with feconds,knows no art,
But mutuall render,onely me for thee.
Hence,thou fubbornd *Informer*, a trew foule
When moft impeacht,ftands leaft in thy controule.

Were't aught to me I bore the canopy,
With my extern the outward honouring,
Or laid great bases for eternity,
Which proves more short than waste or ruining?
Have I not seen dwellers on form and favour
Lose all, and more, by paying too much rent,
For compound sweet forgoing simple savour,
Pitiful thrivers, in their gazing spent?
No, let me be obsequious in thy heart,
And take thou my oblation, poor but free,
Which is not mixed with seconds, knows no art
But mutual render, only me for thee.
Hence, thou suborned informer! A true soul
When most impeached stands least in thy control.

SHAKESPEARE seems to be making puns of doublets here. Some are English *(seen/gazing);* some are Anglo-Latin *(extern/outward, waste/spend, impeached [im-***ped***icare]/stand);* some are Latin (*form/informer, compound/mixed, rent/render*—both from the Latin *rendere*); some are "false" *(bore/su****born****ed);* some are etymological (*oblation* is derived from the Latin word for "to bear" [ferro, ferre, tuli, *latus*] and is therefore connected etymologically to the preterite *bore*); some are conceptual (*dwellers* pay *rent*).

One aesthetic strategy of 125—seen at its height in the ostentatiously Latinate sequence *obsequious . . . oblation*—is to alternate Latinity with simplicity, the *compound* with the *simple.* This is the reason for such an early foregrounded linguistic contrast as *extern/outward,* which no reader can overlook.

Thematically, 125 expresses unequivocally its preference for the simple. Nonetheless, when it engages in its self-offering to the beloved (Q_3), it surprisingly uses Latinate phrases, not only *obsequious* and *oblation* but the conclusive phrase *mutual render.* However, it either "translates" such phrases (as it translates the Latin *mutual render* into the English *me for thee*) or follows them up with immediately designifying modifiers; the speaker will be Latinately *obsequious* ["following after"] only invisibly, *in thy heart;* and his *oblation* will be inconspicuous and of no monetary value, *poor but free.* The English *true soul* of the couplet could not be more different from the Latinate *suborned informer* [< *sub* + *ornatus,* "adorned," and *informare,* "to give a form to a legal charge against someone"]. The struggle between the informer's (Latinate) attempts to *impeach* [< *impedicare,* "fetter the feet of"] and *control* [< *contra* + *rotulus,* "check the account of"] and the true soul's victoriously English continuing to *stand* sums up the final contest. The couplet's declaration that it is when the Latinate is being *most* Latinate that the English is *least* threatened shows the relation between the two linguistic usages to be one of inverse proportionality rather than one of equality.

In retrospect, one can perceive the abrupt jolts from "Latinity" to "Anglicism" throughout, as *great bases for eternity* jolts into *more short than waste;* as *form and favour* jolts into *lose all and more.* The poem, it turns out, is an anathema: "Hence, thou evil one!" and its form of "exorcism" is either to turn away from "Latin" into "English" (*extern* to *outward*) or to translate or denature Latinity (which belongs by definition to conspicuous consumption) into a modest and "English" internal version of itself. In this way, the young man still receives the ceremony (*obsequious[ness]* + *oblation*) that is his due, but receives it in an inward, "English" way. The final "foot" pun, *impeached/stands*, shows how quickly, and how deftly, the speaker can "disarm" and "Anglicize" any word thrown at him by the corrupt Latinate court and its canopied ceremonies.

The couplet intimates that someone—an "informer"—has said that the speaker's motives in cultivating the young man are mercenary—that he wants to curry *favour*, to *thrive*, *to bear the canopy*. Against the whispers of this slanderer standing by, the speaker addresses the young man directly, disclaiming all base motives (those associated with Latinity) and defending his own "English" troth. Yet he pays a price for this stance: he (willingly) forfeits his eternizing habit, *laying great bases for eternity*, because he has lost faith in that eternity. In words reminiscent of earlier sonnets, he condemns eternity because it *proves more short than waste or ruining*. He thereby forgoes eternizing art, placing it among other memorial monuments, and relinquishes the consolations of art's *eternal summer*. In turning back to *simple savour*, away from *compound sweet*, the speaker prefers the ethical to the *gazing* aesthetic, and offers an oblation of punning double denial, one that "*knows no* art." The "*Retro me, Satanas!*" of the couplet confirms the ethical position. Perhaps there was no way to bid farewell to the *lovely boy* (126) without this repudiation of the aesthetic gaze and its *compound sweet*, Latinity.

Couplet Tie: *bor* [-*e*], *su**bor**ned* (1, 13) [a "false" etymology]
form, *in**form**er* (5, 13)
and perhaps
more [*most*] (4, 6, 14)

126

O Thou my louely Boy who in thy power,
Doeſt hould times fickle glaſſe,his ſickle,hower:
Who haſt by wayning growne,and therein ſhou'ſt,
Thy louers withering,as thy ſweet ſelfe grow'ſt.
If Nature(ſoueraine miſteres ouer wrack)
As thou goeſt onwards ſtill will plucke thee backe,
She keepes thee to this purpoſe,that her skill.
May time diſgrace,and wretched mynuit kill.
Yet feare her O thou minnion of her pleaſure,
She may detaine,but not ſtill keepe her treſure!
Her *Audite*(though delayd)anſwer'd muſt be,
And her *Quietus* is to render thee.
(   )
(   )

O thou my lovely boy, who in thy power
Dost hold Time's fickle glass, his sickle, hour;
Who hast by waning grown, and therein show'st
Thy lovers withering, as thy sweet self grow'st;
If Nature (sovereign mistress over wrack),
As thou goest onwards still will pluck thee back,
She keeps thee to this purpose, that her skill
May Time disgrace, and wretched minutes kill.
Yet fear her, O thou minion of her pleasure,
She may detain, but not still keep, her treasure!
Her audit (though delayed) answered must be,
And her quietus is to render thee.
(   )
(   )

THIS odd six-couplet poem "feels like" a sonnet because the first eight lines—a single sentence—become a perfect octave in sentiment, if not in rhyme. Lines 9–12 read as the "sestet," introduced as a reprise by a repetition (line 9) of the *O thou* with which the poem begins. In this farewell to the *lovely boy,* the sovereignty of Time over even Nature herself is the philosophical point, but the psychological point is to show the boy as a catspaw in the unequal power game between Time and Nature. As long as she can, Nature keeps back her choicest morsel (one of *the rarities of nature's truth;* 60), but must surrender him at last to the superior power of Time. The endgame is *delayed* and *detained* in this poem as long as possible—*render thee* being the last two words—and is sustained by the complex retarding mechanisms of the opening address, with its several dependent clauses, which themselves have compound objects and compound verbs. The kernel structure of the octave addressing the boy is: "O thou [who, etc.], if Nature still will pluck thee back [as thou goest onwards], she keeps thee that her skill may disgrace and kill Time." Though *Nature* is the subject of the whole sentence, she does not appear in "Q_1," so that the young man seems to be the sole agent of power there: he *holds,* he *has grown,* he *shows,* and he *grows.* In "Q_2," Nature is the agent of power: she *plucks back,* she *keeps,* she [acts in order that she] *may disgrace* and *kill.* The subsequent effect, in "Q_3," of the defeat of the agency of *both* boy and Nature is eerie because Time is never invoked there by name. The last uses of *her* show agency shifting from Nature to an (unnamed) power, who can demand of her both an audit (the audit *of* her) and a quietus (the quietus *from* her). The other possessive *her*'s in the poem (*her* skill, *her* pleasure, *her* treasure) mean "belonging to Nature, possessed by Nature," but the *her*'s attached to *audit* and *quietus* show her as the debtor to Time: she owes, she does not own.

There are two remarkable technical features to this "sonnet." One is the extraordinarily dense texture of alliteration and assonance joining almost every word to one or several other words. The second is the noticeable presence of disyllabic words, a presence affecting our scansion of the poem.

On the following page is a map of the chief phonetic interrelations, including the rhymes. It will be seen that the deadly word *quietus* participates in four phonetic groups that precede its own appearance: the *k* group of *sickle/fickle/pluck/back*, the large *ī* and *ē* groups, and the *-s* group, making it possess a conclusive set of anticipated phonemes. *Render*, by connecting to *wretched/wrack*, gains a meaning wholly different from its meaning in the preceding sonnet, 125, where it appeared (contrasted with *rent*) in *mutual render, only me for thee*. Here in 126, *render* is likely to call up *rend* ("rend asunder"), as devouring Time seizes the lovely boy for his own. Shakespeare's only other use of *quietus* is in Hamlet's famous soliloquy, where it acts as a synonym for death—an overtone it possesses here, too, for the rend[er]ing of the boy.

If we ask the reason for the sonnet's exceptionally dense interphonetic relations, we see that *audit* and *answered* are the only significant words remaining relatively unpartnered phonetically, and are thereby foregrounded as nonce events. The seamless phonetic web of time's onward passage, in which the lovely boy flourishes, paradoxically waxing even when waning, is interrupted by the last trump of the *audit* (*Audite*, "hear ye," the oral demand of bookkeeping) and Nature's unwilling *answer*. Because two lines have already begun with an amphibrach followed by a caesura—

Ĭf nátŭre //   and   *Yĕt féar hĕr* //

—the ring of *Hĕr áudĭt* comes as a fatal confirmation of both the futility of natural tenacity and the ominous warning. There are (by my count) nine other amphibrachic feet besides these three, and their presence serves to highlight the amphibrachic conclusive word *quĭétŭs*.

Because of the number of significant disyllabic words accented on the first syllable, such as *answer* and *audit*, the poem falls into a trochaic and amphibrachic rather than an iambic pattern. (I say this because given the two possible scansions of, say, line 5—

Iambic: If Na-/ture sove-/reign mis-/tress o-/ver wrack
Trochaic: If / Nature / sovereign / mistress / over / wrack

—I prefer the one which keeps words intact.) On this principle—and noticing how many of the first syllables of these lines are negligible in relation to the import of the second and following syllables—I would scan the lines as follows, italicizing the amphibrachs:

O thou // my love / ly boy // who in / thy power
Dost / hold Time's / fickle / glass // *his sickle* / hour
Who hast / *by waning* / grown // *and therein* / show'st
Thy lovers / with'ring // as thy / sweet self / grow'st
If Nature // sovereign / mistress / over / wrack
As thou / *goest onwards* / still will / pluck thee / back
She keeps thee / to this / purpose // that her / skill
May Time / disgrace // *and wretched* / minutes / kill
Yet fear her // O thou / minion / of her / pleasure
She may / detain // but not / still keep / *her treasure*
Her audit // though de / layed // answered / must be
And her / *quietus* // is to / render / thee.

The effect of the prosody is to suggest that easy conversational intonation in which Shakespeare excels all other poets. The enjambments of lines 1 and 3 enact the ongoingness *(as thou goest onwards)* of the young man's apparently self-propelled growing, and that of line 7 the ongoingness of Nature's resolve to keep him for herself (the true cause of his beauty's preservation until now). But the strong caesuras of lines 9–11, which check the lines' onwardness, show these forward impulses of momentum being met by a powerful, and ultimately victorious, counterforce. The two more regular lines closing both "octave" and "Q_3"—line 8 and line 12—reestablish the status quo of Time's dominion. The combination of extreme felicity of diction—in which almost every phoneme chimes musically with another—and the prosodic dis-ease (with the checking of momentum) provokes our sense that this poem is at once elegiac and necessitarian. The boy whose *power* is apparently celebrated at the outset is, at the end, a rendered *minion,* the creature of a *minute.* The speaker's voice—apparently, at the beginning, the voice of indulgent love—is by "Q_3" the voice of Time itself, speaking the discourse of necessity: the audit "answered *must* be." Rarely has a speaker's voice so altered toward its love-object in the course of twelve short lines.

Phonetic Interrelations in Sonnet 126

ō	*ou*	*ī*	*ē*	*ĭ*
O	thou	my	thee	in
hold	thou	thy	she	fickle
over	thou	Time's	keeps	his
O		by	thee	sickle
though		thy	see	withering
grown		thy	detain	if
show'st		Time	keep	mistress
grow'st			delayed	still
goest			be	will
over			thee	skill
		quietus	quietus	disgrace
				minutes
				kill
				minion
				still
				audit
				is

m	*l*	*b*	*f*	*p*
my	lovely	boy	fickle	power
may	lovers	back	fear	pluck
may				purpose
mistress				pleasure
minutes				
minion				

g	*k*	*h*	*th*	*w*
glass	fickle	hold	therein	waning
grown	sickle	hast	this	withering
grow'st	pluck		that	[on]wards
goest	quietus			
[dis]grace				

s	*r*	*sh*	*t*	*d*
sweet	wrack	she	Time	disgrace
self	wretched	show'st	Time's	detain
sovereign	render	she	treasure	delayed

Phonetic Interrelations in Sonnet 126 (continued)

-st	*-our*	*-ack*	*-ezhur*
dost	power	wrack	pleasure
hast	hour	back	treasure
show'st			
grow'st			
goest			
must			

-r	*-s*
Nature	glass
pleasure	mistress
treasure	keeps
render	this
power	purpose
hour	minutes

Couplet Tie: None, since no couplet exists. But its absence is compensated for by the extreme phonemic resonances listed above. The Quarto's two sets of eloquently silent parentheses (which I retain) emphasize the reader's desire for a couplet and the grim fact of its lack. Inside the parentheses there lies, so to speak, the mute effigy of the rendered youth.

127

IN the ould age blacke was not counted faire,
Or if it weare it bore not beauties name:
But now is blacke beauties ſucceſſiue heire,
And Beautie ſlanderd with a baſtard ſhame,
For ſince each hand hath put on Natures power,
Fairing the foule with Arts faulſe borrow'd face,
Sweet beauty hath no name no holy boure,
But is prophan'd, if not liues in diſgrace.
Therefore my Miſterſſe eyes are Rauen blacke,
Her eyes ſo ſuted, and they mourners ſeeme,
At ſuch who not borne faire no beauty lack,
Slandring Creation with a falſe eſteeme,
Yet ſo they mourne becomming of their woe,
That euery toung ſaies beauty ſhould looke ſo.

In the old age black was not counted fair,
Or if it were it bore not beauty's name;
But now is black beauty's successive heir,
And beauty slandered with a bastard shame:
For since each hand hath put on Nature's power,
Fairing the foul with art's false borrowed face,
Sweet beauty hath no name, no holy bower,
But is profaned, if not lives in disgrace.
Therefore my mistress' eyes are raven black,
Her eyes so suited, and they mourners seem
At such who not born fair no beauty lack,
Sland'ring creation with a false esteem:
Yet so they mourn, becoming of their woe,
That every tongue says beauty should look so.

THIS first of the Dark Lady sonnets is in effect a myth of origin: How did a black-haired, black-eyed woman come to be the reigning heir of beauty? Rephrased as prose, the little myth would go as follows:

> Once upon a time, "in the old age," the archetype of beauty was the unretouched fair woman. Then cosmetics were invented, and now every ugly woman can make herself into a fair woman. In shame, slandered "true" beauty "lives in disgrace," displaced from her wonted shrine ("profaned" [*pro-fanum*, "outside the temple"]). A devotee has arisen to mourn this bastardizing of beauty; this devotee has black eyes to symbolize mourning. She mourns because the natural order of creation has been slandered by those who, though not fair by birth, have acquired all beauty by art. The woe of the mourner is so becomingly expressed by her black eyes that public opinion has now seen how beautiful "dark" beauty can be, and therefore the type of the beautiful has been entirely revised: the new archetype is the "black" form of beauty.

This myth of origin corresponds to that of sonnet 20, which explained how the object of the speaker's affections happened to have a penis though the rest of him was so feminine. In each case, there is something amiss about the love-object that needs to be explained. In 20, the undeniable sexual attraction the speaker feels for the fair youth is explained by the fact that Nature originally made the fair youth a woman, with all the feminine attributes; the penis was a late addition, to make the youth a suitable paramour for herself. It is Nature, then, who had had the disorderly passion; she, as a woman, fell in love with the woman she had created—and added the penis more or less as an organic dildo. The speaker of 20, on the other hand, has perfectly "seemly" heterosexual desires—seeing a womanly object, he fell in love with it and desired it, but was defeated of his understandable aim (sexual possession) by Nature's addition of a penis to the "woman."

Now the speaker finds himself attracted not to a conventionally beautiful fair woman, but to a dark-eyed woman, and must explain this aesthetically anomalous choice. He decides in this case, too, to declare that his choice is not (or at least no longer) aesthetically anomalous: *every tongue* agrees with him. He disposes of other candidates for his approval by saying sophistically that in these days of cosmetic alteration one can no longer tell which are true beauties and which are false beauties, made so by art. The whereabouts of true beauty are dubious; she is nameless, ousted from her holy bower, deshrined, living somewhere out of favor.

The words placing the sonnet in the genre of myth-of-origin are *therefore* (logical explanation) and *suited* (ascribing agency to the creator that made the eyes black to symbolize mourning). This fact may even explain the repetition (and correction) of the description of the lady's *eyes:* first it is said that they *are* black, then that they are *suited so* (as by design, corresponding with the use of *therefore*). (Some editors have unnecessarily emended one of the *eyes* to *hair* or *brows.*)

The imaginative impulse toward the invention of the myth of origin accounts for the then/now construction of the octave, and the logical *therefore* of the sestet, as well as for the "folkloric" inclusion of *in the old age* and *every tongue says.* But it alone does not account for the odd disposition of materials within these parts. The false beauties, troubling to the mind, keep cropping up as if they cannot be discounted, and their persistence from octave to Q_3 is foregrounded by the reinscription in Q_3 of "their" words, *slander (-ed, -ing)* and *false*, first appearing in lines 4 and 6. (As Booth points out, the line "*Fai*ring the *foul* with art's *false* borrowed *face*" enacts the artificiality of cosmetic beauty.) Though the announced intent of 127 is praise of *raven* beauty, praise breaks out, so to speak, only in lines 9–10 and the couplet: the rest of the sonnet worries about change in aesthetic standards and the unsettling democratic acquisition of *nature's power* by *each hand.* There is no hope, apparently, of restoring the old sacred aesthetic standard; *sweet beauty* has no chance of regaining her name and holy bower. The final description of false beauties, made from the point of view of the viewing public, gives them, from that point of view, unequivocal aesthetic value: they are *such who no beauty lack.* It is true that this essential description is ringed round with qualifiers: they were *not born fair,* and (according to a metaphysical norm of judgment) they are *sland'ring creation with a false esteem.* But to the senses, to the eye, to the perception, they *no beauty lack.* This is a very different description from that in the octave, where the norm of X-ray judgment prevails ("fairing *the foul*"). The only "victory" the sonnet can provide is the loss, by the false beauties, of their position in the socio-aesthetic scale. They are beautiful (undeniably) to look at, but their *kind* of beauty is no longer admired; instead, blackness has come into fashion, and the *consensus gentium* *(every tongue)* ratifies it. Nonetheless, this (potentially fickle) elevation of an alternate aesthetic standard is no real consolation for the absolute inability of the world to tell true beauty from false beauty, where "fair" looks are concerned. (See *Love's Labour's Lost*, IV, iii, 243–267.) The climactic phrase *no beauty lack* points up the connection between *lack* and *black* (also rhymed in *Love's Labour's Lost*) as though only by its *lack* (of deceptive possibility) could *black* become fashionable. This (unpleasant) conclusion is smoothed over by the aesthetic harmony between inner *woe*, eyes' *mourn[ing]*, and outer *black[ness]*, in the elevation of the (putative) new standard. But the distress at the perfection to which aesthetic deception has been brought, bursting out in Q_3, is the real motive of the myth of origin, a distress reinforced by the Couplet Tie.

KEY WORD:	BEAUTY
DEFECTIVE KEY WORD:	FAIR (missing in C, where the falsely fair women have disappeared)
Couplet Tie:	*mourn* [*-ers*] (10, 13) *beauty* [*-'s*] (2, 3, 4, 7, 11, 14) *so* (10, 13, 14)

128

HOw oft when thou my muſike muſike playſt,
Vpon that bleſſed wood whoſe motion ſounds
With thy ſweet fingers when thou gently ſwayſt,
The wiry concord that mine eare confounds,
Do I enuie thoſe Iackes that nimble leape,
To kiſſe the tender inward of thy hand,
Whilſt my poore lips which ſhould that harueſt reape,
At the woods bouldnes by thee bluſhing ſtand.
To be ſo tikled they would change their ſtate,
And ſituation with thoſe dancing chips,
Ore whome their fingers walke with gentle gate,
Making dead wood more bleſt then liuing lips,
   Since ſauſie Iackes ſo happy are in this,
   Giue them their fingers, me thy lips to kiſſe.

How oft, when thou my music music play'st
Upon that blessèd wood whose motion sounds
With thy sweet fingers when thou gently sway'st
The wiry concord that mine ear confounds,
Do I envý those jacks that nimble leap
To kiss the tender inward of thy hand,
Whilst my poor lips, which should that harvest reap,
At the wood's boldness by thee blushing stand!
To be so tickled they would change their state
And situation with those dancing chips
O'er whom thy fingers walk with gentle gait,
Making dead wood more blest than living lips.
   Since saucy jacks so happy are in this,
   Give them thy fingers, me thy lips to kiss.

THIS apparently playful sonnet depends on synecdoche, the trope *par excellence* of reduction. The sonnet finds in synecdoche a solution to the aesthetic problem of how one represents sexual jealousy in comic rather than tragic or satiric terms. By understanding that a problem is being solved, we can understand the aesthetic gaiety of the comic solution, and we end by conceiving of this sonnet not as a frigid triviality (as the more solemn commentators would have it) but rather as a triumphant *jeu d'esprit* on the dangerous subject of sexual infidelity.

We recall Romeo's wish that he could be a glove upon the hand of Juliet so that he might touch her cheek. Here, the speaker's wish to be a musical *jack* or key touched by his mistress's hand is not taken literally, any more than Romeo's wish to be a glove. Readers can become impatient with such a conceit; they feel they are being asked to concur in language inappropriate to a "grown man." But in fact there is no such "real" wish; the object in the conceit serves as a miniature surrogate actor playing on an invented stage the drama of physical touch that the lover wishes to act out in "real life." The absurdity of the drama of reduction (in which a glove or keyboard plays the role desired by the lover) lends the fantasy its aesthetic interest. Shakespeare prolongs his conceit for fourteen lines, and uses it to deflect feelings of sexual competition too painful for direct utterance.

When Shakespeare's playlet opens, the lover is standing by his mistress as she plays the virginals, wishing that he could be the *blessèd wood* that resounds under the touch of her *sweet fingers.* The conceit of the poem is apparently so brief—"I envy the wood that kisses your hand"—that one principal aesthetic project here must simply be to keep invention going. In the first quatrain, only tender words are addressed to the mistress. She is herself her lover's music, her fingers are sweet, her playing gentle, and her touch a blessing. Scarcely a line passes without the interjection of some melting word of praise. (In fact, the whole body of the poem, before the couplet, is bracketed by the two loving words *blest* and *gentle:* the *blessèd wood* becomes *wood more blest*, and the concord *gently* swayed engenders the *gentle* gait near the close.)

To reinforce the apparent semantic tenderness, a mimic conjunction of lover and lady is played out in the poem by antiphonal pronominal kisses—*my* music, *thy* fingers; *mine* ear, *thy* hand; *my* lips, *thy* fingers; *thy* fingers, *me*, *thy* lips—thereby exhibiting the private, but frustrated, desire for union which has engendered the speaker's mock jealousy of the instrument's *saucy jacks*. The bracketing of the drama early and late by *blest* and *gentle* and *fingers* tells us that the fictional situation does not change between lines 1 and 12: the wood is still *blest* because of the continued *gentle* playing of the lady's *fingers* upon it. The central project of invention, then, is to modify, during twelve lines, the lover's response to an unchanging situation. It is a project so fragile that too heavy a hand will wreck it.

Shakespeare schematizes the scene, as I have said, by reduction through synecdoche. He reduces the lady, seated, to a hand and fingers; he reduces the lover, standing beside her, to an eye, an ear, and lips. The courting-concert has been a rich subject for genre paintings; if we think of the amount of decorative incident and appropriate ornament that can be given to a room, a lady, a gentleman, and a musical instrument, we become keenly aware of Shakespeare's drastic reduction of the scene to bodily synecdoche. At first, the speaker is an ear, an implied eye watching the lady, a self referred to as *I*, and a pair of lips; his ear, he tells us, is confounded, his eye watches the nimble jacks as they leap, he envies the wood, and his lips blush at the wood's boldness. The first eight lines of the sonnet are a sketch, then, in which a complex human scene is reduced to its very few active elements. We might conceive of such a poem as a drawing in which an image has been reduced to the minimum number of barely descriptive strokes.

But there is even a reduction of this reduction. In the third quatrain the lover is further reduced to nothing but a pair of lips, the lady to nothing but a set of fingers. Here, the lover also abandons the first person, and speaks of his lips in the third person, thereby affecting an impartial "outside" judgment on her fingers and his lips alike. This third-quatrain narrowing and reconceiving of the conceit, done of course in the service of erotic argument (so that the lover and the lady can equally be spectators of the poor disenfranchised lips) turns the poem from present-time habitual retrospect *(How oft)* to conditional-mood hopeful prospect *(To be so tickled, [my lips] would change their state / And situation with those dancing chips)*.

Finally, in the couplet, the continuing synecdoche for the lady (her fingers) is suddenly and winningly changed to an element (lips) that the lover has already been said to own, but which the lady has not yet been mentioned as possessing. And the lover (who in the couplet resumes his first-person account) has so recently been represented by his lips alone that the plea *Give . . . me thy lips* is itself, by the conjunction of *me* and *thy lips*, that desired kiss of lips to lips toward which the poem has been aspiring and on which it ends. The poem is a kiss deferred and, finally, a kiss verbally enacted; one aesthetic problem of the sonnet, successfully solved, is that of finding a way to enact the lover's yearning to kiss, and its final implied success.

I have neglected till now the introductory metaphor of the sonnet, the metaphor of music. The tonic note is sounded in the opening sigh, *How oft, when thou my music music play'st.* The rest of the poem exists to amplify the sense in which, by synecdoche, the lady can be called the lover's music. What is emphasized about music here is the erotic reciprocity between player and instrument (one of the countless images of reciprocity in the *Sonnets*, reciprocity being one of their directing metaphors). This reciprocity at first opposes a conventional female gentleness to an equally conventional male bold *leap to kiss;* but it later adds, we should notice, a female provocative tickling and a male responsive dancing, suggesting the lady's deliberate unchastity. *Music* as we see it here is an affair of a body that both initiates and responds, offering concord and confusion at once.

In the throes of his mock jealousy of the jacks, the lover will refer self-deprecatingly to *my poor lips;* but as he prepares to argue his own case, he calls the jacks *dead wood*, while he, by contrast, possesses *living lips.* Until this moment, he had ostensibly hoped only that the lady's *fingers* might stray away from the nimble jacks and toward his lips; but now his mock-envy turns to a mock-largesse, as he invents a more fitting cessation to the drama. Let the music continue, he suggests, thereby satisfying the jacks and granting the lady her desire to continue "tickling" them; but let a kiss be offered in the lover's direction: *Since saucy jacks so happy are in this, / Give them thy fingers, me thy lips to kiss.* The jacks are allocated the fingers as their portion; the lover hopes for the surprising lips (which until this moment the lady did not verbally possess). The distribution of benefits is announced, it would seem, with a happiness which is delighted that all concerned can be satisfied at once. (Here, as elsewhere, I accept the usual emendation of the Quarto *their* to *thy*.)

But behind the mock-envy, the mock-largesse, and the animated fiction of the jacks that leap across the line-break to kiss; behind the self-deprecation of mock-modesty as the timid lover stands blushing at the sexual audacity of the jacks, there lies the recollection—ironic, of course but touching—of the hyperbolic treasuring in adolescence of all proximity to the beloved. Doting is an emotion not much described in verse:

adults are ashamed to dote. But this is a poem content to be abject in doting—longing to blush, to be tickled, to dance, to kiss, to worship every motion of the beloved, even at the price of sharing her with other lovers.

The metamorphosis proposed by the lover—that his lips should themselves change state and situation and become dancing chips in order to receive the favors of the lady—never has to take place, but it serves to enact the hopeless intensities of sexual jealousy on a comically reduced plane. The jacks reap the harvest that rightfully belongs to the lover. The lady shows no disposition to give up the kisses of the jacks—on the contrary, she deliberately tickles the jacks into their responsive leaps. The first thirteen lines of the poem are, we realize at the end, an elaborate pretext to justify the prayer of the fourteenth; and the fourteenth rings as conclusively as it does because it is a phonetic reinscription. It inscribes over *leap / To kiss* (the action of the jacks) the homonymic phrase *lips to kiss* (the hope of the lover).

In Shakespeare's reduction, the erogenous zones (including here the ear and the fingers, as well as the palm and the lips) eventually take on such importance that the other parts of the body, and all surrounding items, pale into insignificance. In the final totalization of the original synecdoche, she is all fingers and lips, he entirely a yearning pair of living lips. And only one action is permitted to exist—the touch of one element to another, the kiss of fingers to wood, or lips to lips.

The problem of conveying, in a comic mode, the eroticized and tormented state of the sensibility of the jealous lover has been solved both economically and elegantly, with a leavening of bitter humor that permits sexual suggestiveness while aestheticizing it in the convention of courtship by music. The terrors of infidelity, jealousy, promiscuity, and sexual mistress-sharing are brought down to manageable proportions. Shakespeare's brilliant verbal solution has the tact to remain at the playful level of the set problem—the "correct" distribution of the lady's erotic energies. The final verbal kiss satisfies both the lady's free will (she can still give her fingers to the jacks) and the lover's yearning. It is probably no accident that this displacement of jealousy into comedy is followed, in sonnets 129 (on lust) and 131 (on the lady's *black* deeds), by the furious return of the repressed.

The usefulness of the figure of synecdoche lies not only in its reducing to manageability the agonies of love. It lies as well in what this trope manages to exclude. Fixing, as it does, on one or two elements—here, fingers and lips—it succeeds in excluding the whole world of other, competing, objects and essences. It suggests, in miniature, what the aesthetic of the sonnet sequence itself must be, as it reduces the world to a very few personages—the lover, his beloved, his rivals. To those accustomed to the wide social sweep of fiction, this reduction may seem a defect. But it is a mistake to think of the lyric as acting in a world smaller than that of other literary fictions. On the contrary, it acts in the only world there is—the world extending vertically from the Trinity (105) to hell (129), and horizontally from east to west (132). Lyric enlarges its personae to fill that cosmic space: the personages in lyric are so great that the world can contain only two or three of them at once. They usurp all available space. The speaker says of his love that it fears not policy, "but all alone stands *hugely* politic" (124). Shakespeare's need to reduce suggests the anterior daunting immensity of his theme; his frequent turn from reduction to hyperbole implies that the innate grandeur of love will make itself felt, even when reduced to a set of eyes, lips, or fingers. What is implicit, in this raising of the human figure to the scale of all that exists, is the vastness, to human consideration, of the self and its immediate concerns.

DEFECTIVE KEY WORD: LIPS (missing in Q_1, which has not yet arrived at the conceit of the jacks' kiss)

Couplet Tie: *jacks* (5, 13)
thy fingers (3, 11, 14)
lips [*leap*] (5, 7, 12, 14)
kiss (6, 14)
leap / To kiss [*lips to kiss*] (5–6, 14)

129

TH'expence of Spirit in a waſte of ſhame
Is luſt in action,and till action , luſt
Is periurd,murdrous,blouddy full of blame,
Sauage,extreame,rude,cruell,not to truſt,
Inioyd no ſooner but diſpiſed ſtraight,
Paſt reaſon hunted, and no ſooner had
Paſt reaſon hated as a ſwollowed bayt,
On purpoſe layd to make the taker mad.
Made In purſut and in poſſeſſion ſo,
Had,hauing,and in queſt,to haue extreame,
A bliſſe in proofe and proud and very wo,
Before a ioy propoſd behind a dreame,
All this the world well knowes yet none knowes well,
To ſhun the heauen that leads men to this hell.

Th'expense of spirit in a waste of shame
Is lust in action, and till action, lust
Is perjured, murd'rous, bloody, full of blame,
Savage, extreme, rude, cruel, not to trust;
Enjoyed no sooner but despisèd straight,
Past reason hunted, and no sooner had,
Past reason hated as a swallowed bait
On purpose laid to make the taker mad:
Mad in pursuit and in possession so,
Had, having, and in quest to have, extreme;
A bliss in proof, and proved, a very woe,
Before, a joy proposed, behind, a dream.
All this the world well knows yet none knows well
To shun the heaven that leads men to this hell.

SONNET 129, though impersonally phrased, is best accounted for by seeing it as a representation of decisive changes of mind about the experience it treats, changes predicated of a single sensibility: that is, the text encourages us to invent such a sensibility and its changes of heart. But if we treat it, as I want to here, as a problem of construction for the artist, we see that the artist's first choice must be whether to represent his psychological narrative of submission to lust passionally and chronologically—just as it sequentially happened from initial excitement to shame and analysis—or analytically and retrospectively, as one looks back on that submission in later evaluation. Shakespeare seems at first to reject the chronological account—attraction, appetite, enjoyment, disgust, repentance, excuse, analysis—in favor of the more explosive possibilities of the retrospective vision—the awaking to shame, blame, and self-reproach, in a judgmental, "morning-after" account of the experience. In this respect, 129 resembles 119 *(What potions have I drunk)*.

Shakespeare chose as his aesthetic problem the representation of one's changing responses to lust, and decided to enact the changes by showing three different sorts of retrospection: personal-judgmental, personal-chronological, and universal-analytic. He did this rather than demonstrate, about lust, solely a chronological recollection, solely a judgmental self-blame, solely an analytic totalization, or any other possible model (for example, a rapid alternation from blame to excuse and back again, a binary model). Shakespeare also had the choice in this sonnet of using a first-person model (his usual one for sonnets) but chose, unusually, to speak in an impersonal voice which, though it initially mimics a philosophical or homiletic tone, soon loses its initial defensive distance and becomes uncontrolled in its spate of adjectives of social trespass. By the third quatrain, any pretense of the homiletic has been discarded; a cleric might be conceived of as pronouncing the octave, but not the sestet, which certifies lust as *a bliss in proof, a dream*, and a *heaven*.

Reading along an axis of similarity, as most critics have done, one can see similarity displayed in the persistence, throughout the three quatrains, of the definitional syntactic matrix "Lust is X," from *expense of spirit* to *joy* and *dream*. Reading for difference, however, we note the contrasts among the quatrain-definitions of lust, and therefore see the position of the speaker as one that changes over time. The wish to define—represented by the syntax—does not change. The substance of the definition, however, *does* change—from disgusting act to dream. It is the axis of difference that drives us to postulate a change of heart; the axis of similarity ("Lust is . . . lust is . . . lust is . . .") could belong to an impersonal treatise, such as that of Ravisius Textor, to which some have compared this sonnet. I should add that Shakespeare also chooses an analytic rather than a descriptive model of definition; his is a philosophical model of the mean and the extremes, of cause and effect, of before and after, of relations to self and to others. There are of course reasons that we can imagine for such compositional choices, as I will suggest.

To choose a retrospective judgmental view with which to begin the sonnet is, as I have said, more dramatic than to choose a chronological revisiting of the experience. However, in Q_2 chronological reverie begins to *supplant* the retrospective judgment of Q_1 (only to be supplanted in *its* turn by the totalizing view of the couplet, which encompasses both the chronological reenactment of the act and one's retrospective judgment on it). Shakespeare may also have chosen the retrospective judgmental view as his beginning because it is the only angle of vision from which an analytic perspective becomes plausible.

The speaker's choice of definition and division into parts in the deceptively scholastic beginning ("Th'expense of spirit in a waste of shame / Is lust *in action*, and *till action*, lust / Is perjured," etc.) shows us the first defense of the speaker: to divide his unsettling topic into three apparently rational parts, to distinguish its phases along a temporal axis—lust un*til action*, lust *in action*, and lust [after action], when of course it has ceased to exist. The ego has here a vested interest in distinguishing the present self-in-repentance from the former self-in-sin (in the model representing the common conversion schema), and therefore it launches itself, after its putatively tripartite beginning (in which "after action" remains an unexamined ghost part) into its rigid binary antitheses of before and after, tending more and more to obliterate both the actual moment of lust in action and the initial postulated division into three phases. We soon move into the binary schemes of *enjoyed* and *despisèd*, *hunted* and *hated* (the latter retaining a semantic and prosodic overtone of the original tripartite scheme by including *had* in its triplet of *hunted*, *had*, *hated*, while the syntax reinforces the binary model, reinforced as well by the repetition of *past reason*).

Of course both schemata—the "scholastic" one of tripartite division along a temporal axis, and the subsequent "repentant" conversion scheme of binary form—disappear in the double knot where the poem is aesthetically knitted together, in which all divisions collapse and in which the original dramatic passion of self-reproach is itself at last judged: lust has made "the *taker mad: / Mad* in *pursuit* and in *possession* [*mad*]"; lust is "*had, having*, and *in quest to have, extreme.*" After this has been said, nothing can be the same. While the first adverse totalizing judgment has been made on a psychological basis—the subject is *mad* before, during, and after taking the bait—the second adverse totalizing judgment—*extreme*—has been made on a philosophical or classical basis of means and extremes, rather than on the basis of the social or religious or psychological objections earlier displayed in the poem. Socially, lust is of course savage in its pursuit of its object, perjuring itself, untrustworthy, and so on; religiously, it may be an expense of spirit on base matter; psychologically, it may be the occasion of shame and madness. But philosophically, it is *extreme*, going past the mean of reason in all directions. I call this final totalizing judgment philosophical rather than ethical because the vocabulary of purely ethical judgment includes words far less neutral than Shakespeare's carefully chosen word "extreme." (He might have said "bestial," or "ungoverned," or "childish," for instance, and still remained within an ethical vocabulary.)

In running through the whole gamut of retrospective experience—from apparent detachment to violent self-blame and blaming of the other (who laid the swallowed bait on purpose)—and knitting it up finally under the single rubric *extreme*—the word itself remembered, or rather retrieved from line 4, as the only aesthetically productive word from the early torrent of self-accusation—the octave is able to set out, in little, what it is to have an extreme experience and to emerge from it full of self-hatred and hatred of the temptress-other.

Then the poem can move on to its moment of aesthetic difference—to a different view of lust, representing it *as it was felt at the time.* It can then move, in the couplet, to a totalizing encompassing of its previous differentiations.

Let me explain. The word *extreme*, knitting the three temporal phases together under a neutral rubric, enables the second part of the poem to reverse the morning-after model of the octave. The correction proper can now take place (though it has been in itself already a reconceiving to see the action of lust philosophically, as *extreme*, instead of homiletically or socially). The poem now, in Q_3, sees the action of lust (lines 11–12) not from the perspective of an aftermath of shame, in an alienated fashion, but rather affectively—how the action seemed *while it was being lived.* First it seemed like a *bliss*, and later it turned into *woe;* first it seemed like a *joy*, but later it seemed unreal, like a *dream.* This correction—as affective chronology corrects judgmental alienation from one's own past, as *how it felt* corrects *what was done*—is, roughly speaking, the major aesthetic choice of the writer. The poem gives us, in short, two absolutely incompatible yet two absolutely reliable retrospective accounts of lust—the earlier alienated judgment given in nominal and adjectival inventory *(expense, waste; savage, extreme)*, and the late chronological affective tale given in a series of nouns *(bliss, woe, joy, dream)*, which "correct" the earlier ones, *expense*, *waste*, and *shame.* It thus presents us with two models of experience, both of which we know intimately: the model of "What I think of it now that I look back" and the model of "How it felt while it was happening." Usually, in simpler poems, one of these models expels the other. To keep both in suspension, as Shakespeare does here by his cyclical couplet thematizing the preceding two models, is to say that both are equally true. The poem corrects its first judgmental telling by a second, affective one, but, unlike an overpainted painting, does not entirely obliterate the first sketch. The couplet sums up the incompatibility between chronologically lived affective life—the heaven that leads to hell—and the retrospective analytical life—what the world well knows.

We see now the necessity of the authorial choice of the impersonal mode for the purposes of this sonnet. Any existential subject would tend to represent himself at the moment of utterance—the "now" of the poem—as living his retrospection either judgmentally *or* affectively, and this would privilege one point of view over the other. The impersonal mode allows for the habitual incompatibility and the perpetual sequentiality of both models. The couplet ironizes both models, ultimately, putting both their mutual incongruity and repetitive sequentiality in a larger cyclical totalization in which one is only the obverse of the other, both existing in a mutual temporal dependency, represented formally by the chiastic *well knows* and *knows well.* (The poem also comes full circle in its deictic "*this* hell," indicating that the speaker is back where he started in line 1.) For all that, the major aesthetic move of the sonnet is to paint over our first impression—the shame and blame of lust—with a second, the joy and sorrow and unreality of lust; and then to paint over that with the ironizing and totalizing third—that no matter how much we know of the aftermath, we will be unable to shun the joy. Through the third layer of ironic knowledge we see still the two underpaintings—the pentimenti—the first of a post-erotic hell, the second of a brief erotic heaven. Thus, reading for difference among the quatrains and couplet provides a far more interesting—and I could say more "worthy"—shape for this poem than the shape—an unvaried condemnation of lust—offered by those who read the poem along the axis of similarity (see, e.g., Kerrigan).

A superior aesthetic value is normally ascribed to the last stage of a painting exhibiting pentimento; and we do perhaps tend to ascribe a higher epistemological value to the most comprehensive account in a poem of the phases of experience that it treats. But we must recall that in aesthetic terms we ascribe final value not to any one set of lines, but rather to the entire sonnet. The aim of this sonnet has been to solve the problem of representing the various mental phases aesthetically deployed here: judgmental disgust, affective memory, and the ironic totalizing of both. We value Shakespeare's success in representing each, and we admire as well the successive motivations by which each believably replaces its predecessor stage(s). We are drawn to notice the three models because the first careens from nouns into adjectives, the second (Q_3) reverts to nouns, and the third (C) retreats into proverbial diction (among other differences). It is these grammatical and discursive differences that warn us that we must read along an axis of difference, if we are to understand the poem at all. An account of 129 that never asks why its initial contained scholastic and individual definition hurtles into a spate of adjectives of social trespass; or why the initial nouns and adjectives suddenly are displaced by past participles; or why the past participles are then displaced by a pointed return to four nouns *(bliss, woe, joy, dream)* refuting the opening's four nouns (*expense*, *spirit*, *waste*, and *shame*)—an account not following the conspicuous signals afforded by the poem concerning its own phases of difference—will never see the functional aesthetic dynamic of the poem.

Couplet Tie: *shun* [*ac**tion***, *posses**sion***] (2, 9, 14)

130

MY Miſtres eyes are nothing like the Sunne,
Currall is farre more red,then her lips red,
If ſnow be white,why then her breſts are dun:
If haires be wiers,black wiers grow on her head:
I haue ſeene Roſes damaskt,red and white,
But no ſuch Roſes ſee I in her cheekes,
And in ſome perfumes is there more delight,
Then in the breath that from my Miſtres reekes.
I loue to heare her ſpeake,yet well I know,
That Muſicke hath a farre more pleaſing ſound:
I graunt I neuer ſaw a goddeſſe goe,
My Miſtres when ſhee walkes treads on the ground.
And yet by heauen I thinke my loue as rare,
As any ſhe beli'd with falſe compare.

My mistress' eyes are nothing like the sun;
Coral is far more red than her lips' red;
If snow be white, why then her breasts are dun;
If hairs be wires, black wires grow on her head.
I have seen roses damasked, red and white,
But no such roses see I in her cheeks,
And in some perfumes is there more delight
Than in the breath that from my mistress reeks.
I love to hear her speak, yet well I know
That music hath a far more pleasing sound;
I grant I never saw a goddess go—
My mistress when she walks treads on the ground.
And yet by heaven I think my love as rare
As any she belied with false compare.

THIS sonnet is a reply-poem to a poet who has just written a sonnet to his mistress, which reads, more or less:

My mistress' eyes are brilliant as the sun,
And coral's colour matches her lips' red;
Her snowy breasts are like to others none,
And golden wires ornament her head.
A bed of damask roses, red and white,
I find within the confines of her cheeks,
And perfume's self, conferring all delight,
Breathes in the breath that from my mistress reeks.
I love to hear her speak, and well I know
That only music hath such pleasing sound;
In walking she doth like a goddess go,
Her dainty feet scarce printing on the ground.
In all, by heaven I think my love as rare
As any she conceivèd for compare.

Shakespeare's speaker retorts, "I don't know about *your* mistress, but *my* mistress is nothing like that: she's a real woman, and doesn't need any *false compare* to distort her attractions." And so he launches into a series of contrastive comparisons: "*My* mistress' eyes are nothing *like* the sun." The speaker's contrastive comparisons—"russet yeas and honest kersey noes," to use Berowne's phrase when he forswears "three-piled hyperboles" (*Love's Labour's Lost*, V, ii, 407, 413)—are deliberately down-to-earth, but his concluding words, "*I think my love as rare* as any you've made hyperboles about" shows him to be "sincere" in love. This mock-blazon pretends to be a denigration, but is in fact a defense of the woman as she is, as *rare* as any.

The structure of the poem changes in each part. Q_1 simply denies the supposed antecedent hyperbole, but each line is an ingenious variant on denial:

1. eyes—sun *(nothing like);*
2. coral—lips *(far more red);*
3. *If snow is your standard* for whiteness, breasts = dun;
4. If one can call hairs (by metaphor) wires, hers are *black* wires.

In the cleverness of this "baring the device," Shakespeare shows that the familiar resorts of contemporary love-poets—(1) comparison by simile, (2) hierarchizing, (3) valuing by a standard, (4) metaphorizing—can be preposterous when called to the bench of accuracy.

Q_2 is divided between personal observation *(I have seen . . . see I)* and impersonal observation *(there is).* The latter reorders hierarchy against the mistress, saying perfume is sweeter than her breath, while the former denies metaphor altogether, saying cheeks are nothing like roses.

Affect at last enters in Q_3—*I love to hear her speak*—and continues in C—*I think my love as rare as any.* The rehierarchizing begun with perfume and breath continues with music and speech, a goddess' locomotion and the mistress' treading. Here the hierarchizing reaches its humorous climax: "Personally I've never set eyes on a goddess, unlike your privileged self. You say your mistress glides like a goddess; well, *my* mistress, when *she* walks, treads on the ground."

The speaker's submerged irritation at the excesses of love-lyric bursts out in his final oath—*And yet by heaven*—and in his dismissal of his fellow poets' simile-making as he calls it *false.*

Shakespeare's mock-blazon has sometimes been thought misogynistic, in part because readers have formed their idea of it from its octave, where nothing positive is predicated of the mistress. (Of course, nothing negative is predicated of her either.) In the sestet, as I've said, love enters *(I love to hear her speak);* and the fact that music is said to be *far more pleasing* than her speech (or anyone's speech) need not be thought of as a criticism. Speech cannot rival the aesthetic power of music, nor can anyone walk like a goddess. His beloved, the speaker ends by saying, is *as rare as* anyone else's, the more so since the other women are actively *mis*represented *(belied)* in their sycophants' verses.

When the poem is read as simple statement without contrastive emphasis—"My mistress' eyes are X, her breasts are Y"—it sounds, as some have said, like a denigration. But the couplet, in its contrastive force and its oath, shows us how to read the body of the poem contrastively: "*My* mistress' eyes, whatever you say about *your* mistress' eyes, are *not* like the sun." This is another case in which perceiving the accurate nature of the speech-act mimicked by the sonnet is indispensable to a correct understanding of the poem.

Couplet Tie: *love* (9, 13)
more (2, 7, 10)
A witty summation of the point of the poem: the evils of hyperbole versus the tempered nature of believable praise.

Note: Shakespeare is extraordinarily close to the poems he parodies. See, e.g., one such model, from Thomas Watson's 1581 *Hekatompathia:*

Harke you that list to heare what sainte I serve:
Her yellowe lockes exceede the beaten goulde;
Her sparkeling eies in heav'n a place deserve;
Her forehead high and faire of comely moulde;
  Her wordes are musicke all of silver sounde;
  Her wit so sharpe as like can scarce be found:
Each eybrowe hanges like *Iris* in the skies;
Her *Eagles* nose is straight of stately frame;
On either cheeke a *Rose* and *Lillie* lies;
Her breath is sweete perfume, or hollie flame;
  Her lips more red than any *Corall* stone;
  Her necke more white, then aged *Swans* yt mone;
Her brest transparent is, like *Christall* rocke;
Her fingers long, fit for *Apolloes* Lute;
Her slipper such as *Momus* dare not mocke;
Her vertues all so great as make me mute:
  What other partes she hath I neede not say,
  Whose face alone is cause of my decaye.

Thomas Watson, *The Hekatompathia or Passionate Centurie of Love* (London: reprinted from the original edition of circa 1581 by the Spenser Society, n.d.), VII, p. 21.

131

THou art as tiranous,ſo as thou art,
As thoſe whoſe beauties proudly make them cruell;
For well thou know'ſt to my deare doting hart
Thou art the fai:eſt and moſt precious Iewell.
Yet in good faith ſome ſay that thee behold,
Thy face hath not the power to make loue grone;
To ſay they erre,I dare not be ſo bold,
Although I ſweare it to my ſelfe alone.
And to be ſure that is not falſe I ſweare
A thouſand grones but thinking on thy face,
One on anothers necke do witneſſe beare
Thy blacke is faireſt in my iudgements place.
In nothing art thou blacke ſaue in thy deeds,
And thence this ſlaunder as I thinke proceeds.

Thou art as tyrannous, so as thou art,
As those whose beauties proudly make them cruel;
For well thou know'st to my dear doting heart
Thou art the fairest and most precious jewel.
Yet in good faith some say that thee behold,
Thy face hath not the power to make love groan;
To say they err, I dare not be so bold,
Although I swear it to myself alone.
And to be sure that is not false I swear,
A thousand groans but thinking on thy face
One on another's neck do witness bear
Thy black is fairest in my judgement's place.
In nothing art thou black save in thy deeds,
And thence this slander as I think proceeds.

"SINCE you are so beautiful *(fair)*—even if you are a brunette—why do some people say that no one could fall in love with you *(thy face hath not the power to make love groan)?* The only bad *(black)* thing about you is how cruel *(tyrannous)* you are to me, and it is these *black deeds* against me that make people say (*slandering* you) that your face is unlovable."

What, we can reasonably ask, would be the speaker's motive for saying this to the lady? Surely it is to make her behave better toward him so that the world will forgive her and enroll her among those attractive enough to provoke love. He appeals, therefore, to her social self-interest to make her cease tormenting him. (This act implies that any altruistic reason would not appeal to her.) The speaker also represents himself as too timid to stand up for her in public *(I dare not be so bold)*, so that if she wants the slander to end, she will have to begin to act lovable instead of *tyrannous*.

This elaborately summoned-up smokescreen of the social world—incorporating proud fair beauties, their lovers to whom they are tyrannous, and the "some" who criticize the dark lady—acts to conceal the "real" motivation of the poem: "Please stop being so cruel to me." It will not move the lady simply to say, "I am burdened by a thousand groans of frustrated love." A reason for talking about the inner groans has to be presented, and therefore the speaker invents the putative remark by *some that behold* her, "Her face has not the power to make love groan." He also invents his own social timidity, his consequently private counterswearing, and the juridical *witness* of the groans to prove he has not perjured himself. The (actual and factual) groans are thus inserted into a whole invented public/private scenario—and all to say, "I am unhappy, you are cruel to me, please change your deeds with respect to me." To say all this, that is, without appearing abject, and while offering the lady a self-interested reason to be kind to him.

The speaker, to persuade the lady, divides himself into lover, oath taker, thinker, and judge: she is of course *fairest* to his *heart*, but public denigration of her looks forces him privately to *swear* that her face can make love groan; he *thinks on* her face, and the groans testify that her coloring is *fairest*—not to his heart, as he said earlier (line 4), but to his *judgement*. He is thus making a quadruple asseveration of his fidelity via the little narrative of public *slander*.

The division of quatrains bears out the invented nature of the public *slander.* Q_1 simply sets the speaker's dilemma: "Though I love you best, you are tyrannous toward me." His invention of a self-interested reason for her to stop her tyranny generates Q_2, allowing for the expression, in Q_3, of his true inner state of groaning frustration. The *q.e.d.* of the couplet simply draws the moral. I do not believe that *thy deeds* has a wider reference than "thy tyranny toward me," since the *slander* (her face is not lovable) has no moral content. "Fair" beauties can be tyrannous with impunity, but "black" beauties must behave gently to be thought lovable.

In such a sonnet, propositions mean nothing; they are as likely to be made up *(some say . . . I swear [they err])* as to be reliable. Strategy, by contrast, means everything; and solving the *motivation* of propositions ("Why is the speaker making up his little slander-story?") is crucial to understanding both tone and structure.

Couplet Tie: *thou art* [*art thou*] (1, 1, 3, 13)
black (12, 13)
think [*-ing*] (10, 14)

132

THine eies I loue,and they as pittying me,
Knowing thy heart torment me with diſdaine,
Haue put on black,and louing mourners bee,
Looking with pretty ruth vpon my paine.
And truly not the morning Sun of Heauen
Better becomes the gray cheeks of th' Eaſt,
Nor that full Starre that vſhers in the Eauen
Doth halfe that glory to the ſober Weſt
As thoſe two morning eyes become thy face:
O let it then as well beſeeme thy heart
To mourne for me ſince mourning doth thee grace,
And ſute thy pitty like in euery part.
Then will I ſweare beauty her ſelfe is blacke,
And all they foule that thy complexion lacke.

Thine eyes I love, and they, as pitying me,
Knowing thy heart torment me with disdain,
Have put on black, and loving mourners be,
Looking with pretty ruth upon my pain.
And truly not the morning sun of heaven
Better becomes the grey cheeks of the east,
Nor that full star that ushers in the even
Doth half that glory to the sober west
As those two mourning eyes become thy face.
O let it then as well beseem thy heart
To mourn for me, since mourning doth thee grace,
And suit thy pity like in every part.
Then will I swear beauty herself is black,
And all they foul that thy complexion lack.

THE *swear[ing]* of 131 continues here, but whereas in 131 the speaker swore that his mistress' face had the power to make love groan, here he promises to swear that *beauty herself is black,* raising blackness to the level of Platonic form. Once again, this is a strategic sonnet, in which he wants the lady to change the disposition of her heart toward him. At present, her heart *torment[s] [him] with disdain;* she is still being tyrannous. Since his previous (public) scenario in 131 has apparently failed, he now invents another self-interested reason for her to change—it will increase her attractiveness if she suits her heart in mourning to harmonize with the mourning guise of her black eyes. By creating a new decorum of harmonized and aestheticized selfhood, she will ascend to the level of a Platonic form, disadvantaging all competition.

This strategy is enunciated only in the second line of Q_3, with the plea, *O let it then as well beseem thy heart to mourn for me.* The octave disguises the poem's real speech-act (a plea) in its presenting genre, that of praise, praise so lavish it "spills over" its putative limit, the octave, and takes up the first line of Q_3, thereby curtailing the plea from its proper four lines to only three—tucking it in, as it were, between the copious praise and the hyperbolic closing promise *(Then will I swear).*

The pathos of these two sonnets resides of course in their conveying, by their convoluted aesthetic strategies, the speaker's certainty that a "straight" plea would have no effect on the woman. Only self-interest will change her behavior.

The little myth-of-origin in Q_1—because the mistress pities her lover, she has garbed her eyes in black so they might mourn his pain—suggests that her eyes were once blue but have darkened with *pretty ruth* on his behalf. This small—but to the speaker large—token of sympathy on her part (wholly invented, of course, by himself) causes the enormous dilation of gratitude *(and truly)* which causes the cosmic metaphors, their two enjambments, and their emphatic trochees and spondees, which subside to iambs only at the close:

Ănd trúlў, nŏt thĕ mórnĭng sún ŏf héavĕn
Béttĕr bĕcómĕs thĕ gráy chéeks ŏf thĕ éast,

Nor that full star that ushers in the even
Doth half that glory to the sober west
As those two mourning eyes become thy face.

The plea (lines 10–12) distinguishes itself from the praise by its "logical" evenness of iambic rationality:

O let it then as well beseem thy heart
To mourn for me, since mourning doth thee grace,
And suit thy pity like in every part,

The promise (lines 13–14) is distinguished by its trochaic reversals—

Then will I swear beauty herself

before it subsides to a largely iambic close:

is black,
And all they foul that thy complexion lack.

The pun on *morning* and *mourning*, the play on *becomes/become/beseem*, the dividing of the lady into heart and eyes in order to plead for a reconciling decorum of pity in both parts, are all playful aspects of the poem, part of *its* "pretty ruth." On the other hand, the swelling comparisons by which those two (the number emphasized by being—unnecessarily—specified) eyes are rated as equal to the sun and doubly superior to Venus represent a moment of liberty in the poem, in which it almost "forgets" that it has a strategy, and wanders freely in feeling.

The poem would be complete if it ended with *Then will I swear beauty herself is black*. Why draw in other beauties in line 14 in a negative comparison? One reason is the persistent wish to rhyme *black* and its "opposite," *lack* (as if to prove that *black*, by containing *lack*, cannot embody it). Another is perhaps to continue the social reference found in sonnet 131. But chiefly, I think, the other beauties are brought in so that the entire female world can be divided into two under the patronage of Platonic *beauty herself*, which should perhaps be written *Beauty herself:* the sheep and goats of the division are the fair black beauties and the foul lack-black others.

This cosmic division of the (female) world matches the cosmic comparisons to the sun and Venus earlier, and ends the poem on the macrocosmic scale of Idea and value.

Couplet Tie: *black* (3, 13)

133

BEſhrew that heart that makes my heart to groane
For that deepe wound it giues my friend and me;
I'ſt not ynough to torture me alone,
But ſlaue to ſlauery my ſweet'ſt friend muſt be.
Me from my ſelfe thy cruell eye hath taken,
And my next ſelfe thou harder haſt ingroſſed,
Of him,my ſelfe,and thee I am forſaken,
A torment thrice three-fold thus to be croſſed:
Priſon my heart in thy ſteele boſomes warde,
But then my friends heart let my poore heart bale,
Who ere keepes me,let my heart be his garde,
Thou canſt not then vſe rigor in my Iaile.
  And yet thou wilt,for I being pent in thee,
  Perforce am thine and all that is in me.

Beshrew that heart that makes my heart to groan
For that deep wound it gives my friend and me;
Is't not enough to torture me alone,
But slave to slavery my sweet'st friend must be?
Me from my self thy cruel eye hath taken,
And my next self thou harder hast engrossed;
Of him, my self, and thee I am forsaken,
A torment thrice threefold thus to be crossed.
Prison my heart in thy steel bosom's ward,
But then my friend's heart let my poor heart bail;
Whoe'er keeps me, let my heart be his guard,
Thou canst not then use rigour in my jail.
  And yet thou wilt, for I, being pent in thee,
  Perforce am thine, and all that is in me.

THIS sonnet of the lady's infidelity with the speaker's friend has driven Ingram and Redpath to a diagram and to a comparison with "Chinese boxes." The word *torment* (reinforced by *torture*) is reused from 132, and *groan* from 131, but by the time the speaker reaches the couplet, he has abandoned his strategy of plea, visible—in however convoluted a form—in 131 and 132, and present in the body of 133. Here, the plea is entered not for the self but for the friend, the young man now caught in the lady's toils.

Ingram and Redpath's diagram, which represents the speaker as still whole at the end of the octave—though having lost a part of himself called *myself*—seems to me too sanguine. (I believe one should retain, for the fiction of this poem to be intelligible, the Quarto spelling, *my self.*) The crucial proposition is *I am forsaken of him, my self, and thee.* What existential status is, or can be, ascribed to the *I*—missing his self—who is the speaker of this statement? Such a paradox drives us to trace the evolution of the *I* in the sonnet, "a process in stages" (as Ingram and Redpath call it) which led them to their diagrams.

As I see it, these are the stages of the octave:

1. I am separate from her: *that heart* (of hers) makes *my heart* groan.
2. I am inseparable from my friend: when she wounds, she wounds us both at once, *my friend and me.*
3. He was once separate from her, when she tortured *me alone.* Presumably at that time he and I were one, without reference to her.
4. The friend is now en*slave*d by her.
5. Her cruel eye has taken the speaker from himself *(me from my self).*
6. She has even more powerfully captured the speaker's *next self,* the young man.
7. In so doing, she has forsaken the speaker as her erotic object.

As I see these narrated stages, they represent a pathetic attempt by the speaker to preserve a selfhood in the present-tense moment of disintegration (Q_1). *My heart, me, me*—the self-namings in Q_1—maintain the fiction of an integrated self. But when the ego separates into *me, my self, I, my next self* in Q_2—in its frantic attempts to adjust to the joint love-wound, the solo torture, and the friend's slavery—it can no longer represent itself as whole. Its disseminated fragments, under this triple insult, constitute only a ghost self. What is left after *the torment thrice threefold* when one is forsaken by one's self, one's next self, and one's beloved? Hardly an outline in the air where once a body was. (The visual and phonetic alliteration of ***th**rice **th**reefold **th**us* is the poet's "hard engrossing" of this torture.)

A massive attempt to reassemble the fragments in a more ego-satisfying fashion organizes Q_3. They are repackaged as a series of concentric spaces: imprisoned inside the lady's *steel bosom* will be the speaker's *heart;* and inside *his* heart will lodge, in *his* prison, the friend's heart. Theoretically, this is to benefit the friend *(let my heart be his guard)*, but since the speaker's heart is also a jail (as we know from *bail*), he has the pleasures of intimate wardenship, and is "closer" to the friend than is the lady.

In the couplet, the implied previous resistance and plea ("*Thou* canst not then use rigour in *my* jail") collapses: *And yet thou wilt.* The speaker is *per**force*** hers, causing him to be ***fors**aken.* The relation of cause and effect—as *force* causes *forsaken*—makes the result seem inevitable.

The model of thought exhibited in 133—that of a (relatively) simple account of bad things (Q_1) followed by an intolerable complication of effect (Q_2), which forces a request for relief and intelligibility (Q_3), which subsides in a helpless giving-up (C)—is a small replica of the torture chamber itself with its tightening of the screws. Initial cursing *(beshrew that heart)* gives way to protesting questions (lines 3–4); accusation (5–6) produces hopeless knotted realization (7–8); and a lost hope of negotiation (9–12) finally collapses utterly. This psychological mimicry of torment—by the speaker's successive speech-acts of cursing, interrogating, accusing, narrating *(am forsaken)*, pleading, negotiating, conceding *(whoe'er keeps me)*, conjecturing *(thou canst not then use rigour)*, prophesying, and acknowledging—makes the sonnet a torment to the reader as well. The poem marks, by its use of words like *wound, torture, slave, slavery, cruel, harder, torment, crossed, prison, steel,* and *rigour,* the first presentation of the dark lady as without redeeming qualities of beauty or "pretty ruth."

Couplet Tie: [*per-*]*force, fors*[*-aken*] (7, 14)

134

SO now I haue confeſt that he is thine,
And I my ſelfe am morgag'd to thy will,
My ſelfe Ile forfeit,ſo that other mine,
Thou wilt reſtore to be my comfort ſtill:
But thou wilt not,nor he will not be free,
For thou art couetous,and he is kinde,
He learnd but ſuretie-like to write for me,
Vnder that bond that him as faſt doth binde.
The ſtatute of thy beauty thou wilt take,
Thou vſurer that put'ſt forth all to vſe,
And ſue a friend,came debter for my ſake,
So him I looſe through my vnkinde abuſe.
Him haue I loſt, thou haſt both him and me,
He paies the whole,and yet am I not free.

So now I have confessed that he is thine,
And I myself am mortgaged to thy will,
Myself I'll forfeit, so that other mine
Thou wilt restore to be my comfort still:
But thou wilt not, nor he will not be free,
For thou art covetous, and he is kind;
He learned but surety-like to write for me
Under that bond that him as fast doth bind.
The statute of thy beauty thou wilt take,
Thou usurer that put'st forth all to use,
And sue a friend came debtor for my sake,
So him I lose through my unkind abuse.
Him have I lost, thou hast both him and me;
He pays the whole, and yet am I not free.

MANY poems, of which this is one, end where they began; they "get nowhere." Such a structure puts particular stress on what happens in the middle, since every poem has a natural pressure to "get somewhere," and a poem's struggle against a defeated conclusion makes for interesting strategies.

Sonnet 134 takes stock of the torment of the affair between the friend and the mistress announced in 133. The truth has settled in: *So now I have confessed that he is thine*, says the speaker as the poem opens; and he closes, after all his strategic struggles, once more confessing *Him have I lost.* What has motivated the struggles in between, and how are they deployed?

The motive for the tortuous middle is the attempt to rationalize the young man's defection. In 133, he has *forsaken* (a verb implying free will) the speaker; yet he is tautologically *slave* to *slavery*, an involuntary subject of the regime of slavery imposed by the mistress. The little fantasy in 133 of concentric jails (the young man inside the speaker's heart, the speaker's heart in the *steel bosom* of the mistress) has not survived its small and futile moment of hope. Sonnet 134 admits the speaker's definitive separation from the young man, who now is united to the mistress: *he is thine*. The speaker's new metaphor for himself is that he is a mortgaged debtor for whom the young man has stood surety, becoming himself forfeit. No matter how much the speaker wants to reverse the situation and forfeit himself instead, he is powerless: the *bond* now *bind[s]* the young man as well as the speaker. The speaker has been allowed his mortgage by the young man's standing surety for him; perhaps the images of prison in 133 suggested the debt metaphor of 134. Because the mistress now has two sources of repayment instead of one, she exacts the sexual debt from the young man, who pays. It is her beauty that gives her legal rights to the debt of love, yet to collect the debt in this way makes her a "money-lender," a promiscuous sexual *usurer that put[s] forth all to use*, and then collects her interest.

Use, its compound *abuse*, its anagram *sue*, and its agency-noun *usurer* (along with words like ***surety*** and ***statute*** and ***lose***) organize the music of the latter part of the poem, rising to a climax in Q_3, which foregrounds *use* and *abuse* as rhyme-words: *The statute of thy beauty thou wilt take, / Thou* *usurer that put'st forth all to use, / And sue a friend . . . / So him I lose through my unkind abuse*. This music is introduced in Q_2 with *surety* and concluded in C with the past participle of "lose," *lost*. The music of the first six lines is dominated by the *-or-*, *-ort* and *-for[t]* of ***mort**gaged*, ***for**feit*, *rest**ore***, *com**fort***, *n**or** **for***, ***for***. And there is another set of octave-sestet links in *k: confessed, comfort, covetous, kind, take, came, sake, unkind*. Q_2 and C "illegally" rhyme on the same words reversed—*free/me; me/free*—making an internal chiastic "jail." And the Couplet Tie, which embraces both *free* (5, 14) and *lose* [*lost*] (12, 13) has a double recall-value in its twinned phrases: *he will not be free . . . and yet I am not free; him I lose . . . him have I lost.*

The asymmetry between these two doublets puts into relief the various agents in the poem: agency is ascribed by the speaker to himself, to the friend, and to the woman. Yet this agency is confused by the speaker's calling the friend "that other *mine*," and averring that the friend learned "to write *for me*." A "bond . . . *as fast*" binds both the speaker and the friend, who came "debtor *for my sake*." The opening acknowledgment, *he is thine*, hopes to find itself false by means of all the above asseverations of bondedness and identity between the two men. Even in the prophecy *The statute of thy beauty thou wilt take*, the consequent *So him I lose*, though apparently in the present, is really in the envisaged future. It is only in the couplet that all the strategies intervening between line 1 and line 13 are known as futile: *him have I lost*, says the speaker in the present perfect, before returning to the present tense of line 1—*thou hast both him and me.*

All these strategies are ways of blaming the woman, rather than the young man, for the affair. The speaker is certainly hers by his own (apparently voluntary) transaction by which he became *mortgaged to [her] will*. But after the opening statement in lines 1–2, the imagination of the speaker begins to conjure up an ingenuously metaphorical excuse for the young man's behavior: as I have said earlier, he acted as surety, and since the speaker could not pay, the young man became a debtor for the speaker's sake, and now pays all. This description of the behavior "enforced" upon the young man might convince, except for two of the clauses also predicated of the young man: *he will not be free* and *he is kind*, both of them interpretable as indications of collusion on the young man's part. Yet each is ambiguous enough to be taken as another instance of enforcement. The painful oscillation of the speaker between acknowledging (however ambiguously) the young man's free will and sustaining the complex *bond/surety/debtor* metaphor gives the sonnet its emotional tension. The *mortgaged* speaker offers, futilely, to *forfeit* himself (but, being mortgaged, he is already forfeit, since he cannot pay).

Shakespeare's language for human transactions here, as elsewhere in the *Sonnets*, is ruthlessly legal, proffering words like *statute* and *bond* and *pay* as appropriate terms for a certain sort of human relation. For this sort of sex, he implies, the secular language of obligation in law, contracts, debts, and forfeits offers the most plausible description. At the same time, this cold language is internally rebuked by vestiges of the old moral theology (*covetous[ness]* is one of the seven deadly sins) and of the old courtly vocabulary of love *(comfort, kind);* the speaker is casting about within his mind for the proper discourse to use.

Or, in the absence of a vanished moral theology, one can set up an alternative system of absolutes. Here, the substituted absolute is *beauty*, that self-justifying *statute* (the locus of appeal in law). In 133, we saw relations of love rephrased in terms not of contract law but of feudal power *(torture, slavery, jail)*. Available social models are inadequate to this sexual triangle (cf. the nutritional/medical model in 118 for another searching-out of similes for socially dubious love-relations). The repeated attempts in the earlier sonnets to seek models in the natural world (e.g., 18's *summer's day*) are vitiated in the second sequence by the monstrousness of the love-relation for which figures are being sought.

Here in 134, there seems to be a Latin pun on the sounds of *utor, uti, usus sum: sta**tute**, **beaut**y, use*, etc. In the interweaving of agency, *she sues, he pays, I lose;* she is *covet**ous***, and puts forth all to *use;* I *lose* through *abuse*. He is *kind*, my abuse is *unkind*. One must follow these and other such echoes through a pronominal maze. The shuttle of relation darts back and forth from party to party in this text of tangled anguish, with one mysterious dart out to the "objective" *bond that . . . doth bind*, as though that bond were external to all participants, though it must be the voluntary mortgage by which the speaker has enslaved himself to beauty.

The poem is not improved, I think, by the sexual pun some commentators insist on seeing in the word *whole*. Surely Kerrigan is wrong when he identifies the *usurer* as the young man; it is the woman who is being addressed in line 10.

Couplet Tie: *free* (5, 14): *nor he will not be free; and yet I am not free*
lose [*lost*] (12, 13): *him I lose; him have I lost*
This is a Couplet Tie of exceptionally close echoes of whole phrases.

135

WHo euer hath her wiſh,thou haſt thy *Will*,
And *Will* too boote,and *Will* in ouer-plus,
More then enough am I that vexe thee ſtill,
To thy ſweet will making addition thus.
Wilt thou whoſe will is large and ſpatious,
Not once vouchſafe to hide my will in thine,
Shall will in others ſeeme right gracious,
And in my will no faire acceptance ſhine:
The ſea all water,yet receiues raine ſtill,
And in aboundance addeth to his ſtore,
So thou beeing rich in *Will* adde to thy *Will*,
One will of mine to make thy large *Will* more.
Let no vnkinde,no faire beſeechers kill,
Thinke all but one,and me in that one *Will*.

Whoever hath her wish, thou hast thy Will,
And Will to boot, and Will in overplus;
More than enough am I that vex thee still,
To thy sweet will making addition thus.
Wilt thou, whose will is large and spacious,
Not once vouchsafe to hide my will in thine?
Shall will in others seem right gracious,
And in my will no fair acceptance shine?
The sea, all water, yet receives rain still,
And in abundance addeth to his store;
So thou being rich in Will add to thy Will
One will of mine to make thy large Will more.
Let no unkind, no fair beseechers kill;
Think all but one, and me in that one Will.

THIS perplexing, even maddening sonnet is full of implications of a divided subjectivity teased out, notably, by Joel Fineman in *Shakespeare's Perjur'd Eye*, where he treats it together with its companion "Will" sonnets. Though it begins in statement, it quickly becomes, from line 5 on, a prayer; in fact, in another poem, lines 5–10 could be addressed to God: *wilt thou . . . not once vouchsafe . . . right gracious . . . acceptance shine . . . in abundance addeth*. Such echoes of liturgical prayer make the sonnet one of several blasphemously parodying an alternate discourse. Against the discourse of divine generosity Shakespeare sets a mercantile discourse of *addition (addeth, add)* and surplus (*overplus, rich, large*, and *more*). Mediating between the "divine" discourse and the mercantile discourse is the discourse of what might seem, as Booth suggests, natural and/or proverbial exemplum: *the sea, all water, yet receives rain still.* (In fact, the sea, though the speaker's phrasing is proverbial, may come from Ecclesiastes 1:6–7, "All the rivers run into the sea; yet the sea is not full.") The second line of the exemplum uses all three discourses: "*And* [the (proverbial) sea] *in* [divine] *abundance addeth* [the linking word used in all three discourses] *to his store* [mercantile]."

The difficulties raised by the conjunction of these three discourses suggest the ontological confusions with respect to the woman. Is she an idealized Petrarchan goddess, above good and evil? Is she a natural essence, like the ocean? Or is she a calculating accumulator of goods? The speaker perceives his own superfluity very clearly in Q_1: *More than enough am I that vex thee.* This superfluity is enacted by the cloying superfluity of the rhyme in *-ill*, appearing in Q_1, Q_3 and C, and even more by the superfluity, within this rhyme scheme, of the word *will* as end-rhyme (lines 1, 11, 14) as well as its presence as internal rhyme (2, 2, 4, 5, 6, 7, 8, 11, 12, 12). The presence of thirteen uses of *will* in a fourteen-line poem suggests, perhaps, that the woman, even to the end, has not accepted the speaker's will (which, if she had, would add one will, making a perfect parity of lines and *will*). (If, on the other hand, one counts the secret "will" in ***wilt***, the parity hoped for is hidden in the poem.) Q_1 and Q_3 use the same rhyme reversed: *Will/still, still/Will*, proposing a happy outcome; but the devastating reversal in C—*kill/Will*—forbodes a worse ending, however much the speaker implores the reverse.

The superfluity of *-ill* in the rhyme is matched by the superfluity of the sound *-ous*, as both Q_1 and Q_2 rhyme in that sound *(-plus, thus, spacious, gracious)*, which, together with their identical rhymes in *-ill* makes them seem a double-quatrain parody of "overplus." Q_2 is composed of two ironic rhetorical questions, one mirroring the ontological grandeur of the addressee, the other her generous benevolence toward others. The Q_3 exemplum of the sea reinforces them both, the first by *the sea*, *all water* (ontology), the second by *receives rain* (which is connected by alliteration to line 11's *rich*). The conclusion of Q_3, *So thou*, repeats the pattern of the exemplum: she is ontologically *rich in Will*, and can therefore generously add *one [other] will*, the speaker's own.

The couplet, by a repetition of an earlier word, *fair*, suggests that "*fair* beseechers" (line 13) deserve "*fair* acceptance" (line 8). (The parallel is made more noticeable by having both of the twin phrases prefaced by *no*.) But the outcome of the plea is left in abeyance.

The alternatives after all, from the rhymes, are either *kill Will* or *still Will*, and if *still Will* wins, two to one, yet *kill Will* has the last word. (I agree with Evans' support for the reading, "Let no unkind [persons] kill no fair beseechers," as more consonant with the Quarto's punctuation.)

The conspicuous urbanity of this sonnet can be appreciated only when measured against the humiliation of its putative occasion: the lover is refused access by his mistress, though she is freely receiving at least one other sexual partner. The "normal" requests arising in such a condition would be either that she should dismiss the other lover or that she should at least afford her previous lover a turn at her "rich will. " However, the speaker's request is neither of these: it is that she can cram him in as well, as lines 11–12 explicitly say. This shocking plea—shocking if it were said less lightly—argues for the view that the speaker is aroused by participating vicariously in the promiscuity of the mistress.

KEY WORD: WILL

Couplet Tie: *will* (passim) 13 times, and perhaps meant to be seen in *wilt*
no fair (8, 13)

136

IF thy ſoule check thee that I come ſo neere,
Sweare to thy blind ſoule that I was thy *Will*,
And will thy ſoule knowes is admitted there,
Thus farre for loue, my loue-ſute ſweet fullfill.
Will, will fulfill the treaſure of thy loue,
I fill it full with wils, and my will one,
In things of great receit with eaſe we prooue.
Among a number one is reckon'd none.
Then in the number let me paſſe vntold,
Though in thy ſtores account I one muſt be,
For nothing hold me, ſo it pleaſe thee hold,
That nothing me, a ſome-thing ſweet to thee.
Make but my name thy loue, and loue that ſtill,
And then thou loueſt me for my name is *Will*.

If thy soul check thee that I come so near,
Swear to thy blind soul that I was thy Will,
And will thy soul knows is admitted there;
Thus far for love, my love-suit, sweet, fulfil.
Will will fulfil the treasure of thy love,
Ay, fill it full with wills, and my will one.
In things of great receipt with ease we prove
Among a number one is reckoned none:
Then in the number let me pass untold,
Though in thy store's account I one must be;
For nothing hold me, so it please thee hold
That nothing me, a something sweet to thee.
Make but my name thy love, and love that still,
And then thou lovest me for my name is Will.

OF THE several curious things in this sonnet of number, the most cunning is the difference between Q_3 (the *nothing* quatrain) and the other three parts of the poem. That is, the words *love* and *will*, which are prominent in Q_1, Q_2, and C, and reinforced there by words rhyming with both *will (fulfil, fulfil, fill, still)* and with *love (prove)*, do not appear at all in Q_3, where the argument speciously suggests that there is a way in which to *love will* can be considered a *nothing*. It is as though Q_1, Q_2, and C were all composed around a major chord, of which no trace can be found in Q_3. (The word *number* is thought to refer only to plurals, so that *one* is no number; this quibble is the substance of Q_3.)

Other structures are even more salient here than quatrain structure. The first part of the poem—about *will*—takes up six lines, of which the first four are adjurations to the mistress *(swear, fulfill)* and the next two the speaker's third-person promise *(Will will fulfil)*. After that, in line 7, the scherzo on *one* and *none* begins, starting with a sophistic general proposition *(we prove . . . one is . . . none)*, followed by a series of first-person pleas *(let me pass untold, for nothing hold me, make but my name thy love, love that still)*.

There are, then, several overlapping ways of representing the structural divisions of the sonnet:

1. By *will/love*, 6-6-2
   (the inner six lines have no *will* or *love*)
2. By speech acts, 4-2-2-5-1
   adjuration (1–4)
   promise (5–6)
   proposition (7–8)
   plea (9–13)
   result-conclusion (14)
3. Pronominal, 6-2-6
   I (1–6)
   we (7–8)
   I (9–14)

These overlapping structures are sensed as "turns" in the poem and therefore as moments of emotional change in the speaker. For each "turn" the reader is prompted, therefore, to invent a motivation explaining why the speaker has veered, now this way, now that. This pressure on Shakespeare's part exerted on the creative invention of the reader is one factor in the greatness of the *Sonnets.* The biggest "turn" comes at lines 6–7, where the language turns away from the fantastic private artifice of copiousness in lines 5–6, and becomes suddenly public *(we)*—propositional, arithmetical, and plain (if paradoxical).

The second conspicuous "turn" comes at the couplet with the recurrence of *love* and *Will.* Because *will* and *one* alliterate phonetically in *w,* and because they are juxtaposed in line 6 ("my *will one*"), *one* becomes the "stand-in" for *will* in lines 7–10; and once "one" has been proved to be *none* (line 8), *nothing* becomes the placeholder for *will* and *one* in lines 11–12, where the juxtaposition *nothing me* recalls *my will one. Nothing* is then "replaced" by *its* alliterative place-holder, *name*, which is then triumphantly revealed to be *Will,* bringing us back to where we started in line 2. This series—*will/one/none/nothing/name/Will*—organizes this daisy-chain of a poem. The daisy-chain effect is reinforced by the ridiculous number of word-doublings, done often almost immediately, rarely with a delay. The tally of multiples is as follows: *thy soul* (3); *love* [*-st*] (6); *will* [*-s*] (6); *fulfil* [*full/fill*] (4); *sweet* (2); *one* (3); *thing* [*-s*] [*some-*, *no-*] (4); *number* (2); *hold* (2); *name* (2). This takes no account of near repetitions such as *suit/sweet* or *great/receipt/ease.* This sonnet, implicitly, asks with how few counters one can make up an *account.* (A pun on *cunt* may be intended, along with the puns on *will:* see Booth.)

The odd initial appearance of the mistress' *soul* begs some explanation, since the soul drops out as a *dramatis persona* after line 3. As I see it, the opening of the poem reads like a rejoinder. The lady has said: "Come not so near—my soul rebuffs thy will," and the speaker answers, "If thy soul check thee that I come so near, thy soul is blind. Will is a faculty of the soul (along with intellect); and thy soul *knows* (not having lost its other faculty, intellect) that *will* belongs in the soul too." After dismissing her objection (*soul* is *her* word, not his) the speaker never reverts to it, but speaks instead of his will finding a place not in her soul but where he would much rather be: in the *treasure* of her love. This too is logical, since the will's function (in faculty psychology) was to love the *good.* The poem wittily transfers the philosophical function of the will in pursuit of the good into an erotic function—*fil[ling] full.* The slippage from the spiritual *(soul)* to the philosophical *(will . . . is admitted there)*, and thence to the erotic *(will will fulfil)* is the major aesthetic gambit of lines 1–6. The erotic then becomes the arithmetical, in the play on number, until the erotic is restored via *sweet* in line 12. The rabbit-out-of-the-hat fillip at the end, by which the original plea—"love my will"—is reduced to "love my name" and then the two are shown to be one, is naively triumphant (as though the mistress hadn't known all along what his name is).

Is there anything serious about this sonnet? Surely there is a way to read it that makes it heartbreaking, for all its playfulness. The poignant note, I think, is introduced by the two apparently vocative uses of *sweet.* (Though it is true, as Booth says, that they don't have to be vocatives but can be post-positioned adjectives—meaning a "sweet love-suit," a "sweet something"—the vocative seems to me a far more likely reading in line 4 because the speaker is modestly unlikely to characterize his own love-suit as *sweet* (that would be for the woman to decide); and the vocative also seems more likely in line 12 because of the parallelism between a *nothing* and a *something.*) The pathos of the double vocative *sweet,* in the face of the lady's outright originating rebuff, comes from the abjectness of the speaker, who professes constancy even in pain. He does not say, "Swear to thy soul that I *am* thy Will"; rather, he puts it in the pathetic past imperfect (as I understand it)—"I was [used to be] thy Will." To urge "Thus far, *for love,* indulge me" and to call her *Sweet*—when she has shown no love, no sweetness—is to try to recall to her mind her recent more favorable disposition. This abjectness continues in the plea to pass untold, to be held a nothing, to be loved not as a person but only as a name. The "triumph" at the end then becomes a wan joke, its odd "present" tense *lovest* a wish-fulfillment rather than a will-fulfillment. Although sexual puns are present here as in 135, the reduction-to-nothing of selfhood, and then its replacement by verbal selfhood *(my name),* are less contrived than the proposal (repeated from 135 in lines 5–6 of this sonnet) to *fill [her treasure of love] full with wills and my will one.* Since a name cannot enter that sexual *treasure,* actual sexual conquest seems forgone by the end of the sonnet, in spite of the name's being Will. A name can be more easily admitted to her soul (as the first quatrain requests) than a fleshly *will* to her *treasure.* The fantasy of multiple lovers joining together to *fulfil* the mistress' *will* disappears after these two poems.

DEFECTIVE KEY WORDS: LOVE (missing in Q_3)
WILL (missing in Q_3)
Both these speaker-words *have* to be missing in the third quatrain, where the speaker becomes *a nothing.*

Couplet Tie: *love* [*-st*] (4, 4, 5, 13, 13, 14)
will (2, 3, 5, 5, 6, 6, 14)

137

Thou blinde foole loue, what dooſt thou to mine eyes,
That they behold and ſee not what they ſee:
They know what beautie is, ſee where it lyes,
Yet what the beſt is, take the worſt to be.
If eyes corrupt by ouer-partiall lookes,
Be anchord in the baye where all men ride,
Why of eyes falſehood haſt thou forged hookes,
Whereto the iudgement of my heart is tide?
Why ſhould my heart thinke that a ſeuerall plot,
Which my heart knowes the wide worlds common place?
Or mine eyes ſeeing this, ſay this is not
To put faire truth vpon ſo foule a face,
In things right true my heart and eyes haue erred,
And to this falſe plague are they now tranſferred.

Thou blind fool, Love, what dost thou to mine eyes,
That they behold and see not what they see?
They know what beauty is, see where it lies,
Yet what the best is take the worst to be.
If eyes, corrupt by over-partial looks,
Be anchored in the bay where all men ride,
Why of eyes' falsehood hast thou forgèd hooks,
Whereto the judgement of my heart is tied?
Why should my heart think that a several plot,
Which my heart knows the wide world's common place?
Or mine eyes seeing this, say this is not,
To put fair truth upon so foul a face?
In things right true my heart and eyes have erred,
And to this false plague are they now transferred.

SONNETS 137 and 148 are in a sense the "same" poem. They share an address to Love *(Thou blind fool, Love; O cunning Love)*, and they have in common the following words and homonyms: *blind, love, eyes, all men, false, judgement, see*[*-ing*], *fair, true*[*-th*], *foul, no* [*know*], *take* [*mistake*], *is not, ride* [*aright*]. They also share the *if*-clause and a series of persistent questions (the two in 137 usually emended to four, and four in 148). The most interesting verbal differences between them are the disappearance of the word *heart* in 148, and the transferral of blindness from Love to the lover. But the great imaginative difference between them is the overt presence of moral (especially sexual) opprobrium in 137, and its relative concealment within the more explicitly perceptual and aesthetic concerns of 148, which I will discuss in the commentary on that sonnet. The chief rhetorical difference between the two sonnets can be seen in the growth of *if*'s (from one in 137 to three in 148).

Sonnet 137, introducing into the Dark Lady series the concept of the deceiving eye familiar from the Young Man series, is a new version of the eye/heart sonnet (cf. 24, 46, 47, 93, 141, 148). (The puns critics have inferred from the presence of the words *bay* and *anchored* (*see*/sea, *tied*/tide) do not seem to me helpful to the poem, concerned as it is with eyes' sight and heart's judgment, nor do they pass the test for an adequate pun—that it be grammatically substitutable in the place of the word it puns on.) The *judgement* of the heart is not reliable judgment (which is performed only by reason). The heart not only judges here, it also *think[s]* and *knows;* the eyes not only *see* but also *know* and *say.* Thus, both heart and eyes can be said to *err*—a word normally used for reason but here, in its full moral meaning of "being errant," applicable to these faculties of sight and feeling which have usurped the functions of the mind (reason) and of speech.

The desperate confusions of 137 are made visible not only by its frantic questions and hypothesis and alternative proposals, but even more so by its division into two parts: the octave blames Love, but the sestet turns to blaming the speaker's own eyes and heart, and Love has dropped out of sight (Love's reappearance at the close of 148 is one reason for seeing that sonnet as a sequel or "completion" of 137). The other strikingly imagined feature of 137 is its insistent changes of focus from clause to clause. The first quatrain—appearing as one sentence in the Quarto—makes the indirect object *(eyes)* of the first verb *(dost)* the subject of the next five main verbs, *behold*, *see not*, *know*, *see*, and *take*. The second sentence (Q_2) uses one subject *(eyes)* for its antecedent and a different one (*thou* [Love]) for its consequent, with this confusion compounded by two dependent clauses, each with yet another subject *(all men; judgement)*. The antitheses in Q_1 have been constituted in words in fairly parallel syntactic positions (*behold* and *see not; best* and *worst*), but in Q_2 *the judgement of my heart* (a subject) is not grammatically parallel to its paired phrase, *eyes' falsehood* (object of a preposition). These confusions are furthered by the multiple vague reference of the repeated *this* in line 11 and the wholly unexplained reference of *things right true* in line 13.

In short, this is Shakespeare's invention of a discourse that he will characterize in 147:

> *[I am] frantic mad with evermore unrest;*
> *My thoughts and my discourse as madmen's are,*
> *At random from the truth vainly expressed.*

To have invented a frantic discourse of unrest is one of Shakespeare's chief accomplishments in the Dark Lady subsequence. This discourse is formed not only by the rhetorical, syntactic, and referential confusions sketched above, but also—and chiefly, in 137—by the catachresis, or mixed metaphor, in Q_2, where the "philosophical" discourse of Q_1 is suddenly submerged in an incoherent mixture of gazing, corruption, judgment, and iron-forging. Q_2 spurts up as in a geyser of released feeling (after the repressive "analytic" and carefully absolutist diction of *see not / see; best / worst* of lines 2–4). The last agent of confusion in Q_2 is the repeated (said and implied) *Why*, which might be thought to introduce parallel queries but which in fact ushers in very different sorts of questions, each with a different grammatical subject:

> Why hast *thou* forged hooks of eyes' falsehood?
> Why should *my heart* think that a several plot?
> [Why do] *my eyes*, seeing this, say this is not?

After this linguistic reproduction of his "random" disjointed anxiety and self-blame, the speaker subsides into (apparently) virtuous self-judgment in the couplet, in which he, now alienated from his own heart and eyes, twice chastises them as sinners (in ***erred*** and *transf**erred***). We can tell from the sententiousness of line 13's "virtuous" alienation how unalienated the speaker was earlier, when in speaking of his heart and eyes he was one (in his linguistic distress) with their errancy, even when judging them *corrupt.*

To *transfer* heart and eyes to a *false plague* is another catachresis, marking the (newly virtuous) speaker's reawakened agitation of feeling. The word *plague* seems chosen as the last term in the alliterating sequence *plot, place, ______ ;* and also, in its ending *-ue,* to act as an antonym of ***true*** in the preceding line; the word *ague,* visually (though not phonetically) incorporated in ***plague*** may also have pleased Shakespeare, given that "My love is as a *fever*" (147); he would have been aware of the derivation of *ague* from *fièvre aigue,* or "sharp fever." The word *plague* itself, by its derivation from *plaga* ("wound") may have seemed apposite to an effect of Cupid's arrow (cf. 139, "*Wound* me not with thine eyes . . . / *wound* with cunning"). Or *plaga*/wound may suggest the vulva.

KEY WORD: EYES

DEFECTIVE KEY WORD: HEART (missing in Q_1, the quatrain of the *eyes,* before the speaker realizes that love has also corrupted his *heart.*)

Couplet Tie: *eyes* (1, 5, 7, 11, 13)
heart (8, 9, 10, 13)
truth [*true*] (12, 13)
false [*-hood*] (7, 14)

138

WHen my loue ſweares that ſhe is made of truth,
I do beleeue her though I know ſhe lyes,
That ſhe might thinke me ſome vntuterd youth,
Vnlearned in the worlds falſe ſubtilties.
Thus vainely thinking that ſhe thinkes me young,
Although ſhe knowes my dayes are paſt the beſt,
Simply I credit her falſe ſpeaking tongue,
On both ſides thus is ſimple truth ſuppreſt:
But wherefore ſayes ſhe not ſhe is vniuſt?
And wherefore ſay not I that I am old?
O loues beſt habit is in ſeeming truſt,
And age in loue, loues not t'haue yeares told.
Therefore I lye with her, and ſhe with me,
And in our faults by lyes we flattered be.

When my love swears that she is made of truth,
I do believe her though I know she lies,
That she might think me some untutored youth,
Unlearnèd in the world's false subtleties.
Thus vainly thinking that she thinks me young,
Although she knows my days are past the best,
Simply I credit her false-speaking tongue:
On both sides thus is simple truth suppressed.
But wherefore says she not she is unjust?
And wherefore say not I that I am old?
O love's best habit is in seeming trust,
And age in love loves not to have years told.
Therefore I lie with her, and she with me,
And in our faults by lies we flattered be.

ONE might see sonnet 138 psychologically as a possible "resolution" of the frantic disjunction between reason and passion in 137. It is easier to suppress "simple truth" and let the rhetoric of sophistry reign. Yet, though 138 ends where it began, with acknowledged lies *(I know she lies . . . / Therefore I lie with her, and she with me)*, it exposes an abyss of truth at its very center, foregrounded by its expression in questions (while the rest of the sonnet consists of statements):

But wherefore says she not she is unjust?
And wherefore say not I that I am old?

These devastating questions are, interestingly, mediated through reported discourse. They could have read, in direct discourse:

[*But wherefore says she not "I am unjust"?*
And wherefore say not I "I am [now] old"?]

This "bared device" of the questions makes us realize that the whole sonnet depends on reported discourse from the beginning: Not [*When my love swears "O, I am made of truth,"*] but rather *swears that she is made of truth.* This habit of the poem puts into relief, over against its reported discourse, the actual habitual present-tense actions of the couple, presented, till the close, in a zigzag between man and woman:

[*She*] swears
I do believe her
I know
She lies
She might think
She thinks
She knows
I credit
I lie
She [lies]
We flattered be

The one thing they both *don't* do in the actual present is *say*, the simple verb of the suppressed questions, the verb that almost burns a hole in the sonnet in the two lacerating implied statements of the silent *simple truth: she is unjust, I am old.* We notice, when the "simple truth" is written out in this way, that the two imagined utterances are not parallel: the more natural thing for the lady to say (if she were about to tell the truth) would be, "I am false." It is the speaker, wounded by her infidelity, who projects onto her imagined speech an adjective he would like to predicate of her himself: "She is unjust."

The fulcrum of the poem, then, consists of the questions in which the unspeakable simple truth is imagined as statements actually uttered; even the imagining of this rupture with sophistry undoes the diction of the octave. The couplet, which at first seemed a reiteration of that earlier diction, must now be differently understood; and the bridge to that different understanding is given by the "proverbial wisdom" in lines 11–12. The first "proverb" is introduced by the "O," which implies that lines 11–12 offer an answer to the previous questions. "Why don't we say the true sentences? O, it's because . . ." The two statements of lines 11–12 are identified as "proverbial" by axiomatic form *(best habit / seeming trust)* and nugget-like chiasmus *(age/love/loves/years).*

Now, proverbs "let one off the hook," so to speak, saying "'Twas ever thus." Both "proverbs" refer to the speaker rather than to the woman, and are a solution to his bad faith in the octave. In that octave, the speaker and the woman were on different "sides": "*On both sides* thus is simple truth suppressed." But in the couplet, though we see first the *I* and the *she* representing the two sides, they are given a single mutual verb, *lie,* and by the next line they have fused (for the first time in the poem) into a *we* with common *(our)* faults. The zigzag movements of the octave (*she/I/she/I,* etc.) are thus, via the bridge of resigned acceptance of common proverbial accommodation, resolved into the speaker's subsidence in the couplet.

Critical opinion on this sonnet sees it either as a depraved picture of cynical partners or as a sophisticated rendition of the (ultimately comic) way in which all lovers flatter each other. Each reading draws more heavily on one part of the sonnet than on another, the depravity-readers favoring the octave, the comedy-readers favoring the sestet. If one sees, as I do, the speaker's gradual revision of his view (as in 129) as the dynamic mainspring of the poem, then the bitter paradoxes of the octave, the imaginative reconstruction of the unutterable in the questions, the recognition (via the excursus into proverbs) of the *general* unspeakability of certain sentences among *all* lovers, and the subsidence into mutual (false) *faults* can be seen to inscribe a curve of feeling beginning in anger ("She is unjust to me in being unfaithful"), continuing in suppressed anger (*not* saying, "You are unjust"), game-playing ("Simply I credit"), a recognition of the absurdity of the demand for truth-telling at any cost, and an admission that they are both flattered by the status quo of suppression of frank speech in favor of "lying" to and with each other. Her *truth* and his *youth* are both equally *lies*, and his euphemism "she knows my days are *past the best*" shows that he even wants to lie to himself, not merely have the woman lie to him.

DEFECTIVE KEY WORD: FALSE [FAULTS] (missing in Q_3, the quatrain of *simple truth*)

Couplet Tie: *lie* [*-s*] (2, 13, 14)
false [*faults*] (4, 7, 14)

Note: Printed in a slightly different form in *The Passionate Pilgrim* (1599), sonnet 138 has seemed to some a place where we can see Shakespeare reworking an earlier draft. I, like others, think the illogical *(she is young)* version in *The Passionate Pilgrim* was reconstructed by someone with a faulty memory. Here is the first printing (reproduced from Rollins, *Variorum*, I, 353–354):

When my Love sweares that she is made of truth,
I do beleeve her (though I know she lies)
That she might thinke me some untutor'd youth,
Unskilful in the worlds false forgeries.
Thus vainly thinking that she thinkes me young,
Although I know my yeares be past the best:
I smiling, credite her false speaking toung,
Outfacing faults in love, with love's ill rest.
But wherefore sayes my love that she is young?
And wherefore say not I, that I am old:
O, Love's best habit's in a soothing toung,
And Age in love, loves not to have yeares told.
Therefore I'le lye with Love, and love with me,
Since that our faultes in love thus smother'd be.

139

O Call not me to iuſtifie the wrong,
That thy vnkindneſſe layes vpon my heart,
Wound me not with thine eye but with thy toung,
Vſe power with power,and ſlay me not by Art,
Tell me thou lou'ſt elſe-where;but in my ſight,
Deare heart forbeare to glance thine eye aſide,
What needſt thou wound with cunning when thy might
Is more then my ore-preſt defence can bide?
Let me excuſe thee,ah my loue well knowes,
Her prettie lookes haue beene mine enemies,
And therefore from my face ſhe turnes my foes,
That they elſe-where might dart their iniuries:
  Yet do not ſo,but ſince I am neere ſlaine,
  Kill me out-right with lookes,and rid my paine.

O call not me to justify the wrong
That thy unkindness lays upon my heart;
Wound me not with thine eye but with thy tongue;
Use power with power, and slay me not by art.
Tell me thou lov'st elsewhere; but in my sight,
Dear heart, forbear to glance thine eye aside;
What need'st thou wound with cunning when thy might
Is more than my o'erpressed defence can bide?
Let me excuse thee: "Ah, my love well knows
Her pretty looks have been mine enemies,
And therefore from my face she turns my foes,
That they elsewhere might dart their injuries."
  Yet do not so, but since I am near slain,
  Kill me outright with looks, and rid my pain.

As readers have noticed, the speaker, after saying *O call not me to justify the wrong [that you do me in looking amorously at others]*, capitulates and in Q_3 utters precisely that justification: *Let me excuse thee.* What causes this sophistical capitulation? In the capitulation itself, the mistress' *wrong* (turning her eyes away from the speaker) is ingeniously interpreted by the speaker as an act of charity: knowing her love-looks have wounded the speaker, she turns them elsewhere to injure others. The speaker can therefore offer not an *excuse* for *wrong* but rather a praise for his mistress' solicitude. In fact, *unkindness* thus evaporates altogether and love remains unbreached.

The problem of the couplet now presents itself. Will it return to the adjurations of the octave *(call not me, wound me not, use, slay me not, tell me, forbear);* and if so, how? We see that in form it does: *do not, kill me, rid.* But the dramatic pretext of the octave—that the lady is unkind—has been voided by the conjecturing of her kind motive in Q_3—and so the new adjurations urge her to continue her kindness by letting her (returned) love-looks kill him. He will expire happy in her renewed glances.

My account renders 139 more coherent than it seems as one reads it. One source of its incoherence is its implied statement that the lady's eyes can wound in two ways: by commission (the *dart[s]* of her eye-beams piercing the speaker) and by omission (by neglecting to glance at him, by directing her eye-beams toward others). It has become evident to the speaker that painful though the eye-darts are, their withdrawal is even more painful. In between these two levels of the hierarchy of pain is situated (putatively) the pain conveyed by the tongue when it says, "I love elsewhere"; and above all three is a pain so acute it brings death, conveyed by false love-looks:

worst pain — return of (killing) false love-looks
↑
still worse pain — absence of love-looks
↑
worse pain — "I love elsewhere"
↑
pain — love-looks

The wit of the closing line, which makes the least painful element (real love-looks) into the most painful (returned false love-looks) paradoxically lets the killingly painful looks, in their murderous return, rid the speaker of all pain by causing his extinction. In this flux of commission-omission-commission (never directly expounded) lies the mobility of the sonnet, following the mobility of the lady's fluctuating looks. The "incoherence" of 139 also derives in part from the alternation of positive adjuration with negative adjuration; and it arises as well from the "interruption" of the "rational" speech-act pattern adjuration/excuse/adjuration by the interesting lapse, at the climax of the octave, into interrogation: "Why do you need to use *cunning* when your weapon of *might* is already more than adequate?" The foregrounding here—in the anomalous interrogative speech-act—of the opposition *cunning/might* brings into relief the preceding oppositions *eye/tongue*, *power/art*, and suggests the triple parallel *tongue-might-power / eye-cunning-art. Wound me . . . with thy tongue; use power; tell me*, the speaker urges. "Call not *me* to justify [your] wrong [-doing]; *you* are the one who should speak up and justify yourself."

Such has been the speaker's implied train of thought in the octave. But between octave and sestet comes the terrible unspoken question, "What if she should obey me, and indeed *tell* me she loves elsewhere?" This question is, so to speak, prepared for by the "harmless" question about cunning and might, substituted for it in lines 7–8. It is the "real" question, hiding behind the innocuous one, which prompts the speaker's hasty self-reversal; rather than have her tell *him*, *he* will tell her the new construction he puts upon her averting of her looks: that she averts them out of solicitude for his happiness. The "solution" he offers her "satisfies" them both: he will bask in her restored love-looks (though expiring because of their falsity), and she will be rid of her inconvenient lover and be free to love elsewhere.

There is a macabre comedy in all this, reminiscent of "Now *see* what good turns eyes for eyes have done" (24). The sophistry by which this legerdemain is carried on is belied by the pathos in the lapse into the vocative of affection, *dear heart*, in the plea for decent behavior—"[At least] in my sight, / *Dear heart*, forbear [temporarily] to glance thine eye aside." It has the same futility as Hamlet's plea to his mother that she should at least tonight forbear to share the king's bed.

Couplet Tie: *looks* (10, 14)
slay [*slain*] (4, 13)

140

BE wiſe as thou art cruell, do not preſſe
My toung-tide patience with too much diſdaine:
Leaſt ſorrow lend me words and words expreſſe,
The manner of my pittie wanting paine.
If I might teach thee witte better it weare,
Though not to loue, yet loue to tell me ſo,
As teſtie ſick-men when their deaths be neere,
No newes but health from their Phiſitions know.
For if I ſhould diſpaire I ſhould grow madde,
And in my madneſſe might ſpeake ill of thee,
Now this ill wreſting world is growne ſo bad,
Madde ſlanderers by madde eares beleeued be.
    That I may not be ſo, nor thou be lyde,   (wide.
    Beare thine eyes ſtraight, though thy proud heart goe

Be wise as thou art cruel, do not press
My tongue-tied patience with too much disdain,
Lest sorrow lend me words, and words express
The manner of my pity-wanting pain.
If I might teach thee wit, better it were,
Though not to love, yet, love, to tell me so—
As testy sick men, when their deaths be near,
No news but health from their physicians know.
For if I should despair I should grow mad,
And in my madness might speak ill of thee;
Now this ill-wresting world is grown so bad,
Mad slanderers by mad ears believèd be.
    That I may not be so, nor thou belied,
    Bear thine eyes straight, though thy proud heart go wide.

IN SONNET 139, the speaker had at first entreated the mistress to *tell* with her *tongue*, rather than with her averted *looks*, that she loves elsewhere. Terrified lest she tell him indeed, he backed away from his demand, restricting himself only to a plea for the return of her *looks*. Now, in 140, he is afraid of what *his* tongue might say in anger; and he advises her not to speak out her true feelings but rather to dissemble and pretend she loves him: "*better it were*, / Though not to love, yet, love, to *tell* me so."

The unusual KEY WORD here, *be*[-], (1, 7, 12, 12, 13, 13, 14) draws attention by its ordinariness in lines 1 and 7 to the complexity of its occurrence as the poem closes: *believèd be . . . be . . . belied . . . bear.* Alerted by the chain of *be*'s, we pick up the other chains that ornament the poem, especially those chains of verbal and moral consequence that occur both in Q_1 *(sorrow ⟶ words; words ⟶ manner of pain)* and in Q_3 *(despair ⟶ grow mad; madness ⟶ speak ill; ill world ⟶ grown bad ⟶ mad by mad believèd).* These undeflectable chains stand symbolically for the absence of free will. If a certain spring is touched (if too much disdain is manifested by the lady, for instance) everything else follows in a cascade—sorrow, words, expression of pain, despair, madness, ill speech, believed slander. In short, all power is ceded to the lady; she and she alone will be responsible for exposing her reputation to such disaster. Naturally, this is in fact a threat: the speaker promises the results he envisages. The *wit* and *wis[dom]* he affects to teach the lady are prudential rather than moral, and he acknowledges the inevitable straying of her *proud heart.* The hypocrisy she is urged to practice consists of bearing her eyes straight and telling the speaker she loves him, lying after the manner of physicians' "white lies" to dying men.

The "prudential" diction of the octave gives way in Q_3 to a pathological picture of the world in which both speaker and audience are conceded to be mad: *Mad slanderers by mad ears believèd be.* The easy slippage from *believèd* to *belied* (by the deletion of *v* and the superimposition of the two *e*'s) suggests how insidious the chain is from fault to slander. From *manner* to *madness* is such a slippage, as is *press* to *express*, as is *not to love . . . love to tell*, and *disdain . . . despair*, and *no news . . . know*. In suggesting that his future actions are out of his own control, the speaker has abandoned the cool ironies of "choice" in 138.

KEY WORD: BE

Couplet Tie: *be* [*-lievèd*] [*-lied*] [*-ar*] (1, 7, 12, 12, 13, 13, 14) (line 14 possesses the purely graphic Couplet Tie *bear*)

141

IN faith I doe not loue thee with mine eyes,
For they in thee a thouſand errors note,
But 'tis my heart that loues what they diſpiſe,
Who in diſpight of view is pleaſd to dote.
Nor are mine eares with thy toungs tune delighted,
Nor tender feeling to baſe touches prone,
Nor taſte, nor ſmell, deſire to be inuited
To any ſenſuall feaſt with thee alone:
But my fiue wits,nor my fiue ſences can
Diſwade one fooliſh heart from ſeruing thee,
Who leaues vnſwai'd the likeneſſe of a man,
Thy proud hearts ſlaue and vaſſall wretch to be:
  Onely my plague thus farre I count my gaine,
  That ſhe that makes me ſinne,awards me paine.

In faith, I do not love thee with mine eyes,
For they in thee a thousand errors note,
But 'tis my heart that loves what they despise,
Who in despite of view is pleased to dote.
Nor are mine ears with thy tongue's tune delighted,
Nor tender feeling to base touches prone,
Nor taste, nor smell, desire to be invited
To any sensual feast with thee alone;
But my five wits nor my five senses can
Dissuade one foolish heart from serving thee,
Who leaves unswayed the likeness of a man,
Thy proud heart's slave and vassal wretch to be.
  Only my plague thus far I count my gain,
  That she that makes me sin awards me pain.

THE logical argument of the body of this sonnet says that although ten forces (the *five senses* and the *five wits*—imagination, memory, etc.) are arrayed against the single *(one)* heart, they cannot dissuade the heart from its folly. The couplet, as Booth says, seems curiously disjoined from this argument, but contains words (*only, sin*) that connect with words in the body of the sonnet (*alone, one; sensual, senses*).

The imaginative arrangement of the "logical" argument alternates, in an asymmetrical way, portions on the senses (lines 1–2, 5–9) with portions on the heart (lines 3–4, 10–12), appending to this seesaw an apparently unrelated couplet, in which the second-person address *(thee)* of the body of the poem is discarded in favor of third-person reference ("*she* that makes me sin"). The senses/heart structure is thus 2-2-5-3-2 (eyes / heart / other senses / heart / sin), while the pronominal structure is 12-2; the pronominal division 12:2 also marks a rhetorical change from assertion of erotic slavery to evaluation of assets and liabilities. Yet another structure, 8-4-2, is created by the radical changes of the speaker's self-image. In the octave the speaker is a *lover;* in Q_3 a *serv[itor]/slave/vassal wretch;* in C he is a more complex mixture of a plague victim, a sinner, a sufferer *(pain)*, and a beneficiary who can *count [his] gain.*

We are alerted to these changes in self-representation chiefly, I think, from the unexpected substitution in line 10 of the word *serving* for the word *loving.* "Nothing, not even ten faculties united," says the speaker, "can dissuade one foolish heart from—" (and, prepared by "'tis my *heart* that *loves*" earlier, we fill in) "—from [*loving*] thee." We find we are mistaken; and the self-degradation almost invisible in the courtier-like *serving* rapidly betrays itself in the self-demotion to the almost-anagrammatic *slave* and *vassal.* Self-hatred is openly expressed in the speaker's admission that his debased status has made his soul leave *the likeness of a man* to become a *slave.* (Like Circe, the lady makes her lovers less than free men.)

The negative anaphoric enumeration of sense-response organizes the body of the poem *(I do not . . . nor . . . nor . . . nor . . . nor)*, while the couplet is phrased positively (if paradoxically) as *gain* by *pain.* These closing rhyme-words conclude a series in *ā* that begins in line 6 with *base* and continues with *taste, dissuade, unswayed, slave, plague, gain, makes,* and *pain.*

This we could call (for the purposes of this sonnet) the sound of folly, of the foolish heart. But the *foolish heart* has another song, placed in counterpoint to its baseness, and this is a song in *d: de-spise, de-spite, dote, delighted, de-sire, dis-suade.* The *d*'s disappear as *dis-suade* metamorphoses in its first syllable and becomes *un-swayed;* the causal link between succumbing to temptation and becoming subhuman is emphasized by the etymologically distinct but phonetically identical second syllable of these two words: *dis-suade* (< *suavis,* smooth) versus *un-swayed* (< *swey,* to fall). There is a decrescendo in *d* and a crescendo in *ā* as the poem declines from *doting* to increasing *sl**a**very* and *p**a**in.* In view of other such puns (*richer* and *wretched* in 91), we may see the *vassal wretch* as also a "vassal rich"; it is this pun that makes the speaker evaluate his *gain.* "Unpacking" the phrase "vassal rich" means finding some *gain* in the *plague/plaga/ague* (cf. 137); it is as though Shakespeare were confident that an unwitting or casual pun could be mined for significance. The couplet reinforces the masochism of the sonnet: *pain* is a *gain.* (Samuel Butler's suggestion of time remitted in Purgatory, approved by Booth, seems to me highly unlikely, given the speaker's avoidance in the *Sonnets* of Christian doctrine about a personal afterlife for himself.)

The "right relation" of the faculties—implied by the painfully disordered relations the speaker perceives in himself—would be one in which the five wits and the five senses (by reporting what they find delightful and true) cause the heart to be inclined to *dote;* yet this consonance between heart and senses is, in the "right" relation, to be submitted to the reason for judgment. If reason finds no prudential or ethical obstacle, the lover may love and retain his status as fully human. It is both the dissonance between senses and heart here, *and* the absence of any recourse to reason, that suddenly cause the speaker to demote himself from lover—and even server—to *slave* and *vassal wretch,* one who no longer retains his own self-governance by reason. He still invokes the excuse of Adam: *she . . . makes me sin* (line 14). I cannot agree with Booth's suggestion that "the speaker's body is left unswayed—he is left a shell of a man—because his heart has left—has departed, has gone away—to live in his lady's bosom as a slave." Rather, his body is unswayed by reason; he has become less than human.

Couplet Tie: al-[*one*], *one, on* [-ly] (8, 10, 13)
sin, [*sen*]-*sual,* [*sen*]-*ses* (8, 9, 14)

142

Loue is my ſinne, and thy deare vertue hate,
Hate of my ſinne, grounded on ſinfull louing,
O but with mine, compare thou thine owne ſtate,
And thou ſhalt finde it merrits not reproouing,
Or if it do, not from thoſe lips of thine,
That haue prophan'd their ſcarlet ornaments,
And ſeald falſe bonds of loue as oft as mine,
Robd others beds reuenues of their rents.
Be it lawfull I loue thee as thou lou'ſt thoſe,
Whome thine eyes wooe as mine importune thee,
Roote pittie in thy heart that when it growes,
Thy pitty may deſerue to pittied bee.
　　If thou dooſt ſeeke to haue what thou dooſt hide,
　　By ſelfe example mai'ſt thou be denide.

Love is my sin, and thy dear virtue hate,
Hate of my sin, grounded on sinful loving.
O but with mine compare thou thine own state,
And thou shalt find it merits not reproving,
Or if it do, not from those lips of thine,
That have profaned their scarlet ornaments,
And sealed false bonds of love as oft as mine,
Robbed others' beds' revénues of their rents.
Be it lawful I love thee as thou lov'st those
Whom thine eyes woo as mine impórtune thee;
Root pity in thy heart, that when it grows,
Thy pity may deserve to pitied be.
　　If thou dost seek to have what thou dost hide,
　　By self-example mayst thou be denied.

BOTH 142 and 143 represent chains of desire, 142 in bitter terms of human beings (A desires B, who desires C), 143 in the putatively comic terms of a little allegory of a housewife chasing a fowl, while she herself is chased by her baby. Both sonnets enact their overlapping pursuits in chains of self-mirroring language. In 142 this happens in Q_3 and C; in 143, throughout.

Sonnet 142 (which begins with the speaker's *sin*, where 141 closed) exhibits no clear verbal Couplet Tie, but the *hide* and *seek* of line 13 direct attention back to *find* in line 4, and so some care has been taken to attach the couplet to the body of the sonnet semantically (it is linked referentially by its own version of the chain of pursuit). The third-person "alienated" couplet of 141 seems at first to have no counterpart in 142, which continues in second-person address throughout; but then we notice the number of aspectual descriptions of the lady:

thy dear virtue
thine own state
those lips of thine
their scarlet ornaments
thine eyes
thy heart
thy pity
self-example

The distancing effect of the deictic "*those* lips of thine" spreads to all the speaker's alienated references to the lady, as he points out her state, her roving eyes, her not-yet-rooted pity. In this atmosphere we can read *thy dear virtue* only ironically. The lady's hypocrisy is at first apparently believed ("Your virtuous self hates—legitimately—my sinful loving"), but then exposed. His state *may* merit reproving, the speaker concedes, but not from *her* profaned lips. The blasphemy on the Song of Solomon suggested by the phrase *their scarlet ornaments* and the word *seal* intimates bitterness even before the speaker descends into the language of commercial transactions to characterize the lady's sexual voracity.

In Q_3, a new *law (bond)* is proposed, the law of parallel sexual irregularity, phrased in the language of *la ronde:* "Let me love you as you love those whom your eyes woo as mine woo you." Once again the *ronde* is repeated, but this time as a warning: "Some day you'll need pity, so cultivate pity for me now so that when you become pitiful you may deserve to be pitied by others." And the couplet does the *ronde* one last time, but shows it negatively: the mistress now hides pity (for him) but will later seek to have it (for herself) but may be denied it (for herself) by those who cite her own cruel former practice as precedent. One can imagine Shakespeare's satisfaction in making the *ronde* happen three times in six lines, once with love, once with pity, and once with cruelty.

This sonnet departs from the notion of an eternal and universal moral law, which judges everyone equally, and can be invoked by anyone. (In theological terms, it makes no difference if I myself am a sinner: my condemnation of your sin is still accurate and just. It is not the morals of the accuser, but the tablets of the Law, that sanction the accusation.) Here, however, sin is reduced to "personal offense": "You can't accuse me, since you're guilty too." The erection of this new morality in place of the old is advocated in Q_3: "*Be it lawful* I love thee as thou lov'st those . . ." It is continued in the further quasi-legal formulations *may deserve to pitied be* and *by self-example mayst thou be denied.* A series of new "laws" are deducible from these remarks:

1. It is lawful for you, the speaker, to love A if A loves B the way you love A;
2. It is to A's advantage to pity you now so that her eventual pitifulness will deserve a counter-pity from you;
3. It will be lawful to deny pity to A when she seeks it from you if she has hidden it from you when you pleaded for it.

These laws of tit-for-tat are, once again, a parody of the true reciprocity-in-love that is the ideal behind the Young Man subsequence and the Dark Lady subsequence alike.

Couplet Tie: None

143

LOe as a carefull huſwife runnes to catch,
One of her fethered creatures broake away,
Sets downe her babe and makes all ſwift diſpatch
In purſuit of the thing ſhe would haue ſtay:
Whilſt her neglected child holds her in chace,
Cries to catch her whoſe buſie care is bent,
To follow that which flies before her face:
Not prizing her poore infants diſcontent;
So runſt thou after that which flies from thee,
Whilſt I thy babe chace thee a farre behind,
But if thou catch thy hope turne back to me:
And play the mothers part kiſſe me,be kind.
  So will I pray that thou maiſt haue thy *Will*,
  If thou turne back and my loude crying ſtill.

Lo, as a careful huswife runs to catch
One of her feathered creatures broke away,
Sets down her babe and makes all swift dispatch
In púrsuit of the thing she would have stay,
Whilst her neglected child holds her in chase,
Cries to catch her whose busy care is bent
To follow that which flies before her face,
Not prizing her poor infant's discontent:
So runn'st thou after that which flies from thee,
Whilst I, thy babe, chase thee afar behind;
But if thou catch thy hope, turn back to me,
And play the mother's part, kiss me, be kind.
  So will I pray that thou mayst have thy Will,
  If thou turn back and my loud crying still.

CLEARLY a variant on 142, sonnet 143 enacts *la ronde* in even more patterned form. The octave presents the simile *(Lo, as)* of the housewife pursuing the fowl while being pursued by her child; the sestet, with no apparent sense of ridiculousness, applies this simile *(So . . . thou . . . whilst I)* to the lady pursuing her new lover while the speaker pursues her. The verbal parallels between octave and sestet are numerous and ostentatious, and create the concatenation which is the expectable chief trope of the poem: *runs/runn'st; catch/catch; babe/babe; chase/chase; cries/crying; that which flies / that which flies; have/have.*

But aside from these links, both octave and sestet exhibit internal links within themselves: in the octave, *careful/care, catch/catch;* in the sestet, *if thou / if thou, turn back/turn back.* There are other linking devices such as the visibly mimetic alliteration in *c* and *ch;* and the whole body of the sonnet, preceding the couplet, is one unstoppable sentence.

What is the point of this preposterous little allegory? It is of course a transparently implausible attempt to justify the lady's infidelity. The housewife has presumably the right to set down the child she has been carrying in order to catch her runaway creature, but such a domestic interruption offers no real analogy to sexual infidelity. The only thing the tenor and vehicle have in common is the crying baby; and though some commentators have seen here a revelation of Shakespeare's Oedipus complex, I prefer to see it as an example of authorial irony: the sonnet is evidence of the speaker's psychological reduction to infantile and irrational status.

The absurdity of likening the lady's new lover to a hen causes the conspicuous series of evasive descriptions of that object of the housewife's and lady's pursuits; in fact, the secondary trope of the sonnet, after concatenation, is periphrasis:

one of her feathered creatures
the thing she would have stay
that which flies before her face
that which flies from thee
thy hope
thy Will

As these variations mount, so do the variations on the abandoned one left behind:

her babe
her neglected child
her poor infant
thy babe
me

The instability caused by the vagueness with respect to the pursued new lover and the variations in the figure of the pursuing child make the inapplicability of hen-vehicle to love-tenor only too obvious.

The couplet is given pathos because the word *catch*, hitherto appearing in each member of the sonnet (Q_1, Q_2, Q_3) does not make its expected appearance (as KEY WORD) in the couplet. Substituted for it is the word *have* in the subjunctive, preventing the mistress' catching her lover, at least in the poem. The echo of the diphthong of *thou* in *loud* tells us what the crying longs for. A ***kind ki**ss* will undo the ***cr**ying*, the speaker promises, but the *ménage à trois* he envisages is not promising.

Just as sonnet 33 *(Full many a glorious morning have I seen)* offered an epic simile followed by an application, so does 143. But 33 did not "tag" its epic simile at the beginning with *Lo, as* in the way that 143 does. Consequently, though both are "double-exposure" poems, we read them differently. The "literal level" in 33 *seems* to be a story about dawn, but that story is subsequently *(Even so)* revealed in fact to be the metaphorical level, and the literal level is a story of betrayal. Here in 143, the initial *Lo, as* flags the octave as metaphorical, and prepares us for the literal sestet. Even in such small ways, we can see Shakespeare "trying on" different techniques for the same end—here, the verbal overlay corresponding to the (later) photographic effect of double exposure.

At the end of 143, the plaintive lover changes his plea. Originally, his plea was "Leave off chasing my rival; let him go, and let me repossess you." But having despaired of success with that plea, he changes his tune in line 10 and formulates a different plea: "Once you catch him and are satisfied, turn back to me." This four-line plea—phrased hypothetically, since in the stopped caricature of the simile the housewife is still suspended in pursuit of her hen—is also written as a small double exposure, reinforcing the earlier double exposure of the chase:

if thou catch	thy hope	turn back to me	and . . . kiss me
thou mayst have	thy Will	turn back	and . . . still my crying

To see the betrayed speaker vowing to pray that his mistress may have her lover providing she will include him in her ménage is to realize the humiliation that prompts his ironic self-image as an infant.

DEFECTIVE KEY WORD: CATCH (missing in C, so that the mistress never catches her lover)

Couplet Tie: *have* (4, 13)
cries [*crying*] (6, 14)
turn back (11, 14)
if thou (11, 14)

144

TWo loues I haue of comfort and diſpaire,
Which like two ſpirits do ſugieſt me ſtill,
The better angell is a man ri ht faire:
The worſer ſpirit a woman collour'd il.
To win me ſoone to hell my femall euill,
Tempteth my better angel from my ſight,
And would corrupt my ſaint to be a diuel:
Wooing his purity with her fowle pride.
And whether that my angel be turn'd finde,
Suſpect I may, yet not directly tell,
But being both from me both to each friend,
I geſſe one angel in an others hel.
  Yet this ſhal I nere know but liue in doubt,
  Till my bad angel fire my good one out.

Two loves I have, of comfort and despair,
Which like two spirits do suggest me still:
The better angel is a man right fair;
The worser spirit a woman coloured ill.
To win me soon to hell my female evil
Tempteth my better angel from my side,
And would corrupt my saint to be a devil,
Wooing his purity with her foul pride.
And whether that my angel be turned fiend
Suspect I may, yet not directly tell,
But being both from me, both to each friend,
I guess one angel in another's hell.
  Yet this shall I ne'er know, but live in doubt,
  Till my bad angel fire my good one out.

THE FOLLOWING remarks are equally true if one uses the Quarto spelling.

The easy slippage between the rhyme-words *fiend* and *friend*, and the persistence of *ill*, *evil*, and *hell* in the rhymes and within each quatrain, tell the thematic story here. *Still*, *angel*, ***ill***, ***hell***, ***evil***, *angel*, ***devil***, *angel*, ***tell***, *angel*, ***hell***, ***live*** (the anagram for *evil*), *angel*—this chain of words reveals how *angel* rhymes with *hell*, and how to *live* in doubt is to know *evil*.

Behind this literal story is the common medieval drama on which it is predicated, in which good and evil angels contend for a man's soul: at the end, the man goes off either to heaven with the good angel or to hell's mouth with the bad. In his witty "rewriting" of this drama, Shakespeare imagines a new ending, in which the good angel and the bad angel go off together, linked in mutual sexual appetite, leaving behind the man, the original object of their contention, who remains, gaping, at a loss.

This is the sonnet of which the poet John Berryman remarked, in his comments on Lowell in *The Freedom of the Poet*, "When Shakespeare wrote, 'Two loves I have,' reader, he was *not kidding*." And truly, the least strained hypothesis about the *Sonnets* is that they are, roughly speaking, psychologically and dramatically "true." Sonnet 144 has an air of confession to an unspecified other: "Let me describe for you the predicament I find myself in."

Q_1 offers the familiar Christian model of the better angel and the worser spirit, both prompting the speaker, but transforms these spirits into *loves*, and gives them names deriving from theology: *comfort* (salvation) and *despair* (the unforgivable sin). (*Dis-pair*, in the Quarto spelling, is wittily if unetymologically placed between *two . . . two*.) The iconographic description *fair / colored ill* supports the Christian model of angel and devil.

Q_2, while beginning within the Christian presumption that the bad angel wants *to win [the speaker] soon to hell*, slides away from that motive in lines 7–8, as a witty new version of the old plot emerges; the bad angel loses interest in the speaker, and turns her interest to the better spirit. Still, the speaker maintains the essential uprightness of his *man right fair:* he is *my better angel*, and *my saint;* he possesses *purity*.

In the sestet, the speaker loses the narrative certainty of the octave; he can only *suspect*, *guess*, and *live in doubt* until some future revelation of fact. The sestet of suspicion completes the change from the Christian model: in Q_3, the two spirits have, it is suspected, set up a liaison together, abandoning their separate intentions upon the speaker's soul. Yet the speaker continues to refer to the man right fair as an *angel:* "And whether that my *angel* be turned fiend, / Suspect I may"; but the suspicion is once more resisted—"I guess one *angel* in another's hell." For the first time, here in line 12, the two spirits are implicitly given the same name, *angel* ("one *angel* in another [angel]'s hell"). Rather than say his friend has turned *fiend*, the speaker prefers to turn the *worser spirit* into hell's *angel.* By this manipulation is the couplet made possible, in which the bad angel and the good angel are equally named as angels; the decline is marked by the degradation of *fair* (line 3) to *fire* (line 14), by which we infer the *friend* has indeed turned *fiend.*

The considerable shock of aesthetic surprise in the "rewriting" of the contention of angel and fiend for the soul of Everyman is the chief accomplishment of the poem, but the passage from the narrative of fact (octave) to the narrative of suspicion (Q_3) to the prophecy of continued anxiety (C) is another successful source of the evolving momentum of the whole.

The rigid antitheses of the sonnet are played out in its sentence arrangements, in which at first on the left (mentioned first, line 3) we find the man right fair; on the right (mentioned second, line 4), the woman colored ill. Soon, however, lines *about* the good angel begin to open with *words* belonging to the bad angel: *Tempteth / And would corrupt / Wooing.* Soon, the good angel begins to lean to the right of the line: *my angel . . . turned fiend; one angel in another's hell.* A reversal of this directed movement is thematically suggested in the last line, by which the "good" angel will be cast out from the hell fire into which he earlier slid; but the syntax (left to right, directionally speaking), leaving the *good one* still in the right half (of the line), suggests no change from the *angel turned fiend*, the *angel in hell.*

KEY WORD and Couplet Tie: ANGEL (3, 6, 9, 12, 14)

145

THose lips that Loues owne hand did make,
Breath'd forth the ſound that ſaid I hate,
To me that languiſht for her ſake:
But when ſhe ſaw my wofull ſtate,
Straight in her heart did mercie come,
Chiding that tongue that euer ſweet,
Was vſde in giuing gentle dome:
And tought it thus a new to greete:
I hate ſhe alterd with an end,
That follow'd it as gentle day,
Doth follow night who like a fiend
From heauen to hell is flowne away.
I hate,from hate away ſhe threw,
And ſau'd my life ſaying not you.

Those lips that Love's own hand did make
Breathed forth the sound that said "I hate"
To me that languished for her sake:
But when she saw my woeful state,
Straight in her heart did mercy come,
Chiding that tongue that ever sweet
Was used in giving gentle doom,
And taught it thus anew to greet:
"I hate" she altered with an end
That followed it as gentle day
Doth follow night, who like a fiend
From heaven to hell is flown away.
"I hate" from hate away she threw,
And saved my life, saying "not you."

IN THE contorted opening sentence that constructs itself over the first twelve lines of this two-sentence tetrameter "sonnet," there are no less than fourteen subjects and verbs, a disproportion so grotesque as to render the sentence entirely unidiomatic. The sentence itself is a tripartite one, separating its three parts with the adversative conjunction *but* and the coordinate conjunctive *and:*

> lips breathed forth sound
> *but* mercy did come
> *and* taught [tongue] to greet anew, [as] she altered [the sound]

This skeleton is festooned with six relative clauses (five with *that* and one with *who*). The total list of fourteen subjects and verbs (main and subordinate) in this first sentence follows; though there are some repeats among the subjects (three *I*'s, two *she*'s, two *mercy*'s), the total number of different subjects—ten—is still very large.

> Love's hand did make [lips]
> lips breathed forth sound
> [sound] that said
> I hate
> [me] that languished
> she saw
> mercy did come
> [tongue] that was used
> [mercy] taught tongue
> I hate
> she altered
> [end] that followed it
> day doth follow night
> [night] who is flown away

This preposterous syntactic stringing-along (which does not even include the other verbals, like *giving* and *to greet*) is made more bizarre by its six *that*'s, one of them confusing the issue by being a demonstrative adjective *(that tongue)* rather than, like all the rest, a relative pronoun.

The long first sentence, with its several dependent clauses (five in *that*, one in *when*, one in *as*, one in *who*) and its dependent verb-phrase *chiding*, is further complicated by its double simile in *as* and *like*, and its "irrational" doubling of *gentle* (in two different senses) in *gentle doom* and *gentle day*. The woman is sometimes referred to by synecdoche *(those lips, her heart, that tongue)* and sometimes simply as *she;* the same complication of reference is used of the speaker *(me, my state, my life)*, vexing reference even further. The rhymes are—by the standards of the usual Shakespearean accomplishment—"wrong": the alternate rhymes of Q_1 *(make, hate, sake, state)* phonetically resemble each other too closely for comfort, especially since the first word of Q_2 *(straight)* "rhymes" with these as well. *Sweet* and *greet* are too close to *hate, state,* and *straight* (especially considering the possible Renaissance pronunciation of *swāte* and *grāte*, and indeed the same rhyme-vowel *ā* is preserved in one set of the rhymes of Q_3—*day* and *away*—with the continued internal rhymes of *hate* and (in the couplet) *hate, hate, away, saved, saying.* The effect is one of cacophony, not euphony, since rhymes recur faster in tetrameters than in pentameters.

The octave is deliberately awkward as well in the noncoincidence of its rhyme-units (4-4) with its syntactic units (3-5). And, though it can be manipulated into logic, the double simile is initially confusing: at first the motion goes from bad to good, as the good *end* that follows *I hate* follows it as gentle day follows night. So far so good; but then the motion is reversed, as night, like a fiend, is flown from heaven to hell (a bad end following a good earlier state). This nocturnal reversed good-to-bad confuses the earlier bad-to-good of the dawn.

The concatenation principle visible in the syntax is extremely strong in the perversely linked members of the quatrains. The disjunction principle (throwing *I hate* away from *hate*) governs the couplet logically; but in construction, it too follows the principle of concatenation as the woman makes *not you* "follow" *I hate.*

This is one of the sonnets that "ought to be" a KEY WORD sonnet: the phrase *I hate* turns up in Q_1, Q_3, and C, but is "missing" from Q_2, precisely the quatrain of relenting and "mercy" where the tongue is *taught anew.* The phrase *to me that languished for her sake* puts the sonnet into the tradition of *Quia amore langueo*, and makes it more like a madrigal than a sonnet, to my mind. The conjecture by Andrew Gurr that *hate away* is a witty pun on "Hathaway" (see Booth) is a convincing one.

DEFECTIVE KEY WORD: I HATE (missing from Q_2, as the mistress relents)

Couplet Tie: *I hate* (2, 9, 13)
away (12, 13)
[say] *said, saying* (2, 14)

146

POore ſoule the center of my ſinfull earth,
My ſinfull earth theſe rebbell powres that thee array,
Why doſt thou pine within and ſuffer dearth]
Painting thy outward walls ſo coſtlie gay?
Why ſo large coſt hauing ſo ſhort a leaſe,
Doſt thou vpon thy fading manſion ſpend?
Shall wormes inheritors of this exceſſe,
Eate vp thy charge?is this thy bodies end?
Then ſoule liue thou vpon thy ſeruants loſſe,
And let that pine to aggrauat thy ſtore;
Buy tearmes diuine in ſelling houres of droſſe:
Within be fed, without be rich no more,
So ſhalt thou feed on death,that feeds on men,
And death once dead,ther's no more dying then.

Poor soul, the center of my sinful earth,
Feeding these rebel pow'rs that thee array,
Why dost thou pine within and suffer dearth,
Painting thy outward walls so costly gay?
Why so large cost, having so short a lease,
Dost thou upon thy fading mansion spend?
Shall worms, inheritors of this excess,
Eat up thy charge? Is this thy body's end?
Then, soul, live thou upon thy servants' loss,
And let that pine to aggravate thy store;
Buy terms divine in selling hours of dross;
Within be fed, without be rich no more:
So shalt thou feed on death, that feeds on men,
And death once dead, there's no more dying then.

BOOTH'S interesting discussion of the contrary pulls of this sonnet is perhaps too greatly concerned with meaning alone. He argues that Christian and non-Christian views of the sonnet both find warrant in its lines, the first from the religious allusions, the second from the absence of any reference to Christ, the Resurrection, or an afterlife. This is true enough, but it is only globally true; that is, it is true if one wants to "sum up" the "meaning(s)" of the poem. But such a desire is intellectual and expository. I am more concerned with the aesthetic experience one encounters temporally as one reads the sonnet. It certainly pronounces itself to be by genre a homily to the soul (leading the reader to expect moral or religious content). Progressively more abrupt hectoring questions are addressed in the octave to the speaker's *poor soul: Why dost thou pine? Why dost thou spend? Shall worms eat up thy charge? Is this thy body's end?* In the second "movement," Q_3, adjurations follow the vocative, *soul,* repeated from the octave: *Then, soul, live thou; let that pine; buy terms divine; be fed; be rich no more.* Finally, the homiletic rhetoric concludes in the couplet with the promise *so shalt thou* (comparable to religious promises such as "This day *thou shalt* be with me in Paradise"). Only the last epigrammatic line—*And death once dead, there's no more dying then*—departs from the homiletic model, which would inevitably mention redemption, resurrection, or heaven. The combination of the homiletic model and the religious references to *soul, sinful, fading mansion, worms, body's end, servants, terms divine* suffices to convince some readers that they have read a conventionally religious and unproblematic poem (one, incidentally, which would lack any element of aesthetic originality—a characteristic perhaps preferred by some devout readers).

The corrupt second line in the Quarto (repeating *my sinfull earth*) has made the poem tantalizingly incomplete. I would like to argue for *feeding* as the missing word, chiefly because it "explains" the presence of the word *fading* used of the mansion. Once *feeding* is in place, the sonnet becomes one exhibiting a KEY WORD, "FEED [FADE]": Q_1 *feeding;* Q_2 *fading;* Q_3 *fed;* C *feed, feeds.* Shakespeare's attraction to such structures is amply evident, and it is oddly unidiomatic (and otherwise inexplicable) to speak of a *mansion* as subject to *fading.*

The other unusual word in the sonnet is *aggravate*, possibly present by contamination from a poem from Bartholomew Griffin's 1596 *Fidessa* (as Kerrigan suggests) in which the body is addressed as "Untoward subject of the last aggrievance!"—though it is hard to believe Shakespeare found such a line worthy of imitation. I prefer to think *aggravate* is used to suggest the awaiting grave. Booth has noticed the presence of *death* in *dearth* and *man* in *mansion*, and I would add the quasi-presence of *grave* in *aggravate*, and of *end* in *spend*, and the resemblance of *lease* to *loss*, *large* to *charge*.

The poem works by antitheses and by repetitions, of which the chief are shown in the diagram. Encircling chiastic repetitions are particularly marked in the sestet *(Then . . . And . . . no more; And . . . no more . . . then)*, while *traductio* and concatenation are the tropes of the Pauline couplet.

Antitheses and Repetitions in Sonnet 146

poor/rich					
earth dearth death dead dying	dost thou dost thou	pine painting pine	within / outward within / without		costly cost rich buy
[feeding] fading fed feed feeds	why why buy	soul soul	buy / sell	powers hours	man-sion men
no more no more	then then	array aggravate	then then	[soul] [soul] sell[ing] shal[t]	large charge

We might ask (of the emended [*feeding*] sonnet) when the reader begins to be surprised, since it is the mark of any good poem to be surprising. One is not surprised by the rebel (sensual) powers of the body, nor by the reversal of the proper relation of subordination of body to soul: these are conventional notions. The appetites demand to be fed, and the soul's own nurture has been diverted to them (to be rediverted to its proper destination in *within be fed, without be rich no more*). The speaker assumes in line 12 that external riches bestowed on the sensual body are inversely proportionate to the proper feeding of the soul—an argument for inserting *feeding* in Q_1 to match *costly gay*. The religious paradoxes (*large cost /*

short lease; buy terms divine / selling hours of dross; rebel powers / servants; etc.) animate the homiletic solemnity of the poem, and are expectable in this context—even the "buying" of terms divine is not unexpected, given the medieval practice of buying indulgences.

It is in the eating-chain that the poem becomes disturbing. The soul has been feeding its rebel powers instead of itself, and consequently it pines within. The rebel powers eat up its store. And when the body those powers inhabit falls victim to mortality, worms will *eat up* the soul's charge, and profit from its excess. The proposed reversal is: let thy servants' excess pine to aggravate thy store, so that then thou mayst *live* and *be fed.* Though we are coming close to materializing the soul here, the verbs *live* and *be fed* (passive voice) can remain—just barely—on a metaphysical level (in this poem of repeated materialization of spiritual relations into dearth, paint, walls, cost, inheritors, rebel powers (servants), store, buying and selling, poor and rich).

But the active-voice verb *shalt feed on,* used of the soul, is hopelessly material, especially when it is repredicated of *Death that feeds on men,* recalling the worms who *eat up* the body and the rebel powers that (as I believe) feed on the soul's store. The eating-chain—first death (the worm) feeds on men, then the soul will feed on death—puts the soul in the position of ingesting the death-worm and his ingested men. In this little proposed counternarrative, death pines along with the starved and digested body, and the soul is correspondingly advantaged. "Who will deliver me from the body of this death?" says Saint Paul, linking body and death as a double prison.

Line 13 is, as I have said, conventionally phrased in the future tense of religious promise: *So shalt thou feed on death.* But the rest of the couplet consists of tense-manipulations:

so shalt thou feed	:	*Future*
death that feeds	:	*Habitual Present*
death once dead	:	*Past Participle* (completed action erasing habitual present)
there's	:	*Future Masquerading as Habitual Present*
no more dying	:	*Gerund:* "tenseless" verbal noun *dying* canceled by *no more,* but with overtones of continual process; "dying" exists in the present, not yet negated by the fulfillment of the promise.

The domination of the word *dying* in the close, joined immediately to *no more* on the left and *then* on the right, means that whatever will happen *then* (in the future), the present is nothing *but* dying. *Feeding, painting,* and *selling* (the participles and gerund resembling in their suffix the gerund *dying*) and the participial adjective *fading* are in effect cover-ups for *dying,* revealed apocalyptically as the "true" present-tense action of the poem. There's no more dying *then*—but there is only dying *now. Live thou* (by the hoped-for reversal), the speaker says to his soul, but as things now stand, *[thou art] dying.*

The speaker's exhortations may or may not be obeyed by the soul; it is, however, certain that as of now, death is feeding on men and the soul is pining and suffering dea[r]th. The gloominess of this sonnet has little of the radiance of Christian hope. *Buy terms divine* the speaker says, but (as Booth notes) the divine is infinite and has no terms (limits). The divine is quickly obscured by the Dantesque linked rapacity of the couplet. *death once dead* is an encouraging remark, rather than a prophecy. Certainly once death is dead, there's no more dying; but will feeding on death by starving the body kill him?

The alternation in metaphor of feeding a crew of *powers* and decorating a *mansion* (the *fed/rich* axis and the *pine/paint* axis) suggests that when the soul is wholly well-fed by feeding on death, there will be a consequent state of internal riches better than the *costly gay* material riches of the body. But no positive information about this future state is available; it is describable only by optatives *(buy, be fed),* and by negatives—"There's *no more* dying then." There is no passing through, even in the imagination, to the other side of death. The *terms divine* are given no imaginative realization; the corporeal and incorporeal ingestion by worms and by death and by the soul show the imagination stopped at a dark consuming. However, for this very reason, the poem becomes more humane as it progresses, leaving behind its tone of superiority as it concludes in a meditation on the universality of death and the incorrigible materiality of the body.

The rhythmic variants of 146 are of special interest. As the severe inquisition of Q_1 modulates into the hectoring questions of Q_2 and the adjurations of Q_3, there are many initial trochaic substitutions and initial spondees to give point to reproaches, questions, and adjurations:

Póor sóul

Féedin̆g

Whý dŏst

Páintĭng

Whý só

Thén, sóul

Só shălt

The lines in the body of the poem, when they exhibit caesura, shift the caesural position. It occurs after syllable 1 *(Then)*, after syllable 2 *(poor soul; shall worms; then, soul)*, after syllable 4 *(why so large cost; eat up thy charge; within be fed)*. Even when there is no obvious caesura, the word-groupings in lines of comparable rhythm vary, as in lines 3–4:

Why dost thou	*pine within*	*and suffer death*
3 syllables	3 syllables	4 syllables
3 words	2 words	3 words
Painting	*thy outward walls*	*so costly gay*
2 syllables	4 syllables	4 syllables
1 word	3 words	3 words

Only in the closing couplet is there an almost perfect chiastic symmetry, giving it its lulling air of promise:

by syllables	line 13:	6 // 4	by words	line 13:	6 // 4
	line 14:	4 // 6		line 14:	4 // 5

Thomas Roche, in "Shakespeare and the Sonnet Sequence" (p. 84, n. 1), thanks Walton Litz for pointing out in conversation a structural feature of 146 that seems to me undeniably present: it is that lines 1–2 generate line 9; lines 3–4 generate line 10; lines 5–6 generate line 11; and lines 7–8 generate line 12. Let me reproduce the sonnet following this model:

Poor *soul*, the center of my sinful earth, Feeding these rebel pow'rs that thee array,	Then, *soul*, live thou upon thy servant's loss.
Why dost thou *pine* within and suffer dearth, Painting thy outward walls so costly gay?	And let that *pine* to aggravate thy store;

Why so large cost, having so short a lease,
Dost thou upon thy fading mansion *spend?*
Shall worms, inheritors of this excess,
Eat up thy charge? Is this thy body's end?

Buy terms divine in selling hours of dross,

Within be *fed*, without be rich no more.

(If this structure seems a plausible one, it could be thought to resemble somewhat the "split" structure of 94, in which the octave generates line 13, and Q_3 generates line 14. Such "distributive" structures are more spatial than linear.)

The word *death*, so carefully suppressed in the body of 146 (though lurking in *dearth*) grows like a cancer in the couplet, quadrupling itself *(death, death, dead, dying).* Aside from the estimable Pauline statement being made, on which commentators have relied rather too heavily for their orthodox views of the sonnet, I find the proliferation of "deaths" unnervingly reiterative, especially after the arm's-length euphemisms *thy fading mansion* and *thy body's end* which have preceded the outburst of the fatal word.

KEY WORD: FEED[-S] [FED] [FEEDing] [FADing]

Couplet Tie: *feed* [*-s*], *fed*, *feeding*, *fad* [*-ing*] ([2], 6, 12, 13, 13)
no more (12, 14)
then (9, 14) [foregrounded by being the first and last word of the sestet]
death, [*dea(r)th*], *dying* (3, 13, 14, 14)
men, *man*[*-sion*] (6, 13)

147

MY loue is as a feauer longing ſtill,
For that which longer nurſeth the diſeaſe,
Feeding on that which doth preſerue the ill,
Th'vncertaine ſicklie appetite to pleaſe:
My reaſon the Phiſition to my loue,
Angry that his preſcriptions are not kept
Hath left me,and I deſperate now approoue,
Deſire is death,which Phiſick did except.
Paſt cure I am,now Reaſon is paſt care,
And frantick madde with euer-more vnreſt,
My thoughts and my diſcourſe as mad mens are,
At randon from the truth vainely expreſt.
  For I haue ſworne thee faire,and thought thee bright,
  Who art as black as hell,as darke as night.

My love is as a fever longing still
For that which longer nurseth the disease,
Feeding on that which doth preserve the ill,
Th'uncertain sickly appetite to please.
My reason, the physician to my love,
Angry that his prescriptions are not kept,
Hath left me, and I desperate now approve
Desire is death, which physic did except.
Past cure I am, now reason is past care,
And frantic mad with evermore unrest;
My thoughts and my discourse as madmen's are,
At random from the truth vainly expressed:
  For I have sworn thee fair, and thought thee bright,
  Who art as black as hell, as dark as night.

THE *feeding* I have proposed for the initial position of line 2 of 146 opens line 3 of 147, pleasing the *sickly appetite*—one of those *rebel pow'rs* of 146. The struggle between the pining soul and the prosperous body of 146 has been reimagined as a struggle between the prescribing/proscribing physician Reason and a diseased patient. The account of worsening symptoms—*My love is as a fever . . . Past cure I am . . . My thoughts and my discourse as madmen's are*—is interrupted by a diagnostic "explanation": Reason, the physician, has abandoned his disobedient patient, who has refused the prescribed medicine.

The body of the sonnet contains two symptomatic emphases (separated by the account of Reason): the first is physical *(fever, disease, ill[ness], sickly appetite)*, the second, more serious, is mental *(frantic mad; evermore unrest; thoughts and discourse as madmen's are; at random from the truth vainly expressed)*. The gradually intensifying situation—as *desire* becomes *death*, *longing* becomes *desperat[ion]*, and madness supervenes on fever—reaches its climax as both thought and speech, inner and outer expression, veer from the truth, and—worst of all—not in a predictable way but at random. (Booth points out the underlying French and Latin puns in *randonnée / running away* and *currere / dis-course*.)

After the elaborate Latinity of diagnosis and explanation *(preserve, uncertain, appetite, physician, prescription, desperate, approve, desire, except, cure, reason, care, discourse, random, vainly, expressed)*, the predominantly Anglo-Saxon lexicon of the couplet comes as an enormous surprise. The couplet is offered as an instance of how far from sanity the speaker's thoughts and discourse have gone; the *proof* that he is mad is that he has (mentally) *thought* her bright and (by discourse) *sworn* her to be fair. The direct second-person accusation of the last line departs from the self-diagnostic pose of the rest, while the perfect syllabic balance—6, 4, 6, 4—of the closing two lines, coming after the irregular desperation of the diagnosis, suggests a complete and "perfected" knowledge lying behind the "madness" of thought and expression.

The central sentence in the whole poem is *I desperate now approve / Desire is death*. The graphic overlap among the three key words—

desperate	*desperate*	*desire*
desire	*death*	*death*

—"proves" the assertion.

Booth and others have remarked the prolongation accomplished by *longing . . . longer*, the encapsulation of *ill* in *still*, and the witty rewriting of the proverbial *Past cure, past care* from its original meaning to its new role in the allegory of the defecting physician Reason. The surprise comes in the address of the couplet—which turns away from the anguished self *in extremis* and casts a bitter glance both on past self-deception and on the present corrupt mistress. The late introduction of direct address now "explains" the illness to the woman rather than to the self. What motivates this gesture? It is the single most salient aesthetic choice of the poem—to turn to address the woman (a gesture shared by 148). One suspects that the anger ascribed to Reason against his unreasonable patient is displaced from the patient's anger against his deceiving mistress—and that that anger finally erupts as the self-enclosure of the sickroom is broken for one final *j'accuse*.

Here, as elsewhere, certain parallels in rhythm "foreground" conceptual resemblances. The subject phrase *My reason* matches rhythmically and positionally its verb phrase *hath left me; Desire is death* nearly matches, rhythmically and positionally, its parallel *past cure I am.* The alliterating "semantic chain" *disease, desperate, desire, death, discourse, dark* tells in brief the story of the poem. The double use of *now* linking Q_2 and Q_3 sets the present-tense moments *(approve, am)* against the three present-perfect verbs: "My reason *hath left* me," "I *have sworn* . . . and *[have] thought.*" The contrast between past-extending-into-present and the present of "now" gives the poem its sense of temporal extension marking character disintegration. The "clarity" of the couplet suddenly confers a kind of nobility on the *frantic mad* speaker, who suddenly enters a moment of utter lucidity even while he is offering an instance of his own past madness.

The paradox of the sonnet is that this "madman" is perfectly clear about what the truth is: he knows that his thoughts and his discourse are "at random from *the truth.*" He knows that his appetite is *uncertain* and *sickly* (rather than thinking it healthy or good). Though he tells us Reason has left him, we cannot believe him. He comes closer to the truth in line 9, where he says Reason is *past care;* he knows what Reason says, but he no longer cares to observe its mandates. As soon as he says he *is* "frantic mad" he corrects himself, saying that his words are "*as* madmen's are." Such instant self-corrections—from *hath left* to *past care*, from *mad* to *as madmen's*—refuse the flattering unction of madness, and judge the self culpable rather than excusing it.

Couplet Tie: *thought* [*-s*] (11, 13)

148

O Me! what eyes hath loue put in my head,
Which haue no correſpondence with true ſight,
Or if they haue,where is my iudgment fled,
That cenſures falſely what they ſee aright?
If that be faire whereon my falſe eyes dote,
What meanes the world to ſay it is not ſo?
If it be not,then loue doth well denote,
Loues eye is not ſo true as all mens:no,
How can it? O how can loues eye be true,
That is ſo vext with watching and with teares?
No maruaile then though I miſtake my view,
The ſunne it ſelfe ſees not, till heauen cleeres.
　O cunning loue,with teares thou keepſt me blinde,
　Leaſt eyes well ſeeing thy foule faults ſhould finde.

O me! what eyes hath love put in my head,
Which have no correspondence with true sight?
Or if they have, where is my judgement fled,
That censures falsely what they see aright?
If that be fair whereon my false eyes dote,
What means the world to say it is not so?
If it be not, then love doth well denote
Love's eye is not so true as all men's: no,
How can it? O how can love's eye be true,
That is so vexed with watching and with tears?
No marvel then though I mistake my view:
The sun itself sees not till heaven clears.
　O cunning love, with tears thou keep'st me blind,
　Lest eyes well seeing thy foul faults should find.

SONNET 148 has many words in common with 137: *blind, love, eyes, all men, false, judgment, see[ing], fair, true [truth], foul.* Such an overlap sometimes suggests that one poem is a "rewrite" of the other. (Sonnet 149 also uses *blind, love, all, eyes,* and *see;* 152 uses *love, all, truth, eye(s), blindness, see, fair, foul.* These, too, fall into this group concerning blindness, but as developments rather than as revisions.) If we look into the relations between 137 and 148, we see that 137, though first ascribing blame to Cupid in the octave, becomes chiefly preoccupied with self-condemnation. The agency of Cupid is dropped after line 1, and agency is then ascribed to heart and eyes, which have *erred.* Agency is thus continually displaced from the integrated self, first by being transferred mythologically to Cupid and second by synecdoche to eyes and heart. The integrated *I* never appears to assume blame.

In Sonnet 148, some of the same strategies are followed (agency is initially and briefly ascribed to *love,* but passes far more rapidly to *eyes* and *judgement*). However, the integrated *I* eventually appears: showing up in disguise as *eye* in line 8 (repeated in line 9), it finally takes on its "true" shape as *I* in line 11 and as *me* in line 13. (The explicit version of the pun will arrive in 152: "For *I* have sworn thee fair: more perjured *eye.*") In short, 148 goes narratively further than 137; instead of stopping at self-condemnation, it goes on to self-excuse. The excuse is triply phrased: allegorically, personally, and cosmically.

Allegorically:	O how *can* love's *eye* be true, / That is so vexed with watching and with tears?
Personally:	No marvel then though *I* mistake *my* view.
Cosmically:	The *sun itself* sees not till heaven clears.

The return to the agency of love in C substitutes the woman (as "*cunning* love," the obscene pun fixing the reference) for Cupid (if we interpret the original *love* that has put misleading eyes in the speaker's head as Cupid) and for allegorical love (love's eye). As the reference of the word *love* shifts, so does agency. At first the speaker is a victim of the love that has put *false eyes* in his head; next, he is the allegorical lover, bearing love's personified eye, *vexed with watching and with tears.* Finally agency shifts to the *cunning love* who keeps him blind. He still ascribes ill-seeing to his eyes, but has dropped words like *false* and *true* in reference to them, and has transferred falsity to the woman in the punning phrase "thy foul *faults.*"

Booth notes, in lines 7–9, "the phonetically related words *not, -note, no,* and *O,*" and mentions the bawdy potential of *O* as construed by Partridge. In fact, the sound and letters of *O* and *no,* along with *eye, I,* and the pun on *aye,* appear prominently throughout:

1. ***O eyes*** *love*
2. ***no*** *corresp**on**dence*
3. ***O**r*
5. *where**on** **eyes** dote*
6. *world **to** **not** **so***
7. ***not**, love doth de**no**te*
8. *Love's **eye** **not** so **no***
9. *How **O** how love's **eye***
10. *S**o***
11. ***No** though **I***
12. ***not***
13. ***O** love thou*
14. ***eyes** foule should*

The sound of *o* and the letter *o,* in their frequent occurence, are foregrounded by often appearing in the initial word (1, 3, 8, 9, 11, 13) or final word (5, 6, 7, 8) of the line. And the fact that Q_2 rhymes solely in *ō* calls the letter and sound to our attention.

The rhetoric of 148 is—after the lexical overlap with other sonnets and the insistent presence of *ī* and *ō*—the feature that most prominently thrusts itself forward. The self-hectoring questions and exclamations recall those of 146, but the chop-logic *(if they have, if that be fair, if it be not)* is foreign to the more solemn 146. The "blind" speaker of 137, 138, 149, 150, and 152, exploring his self-delusion, brings many defenses to bear (as he blames Cupid, the woman, his own false eyes, his judgment, his heart, and even natural law). The specific measuring stick in 137 was an internal Platonic perpendicular: the speaker's eyes *know where beauty is, see where it lies* and yet take the worst to be what the best is. The speaker's *heart knows [the woman's body to be] the wide world's common place* and yet *think[s it] a several plot.* His eyes *see* this, yet *say this is not.* All the standards are within the speaker, and *right true,* as he admits. The word *erred* in 137 is not to be taken as meaning "made a mistake, been deceived," but as meaning *wandered from the moral way*, and the pun on ***erred*** (< *errare*) and *trans**ferred*** (< *ferre*) makes the spatial point again, while invoking as defense the passive manipulation of the speaker's faculties:

> In things right true my heart and eyes have erred,
> And to this false plague *are* they now *transferred.*

Line 13 of 137 is in the present perfect of contrition: *[I] have erred.* But the second line of the couplet, with its lyric *now,* is in a passive present tense vaguely unascribed to any agency. The common *place* of line 10 contains a *plague* (line 14) to which eyes and heart are now subject.

By 148, the inner standard has been so shaken that the speaker now looks in Q_2 to an external measure—what *the world* says, what all men's *eyes (ayes)* affirm as true. The poem, it is true, opens with a reference to *true sight* (the inner perpendicular), and it is even conjectured that the speaker's eyes still have a correspondence with that measuring standard *(if they have).* But even if they *see aright* the woman's lack of beauty, his judgment errs in its censure (*sin-sure,* as Booth remarks) affirming the object of sight to be beautiful. The speaker's eyes certainly *dote:* and he can only conclude, in Q_3, that his eye *(Love's eye)* is in the wrong, so clouded with tears is it by the agency of *cunning love.* By the end, he is not only blind, but durably kept blind, and the knowledge of her *foul faults* is ascribed not to himself but to the woman herself, who has therefore blinded him lest he find her out.

These are sophistries, yet they continue to admit one trustworthy measure—the world's external "true" censure—even if the speaker has lost true sight or, perhaps, true judgment. By 149, even the world's measure will be lost, and the speaker will align himself, in all his judgments, with the woman, still claiming blindness for his own portion. In 150, the inner perpendicular is again present, and the speaker knows himself to be clearly perjured as he *give[s] the lie* to his *true sight.* The focus changes there, from the speaker's sin to the woman's power. And finally, as we shall see, in 152 the emphasis is no longer on inner judgment but on the verbal betrayal of just discourse, to *swear against the truth.*

In 148, as elsewhere in the *Sonnets,* Shakespeare has his speaker run through a series of logical "places" (here, *eyes, head, sight, judgement, Love's eye, the sun, heaven*). Each of these nouns summons up a host of possible modifiers and verbs, as a whole grid of Renaissance psychology and cosmology comes into play. Since all of this vocabulary about eyes, true sight, judgment, love-blindness, and so on is common coin in Renaissance poetry, we must ask how Shakespeare vivifies it here. In these later sonnets on heart and eyes, he does it in part by departing so conspicuously from the fanciful tone of the earlier heart/eye sonnets, by refusing contrition, and by substituting for contrition various agitations and defenses (realized by punctuation and rhythm as well as by larger means). The speaker's confession of fault (by the Platonic standard of *true sight*, by the vaguely religious standard of *error* and *plague*, or by the worldly standard of *all men's eyes*) normally would lead to the sort of repentance exemplified by Petrarch and Sidney in their sequences. Shakespeare's speaker does not repent. He remains—no matter how perjured—confirmed in his choice, preferring, he defiantly declares, to *err*, to have his heart and eyes transf*erred* to a *false plague*, to *mistake [his] view*, to be *blind*, to be a *tyrant . . . against [him]self*, *to give the lie to [his] true sight*, *to betray [his] nobler part to [his] gross body's treason*, and finally *to swear against the truth so foul a lie*. At the end there is no self-deception left, no excuses about the agency of others or mistake or blindness. There is something heroic about sonnet 152, as the speaker abandons all defenses and accepts the degrading equation of "love" and clear-eyed perjury. Eyes now have no need of a postulated inner perpendicular at all, nor of an external standard, to enable them to judge what they see. Perception is self-ratifying. All along, his eyes saw the foul faults of the lady; but he swore against the thing his eyes saw. Sight is undeniable, and "blindness" is only a smokescreen. It is perjury the speaker is guilty of. This is the sin against accuracy of discourse, the only mortal sin for a writer. Conformity of speech to what he sees is the writer's chief moral obligation. Mis-representation is his evil. The soul who speaks in 152 is damned as a writer, if still precariously alive as a lover.

It is in such groupings as that of 137, 147 (where the false swearing that will end the cluster enters it), and 148–152 that the power of Shakespeare's use of the sequence-form is felt. Each of these poems gains sinister strength from its fellows in the cluster. A psychological dynamic larger than what can be represented in fourteen lines binds the poems. The final clear-sighted and dry-eyed embrace of complete, voluntary perjury would lack full effect if it had not been preceded by self-deception, displacements of agency, and tears.

In forsaking, in these poems, the sexual triangle, Shakespeare mimics erotic bondage in its pure form, where infidelities with others, on either side (see 152), are not at all the heart of the matter. The moral crux is the fact that one "loves" the agent of degradation more than one hates self-degradation.

The Couplet-Tie words in 148 are so numerous (*eye* [*-s*]; *love* [*-'s*];

see[*-ing*]; [*sees*]; [*sight*]; *O; false*[*-ly*] [*faults*]; *well; tears*) that one is led to suspect the presence of one or more KEY WORDS (appearing at least once in Q_1, Q_2, Q_3, and C), and in fact there are two clear ones:

EYE [-S] [-'S] (1, 5, 8, 9, 14)
LOVE [-'S] (1, 7, 8, 9, 13)

Finally, the repetition of *true*, *false*, and *see* [*-s*] [*-ing*] [*sight*] suggests they may play the roles of DEFECTIVE KEY WORDS, appearing in three out of four parts of a sonnet, but suppressed in one member. This proves to be the case. *True* is present in Q_1, Q_2, and Q_3 but suppressed in C; *false* is present in Q_1 as *falsely*, in Q_2 as *false*, and in C as *faults*. It is clear that *true* must be suppressed in the couplet where the speaker, kept blind, can see nothing true. But why is *false* suppressed in Q_3? This is, we note, the quatrain of self-exculpation: for the word *false* the speaker has substituted (in line 8) the euphemism *not so true as all men's*. By exclaiming, "How *can* such a vexed eye be true?" and by saying he *mistakes* his view, the speaker protects himself against both his previously named *false* eyes and *falsely* censuring judgment. Though he has successfully suppressed the word in Q_3, it recurs (but diverted to the woman) in C, in a perfect and violent return of the repressed (the violence contributed by the conspicuous alliteration *foul faults . . . find*). The word *see* is missing in Q_2, which deserts external narration for inner debate.

One reason for thinking the suppression of a word is deliberate is that Shakespeare, here, could perfectly well have inserted *see* into his quatrain of inner debate: ["If I *see* fair whene'er my false eyes dote"] or ["love's *sight* is not so true as all men's"]. The principle of inertia in writing always presses the writer to continue in the vein in which he began. Shakespeare plays off this principle (which leads to both KEY WORDS *and* DEFECTIVE KEY WORDS) against his even stronger principle: that a poem should constantly surprise by resisting its inertial momentum. In Q_2, he marks his departure from alternative constatation of fact ("Either love has put eyes in my head that have not true *sight*, or they *see* truly, but my judgment is amiss") to social speculation by avoiding the *see* of visual perception in favor of the words *eyes dote* and *love's eye*, which clearly denote not simple perception but biased judgment. *See* does not return until we meet the fact that the sun shines only in clear weather. In the last appearance of *see*, we are told that no visually factual *seeing* has ever taken place at all, because the lover is *blind*.

In the emotional tonality of 148, the agitated self-judging questions and exclamations give way, after the invoking of the world's judgment, to an apparent critique of the unreliability of love's eye. This wonderful "turn" is marked in a number of ways:

1. by the odd Quarto punctuation of line 8;
2. by the potential phonetic pun on *no* and *eye* [*aye*];
3. by defensive exact reiteration: "N*o*, / *How can* it? *O how can* . . .";
4. by the spondaic *is so vexed;*
5. by the grammatical "mistake" in paralleling a gerund *(watching)* to a "true noun" *(tears)*—instead of [*with watching and with weeping*].

Shakespeare's turn in mid-sonnet to pathos and helplessness *(O how can)* will be remembered by Yeats in "Leda and the Swan":

> *How can* those terrified vague fingers push
> The feathered glory from her loosening thighs?
> *And how can* body, laid in that white rush,
> But feel the strange heart beating where it lies?

Had Shakespeare's sonnet ended with the almost complacent ["No marvel then though *I* mistake *my* view / [Why,] The sun *itself* sees not till heaven clears"], it would have rested in self-justification, in pathos and self-pity buttressed by natural law ("How can *I* if the sun can't?"). Why does the couplet not continue in the same complacent vein? When we pose this question, we notice that it is only in Q_3 that tears of physical weakness are introduced as the explanation of ill-seeing. Any overtired and grieving eye *vexed with watching and with tears* will be unreliable. But this phrase suggests only the proximate, bodily cause of unreliability. The physical eye has been unmanned (and led to vigils and weeping) by the cunning beloved, the remote efficient cause of the speaker's blindness, designedly stimulating his tears so as to hide her foul faults.

The true structure of the poem, then, is a circular one:

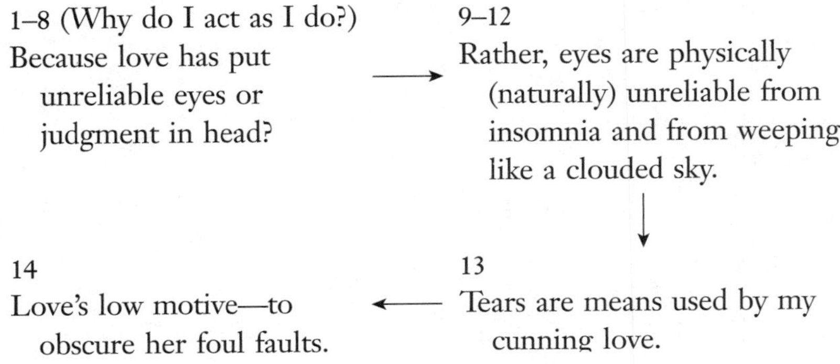

1–8 (Why do I act as I do?)
Because love has put unreliable eyes or judgment in head?
9–12
Rather, eyes are physically (naturally) unreliable from insomnia and from weeping like a clouded sky.
13
Tears are means used by my cunning love.
14
Love's low motive—to obscure her foul faults.

The couplet acts as a late half of a rough chiasmus:

eyes / bad sight : love and tears :: love and tears : eyes / bad sight.
1–8 : 9–12 :: 13 : 14

KEY WORDS:	EYE [-S] [-'S] LOVE [-'S]
DEFECTIVE KEY WORDS:	TRUE (missing in C) FALSE [-LY], [FAULTS] (missing in Q_3) SEE [-S] [-ING], SIGHT (missing in Q_2) One could make SEE into a true KEY WORD if one were willing to include the phonetically hidden but graphically visible *see* in ***false eyes*** (line 5). Cf. the similar *slo* in 51's ***perfects love***.
Couplet Tie:	*eye* [-*s*] [-*'s*] (1, 5, 8, 9, 14) *love* [-*'s*] (1, 7, 8, 9, 13) *see* [-*s*] [-*ing*] *sight*, and perhaps [***false eyes***], (2, 4, [5], 12, 14) *O* (1, 9, 13) *false* [-*ly*] [*faults*] (4, 5, 14) *well* (7, 14) *tears* (10, 13)

149

Canſt thou O cruell,ſay I loue thee not,
When I againſt my ſelfe with thee pertake:
Doe I not thinke on thee when I forgot
Am of my ſelfe, all tirant for thy ſake?
Who hateth thee that I doe call my friend,
On whom froun'ſt thou that I doe faune vpon,
Nay if thou lowrſt on me doe I not ſpend
Reuenge vpon my ſelfe with preſent mone?
What merrit do I in my ſelfe reſpect,
That is ſo proude thy ſeruice to diſpiſe,
When all my beſt doth worſhip thy defect,
Commanded by the motion of thine eyes.
  But loue hate on for now I know thy minde,
  Thoſe that can ſee thou lou'ſt,and I am blind.

Canst thou, O cruel, say I love thee not,
When I against myself with thee partake?
Do I not think on thee when I forgot
Am of myself, all, tyrant, for thy sake?
Who hateth thee that I do call my friend?
On whom frown'st thou that I do fawn upon?
Nay, if thou lour'st on me, do I not spend
Revenge upon myself with present moan?
What merit do I in myself respect
That is so proud thy service to despise,
When all my best doth worship thy defect,
Commanded by the motion of thine eyes?
  But, love, hate on, for now I know thy mind:
  Those that can see thou lov'st, and I am blind.

THE reply-genre that we have seen in the sonnets to the young man returns here. The woman has said, "You do not love me," and the speaker exclaims *Canst thou, O cruel, say I love thee not . . . ?* The body of the sonnet is a series of "proofs of love": the speaker voices them as indignant self-defending questions, which we can rephrase as assertions:

I partake with thee against myself;
I am forgot of myself, thinking on thee, all for thy sake;
I call no one my friend who hates thee;
I fawn on no one thou frown'st on;
Nay, if thou lour'st on me I spend revenge upon myself with present moan;
I respect no merit in myself that would, out of pride, despise serving thee;
All my best worships thy defect, commanded by the motion of thine eyes.

In this masochistic narrative, the speaker goes from self-criticism to self-neglect, to social slavery, to self-cruelty, to self-degradation, ending in the posture where *all* his *best* worships her *defect*, a superlative abasing itself before a negative.

The narrative gradually focuses on seeing: She *frowns on* someone, she *lours on* the speaker. As for him, two verbs associated with him in Q_3 are *respect* (< *re-spicere*) and *despise* (< *de-spicere*)—both deriving from *spectare*, to look at—and it is her *eyes* that command him. (Even the verb *spend* ascribed to the speaker takes on, by its *sp-* alliance with *re**sp**ect* and *de**sp**ise*, a "false" cognate status with the eye-words.)

The variation in length of the accusatory questions (2, 2, 1, 1, 2, 4) is part of Shakespeare's accuracy in the dramatic mimesis of speech, while his "partnering" the questions two by two, or one by one, reveals his impulse to aesthetic stylization.

The self-characterization of the couplet *(I am blind)* has been prepared for by the speaker's denying that he *respects* or *despises.* By refusing to *re-spicere* or *de-spicere* he has lost the right to *spectare,* or look upon. The very definition of moral blindness is to forgo the right to despise and respect.

In the groveling of Q_3 is prepared the conclusive self-diagnosis of blindness. The speaker is, paradoxically, only now enlightened enough to see that his mistress' motive for saying (line 1) *he* doesn't love *her* is that *she* hates *him: But, love, hate on.* The *now* of ***knowing*** (line 13) replaces the *then* of thinking he was beloved. She can only love independent minds—those that can *see, respect* their own merit, *despise* slavery in service. He has lost her love by loving her unto the very blindness she provoked in him as he practiced (but on himself) her cruelty and tyranny to him, in a grotesque parody of love's tendency to imitation, reproduction, and reciprocity. If another person (X) hates her, the speaker (therefore) hates X; she (therefore) hates the speaker for his spinelessness.

Couplet Tie: *love* [*-'st*] (1, 13, 14)
hate [*-th*] (5, 13)
and possibly (in the Quarto): *lov'st* [*lowrst*] (7, 14)
The play on *thou lour'st* and *thou lov'st* sums up, in little, the speaker's fall from grace.

150

OH from what powre haſt thou this powrefull might,
VVith inſufficiency my heart to ſway,
To make me giue the lie to my true ſight,
And ſwere that brightneſſe doth not grace the day?
Whence haſt thou this becomming of things il,
That in the very refuſe of thy deeds,
There is ſuch ſtrength and warranti ſe of skill,
That in my minde thy worſt all beſt exceeds?
Who taught thee how to make me loue thee more,
The more I heare and ſee iuſt cauſe of hate,
Oh though I loue what others doe abhor,
VVith others thou ſhouldſt not abhor my ſtate.
  If thy vnworthineſſe raiſd loue in me,
  More worthy I to be belou'd of thee.

O from what pow'r hast thou this pow'rful might,
With insufficiency my heart to sway,
To make me give the lie to my true sight,
And swear that brightness doth not grace the day?
Whence hast thou this becoming of things ill,
That in the very refuse of thy deeds
There is such strength and warrantise of skill
That in my mind thy worst all best exceeds?
Who taught thee how to make me love thee more,
The more I hear and see just cause of hate?
O, though I love what others do abhor,
With others thou shouldst not abhor my state:
  If thy unworthiness raised love in me,
  More worthy I to be beloved of thee.

"ALL MY best doth *worship* thy defect," declared the speaker in 149, using the word normally reserved for veneration addressed to God alone, but exceptionally included in the marriage service: "With my body I thee *worship*." The verb *worship* derives from the noun *worth*, which in two forms replaces it, so to speak, in the couplet of 150—first, in its negative form, *unworthiness* as synonym to what 149 called the woman's *defect;* second, in a paradoxical use of its adjectival positive form, *worthy*, to imply moral "unworthiness":

All my best doth *worship thy defect* (149);

If thy *unworthiness* [thy worshiped defect] raised love in me,
More *worthy* [in my love for even your defects] I to be beloved of thee.

The mystery of the woman's powerful defect is in fact the opening gambit of 150: her *insufficiency* has *might*. But 150 centrally concerns, like the other sonnets of its group, *giv[ing] the lie to true sight*. Because the speaker is not yet ready to blame himself (as he will in 152), he here displaces the blame onto the woman's quasi-magical might, bestowed on her by some yet more powerful agency, so that even she acts only as the conduit of a force greater than herself. In this construction of his state, the lover is indeed wholly overpowered.

The octave of the sonnet is private; Q_3 is social (as he loves what *others* abhor; as she, with *others*, abhors him); and the couplet is once again apparently private, given its manifest Couplet Tie of *love* [*beloved*]. Yet even as we note the apparent anomalous social reference of Q_3 (with its suspicious double introduction of unnamed *others* outside the lovers' dyad), the very presence of the "extra" people makes us alert to the periphrases and euphemisms—are they not social in reference also?—of Q_2:

Whence hast thou *this becoming of things ill*,
That in the very *refuse of thy deeds*
There is such *strength and warrantise of skill*
That in my mind thy *worst all best exceeds*.

Covert social reference is everywhere. (Compare Q_2 of 148.) What are the ill things she makes lovely, the deeds in which she shows such strength, such guaranteed skill? Who are the shadowy figures possessing *all best* qualities who are outclassed (to the speaker's mind) by her *worst?* What are those worst deeds?

No one knows better than Shakespeare how to prepare a dramatic effect. The dark hints in Q_2 are of course subordinated to its ostensible intent—to ask again the source of the woman's might—but this time under the rubric of the way her presence in the social world aestheticizes evil, *this becoming of things ill.* Because of the sinister periphrases of Q_2, we are not surprised to find the speaker alleging that he has *just cause of hate*, that *others* are involved in her rejection of him, and that whoredom is at the bottom of it all, first as he is *abhor[red]* by the social world for his enslavement to a whore, and second as she, with them, *abhors* him (perhaps by playing the whore with those very *others*).

We now see the complex play—stimulated by the couplet's foregrounding of the word *worth*—on *worst* (8), *abhor/[whore]* (11, 12), and [*worth*] [*-y*] [*-iness*] (13, 14), manifesting the letters *wor-/-hor/wor-h-*, which, together with the phoneme *hōr*, make the word *whore* flicker through the poem.

The oddity of the sonnet is that the insistent interrogations of its first ten lines receive no implied answer from the woman. The rhetorical structure of the sonnet (10-2-2), departing from the two "normal" Shakespearean rhetorical structures (4-4-4-2 and 8-4-2), demands that we look into these repeatedly pressed questions about the source of the woman's power. *O from what power? . . . Whence hast thou? . . . Who taught thee how?* I will come in a moment to the odd substance of each of these queries, but first we must notice their outcome. Balked of an answer to his first ten lines, the speaker skitters aside and pulls in the red herring of *others* (lines 11–12), who play, in his mind, the contradictory parts of abhorring his mistress and helping her abhor him. It is only in the couplet that the speaker gives up on ascribing the mistress' uncanny power to some superior force, admitting that he loves her not in spite of, but *because of*, her ill deeds. This insight (like its concessive predecessor, *though I love what others do abhor*) is admitted only in hypothetical form *(if)*, but its conclusive position in the couplet, and its self-blame, give it power over the former (fanciful) suppositions of magical power in the woman: on the contrary, not her might but her *unworthiness raised love in me.* The couplet's bitter recognition that the speaker's arousal depends on her promiscuity—making, as I've said, the word *worthy* resonant with irony, and vitiating the very presence of the courtly reciprocal *love/beloved*—prepares the way for the speaker's final recognition of his own double immorality of word and deed in 152.

I return to the substance of the three self-deceiving questions comprising lines 1–10. The first ratifies *true sight,* and openly admits that the speaker's *lie* is worsened by perjury, a false oath: "[I] *swear* that brightness doth not grace the day." This is of course a self-allusion to sonnet 28:

> I tell the *day* to please him thou art *bright*
> And *dost* him *grace* when clouds do blot the heaven.

Even when the day was cloudy, the young man was sufficient, in the poet's eye, to supply the absence of the sun. A negative version of this compliment—now classed as a *lie*—is turned to the benefit of the woman of the night: because she is dark, day and its brightness must be denigrated.

The second quatrain—in its hyperbole the most powerful—establishes a scale of comparative value. The "simple" opposition of dark and bright organizing Q_1 (and remembered from 147) is replaced by a grotesque, further differentiated, hierarchy of value. At the bottom is the human good, then above it the human better, then the human best; and above them all towers the mistress' *worst.* This internal transvaluation of moral values *(in my mind)* is "worse," morally speaking, than a refusal of accurate perception (giving the *lie to true sight*) prompted by the affections of the *sway[ed] heart.*

How is the third quatrain related to these investigations of the faults of (a) the heart and perception, and (b) the mind and judgment? The third question, significantly, abandons the former comparatives ("I deny *the day* brightness because I prefer the night"; "Her worst exceeds *all [other] best*"), and faces not a question of comparative preference but an absolute: the worse she is, the more the speaker loves her, in a "pure" geometric proportionality, as escalating cause of hate = escalating love:

> *Who taught thee how to make me love thee more,*
> *The more I hear and see just cause of hate?*

The "stutter" in this question—*thee more / The more*—suggests the fixity of the speaker in his obsession.

If, as I suggest, the three questions go from a relatively "innocent" lie about the day to a comparative preference for the worst, and thence to an absolute sexual intensification from repeatedly perceived promiscuity, we can see in them the speaker's mounting self-knowledge of his own moral unworthiness, preparing for the sting in the final judgment that he and the woman are indeed birds of a feather in their degradation. But her debasement is primarily sexual; his, being conscious of itself and concerned with personal moral value, is the worser ill. The sexual component of his addiction is set forth in the sardonic phallic phrase *raised love in me*, to be further elaborated in the next sonnet.

The speaker's masochism is most fully expressed in the shameful adoration of lines 5–7, where the naked clash of values is laid bare:

Whence hast thou this becoming of things ill,
That in the very refuse of thy deeds
There is such strength and warrantise of skill
That in my mind thy worst all best exceeds?

Sweetest things turn sourest by their deeds (94), we recall, and there is a suggestion of 94's festered lilies in the phrase "*the very refuse* of thy *deeds*." The image cluster evoked by *deeds*, *strength*, and *warrantise of skill* is certainly masculine, and places the lover in a position of relative-weakness-admiring-strength. This classically "female" position is provoked, at least in part, by the speaker's retreat from responsibility for his own actions, which is embodied in his "helpless" questions.

Couplet Tie: *love* [*beloved*] (9, 11, 13, 14)
and possibly: *worst* [*worth*] [*-iness*] [*-y*] (8, 13, 14)

151

LOue is too young to know what conſcience is,
Yet who knowes not conſcience is borne of loue,
Then gentle cheater vrge not my amiſſe,
Leaſt guilty of my faults thy ſweet ſelfe proue.
For thou betraying me, I doe betray
My nobler part to my groſe bodies treaſon,
My ſoule doth tell my body that he may,
Triumph in loue,fleſh ſtaies no farther reaſon.
But ryſing at thy name doth point out thee,
As his triumphant prize,proud of this pride,
He is contented thy poore drudge to be
To ſtand in thy affaires,fall by thy ſide.
  No want of conſcience hold it that I call,
  Her loue,for whoſe deare loue I riſe and fall.

Love is too young to know what conscience is,
Yet who knows not conscience is born of love?
Then, gentle cheater, urge not my amiss,
Lest guilty of my faults thy sweet self prove.
For thou betraying me, I do betray
My nobler part to my gross body's treason;
My soul doth tell my body that he may
Triumph in love; flesh stays no farther reason,
But rising at thy name doth point out thee
As his triumphant prize; proud of this pride,
He is contented thy poor drudge to be,
To stand in thy affairs, fall by thy side.
  No want of conscience hold it that I call
  Her "love" for whose dear love I rise and fall.

LOVE and *conscience*, *rise* (and its variants) and *fall* are, unsurprisingly, the Couplet Tie of this enigmatic sonnet, which thematizes the conflict openly represented in all the poems concerning the dark lady, and at least covertly present in those concerning the young man. The idealization of the young man led to grief, as did the idealization of the mistress. Shakespeare recognizes unblinkingly the enhancement of ego produced in his speaker by the idealization of the other: "*proud* of this *pride*, [flesh] is contented thy poor drudge to be . . .," or, earlier, "Thy sweet love remembered such *wealth* brings, / That then I scorn to change my state with *kings*" (29).

Because the sonnets show the cycle of idealization, infatuation, and inevitable disillusion twice over, once with a male love-object and once with a female (exhausting both possibilities for their speaker) their human psychological import is essentially tragic. (The two mythical sonnets closing the entire sequence treat the cycle in the eternal comedy of Anacreontic parable.) But the moral import of the sequences is mixed. The speaker never recovers from his attachments: the last sonnet to the woman begins *In loving thee*, and the last sonnet to the man opens with *O thou my lovely boy*. In Christian terms, the speaker shows no "firm purpose of amendment" for sexual sin in the second sequence, nor does he exhibit, in the first sequence, a resolve to love more wisely in the future. His eye, helpless before the snare of physical beauty, and his soul, sexually aroused by promiscuity itself, are *past cure*. Reason seems unlikely to resume governance of either addicted eye or addicted soul.

The end of the physical body, in both sequences, is the worm:

Be not self-willed, for thou art much too fair
To be death's conquest and make worms thine heir
(sonnet 6)

Shall worms, inheritors of this excess,
Eat up thy charge? Is this thy body's end?
(sonnet 146)

Though sonnet 146 suggests that *terms divine* might be had for the buying, the soul shows no disposition in later sonnets to sell its hours of dross: on the contrary, according to the speaker of 151, the soul is regularly betrayed, and betrays itself by urging the body on. This is one of two crucial statements in 151: *My soul doth tell my body that he may / Triumph in love.* The previous crucial statement is the axiom (said to be known to all) that *conscience is born of love.* Eros is the cause of self-awareness through self-reproach, and awareness points out future erotic possibility to flesh, which responds involuntarily with erection. This is to simplify Shakespeare (by leaving out the self's antecedent betrayal of the soul), but it is nonetheless true as far as it goes.

Shakespeare here admits the libidinal base of adult consciousness itself. The subject had interested him in *Romeo and Juliet,* in which love (not simply lust, as we see from the cognitively ineffectual presence of Romeo's former penchant for Rosaline) awakens the full spectrum of moral awareness and personal conviction in its two young protagonists. (There is another Shakespearean form of awareness—Mercutio's, Ariel's—not caused by love; but it is aesthetic, nonmoral, and nonrelational, constructive of its own fantastic world rather than immediately derived from the human and social environment.)

The triple verbal play embodied in the word *conscience*—as "consciousness" and "moral judgment" and "knowledge of cunt"—governs each of its three appearances in this sonnet and draws magnetically to it its sister word, *contented*/"cuntented." Certainly in the first two lines the word *conscience* possesses fully all three of its meanings (its meaning in line 13 is more dubious).

The second-person address ("thou") of this poem begins visibly in line 3, and seems to end with line 12, since the couplet refers to the woman in the third person *(Her).* But we cannot help seeing that this is a reply-sonnet: the woman—herself a *gentle cheater,* the speaker reminds her in his retort—has complained of some *amiss* on the speaker's part, which turns out to be his addressing her as "love." "Doesn't your *conscience* reproach you," she says, "when you call me '*love*'? I hardly think that what you feel for me justifies that word." The poem begins with the speaker's evasive reply: *Love* [being a babe, cf. 115] *is too young to know what conscience is.* This reply (with its subsequent threat of counteraccusations) continues grammatically through line 12 ("fall by *thy* side"). Logic makes us confident that the same person is addressed in the couplet "[Do not thou] *hold it* a want of conscience that I call"—and we expect *thee* instead of *her.* "Don't think it wrong of me to call the person for whom I rise and fall 'love,'" says the speaker, putting his case "impersonally" and "logically." "Doesn't everyone call his sex partner 'love'? Haven't I a right, exposing myself to falls for the sake of her socially discredited love, to use the word 'love'? Can one disentangle appetite from love? Can I? Can you?"

The technical aim of the sonnet is to enact appetite and orgasm, and to that end it might be wise to keep the Quarto's division of the poem into only three sentences. After Q_1 (the Quarto's first sentence), Q_2 and Q_3 make one long sentence in the Quarto, and it is certainly a mistake, in aesthetic terms, to break up this breathless sentence with periods, or even (as Booth does) with a dash. The point of orgasm—*prize/proud/pride*—especially needs concatenation. The *p*'s obtrude themselves, beginning in *prove* and *part*, climaxing at *point*, *prize*, *proud*, and *pride*, and falling off in *poor* (with graphic reinforcement of *p* in *triumph* and *trium**ph**ant*). The unstoppability of orgasm is certainly imitated here, with "ejaculation" occuring in the redundancy of *proud of this pride;* and orgasm is reinforced by the flurry of sounds reinforcing the phonemes of "rising," "raise," and "ride": bet***raying***, *be**tray***, ***treason***, ***tr**iumph*, ***reason***, ***rising***, ***tr**iumphant*, *p**ri**ze*, ***pride***, ***rise***. (Between *triumph* and *triumphant* we even find the link *but **ris**ing*.)

Detumescence is represented not only by the semantic decline from *proud* to *poor* but also from *tr-iu-mph* to *dr-u-dge*, words which, with their initial double consonants, triple final letters and common *u* in the middle, seem to be some sort of graphic cousins. Post-coital quiet comes in *con/[cunt]/tented*, followed by an analytic third-person treatment of both the mistress *(her)* and the phallus (*thy poor drudge*, a phrase completing the turn from "*my* body" to independent third-person *flesh*, thence to possession by the other, "*thy* drudge").

I have so far omitted, in this account, the disturbing Q_2. It becomes violently subordinated to the triumph of the flesh in Q_3 and the subsequent urbane and bitter couplet-conclusion about one's rise and fall at the expense of *dear* love. In Q_2, the sexual (because "unstoppable") trope of concatenation, ending in *poor drudge*, has begun with double betrayal: the woman betrays the speaker, and he betrays his *nobler part*. The soul advises the body of his opportunity, the flesh rises to the chance, and the triumphant ejaculation occurs in *prize/proud/pride*. The originating word *betraying* spawns *betray; treason* is shown to contain *reason;* and *treason*, *reason*, and *rising* in turn act out lexically, etymologically, phonemically, and graphically the trope of concatenation (seen earlier in 129). Formally, the poem's structure is 4-8-2, with the eight-line group acting out tumescence and detumescence, itself bordered fore and aft by the speaker's reformulation of the woman's reproach.

The woman is still blamed in Q_2; her betrayal initiates that of himself by the man. It is not fanciful, perhaps, to see this as a reenactment of the primal Adamic *fall* (the word twice repeated, employed as a Couplet Tie, and the last word in the poem). Though the woman first betrays the speaker (presumably sexually), his appetite is aroused by her very promiscuity—and he betrays himself, an act worse than betraying another.

Nonetheless, some blame is still apportioned here to the woman, and the speaker's shame is covered up in the grimly "libertine" ending, in which his *nobler part* has vanished, along with any remnant of the moral sense of *conscience.* It is not until the next sonnet that the speaker blames himself more than the woman, both for his moral fault and for his betrayal of discourse itself.

DEFECTIVE KEY WORD: LOVE (missing in Q_3, the quatrain of erection, ejaculation, and detumescence)

Couplet Tie: *love* (1, 2, 8, 14, 14)
conscience (1, 2, 13)
rise [*-ing*] [*p-rize*] (9, 10, 14) and perhaps
[*t-reason*] [*reason*] (6, 8)
fall (12, 14) (and perhaps *faults*, 4)

152

IN louing thee thou know'ſt I am forſworne,
But thou art twice forſworne to me loue ſwearing,
In act thy bed-vow broake and new faith torne,
In vowing new hate after new loue bearing:
But why of two othes breach doe I accuſe thee,
When I breake twenty:I am periur'd moſt,
For all my vowes are othes but to miſuſe thee:
And all my honeſt faith in thee is loſt.
For I haue ſworne deepe othes of thy deepe kindneſſe:
Othes of thy loue,thy truth,thy conſtancie,
And to inlighten thee gaue eyes to blindneſſe,
Or made them ſwere againſt the thing they ſee.
  For I haue ſworne thee faire::more periurde eye,
  To ſwere againſt the truth ſo foule a lie.

In loving thee thou know'st I am forsworn,
But thou art twice forsworn to me love swearing:
In act thy bed-vow broke, and new faith torn
In vowing new hate after new love bearing.
But why of two oaths' breach do I accuse thee,
When I break twenty? I am perjured most,
For all my vows are oaths but to misuse thee,
And all my honest faith in thee is lost.
For I have sworn deep oaths of thy deep kindness,
Oaths of thy love, thy truth, thy constancy,
And to enlighten thee gave eyes to blindness,
Or made them swear against the thing they see:
  For I have sworn thee fair: more perjured eye,
  To swear against the truth so foul a lie.

WITH this enormously comprehensive poem, the sequence of the dark mistress is brought to an end. The fruit of erotic experience, here as in the earlier sequence, is greater self-knowledge; in 151 and 152 it provokes a bitterly shaming acknowledgment of one's own least acceptable sexual proclivities. To realize that one requires promiscuity in the mistress in order to be sexually aroused is in itself horrifying, especially when "consciously" one detests the fact that the mistress is *the bay where all men ride* (137). The whole second sequence can be read as the speaker's gradual discovery that it is not an accident that he has found himself infatuated with a promiscuous woman; his own complicity is what shocks him, as he discovers that it is precisely her *unworthiness* that raises "love" in him. This is the speaker's discovery as a lover; but he has a further shame to express. As a user of language, his obligation is to accuracy and truth; his addiction has led him not only to corporeal abasement but also to abuse of language, for a writer the profounder corruption.

Masculine and feminine rhymes alternate in the quatrains of 152—mfmf; fmfm; fmfm; the couplet has masculine rhymes, mm. The whole makes up a somewhat chiastic pattern, with masculine rhymes opening Q_1 and C, while the two inner parts are initiated by feminine rhymes. The unpredictability of this form, by comparison with the other two sonnets with a substantial number of feminine rhymes—20 (all feminine) and 87 (with only two masculine rhyme-words)—enacts unpredictability itself, in formal terms. A perjurer is, the form would seem to say, unreliable in his procedures.

In terms of chronology, the poem is structured from the perjured "now" to the naive "then" and back again. If we reconstruct the speaker's chronology as it happened, we have this scheme:

1. I (originally) swear thee fair;
2. I swear deep oaths of thy deep kindness, oaths of thy love, thy truth, thy constancy [protesting too much, perhaps, given the double intensive *deep*];
3. I perceive thou art forsworn (thy marital bed-vow broke) in performing the act with me;

4. I perceive thou art twice forsworn, swearing love to me and then vowing hate toward me;
5. I accuse thee of being doubly forsworn, but
6. I accuse myself of being twenty times forsworn, because twenty times I have vowed to misuse thee, and I break my vow each time by continuing to love thee;
7. In the contest of perjury, of "forswornness," I am the winner;
8. I see thy falsity and foulness, and I have lost all my honest faith in thee, and yet I continue to love thee.

In the poem we meet this chronology scrambled, and the means of confusion are chiefly grammatical ones: the poem deliberately intertwines various forms of presentness (present participles—*loving*, *swearing*, *vowing*, *bearing*—and present tenses—*I accuse*, *I break*, *my vows are oaths*) with various forms of pastness (past participles—*broke*, *torn*—and past tenses—*I gave*, *[I] made them swear*). Among these are intermingled forms of the reflexive verbs *to forswear oneself* and *to perjure oneself*; these forms are composed of a present-tense auxiliary and a past participle, giving them the curious appearance of present pastness or past presentness: *I am forsworn; thou art forsworn; I am perjured.* To this mix are added present perfect forms carrying a past action into present view *(I have sworn . . . I have sworn)* and infinitives *(to misuse, to enlighten, to swear):* these infinitives apply respectively to the future, the past, and the metaphysical present. A form like *is lost* sums up the pastness of the present view, in its combining of a present tense and a past participle.

This sonnet, then, offers perhaps the best example of the "mad" verbal randomness feared by the speaker in 147. Besides zigzagging unsettlingly between the present and the past, the speaker returns obsessively to the same words over and over: *swear* and its variants *(swore, forsworn, swearing)* alone occur seven times (1, 2, 2, 9, 12, 13, 14); *oaths* four times (5, 7, 9, 10); *vow(s)* (3, 4, 7), *love* (2, 4, 10), and *new* (3, 4, 4) thrice; and the punning *I/eye* [*-s*] appears eight times (1, 5, 6, 6, 9, 11, 13, 13). *Perjured* (6, 13), *truth* (10, 14), *faith* (3, 8), and *deep* (9, 9) are each repeated once. But *the distraction of this madding fever* (119) appears as well in the apparent incoherence of the rebuke about new faith, new hate, and new love, and in the confusion about topics suitable for oaths. It may be common to swear that one's beloved is constant and true in love; it seems distinctly odd to swear *deep oaths* of her *deep kindness*—and as for whether she is fair, that is usually taken as self-evident, not a matter for oath-taking. Sonnet 152 is, of course, remembering 131; when bystanders said the woman's face had not *the power to make love groan*, the lover was not bold enough to correct them outright, but took an oath on it privately: *I swear it to myself alone. / And to be sure that is not false I swear, / A thousand groans . . . do witness bear.* And 152 is also recalling, in its *I have sworn thee fair,* 147: *For I have sworn thee fair, and thought thee bright, / Who art as black as hell, as dark as night.* The swearing reaches its apogee, and is named climactically as an outright lie, as the lyric sequence proper comes to a close.

Blame of the woman has faded in view of the greater blame with which the speaker castigates himself. The self-lacerating intelligence in the later sonnets produces a voice so undeceived about reality *(the truth)* and himself (his *perjured eye*) that the reader admires the clarity of mind that can so anatomize sexual obsession while still in its grip, that can so acquiesce in humiliation while inspecting its own arousal, that can lie freely while acknowledging the truth. To represent such a voice in all its paradoxical incapacity and capacity is the victory of Shakespeare's technique in the second subsequence.

KEY WORD: EYE [-S], I (Normally, *I* would not qualify as a foregrounded word, but the pun with *eye* brings it forward.)

DEFECTIVE KEY WORD: SWEAR (missing in Q_2, the quatrain of broken oaths)

Couplet Tie: *eye* [*-s*], *I* (1, 5, 6, 6, 9, 11, 13, 13)
swear [*-ing*], *sworn*, *forsworn* (1, 2, 2, 9, 12, 13, 14)
perjured (6, 13)
truth (10, 14)

153

CVpid laid by his brand and fell a ſleepe,
A maide of *Dyans* this aduantage found,
And his loue-kindling fire did quickly ſteepe
In a could vallie-fountaine of that ground:
Which borrowd from this holie fire of loue,
A datelеſſe liuely heat ſtill to indure,
And grew a ſeething bath which yet men proue,
Againſt ſtrang malladies a ſoueraigne cure:
But at my miſtres eie loues brand new fired,
The boy for triall needes would touch my breſt,
I ſick withall the helpe of bath deſired,
And thether hied a ſad diſtemperd gueſt.
    But found no cure, the bath for my helpe lies,
    Where *Cupid* got new fire; my miſtres eye.

Cupid laid by his brand and fell asleep:
A maid of Dian's this advantage found,
And his love-kindling fire did quickly steep
In a cold valley-fountain of that ground;
Which borrowed from this holy fire of Love
A dateless lively heat, still to endure,
And grew a seething bath, which yet men prove
Against strange maladies a sovereign cure.
But at my mistress' eye Love's brand new fired,
The boy for trial needs would touch my breast;
I, sick withal, the help of bath desired,
And thither hied, a sad distempered guest;
    But found no cure: the bath for my help lies
    Where Cupid got new fire—my mistress' eyes.

154

THe little Loue-God lying once a ſleepe,
Laid by his ſide his heart inflaming brand,
Whilſt many Nymphes that vou'd chaſt life to keep,
Came tripping by,but in her maiden hand,
The fayreſt votary tooke vp that fire,
Which many Legions of true hearts had warm'd,
And ſo the Generall of hot deſire,
Was ſleeping by a Virgin hand diſarm'd.
This brand ſhe quenched in a coole Well by,
Which from loues fire tooke heat perpetuall,
Growing a bath and healthfull remedy,
For men diſeaſd,but I my Miſtriſſe thrall,
Came there for cure and this by that I proue,
Loues fire heates water,water cooles not loue.

The little Love-god lying once asleep
Laid by his side his heart-inflaming brand,
Whilst many nymphs that vowed chaste life to keep
Came tripping by; but in her maiden hand
The fairest votary took up that fire
Which many legions of true hearts had warmed,
And so the general of hot desire
Was sleeping by a virgin hand disarmed.
This brand she quenchèd in a cool well by,
Which from Love's fire took heat perpetual,
Growing a bath and healthful remedy
For men diseased; but I, my mistress' thrall,
Came there for cure, and this by that I prove:
Love's fire heats water, water cools not love.

SONNETS 153 and 154 are close in plot, but not identical. Each is an Anacreontic narrative about the unquenchability of love. According to 153, if Cupid's torch is put out, he can get new fire from a *mistress' eye*, which is the ultimate cure for love-sickness. Sonnet 154 omits Cupid's seeking new fire, and the speaker's hope to be cured by his mistress' eyes, but tells the original Greek love-story common to both poems: a nymph-votaress of Diana, vowed to chastity, quenches the sleeping Cupid's torch in a nearby fountain/well, which, taking on heat from the torch, becomes a curative bath for diseased men. Both 153 and 154, unlike the epigram from which they descend, tell two stories: the first is Cupid's story, the second the lover's story. In 153 Cupid occupies the octave, the speaker the sestet, where he becomes a "living torch," inflamed by Cupid's new-fired brand. The speaker-torch goes to quench himself in the water where the Cupid-torch was quenched but finds no cure there, and can only hope for cure from his mistress' eyes. The first of these two poems, then, gives equal time to both stories. In 154, however, the lyric speaker enters very late, cramming his story into the last two-and-one-half lines:

I, my mistress' thrall,
Came there for cure, and this by that I prove:
Love's fire heats water, water cools not love.

Retelling the Anacreontic parable becomes an exercise in hermeneutics, as each personal "application" reinterprets the phallic myth. The myth represents a contest of chastity against passion in which passion wins, its heat transferred to the water that quenches it. But the "application" in 153 represents Cupid's brand as once more reignited, after being quenched, and the curative bath as inefficacious in the speaker's case. The brief "application" in 154 leaves the original myth undisturbed, and repeats the inefficacy of the bath. In both the original epigram and in 154's interpretation of it, phallic heat is transferrable but not reignitable; in 153's interpretation, phallic heat is an ever-renewable phoenix-fire whose enduring seat is the mistress' eye, rather than the phallus itself. Both applications agree on the invalidity of the Greek comic myth; the bath finds at least one diseased man whom it cannot cure. Sonnet 153 envisages an ultimate cure for love (the mistress' eye) while not obtaining it, but 154 envisages no cure at all.

The triviality of expression in these twinned poems has made them seem odd envoys to the second subsequence, less successful surely than was 126 as an envoy to the first. Yet the very triviality and ancientness of these little myths—and the comic and frivolous tone with which they treat the whole question of passion—cool down the *deep oaths* of the rhetorically fevered lyric poems. The representative mythical *I* of 153 and 154 is far from the historical *dramatis persona* who could urge the young man to get a son, or could watch a woman playing the virginals. Comic distance is thereby gained on the realm of Eros and even on its enemy, Diana. The poems de-Christianize the sequence, putting chastity and passion in a pre-Christian long focus.

Both poems resemble 145 in style, in that they are made of long chains of coordinate and dependent clauses, with connectives like *and* and *but.* In 153, the chain runs, "A maid found . . . *and* did steep in fountain *which* borrowed heat, *still* to endure, *and* grew a bath *which* men prove . . . *But* the boy would touch . . . ; I help desired, *and* tried, *but* found no cure." In 154, the similar chain is, "Love-god laid by brand, *whilst* nymphs *that* vowed came by, *but* fairest took fire *which* had warmed, *and so* general was disarmed. She quenched brand in well *which* took heat, *growing* a bath, *but* I came, *and* this I prove." This linear and additive dependency chain, rarely broken by a full stop, does not represent the Shakespearean colloquial speech-pattern, formed by dramatic writing, which prevails in the other sonnets. My own guess would be that the Anacreontics (like 145) were early work (on loose sheets, so to speak) and were inserted as a plausible and conventional end-note to the abruptly terminated Dark Lady subsequence (perhaps because the Young Man subsequence had already been given a formal ending by 126).

I accept (for the rhyme's sake) the emendation of *eye* to *eyes* in line 14 of 153.

For sonnet 153

KEY WORD: FIRE [-D] (3, 5, 9, 14)

DEFECTIVE KEY WORD: BATH (missing in Q_1 before growth of bath)

Couplet Tie: *found* (2, 13)
cure (8, 13)
bath (7, 11, 13)
help (11, 13)
Cupid (1, 14)
new (9, 14)
fire [-*d*] (3, 5, 9, 14)
my mistress' eye [-*s*] (9, 14)

For sonnet 154

DEFECTIVE KEY WORDS: LOVE (missing in Q_2, the quatrain of virgin chastity)
FIRE
HEAT [-S] [HOT]
(missing in Q_2, where Cupid lays by his brand)

Couplet Tie: *came* (4, 13)
love (1, 10, 14, 14)
fire (5, 10, 14)
heat [-*s*] [*hot*] (7, 10, 14)
cool [-*s*] (9, 14)

APPENDIXES

WORKS CONSULTED

INDEX OF FIRST LINES

APPENDIX 1

KEY WORDS

7. LOOK [-S] [unLOOKed]
10. SELF
15. YOU (It could be argued that this word is not present in Q_1, but I suggest it is phonetically hiding in "HUge," chosen precisely for its anticipation of YOU.)
20. WOMAN [WOMEN]
24. EYE [-S]
26. SHOW
30. WOE [-S] (the last is a pun: sor-WOES)
31. LOVE [-'S] [-RS] [-D]
32. LOVE [-R] [LOVING]
42. LOVE
43. DAY [-S]; SEE [unSEEing] [SIGHT]
46. EYE [-S] [-'S]; HEART
50. ON
51. SLOW [SLO]
52. BLESSÈD [BLEST] [PLACÈD]
53. If one is prepared to find it orthographically hiding, as well as phonetically present, it is ONE [ON]: milliONs (2), ONE (4), AdONis (5), ON (7), foisON (9), ONE (10), nONE (14), cONstant (14).
55. LIVE [outLIVE] [LIVING] [obLIVious]
56. BE [-ING] (Normally, a word as common as *be* is not sufficiently foregrounded by the poem to take on salience in the reader's mind. In this sonnet, however, it is initially foregrounded by a spondaic rhythm—*Sweet love, renew thy force, be it not said*—and later by alliteration: *blunter be, blest may be*. It is also used as the rhyme-word in line 9.)
62. SELF (The Quarto prints *self-love* as one hyphenated word, but *my self* and *self loving* as two words. Following Evans, I retain the two-word *my self* only in line 13.)
64. HAVE (foregrounded because of pun on auxiliary and full use)
68. BEAUTY [-'S]
74. Here, more properly, a KEY PHRASE, for which the formula is "preposition-plus-*thee*":

with
to
of
with } THEE (4, 6, 12, 14)

98. YOU [YOUTH] (Q_1); HUE (Q_2); YOU (Q_3, C)
99. STEAL [STOL'N]
100. TIME/MIGHT [TĪM/MĪT] (possible anagrammatic KEY WORD)
103. MORE/MAR (if the near-homophone is allowed)
105. ONE [alONE] [WONdrous]
106. PRAISE [-S] [exPRESS'd]
108. LOVE [-'S] [halLOWÈD]
115. SAY [SAID] [SAcred] (possible KEY WORD)
119. ILL (if one accepts its "hidden" forms)
127. BEAUTY
135. WILL
137. EYES
140. BE
144. ANGEL
146. FEED [-S] [FED] [FEEDing] [FADing]
148. EYE [-S] [-'S]; LOVE [-'S]
152. EYE [-S], I (Normally, *I* would not qualify as a foregrounded word, but the pun with *eye* brings it forward.)
153. FIRE [-D]

APPENDIX 2

DEFECTIVE KEY WORDS

23. LOVE (absent from the "speechless" Q_1)
29. STATE (missing in Q_2, which describes the state of others, not his own)
31. ALL (missing in Q_2, which concerns absence and removal, rather than presence)
36. LOVE [-S] (missing in Q_3)
47. EYE, HEART (missing in Q_3)
51. EXCUSE (missing in C, except conceptually as *leave to go*)
65. HOLD, STRONG [-ER] (missing in C, as representing the organic order)
67. LIVE [-S] [-ING] (missing in C)
69. EYE [-S] (missing in C)
72. LOVE (missing in Q_2)
76. NEW (missing in Q_2); STILL (missing in Q_1)
85. WORDS, THOUGHT [-S] (missing in Q_1, the quatrain representing the Muse's *tongue-tied still[ness]* while listening to others' comments)
87. GIFT [GIVES] [GAV'ST] (missing in C)
91. ALL (missing in Q_1)
92. LIFE (missing in C)
93. LOOKS, HEART (missing in C)
94. DO [DEEDS] (missing in Q_3, the flower quatrain)
100. TIME [-'S] (missing in Q_1)
101. MUSE (missing in Q_3)
115. THEN, LOVE (both missing in Q_2, the quatrain interrupting the narrative of *love* as it was *then*)
116. LOVE [-D] (missing in Q_2) (Since I can see no cause for its absence in Q_2, I conclude this effect may be accidental.)
118. SICK [-EN] [-NESS] (missing in Q_3, the quatrain describing the state anterior to the ingestion of the sickness-producing drugs)
124. TIME (missing in the "immutable" Q_3)
127. FAIR (missing in C, where the falsely fair women have disappeared)
128. LIPS (missing in Q_1, which has not yet arrived at the conceit of the jacks' kiss)
136. LOVE (missing in Q_3); WILL (missing in Q_3)
137. HEART (missing in Q_1, the quatrain of the *eyes*, before the speaker realizes that love has also corrupted his *heart*)
138. FALSE [FAULTS] (missing in Q_3, the quatrain of *simple truth*)

143. CATCH (missing in C, so that the mistress never catches her lover)
145. I HATE (missing from Q_2, as the mistress relents)
148. TRUE (missing in C); FALSE [-LY], [FAULTS] (missing in Q_3); SEE [-S] [-ING], SIGHT (missing in Q_2)
151. LOVE (missing in Q_3, the quatrain of erection, ejaculation, and detumescence)
152. SWEAR (missing in Q_2, the quatrain of broken oaths)
153. BATH (missing in Q_1 before growth of bath)
154. LOVE (missing in Q_2, the quatrain of virgin chastity); FIRE and HEAT [-S] [HOT] (which are missing in Q_2, where Cupid lays by his brand)

Note:

The nine sonnets containing both one or more KEY WORDS(S) *and* one or more DEFECTIVE KEY WORD(S) are: 31, 51, 100, 115, 127, 137, 148, 152, and 153.

The nine sonnets lacking a Couplet Tie are 3, 21, 25, 34, 37, 40, 44, 126 (since it has no final couplet), and 142.

WORKS CONSULTED

Adorno, Theodor. *Aesthetic Theory.* London: Routledge and Kegan Paul, 1986.

———*Notes to Literature: Vols. I–II.* Ed. Rolf Tiedemann, trans. Shierry Weber Nicolsen. New York: Columbia University Press, 1992.

Andrews, Michael Cameron. "Sincerity and Subterfuge in Three Shakespearean Sonnet Groups." *Shakespeare Quarterly* 33 (Autumn 1982): 314–327.

Atkins, G. Douglas, and David M. Bergeron. *Shakespeare and Deconstruction.* New York: Peter Lang, 1988.

Auden, W. H. *"The Dyer's Hand" and Other Essays.* New York: Viking, 1968.

Bahktin, Mikhail [writing as V. Voloshinov]. "Discourse in Life and Discourse in Poetry: Questions of Sociological Poetics." Trans. John Richmond. In *Bakhtin School Papers*, ed. Ann Shukman. *Russian Poetics in Translation* 10 (1983): 5–30.

Barber, C. L., and Richard P. Wheeler. *The Whole Journey: Shakespeare's Power of Development.* Berkeley: University of California Press, 1986.

Barrell, John. "Editing Out the Discourse of Patronage and Shakespeare's Twenty-ninth Sonnet." In *Poetry, Language and Politics.* New York: University of Manchester Press, 1988.

Bate, Jonathan. "Ovid and the Sonnets; Or, Did Shakespeare Feel the Anxiety of Influence?" *Shakespeare Survey* 42 (1989): 65–76.

Bates, Catherine. *The Rhetoric of Courtship in Elizabethan Language and Literature.* Cambridge: Cambridge University Press, 1992.

Bearn, Gordon C. F. "Still Looking for Proof: A Critique of Smith's Relativism." In *Journal of Aesthetics and Art Criticism* 49 (Fall 1991): 297–306.

Bergeron, David M., and Gerlado U. de Sousa. *Shakespeare: A Study and Research Guide.* Lawrence: University Press of Kansas, 1987.

Bermann, Sandra. *The Sonnet over Time: A Study in the Sonnets of Petrarch, Shakespeare, and Baudelaire.* Chapel Hill: University of North Carolina Press, 1988.

Bernard, John D. "To Constancie Confin'de: The Poetics of Shakespeare's Sonnets." *PMLA* 94 (1979): 77–90.

Berryman, John. "Shakespeare at Thirty." In Berryman, *The Freedom of the Poet.* New York: Farrar, Straus and Giroux, 1976.

Bishop, Elizabeth. *One Art: Letters.* Ed. Robert Giroux. Farrar, Straus and Giroux, 1994. Letter to Donald Stanford, November 1933.

Blackmur, R. P. "A Poetics of Infatuation." In Edward Hubler, ed., *The Riddle of Shakespeare's Sonnets.* New York: Basic Books, 1962.

Booth, Stephen. *An Essay on Shakespeare's Sonnets.* New Haven, Conn.: Yale University Press, 1969.

———ed. *Shakespeare's Sonnets.* New Haven, Conn.: Yale University Press, 1977.

Bradshaw, Graham. "Sequential Readings." Review of *Shakespeare: "The Sonnets" and "A Lover's Complaint,"* ed. John Kerrigan (London: Penguin, 1987). *Times Literary Supplement* (October 30-November 5, 1987): 1199.

Bray, Alan. *Homosexuality in Renaissance England.* London: Gay Men's Press, 1982.

Bredbeck, Gregory W. *Sodomy and Interpretation: Marlowe to Milton.* Ithaca, N.Y.: Cornell University Press, 1991.

Brower, Reuben, Helen Vendler, and John Hollander, eds. *I. A. Richards: Essays in His Honor.* Oxford: Oxford University Press, 1973.

Bunting, Basil. Annotations in his copy of Shakespeare's *Sonnets* (Leipzig: Insel Verlag, n.d.). Copy in the possession of Professor Massimo Bacigalupo, University of Genoa, Italy.

Burto, William, ed. *Shakespeare: The Sonnets.* New York: NAL Penguin, 1988.

Bush, Douglas, and Alfred Harbage, eds. *William Shakespeare: The Sonnets.* New York: Penguin, 1970.

Butler, Christopher. *Interpretation, Deconstruction and Ideology.* Oxford: Clarendon, 1984.

Cady, Joseph. "Renaissance Awareness and Language for Heterosexuality: 'Love' and 'Feminine Love.'" In *Renaissance Discourses of Desire*, ed. Claude J. Summers and Ted-Larry Pebworth. Columbia, Mo.: University of Missouri Press, 1993.

Cavell, Stanley. "Aesthetic Problems of Modern Philosophy." In Cavell, *Must We Mean What We Say?* Cambridge: Cambridge University Press, 1969; rpt. 1976.

Coetzee, J. M. "Speaking for Language." *New York Review of Books* 43 (February 1, 1996): 28–31.

Colie, Rosalie. *Shakespeare's Living Art.* Princeton: Princeton University Press, 1974.

Copenhaver, Brian P., and Charles B. Schmitt. *Renaissance Philosophy.* Oxford: Oxford University Press, 1992.

Crockett, Bryan. "Word Boundary and Syntactic Line Segmentation in Shakespeare's Sonnets." In *Style* 24 (Winter 1990): 600–610.

Crosman, Robert. "Making Love out of Nothing at All: The Issue of Story in Shakespeare's Procreation Sonnets." *Shakespeare Quarterly* 41 (Winter 1990): 470–488.

de Grazia, Margreta. "Babbling Will in *Shake-speares Sonnets* 127 to 154." *Spenser Studies* 1 (1980): 121–134.

———*Shakespeare Verbatim: The Reproduction of Authenticity and the 1790 Apparatus.* Oxford: Clarendon, 1991.

de Man, Paul. *Allegories of Reading: Figural Language in Rousseau, Nietzsche, Rilke, and Proust.* New Haven, Conn.: Yale University Press, 1979.

———*Blindness and Insight: Essays in the Rhetoric of Contemporary Criticism.* Minneapolis: University of Minnesota Press, 1983.

———*The Rhetoric of Romanticism.* New York: Columbia University Press, 1984.

———*The Resistance to Theory.* Minneapolis: University of Minnesota Press, 1986.

———*Critical Writings, 1953–1978.* Ed. Lindsay Waters. Minneapolis: University of Minnesota Press, 1989.

Derrida, Jacques. *Of Grammatology.* Trans. Gayatri Chakravorty Spivak. Baltimore: Johns Hopkins University Press, 1976.

Diehl, Patrick S., trans. *Dante's Rime.* Princeton, N.J.: Princeton University Press, 1979.

Dollimore, Jonathan. *Radical Tragedy: Religion, Ideology and Power in the Drama of Shakespeare and His Contemporaries.* Chicago: University of Chicago Press, 1987.

Drakakis, John, ed. *Shakespearean Tragedy.* London: Longman, 1992.

Dubrow, Heather. *Captive Victors: Shakespeare's Narrative Poems and Sonnets.* Ithaca, N.Y.: Cornell University Press, 1987.

Duncan-Jones, Katherine. "Was the 1609 *Shake-speares Sonnets* Really Unauthorized?" *Review of English Studies* 34 (May 1983): 151–171.

Durling, Robert M., ed. and trans. *Petrarch's Lyric Poems: The "Rime sparse" and Other Lyrics.* Cambridge, Mass.: Harvard University Press, 1976.

Eagleton, Terry. *The Shakespeare Myth.* Ed. Graham Holderness. New York: Manchester University Press, 1988.

Ellrodt, Robert. "Shakespeare the Non-Dramatic Poet." In *The Cambridge Companion to Shakespeare Studies,* ed. Stanley Wells. London: Cambridge University Press, 1986.

Engle, Lars. "Afloat in Thick Deeps: *Shakespeare's Sonnets* on Certainty." *PMLA* 104, no. 5 (October 1989): 832–843.

Evans, G. B., ed. *Shakespeare's Sonnets.* Cambridge: Cambridge University Press, 1996.

Everett, Barbara. "Shakespeare's Greening." *Times Literary Supplement* (July 8, 1994): 11–13.

Faas, Ekbert. *Shakespeare's Poetics.* Cambridge: Cambridge University Press, 1986.

Fabricius, Johannes. *Syphilis in Shakespeare's England.* London: Kingsley, 1995.

Farber, Lianna. "The Logic of Agency in Shakespeare's 'Dark Lady' Sonnets." Unpublished typescript, 1994.

Felperin, Howard. "The Dark Lady Identified, or What Deconstruction Can Do for Shakespeare's *Sonnets*." In *Shakespeare and Deconstruction*, ed. G. Douglas Atkins and David M. Bergeron. New York: Peter Lang, 1988.

Felstiner, John. "Translating Celan: Translating Shakespeare." *Parnassus: Poetry in Review* 16 (1990): 174–194.

Ferris, David. "'Truth Is the Death of Intention': Benjamin's Esoteric History of Romanticism." *Studies in Romanticism* 31 (Winter 1992): 455–480.

Fineman, Joel. *Shakespeare's Perjured Eye*. Berkeley: University of California Press, 1986.

Firenzuola, Agnolo. *On the Beauty of Women*. Trans. and ed. Konrad Eisenbichler and Jacqueline Murray. Philadelphia: University of Pennsylvania Press, 1992.

Flood, John L. "The Winchester Geese." Review of Johannes Fabricius, *Syphilis in Shakespeare's England* (London: Kingsley, 1995). *Times Literary Supplement* (January 13, 1995): 12.

Foster, Donald W. "Master W.H., R.I.P." *PMLA* 102 (January 1987): 42–54.

———*Elegy by William Shakespeare: A Study in Attribution*. Newark: University of Delaware Press, 1989.

———"Reconstructing Shakespeare." *Shakespeare Newsletter* (Fall 1991): 26–27.

Foucault, Michel. *The Archaeology of Knowledge and the Discourse of Language*. Trans. A. M. Sheridan Smith. New York: Pantheon, 1972.

Fowler, Alastair. *Triumphal Forms: Structural Patterns in Elizabethan Poetry*. Cambridge: Cambridge University Press, 1970.

Fraistat, Neil, ed. *Poems in Their Place: The Intertexuality and Order of Poetic Collections*. Chapel Hill: University of North Carolina Press, 1986.

Fraser, Russell. "George Herbert's Poetry." *Sewanee Review* 95 (Fall 1987): 573–574.

Freud, Sigmund. "A Special Type of Choice of Object Made by Men" [1910] and "On the Universal Tendency to Debasement in the Sphere of Love" [1912]. Parts I and II of "Contributions to a Psychology of Love." In *Complete Psychological Works of Sigmund Freud*, trans. James Strachey, ed. James Strachey in collaboration with Anna Freud, 24 vols. London: Hogarth, 1953–1974.

Gadamer, Hans-Georg. "The Eminent Text and Its Truth." In *The Horizon of Literature*, ed. Paul Hernadi. Lincoln: University of Nebraska Press, 1982.

Gardner, C. O. "Some Reflections on Shakespeare's Sonnets No. 33, 34, and 35." *Theoria* 42 (1974): 43–55.

Gasché, Rodolphe. "The Sober Absolute: On Benjamin and the Early Romantics." *Studies in Romanticism* 31 (Winter 1992): 433–453.

Genette, Gérard. *Figures of Literary Discourse.* New York: Columbia University Press, 1982.

di Girolamo, Costanzo. *A Critical Theory of Literature.* Madison: University of Wisconsin Press, 1981.

Giroux, Robert. *The Book Known as Q: A Consideration of* Shakespeare's Sonnets. New York: Atheneum, 1982.

Goethe, Johann Wolfgang von. *Conversations with Eckermann.* Washington, D.C.: M. Walter Dunne, 1901.

Goldberg, Jonathan. *Endlesse Worke: Spenser and the Structures of Discourse.* Baltimore: Johns Hopkins University Press, 1981.

———*Voice Terminal Echo.* New York: Methuen, 1986.

———*Sodometries.* Stanford, Calif.: Stanford University Press, 1992.

Goldsmith, Ulrich K. "Words out of a Hat? Alliteration and Assonance in Shakespeare's Sonnets." In *Studies in Comparison* ed. Hazel E. Barnes, William M. Calder III, and Hugo Schmidt. New York: Peter Lang, 1989.

Grady, Hugh. *The Modernist Shakespeare: Critical Texts in a Material World.* Oxford: Clarendon, 1991.

Graziani, Rene. "The Numbering of Shakespeare's Sonnets: 12, 60, and 126." *Shakespeare Quarterly* 35 (Spring 1984): 79–82.

Green, Martin. "Wriothesley's Roses." In *Shakespeare's Sonnets, Poems and Plays.* Baltimore: Clevedon Books, 1993.

Greene, Thomas M. "Anti-Hermeneutics: The Case of Shakespeare's Sonnet 129." In *Poetic Traditions of the English Renaissance,* ed. Maynard Mack and George deForest Lord. New Haven, Conn.: Yale University Press, 1982.

———"Pitiful Thrivers: Failed Husbandry in the Sonnets." In *Shakespeare and the Question of Theory* , ed. Patricia Parker and Geoffrey Hartman. New York: Methuen, 1985.

Greenblatt, Stephen J., ed. *Allegory and Representation: Selected Papers from the English Institute, 1979–80.* Baltimore: Johns Hopkins University Press, 1981.

Gurr, Andrew. "Shakespeare's First Poem: Sonnet 145." *Essays in Criticism: A Quarterly Journal of Literary Criticism* 21 (1971): 221–226.

———"You and Thou in Shakespeare's Sonnets." *Essays in Criticism: A Quarterly Journal of Literary Criticism* 32 (1982): 9–25.

Hamburger, Käte. *The Logic of Literature.* Trans. Marilyn J. Rose. 2nd ed. Bloomington: Indiana University Press, 1973.

Hapgood, Robert. "The Transcendent Bard in Transition." *Times Literary Supplement* (August 25–31, 1989): 927–928.

Harder, Kelsie. "Southern Formalism at Shakespeare: Ransom on the Sonnets." In *Shakespeare and Southern Writers: A Study in Influence.* Jackson: University Press of Mississippi, 1985.

Harvey, Elizabeth D., and Katharine Eisaman Maus, eds. *Soliciting Interpretation: Literary Theory and Seventeenth-Century English Poetry.* Chicago: University of Chicago Press, 1990.

Hedley, Jane. *Power in Verse: Metaphor and Metonymy in the Renaissance Lyric.* University Park: Pennsylvania State University Press, 1988.

Heninger, S. K., Jr. "Sequences, Systems, Models: Sidney and the Secularization of Sonnets." In *Poems in Their Place: The Intertextuality and Order of Poetic Collections,* ed. Neil Fraistat. Chapel Hill: University of North Carolina Press, 1986.

———*The Subtext of Form in the English Renaissance: Proportion Poetical.* University Park: Pennsylvania State University Press, 1994.

Hieatt, A. Kent. "The Genesis of *Shakespeare Sonnets:* Spenser's Ruines of Rome." *PMLA* 98 (October 1983): 800–814.

———, Charles W. Hieatt, and Anne Lake Prescott. "When Did Shakespeare Write *Sonnets* 1609?" *Studies in Philology* 88 (Winter 1991): 69–109.

Hill, Geoffrey. *The Lords of Limit: Essays on Literature and Ideas.* London: A. Deutsch, 1984.

Hosek, Chaviva, and Patricia Parker, eds. *Lyric Poetry: Beyond New Criticism.* Ithaca, N.Y.: Cornell University Press, 1985.

Hubler, Edward, ed. *The Riddle of Shakespeare's Sonnets.* New York: Basic Books, 1962.

Ingram, W. G., and Theodore Redpath, eds. *Shakespeare's Sonnets.* London: Hodder and Stoughton, 1978.

Jackson, Berners A. W., ed. *William Shakespeare: The Two Gentlemen of Verona.* Baltimore: Penguin, 1964.

Jackson, MacDonald P. "How Many Horses Has Sonnet 51? Textual and Literary Criticism in Shakespeare's Sonnets." *English Language Notes* 27 (March 1990): 10–19.

Kamps, Ivo, ed. *Shakespeare Left and Right.* New York: Routledge, Chapman, and Hall, 1991.

Kernan, Alvin. "Shakespeare's Sonnets and Patronage Art." In *Shakespeare, the King's Playwright: Theater in the Stuart Court, 1603–1613.* New Haven, Conn.: Yale University Press, 1995.

Kerrigan, John, ed. "*The Sonnets*" *and* "*A Lover's Complaint.*" New York: Penguin, 1986.

Kerrigan, William, and Gordon Braden. *The Idea of the Renaissance.* Baltimore: Johns Hopkins University Press, 1989.

Kott, Jan. Introduction to William Shakespeare, *Sonnets,* ed. Jerzy S. Sito. Warsaw: Panstwowy Instytut Wydawniczy, 1964.

Kuin, Roger. "The Gaps and the Whites: Indeterminacy and Undecideability in the Sonnet Sequences of Sidney, Spenser, and Shakespeare." *Spenser Studies* 8 (1987): 251–285.

Kristeva, Julia. *Semeiotiké: Recherches pour une sémanalyse.* Paris: Seuil, 1969.

Lacoue-Labarthe, Philippe. "Introduction to Walter Benjamin's *The Concept of Art Criticism in the German Romantics.*" *Studies in Romanticism* 31 (Winter 1992): 421–432.

Lanham, Richard A. *The Motives of Eloquence: Literary Rhetoric in the Renaissance.* New Haven, Conn.: Yale University Press, 1976.

Leishman, J. B. *Themes and Variations in Shakespeare's Sonnets.* New York: Harper and Row, 1963.

Lever, J. W. *The Elizabethan Love Sonnet.* London: Methuen, 1966.

Lifson, Martha R. "The Rhetoric of Consolation: Shakespeare's Couplets." In *Assays: Critical Approaches to Medieval and Renaissance Texts* 2 (1982): 95–114.

MacDonald, Russ, ed. *Shakespeare Reread.* Ithaca: Cornell University Press, 1994.

Mack, Maynard, and George deForest Lord, eds. *Poetic Traditions of the English Renaissance.* New Haven, Conn.: Yale University Press, 1982.

Mailloux, Steven. "Rhetorical Hermeneutics." *Critical Inquiry* 11 (1985): 620–641.

McIver, Bruce, and Ruth Stevenson, eds. *Teaching with Shakespeare.* Newark: University of Delaware Press, 1994.

Marcuse, Herbert. *The Aesthetic Dimension: Toward a Critique of Marxist Aesthetics.* Boston: Beacon, 1978.

Marotti, Arthur F. "'Love Is Not Love': Elizabethan Sonnet Sequences and the Social Order." *ELH* 49 (Summer 1982): 396–428.

———"Shakespeare's Sonnets as Literary Property." In *Soliciting Interpretation: Literary Theory and Seventeenth-Century English Poetry,* ed. Elizabeth D. Harvey and Katharine Eisaman Maus. Chicago: University of Chicago Press, 1990.

Martin, Christopher. *Policy in Love: Lyric and Public in Ovid, Petrarch and Shakespeare.* Pittsburgh: Duquesne University Press, 1994.

McGann, Jerome J. *The Romantic Ideology.* Chicago: University of Chicago Press, 1983.

McGuire, Philip C. "Shakespeare's Non-Shakespearean Sonnets." *Shakespeare Quarterly,* 38 (Autumn 1987): 304–319.

Meier, Hans H. "Shakespeare Restored: Sonnets 51.11 and 146.2." *English Studies* 4 (1991): 350–354.

Moss, Howard. "Modified Sonnets." In Moss, *A Swimmer in the Air.* New York: Scribner, 1957.

Neely, Carol Thomas. "Detachment and Engagement in Shakespeare's Sonnets: 94, 116, and 129." *PMLA* 92 (1977): 83–95.

Nejgebauer, A. "The Sonnets." *Shakespeare Survey* 15 (1962): 10–61.

Nelson, Lowry, Jr. "The Matter of Rime: Sonnets of Sidney, Daniel, and Shakespeare 123–142." In *Poetic Traditions of the English Renaissance,* ed.

Maynard Mack and George deForest Lord. New Haven, Conn.: Yale University Press, 1982.

Nohrnberg, James. *The Analogy of the Faerie Queene.* Princeton, N.J.: Princeton University Press, 1976.

Norbrook, David. *Poetry and Politics in the English Renaissance.* London: Routledge and Kegan Paul, 1984.

Nowottny, Winifred. *The Language Poets Use.* New York: Oxford University Press, 1962.

———"Some Features of Form and Style in Sonnets 97–126." In *New Essays on Shakespeare's Sonnets,* ed. Hilton Landry. New York: AMS Press, 1976.

Obler, Loraine K., and Lise Menn, eds. *Exceptional Language and Linguistics.* New York: Academic Press, 1982.

O'Connor, M. P. "'Unanswerable the Knack of Tongues': The Linguistic Study of Verse." In *Exceptional Language and Linguistics,* ed. Loraine K. Obler and Lise Menn. New York: Academic Press, 1982.

Ong, Walter J. "Commonplace Rhapsody: Ravisius Textor, Zwinger and Shakespeare." In *Classical Influences on European Culture, A.D. 1500–1700.* Cambridge: Cambridge University Press, 1976.

Parker, Patricia, and Geoffrey Hartman, eds. *Shakespeare and the Question of Theory.* New York: Methuen, 1985.

Parker, Patricia and David Quint, eds. *Literary Theory / Renaissance Texts.* Baltimore: Johns Hopkins University Press, 1986.

Pequigney, Joseph. *Such Is My Love: A Study of Shakespeare's Sonnets.* Chicago: University of Chicago Press, 1985.

Perkins, David. "Romantic Lyric Voice: What Shall We Call the 'I'?" *Southern Review* 29 (Spring 1993): 225–238.

Pirkhofer, Anton M. "The Beauty of Truth: The Dramatic Character of Shakespeare's Sonnets." In *New Essays on Shakespeare's Sonnets,* ed. Hilton Landry. New York: AMS Press, 1976.

Ransom, John Crowe. "Shakespeare at Sonnets." In Ransom, *The World's Body.* New York: Scribner's 1938.

———"Postscript on Shakespeare's Sonnets." *Kenyon Review* 30 (1968); 523–531.

Ricks, Christopher, ed. *New History of Literature, II: English Poetry and Prose, 1540–1674.* New York: Peter Bedrick, 1987.

Roche, Thomas P. "Five Books on Shakespeare's Sonnets." Book review. *Shakespeare Quarterly* 29 (1978): 439–448.

———"Shakespeare and the Sonnet Sequence." In *New History of Literature, II: English Poetry and Prose 1540–1674,* ed. Christopher Ricks. New York: Peter Bedrick, 1987.

———*Petrarch and the English Sonnet Sequence.* New York: AMS Press, 1989.

Roessner, Jane. "Double Exposure: Shakespeare's Sonnets 100–114." *ELH* 46 (1979): 357–378.

———"The Coherence and the Context of Shakespeare's Sonnet 16." *Journal of English and Germanic Philology* 81 (July 1982): 331–346.

Rollins, Hyder Edward, ed. *New Variorum Shakespeare: The Sonnets.* 2 vols. Philadelphia: Lippincott, 1944.

Rosmarin, Adena. "Hermeneutics versus Erotics: Shakespeare's *Sonnets* and Interpretive History." *PMLA* 100 (January 1985): 20–37.

———*The Power of Genre.* Minneapolis: University of Minnesota Press, 1985.

Røstvig, Maren-Sofie. *Fair Forms: Essays in English Literature from Spenser to Jane Austen.* Cambridge: D. S. Brewer, 1975.

———"A Frame of Words on the Craftsmanship of Samuel Daniel." *English Studies* 60 (April 1979): 122–137.

Rutelli, Romana. *Saggi sulla connotazione: Tre sonetti de Shakespeare.* Turin: G. Giappichelli, 1982.

Santayana, George. "Shakespeare's Sonnet 29 Translated into Modern American." *The New Republic* II (Feb. 27, 1915): 17. Rpt. in *The Genteel Tradition: Nine Essays by George Santayana*, ed. Douglas L. Wilson. Cambridge, Mass.: Harvard University Press, 1957.

Sedgwick, Eve. *Between Men: English Literature and Male Homosocial Desire.* New York: Columbia University Press, 1985.

Shakespeare, William. *New Variorum Shakespeare: The Sonnets.* Ed. Hyder Edward Rollins. 2 vols. Philadelphia: Lippincott, 1944.

———*Shakespeare's Sonnets.* Ed. W. G. Ingram and Theodore Redpath. London: Hodder and Stoughton Educational, 1978. Orig. pub. 1964.

———*Sonnets 1609.* Menston, England: Scolar Press, 1968.

———*Shakespeare's Sonnets.* Ed. Stephen Booth. New Haven, Conn.: Yale University Press, 1977.

———*"Sonnets" and "A Lover's Complaint."* Ed. John Kerrigan. New York: Penguin, 1986.

———*Sonnets.* Ed. G. B. Evans. Cambridge: Cambridge University Press, 1996.

Simonds, Peggy Munoz. "Eros and Anteros in Shakespeare's Sonnets 153 and 154: An Iconographical Study." *Spenser Studies* 7 (1986): 261–323.

Sinfield, Alan. *Faultlines: Cultural Materialism and the Politics of Dissident Reading.* Oxford: Clarendon, 1992.

Smith, Barbara Herrnstein. *On the Margins of Discourse: The Relation of Literature to Language.* Chicago: University of Chicago Press, 1978.

Smith, Bruce R. *Homosexual Desire in Shakespeare's England.* Chicago: University of Chicago Press, 1991.

Spiller, Michael R. G. *The Development of the Sonnet: An Introduction.* New York: Routledge, 1992.

Stallybrass, Peter. "Editing as Cultural Formation: The Sexing of Shakespeare's Sonnets." *Modern Language Quarterly* 54 (March 1993): 91–104.

Stanford, Donald E. "Robert Bridges and Samuel Butler on Shakespeare's

Sonnets: An Exchange of Letters." *Shakespeare Quarterly* 22 (Autumn, 1971): 329–335.

Starbuck, George. *Space-Saver Sonnets.* Cleveland: Bits Press, 1986.

Summers, Claude J., and Ted-Larry Pebworth. *Renaissance Discourses of Desire.* Columbia, Mo.: University of Missouri Press, 1993.

Swir, Anna. *Talking to My Body.* Trans. Czeslaw Milosz and Leonard Nathan. Port Townsend, Wash.: Copper Canyon Press, 1996.

Szondi, Peter. "The Poetry of Constancy: Paul Celan's Translation of Shakespeare's Sonnet 105." In Szondi, *On Textual Understanding and Other Essays,* trans. Harvey Mendelsohn. Minneapolis: University of Minnesota Press, 1986.

Taylor, Gary. "Shakespeare's Sonnets: A Rediscovery." *Times Literary Supplement* (April 19, 1985): 450.

———"Some Manuscripts of Shakespeare's Sonnets." *Bulletin of the John Rylands Library* 68 (Autumn 1985): 210–246.

Todorov, Tzvetan, ed. *French Literary Theory: A Reader.* Trans. R. Carter. Cambridge: Cambridge University Press, 1982.

Trousdale, Marion. *Shakespeare and the Rhetoricians.* Chapel Hill: University of North Carolina Press, 1982.

Tuve, Rosemond. *Elizabethan and Metaphysical Imagery: Renaissance Poetic and Twentieth-Century Critics.* Chicago: University of Chicago Press, 1947.

Vendler, Helen. "Jakobson, Richards, and Shakespeare's Sonnet 129." In *I. A. Richards: Essays in His Honor,* ed. Reuben Brower, Helen Vendler, and John Hollander. New York: Oxford University Press, 1973.

———"Shakespeare's Sonnets: Reading for Difference." *Bulletin of the American Academy of Arts and Sciences* 47 (March 1994): 33–50.

———"Reading Stage by Stage: Shakespeare's *Sonnets.*" In *Shakespeare Reread,* ed. Russ MacDonald. Ithaca, N.Y.: Cornell University Press, 1994.

———"Reading for Difference: *The Sonnets.*" In *Teaching with Shakespeare,* ed. Bruce McIver and Ruth Stevenson. Newark: University of Delaware Press, 1994.

Vickers, Brian. *Classical Rhetoric in English Poetry.* Carbondale: Southern Illinois University Press, 1970.

———"Rhetoric and Feeling in Shakespeare's *Sonnets.*" In *Shakespeare Today: Directions and Methods of Research,* ed. Keir Elam. Florence: La Casa Usher, 1984.

———"Bard-Watching." *Times Literary Supplement* (August 26-September 1, 1988): 933–935.

———*Appropriating Shakespeare: Contemporary Critical Quarrels.* New Haven, Conn.: Yale University Press, 1993.

Waddington, Raymond B. "The Poetics of Eroticism: Shakespeare's 'Master

Mistress.'" In *Renaissance Discourses of Desire*, ed. Claude J. Summers and Ted-Larry Pebworth. Columbia, Mo.: University of Missouri Press, 1993.

Waller, Gary. "Decentering the Bard: The Dissemination of the Shakespearean Text." In *Shakespeare and Deconstruction*, ed. G. Douglas Atkins and David M. Bergeron. New York: Peter Lang, 1988.

Warren, Charles. *T. S. Eliot on Shakespeare.* Ann Arbor, Mich.: UMI Research Press, 1987.

Watson, Thomas. *The Hekatompathia, or Passionate Centurie of Love.* London: Spenser Society, 1869; reprinted from the original edition of ca. 1581.

Weimann, Robert. "Shakespeare (De)Canonized: Conflicting Uses of 'Authority' and 'Representations.'" *New Literary History* 20 (Autumn 1988): 65–81.

Weiser, David K. "'I' and 'Thou' in Shakespeare's *Sonnets.*" *Journal of English and Germanic Philology* 76 (1977): 506–524.

———*Mind in Character: Shakespeare's Speaker in the Sonnets.* Columbia, Mo.: University of Missouri Press, 1987.

Wells, Stanley. "New Readings in Shakespeare's Sonnets." In *Elizabethan and Modern Studies*, ed. J. P. Motten. Ghent: Seminarie voor English and American Literature, Rijksuniversiteit Gent, 1985.

———ed. *The Cambridge Companion to Shakespeare Studies.* Cambridge: Cambridge University Press, 1986.

———ed. *Shakespeare: A Bibliographical Guide.* Oxford: Clarendon, 1990.

Wilson, John Dover. *An Introduction to the Sonnets of Shakespeare for the Use of Historians and Others.* New York: Cambridge University Press, 1964.

Wright, George T. *Shakespeare's Metrical Art.* Berkeley: University of California Press, 1988.

Wyndham, George, ed. *Poems of Shakespeare.* London: Methuen, 1898.

Zumthor, Paul. "On the Circularity of Song." In *French Literary Theory Today: A Reader*, ed. Tzvetan Todorov, trans. R. Carter. Cambridge: Cambridge University Press, 1982.

INDEX